Beelzebub's Tales: Book One

The Side by Side Comparison

Edited by Robin Bloor

KARNAK PRESS

Austin, Texas

Beelzebub's Tales: Book One
The Side by Side Comparison

ISBN 978-1-957278-08-7

First Edition, First Publication 2024

Published in the United States of America

KARNAK PRESS

Dedicated to:

Alfred R Orage,
Gurdjieff's timeless editor

Introduction

Ostensibly, there are two legitimate versions of Gurdjieff's magnum opus, *An Objectively Impartial Criticism of the Life of Man or Beelzebub's Tales to His Grandson*: the officially published version that first appeared in 1950, and *The 1931 Manuscript*, which was a completed draft that Gurdjieff updated in the intervening years.

Gurdjieff allowed Alfred Orage to publish and sell *The 1931 Manuscript* to a select group of his American pupils in order to raise much needed funds. One hundred mimeographed copies were made of the manuscript, which were sold for $10.00 each (equivalent to about $186 in 2024 dollars). From 1926 to 1930, Orage had been holding group meetings to study and discuss some of the draft chapters of The Tales – he was, at the same time, editing and refining the text of *The Tales* with Gurdjieff.

Notes on those meetings were published, in edited form, by C. S. Nott in his book *Teachings of Gurdjieff: A Pupil's Journey* and more recently by Book Studio, in a book entitled *Orage's Commentary on Gurdjieff's "Beelzebub's Tales To His Grandson,"* the text of which is taken from the meeting notes taken by Lawrence Morris and Sherman Manchester.

Students of The Work who read either or both of those books could be forgiven for assuming that the comments made during those meetings relate to the 1950 published version of *The Tales*. However, they do not, nor do they necessarily refer to the text of *The 1931 Manuscript* published here. Orage likely worked from earlier versions of the text.

The Virtues of The 1931 Manuscript

Readers who enjoy reading *The Tales* usually enjoy reading *The 1931 Manuscript* as well. Despite the differences between the two, the text bears the mark of Gurdjieff. It's permeated with his rhythm and style. In some chapters, the text of the two versions is very similar, while others show clear differences. When reading those different chapters, you often get the impression you're reading a Gurdjieff book you haven't encountered before. The subject matter may be familiar, but the text feels "new."

Our experience suggests that *The 1931 Manuscript* has a similar impact on the reader as the 1950 publication, when read in the first or second ways Gurdjieff recommends, which are:

"at least as you have already become mechanized to read all your contemporary books and newspapers" (the first way), and:

"as if you were reading aloud to another person" (the second way).

The third mode of reading Gurdjieff recommends to the reader, is to: "try and fathom the gist of my writings."

Our experience suggests you'll find *The 1931 Manuscript* useful for this endeavor. Importantly, it offers a valid alternative version of the text. Both versions are unquestionably legitimate, as they were both authored by Gurdjieff. However, when read carefully word-for-word, they can offer different perspectives on the meaning.

If you discover any apparent contradiction between the two texts, resolving it is straightforward, as the 1950 publication is undoubtedly the definitive version. However, this rarely occurs. The more common outcome of reading both versions is that Gurdjieff's intended meaning seems to emerge with greater clarity.

Here, we suspect a very simple psychological mechanism at play. When we have only one version of a particular sentence or paragraph, we may attach a slightly distorted meaning to it, simply due to what Gurdjieff calls "mentation by form." However, when we have two versions of the text, the likelihood of such internal distortion is reduced.

In summary, then, there are two main reasons why someone might choose to read *The 1931 Manuscript*.

1)   For the sheer joy of reading unfamiliar text written by Gurdjieff

2)   As part of an effort to "try and fathom the gist" of *The Tales*.

Of course, it's the second of these activities that this book has been designed to facilitate, making the direct comparison of the two texts as easy as possible.

The Layout of This Book

This book's layout is designed to let you compare the two versions of *The Tales* paragraph by paragraph and line by line. For the sake of cost and usability, we also chose a layout and typeface that kept the page count below 550.

The 1950 version of *The Tales* is printed on he left-hand side of each spread, while *The 1931 Manuscript* is on the right. Page numbers for the 1950 version are shown with dotted lines and a number. On the right side, dotted lines only indicate a page change in the 1950 version.

This layout allows you to read *The Tales* paragraph by paragraph, comparing the versions side-by-side. Readers have found this approach to reading helpful in enriching the text's meaning.

Differences Between The Two Versions in Overview

Between 1931 and 1950, the book underwent significant revisions. Extensive new text was added, and the original content was modified, mostly minor edits but with some substantial changes. *The 1931 Manuscript*, at roughly 290,000 words, is only 80% the length of the final book, which clocks in at around 360,000 words. Here's a breakdown of the reasons for this difference:

- Gurdjieff added minor details and occasionally reworked passages to improve the text's rhythm.

- In some sections, he made the text more verbose, potentially hindering comprehension.

- He added new stories or expanded existing ones with significant details in specific parts.

- The book's structure was reworked in a few places. Notably, chapters 39 (The Holy Planet Purgatory) and 40 (Heptaparaparshinokh) were significantly altered, with some text moving from chapter 40 to 39. Ultimately, both chapters were lengthened. Additionally, the order of chapters 44, 45, and 46 was changed, and new text was included.

- Gurdjieff removed minimal text from *The 1931 Manuscript*, though he did eliminate a few pages that largely duplicated earlier content.

The Editing of the 1931 Manuscript

Our source for *The 1931 Manuscript* was a digital copy (PDF) that circulated online for years. It contained many typos, which we corrected to create a text that was "easy to read and study." This book replicates exactly the text from our 2014 publication. Here's a breakdown of our editing approach:

- **Typos and Spelling:** The original manuscript was clearly rushed into production and contained numerous typos. These were easy to identify and correct. However, we treated every word as significant (as each was chosen by Gurdjieff). Even for seemingly obvious errors, the editing process was meticulous. Whenever possible, we compared discrepancies with the 1950 publication's text and used common sense to determine the intended meaning.

- **Spelling Standard:** The original manuscript used British English spelling (e.g., labour, centre). Since the book was published in the US, we adopted American English conventions (e.g., labor, center).

- **Gurdjieff's Neologisms:** The manuscript presented a particular challenge with Gurdjieff's invented words (neologisms) and names. Their spellings often differed from the 1950 publication. While we could have left them unchanged, this would have confused readers familiar with the 1950 text. To avoid confusion, especially with frequently used words like "Triamazikamno" (sometimes "Triamonia") and "Heptaparaparshinokh" (sometimes "Eftologodiksis"), we adopted the spellings used in the 1950 publication. Inconsistencies in the original manuscript, with these words spelled differently across chapters and typos further supported this decision.

- **Punctuation:** The punctuation in *The Tales*, particularly quotation marks, is complex in certain sections. The original manuscript lacked proper punctuation in this regard. We edited it to match the 1950 publication's punctuation, which follows these conventions:

- ○ Beelzebub's words have opening quotation marks at the beginning of each paragraph but closing quotation marks only at the end of the final paragraph.

- ○ When Beelzebub reports conversations, quotations are nested (quotation marks within quotation marks). Here, we alternate between double and single quotation marks for clarity.

- ○ In rare instances, Beelzebub reports someone else reporting yet another conversation. These nested quotations become even more intricate.

- **Quotation Marks:** Gurdjieff sometimes uses quotation marks for emphasis, as in "they therefore kept on demanding what they call 'money' from the ordinary beings of their community," highlighting the specific word "money" for the reader's attention. We preserved Gurdjieff's original choices regarding emphasis quotations in the 1931 text.

- **Capitalization:** Gurdjieff's capitalization style differed between the manuscript and the 1950 publication. The 1950 version consistently capitalizes all direct references to God (the Absolute), while rarely capitalizing other words. *The 1931 Manuscript* lacked consistency. To maintain consistency, we adopted the 1950 publication's approach for mentions of God, editing the text accordingly.

- **Initial Capitalization:** Gurdjieff occasionally capitalizes the first letter of a word, to suggest a subtle difference in meaning. For instance, "Reason" might hold a slightly different meaning than "reason." These capitalization choices differed between the manuscript and the 1950 publication. We opted to preserve Gurdjieff's original choices in this regard.

- **Hyphenation:** Gurdjieff frequently hyphenates words together to indicate they form a single concept. There are instances where his hyphenation choices differed between the manuscript and the 1950 publication. We respected Gurdjieff's original decisions and did not alter these hyphenations.

Our "word-by-word" editing approach for *The 1931 Manuscript* prioritized preserving the original text. We addressed errors and adopted American English conventions for punctuation and spelling. Additionally, we followed the 1950 publication's capitalization for mentions of God and standardized the neologisms' spellings.

Significant Changes Made To The Text

The 1931 Manuscript contained some structural issues beyond simple typos. Readers might encounter occasional gaps or inconsistencies in the text's flow. We addressed these issues in the following ways, focusing on Books Two and Three (no changes were made to Book One):

Here's a breakdown of how we addressed structural issues in the manuscript for Book Two and Three:

- **Missing Chapter:** In Book Two, Chapter 35, "A Change in the Appointed Course of the Falling of the Trans-space Ship Karnak," was entirely missing. We incorporated this missing text verbatim from the 1950 publication.

- **Combined Chapters:** In Book Two, Chapters 36 and 37 were merged under one title. We separated the chapters but inserted the title "France" for Chapter 37 to maintain clarity.

- **Missing List:** In Book Three, Chapter 40 ("Heptaparaparshinokh") lacked the list of 42 "active elements of opium." We included this list from the 1950 publication.

- **Inseparable Chapters:** Book Three, Chapters 44 ("Form & Sequence") and 45 were combined under a single title. Due to interwoven text, separating them proved impractical.

- **Incomplete Chapter:** Book Three, Chapter 46 ("Electricity") ended abruptly. We added the six missing pages from the 1950 publication.

- **Missing Context:** Book Three, Chapter 44 began with a reference to a "moving event" not present in the preceding chapter. We added two relevant paragraphs from the 1950 publication to provide continuity.

- **Chapter Order:** Be aware that the order of Chapters 44, 45, and 46 differs between the 1931 Manuscript and the 1950 publication.

- **Chapter Titles:** In the original manuscript the chapter titles at the start of the manuscript did not match the chapter titles as they occurred in the text. We replace the original contents list with one that matched the text.

- **Removed Text:** We removed almost two pages of text that occurred, disjointedly, at the end of Chapter 34 *Russia*. These pages duplicated content from earlier in that chapter, so they seemed superfluous.

G. GURDJIEFF

All and Everything

Ten Books, in Three Series
of which this is the First Series

Volume 1

G. GURDJIEFF

The 1931 Manuscript

of

An Objectively Impartial Criticism of the Life of Man

or

Beelzebub's Tales to His Grandson

Volume 1

Original written in Russian and Armenian.
Translations into other languages have been
made under the personal direction of the author, by a group of translators chosen by him
and specially trained according to their
defined individualities, in conformity with the
text to be translated and in relation to the
philological particularities of each language.

FIRST SERIES: Three books under the title of *"An Objectively Impartial Criticism of the Life of Man,"* or, *"Beelzebub's Tales to His Grandson."*

SECOND SERIES: Three books under the common title of *"Meetings with Remarkable Men."*

THIRD SERIES: Four books under the common title of *"Life is Real Only Then, When 'I Am.'"*

All written according to entirely new principles of logical reasoning and strictly directed towards the solution of the following three cardinal problems:

FIRST SERIES: To destroy, mercilessly, without any compromises whatsoever, in the mentation and feelings of the reader, the beliefs and views, by centuries rooted in him, about everything existing in the world.

SECOND SERIES: To acquaint the reader with the material required for a new creation and to prove the soundness and good quality of it.

THIRD SERIES: To assist the arising, in the mentation and in the feelings of the reader, of a veritable, non-fantastic representation not of that illusory world which he now perceives, but of the world existing in reality.

Friendly Advice

*[Written impromptu by the author on delivering this
book, already prepared for publication, to the printer.]*

ACCORDING TO the numerous deductions and conclusions made by me during experimental elucidations concerning the productivity of the perception by
contemporary people of new impressions from what is heard and read, and also according to the thought of one of the sayings of popular wisdom I have just remembered, handed down to our days from very ancient times, which declares:

"Any prayer may be heard by the Higher Powers and a corresponding answer obtained only if it is uttered thrice:

Firstly—for the welfare or the peace of the souls of one's parents.

Secondly—for the welfare of one's neighbor.

And only thirdly—for oneself personally."

I find it necessary on the first page of this book, quite ready for publication, to
give the following advice:

"Read each of my written expositions thrice:

Firstly—at least as you have already become mechanized to read all your contemporary books and newspapers.

Secondly—as if you were reading aloud to another person.

And only thirdly—try and fathom the gist of my writings."

Only then will you be able to count upon forming your own impartial judgment,
proper to yourself alone, on my writings. And only then can my hope be actualized
that according to your understanding you will obtain the specific benefit for yourself which I anticipate, and which I wish for you with all my being.

AUTHOR

Contents

Contents

✻

FIRST BOOK

✻

*

FIRST BOOK

*

The Arousing of Thought

AMONG other convictions formed in my common presence during my re-sponsible, peculiarly composed life, there is one such also—an indubitable conviction—that always and everywhere on the earth, among people of every degree of development of understanding and of every form of manifestation of the factors which engender in their individuality all kinds of ideals, there is acquired the tendency, when beginning anything new, unfailingly to pronounce aloud or, if not aloud, at least mentally, that definite utterance understandable to every even quite illiterate person, which in different epochs has been formulated variously and in our day is formulated in the following words: "In the name of the Father and of the Son and in the name of the Holy Ghost. Amen."

That is why I now, also, setting forth on this venture quite new for me, namely, authorship, begin by pronouncing this utterance and moreover pronounce it not only aloud, but even very distinctly and with a full, as the ancient Toulousites defined it, "wholly-manifested intonation"—of course with that fullness which can arise in my entirety only from data already formed and thoroughly rooted in me for such a manifestation; data which are in general formed in the nature of man, by the way, during his preparatory age, and later, during his responsible life engender in him the ability for the manifestation of the nature and vivifyingness of such an intonation.

Having thus begun, I can now be quite at ease, and should even, according to the notions of religious morality existing among contemporary people, be beyond all doubt assured that everything further in this new venture of mine will now proceed, as is said, "like a pianola."

------------------------------ 3 ------------------------------

In any case I have begun just thus, and as to how the rest will go I can only say meanwhile, as the blind man once expressed it, "we shall see."

First and foremost, I shall place my own hand, moreover the right one, which—although at the moment it is slightly injured owing to the misfortune which recently befell me—is nevertheless really my own, and has never once failed me in all my life, on my heart, of course also my own—but on the inconstancy or constancy of this part of all my whole I do not find it necessary here to expatiate—and frankly confess that I myself have personally not the slightest wish to write, but attendant circumstances, quite independent of me, constrain me to do so—and whether these circumstances arose accidentally or were created intentionally by extraneous forces, I myself do not yet know. I know only that these circumstances bid me write not just anything "so-so," as, for instance, something of the kind for reading oneself to sleep, but weighty and bulky tomes.

However that may be, I begin . . .

But begin with what?

Oh, the devil! Will there indeed be repeated that same exceedingly unpleasant and highly strange sensation which it befell me to experience when about three

13

CHAPTER I

WARNING (Instead of a Preface)

EVERYWHERE on the Earth, before beginning anything new, it is customary first of all, to pronounce aloud, or, at least mentally, the following words understandable by every contemporary even quite illiterate person—namely:

"In the name of the Father and of His Son and in the name of that Holy Ghost who, if not understood by all ordinary mortals, is, at any rate, understood and beyond all doubt known by our priests and theologians.

That is why I also, setting out on this for me new venture, namely, authorship, begin with these same words and even pronounce them aloud very distinctly and with the proper intonation, with the intonation, of course, arising from the data crystallized in my common presence in the course of my life, those data, which, in general, engender in a man's Being, a quality of intonation manifest of the impulses of "faith," "doubt," "superstition" and so on.

"In the name of the Father and of the Son and of the Holy Ghost, Amen."

Having begun in this way, I ought to be quite assured and to be able to count without any essence anxiety, upon everything further now gliding along, as is said, "on-oil-to-an-Italian-hurdy-gurdy-accompaniment."

- -

I shall begin by placing my own hand—though somewhat injured through a misfortune which recently befell me, yet nevertheless indeed my own—upon my heart, of course also my own, and frankly confess that, for myself, I have not the slightest wish to write; but unfortunately for me, I am constrained to do so by surrounding circumstances, not dependent on my individuality, which have either arisen accidentally, or perhaps have been intentionally created by an outside force, and which constrain me to write not just "so-so" but "weighty-fat-tomes."

And so I begin. But how?

Just in this case, experienced people, "who-know-what's-what," always talk about "being-on-three-horns-of-a-dilemma."

weeks ago I was composing in my thoughts the scheme and sequence of the ideas destined by me for publication and did not know then how to begin either?

This sensation then experienced I might now formulate in words only thus: "the-fear-of-drowning-in-the-overflow-of-my-own-thoughts."

To stop this undesirable sensation I might then still have had recourse to the aid of that maleficent property existing also in me, as in contemporary man, which has become inherent in all of us, and which enables us, without

---------------------------------- 4 ----------------------------------

experiencing any remorse of conscience whatever, to put off anything we wish to do "till tomorrow."

I could then have done this very easily because before beginning the actual writing, it was assumed that there was still lots of time; but this can now no longer be done, and I must, without fail, as is said, "even though I burst," begin.

But with what indeed begin . . . ?

Hurrah! . . . Eureka!

Almost all the books I have happened to read in my life have begun with a preface.

So in this case I also must begin with something of the kind.

I say "of the kind," because in general in the process of my life, from the moment I began to distinguish a boy from a girl, I have always done everything, absolutely everything, not as it is done by other, like myself, biped destroyers of Nature's good. Therefore, in writing now I ought, and perhaps am even on principle already obliged, to begin not as any other writer would.

In any case, instead of the conventional preface I shall begin quite simply with a Warning.

Beginning with a Warning will be very judicious of me, if only because it will not contradict any of my principles, either organic, psychic, or even "willful," and will at the same time be quite honest—of course, honest in the objective sense, because both I myself and all others who know me well, expect with indubitable certainty that owing to my writings there will entirely disappear in the majority of readers, immediately and not gradually, as must sooner or later, with time, occur to all people, all the "wealth" they have, which was either handed down to them by inheritance or obtained by their own labor, in the form of quieting notions evoking only naive dreams,

---------------------------------- 5 ----------------------------------

and also beautiful representations of their lives at present as well as of their prospects in the future.

Professional writers usually begin such introductions with an address to the reader, full of all kinds of bombastically magniloquent and so to say "honeyed" and "inflated" phrases.

Just in this alone I shall follow their example and also begin with such an address, but I shall try not to make it very "sugary" as they usually do, owing particularly to their evil wiseacring by which they titillate the sensibilities of the more or less normal reader.

Thus . . .

Hurrah! Eureka!
Most of the books I have chanced to read in my life have begun with a preface.
So, I, too, shall begin with something of the kind.
I say "of-the-kind" because in the process of my life, I have so far in general
done absolutely everything not as other similar biped beings do, so that, in writing now, I must also begin not as any writer would.

In the present instance, instead of the required conventional preface, I shall begin quite simply with a Warning.
Beginning with a Warning will not only not be contrary to those of my already
thoroughly fixed principles which have now become, as it were, natural inherencies, but from my point of view—ensuing from the totality of those aims upon
which I intend to base my proposed writings—it will be more honest, of course,
in the objective sense.

Professional writers usually begin such introductions with an address to the
reader full of all kinds of "sugary," magniloquently bombastic what are called
"blown-up-phrases."
Just in this alone, I shall follow their example and also begin with an address,
but, of course, not with a very, as is said, "mellifluous" one, as they usually do.

Thus . . .

My dear, highly honored, strong-willed and of course very patient Sirs, and my much-esteemed, charming, and impartial Ladies—forgive me, I have omitted the most important—and my in no wise hysterical Ladies!

I have the honor to inform you that although owing to circumstances that have arisen at one of the last stages of the process of my life, I am now about to write books, yet during the whole of my life I have never written not only not books or various what are called "instructive-articles," but also not even a letter in which it has been unfailingly necessary to observe what is called "grammaticality," and in consequence, although I am now about to become a professional writer, yet having had no practice at all either in respect of all the established professional rules and procedures or in respect of what is called the "bon ton literary language," I am constrained to write not at all as ordinary "patented-writers" do, to the form of whose writing you have in all probability become as much accustomed as to your own smell.

In my opinion the trouble with you, in the present instance, is perhaps chiefly due to the fact that while still in childhood, there was implanted in you and has now become ideally well harmonized with your general psyche, an excellently working automatism for perceiving all kinds

————————————————————— 6 —————————————————————

of new impressions, thanks to which "blessing" you have now, during your responsible life, no need of making any individual effort whatsoever.

Speaking frankly, I inwardly personally discern the center of my confession not in my lack of knowledge of all the rules and procedures of writers, but in my non-possession of what I have called the "bon ton literary language," infallibly required in contemporary life not only from writers but also from every ordinary mortal.

As regards the former, that is to say, my lack of knowledge of the different rules and procedures of writers, I am not greatly disturbed.

And I am not greatly disturbed on this account, because such "ignorance" has already now become in the life of people also in the order of things. Such a blessing arose and now flourishes everywhere on Earth thanks to that extraordinary new disease of which for the last twenty to thirty years, for some reason or other, especially the majority of those persons from among all the three sexes fall ill, who sleep with half-open eyes and whose faces are in every respect fertile soil for the growth of every kind of pimple.

This strange disease is manifested by this, that if the invalid is somewhat literate and his rent is paid for three months in advance, he (she or it) unfailingly begins to write either some "instructive article" or a whole book.

Well knowing about this new human disease and its epidemical spread on Earth, I, as you should understand, have the right to assume that you have acquired, as the learned "medicos" would say, "immunity" to it, and that you will therefore not be palpably indignant at my ignorance of the rules and procedures of writers.

My dear, highly honored and very patient Sirs, and my highly respected, charming, and of course impartial ladies! Forgive me; I have omitted the most important—and my "in-no-wise-hysterical" Ladies!

I have the honor to inform you that although, with the help of my patron saints and by the permission of the local authorities, and also of course of my "merciless-domestic-tyrant"—a personality, that is, inevitably present in every contemporary household, who has automatically acquired power owing only to the abnormally established conditions of contemporary ordinary life—I am now about to write books, nevertheless, I have not only never during the whole of my life written either books or various what are called "informative-articles," but also never even a letter in which the rules of what is called "bon-ton-grammaticality," prevalent in contemporary civilization, should be observed; and having, in consequence of this, no practice at all in so to say "automatic-twaddle," therefore although I have now to become a writer, I am now in respect of all the accepted rules and procedures of professional writers and also in respect of what is called the "literary-language-of-the-intelligentsia" a complete as is said "booby," or as certain contemporary so-styled "well-read" people would call me, "an-ignoramus-on-the-zigzag-plane-squared"—in consequence of all which, I am not going

- -

to write at all like the "Patented-professional-writers," to whose form of writing you are undoubtedly already well accustomed; and I must add that of course in you also, an ideally well working automatism has already been acquired and permanently fixed for perceiving as well as for as is said "digesting," thanks to which "blessing" no individual effort whatsoever is ever required of you.

I particularly warn you about the latter, namely, what I have called the "literary-language-of-the-intelligentsia."

This understanding of mine bids me inwardly to make the center of gravity of my warning my ignorance of the literary language.

In self-justification, and also perhaps to diminish

--- 7 ---

the degree of the censure in your waking consciousness of my ignorance of this language indispensable for contemporary life, I consider it necessary to say, with a humble heart and cheeks flushed with shame, that although I too was taught this language in my childhood, and even though certain of my elders who prepared me for responsible life, constantly forced me "without sparing or economizing" any intimidatory means to "learn by rote" the host of various "nuances" which in their totality compose this contemporary "delight," yet, unfortunately of course for you, of all that I then learned by rote, nothing stuck and nothing whatsoever has survived for my present activities as a writer.

And nothing stuck, as it was quite recently made clear to me, not through any fault of mine, nor through the fault of my former respected and non-respected teachers, but this human labor was spent in vain owing to one unexpected and quite exceptional event which occurred at the moment of my appearance on God's Earth, and which was—as a certain occultist well known in Europe explained to me after a very minute what is called "psycho-physico-astrological" investigation—that at that moment, through the hole made in the windowpane by our crazy lame goat, there poured the vibrations of sound which arose in the neighbor's house from an Edison phonograph, and the midwife had in her mouth a lozenge saturated with cocaine of German make, and moreover not "Ersatz," and was sucking this lozenge to these sounds without the proper enjoyment.

Besides from this event, rare in the everyday life of people, my present position also arose because later on in my preparatory and adult life—as, I must confess, I myself guessed after long reflections according to the method of the German professor, Herr Stumpsinschmausen—I always avoided instinctively as well as

--- 8 ---

automatically and at times even consciously, that is, on principle, employing this language for intercourse with others. And from such a trifle, and perhaps not a trifle, I manifested thus again thanks to three data which were formed in my entirety during my preparatory age, about which data I intend to inform you a little later in this same first chapter of my writings.

However that may have been, yet the real fact, illuminated from every side like an American advertisement, and which fact cannot now be changed by any forces even with the knowledge of the experts in "monkey business," is that although I, who have lately been considered by very many people as a rather good teacher of temple dances, have now become today a professional writer and will of course write a great deal—as it has been proper to me since childhood whenever "I do anything to do a great deal of it"—nevertheless, not having, as you see, the automatically acquired and automatically manifested practice necessary for this, I shall be constrained to write all I have thought out in ordinary simple everyday language established by life, without any literary manipulations and without any "grammarian wiseacrings."

- -

Concerning this language it must be said that although I too was taught it in my childhood, and some of my elders who were preparing me for responsible life even constantly compelled me to "learn-by-rote" the multitude of various nuances which compose this "contemporary delight," yet unfortunately—in this case obviously for you—nothing of all I then learnt by rote stuck, and nothing now survives for my writing activities.

And according to the very minute investigations and elucidations of a meteorologist very well known at the present time on the continent of Europe, with whom I chanced to become what is called "bosom-friends" owing to frequent meetings in the nocturnal restaurants of Montmartre, it was not assimilated for the reason that even in my childhood my instinct already contained a certain, as he defined it, "something" which did not permit my Being to absorb this contemporary high-wisdom, and also because, owing to various fortuitous surrounding conditions of my later life, I neither automatically nor semiconsciously, nor even at times, I confess, on principle, that is to say, consciously, employed that language for intercourse with others.

- -

As a result of all this, esteemed buyer of my writings, though I now intend to become a professional writer, yet having, as you see, none of the mentioned "automatic experience" for it, I am already willy-nilly compelled to disregard—and if you like, I again confess, I will even, as if intentionally disregard—that language and write in the ordinary simple everyday language established by life, without any so-to-say "grammarian wiseacrings."

But the pot is not yet full! . . . For I have not yet decided the most important question of all—in which language to write.

Although I have begun to write in Russian, nevertheless, as the wisest of the wise, Mullah Nassr Eddin, would say, in that language you cannot go far.

(Mullah Nassr Eddin, or as he is also called, Hodja Nassr Eddin, is, it seems, little known in Europe and America, but he is very well known in all countries of the continent of Asia; this legendary personage corresponds to the American Uncle Sam or the German Till Eulenspiegel. Numerous tales popular in the East, akin to the wise sayings, some of long standing and others newly

- 9 -

arisen, were ascribed and are still ascribed to this Nassr Eddin.)

The Russian language, it cannot be denied, is very good. I even like it, but . . . only for swapping anecdotes and for use in referring to someone's parentage.

The Russian language is like the English, which language is also very good, but only for discussing in "smoking rooms," while sitting on an easy chair with legs outstretched on another, the topic of Australian frozen meat or, sometimes, the Indian question.

Both these languages are like the dish which is called in Moscow "Solianka," and into which everything goes except you and me, in fact everything you wish, and even the "after-dinner *Cheshma*"* of Scheherazade.

It must also be said that owing to all kinds of accidentally and perhaps not accidentally formed conditions of my youth, I have had to learn, and moreover very seriously and of course always with self-compulsion, to speak, read, and write a great many languages, and to such a degree of fluency, that if, in following this profession unexpectedly forced on me by Fate, I decided not to take advantage of the "automatism" which is acquired by practice, then I could perhaps write in any one of them.

But if I set out to use judiciously this automatically acquired automatism which has become easy from long practice, then I should have to write either in Russian or in Armenian, because the circumstances of my life during the last two or three decades have been such that I have had for intercourse with others to use, and consequently to have more practice in, just these two languages and to acquire an automatism in respect to them.

O the dickens! . . . Even in such a case, one of the aspects of my peculiar psyche, unusual for the normal man,

- 10 -

has now already begun to torment the whole of me.

And the chief reason for this unhappiness of mine in my almost already mellow age, results from the fact that since childhood there was implanted in my peculiar psyche, together with numerous other rubbish also unnecessary for contempor-

----

* *Chesma* means veil

But the pot is not yet full. For I have not yet decided the most important item of all—in which language to write.

Although I have begun to write in Russian, nevertheless as the wisest of the wise, Mullah Nassr Eddin would say, in that language "you-cannot-go-far."

I recalled this saying from among the many "infallible" and "indisputable" sayings of that, in my opinion, universal teacher, the wisest of all the terrestrial sages, one whom I particularly esteem, and one who, again, of course, in my opinion, ought to be esteemed and respected by everybody without exception—Mullah Nassr Eddin—and I have set it down at this point in my Warning, because of my

- -

proposed subsequent writings I intend often to touch upon philological questions also.

The said Russian language is, it cannot be denied, very good. I even like it, but . . . only for swapping anecdotes in the cooling room of that "Hamman" of mine, which I especially constructed on a spot in that place which by the Will of Fate has become my refuge, like a second "native-land."

The Russian language is like the English, which language is also very good . . . for discussing on the easy sofas of what are called "smoking-rooms," the topic of "Australian-frozen-meat" or, sometimes, the "Indian question."

Both these languages are like the dish which is called in Moscow "Solianka," into which everything goes, dear buyer of my wiseacring, except just you and me.

I think I might as well say here also that although the surrounding circumstances and conditions of my life during both my preparatory age and also my maturity have been such that I have had to speak, read and write in many languages, yet circumstances have so fallen out that in recent years I have had practice mostly in Russian and in Armenian.

- -

ary life, such an inherency as always and in everything automatically enjoins the whole of me to act only according to popular wisdom.

In the present case, as always in similar as yet indefinite life cases, there immediately comes to my brain—which is for me, constructed unsuccessfully to the point of mockery—and is now as is said, "running through" it that saying of popular wisdom which existed in the life of people of very ancient times, and which has been handed down to our day formulated in the following words: "every stick always has two ends."

In trying first to understand the basic thought and real significance hidden in this strange verbal formulation, there must, in my opinion, first of all arise in the consciousness of every more or less sane-thinking man the supposition that, in the totality of ideas on which is based and from which must flow a sensible notion of this saying, lies the truth, cognized by people for centuries, which affirms that every cause occurring in the life of man, from whatever phenomenon it arises, as one of two opposite effects of other causes, is in its turn obligatorily molded also into two quite opposite effects, as for instance: if "something" obtained from two different causes engenders light, then it must inevitably engender a phenomenon opposite to it, that is to say, darkness; or a factor engendering in the organism of a living creature an impulse of palpable satisfaction also engenders without fail non-satisfaction, of course also palpable, and so on and so forth, always and in everything.

Adopting in the same given instance this popular wisdom

---------------------------------- *11* ----------------------------------

formed by centuries and expressed by a stick, which, as was said, indeed has two ends, one end of which is considered good and the other bad, then if I use the aforesaid automatism which was acquired in me thanks only to long practice, it will be for me personally of course very good, but according to this saying, there must result for the reader just the opposite; and what the opposite of good is, even every non-possessor of hemorrhoids must very easily understand.

Briefly, if I exercise my privilege and take the good end of the stick, then the bad end must inevitably fall "on the reader's head."

This may indeed happen, because in Russian the so to say "niceties" of philosophical questions cannot be expressed, which questions I intend to touch upon in my writings also rather fully, whereas in Armenian, although this is possible, yet to the misfortune of all contemporary Armenians, the employment of this language for contemporary notions has now already become quite impracticable.

In order to alleviate the bitterness of my inner hurt owing to this, I must say that in my early youth, when I became interested in and was greatly taken up with philological questions, I preferred the Armenian language to all others I then spoke, even to my native language.

This language was then my favorite chiefly because it was original and had nothing in common with the neighboring or kindred languages.

As the learned "philologists" say, all of its tonalities were peculiar to it alone, and according to my understanding even then, it corresponded perfectly to the

- -

I can now write in either of these languages with ease, but to my pained regret, the niceties of philosophical questions cannot be expressed in Russian, while, to the misfortune to all contemporary Armenians, although this is possible in Armenian, it has now become quite impossible to employ that language for contemporary questions.

In my early youth, when I first became interested in and was much absorbed in philological questions, I preferred the Armenian language above all others I spoke.

This language was then my favorite chiefly because it was original and had nothing in common with the neighboring languages, of which there is today an innumerable host.

All of its tonalities were peculiar to it alone, and according to my understanding then, based of course, as is characteristic of young people who have not yet

psyche of the people composing that nation.

But the change I have witnessed in that language during the last thirty or forty years has been such, that instead of an original independent language coming to us from the remote past, there has resulted and now exists one,

------------------------------ *12* ------------------------------

which though also original and independent, yet represents, as might be said, a "kind of clownish potpourri of languages," the totality of the consonances of which, falling on the ear of a more or less conscious and understanding listener, sounds just like the "tones" of Turkish, Persian, French, Kurd, and Russian words and still other "indigestible" and inarticulate noises.

Almost the same might be said about my native language, Greek, which I spoke in childhood and, as might be said, the "taste of the automatic associative power of which" I still retain. I could now, I dare say, express anything I wish in it, but to employ it for writing is for me impossible, for the simple and rather comical reason that someone must transcribe my writings and translate them into the other languages. And who can do this?

It could assuredly be said that even the best expert of modern Greek would understand simply nothing of what I should write in the native language I assimilated in childhood, because, my dear "compatriots," as they might be called, being also inflamed with the wish at all costs to be like the representatives of contemporary civilization also in their conversation, have during these thirty or forty years treated my dear native language just as the Armenians, anxious to become Russian intelligentsia, have treated theirs.

That Greek language, the spirit and essence of which were transmitted to me by heredity, and the language now spoken by contemporary Greeks, are as much alike as, according to the expression of Mullah Nassr Eddin, "a nail is like a requiem."

What is now to be done?

Ah . . . me! Never mind, esteemed buyer of my wiseacrings. If only there be plenty of French armagnac and "Khaizarian bastourma," I shall find a way out of even this difficult situation.

------------------------------ *13* ------------------------------

I am an old hand at this.

In life, I have so often got into difficult situations and out of them, that this has become almost a matter of habit for me.

Meanwhile in the present case, I shall write partly in Russian and partly in Armenian, the more readily because among those people always "hanging around" me there are several who "cerebrate" more or less easily in both these languages, and I meanwhile entertain the hope that they will be able to transcribe and translate from these languages fairly well for me.

In any case I again repeat—in order that you should well remember it, but not as you are in the habit of remembering other things and on the basis of which are accustomed to keeping your word of honor to others or to yourself—that no mat-

tasted the "delights-of-life," upon the impulses of "self-imagining," "self-enthus-ing," "self-puffing-up" and so on, it responded perfectly to the psyche of the people composing that nation.

But I have witnessed during the last thirty or forty years, such a change in that language, that instead of an original independent language, there has resulted and now exists—although similarly original and independent—what might be

defined as a "kind-of-motley-pot-pourri-of-languages," the totality of whose con-sonances, falling on the ear of a more or less conscious listener, rings just like the tones of Turkish, Persian, Kurd, French and Russian words, together with various other completely "indigestible" inarticulate noises.

As for my native language, namely, the Greek which I spoke in childhood, and as might be said, the "taste-of-the-automatic-associative-power-of-which" I still retain, I could now, I dare say, express anything I wish in it, but I cannot employ it for writing, for the following for me very serious reasons.

For must not someone transcribe my writings and translate them into the lan-guage I desire? And who can do this?

Even the most learned-philologist of modern Greek would understand simply nothing of what I should write in the native language I assimilated in childhood, because my dear compatriots being also inflamed with the wish at all costs to be like the representatives of contemporary civilization also in their conversation have, as a consequence, in the mentioned flow of time, treated my dear native lan-guage just as the Armenians, anxious to become Russian intelligentsia, have treated theirs.

That Greek language, the spirit and essence of which were transmitted to me by heredity, and the language now spoken by contemporary Greeks, are as much alike, as, according to the expression of Mullah Nassr Eddin, "a-nail-is-like-a-re-quiem."

What is to be done?

Eh . . . Eh . . . Ekh! Never mind, esteemed buyer of my writings.

If only there be plenty of French "Armagnac" and "Khaizarian-basturma"—I shall find a way out of even this difficult situation.

I am an old hand at this!

During the period of the process of my life, I have so many times got into difficult situations and out of them, that this has for me become almost a matter of habit.

In the present case, I shall meanwhile write partly in Russian and partly, where it is necessary, so to say, to "philosophize," in Armenian, the more readily because there are people near to me and always at hand who "cerebrate" more or less in both languages, and I entertain the hope that they will be able to transcribe and translate from these languages fairly well for me.

But, of course, whatever language I use, you must know that I shall always dis-regard the aforesaid "bon-ton-language."

ter what language I shall use, always and in everything, I shall avoid what I have called the "bon ton literary language."

In this respect, the extraordinarily curious fact and one even in the highest degree worthy of your love of knowledge, perhaps even higher than your usual conception, is that from my earliest childhood, that is to say, since the birth in me of the need to destroy birds' nests, and to tease my friends' sisters, there arose in my, as the ancient theosophists called it, "planetary body," and moreover, why I don't know, chiefly in the "right half," an instinctively involuntary sensation, which right up to that period of my life when I became a teacher of dancing, was gradually formed into a definite feeling, and then, when thanks to this profession of mine I came in contact with many people of different "types," there began to arise in me also the conviction with what is called my "mind," that these languages are compiled by people, or rather "grammarians," who are in respect of knowledge of the given language exactly similar to those biped animals whom

—————————————————————— *14* ——————————————————————

the esteemed Mullah Nassr Eddin characterizes by the words: "All they can do is to wrangle with pigs about the quality of oranges."

This kind of people among us who have been turned into, so to say, "moths" destroying the good prepared and left for us by our ancestors and by time, have not the slightest notion and have probably never even heard of the screamingly obvious fact that, during the preparatory age, there is acquired in the brain functioning of every creature, and of man also, a particular and definite property, the automatic actualization and manifestation of which the ancient Korkolans called the "law of association," and that the process of the mentation of every creature, especially man, flows exclusively in accordance with this law.

In view of the fact that I have happened here accidentally to touch upon a question which has lately become one of my so to speak "hobbies," namely, the process of human mentation, I consider it possible, without waiting for the corresponding place predetermined by me for the elucidation of this question, to state already now in this first chapter at least something concerning that axiom which has accidentally become known to me, that on Earth in the past it has been usual in every century that every man, in whom there arises the boldness to attain the right to be considered by others and to consider himself a "conscious thinker," should be informed while still in the early years of his responsible existence that man has in general two kinds of mentation: one kind, mentation by thought, in which words, always possessing a relative sense, are employed; and the other kind, which is proper to all animals as well as to man, which I would call "mentation by form."

The second kind of mentation, that is, "mentation by form," by which, strictly speaking, the exact sense of all

—————————————————————— *15* ——————————————————————

writing must be also perceived, and after conscious confrontation with information already possessed, be assimilated, is formed in people in dependence upon the conditions of geographical locality, climate, time, and, in general, upon the whole environment in which the arising of the given man has proceeded and in

Why from my earliest childhood I have always disliked this "language-of-the-intelligentsia" I do not know—apparently simply because at the moment of my appearance here below there was being played in our neighbor's house a "phonograph" and at the same time the "midwife" had in her mouth a lozenge dipped in cocaine.

While still a youth, I felt that the whole of my, as the ancient Theosophists called it, "planetary-body," and moreover—why I don't know—chiefly with the right-half, and in later years—particularly when I became a "teacher-of-dancing" and came in contact with people of different "types"—I became gradually convinced of it also with my what is called "mind,"—that the so-styled "grammar" of any language is compiled by people who not only in respect of knowledge of the given language are those biped "somethings" which His Uniqueness Mullah Nassr

Eddin characterizes by the words "all-they-can-do-is-to-wrangle-with-pigs-about-the-quality-of-oranges," but, who furthermore, have not even any approximate representation of the screamingly obvious fact that during the preparatory age there is required in the brain-functioning of every creature, and, of man, of course, also, a particular and definite property, the automatic actualization and manifestation of which the ancient Korkolans called the "law-of-association," and that the process of the mentation of every "life," including the "life" of man, proceeds exclusively in accordance with this law.

From the very beginning on the Earth it has become usual that every man who, so to say, "devotes-himself-to-the-field-of-a-conscious-thinker" should be well informed while still in the early years of his responsible existence, that man has in general two kinds of mentation; one kind, by thoughts, for the expression of which, subjective words, possessing always a relative sense, are employed; and another kind, proper to man as well as to all animals, called by those same ancient Korkolans "mentation-by-form."

The second kind of mentation, by which, strictly speaking, the exact sense of all

writing must also be perceived, is formed in dependence upon the conditions of geographical locality, climate, time and, in general, upon the whole environment in which the arising of the given man has proceeded and in which his existence has flowed up to maturity.

which his existence has flowed up to manhood.

Accordingly, in the brains of people of different races and conditions dwelling in different geographical localities, there are formed about one and the same thing or even idea, a number of quite independent forms, which during functioning, that is to say, association, evoke in their being some sensation or other which subjectively conditions a definite picturing, and which picturing is expressed by this, that, or the other word, that serves only for its outer subjective expression.

That is why each word, for the same thing or idea, almost always acquires for people of different geographical locality and race a very definite and entirely different so to say "inner content."

In other words, if in the entirety of any man who has arisen and been formed in any locality, from the results of the specific local influences and impressions a certain "form" has been composed, and this form evokes in him by association the sensation of a definite "inner content," and consequently of a definite picturing or notion for the expression of which he employs one or another word which has eventually become habitual, and as I have said, subjective to him, then the hearer of that word, in whose being, owing to different conditions of his arising and growth, there has been formed concerning the given word a form of a different "inner content," will always perceive and of course infallibly understand that same word in quite another sense.

This fact, by the way, can with attentive and impartial

- *16* -

observation be very clearly established when one is present at an exchange of opinions between persons belonging to two different races or who arose and were formed in different geographical localities.

And so, cheerful and swaggering candidate for a buyer of my wiseacrings, having warned you that I am going to write not as "professional writers" usually write but quite otherwise, I advise you, before embarking on the reading of my further expositions, to reflect seriously and only then to undertake it. If not, I am afraid for your hearing and other perceptive and also digestive organs which may be already so thoroughly automatized to the "literary language of the intelligentsia" existing in the present period of time on Earth, that the reading of these writings of mine might affect you very, very cacophonously, and from this you might lose your . . . you know what? . . . your appetite for your favorite dish and for your psychic specificness which particularly titillates your "inside" and which proceeds in you on seeing your neighbor, the brunette.

For such a possibility, ensuing from my language, or rather, strictly speaking, from the form of my mentation, I am, thanks to oft-repeated past experiences, already quite as convinced with my whole being as a "thoroughbred donkey" is convinced of the right and justice of his obstinacy.

Now that I have warned you of what is most important, I am already tranquil about everything further. Even if any misunderstanding should arise on account of my writings, you alone will be entirely to blame, and my conscience will be as clear as for instance . . . the ex-Kaiser Wilhelm's.

Accordingly, in the brains of people of different geographical localities, different races and different conditions, there are formed about one and the same thing or idea, a number of quite independent forms, which in their association evoke in a being some sensation or other which in turn conditions a picturing, and which picturings in their turn are expressed by this, that or the other word that serves for their outer expression.

That is why each word, for the same thing or idea, almost always acquires for people of varying geographical locality and race, entirely different so to say "inner-content."

In other words, suppose that in the common presence of some given man who has arisen and been formed in any given locality, a certain "form" has been crystallized from the results of specific local influences and impressions, and that this form evokes in him by association the sensation of a definite "inner-content" and consequently of a definite image or notion, and he should then employ for the expression of this image or notion some word which has eventually become habitual and subjective to him, then, the hearer of that word—in whose being, owing to the quite other conditions of his arising and formation, there has been crystallized concerning the given word, quite another form of data for the mentioned "inner-content"—will in consequence always perceive and inevitably understand that same word in quite another sense.

This fact, by the way, can with attentive and impartial

- -

observation be very clearly constated when one is present at an exchange of opinions between persons belonging to different nations.

And so, esteemed buyer of my writings, I warn you that I am going to write not as "professional-writers" usually write, but quite otherwise. So before embarking on the reading of my further "wiseacrings," first reflect seriously, and only then undertake it. Maybe your hearing and other perceptive organs are already so thoroughly automatized to the "literary-language-of-the-intelligentsia," that the reading of these writings of mine might affect you frightfully cacophonously, as a result of which you might lose your . . . you know what? . . . your relish for your favorite dish.

I consider it my duty to say, that thanks to oft-repeated past experiences, I am already quite as convinced with my whole being of this possibility ensuing from my language or rather from the form of my mentation, as a "thoroughbred-donkey" is convinced of the right and justice of his obstinacy.

Now that I have given you warning of the most important thing, I am already tranquil about everything further, because if any misunderstanding should arise on account of my writings, you alone will be entirely to blame, and my own conscience will be as clear as the Ex-Kaiser Wilhelm's.

In all probability you are now thinking that I am, of course, a young man with an auspicious exterior and, as some express it, a "suspicious interior," and that, as a

novice in writing, I am evidently intentionally being eccentric in the hope of becoming famous and thereby rich.

If you indeed think so, then you are very, very mistaken.

First of all, I am not young; I have already lived so much that I have been in my life, as it is said, "not only through the mill but through all the grindstones"; and secondly, I am in general not writing so as to make a career for myself, or so as to plant myself, as is said, "firm-footedly," thanks to this profession, which, I must add, in my opinion provides many openings to become a candidate d-i-r-e-c-t for "Hell"—assuming of course that such people can in general by their Being, perfect themselves even to that extent, for the reason that knowing nothing whatsoever themselves, they write all kinds of "claptrap" and thereby automatically acquiring authority, they become almost one of the chief factors, the totality of which steadily continues year by year, still further to diminish the, without this, already extremely diminished psyche of people.

And as regards my personal career, then thanks to all forces high and low and, if you like, even right and left, I have actualized it long ago, and have already long been standing on "firm feet" and even maybe on very good feet, and I moreover am certain that their strength is sufficient for many more years, in spite of all my past, present, and future enemies.

Yes, I think you might as well be told also about an idea which has only just arisen in my madcap brain, and namely, specially to request the printer, to whom I shall give my first book, to print this first chapter of my writings in such a way that anybody may read it before cutting the pages of the book itself, whereupon, on learning that it is not written in the usual manner, that is to say, for helping to produce in one's mentation, very smoothly and easily, exciting images and lulling reveries, he may, if he wishes,

without wasting words with the bookseller, return it and get his money back, money perhaps earned by the sweat of his own brow.

In all probability you are now thinking that, as a novice in writing, I am obviously trying to be eccentric, in the hope of becoming famous and thereby rich.

And of course you also think that I am a young man with a pleasing exterior and, as some express it, "suspicious-interior."

If you indeed think so, then you are mightily mistaken.

First of all, I am not young. I have already lived so much that I have been through even more than one mill in my life; and secondly, I am not trying to be eccentric nor do I intend to make my career or to plant myself in this profession—a profession which, I must add, in my opinion provides many opportunities for candidates d.i.r.e.c.t. . . . for "Hell," assuming of course, that such people can in general by their Being perfect themselves to that extent—for the reason that knowing nothing whatsoever themselves, they write all kinds of "claptrap," and acquiring authority thereby, they become, of course unconsciously, what are called "automatically-working-factors" for the diminution of the without this already sufficiently diminished psyche of those around them.

And as regards my personal career, then thanks to all forces high and low and, if you like, even right and left, I have actualized it long ago, and have already long been standing on "firm-feet," and maybe on very good feet; and moreover, I am certain that their strength is sufficient for many more years, in spite of all my past and future enemies.

But enough of trifling, old fellow, one must write.

Yes . . . I think you might as well be told also about an idea which has only arisen in my brain, and namely, specially to request the printers, to whom I shall give my first book, to print this warning on the opening pages so that anybody may read it before cutting the pages of the book itself, whereupon, on learning that it is not written in the "language-of-the-intelligentsia," he may if he likes,

without wasting words with the bookseller, return it and get his money back, which perhaps he has earned by the sweat of his brow.

While writing and cogitating how to explain this idea to Mr. Printer, there arose unsought in this madcap brain of mine, another idea quite disadvantageous for me personally, namely, the idea to be sure to assign a definite sum of money for the misunderstandings which may arise when the uncut books are returned to the bookseller.

The disadvantage to myself in this idea which has spontaneously arisen in my madcap brain consists chiefly in this; that I shall be forced to take this money from a fund, dependent solely on my own will, free from the advice or disagreement of others, misbegotten busybodies, always around me, and, namely, from what is called my "Crayfish-fund."

Now that I happen to be speaking of this fund of mine, which depends solely on my independent will, objective justice demands that I should not fail, first of

all, to praise and extol with an impulse of great affection and sentiment the names of the noble "Uncle Sam" and "John Bull," and then, with an impulse of gratitude, to remark that during several years, genuine sprigs of those names I have just extolled, who for various objective merits have become worthy to rank as "Crayfish-idiots," have hitherto always punctually and even with unction kept supplied and so far still supply this solitary hearth of my, so to say, hopes and expectations.

It must be allowed that by reducing the number of my so to say "crayfish-parasites," who have become indispensable assistants in what has lately become, as it were, a necessity for my recreation, I ought to be able also to provide that sum of money from this fund, but owing to that specific and moreover terrible disease, always chronic and, lately, on the increase among the poor and wretched money-changers, which disease has become well known on the Earth under the description of being "hell-bent," not even such a self-deprivation can save me, because on account of this terrible disease, it has already now become extremely difficult for me to make both ends meet.

Eh . . . Ekh! . . . unfortunate me, hapless victim of a combination of planetary influences at the moment of my appearance here below!

This time also it is already beyond doubt—as it has happened to me many a time before my arrival in Europe—that on account of this altruistic intention which spontaneously arose in me, all the rest of the parts of my entire whole will once again "totally-unexpectedly" be made the "scapegoats."

It has always been so; no sooner does an idea arise in my madcap brain, but it inexorably compels the whole of me to carry it out at any cost, as for instance in the present case, to assign without fail the said sum of money, when, in fact, I have none, nor are there in sight any likely "fat-sheep-for-shearing."

The data engendering just this feature of my character, on account of which on all occasions, all kinds of factors for the formation of diverse for me personally "indigestible-consequences" always arise, were crystallized in my common presence from an impression perceived by me in my early youth, thanks to a story I heard about what happened to a certain "Transcaucasian Kurd."

Of course I must not fail to confess here, that it was only recently that I made clear to my pure Reason when precisely these data for my psyche were formed in me and all the details of their crystallization—that is to say, it was only after I had forced myself to spend a certain time punctiliously following all the indications of the Yogis and after I had later thoroughly studied from all sides that perfectly bewitching branch of "contemporary science" now existing everywhere under the name of "Psycho-analysis."

These specific data together with other similar data which constitute and manifest my present individuality, and which had in their formation decidedly nothing issuing from my essence and which were crystallized in my common presence owing only to various fortuitous surrounding conditions of my life, not only became thereafter, for the whole of me for the rest of my life, almost the dominant what is called "initiating-factor" in the begetting of always the same "indigestible consequences," but also, during their, as the learned psychiatrists would say, "gravity-center-functioning," which proceeds in general under the influence of a

I shall do this without fail, moreover, because I just now again remember the story of what happened to a Transcaucasian Kurd, which story I heard in my quite early youth and which in subsequent years, whenever I recalled it in corresponding cases, engendered in me an enduring and inextinguishable impulse of tenderness. I think it will be very useful for me, and also for you, if I relate this story to you somewhat in detail.

It will be useful chiefly because I have decided already to make the "salt," or as contemporary pureblooded Jewish businessmen would say, the "Tzimus" of this story, one of the basic principles of that new literary form which I intend to employ for the attainment of the aim I am now pursuing by means of this new profession of mine.

This Transcaucasian Kurd once set out from his village on some business or other to town, and there in the market he saw in a fruiterer's shop a handsomely arranged display of all kinds of fruit.

In this display, he noticed one "fruit," very beautiful in both color and form, and its appearance so took his fancy and he so longed to try it, that in spite of his having scarcely any money, he decided to buy without fail at least one of these gifts of Great Nature, and taste it.

Then, with intense eagerness, and with a courage not customary to him, he entered the shop and pointing with his horny finger to the "fruit" which had taken his fancy he asked the shopkeeper its price. The shopkeeper replied that a pound of the "fruit" would cost two cents.

Finding that the price was not at all high for what in his opinion was such a beautiful fruit, our Kurd decided to buy a whole pound.

------------------------------ *19* ------------------------------

Having finished his business in town, he set off again on foot for home the same day.

Walking at sunset over the hills and dales, and willy-nilly perceiving the exterior visibility of those enchanting parts of the bosom of Great Nature, the Common Mother, and involuntarily inhaling a pure air uncontaminated by the usual exhalations of industrial towns, our Kurd quite naturally suddenly felt a wish to

corresponding association, they evoke in me almost every time the experiencings called in ancient Indian philosophy "commiseration-with-impartial-affection."

Thanks to this feature of my character, on account of which especially in recent years, I find myself already quite incapable of refraining from actualizing in practice every idea, however personally disadvantageous to me, so in this case also, the whole of my common presence will be inexorably compelled to follow this solicitous procedure, merely in order to caution you, just you a person wholly alien to me, against falling a victim to cunning through the effect upon you of the usual "honeyed-words" of the bookseller; I repeat that I do this in spite of the fact that this measure, as you see for yourselves will mean a considerable loss for me personally.

To fret about it now and to think up some measure less detrimental for me, it is already too late.

So it pleases Fate.

But meanwhile, I think it will not be useless and may perhaps be productive for me as well as instructive for you, if I relate to you somewhat in detail the story of what happened to the mentioned Transcaucasian Kurd.

And it may be productive for me and instructive for you because I have already categorically decided to make use in my proposed writings of the very "Tzimmuss" of this story also for the actualization of the aims I have in view.

This Transcaucasian Kurd once set out from his village on some business or other to town, and there in the market he saw in a fruiterer's shop, a handsomely arranged display of all kinds of fruit.

In this display he noticed one fruit, very beautiful in both color and form, and its appearance so took his fancy and he so longed to try it, that, in spite of his having scarcely any money, he decided that he couldn't not buy at least just one of these fruits, and try it.

With intense eagerness and with an audacity not common to him, he entered the shop and pointing with his horny finger at the fruit which had taken his fancy, he asked the shopkeeper its price.

The shopkeeper replied that a pound of the fruit would cost "six-groschen."

Finding that this price was not at all high, our Kurd decided to buy a whole pound.

Having finished his business in town, he set off for home the same day.

Walking at sunset over the hills and dales, and perceiving the exterior visibility of those enchanting scenes of the bosom of Great Nature, the common mother, and there inhaling a pure air uncontaminated by the usual exhalations of industrial towns, our Kurd quite naturally suddenly felt a wish to gratify himself with gratify himself with some ordinary food also; so sitting down by the side of the road, he took from his provision bag some bread and the "fruit" he had bought which had looked so good to him, and leisurely began to eat.

But . . . horror of horrors! . . . very soon everything inside him began to burn. But in spite of this he kept on eating.

And this hapless biped creature of our planet kept on eating, thanks only to that particular human inherency which I mentioned at first, the principle of which I intended, when I decided to use it as the foundation of the new literary form I have created, to make, as it were, a "guiding beacon" leading me to one of my aims in view, and the sense and meaning of which moreover you will, I am sure, soon grasp—of course according to the degree of your comprehension—during the reading of any subsequent chapter of my writings, if, of course, you take the risk and read further, or, it may perhaps be that even at the end of this first chapter you will already "smell" something.

And so, just at the moment when our Kurd was overwhelmed by all the unusual sensations proceeding within him from this strange repast on the bosom of Nature, there came along the same road a fellow villager of his, one reputed by those who knew him to be very clever and experienced; and, seeing that the whole face of the Kurd was aflame, that his eyes were streaming with tears, and

-------------------------------- 20 --------------------------------

that in spite of this, as if intent upon the fulfillment of his most important duty, he was eating real "red pepper pods," he said to him:

"What are you doing, you Jericho jackass? You'll be burnt alive! Stop eating that extraordinary product, so unaccustomed for your nature."

But our Kurd replied: "No, for nothing on Earth will I stop. Didn't I pay my last two cents for them? Even if my soul departs from my body I shall still go on eating."

Whereupon our resolute Kurd—it must of course be assumed that he was such—did not stop, but continued eating the "red pepper pods."

After what you have just perceived, I hope there may already be arising in your mentation a corresponding mental association which should, as a result, effectuate in you, as it sometimes happens to contemporary people, that which you call, in general, understanding, and that in the present case you will understand just why I, well knowing and having many a time commiserated with this human inherency, the inevitable manifestation of which is that if anybody pays money for something, he is bound to use it to the end, was animated in the whole of my en-

some ordinary food also; so sitting down by the side of the road he took from his provision-bag some bread and fruit he had brought that had looked so good to him and began to eat.

But ... oh horror! ... very soon, everything inside him began to burn.

But in spite of this he kept on eating.

And this hapless biped creature of our planet kept on eating only thanks to that same particular human inherency which I first mentioned, and which was just what I had in view when I began to relate the present story, and the sense and meaning of which moreover you will, I am sure soon grasp—of course, according to the degree of your resourcefulness—during the reading of any subsequent chapter of my writings, assuming, of course, that you take the risk and read further, or, it may perhaps be that you will even already "smell" something at the end of this warning of mine.

Meanwhile I boldly or, if you like, impudently, take it upon myself in advance to advise you to absorb with, as might be said, an "intensive-mobilization" of all your perceptive organs, the information elaborating the rest of this story, in order that the crystallization in you of the new impression may proceed normally and not in the manner in which it has already become habitual for this to proceed, that is to say, as the great sage Mullah Nassr Eddin defines and expresses it:

"One part is used up for one's own welfare, and that only for today, while all the rest going in at one ear, is exhausted in the process of trying to get out at the other."

Well then, just at the moment when our Kurd was overwhelmed by all the unusual sensations proceeding within him from this strange repast on the bosom of Nature, there came along the same road a fellow-villager of his, once reputed by those who knew him to be very clever and experienced; and seeing that the whole face of our Kurd was aflame, that his eyes were streaming with tears, and that in

spite of this, as if intent upon the fulfilment of his most important duty, he was eating real "red-pepper-pods," he said to him:

"What are you doing, you jackass! You'll be burnt alive! Stop eating that extraordinary and, for your nature, unaccustomed product."

But our Kurd replied:

"No, not for anything on Earth will I stop. Didn't I pay my last 'six-groschen' for them? Even if my soul leaves my body, I shall go on eating."

Whereupon our resolute Kurd—it must, of course, be assumed that he was such—did not stop, but continued eating the "red-pepper-pods."

After what you have just perceived, esteemed buyer of my writings, I hope—of course only faintly—that there may already be arising in your mentation a corresponding association which should, as a result, bring about as it happens sometimes to some people, what you call an understanding, and that in the present case you will understand just why I, well knowing and having many a time commiserated with this human inherency—whose inevitable manifestation takes the form that if anybody pays money for something he is bound to use it to the end—

tirety with the idea, arisen in my mentation, to take every possible measure in order that you, as is said "my brother in appetite and in spirit"—in the event of your proving to be already accustomed to reading books, though of all kinds, yet nevertheless only those written exclusively in the aforesaid "language of the intelligentsia"—having already paid money for my writings and learning only afterwards that they are not written in the usual convenient and easily read language, should not be compelled as a consequence of the said human inherency, to read my writings through to the end at all costs, as our poor Transcaucasian Kurd was compelled to go on with his eating of what he had

- *21* -

fancied for its appearance alone—that "not to be joked with" noble red pepper.

And so, for the purpose of avoiding any misunderstanding through this inherency, the data for which are formed in the entirety of contemporary man, thanks evidently to his frequenting of the cinema and thanks also to his never missing an opportunity of looking into the left eye of the other sex, I wish that this commencing chapter of mine should be printed in the said manner, so that everyone can read it through without cutting the pages of the book itself.

Otherwise the bookseller will, as is said, "cavil," and will without fail again turn out to act in accordance with the basic principle of booksellers in general, formulated by them in the words: "You'll be more of a simpleton than a fisherman if you let go of the fish which has swallowed the bait," and will decline to take back a book whose pages you have cut. I have no doubt of this possibility; indeed, I fully expect such lack of conscience on the part of the booksellers.

And the data for the engendering of my certainty as to this lack of conscience on the part of these booksellers were completely formed in me, when, while I was a professional "Indian Fakir," I needed, for the complete elucidation of a certain "ultra-philosophical" question also to become familiar, among other things, with the associative process for the manifestation of the automatically constructed psyche of contemporary booksellers and of their salesmen when palming off books on their buyers.

Knowing all this and having become, since the misfortune which befell me, habitually just and fastidious in the extreme, I cannot help repeating, or rather, I cannot help again warning you, and even imploringly advising you, before beginning to cut the pages of this first book of mine, to read through very attentively, and even more than once, this first chapter of my writings.

- *22* -

But in the event that notwithstanding this warning of mine, you should, nevertheless, wish to become acquainted with the further contents of my expositions, then there is already nothing else left for me to do but to wish you with all my "genuine soul" a very, very good appetite, and that you may "digest" all that you read, not only for your own health but for the health of all those near you.

I said "with my genuine soul" because recently living in Europe and coming in frequent contact with people who on every appropriate and inappropriate occa-

was seized with the idea, to take every possible measure in order that you, my "neighbor"—in the event that you should prove to be already accustomed to reading books, though of any kind yet nevertheless only those written exclusively in the mentioned "language-of-the-intelligentsia"—having already paid money for my writings and learning only afterwards that they are not written in the usual easily and comfortably read language, should not be compelled, as a consequence of the said human inherency, to read my writings through to the end at all costs, as our poor Transcaucasian Kurd was compelled to continue eating what he had taken a

- -

fancy to from its appearance alone—that "not-to-be-joked-with" noble "red-pepper."

For the purpose of avoiding any misunderstanding through this inherency in man, I wish that this warning of mine may be printed in the said manner, so that everyone can read it through without cutting the pages of the book itself.

Otherwise I am very much afraid that the bookseller may, in that case also, try to make a profit for himself and decline to take back a book whose pages had once been cut.

I have no doubt of this possibility, and I fully expect such unconscionableness on their part.

And the data for the engendering of my certainty as to their unconscionableness were acquired in me just when, while I was a professional "Indian-fakir," I happened to become familiar also with, among other things the various aspects of the psyche of contemporary booksellers and particularly with that of their clerks when palming off books on their buyers, and now, having become, since the misfortune which befell me, by nature just, in the maximum degree, I cannot help repeating, that is to say, I cannot help again warning you and even imploringly advising you before beginning to cut the pages of my first book, to read through very attentively and even more than once this Warning of mine.

- -

But in case you decide and notwithstanding this Warning of mine, should wish to become acquainted with the further contents of my "wiseacrings," then there is already nothing else left for me to do but to wish you with all my genuine soul an excellent appetite, and that you may "digest" all that you may read not only for your own health, but also for the health of all those near to you.

I say with my "genuine-soul" because it is a habit of mine to refer often to what is called my "English-soul"; but why it is a habit of mine, I suggest that you puzzle

sion are fond of taking in vain every sacred name which should belong only to man's inner life, that is to say, with people who swear to no purpose, I being, as I have already confessed, a follower in general not only of the theoretical—as contemporary people have become—but also of the practical sayings of popular wisdom which have become fixed by the centuries, and therefore of the saying which in the present case corresponds to what is expressed by the words: "When you are in Rome do as Rome does," decided, in order not to be out of harmony with the custom established here in Europe of swearing in ordinary conversation, and at the same time to act according to the commandment which was enunciated by the holy lips of Saint Moses "not to take the holy names in vain," to make use of one of those examples of the "newly baked" fashionable languages of the present time, namely English, and so from then on, I began on necessary occasions to swear by my "English soul."

The point is that in this fashionable language, the words "soul" and the bottom of your foot, also called "sole," are pronounced and even written almost alike.

I do not know how it is with you, who are already partly candidate for a buyer of my writings, but my peculiar nature cannot, even with a great mental desire, avoid being indignant at the fact manifested by people

of contemporary civilization, that the very highest in man, particularly beloved by our COMMON FATHER CREATOR, can really be named, and indeed very often before even having made clear to oneself what it is, can be understood to be that which is lowest and dirtiest in man.

Well, enough of "philologizing." Let us return to the main task of this initial chapter, destined, among other things, on the one hand to stir up the drowsy thoughts in me as well as in the reader, and, on the other, to warn the reader about something.

And so, I have already composed in my head the plan and sequence of the intended expositions, but what form they will take on paper, I, speaking frankly, myself do not as yet know with my consciousness, but with my subconsciousness I already definitely feel that on the whole it will take the form of something which will be, so to say, "hot," and will have an effect on the entirety of every reader such as the red pepper pods had on the poor Transcaucasian Kurd.

Now that you have become familiar with the story of our common countryman, the Transcaucasian Kurd, I already consider it my duty to make a confession and hence before continuing this first chapter, which is by way of an introduction to all my further predetermined writings, I wish to bring to the knowledge of what is called your "pure waking consciousness" the fact that in the writings following this chapter of warning I shall expound my thoughts intentionally in such sequence and with such "logical confrontation," that the essence of certain real notions may of themselves automatically, so to say, go from this "waking consciousness"—which most people in their ignorance mistake for the real consciousness, but which I affirm and experimentally prove is the fictitious one—into what you call the subconscious, which ought to be in my opinion the real human consciousness,

out for yourself, assuming, of course, that there is or should arise in you any curiosity to learn how easily the very highest and most particularly beloved of our ALL-MAINTAINING CREATOR may unconsciously be taken for the very lowest in man.

- -

The plan and sequence of my intended expositions I have already composed in my "swollen" head, but into what form they will mould themselves upon paper, I frankly confess that I myself do not know with my consciousness, though with the total result of the functioning of my instinct I already definitely feel that on the whole it will all mould itself into "something" so to say "hot," and will have an effect on the common presence of every reader like that which the "red-pepper-pods" had on the poor Transcaucasian Kurd.

Thanks to the data crystallized in me which long ago became the main lever of my individuality, and about which I wish just now to inform you, I shall of course touch in my proposed writings upon questions not only of the everyday life of people, already so to say regularized on the Earth—an everyday life, it must be said, contracted—of course only in my opinion—to the point of wretchedness—but I shall also touch upon questions from which there must inevitably arise unusual sensations and uncommon picturings in all your separate relatively independent parts, which parts the ancient sages characterized as "falsely-ascribing-initiative-to-themselves"; namely, in your thoughts, your feelings, and simply in your body. The process of the beneficent Armagnac proceeding at the present

and there by themselves mechanically bring about that transformation which should in general proceed in the entirety of a man and give him, from his own conscious mentation, the results he ought to have, which are proper to man and not merely to single- or double-brained animals.

I decided to do this without fail so that this initial chapter of mine, predetermined as I have already said to awaken your consciousness, should fully justify its purpose, and reaching not only your, in my opinion, as yet only fictitious "consciousness," but also your real consciousness, that is to say, what you call your subconscious, might, for the first time, compel you to reflect actively.

In the entirety of every man, irrespective of his heredity and education, there are formed two independent consciousnesses, which in their functioning as well as in their manifestations have almost nothing in common. One consciousness is formed from the perception of all kinds of accidental, or on the part of others intentionally produced, mechanical impressions, among which must also be counted the "consonances" of various words which are indeed as is said empty; and the other consciousness is formed from the so to say, "already previously formed material results" transmitted to him by heredity, which have become blended with the corresponding parts of the entirety of a man, as well as from the data arising from his intentional evoking of the associative confrontations of these "materialized data" already in him.

The whole totality of the formation as well as the manifestation of this second human consciousness, which is none other than what is called the "subconscious," and which is formed from the "materialized results" of heredity and the confrontations actualized by one's own intentions, should in my opinion, formed by many years of my experimental elucidations during exceptionally favorably

- 25 -

arranged conditions, predominate in the common presence of a man.

As a result of this conviction of mine which as yet doubtlessly seems to you the fruit of the fantasies of an afflicted mind, I cannot now, as you yourself see, disregard this second consciousness and, compelled by my essence, am obliged to construct the general exposition even of this first chapter of my writings, namely, the chapter which should be the preface for everything further, calculating that it should reach and, in the manner required for my aim, "ruffle" the perceptions accumulated in both these consciousnesses of yours.

Continuing my expositions with this calculation, I must first of all inform your fictitious consciousness that, thanks to three definite peculiar data which were crystallized in my entirety during various periods of my preparatory age, I am really unique in respect of the so to say "muddling and befuddling" of all the notions and convictions supposedly firmly fixed in the entirety of people with whom I come in contact.

Tut! Tut! Tut! . . . I already feel that in your "false"—but according to you "real"—consciousness, there are beginning to be agitated, like "blinded flies," all the chief data transmitted to you by heredity from your uncle and mother, the totality of which data, always and in everything, at least engenders in you the impulse—nevertheless extremely good—of curiosity, as in the given case, to find out

moment in my common presence bids me confess to you and warn you that owing to the aforementioned data, the whole of my common presence, in the present
period of my life, namely, just when from causes not dependent on me, I have
now to become a professional writer, is already such that even with the whole of
my mental categorical decision and desire, and with the help of all my separately
spiritualized and independent parts—those educated of themselves as well as
those educated intentionally by my own will, just that will of mine which flows
from and is based exclusively only on my Pure Reason—which parts constitute in
me as well as in you this common presence of mine—I cannot do otherwise than
as the most exalted great terrestrial sage Mullah Nassr Eddin would say, "tangle-
and-entangle" the whole of you, or as he also sometimes says, "put-you-in-
galoshes," in full face of the fact that I am counting on your help, or rather on your
money, which I shall receive thanks to your purchase of writings; for the full possibility of accomplishing even with a "flourish," my self-imposed and perhaps
from your point of view, purely egoistic aim.

as quickly as possible why I, that is to say, a novice at writing, whose name has not even once been mentioned in the newspapers, have suddenly become so unique.

Never mind! I personally am very pleased with the arising of this curiosity even though only in your "false" consciousness, as I already know from experience that this impulse unworthy of man can sometimes even pass from this consciousness into one's nature and become a

- 26 -

worthy impulse—the impulse of the desire for knowledge, which, in its turn, assists the better perception and even the closer understanding of the essence of any object on which, as it sometimes happens, the attention of a contemporary man might be concentrated, and therefore I am even willing, with pleasure, to satisfy this curiosity which has arisen in you at the present moment.

Now listen and try to justify, and not to disappoint, my expectations. This original personality of mine, already "smelled out" by certain definite individuals from both choirs of the Judgment Seat Above, whence Objective justice proceeds, and also here on Earth, by as yet a very limited number of people, is based, as I already said, on three secondary specific data formed in me at different times during my preparatory age. The first of these data, from the very beginning of its arising, became as it were the chief directing lever of my entire wholeness, and the other two, the "vivifying-sources," as it were, for the feeding and perfecting of this first datum.

The arising of this first datum proceeded when I was still only, as is said, a "chubby mite." My dear now deceased grandmother was then still living and was a hundred and some years old.

When my grandmother—may she attain the kingdom of Heaven—was dying, my mother, as was then the custom, took me to her bedside, and as I kissed her right hand, my dear now deceased grandmother placed her dying left hand on my head and in a whisper, yet very distinctly, said:

"Eldest of my grandsons! Listen and always remember my strict injunction to you: In life never do as others do."

Having said this, she gazed at the bridge of my nose and evidently noticing my perplexity and my obscure understanding of what she had said, added somewhat angrily and imposingly:

- 27 -

"Either do nothing—just go to school—or do something nobody else does."

Whereupon she immediately, without hesitation, and with a perceptible impulse of disdain for all around her, and with commendable self-cognizance, gave up her soul directly into the hands of His Truthfulness, the Archangel Gabriel.

I think it will be interesting and even instructive to you to know that all this made so powerful an impression on me at that time that I suddenly became unable to endure anyone around me, and therefore, as soon as we left the room where the mortal "planetary body" of the cause of the cause of my arising lay, I very quietly, trying not to attract attention, stole away to the pit where during Lent the bran and potato skins for our "sanitarians," that is to say, our pigs, were

And now, my dear, as yet only candidate for my, so to say, future "voluntary-slaves," listen attentively and try your hardest without letting any thing escape you, to transubstantiate in your common presence the information concerning the arising of the original cause and also of those two events whose effects on the whole of me, having become by the Will of Fate, as contemporary scientists and

pious pastors would say, "vivifying," served as factors for the accomplished crystallization in my common presence, of just those specific data on account of which, it may be said, firstly, that I am now an "exceptional-monster" among the many millions of animals similar to me, and secondly, that since in the present period of my existence I must become a professional writer, I am compelled to employ this new profession of mine, at whatever cost, as our esteemed Mullah Nassr Eddin has expressed it, to "tangle-and-entangle" all your, as you call them, "images" and "notions" you have until now acquired, which though they are your own attainments, are nevertheless, even in your frank opinion, "very-suspicious."

And so, my dear and precious future "voluntary-slave."

When I was still only as is said, a "chubby-mite," my dear, now deceased grandmother—may she attain the Kingdom of Heaven—was still living and was a hundred and some years old.

When she was dying, my mother, as was then the custom, took me to her bedside, and as I kissed her right hand, my dear now deceased grandmother placed her dying left hand on my head and in a low voice but very distinctly and even a little imperatively said:

"Eldest of my grandsons!
Listen and always remember my strict injunction to you.
In life never do as others do.
Either do nothing—just go to school—or do something that nobody else does."

Whereupon, she immediately, without hesitation, and with a perceptible impulse of contempt and with commendable self-cognizance, gave her soul directly into the hands of His Truthfulness the Archangel Gabriel.

I think it will interest you and even perhaps be instructive, to know that all this then made so powerful an impression on me, that I suddenly could not hear those similar around me; and when we left the room where the mortal "planetary-body" of the cause of the cause of my arising lay, I very quietly, without attracting

stored, and lay there, without food or drink, in a tempest of whirling and confused thoughts—of which, fortunately for me, I had then in my childish brain still only a very limited number—right until the return from the cemetery of my mother, whose weeping on finding me gone and after searching for me in vain, as it were "overwhelmed" me. I then immediately emerged from the pit and standing first of all on the edge, for some reason or other with outstretched hand, ran to her and clinging fast to her skirts, involuntarily began to stamp my feet and why, I don't know, to imitate the braying of the donkey belonging to our neighbor, a bailiff.

Why this produced such a strong impression on me just then, and why I almost automatically manifested so strangely, I cannot until now make out; though during recent years, particularly on the days called "Shrovetide," I pondered a good deal, trying chiefly to discover the reason for it.

I then had only the logical supposition that it was perhaps only because the room in which this sacred scene

---------------------------------- 28 ----------------------------------

occurred, which was to have tremendous significance for the whole of my further life, was permeated through and through with the scent of a special incense brought from the monastery of "Old Athos" and very popular among followers of every shade of belief of the Christian religion. Whatever it may have been, this fact still now remains a bare fact.

During the days following this event, nothing particular happened in my general state, unless there might be connected with it the fact that during these days, I walked more often than usual with my feet in the air, that is to say, on my hands.

My first act, obviously in discordance with the manifestations of others, though truly without the participation not only of my consciousness but also of my subconsciousness, occurred on exactly the fortieth day after the death of my grandmother, when all our family, our relatives and all those by whom my dear grandmother, who was loved by everybody, had been held in esteem, gathered in the cemetery according to custom, to perform over her mortal remains, reposing in the grave, what is called the "requiem service," when suddenly without any rhyme or reason, instead of observing what was conventional among people of all degrees of tangible and intangible morality and of all material positions, that is to say, instead of standing quietly as if overwhelmed, with an expression of grief on one's face and even if possible with tears in one's eyes, I started skipping round the grave as if dancing, and sang:

"Let her with the saints repose,
Now that she's turned up her toes,
Oi! oi! oi!
Let her with the saints repose,
Now that she's turned up her toes."

---------------------------------- 29 ----------------------------------

. . . and so on and so forth.
And just from this it began, that in my entirety a "something" arose which in

attention, stole away to the pit where the bran for our pigs was stored, and lay there without food or drink in a tempest of whirling and confused thoughts—of which, fortunately for me, I had then in my childish brain still only a very limited number—right until the return from the cemetery of my mother, whose weeping, on finding me gone and after searching for me in vain, recalled me to myself, and I emerged from the pit as if in a state of somnambulism, and, flustered, ran to her and as is said "clung-fast" to her skirts.

Though many times in later years, and somehow or other always during the days we call "Shrove-tide," I have seriously thought and tried to make clear to myself exactly why this event made so strong an impression on me, I have not succeeded to this day.

- -

Perhaps it was only because the room in which occurred this sacred scene, which was to be significant for the whole of my life, was full of the scent of incense from what is called "Old-Athos."

Whatever it may have been, the fact remains a fact.

During the days following this event, nothing particular could have proceeded in my general state, or I should now have remembered it, unless it was perhaps the fact that during these days I walked more often than usual with my feet in the air, that is to say, on my hands.

My first act of obvious discordance with the manifestations of others, occurred exactly on the fortieth day after the death of my dear grandmother, when all our family, our relatives, and all those by whom my dear grandmother, who was loved by everybody, had been held in esteem, gathered in the cemetery according to custom, to perform over her mortal body, reposing in what seemed to me a not very cosy grave, what is called the "requiem-service." Suddenly without any rhyme or reason, instead of observing the conventional what is called "bon-ton-etiquette," that is to say, standing as if overwhelmed, with an expression of grief on one's face and even if possible with tears in one's eyes, I started skipping around the grave as if dancing, and sang:

"Let her with the saints repose
Now that she's turned up her toes . . . "

- -

respect of any kind of so to say "aping," that is to say, imitating the ordinary auto-matized manifestations of those around me, always and in everything engendered what I should now call an "irresistible urge" to do things not as others do them.

At that age I committed acts such as the following.

If for example when learning to catch a ball with the right hand, my brother, sisters and the neighbors' children who came to play with us, threw the ball in the air, I, with the same aim in view, would first bounce the ball hard on the ground, and only when it rebounded would I, first doing a somersault, catch it, and then only with the thumb and middle finger of the left hand; or if all the other children slid down the hill head first, I tried to do it, and moreover each time better and better, as the children then called it, "backside-first"; or if we children were given various kinds of what are called "Abaranian pastries," then all the other children, before putting them in their mouths, would first of all lick them, evidently to try their taste and to protract the pleasure, but . . . I would first sniff one on all sides and perhaps even put it to my ear and listen intently, and then though only almost unconsciously, yet nevertheless seriously, muttering to myself "so and so and so you must, do not eat until you bust," and rhythmically humming correspondingly, I would only take one bite and without savoring it, would swallow it—and so on and so forth.

The first event during which there arose in me one of the two mentioned data which became the "vivifying sources" for the feeding and perfecting of the in-junction of my deceased grandmother, occurred just at that age when I changed from a chubby mite into what is called a "young rascal" and had already begun to be, as is sometimes

------------------------------ *30* ------------------------------

said, a "candidate for a young man of pleasing appearance and dubious con-tent."

And this event occurred under the following circumstances, which were per-haps even specially combined by Fate itself.

With a number of young rascals like myself, I was once laying snares for pi-geons on the roof of a neighbor's house, when suddenly, one of the boys who was standing over me and watching me closely, said:

"I think the noose of the horsehair ought to be so arranged that the pigeon's big toe never gets caught in it, because, as our zoology teacher recently explained to us, during movement it is just in that toe that the pigeon's reserve strength is con-centrated, and therefore if this big toe gets caught in the noose, the pigeon might of course easily break it."

Another boy, leaning just opposite me, from whose mouth, by the way, whenever he spoke saliva always splashed abundantly in all directions, snapped at this remark of the first boy and delivered himself, with a copious quantity of

And just from this it began, that in my common presence a "something" arose which in respect of any kind of so to say "aping," that is the imitation of the ordinary automatized manifestations of those around me—always and in everything engendered what I should now call an "irresistible urge" to do not as others do.

At that age, of course, I did all this as yet unconsciously, that is to say, my what you call "reasonable-consciousness" did not then participate in all these manifestations of mine.

At that age these acts of mine were like the following:

If for example when learning to catch a ball with the right hand, my brother, sisters, and the neighbor's children who came to play with us, threw the ball into the air, I, with the same purpose, would first bounce the ball on the ground, and only on the rebound would I catch it, and then just with the thumb and middle finger of the left hand.

Or if all the other children sledded down hill head first, I would try to do it, and moreover as expertly as possible, as the children then called it, "backside-first."

Or if we children were given various kinds of what are called "Abaranian pastries," then all the other children would first of all lick them, evidently to try their taste before putting them into their mouths; but I . . . would first sniff it and sometimes even put it to my ear and listen intently with the definite instinctive intention of discovering whether there might be in this exterior form some inner peculiarity that would disclose itself, and so on and so forth.

Time passed. From a "chubby-mite" I changed into what in called a "young-rascal."

- -

Just at the end of this age, namely, the age in which one
is sometimes called a "candidate-for-a-young-man-of-pleasing-appearance-and-dubious-content," the first of the mentioned two events occurred, the effect of which enabled the essence of my dear grandmother's behest to take foot in as yet my nature alone.

And this fell out in the following way.

With a number of other young rascals like myself, I was once setting snares for pigeons on the roof of a neighbor's house.

One of the boys, who was watching me closely, said:

"I think the snicker of horsehair ought to be so arranged that the pigeon's big toe never gets caught in it, because, as our zoology teacher recently explained to me, during movement it is just in that toe that the pigeon's greatest strength is concentrated, and it might therefore easily, of course, break the noose."

Another boy, leaning just opposite me, from whose mouth by the way,

saliva, of the following words:

"Shut your trap, you hopeless mongrel offshoot of the Hottentots! What an abortion you are, just like your teacher! Suppose it is true that the greatest physical force of the pigeon is concentrated in that big toe, then all the more, what we've got to do is to see that just that toe will be caught in the noose. Only then will there be any sense to our aim—that is to say, for catching these unfortunate pigeon creatures—in that brain-particularity proper to all possessors of that soft and slippery 'something' which consists in this, that when, thanks to other actions, from which its insignificant manifestability depends, there arises a periodic requisite law-conformable what is called 'change of presence,' then this small so to say 'law-conformable confusion' which should proceed for the animation of

------------------------------ *31* ------------------------------

other acts in its general functioning, immediately enables the center of gravity of the whole functioning, in which this slippery 'something' plays a very small part, to pass temporarily from its usual place to another place, owing to which there often obtains in the whole of this general functioning, unexpected results ridiculous to the point of absurdity."

He discharged the last words with such a shower of saliva that it was as if my face were exposed to the action of an "atomizer"—not of "Ersatz" production—invented by the Germans for dyeing material with aniline dyes.

This was more than I could endure, and without changing my squatting position, I flung myself at him, and my head, hitting him with full force in the pit of his stomach, immediately laid him out and made him as is said "lose consciousness."

I do not know and do not wish to know in what spirit the result will be formed in your mentation of the information about the extraordinary coincidence, in my opinion, of life circumstances, which I now intend to describe here, though for my mentation, this coincidence was excellent material for the assurance of the possibility of the fact that this event described by me, which occurred in my youth, proceeded not simply accidentally but was intentionally created by certain extraneous forces.

The point is that this dexterity was thoroughly taught me only a few days before this event by a Greek priest from Turkey, who, persecuted by Turks for his political convictions, had been compelled to flee from there, and having arrived in our town had been hired by my parents as a teacher for me of the modern Greek language.

I do not know on which data he based his political convictions and ideas, but I very well remember that in all the conversations of this Greek priest, even while explaining to me the difference between the words of exclamation

------------------------------ *32* ------------------------------

in ancient and in modern Greek, there were indeed always very clearly discernible his dreams of getting as soon as possible to the island of Crete and there manifesting himself as befits a true patriot.

Well, then, on beholding the effect of my skill, I was, I must confess, extremely frightened, because, knowing nothing of any such reaction from a blow in that

whenever he spoke, saliva always splashed abundantly in all directions—sneezed at this remark of the first boy and delivered himself, with a copious quantity of saliva, of the following words:

"Shut your trap, you Hottentot bastard, you abortion, just like your teacher!"

"Suppose its true that the greatest physical force of the pigeon is concentrated in that toe, then all the more, all we've got to see is that just that toe will be snickeled."

"Only then will there be any sense for our aim—that is, for the catching of these also unfortunate pigeon creatures—in that brain-particularity proper to all possessors of that soft and "slippery something," namely, in that particularity which, when a little disharmony occurs in it, or so to say "confusion" arises, enables the

center of gravity of the whole functioning in which that particularity plays a very small part to pass temporarily to another place and this at times yields surprising results ridiculous to the point of absurdity."

He "discharged" the last word with such a shower of saliva, that it was as if my face was exposed to the action of the "pulverizer" invented by the Germans for dyeing material with aniline dyes.

This was more than I could endure, and without changing my squatting position, I flung myself at him, and my head, charging him with full force in the pit of his stomach, immediately laid him out and made him lose what is called "consciousness."

Curious and exceedingly peculiar is the coincidence of accidental life-circumstances, that this dexterity should have been thoroughly taught me only a few

days before this event by a Greek priest from Turkey who, persecuted by the Turks for his political convictions, had been compelled to flee from there, and having arrived in our town had been hired by my parents as a teacher for me of the new Greek language. It must be said that he longed to get to the island of Crete and there manifest himself as befits a true patriot.

place, I quite thought I had killed him.

At the moment I was experiencing this fear, another boy, the cousin of him who had become the first victim of my so to say "skill in self-defense," seeing this, without a moment's pause, and obviously overcome with a feeling called "consanguinity," immediately leaped at me and with a full swing struck me in the face with his fist.

From this blow, I, as is said, "saw stars," and at the same time my mouth became as full as if it had been stuffed with the food necessary for the artificial fattening of a thousand chickens.

After a little time when both these strange sensations had calmed down within me, I then actually discovered that some foreign substance was in my mouth, and when I pulled it out with my fingers, it turned out to be nothing less than a tooth of large dimensions and strange form.

Seeing me staring at this extraordinary tooth, all the boys swarmed around me and also began to stare at it with great curiosity and in a strange silence.

By this time the boy who had been laid out flat recovered and, picking himself up, also began to stare at my tooth with the other boys, as if nothing had happened to him.

This strange tooth had seven shoots and at the end of each of them there stood out in relief a drop of blood, and through each separate drop there shone clearly and definitely one of the seven aspects of the manifestation of the white ray.

---------------------------- 33 ----------------------------

After this silence, unusual for us "young rascals," the usual hubbub broke out again, and in this hubbub it was decided to go immediately to the barber, a specialist in extracting teeth, and to ask him just why this tooth was like that.

So we all climbed down from the roof and went off to the barber's. And I, as the "hero of the day," stalked at the head of them all.

The barber, after a casual glance, said it was simply a "wisdom tooth" and that all those of the male sex have one like it, who until they first exclaim "papa" and "mama" are fed on milk exclusively from their own mother, and who on first sight are able to distinguish among many other faces the face of their own father.

As a result of the whole totality of the effects of this happening, at which time my poor "wisdom tooth" became a complete sacrifice, not only did my consciousness begin, from that time on, constantly absorbing, in connection with everything, the very essence of the essence of my deceased grandmother's behest—God bless her soul—but also in me at that time, because I did not go to a "qualified dentist" to have the cavity of this tooth of mine treated, which as a matter of fact I could not do because our home was too far from any contemporary center of culture, there began to ooze chronically from this cavity a "something" which—as it was only recently explained to me by a very famous meteorologist with whom I chanced to become, as is said, "bosom friends" owing to frequent meetings in the Parisian night restaurants of Montmartre—had the property of arousing an interest in, and a tendency to seek out the causes of the arising of every suspicious "actual fact"; and this property, not transmitted to my entirety by heredity, gradually and automatically led to my ultimately becoming a specialist

---------------------------- 34 ----------------------------

On beholding the effect of my skill, I was, I must confess, extremely frightened, because, knowing nothing of any such reaction from a blow in that place, I quite thought I had killed him.

But another boy, his cousin, seeing this, without a moment's pause, and obviously overcome with the feeling called "consanguinity" immediately leapt at me and with a full swing struck me in the face with his fist.

This blow struck sparks from my eyes and at the same time my mouth became as full as if it had been stuffed with the porridge for the artificial fattening of a thousand chickens.

After a little time when both these sensations had died down within me and blood began to ooze out of my mouth, I then actually discovered that in my mouth was some foreign substance and when I pulled it out with my finger, it turned out to be nothing less than a tooth of large dimensions and strange form.

By this time the boy who had been prostrate had recovered and was standing up; and seeing me staring at this extraordinary tooth, he and all the other boys swarmed round me as if nothing had happened and gazed at it with me with utter curiosity and in a strange silence.

This tooth had seven fangs and at the end of each of them realistically stood a

drop of blood, and through each drop there shone clearly, definitely, and separately, all the seven aspects of the white ray.

After this silence, rare among us "young-rascals," the usual hubbub broke out again, and in this clatter it was decided to go at once to the barber, a specialist in extracting teeth and to ask him just why this tooth was like that.

So we all climbed down from the roof and went off to the barber's.

And I, as the "hero-of-the-day" stalked at the head of them all.

The barber, after a casual glance, simply pronounced it a "wisdom-tooth."

From the whole totality of the effect of this event—which became significant for the rest of my life and in the process of which my poor "wisdom-tooth" had become so to say the "exemplary victim"—not only did the essence of my dear grandmother's injunction become definitely instilled into my nature, but also because I did not go to a "qualified-dentist" to have the former cavity of this tooth of mine treated—which as a matter of fact I could not, because our home was too far from any contemporary centers of culture—there began to ooze chronically from this cavity a "something" which had the property of engendering an interest and a tendency to seek out the causes of everything suspicious—as this was made clear to me only recently according to a very minute what is called "psycho-physiological-analysis" made by an occultist well known on the continent of Europe—there was acquired in me an irresistible-urge to become a specialist in the investigation of every kind of "suspicious-phenomenon" which happened to come my way.

in the investigation of every suspicious phenomenon which, as it so often happened, came my way.

This property newly formed in me after this event—when I, of course with the co-operation of our ALL-COMMON MASTER THE MERCILESS HEROPASS, that is the "flow of time," was transformed into the young man already depicted by me—became for me a real inextinguishable hearth, always burning, of consciousness.

The second of the mentioned vivifying factors, this time for the complete fusion of my dear grandmother's injunction with all the data constituting my general individuality, was the totality of impressions received from information I chanced to acquire concerning the event which took place here among us on Earth, showing the origin of that "principle" which, as it turned out according to the elucidations of Mr. Alan Kardec during an "absolutely secret" spiritualistic seance, subsequently became everywhere among beings similar to ourselves, arising and existing on all the other planets of our Great Universe, one of the chief "life principles."

The formulation in words of this new "all-universal principle of living" is as follows:

"If you go on a spree then go the whole hog including the postage."

As this "principle," now already universal, arose on that same planet on which you too arose and on which, moreover, you exist almost always on a bed of roses and frequently dance the fox trot, I consider I have no right to withhold from you the information known to me, elucidating certain details of the arising of just that universal principle.

Soon after the definite inculcation into my nature of the said new inherency, that is, the unaccountable striving to elucidate the real reasons for the arising of all sorts of "actual facts," on my first arrival in the heart of Russia,

35

the city of Moscow, where, finding nothing else for the satisfaction of my psychic needs, I occupied myself with the investigation of Russian legends and sayings, I once happened—whether accidentally or as a result of some objective sequence according to a law I do not know—to learn by the way the following:

Once upon a time a certain Russian, who in external appearance was to those around him a simple merchant, had to go from his provincial town on some business or other to this second capital of Russia, the city of Moscow, and his son, his favorite one—because he resembled only his mother—asked him to bring back a

After this event, with this inherency now rooted in my nature, I began, again of course with the cooperation of our All-Common Master the Merciless Heropass, that is, the "flow-of-time," to grow up into the mentioned young man.

I think that it may be significant for you to know also that according to my later, personal, detailed investigations, none of the results of my manifestations at that age corresponding to the injunction of my deceased grandmother had up to that time any specific effect on what are called the present "corns" of various degree of those around me, only because in my opinion my own so to say "reasonable-consciousness" had not yet begun to participate in these actions of mine.

Furthermore, it must be confessed that even then, although this reasonable-consciousness of mine had not yet begun to participate in these manifestations, I endeavored nevertheless, with an instinctive consciousness of my duty, to perform everything very honorably, without giving way to all my various weaknesses, both those acquired and those transmitted by heredity also.

The second of the mentioned vivifying factors, this time for the complete fusion of my dear grandmother's injunction—may she attain the kingdom of Heaven—with all the data constituting my general individuality, was the totality of impressions received from information I chanced to perceive concerning the story that happened here among us on the Earth, of the arising of that "principle-of-living" which, as it turned out according to data elucidated by Mr. Alan Kardek during an "absolutely secret" spiritualistic séance, subsequently became a "principle" everywhere among beings similar to ourselves arising and existing on all the other planets of our Great Universe as well.

The formulation in words of this now "All-Universal-principle-of-living" is as follows:

"If-you-decide-to-go-on-the-spree-then-go-the-whole-hog-including-the-postage."

As this "principle-of-living" now already universally accepted arose on that same planet on which you too arose and on which, moreover, you exist almost on a bed of roses, and frequently dance the fox-trot, I consider I have no right to withhold from you the information approximately elucidating certain details of the arising of just that universally general fact.

Well then, when I was once actualizing in practice just that specificity of mine, which had already become also an inherency in the whole of my common pres-

ence, namely, the investigation of suspicious phenomena, and I was investigating also Russian legends and sayings, I happened—whether accidentally or as a result of some objective law-conformable successiveness I don't know—to learn among other things the following:

Once upon a time, a certain Russian, who in external appearance was to those around him a simple merchant, had to go from his provincial town on some business or other to the second capital of Russia, the city of Moscow, and his son, furthermore, his favorite one, asked him to bring him a certain book.

certain book.

When this great unconscious author of the "all-universal principle of living" arrived in Moscow, he together with a friend of his became—as was and still is usual there—"blind drunk" on genuine "Russian vodka."

And when these two inhabitants of this most great contemporary grouping of biped breathing creatures had drunk the proper number of glasses of this "Russian blessing" and were discussing what is called "public education," with which question it has long been customary always to begin one's conversation, then our merchant suddenly remembered by association his dear son's request, and decided to set off at once to a bookshop with his friend to buy the book.

In the shop, the merchant, looking through the book he had asked for and which the salesman handed him, asked its price.

The salesman replied that the book was sixty kopecks. Noticing that the price marked on the cover of the book was only forty-five kopecks, our merchant first began pondering in a strange manner, in general unusual for Russians, and afterwards, making a certain movement with his shoulders, straightening himself up almost like a pillar and throwing out his chest like an officer of the

------------------------------------ *36* ------------------------------------

guards, said after a little pause, very quietly but with an intonation in his voice expressing great authority:

"But it is marked here forty-five kopecks. Why do you ask sixty?" Thereupon the salesman, making as is said the "oleaginous" face proper to all salesmen, replied that the book indeed cost only forty-five kopecks, but had to be sold at sixty because fifteen kopecks were added for postage.

After this reply to our Russian merchant who was perplexed by these two quite contradictory but obviously clearly reconcilable facts, it was visible that something began to proceed in him, and gazing up at the ceiling, he again pondered, this time like an English professor who has invented a capsule for castor oil, and then suddenly turned to his friend and delivered himself for the first time on Earth of the verbal formulation which, expressing in its essence an indubitable objective truth, has since assumed the character of a saying.

And he then put it to his friend as follows:

"Never mind, old fellow, we'll take the book. Anyway we're on a spree today, and 'if you go on a spree then go the whole hog including the postage.'"

As for me, unfortunately doomed, while still living, to experience the delights of "Hell," as soon as I had cognized all this, something very strange, that I have never experienced before or since, immediately began, and for a rather long time continued to proceed in me; it was as if all kinds of, as contemporary "Hivintzes" say, "competitive races" began to proceed in me between all the various-sourced associations and experiences usually occurring in me.

At the same time, in the whole region of my spine there began a strong almost

When this truly great merchant, the unconscious author of the "all-universal-principle-of-living," arrived in Moscow, he together with a friend of his became—as used to be and is still usual there—as is said "blind drunk" on genuine "Russian-vodka."

And when these two inhabitants of this most great contemporary grouping had drunk the proper number of glasses of this Russian "blessing," and according to long custom were discussing what is called "public-education," our merchant suddenly remembered by association his dear son's commission and decided to set off to a bookshop at once with his friend—who, it must be said, had become his friend chiefly by the common tie of the said Russian "blessing"—in order to buy the book.

In the shop, the merchant, looking through the book he had asked for and which the clerk handed him, asked its price. On being told by the assistant that the book was sixty kopecks and noticing that the price marked on the cover of the book was only forty-five kopeks, our merchant first began pondering in a strange manner unusual for him, and afterwards, making a certain movement with his shoulders, straightening himself up and throwing out his chest like an officer of the guards when he as is said "becomes-stiff-as-a-poker," he very quietly but with

an intonation in his voice expressing great authority, said after a little pause:

"But it is marked here forty-five kopeks, why do you ask sixty?"

Thereupon the assistant, putting on, as is said the "plasto-oleaginous" expression proper to all shop assistants, replied that the book indeed cost only forty-five kopeks, but had to be sold at sixty because fifteen kopeks were added for the postage.

Upon this, the Russian merchant—pardon me, the most great author of one of the universal "principles-of-living"—fixing his gaze on the ceiling, again cogitated this time seriously perplexed, when, suddenly turning to his friend, he delivered himself of the first verbal information of the very essence of that principle defining an indubitable so to say objective truth.

And he then uttered it to his friend as follows:

"Never mind, old dear! We'll take the book. What's it matter, we're on the spree today, and 'if-you-go-on-the-spree-then-go-the-whole-hog-including-the-postage.'"

As for me, esteemed buyer of my writings, as soon as I had elucidated this to myself, something very strange, that I never experienced before or since, immediately began and for a rather long time continued to proceed in me; it was as if all kinds of so to say "general-postraces" for what are called "peshkash" or, as they call them here in Europe, "great-stakes" began to proceed in me between all the various-sourced associations and experiences usually proceeding in me, and at the same time, without any rhyme or reason, an intense almost intolerable itching

unbearable itch, and a colic in the very center of my solar plexus, also unbearable, and all this, that is these dual, mutually stimulating sensations,

- 37 -

after the lapse of some time suddenly were replaced by such a peaceful inner condition as I experienced in later life once only, when the ceremony of the great initiation into the Brotherhood of the "Originators of making butter from air" was performed over me; and later when "I," that is, this "something-unknown" of mine, which in ancient times one crank—called by those around him, as we now also call such persons, a "learned man"—defined as a "relatively transferable arising, depending on the quality of the functioning of thought, feeling, and organic automatism," and according to the definition of another also ancient and renowned learned man, the Arabian Mal-el-Lel, which definition by the way was in the course of time borrowed and repeated in a different way by a no less renowned and learned Greek, Xenophon, "the compound result of consciousness, subconsciousness, and instinct"; so when this same "I" in this condition turned my dazed attention inside myself, then firstly it very clearly constated that everything, even to each single word, elucidating this quotation that has become an "all-universal life principle" became transformed in me into some special cosmic substance, and merging with the data already crystallized in me long before from the behest of my deceased grandmother, changed these data into a "something" and this "something" flowing everywhere through my entirety settled forever in each atom composing this entirety of mine, and secondly, this my ill-fated "I" there and then definitely felt and, with an impulse of submission, became conscious of this, for me, sad fact, that already from that moment I should willy-nilly have to manifest myself always and in everything without exception, according to this inherency formed in me, not in accordance with the laws of heredity, nor even by the influence of surrounding circumstances, but arising in my entirety

- 38 -

under the influence of three external accidental causes, having nothing in common, namely: thanks in the first place to the behest of a person who had become, without the slightest desire on my part, a passive cause of the cause of my arising; secondly, on account of a tooth of mine knocked out by some ragamuffin of a boy, mainly on account of somebody else's "slobberiness"; and thirdly, thanks to the verbal formulation delivered in a drunken state by a person quite alien to me— some merchant of "Muscovite brand."

If before my acquaintance with this "all-universal principle of living" I had actualized all manifestations differently from other biped animals similar to me, arising and vegetating with me on one and the same planet, then I did so automatically, and sometimes only half consciously, but after this event I began to do so consciously and moreover with an instinctive sensation of the two blended impulses of self-satisfaction and self-cognizance in correctly and honorably fulfilling my duty to Great Nature.

It must even be emphasized that although even before this event I already did everything not as others did, yet my manifestations were hardly thrust before the eyes of my fellow countrymen around me, but from the moment when the es-

broke out over the whole region of my vertebral column, and an also intolerable colic in the very center of my what is called "solar plexus." After a time all this sud-

denly quieted down of its own accord, and when I, that is to say, that uncertain something of mine which in olden times one crank—called by those around him, as we also now call such persons, a scientist—defined as "a-certain-relative-arising-depending-on-the-quality-of-the-functioning-of-thought-feeling-and-organic-automatism"—and which a certain famous Arabian Mal-el-Lel, another ancient scientist, formulated in a definition which was borrowed and repeated in another way by the no less famous Greek scientist Xenophon, as "the-result-of-the-totality-of-consciousness-and-unconsciousness-and-instinct"—well then, when this same "I" directed my confused attention within myself, that is, within the whole of me, I then very clearly constated that the whole substantial result of what I had just made clear with my consciousness about the said "principle-of-living" had, without any residue, fused with the data already crystallized in me long before from the results of my dear grandmother's injunction, and this "I" of mine then very definitely sensed, and, with an impulse of submission simultaneously arising in me, cognized the fact, grievous for me, that from that moment on, I should willy-nilly have to manifest myself always and in everything without exception according to these data which had formed in me and which arose under the influence of three external accidental causes having nothing in common with one another, namely, owing firstly to the arbitrary injunction of a person who had become without any desire whatsoever on my part, the passive cause of the cause of my arising; secondly, through some rascal having knocked out a tooth of mine, chiefly on account of somebody else's "slobbering"; and thirdly, thanks to the verbal formulation issuing from the drunken lips of a personality quite strange to me who existed on the Earth under the name of a "Russian-merchant."

That is why "I" and all the heterogeneous sources of the common presence of this "I" of mine, began from that time on, not only, as before, automatically and only occasionally semiconsciously, to actualize manifestations different from those of other surrounding similar biped beings arising and existing on the same planet as I, but to do so from then on consistently and consciously.

Formerly, that is to say, until my elucidation of the arising of this "principle-of-living" through the lips of the Russian merchant immortalized through objective glory, if indeed I did do everything not as others did, my manifestations were not yet patently thrust before the eyes of my fellow-countrymen around me, but from the moment when to my increased misfortune I made all this clear to myself, not only did I do everything without exception intentionally, and not only was everything also done intentionally through me in accordance with the injunction of my deceased grandmother, but I began carrying out all these actions of mine to the utmost possible limits; and from the very beginning the practice was acquired in me and now continues, on beginning anything new and also at any

sence of this principle of living was assimilated in my nature, then on the one hand all my manifestations, those intentional for any aim and also those simply, as is said, "occurring out of sheer idleness," acquired vivifyingness and began to assist in the formation of "corns" on the organs of perception of every creature similar to me without exception who directed his attention directly or indirectly toward my actions, and on the other hand, I myself began to carry out all these actions of mine in accordance with the injunctions of my deceased grandmother to the utmost possible limits; and the practice was automatically acquired in me on beginning anything new

---------------------------------- 39 ----------------------------------

and also at any change, of course on a large scale, always to utter silently or aloud:
"If you go on a spree then go the whole hog including the postage."

And now, for instance, in the present case also, since, owing to causes not dependent on me, but flowing from the strange and accidental circumstances of my life, I happen to be writing books, I am compelled to do this also in accordance with that same principle which has gradually become definite through various extraordinary combinations created by life itself, and which has blended with each atom of my entirety.

This psycho-organic principle of mine I shall this time begin to actualize not by following the practice of all writers, established from the remote past down to the present, of taking as the theme of their various writings the events which have supposedly taken place, or are taking place, on Earth, but shall take instead as the scale of events for my writings—the whole Universe. Thus in the present case also, "If you take then take!"—that is to say, "If you go on a spree then go the whole hog including the postage."

Any writer can write within the scale of the Earth, but I am not any writer.

Can I confine myself merely to this, in the objective sense, "paltry Earth" of ours? To do this, that is to say, to take for my writings the same themes as in general other writers do, I must not, even if only because what our learned spirits affirm might suddenly indeed prove true; and my grandmother might learn of this; and do you understand what might happen to her, to my dear beloved grandmother? Would she not turn in her grave, not once, as is usually said, but—as I understand her, especially now when I can already quite "skillfully" enter into the position of another—she would turn so many

---------------------------------- 40 ----------------------------------

times that she would almost be transformed into an "Irish weathercock."

Please, reader, do not worry . . . I shall of course also write of the Earth, but with such an impartial attitude that this comparatively small planet itself and also everything on it shall correspond to that place which in fact it occupies and which, even according to your own sane logic, arrived at thanks of course to my guidance, it must occupy in our Great Universe.

I must, of course, also make the various what are called "heroes" of these writings of mine not such types as those which in general the writers of all ranks and epochs on Earth have drawn and exalted, that is to say, types such as any Tom,

change—of course, on a large scale—always to utter silently or aloud:

- -

"If-I-decide-to-go-on-the-spree-then-go-the-whole-hog-including-the-post-age."

And now that owing to circumstances and causes not dependent on me, I happen to be writing books, I am compelled to do so in accordance with that same principle, also.

In the present case I shall begin not by following the practice of all writers, established from the remote past down to the present, of taking as the theme of their various "wiseacrings" events which have, as it were, taken place or are taking place on the Earth, but I shall for my writings take instead the scale of events of the whole World. Thus in the present case also, if "you take, then take"!—that is to say "If-I-decide-to-go-on-the-spree-then-go-the-whole-hog-including-the-postage."

Within the scale of the Earth, any writer can write, but I am not any writer!

Can I confine myself merely to this in the objective sense "paltry-Earth" of ours? Is it for nothing, firstly, that I am the grandson of my dear grandmother, and is it for nothing secondly that that intensive transformation then took place in me for the assimilation without residue of the now already All-universal-principle-of-living?

- -

Please, however, do not worry my dear future and to me very necessary "voluntary-slave . . . " I shall of course also write of the Earth, but with such an impartial attitude and on such a correspondent objective scale that the planet itself and also everything on it may take that position which, in fact, according even to your own sane logic, they do and must occupy in our Great Universe.

Likewise as regards the various what are called "heroes," I intend in these writings of mine to present types not like those which in general the writers of all epochs on the Earth have extolled and still extol, that is to say, like the Toms,

Dick, or Harry, who arise through a misunderstanding, and who fail to acquire during the process of their formation up to what is called "responsible life," anything at all which it is proper for an arising in the image of God, that is to say a man, to have, and who progressively develop in themselves to their last breath only such various charms as for instance: "lasciviousness," "slobberiness," "amorousness," "maliciousness," "chicken-heartedness," "enviousness," and similar vices unworthy of man.

I intend to introduce in my writings heroes of such type as everybody must, as

------------------------------ *41* ------------------------------

is said, "willy-nilly" sense with his whole being as real, and about whom in every reader data must inevitably be crystallized for the notion that they are indeed "somebody" and not merely "just anybody."

During the last weeks, while lying in bed, my body quite sick, I mentally drafted a summary of my future writings and thought out the form and sequence of their exposition, and I decided to make the chief hero of the first series of my writings . . . do you know whom? . . . the Great Beelzebub Himself—even in spite of the fact

that this choice of mine might from the very beginning evoke in the mentation of most of my readers such mental associations as must engender in them all kinds of automatic contradictory impulses from the action of that totality of data infallibly formed in the psyche of people owing to all the established abnormal conditions of our external life, which data are in general crystallized in people owing to the famous what is called "religious morality" existing and rooted in their life, and in them, consequently, there must inevitably be formed data for an inexplicable hostility towards me personally.

But do you know what, reader?

In case you decide, despite this Warning, to risk continuing to familiarize yourself with my further writings, and you try to absorb them always with an impulse of impartiality and to understand the very essence of the questions I have decided to elucidate, and in view also of the particularity inherent in the human psyche, that there can be no opposition to the perception of good only exclusively when so to say a "contact of mutual frankness and confidence" is established, I now still wish to make a sincere confession to you about the associations arisen within me which as a result have precipitated in the corresponding sphere of my consciousness the data which have prompted the whole of my individuality to select as the chief hero for my writings just such an individual as is presented before your inner eyes by this same Mr. Beelzebub.

This I did, not without cunning. My cunning lies simply in the logical supposition that if I show him this attention he infallibly—as I already cannot doubt any more—has to show himself grateful and help me by all means in his command in my intended writings.

Although Mr. Beelzebub is made, as is said, "of a different grain," yet, since He also can think, and, what

------------------------------ *42* ------------------------------

Dicks or Harrys who arise by a misunderstanding and who fail to acquire during the process of their formation up to what is called "responsible-existence" anything at all which is proper to a human-being and not merely to an animal to have, and who during the whole of their responsible existence progressively develop in themselves to their last breath only those various "charms" called "lasciviousness," "mawkishness," "amorousness," "maliciousness," "chicken-heartedness," "enviousness," and so on in the same strain.

I intend, as is said, to "create" personages in my writings whom everybody

must, whether he will or not, sense with his whole Being as something real, and about whom in every reader, even though he has never encountered such "typenesses," data must inevitably be crystallized for the conclusion that they are indeed "something" and not merely "tails-of-donkeys."

About two weeks ago, while I was mentally drafting the summary sketch of these proposed writings of mine, I categorically decided to make what is called my chief hero ... do you know whom? ... Beelzebub himself—even in spite of the fact that this choice of mine might from the very beginning evoke in the mentation of most of my readers an association of so to say "moral-contortions."

But do you know what, reader?

If, in spite of this Warning, you decide to risk familiarizing yourself with my writings and, perceiving them with an impulse of impartiality, will try to understand the essence of my subsequent expoundings, then in view of the fact that a contact of mutual trust must necessarily be established between you and me, I must now frankly confess to you about the associations which have arisen within me and which as a result have precipitated in the corresponding sphere of my individuality the data engendering the deliberate so to say cunning, which has prompted the whole of me to select as the chief hero for my writings just such a type as is presented before your inner eyes by this same Mr. Beelzebub.

My cunning in selecting Mr. Beelzebub as my principal hero is that I expect personal profit for myself from it, on the assumption that if I show him this attention, He will of course without fail—as I for myself am certain with the whole of my left fundament—wish to express his gratitude by helping me with all the means available to Him, in these proposed writings of mine.

Although Beelzebub is made, as is said, "of-a-different-cloth," nevertheless, since He also can think,

is most important, has—as I long ago learned, thanks to the treatise of the famous Catholic monk, Brother Foolon—a curly tail, then I, being thoroughly convinced from experience that curls are never natural but can be obtained only from various intentional manipulations, conclude, according to the "sane-logic" of hieromancy formed in my consciousness from reading books, that Mr. Beelzebub also must possess a good share of vanity, and will therefore find it extremely inconvenient not to help one who is going to advertise His name.

It is not for nothing that our renowned and incomparable teacher, Mullah Nassr Eddin, frequently says:

"Without greasing the palm not only is it impossible to live anywhere tolerably but even to breathe."

And another also terrestrial sage, who has become such, thanks to the crass stupidity of people, named Till Eulenspiegel, has expressed the same in the following words:

"If you don't grease the wheels the cart won't go."

Knowing these and many other sayings of popular wisdom formed by centuries in the collective life of people, I have decided to "grease the palm" precisely of Mr. Beelzebub, who, as everyone understands, has possibilities and knowledge enough and to spare for everything.

Enough, old fellow! All joking even philosophical joking aside, you, it seems, thanks to all these deviations, have transgressed one of the chief principles elaborated in you and put in the basis of a system planned previously for introducing your dreams into life by means of such a new profession, which principle consists in this, always to remember and take into account the fact of the weakening of the functioning of the mentation of the contemporary reader and not to fatigue him with the perception of numerous ideas over a short time.

Moreover, when I asked one of the people always around me who are "eager to enter Paradise without fail

--------------------------------- *43* ----------------------------------

with their boots on," to read aloud straight through all that I have written in this introductory chapter, what is called my "I"—of course, with the participation of all the definite data formed in my original psyche during my past years, which data gave me among other things understanding of the psyche of creatures of different type but similar to me—constated and cognized with certainty that in the entirety of every reader without exception there must inevitably, thanks to this first chapter alone, arise a "something" automatically engendering definite unfriendliness towards me personally.

and besides—as I long ago learned from the treatise of the famous Catholic Monk, Brother Foolon—also has a curled tail, then I conclude, according to the sane-logic formed in my consciousness also owing to education and the reading of contemporary books—that he also must of course possess a good share of vanity and will therefore find it extremely difficult not to help one who is going to advertise His name.

It is not for nothing that our renowned and incomparable Mullah Nassr Eddin frequently says:

"Without-greasing-palms-not-only-is-it-impossible-to-live-anywhere-but-even-to-breathe."

And another also terrestrial sage named Till Eulenspiegel has expressed the same in the following words:

"If-you-don't-grease-the-wheels-the-cart-won't-go."

In accordance with the sayings just quoted, the veracity of which is plain to every contemporary person, I have decided to "grease-the-palm" precisely of Mr. Beelzebub, who, as everyone understands, has means and knowledge, as is said, "enough-and-to-spare" for everything.

All joking, even philosophical joking aside, this Warning of mine has in truth turned out to be rather lengthy.

But this does not matter, I think . . .

It will be no great calamity if you spend an extra twenty or thirty minutes of your time reading it, after I, who in every respect am rather badly "battered," have spent almost two weeks writing it.

The more so, as you—and in this it seems I am not mistaken—value your time and everything else, according to the wise saying of, as always, that same All-Common teacher Mullah Nassr Eddin, which consists in the following words:

"It's-all-the-same-everything-under-the-sun-is-nonsense-and-ha-ha-if-only-the-process-of-digestion-goes-fairly-well-and-the-functioning-of-the-essence-of-our-actual-existence-never-misses-fire."

So good night . . . although morning is already here.

It is already late morning; yet to lie in bed and sleep when normal people have by the sweat of their brow honestly earnt and eaten their breakfast, has already lately become fixed in my mode of living.

And so, I shall try to fall asleep; and you . . . continue to think your usual morning thoughts, probably of the following kind: precisely how many francs must be left just for today for housekeeping; because yesterday one of the members of your family ventured not to consider you and rudely stepped on just that "corn" of yours which already long ago chose its place of existence on the fourth toe of your left foot.

If one has recourse to the priceless definitions of our great Teacher, Teacher above all Teachers, Mullah Nassr Eddin, in this situation in which I, doing nothing, intend to go carefree to bed, while at the same time advising you to think well

To tell the truth, it is not this which is now chiefly worrying me, but the fact that at the end of this reading I also constated that in the sum total of everything expounded in this chapter, the whole of my entirety in which the aforesaid "I" plays a very small part, manifested itself quite contrary to one of the fundamental commandments of that All-Common Teacher whom I particularly esteem, Mullah Nassr Eddin, and which he formulated in the words: "Never poke your stick into a hornets' nest."

The agitation which pervaded the whole system affecting my feelings, and which resulted from cognizing that in the reader there must necessarily arise an unfriendly feeling towards me, at once quieted down as soon as I remembered the ancient Russian proverb which states: "There is no offense which with time will not blow over."

But the agitation which arose in my system from realizing my negligence in obeying the commandment of Mullah Nassr Eddin, not only now seriously troubles me, but a very strange process, which began in both of my recently discovered "souls" and which assumed the form of an unusual itching immediately I understood this, began progressively to increase until it now evokes and produces an almost intolerable pain in the region a little below

-------------------------------- *44* --------------------------------

the right half of my already, without this, overexercised "solar plexus."

Wait! Wait! . . .This process, it seems, is also ceasing, and in all the depths of my consciousness, and let us meanwhile say "even beneath my subconsciousness," there already begins to arise everything requisite for the complete assurance that it will entirely cease, because I have remembered another fragment of life wisdom, the thought of which led my mentation to the reflection that if I indeed acted against the advice of the highly esteemed Mullah Nassr Eddin, I nevertheless acted without premeditation according to the principle of that extremely sympathetic—not so well known everywhere on earth, but never forgotten by all who have once met him—that precious jewel, Karapet of Tiflis.

and honestly to apportion the said francs, he would say:

"Today, for the whole day, I pass . . . and you . . . stir water in a bucket till it is thick."

Just now on concluding, I asked one of those always "hanging-about" me, to read me aloud straight through all that I have written in this first chapter, and thereupon my "I"—of course with the participation of all the results of the data crystallized in my common presence during my past years, which give, by the way, also knowledge and understanding of the psyche of the surrounding diversely-typed fertilizers of such "Nature's-blessings" as wheat, potatoes, horseradish and other similar products which our poor hapless Earth yields with great difficulty—constated and cognized with anxiety that in the common presence of every reader without exception belonging to any of the three sexes, there must inevitably thanks to this chapter alone, arise a "something" engendering so to say "unfriendliness" towards me.

To tell the truth, it is not this which now chiefly worries me, but the fact that at the end of his reading, I also constated that I had manifested myself in this writing contrary to one of the fundamental commandments of that All-Common teacher whom I particularly esteem, Mullah Nassr Eddin, which he formulates in the words:

"Never-stir-up-a-hornets'-nest."

As regards the first qualms that arose in me, they immediately ceased when I remembered an ancient Russian proverb, the truth of which I have many times experienced and verified, and which says:

"Time-grinds-every-grain."

But my agitation from cognizing my negligence in obeying the always irrefragably sound advice of Mullah Nassr Eddin, not only now seriously troubles me, but I experience now, at an accelerating tempo, an impulse of "Remorse-of-Conscience"; and furthermore, after I understood this, a very strange process began and at the present moment continues in both of my recently acquired "souls," which manifests itself in the form of an unusual itching, the result of which

----

evokes and produces an almost intolerable pain in the region a little below the right half of my, already without this, over-exercised "Solar Plexus."

Wait! Wait! . . . This process, it seems, is beginning to slow down, and I am now completely certain that it will cease entirely because, remembering another fragment of life-wisdom, I immediately reflected that if I indeed acted against the advice of the highly esteemed Mullah Nassr Eddin, I, however, acted unintentionally, according to the principle of that extremely sympathetic—though not well known everywhere on the Earth, yet memorable to all who have once met him—that nugget, Karapet.

It can't be helped. . . . Now that this introductory chapter of mine has turned out to be so long, it will not matter if I lengthen it a little more to tell you also about this extremely sympathetic Karapet of Tiflis.

First of all I must state that twenty or twenty-five years ago, the Tiflis railway station had a "steam whistle."

It was blown every morning to wake the railway workers and station hands, and as the Tiflis station stood on a hill, this whistle was heard almost all over the town and woke up not only the railway workers, but the inhabitants of the town of Tiflis itself.

The Tiflis local government, as I recall it, even entered into a correspondence with the railway authorities about the disturbance of the morning sleep of the peaceful citizens.

To release the steam into the whistle every morning was the job of this same Karapet who was employed in the station.

So when he would come in the morning to the rope with which he released the steam for the whistle, he

45

would, before taking hold of the rope and pulling it, wave his hand in all directions and solemnly, like a Mohammedan mullah from a minaret, loudly cry:

"Your mother is a—— , your father is a—— , your grandfather is more than a—— ; may your eyes, ears, nose, spleen, liver, corns . . ." and so on; in short, he pronounced in various keys all the curses he knew, and not until he had done so would he pull the rope.

When I heard about this Karapet and of this practice of his, I visited him one evening after the day's work, with a small boordook of wine, and after performing this indispensable local solemn "toasting ritual," I asked him, of course in a suitable form and also according to the local complex of "amenities" established for mutual relationship, why he did this.

Having emptied his glass at a draught and having once sung the famous Georgian song, "Little did we tipple," inevitably sung when drinking, he leisurely began to answer as follows:

"As you drink wine not as people do today, that is to say, not merely for appearances but in fact honestly, then this already shows me that you do not wish to know about this practice of mine out of curiosity, like our engineers and technicians, but really owing to your desire for knowledge, and therefore I wish, and even consider it my duty, sincerely to confess to you the exact reason of these inner, so to say, 'scrupulous considerations' of mine, which led me to this, and which little by little instilled in me such a habit."

He then related the following:

"Formerly I used to work in this station at night cleaning the steam boilers, but when this steam whistle was brought here, the stationmaster, evidently considering my age and incapacity for the heavy work I was doing, ordered me to occupy myself only with releasing the steam into

46

the whistle, for which I had to arrive punctually every morning and evening.

I think, patient reader, that now that this Preface of mine has turned out to be so long, it will not matter if I spin it out a little more—lead where it may—to tell about this Karapet also.

Twenty or twenty-five years ago, the Tiflis railway station had a "steam-whistle."

It was blown every morning to awaken the railway-workers and station-hands, and as the Tiflis station stood on a hill, this whistle was heard almost all over the town, and woke up not only the railway-workers, but the inhabitants of the town of Tiflis itself.

The Tiflis local government, as I recall it, had even had, as was then the custom, what is called a "long-drawn-out-correspondence" with the railway authorities about the disturbance of the morning sleep of the peaceful citizens.

To release the steam into this whistle every morning was the job of this same Karapet, who was employed in the station.

So when this Tiflis Karapet would come in the morning to the rope with which he released the steam for the whistle, he

would before taking hold of the rope, wave his hand in all directions and solemnly, like a Mohammedan Mullah from a minaret, loudly cry:

"Your mother is a . . . , your father is a . . . , your grandfather is more than a . . . , may your eyes, ears, nose, spleen, corns . . . " and so on; in short, he pronounced in various keys all the curses he knew, and not until he had done so, would he pull the rope.

Having heard of him and of this custom of his, I visited him one evening after the day's work, with a small Boordook of "Kahketeenian-wine," and after performing the local what is called "Toasting-ritual" I asked him, of course in a suitable form and also according to the local "amenities" for relationship, why he did this.

He frankly answered as follows:

"The first week of this new service, I once noticed that after performing this duty of mine, I felt for an hour or two vaguely ill at ease. But when this strange feeling, increasing day by day, ultimately became a definite instinctive uneasiness from which even my appetite for 'Makhokh' disappeared, I began from then on always to think and think in order to find out the cause of this. I thought about it all particularly intensely for some reason or other while going to and coming from my work, but however hard I tried I could make nothing whatsoever, even approximately, clear to myself.

"It thus continued for almost two years and, finally, when the calluses on my palms had become quite hard from the rope of the steam whistle, I quite accidentally and suddenly understood why I experienced this uneasiness.

"The shock for my correct understanding, as a result of which there was formed in me concerning this an unshakable conviction, was a certain exclamation I accidentally heard under the following, rather peculiar, circumstances.

"One morning when I had not had enough sleep, having spent the first half of the night at the christening of my neighbor's ninth daughter and the other half in reading a very interesting and rare book I had by chance obtained and which was entitled Dreams and Witchcraft, as I was hurrying on my way to release the steam, I suddenly saw at the corner a barber-surgeon I knew, belonging to the local government service, who beckoned me to stop.

"The duty of this barber-surgeon friend of mine consisted in going at a certain time through the town accompanied by an assistant with a specially constructed carriage and seizing all the stray dogs whose collars were without

47

the metal plates distributed by the local authorities on payment of the tax and taking these dogs to the municipal slaughterhouse where they were kept for two weeks at municipal expense, feeding on the slaughterhouse offal; if, on the expiration of this period, the owners of the dogs had not claimed them and paid the established tax, then these dogs were, with a certain solemnity, driven down a certain passageway which led directly to a specially built oven.

"After a short time, from the other end of this famous salutary oven, there flowed, with a delightful gurgling sound, a definite quantity of pellucid and ideally clean fat to the profit of the fathers of our town for the manufacture of soap and also perhaps of something else, and, with a purling sound, no less delightful to the ear, there poured out also a fair quantity of very useful substance for fertilizing.

"This barber-surgeon friend of mine proceeded in the following simple and admirably skillful manner to catch the dogs.

"He somewhere obtained a large, old, and ordinary fishing net, which, during these peculiar excursions of his for the general human welfare through the slums of our town, he carried, arranged in a suitable manner on his strong shoulders, and when a dog without its 'passport' came within the sphere of his all-seeing and, for all the canine species, terrible eye, he without haste and with the softness of a panther, would steal up closely to it and seizing a favorable moment when the dog was interested and attracted by something it noticed, cast his net on it and quickly entangled it, and later, rolling up the carriage, he disentangled the dog in

"You see . . . everybody who hears the whistle disturbing his sweet slumbers, will undoubtedly curse me, as the cause of this hellish row, 'by-everything-under-the-sun.'

"One morning when I had not had enough sleep myself, thanks to a christening at the neighbor's, and I was on my way to release the steam, I reflected upon this and decided to curse them all in advance, so that however much all those, as might be said, 'who-lie-in-the-realm-of-idiotism,' that is between sleep and waking, might afterwards curse me—it would have no effect on me."

such a way that it found itself in the cage attached to the carriage.

"Just when my friend the barber-surgeon beckoned me to stop, he was aiming to throw his net, at the opportune

----------------------------- *48* -----------------------------

moment, at his next victim, which at that moment was standing wagging his tail and looking at a bitch. My friend was just about to throw his net, when suddenly the bells of a neighboring church rang out, calling the people to early morning prayers. At such an unexpected ringing in the morning quiet, the dog took fright and springing aside flew off like a shot down the empty street at his full canine velocity.

"Then the barber-surgeon so infuriated by this that his hair, even beneath his armpits, stood on end, flung his net on the pavement and spitting over his left shoulder, loudly exclaimed:

"'Oh, Hell! What a time to ring!'

"As soon as the exclamation of the barber-surgeon reached my reflecting apparatus, there began to swarm in it various thoughts which ultimately led, in my view, to the correct understanding of just why there proceeded in me the aforesaid instinctive uneasiness.

"The first moment after I had understood this there even arose a feeling of being offended at myself that such a simple and clear thought had not entered my head before.

"I sensed with the whole of my being that my effect on the general life could produce no other result than that process which had all along proceeded in me.

"And indeed, everyone awakened by the noise I make with the steam whistle, which disturbs his sweet morning slumbers, must without doubt curse me 'by everything under the sun,' just me, the cause of this hellish row, and thanks to this, there must of course certainly flow towards my person from all directions, vibrations of all kinds of malice.

"On that significant morning, when, after performing my duties, I, in my customary mood of depression, was sitting in a neighboring 'Dukhan' and eating 'Hachi' with garlic,

----------------------------- *49* -----------------------------

I, continuing to ponder, came to the conclusion that if I should curse beforehand all those to whom my service for the benefit of certain among them might seem disturbing, then, according to the explanation of the book I had read the night before, however much all those, as they might be called, 'who lie in the sphere of idiocy,' that is, between sleep and drowsiness, might curse me, it would have—as explained in that same book—no effect on me at all.

"And in fact, since I began to do so, I no longer feel the said instinctive uneasiness."

Well, now, patient reader, I must really conclude this opening chapter. It has now only to be signed.

He who . . .

Stop! Misunderstanding formation! With a signature there must be no joking,

- -

- -

Now, this is indeed already enough.
This warning of mine must be signed.
He who . . .

Stop! Old fellow! With a signature there must be no joking. Otherwise the same otherwise the same will be done to you as once before in one of the empires of Central Europe, when you were made to pay ten years' rent for a house you occupied only for three months, merely because you had set your hand to a paper undertaking to renew the contract for the house each year.

Of course after this and still other instances from life experience, I must in any case in respect of my own signature, be very, very careful.

Very well then.

He who in childhood was called "Tatakh"; in early youth "Darky"; later the "Black Greek"; in middle age, the "Tiger of Turkestan"; and now, not just anybody, but the genuine "Monsieur" or "Mister" Gurdjieff, or the nephew of "Prince Mukransky," or finally, simply a "Teacher of Dancing."

-------------------------------- *50* --------------------------------

will be done to you as was done to you once before in one of the Empires of Central Europe, when you were made to pay ten years' rent for a house you occupied for only three months in all, merely because you had set your hand to a paper undertaking to renew the contract for the house each year.

Of course after this and still other instances from life experience, I must, in any comparable case, in respect of my own signature, be scrupulously careful.

Very well then. He who in early youth was called the "Black-Greek"; in middle age, the "Turkestan-Tiger"; and now, not just anybody, but the genuine "Monsieur" or "Mister Gurdjieff," or the nephew of "Prince Mukransky," or finally, just a "Teacher-of-Dancing."

Introduction

Why Beelzebub Was in Our Solar System

I T WAS in the year 223 after the creation of the World, by objective time-calculation, or, as it would be said here on the "Earth," in the year 1921 after the
birth of Christ.

Through the Universe flew the ship *Karnak* of the "transspace" communication.

It was flying from the spaces "Assooparatsata," that is, from the spaces of the
"Milky Way," from the planet Karatas to the solar system "Pandetznokh," the sun
of which is also called the "Pole Star."

On the said "transspace" ship was Beelzebub with his kinsmen and near attendants.

He was on his way to the planet Revozvradendr to a special conference in
which he had consented to take part, at the request of his friends of long standing.

Only the remembrance of these old friendships had constrained him to accept
this invitation, since he was no longer young, and so lengthy a journey, and the
vicissitudes inseparable from it, were by no means an easy task for one of his
years.

Only a little before this journey Beelzebub had returned home to the planet
Karatas where he had received his arising and far from which, on account of circumstances independent of his own essence, he had passed many years of his existence in conditions not proper to his nature.

This many-yeared existence, unsuited to him, together with the perceptions
unusual for his nature and the experiences not proper to his essence involved in
it, had not failed to leave on his common presence a perceptible mark.

---------------------------------- *51* ----------------------------------

Besides, time itself had by now inevitably aged him, and the said unusual conditions of existence had brought Beelzebub, just that Beelzebub who had had such
an exceptionally strong, fiery, and splendid youth, to an also exceptional old age.

Long, long before, while Beelzebub was still existing at home on the planet
Karatas, he had been taken, owing to his extraordinarily resourceful intelligence,
into service on the "Sun Absolute," where our LORD SOVEREIGN ENDLESS-
NESS has the fundamental place of HIS Dwelling; and there Beelzebub, among
others like himself, had become an attendant upon HIS ENDLESSNESS.

It was just then that, owing to the as yet unformed Reason due to his youth, and
owing to his callow and therefore still impetuous mentation with unequally flowing associations—that is, owing to a mentation based, as is natural to beings who
have not yet become definitely responsible, on a limited understanding—Beelzebub once saw in the government of the World something which seemed to him
"illogical," and having found support among his comrades, beings like himself
not yet formed, interfered in what was none of his business.

Introduction: Why Beelzebub Was In Our Solar System

IT WAS in the year 223 after the creation of the World, by objective time-calculation, or, as it would be said here on the Earth, in the year 1921 after the Birth of Christ.

Through the Universe flew the ship "Karnak" of the "trans-space" communication.

It flew from the spaces "Assooparatsata," that is, from the spaces of the "Milky Way," from the planet "Karatas" to the solar system "Pandetznokh," the sun of which is also called the "Pole Star."

On the said "trans-space ship" was Beelzebub with his kinsmen and near attendants.

He was on his way to the planet "Revozvradendr" for a certain conference in which he had consented to take part, at the request of his friends of long-standing.

Only the remembrance of these old friendships had constrained him to accept this invitation since he was no longer young, and so long a journey, and the contingencies attached to it presented by no means an easy task for one of his years.

Only a little before this journey, Beelzebub had returned home to the planet "Karatas" where he had received his arising, and far from which, on account of circumstances independent of his essence, he had passed many years of his existence in conditions not proper to his nature.

This many-yeared existence, unsuited to him, and the perceptions unusual for his nature, connected with it, and the experiences, inappropriate to his essence, had not failed to leave on his general "presence" a perceptible mark.

In addition, time itself had already aged him, and in the said unusual conditions of existence had brought Beelzebub, just that Beelzebub who had had so exceptionally strong, fiery, and splendid a youth, to an unusual old age also.

Long, long before, when Beelzebub was still existing at home on the planet "Karatas," he had been taken, owing to his exceptionally resourceful intelligence, into service on the "Sun Absolute," where our LORD SOVEREIGN ENDLESSNESS had the fundamental place of HIS dwelling; and there Beelzebub among others like himself, was attached as an attendant upon HIS ENDLESSNESS.

It was just then that, owing to the as yet unformed reason due to his youth, and owing to his callow and therefore still fiery mentation with unequally flowing associations, that is, owing to a mentation based as is natural to beings who have not yet become finally responsible on a narrow understanding, Beelzebub saw in the government of the World something which seemed to him "illogical," and having found support amongst comrades, beings like himself not yet formed, interfered in what was none of his business.

Thanks to the impetuosity and force of Beelzebub's nature, his intervention together with his comrades then soon captured all minds, and the effect was to bring the central kingdom of the Megalocosmos almost to the edge of revolution.

Having learned of this, HIS ENDLESSNESS, notwithstanding his All-lovingness and All-forgiveness, was constrained to banish Beelzebub with his comrades to one of the remote corners of the Universe, namely, to the solar system "Ors" whose inhabitants call it simply the "Solar System," and to assign as the place of their existence one of the planets of that solar system, namely, Mars, with the privilege of existing on other planets also, though only of the same solar system.

-------------------------------- 52 --------------------------------

Among these exiles, besides the said comrades of Beelzebub, were a number of those who merely sympathized with him, and also the attendants and subordinates both of Beelzebub and of his comrades.

All, with their households, arrived at this remote place and there in a short time on the planet Mars a whole colony was formed of three-centered beings from various planets of the central part of our Great Universe.

All this population, extraordinary for the said planet, accommodated itself little by little to its new dwelling place, and many of them even found one or another occupation for shortening the long years of their exile.

They found occupations either on this same planet Mars or upon the neighboring planets, namely, on those planets that had been almost entirely neglected on account of their remoteness from the Center and the poverty of all their formations.

As the years rolled by, many either on their own initiative or in response to needs of general character, migrated gradually from the planet Mars to other planets; but Beelzebub himself, together with his near attendants, remained on the planet Mars, where he organized his existence more or less tolerably.

One of his chief occupations was the arranging of an "observatory" on the planet Mars for the observation both of remote points of the Universe and of the conditions of existence of beings on neighboring planets; and this observatory of his, it may here be remarked, afterwards became well known and even famous everywhere in the Universe.

Although the solar system "Ors" had been neglected owing to its remoteness from the center and to many other reasons, nevertheless our LORD SOVEREIGN had sent from time to time HIS Messengers to the planets of this system, to regulate, more or less, the being-existence of the three-brained beings arising on them, for the co-ordination of

-------------------------------- 53 --------------------------------

the process of their existence with the general World Harmony.

And thus, to a certain planet of this solar system, namely, the planet Earth, there was once sent as such a Messenger from our ENDLESSNESS, a certain Ashiata Shiemash, and as Beelzebub had then fulfilled a certain need in connection with his mission, the said Messenger, when he returned once more to the "Sun Absolute," earnestly besought HIS ENDLESSNESS to pardon this once young and fiery but now aged Beelzebub.

Thanks to the fury and force of Beelzebub's nature, his intervention together with that of his comrades, then soon captured all minds and the effect was almost to bring the central kingdom of the Megalocosmos into revolution.

Having learned of this, HIS ENDLESSNESS, in spite of his All-lovingness and All-forgivingness, was constrained to exile Beelzebub with his comrades to one of the remote corners of the Universe, namely, to the solar system "Ors," whose inhabitants call it simply the "solar system," and HE assigned as the place for their existence one of the planets of that solar system, namely, "Mars," with the privilege of existing on other planets also, although of the same solar system only.

Among these exiles, besides the said comrades of Beelzebub, were a number of those who merely sympathized with him, and also the attendants and subordinates both of Beelzebub and of his comrades.

All, with their households, arrived at this remote place and there in a short time on the planet "Mars" a whole colony was formed of three-centered beings from various planets of the central part of our Great Universe.

All this population, incongruous with the said planet, accommodated itself little by little to its new dwelling place and many of them even found one or another occupation for shortening the long years of their exile.

They found occupations either on this same planet "Mars" or upon the neighboring planets, namely, on those planets that had been almost neglected on account of their remoteness from the center and the poverty of all their formations.

As the years rolled by, many, either voluntarily or in response to needs of a general character, migrated gradually from the planet "Mars" to other planets, but Beelzebub himself, together with his near attendants, remained to exist on the planet "Mars," where he organized his existence more or less tolerably.

One of his chief occupations was the arranging of an "observatory" on the planet "Mars" for the observation of remote points of the Universe and the conditions of existence of beings on neighboring planets; and this observatory of his, it may be remarked, afterwards became well known and even famous everywhere in the Universe.

Although the solar system "Ors" had been neglected owing to its remoteness from the center, and to many other reasons, nevertheless our LORD SOVEREIGN had sent HIS Messengers from time to time to the planets of this system, to regulate, more or less, the being-existence of the three-brained beings arising on them for the coordination

of the process of their existence with the general World Harmony.

And thus, to a certain planet of this solar system, namely, the planet "Earth" as such a Messenger from our ENDLESSNESS there was once sent, a certain Jesus Christ, and as Beelzebub had then fulfilled a certain need in connection with his mission, when the said Messenger returned again to the "Sun Absolute," he ardently besought HIS ENDLESSNESS to pardon this once young and fiery but now aged Beelzebub.

In view of this request of Ashiata Shiemash, and also of the modest and cognoscent existence of Beelzebub himself, our MAKER CREATOR pardoned him and gave him permission to return to the place of his arising.

And that is why Beelzebub, after a long absence, happened now to be again in the center of the Universe.

His influence and authority had not only not declined during his exile, but, on the contrary, they had greatly increased, since all those around him were clearly aware that, thanks to his prolonged existence in the aforementioned unusual conditions, his knowledge and experience must inevitably have been broadened and deepened.

And so, when events of great importance occurred on one of the planets of the solar system "Pandetznokh," Beelzebub's old friends had decided to intrude upon him and to invite him to the conference concerning these events.

And it was as the outcome of this that Beelzebub was now making the long journey on the ship *Karnak* from the planet Karatas to the planet Revozvradendr.

On this big space-ship *Karnak*, the passengers included the kinsmen and attendants of Beelzebub and also many beings who served on the ship itself.

During the period to which this tale of ours refers, all the passengers were occupied either with their duties

------------------------------ 54 ------------------------------

or simply with the actualization of what is called "active being mentation."

Among all the passengers aboard the ship, one very handsome boy was conspicuous; he was always near Beelzebub himself.

This was Hassein, the son of Beelzebub's favorite son Tooloof. After his return home from exile, Beelzebub had seen this grandson of his, Hassein, for the first time, and, appreciating his good heart, and also owing to what is called "family attraction," he took an instant liking to him.

And as the time happened to coincide with the time when the Reason of little Hassein needed to be developed, Beelzebub, having a great deal of free time there, himself undertook the education of his grandson, and from that time on took Hassein everywhere about with him.

That is why Hassein also was accompanying Beelzebub on this long journey and was among the number around him.

And Hassein, on his side, so loved his grandfather that he would not stir a step without him, and he eagerly absorbed everything his grandfather either said or taught.

At the time of this narrative, Beelzebub with Hassein and his devoted old servant Ahoon, who always accompanied him everywhere, were seated on the highest "Kasnik," that is, on the upper deck of the ship *Karnak* under the "Kalnokranonis," somewhat resembling what we should call a large "glass bell," and were talking there among themselves while observing the boundless space.

Beelzebub was talking about the solar system where he had passed long years.

And Beelzebub was just then describing the peculiarities of the nature of the planet called Venus.

During the conversation it was reported to Beelzebub that the captain of their ship wished to speak with him and to this request Beelzebub acceded.

------------------------------ 55 ------------------------------

In view of this request of Jesus Christ and also of the modest and cognoscent existence of Beelzebub himself, our MAKER CREATOR pardoned him and gave him permission to return to the place of his arising.

And that is why Beelzebub, after a long absence, happened now to be again in the center of the Universe.

His influence and authority had not only not diminished during his exile, but, on the contrary, were much increased, since all about him were clearly aware that, thanks to his prolonged existence in the unusual conditions mentioned, his knowledge and experience must inevitably have become both wider and deeper.

And so, when events of great importance happened to occur on one of the planets of the solar system "Pandetznokh," Beelzebub's old friends at once decided to intrude upon him and to invite him to the conference concerning them.

It was as a result of this that Beelzebub was now making the long journey on the ship "Karnak," from the planet "Karatas" to the planet "Revozvradendr."

On this big spaceship "Karnak," there were as passengers the kinsmen and attendants of Beelzebub and also many beings who served on the ship itself.

During the period to which this tale of ours refers, all the passengers were occupied either with their duties,

- -

or they simply actualized what is called "active-being-mentation."

Amongst all the passengers aboard the ship was conspicuous a very handsome boy; he was always near Beelzebub himself.

This was Hassein, the son of the favorite son of Beelzebub, Tooloof. After his return home from exile, Beelzebub had seen this grandson of his, Hassein, for the first time, and appreciating his good heart and also owing to what are called "family ties," he immediately took a liking to him.

And as the time chanced to coincide with the time when the reason of little Hassein needed to be developed, Beelzebub having a great deal of free time there undertook himself the education of his grandson, and from that time on took Hassein everywhere about with him.

That is why Hassein also was accompanying Beelzebub on this long journey and was among the number around him.

And Hassein, on his side, so loved his grandfather that he would not stir a step without him and he eagerly absorbed everything that his grandfather either said or taught.

At the time indicated, Beelzebub with Hassein and his devoted old servant Ahhoon, who always accompanied him everywhere, were seated on the highest "Kasnik," that is, on the upper deck of the ship "Karnak" under the "Kalnokranonis," somewhat resembling what we should call a large "glass-bell," and talking there among themselves while observing the boundless space.

Beelzebub was just then describing the peculiarities of the nature of the planet called "Venus."

During the conversation it was reported to Beelzebub that the captain of their ship wished to speak with him and to this request Beelzebub agreed.

- -

The Cause of the Delay in the Falling of the Ship Karnak

THE captain soon afterward entered and having performed before Beelzebub all the ceremonies appropriate to Beelzebub's rank, said:

"Your Right Reverence, allow me to ask your authoritative opinion upon an 'inevitability' that lies in the line of our course, and which will hinder our smooth falling by the shortest route.

"The point is that if we follow our intended course, then our ship, after two 'Kilprenos*', will pass through the solar system 'Vuanik.'

"But just through where our ship must pass, there must also pass, about a 'Kilpreno' before, the great comet belonging to that solar system and named 'Sakoor' or, as it is sometimes called, the 'Madcap.'

"So if we keep to our proposed course, we must inevitably traverse the space through which this comet will have to pass.

"Your Right Reverence of course knows that this 'Madcap' comet always leaves in its track a great deal of 'Zilnotrago' which on entering the planetary body of a being disorganizes most of its functions until all the 'Zilnotrago' is volatilized out of it.

"I thought at first," continued the captain, "of avoiding the 'Zilnotrago' by steering the ship around these spheres,

------------------------------ *56* ------------------------------

but for this a long detour would be necessary which would greatly lengthen the time of our passage. On the other hand, to wait somewhere until the 'Zilnotrago†' is dispersed would take still longer.

"In view of the sharp distinction in the alternatives before us, I cannot myself decide what to do, and so I have ventured to trouble you, your Right Reverence, for your competent advice."

The captain having finished speaking, Beelzebub thought a little and then said as follows:

"Really, I do not know how to advise you, my dear Captain. Ah, yes . . . in that solar system where I existed for a long time, there is a planet called Earth. On that planet Earth arose, and still continue to arise, very strange three-centered beings. And among the beings of a continent of that planet called 'Asia,' there arose and existed a very wise three-brained being whom they called there 'Mullah Nassr Eddin.'

"For each and every peculiar situation great and small in the existence of the beings there," Beelzebub continued, "this same terrestrial sage Mullah Nassr Eddin had an apt and pithy saying.

"As all his sayings were full of the sense of truth for existence there, I also

---

* The word "Kilpreno" in the language of Beelzebub means a certain period of time, equal approximately to the duration of the flow of time which we call an "hour."

† The word "Zilnotrago" is the name of a special gas similar to what we call "cyanic acid."

The Reason Of The Delay In The Falling Of The "Karnak"

THE CAPTAIN soon afterwards entered and, having performed before Beelzebub all the ceremonies appropriate to Beelzebub's position, said:

"Your Right Reverence, allow me to ask you your authoritative opinion upon an inevitable eventuality that lies in the line of our course, which will hinder our smooth falling by the shortest route.

"The case is, that if we follow our intended course, then our ship, after two 'Kilpreno', will pass through the solar system 'Vuanik.'

"But just through where our ship must pass, there also must pass, about a 'Kilpreno' before, the great comet belonging to that solar system named 'Sakoor' or, as it is sometimes called, the 'Madcap.'

"So if we keep on our arranged course, we must inevitably traverse the space through which the comet will have passed.

"Moreover, Your Right Reverence knows that this 'Madcap' comet always leaves in its track a great deal of 'Zilnotrago', which on entering the 'planetary body' of a being, disorganizes most of its functions until all the 'Zilnotrago' is dispersed from it.

"I thought at first," continued the captain, "to avoid the 'Zilnotrago' by steering the ship around these spheres.

- -

But a long detour would then be necessary which would greatly lengthen the time of our passage.

"On the other hand, to wait somewhere until the 'Zilnotrago' disperses will take still longer.

"In view of the sharp distinction in the alternatives before us I cannot decide now by myself what to do and so I have ventured to trouble you, Your Right Reverence, for your competent advice."

The captain having finished speaking, Beelzebub thought a little and then said as follows:

"Really I do not know how to advise you, my dear captain. Ah, yes . . . in that solar system where I existed for a long time, there is a planet called 'Earth.' On that planet 'Earth' very peculiar three-centered beings arose and still continue to arise. And among the beings of a continent of that planet called 'Asia' there arose and existed a very wise three-brained being whom they called there 'Mullah Nassr Eddin.'

"For each and every peculiar situation, whether great or small in the existence of the beings there, this same terrestrial sage, Mullah Nassr Eddin, had an apt and pointed saying.

"As all his sayings were full of the sense of truth for existence there, I also always used them there as a guide, in order to have a comfortable existence among the beings of that planet.

"And in the given case too, my dear Captain, I intend to profit by one of his wise sayings.

"In such a situation as has befallen us, he would probably say: 'You cannot jump over your knees and it is absurd to try to kiss your own elbow.'

"I now say the same to you, and I add: there is nothing to be done; when an event is impending which arises from forces immeasurably greater than our own, one must submit.

---------------------------- 57 -----------------------------

"The only question is, which of the alternatives you mentioned should be chosen—that is, to wait somewhere or to add to our journey by a 'detour.'

"You say that to make a detour will greatly lengthen our journey but that waiting will take still longer.

"Good, my dear Captain. Suppose that by making the detour we should save a little time, what do you think: Is the wear and tear of the parts of our ship's machinery worthwhile for the sake of ending our journey a little sooner?

"If the detour should involve even the most trifling damage to our ship, then in my opinion we ought to prefer your second suggestion, that is, to stop somewhere until the path is cleared of the noxious 'Zilnotrago.' By that means we should spare our ship useless damage.

"And we will try to fill the period of this unforeseen delay with something useful for us all.

"For instance, it would give me personally great pleasure to talk with you about contemporary ships in general and about our ship in particular.

"Very many new things, of which I still know nothing, have been done in this field during my absence from these parts.

"For example, in my time these big transspace ships were so complicated and cumbersome that it took almost half their power to carry the materials necessary to elaborate their possibility of locomotion.

"But in their simplicity and the freedom on them, these contemporary ships are just embodiments of 'Bliss-stokirno.'

"There is such a simplicity for beings upon them and such freedom in respect of all being-manifestations that at times you forget that you are not on one of the planets.

"So, my dear Captain, I should like very much to know how this boon was brought about and how the contemporary ships work.

---------------------------- 58 -----------------------------

"But now go and make all arrangements necessary for the required stopping. And then, when you are quite free, come to me again and we will pass the time of our unavoidable delay in conversation useful for us all."

When the captain had gone, Hassein suddenly sprang to his feet and began to dance and clap his hands and shout:

"Oh, I'm glad, I'm glad, I'm glad of this."

always used them in order to have a comfortable existence among the beings of that planet.

"In the given case also, my dear Captain, I intend to profit by one of his wise sayings.

"In such a situation as has befallen us he would probably say:

"You cannot jump over your knees and it's absurd to try to kiss your own elbow.

"Now I also say the same to you and add: There is nothing to be done; when an event is foreseen, coming from forces immeasurably superior to us, one must submit.

"The question is only this: which of the two alternatives you mentioned should be chosen, namely, to wait somewhere or to make a roundabout 'detour.'

"You say that to make a detour will greatly lengthen our journey, but that waiting will take still longer.

"Good, my dear captain. Suppose we should make the detour and even save a little time by it, what do you think? Is the wear and tear and working of the parts of our ship's machinery worthwhile for the sake of getting to the end of our journey a little sooner?

"If such a detour involves even trifling damage to our ship, then in my opinion we ought to prefer your second suggestion, that is, to stop somewhere until the path is cleared of the noxious 'Zilnotrago,' thereby at least saving our ship useless damage.

"And the period of this unforeseen delay we will try to fill with something useful for us all.

"For instance, it would give me personally great pleasure to talk with you about contemporary ships in general and our ship in particular.

"Very many new things, as yet quite unknown to me, have been done in this field during my absence from these places.

"I can cite this as an example, that in my time these big trans-space ships were so complicated and cumbersome that almost half their power was spent in carrying the necessary materials to make their locomotion possible.

"But these contemporary ships in their simplicity and the freedom on them are just embodiments of 'Bliss-stokirno.'

"There is such a simplicity upon them for beings and such a freedom in respect of all being-manifestations that you could frequently forget that you were not on one of the planets.

"So, my dear captain, I should very much like to know how this blessing was brought about and how the contemporary ships work.

"And now go and make all the arrangements necessary for the needed stopping. And then, when you are quite free, come to me again and we will pass the time of our unavoidable delay in conversation useful for all of us.

When the captain had gone, Hassein suddenly sprang to his feet and began to dance and clap his hands and shout:

"Oh, I'm glad, I'm glad, I'm glad for this!"

Beelzebub looked with affection on these joyous manifestations of his favorite, but old Ahoon could not restrain himself and, shaking his head reproachfully, called the boy—half to himself—a "growing egoist."

Hearing what Ahoon called him, Hassein stopped in front of him, and, looking at him mischievously, said:

"Don't be angry with me, old Ahoon. The reason for my joy is not egoism but only the coincidence which chances to be happy for me. You heard, didn't you? My dear grandfather did not decide only just to make a stop, but he also promised the captain to talk with him. . . .

"And you know, don't you, that the talks of my dear grandfather always bring out tales of places where he has been, and you know also how delightfully he tells them and how much new and interesting information becomes crystallized in our presences from these tales.

"Where is the egoism? Hasn't he himself, of his own free will, having weighed with his wise reason all the circumstances of this unforeseen event, decided to make a stop which evidently doesn't upset his intended plans very much?

"It seems to me that my dear grandfather has no need to hurry; everything necessary for his rest and comfort is present on the *Karnak* and here also are many who love him and whom he loves.

"Don't you remember he said recently 'we must not

------------------------------ 59 ------------------------------

oppose forces higher than our own' and added that not only one must not oppose them, but even submit and receive all their results with reverence, at the same time praising and glorifying the wonderful and providential works of Our Lord Creator?

"I am not glad because of the misadventure but because an unforeseen event issuing from above has occurred, owing to which we shall be able to listen once more to the tales of my dear grandfather.

"Is it my fault that the circumstances are by chance most desirable and happy for me?

"No, dear Ahoon, not only should you not rebuke me, but you should join me in expressing gratitude to the source of all beneficent results that arise."

All this time Beelzebub listened attentively and with a smile to the chatter of his favorite, and when he had finished said:

"You are right, dear Hassein, and for being right I will tell you, even before the captain's arrival, anything you like."

Upon hearing this, the boy at once ran and sat at the feet of Beelzebub and after thinking a little said:

"My dear Grandfather, you have told me so much about the solar system where you spent so many years, that now perhaps I could continue just by logic alone to describe the details of the nature of that peculiar corner of our Universe.

"But I am curious to know whether there dwell three-brained beings on the planets of that solar system and whether higher 'being-bodies' are coated in them.

Beelzebub looked with affection at these manifestations of his favorite, but old Ahoon could not restrain himself and, shaking his head reproachfully, called the boy—half to himself—a "growing egoist."

Hearing what Ahoon called him Hassein stopped in front of him, looked at him mischievously and said:

"Don't be angry with me, old Ahoon. The reason of my joy is not egoism but only the happy chance coincidence for me. You heard, didn't you? My dear grand-father decided not only just to make a stop but he also promised the captain to talk with him.

"And this you know, that the talks of my dear grandfather always bring out tales of places where he has been, and you know also how well he relates them and that from these tales so much new and interesting information becomes crystallized in our 'presences.'

"Where is the egoism? He has himself of his own free will, having weighed with his wise reason all the circumstances of this unforeseen event, decided to make a stop which evidently doesn't upset his intended plans very much.

"It seems to me that my dear grandfather has no need to hurry; everything ne-cessary for his rest and comfort is present on the 'Karnak' and here also are many who love him and whom he loves.

"Don't you remember he said recently, 'We must not

oppose forces higher than our own,' and added that not only one must not oppose but even submit and receive all their results with reverence, at the same time praising and glorifying the wonderful and providential works of our LORD CRE-ATOR.

"I am not glad because of the misadventure but because an unforeseen event issuing from above has occurred, owing to which we shall be able to listen once more to the tales of my dear grandfather.

"Is it my fault that the circumstances are by chance most desirable and happy for me?

"No, dear Ahoon, not only ought I not to be blamed but I should be joined in rendering gratitude to the source of all beneficent results which arise."

All this time Beelzebub listened attentively and with a smile to the chatter of his favorite and when he had finished said:

"You are right, dear Hassein, and for being right I shall tell you, even before the captain's arrival, anything you like."

Upon hearing this, the boy at once ran and sat at the feet of Beelzebub and after thinking a little said:

"My dear grandfather, you have told me so much about the solar system where you spent so many years that I could now perhaps even continue logically to de-scribe the details of the nature of this peculiar corner of our Universe.

"But I am now curious to know whether there dwell three-brained beings on the planets of that solar system and whether higher 'being-bodies' are coated in them.

"Please tell me now about just this, dear Grandfather," concluded Hassein, looking affectionately up at Beelzebub.

"Yes," replied Beelzebub, "on almost all the planets of that solar system also, three-brained beings dwell, and in almost all of them higher being-bodies can be coated.

-------------------------------- 60 --------------------------------

"Higher being-bodies, or as they are called on some planets of that solar system, souls, arise in the three-brained beings breeding on all the planets except those before reaching which the emanations of our 'Most Holy Sun Absolute,' owing to repeated deflections, gradually lose the fullness of their strength and eventually cease entirely to contain the vivific power for coating higher being-bodies.

"Certainly, my boy, on each separate planet of that solar system also, the planetary bodies of the three-brained beings are coated and take an exterior form in conformity with the nature of the given planet, and are adapted in their details to the surrounding nature.

"For instance, on that planet on which it was ordained that all we exiles should exist, namely, the planet Mars, the three-brained beings are coated with planetary bodies having the form—how shall I tell you—a form like a 'karoona,' that is to say, they have a long broad trunk, amply provided with fat, and heads with enormous protruding and shining eyes. On the back of this enormous 'planetary body' of theirs are two large wings, and on the under side two comparatively small feet with very strong claws.

"Almost the whole strength of this enormous 'planetary body' is adapted by nature to generate energy for their eyes and for their wings.

"As a result, the three-brained beings breeding on that planet can see freely everywhere, whatever the 'Kal-da-zakh-tee,' and they can also move not only over the planet itself but also in its atmosphere and some of them occasionally even manage to travel beyond the limits of its atmosphere.

"The three-brained beings breeding on another planet, a little below the planet Mars, owing to the intense cold there are covered with thick soft wool.

-------------------------------- 61 --------------------------------

"The external form of these three-centered beings is like that of a 'Toosook,' that is, it resembles a kind of 'double sphere,' the upper sphere serving to contain the principal organs of the whole planetary body, and the other, the lower sphere, the organs for the transformation of the first and second being-foods.

"There are three apertures in the upper sphere, opening outwards; two serve for sight and the third for hearing.

"The other, the lower sphere, has only two apertures: one in front for taking in the first and second being-foods, and the other at the back for the elimination from the organism of residues.

"To the lower sphere are also attached two very strong sinewy feet, and on each of these is a growth that serves the purpose of fingers with us.

"There is still another planet, a quite small one, bearing the name Moon, in that solar system, my dear boy.

"During its motion this peculiar little planet often approached very near to our

"Please tell me now just about this, dear grandfather," concluded Hassein, looking affectionately up at Beelzebub.

"Yes," replied Beelzebub, "on almost all the planets of that solar system also, three-brained beings dwell and in almost all of them higher being-bodies can be coated.

- -

"Higher being-bodies or, as on some planets of that solar system they are called, souls only do not arise in the three-brained beings breeding on those planets, before reaching which, the emanations of our most holy 'Sun Absolute' owing to repeated refractions, gradually lose the fullness of their strength and eventually cease to contain the vivific power for coating the higher being-bodies.

"Certainly, my boy, on each separate planet of that solar system also, the 'planetary' bodies of the three-brained beings are coated and take an exterior in conformity with the nature of the given planet, and are adapted in their detail to the surrounding nature.

"For instance, on that planet on which all we exiles had been ordered to exist, namely, the planet Mars, the three-brained beings are coated with planetary bodies having the form . . . how shall I tell you, a form like a 'karoona,' that is to say, they have a long broad trunk, amply provided with fat, and heads with enormous protruding and shining eyes. On the back of this enormous 'planetary-body' of theirs are two large wings, and on the under side two comparatively small feet but having very strong claws.

"Almost the whole strength of this enormous 'planetary body' is adapted by Nature for the transforming of energy for their eyes and wings.

"As a result, the three-brained beings breeding on that planet can see freely everywhere whatever the 'Kal-da-zakh-tee' and they can also move, not only over the planet itself but also in its atmosphere and some of them occasionally even manage to travel beyond its limits.

"The three-brained beings breeding on another planet, a little below the planet 'Mars,' owing to the intense cold there, are covered with thick soft wool.

- -

"The external form of these three-centered beings is like that of a 'Toosook,' that is, it somewhat resembles a 'double-sphere,' the upper sphere serving to contain the principal organs of the whole planetary body, and the other, the lower sphere, for the transformation of food.

"There are three apertures in the upper sphere, one in front opening outwards; two serve for sight and the third for hearing.

"The other, the lower sphere, had only two apertures: one is in front for taking in food and the other at the back for the elimination from the organism of the residue.

"To the lower sphere are also attached two very strong sinewy feet, and on each of these is a growth that serves the purpose of fingers with us.

"There is still another planet, a quite small one, bearing the name 'Moon,' in that solar system, my dear boy.

"During its motion this peculiar little planet often approached very near to our

planet Mars and sometimes during whole 'Kilprenos' I took great pleasure in observing through my 'Teskooano*' in my observatory the process of existence of
the three-brained beings upon it.

"Though the beings of this planet have very frail 'planetary bodies,' they have
on the other hand a very 'strong spirit,' owing to which they all possess an extraordinary perseverance and capacity for work.

"In exterior form they resemble what are called large ants; and, like these, they
are always bustling about, working both on and within their planet.

"The results of their ceaseless activity are now already plainly visible.

"I once happened to notice that during two of our years

- 62 -

they 'tunneled,' so to say, the whole of their planet.

"They were compelled to undertake this task on account of the abnormal local
climatic conditions, which are due to the fact that this planet arose unexpectedly,
and the regulation of its climatic harmony was therefore not prearranged by the
Higher Powers.

"The 'climate' of this planet is 'mad,' and in its variability it could give points to
the most highly strung hysterical women existing on another of the planets of that
same solar system, of which I shall also tell you.

"Sometimes there are such frosts on this 'Moon' that everything is frozen
through and through and it becomes impossible for beings to breathe in the open
atmosphere; and then suddenly it becomes so hot there that an egg can be cooked
in its atmosphere in a jiffy.

"For only two short periods on that peculiar little planet, namely, before and
after its complete revolution about its neighbor—another planet nearby—the
weather is so glorious that for several rotations the whole planet is in blossom and
yields the various products for their first being-food greatly in excess of their general need during their existence in that peculiar intraplanetary kingdom which
they have arranged and where they are protected from all the vagaries of this
'mad' climate inharmoniously changing the state of the atmosphere.

"Nearest to that small planet is another, a larger planet, which also occasionally
approaches quite close to the planet Mars and is called Earth.

"The said Moon is just a part of this Earth and the latter must now constantly
maintain the Moon's existence.

"On the just mentioned planet Earth, also, three-brained beings are formed;
and they also contain all the data for coating higher being-bodies in themselves.

"But in 'strength of spirit' they do not begin to compare with the beings breeding on the little planet aforementioned.

- 63 -

The external coatings of the three-brained beings of that planet Earth closely resemble our own; only, first of all, their skin is a little slimier than ours, and then,
secondly, they have no tail, and their heads are without horns. What is worst
about them is their feet, namely, they have no hoofs; it is true that for protection
against external influences they have invented what they call 'boots,' but this in-

---

* "Teskooano" means "telescope."

planet 'Mars' and sometimes during whole 'Kilprenos' I took great pleasure in observing through the 'Teskooano' in my observatory the process of existence of the three-brained beings upon it.

"Although the beings of this planet have very frail 'planetary bodies,' they have, on the other hand, a very 'strong spirit,' owing to which they all possess an extraordinary perseverance and capacity for work.

"In exterior form they resemble what are called large ants; and, like these, are always bustling about, working both on and within their planet.

"The results of their ceaseless activity are already now plainly visible.

"I once happened to notice that during two of our years

they 'tunneled,' so to speak, the whole of their planet.

"They were compelled to undertake this task on account of the abnormal local climatic conditions which are due to the fact that this planet arose unexpectedly, and the regulation of its climatic harmony was therefore not prearranged by the Higher Powers.

"The 'climate' of this planet is really 'mad,' and in its variability it could give points to the most highly strung hysterical woman existing on another of the planets of that same solar system of which I shall also tell you.

"Sometimes there are such frosts on that 'Moon' that everything is frozen through and through, and it becomes impossible for the beings to breathe in the open atmosphere; and then suddenly it becomes so hot there that an 'egg' can be cooked in its atmosphere in a jiffy.

"For only two short periods on that peculiar planet, namely, before and after its complete revolution about its neighbor—another planet nearby—the weather is so glorious that for several rotations the whole planet is in blossom and yields the various products for their first being-food greatly in excess of their general need for their existence in that peculiar intraplanetary kingdom which they have arranged and where they are protected from all the vagaries of that 'mad' climate which unharmoniously changes the state of the planet's atmosphere.

"Nearest to that small planet is another, a large planet, which also occasionally approaches quite close to the planet 'Mars' and is called 'Earth.'

"The said 'Moon' is just a part of this 'Earth' and the latter must now constantly maintain the Moon's existence.

"On the just mentioned planet 'Earth,' three-brained beings also are formed; and they also contain all the data for coating higher-being-bodies in themselves.

"But in 'strength of spirit' they do not begin to compare with the beings breeding on the little planet before mentioned.

"The external coatings of the three-brained beings of that planet 'Earth' closely resemble our own only, first of all, their skin is a little slimier than ours, and then, secondly they have no tail, and their heads are without horns. What is worst about them is their feet, namely, they have no hoofs; it is true for protection against external influences they have invented what they call 'boots' but this invention is of

vention does not help them very much.

"Apart from the imperfection of their exterior form, their Reason also is quite 'uniquely strange.'

"Their 'being-Reason,' owing to very many causes about which also I may tell you sometime, has gradually degenerated, and at the present time, is very, very strange and exceedingly peculiar."

Beelzebub would have said still more, but the captain of the ship entering at that moment, Beelzebub, after promising the boy to tell him about the beings of the planet Earth on another occasion, began to talk with the captain.

Beelzebub asked the captain to tell him, first, who he was, how long he had been captain, and how he liked his work, and afterwards to explain some of the details of the contemporary cosmic ships.

Thereupon the captain said:

"Your Right Reverence, I was destined by my father, as soon as I reached the age of a responsible being, for this career in the service of our ENDLESS CREATOR.

"Starting with the lowest positions on the transspace ships, I ultimately merited to perform the duties of captain, and it is now eight years that I have been captain on the long-distance ships.

"This last post of mine, namely, that of captain of the ship *Karnak*, I took, strictly speaking, in succession to my father, when after his long years of blameless service to HIS ENDLESSNESS in the performance of the duties of captain

———————————————————— *64* ————————————————————

from almost the very beginning of the World-creation, he had become worthy to be promoted to the post of Ruler of the solar system 'Kalman.'

"In short," continued the captain, "I began my service just when your Right Reverence was departing for the place of your exile.

"I was still only a 'sweeper' on the long-distance ships of that period.

"Yes . . . a long, long time has passed by.

"Everything has undergone change and is changed since then; only our LORD AND SOVEREIGN remains unchanged. The blessings of 'Amenzano' on HIS UNCHANGEABLENESS throughout Eternity!

"You, your Right Reverence, have condescended to remark very justly that the former ships were very inconvenient and cumbersome.

"Yes, they were then, indeed, very complicated and cumbersome. I too remember them very well. There is an enormous difference between the ships of that time and the ships now.

"In our youth all such ships both for intersystem and for interplanetary communication were still run on the cosmic substance 'Elekilpomagtistzen,' which is a totality consisting of two separate parts of the omnipresent Okidanokh.

"And it was to obtain this totality that just those numerous materials were necessary which the former ships had to carry.

"But these ships did not remain in use long after you flew from these parts, having soon thereafter been replaced by ships of the system of Saint Venoma."

———————————————————— *65* ————————————————————

very little use to them.

"Not only is their external form imperfect, but even their reason is quite 'uniquely strange.'

"Their 'being-reason,' owing to very many causes about which also I may tell you sometime, has gradually degenerated, and, at the present time is very very strange and exceedingly peculiar."

Beelzebub would have said still more, but the captain of the ship entering at that moment, Beelzebub, after promising the boy to tell him about the beings of the planet 'Earth' on another occasion, began to talk to the captain.

Beelzebub asked the captain to tell him, first, who he was, how long he had been captain, and how he liked his work, and afterwards to explain some of the details of the contemporary cosmic ships.

Thereupon the captain said:

"Your Right Reverence, I was destined by my father, as soon as I approached the age of a responsible being, for this career in the service of our ENDLESS CRE-ATOR.

"Starting with the lowest positions on the trans-space ships, I ultimately merited to perform the duties of captain, and it is now eight years that I have been captain on the long distance ships.

"This last post of mine, namely, that of captain of the ship 'Karnak' I took, strictly speaking, in succession to my father, when after his long years of blameless service to HIS ENDLESSNESS in the performance of the duties of captain

from almost the very beginning of the World-Building, he was promoted to the post of the Ruler of the solar system 'Kalman.'

"In short," continued the captain, "I began my service just then when Your Right Reverence was departing for the place of your exile.

"I was still only a 'sweeper' on the long distance ships of that period.

"Yes . . . a long, long time has passed by.

"Everything has undergone change and is changed since then; only OUR LORD AND SOVEREIGN remains unchanged. The blessings of 'Amenzano' upon HIS UNCHANGEABLENESS throughout Eternity!

"You, Your Right Reverence, have condescended to remark very justly that former 'ships' were very inconvenient and cumbersome.

"Yes, they were then, indeed, very complicated and cumbersome. I also remember them very well. There is an enormous difference between the ships of that time and the ships now.

"In my youth all these ships both for trans-system and for trans-planetary communication were still run on the cosmic substance 'Elekilpomagtistzen,' which is the totality of the separate parts of the omnipresent active element Okidanokh in a certain proportion and is found chiefly in the atmosphere surrounding planets.

"And it was to obtain this substance that just those numerous materials were necessary which the former ships had to carry.

"But after your flight from these parts these ships did not remain in use long, having soon thereafter been replaced by ships of the system of Saint Venoma."

The Law of Falling

THE captain continued:
     "This happened in the year 185, by objective time-calculation.

"Saint Venoma had been taken for his merits from the planet 'Soort' to the holy planet 'Purgatory,' where, after he had familiarized himself with his new surroundings and new duties, he gave all his free time to his favorite work.

"And his favorite work was to seek what new phenomena could be found in various combinations of already existing, law-conformable phenomena.

"And sometime later, in the course of these occupations, this Saint Venoma first constated in cosmic laws what later became a famous discovery, and this discovery he first called the 'Law of Falling.'

"This cosmic law which he then discovered, St. Venoma himself formulated thus:

"'Everything existing in the World falls to the bottom. And the bottom for any part of the Universe is its nearest "stability," and this said "stability" is the place or the point upon which all the lines of force arriving from all directions converge.

"'The centers of all the suns and of all the planets of our Universe are just such points of "stability." They are the lowest points of those regions of space upon which forces from all directions of the given part of the Universe definitely tend and where they are concentrated. In these points there is also concentrated the equilibrium which enables suns and planets to maintain their position.'

"In this formulation of his, Saint Venoma said further that everything when dropped into space, wherever it

------------------------------ 66 ------------------------------

may be, tends to fall on one or another sun or on one or another planet, according to which sun or planet the given part of space belongs to, where the object is dropped, each sun or planet being for the given sphere the 'stability' or bottom.

"Starting from this, Saint Venoma reasoned in his further researches as follows:

"'If this be so, may it not therefore be possible to employ this cosmic particularity for the locomotion we need between the spaces of the Universe?'

"And from then on, he worked in this direction.

"His further saintly labors showed that although in principle this was in general possible, yet it was impossible fully to employ for this purpose this 'Law of Falling' discovered by him. And it would be impossible owing solely to the atmospheres around most of the cosmic concentrations, which atmospheres would hinder the straight falling of the object dropped in space.

"Having constated this, Saint Venoma then devoted his whole attention to discovering some means of overcoming the said atmospheric resistance for ships constructed on the principle of Falling.

"And after three 'Looniases' Saint Venoma did find such a possibility, and later on when the building of a suitable special construction had been completed

CHAPTER IV

The Law of Falling

THE CAPTAIN continued: "This happened in the year 185 by objective time-calculation.

"Saint Venoma had been taken for his merits from the planet 'Soort' to the holy planet 'Purgatory' where, after he had familiarized himself with his new surroundings and new duties, he gave all his free time to his favorite work.

"And his favorite work was to seek what new phenomena could be found in various combinations of phenomena already existing according to law.

"And some time later, in the course of these occupations, this Saint Venoma constated for the first time in cosmic laws what later became a famous discovery, which discovery he himself first called the 'Law of Falling.'

"This cosmic law which he then discovered, Saint Venoma himself formulated thus:

"Everything existing in the World falls to the bottom. And the bottom for any part of the Universe is its nearest 'stability,' and this said 'stability' is the place or the point upon which all the lines of forces arriving from all directions converge.

"'These points of 'stability' are the centers of all the suns and all the planets of our 'Universe.' They are just the lowest points of those regions of space upon which forces from all directions of the given part of the 'Universe' definitely tend and where they are concentrated. In these points there is also concentrated the equilibrium which enables suns and planets to maintain their position.'

"In this formulation of his, Saint Venoma said further that everything, when dropped in space wherever it

may be, tends to fall on one or another sun, or on one or another planet according to that sun or planet to which the given part of the space belongs where the object is dropped, each sun or planet being for the sphere in question the 'stability' or bottom.

"Starting from this, Saint Venoma reasoned in his further researches as follows:

"'If this is so, may it not therefore be possible to employ this cosmic particularity for the locomotion we need between the spaces of the Universe?'

"And from then on, he worked in this direction.

"His further saintly labors showed that, although in principle this was generally possible, yet for this purpose it was impossible to employ fully this 'Law of Falling' discovered for the first time by him. And it was impossible owing solely to the atmosphere around most of the cosmic concentrations, which atmosphere would prove an obstacle to the straight falling of the object dropped in space.

"Having constated this, Saint Venoma then devoted his whole attention to discovering some means of overcoming the said atmospheric resistance for ships constructed on the principle of falling.

"After three 'Looniases,' Saint Venoma found such a possible means also and later on when the building of a suitable special construction had been completed under his direction, he proceeded to practical trials.

"This special construction had the appearance of a large enclosure, all the walls of which were made of a special material something like glass.

"Then to every side of that large enclosure were fitted things like 'shutters' of a material impervious to the rays of the cosmic substance 'Elekilpomagtistzen,' and these shutters, although closely fitted to the walls of the said enclosure, could yet freely slide in every direction.

"Within the enclosure was placed a special 'battery,'

------------------------------ 67 ------------------------------

generating and giving this same substance 'Elekilpomagtistzen.'

"I myself, your Right Reverence, was present at the first trials made by Saint Venoma according to the principles he had discovered.

"The whole secret lay in this, that when the rays of 'Elekilpomagtistzen' were made to pass through this special glass, then in all the space they reached, everything usually composing the atmosphere itself of planets, such as 'air,' every kind of 'gas,' 'fog,' and so on, was destroyed. This part of space became indeed absolutely empty and had neither resistance nor pressure, so that, if even an infant-being pushed this enormous structure, it would move forward as easily as a feather.

"To the outer side of this peculiar structure there were attached appliances similar to wings, which were set in motion by means of this same substance 'Elekilpomagtistzen,' and served to give the impetus to move all this enormous construction in the required direction.

"The results of these experiments having been approved and blessed by the Commission of Inspection under the presidency of Archangel Adossia, the construction of a big ship based on these principles was begun.

"The ship was soon ready and commissioned for service. And in a short time, little by little, ships of this type came to be used exclusively, on all the lines of intersystem communication.

"Although later, your Right Reverence, the inconveniences of this system gradually became more and more apparent, nevertheless it continued to displace all the systems that had existed before.

"It cannot be gainsaid that although the ships constructed on this system were ideal in atmosphereless spaces, and moved there almost with the speed of the rays 'Etzikolnianakhnian' issuing from planets, yet when nearing

------------------------------ 68 ------------------------------

some sun or planet it became real torture for the beings directing them, as a great deal of complicated maneuvering was necessary.

"The need for this maneuvering was due to the same 'Law of Falling.'

"And this was because when the ship came into the medium of the atmosphere of some sun or planet which it had to pass, it immediately began to fall towards that sun or planet, and as I have already intimated, very much care and considerable knowledge were needed to prevent the ship from falling out of its course.

"While the ships were passing near any sun or planet whatsoever, their speed of locomotion had sometimes to be reduced hundreds of times below their usual

under his direction, he began his practical trials.

"This special construction had the appearance of a large enclosure all the walls of which were made of a special material something like glass.

"Then to every side of that large enclosure were fitted things like 'shutters' of a material impervious to the rays of the cosmic substance 'Elekilpomagtistzen,' and these shutters, although hermetically fitted to the walls of the said enclosure, could yet freely slide in every direction.

"Within that enclosure was placed a special 'battery,'

developing and giving this same substance 'Elekilpomagtistzen.'

"I myself, Your Right Reverence, was present at the first trial made by Saint Venoma according to the principles he had found.

"The whole secret lay in this, that when the rays of 'Elekilpomagtistzen' were made to pass through this special glass, then everything within the space they reached, usually composing the atmosphere itself of the planet, such as 'air,' every kind of 'gas,' 'fog' and so on, was destroyed. This part of space became indeed absolutely empty and had neither resistance nor pressure, so that if even an infant-being pushed this enormous structure, it would be moved forward as easily as a feather.

"To the outer sides of this peculiar structure there were attached appliances similar to wings, which were set in motion by means of this same substance 'Elekilpomagtistzen' and served to give the impetus to move all this enormous construction in the required direction. The results of these experiments having been approved and blessed by the Commission of Inspection under the presidency of Archangel Adossia, the construction of a big ship based on these principles was begun.

"The ship was soon ready and commissioned for service. And little by little in a short time only ships of this type were used on all the lines of trans-system communication.

"Although later, Your Right Reverence, the inconveniences also of this system gradually became more and more apparent, nevertheless it continued to displace all the systems that had existed before.

"It cannot be gainsaid that although the ships constructed on this system were ideal in atmosphereless spaces, and moved there almost with the speed of the rays 'Etzikolnianakhnian' issuing from a planet, yet when nearing

some sun or planet, it became real torture for the beings directing them, as a great deal of complicated maneuvering was necessary.

"The need for this maneuvering was due to the same 'Law of Falling.'

"And this was because when the ship came into the medium of the atmosphere of some sun or planet by which it had to pass, it immediately began to fall towards that sun or planet, and, as I have already stated, very much care and considerable knowledge were needed to prevent the ship from falling out of its course.

"While the ships were passing near any sun or planet whatsoever, their speed of locomotion had sometimes to be reduced by some hundreds of times below the rate.

"It was particularly difficult to steer them in those spheres where there was a great aggregation of 'comets.'

"That is why great demands were then made upon the beings who had to direct these ships, and they were prepared for these duties by beings of very high Reason.

"But in spite of the said drawbacks of the system of Saint Venoma, it gradually, as I have already said, displaced all the previous systems.

"And the ships of this system of Saint Venoma had already existed for twenty-three years when it was first rumored that the Angel Hariton had invented a new type of ship for intersystem and interplanetary communication."

usual rate.

"It was particularly difficult to steer them in those spheres where there was a great aggregation of 'comets.'

"That is why great demands were then made upon the beings who had to direct these ships, and they were prepared for these duties by beings with very high reason.

"But, in spite of the said drawbacks of the system of Saint Venoma, it gradually, as I have already stated, displaced all the previous systems.

"And the ships of this system of Saint Venoma had already existed for twenty three years when it was first rumored that the Angel Hariton had invented a new type of ship for trans-system and trans-planetary communication.

The System of Archangel Hariton

A ND indeed, soon after this rumor, practical experiments open to all, again under the superintendence of the Great Archangel Adossia, were made with this new and later very famous invention.

"This new system was unanimously acknowledged to be the best, and very soon it was adopted for general Universal service and thereafter gradually all previous systems were entirely superseded.

"That system of the Great Angel, now Archangel, Hariton is now in use everywhere at the present day.

"The ship on which we are now flying also belongs to this system and its construction is similar to that of all the ships built on the system of the Angel Hariton.

"This system is not very complicated.

"The whole of this great invention consists of only a single 'cylinder' shaped like an ordinary barrel.

"The secret of this cylinder lies in the disposition of the materials of which its inner side is made.

"These materials are arranged in a certain order and isolated from each other by means of 'amber.' They have such a property that if any cosmic gaseous substance whatever enters the space which they enclose, whether it be 'atmosphere,' 'air,' 'ether,' or any other 'totality' of homogeneous cosmic elements, it immediately expands, owing to the mentioned disposition of materials within the cylinder.

"The bottom of this cylinder-barrel is hermetically sealed, but its lid, although it can be closely shut, yet is so arranged on hinges that at a pressure from within it can be opened and shut again.

"So, your Right Reverence, if this cylinder-barrel is filled with atmosphere, air, or any other such substance,

--------------------------------- *70* ---------------------------------

then from the action of the walls of this peculiar cylinder-barrel, these substances expand to such an extent that the interior becomes too small to hold them.

"Striving to find an outlet from this, for them constricted, interior, they naturally press also against the lid of the cylinder-barrel, and thanks to the said hinges the lid opens and, having allowed these expanded substances to escape, immediately closes again. And as in general Nature abhors a vacuum, then simultaneously with the release of the expanded gaseous substances the cylinder-barrel is again filled with fresh substances from outside, with which in their turn the same proceeds as before, and so on without end.

"Thus the substances are always being changed, and the lid of the cylinder-barrel alternately opens and shuts.

"To this same lid there is fixed a very simple lever which moves with the movement of the lid and in turn sets in motion certain also very simple 'cogwheels'

The System of Archangel Hariton

A ND INDEED soon after this rumor, practical experiments open to all, again under the superintendence of the Great Archangel Adossia, were made with this new and later very famous invention.

"This new system was unanimously acknowledged to be the best, and very soon it was adopted for general-Universal-service and thereafter gradually all the previous systems were entirely superseded.

"That system of the Great Angel, today Archangel Hariton is in use everywhere at the present day.

"The ship on which we are now flying also belongs to this system and its construction is similar to that of all the ships built on the system of the Angel Hariton.

"This system is not very complicated.

"The whole of this great invention consists of only a single 'cylinder' shaped like an ordinary barrel.

"The secret of this cylinder lies in the disposition of the materials of which its inner side is made.

"These materials are arranged in certain order and isolated each from the other by means of 'Amber.' They have such a property that if any cosmic gaseous substance whatever enters into the space which they enclose, whether it be 'atmosphere,' 'air,' 'ether' or any other 'totality' of homogeneous cosmic elements, then, owing to the mentioned disposition of materials within the cylinder, it immediately expands.

"The bottom of this cylinder-barrel is hermetically sealed, but its lid, although it can be closely shut, yet is so arranged on hinges that, at a pressure from within, it can be opened and shut again.

"So, Your Right Reverence, if this cylinder-barrel is filled with atmosphere, air or any other such substance,

-----

then from the action of the walls of this peculiar cylinder-barrel, these substances expand to such an extent that the interior becomes too small to hold them.

"Striving to find an outlet from this, for them, constricted interior, they naturally press also against the lid of the cylinder-barrel, thanks to the said hinges the lid opens and, having allowed these expanded substances to escape, immediately closes again. And as in general, Nature abhors a vacuum, simultaneously with the release of the expanded gaseous substances, the cylinder-barrel is again filled with fresh substances from outside, with which in their turn the same proceeds as before and so on without end.

"Thus the substances are always being changed, and the lid of the cylinder-barrel alternately opens and shuts.

"To this same lid there is fixed a very simple lever which moves with the movement of the lid, and in turn sets in motion certain also very simple 'cog-wheels' which again in their turn revolve the fans attached to the sides and stern of the ship itself.

"Thus, your Right Reverence, in spaces where there is no resistance, contemporary ships like ours simply fall towards the nearest 'stability'; but in spaces where there are any cosmic substances which offer resistance, these substances, whatever their density, with the aid of this cylinder enable the ship to move in any desired direction.

"It is interesting to remark that the denser the substance is in any given part of the Universe, the better and more strongly the charging and discharging of this cylinder-barrel proceed, and in consequence of course, the force of the movement of the levers is also changed.

"But nevertheless, I repeat, a sphere without atmosphere, that is, a space containing only World Etherokrilno, is for contemporary ships also the best, because in such a sphere there is no resistance at all, and the

---------------------------------- *71* ----------------------------------

'Law of Falling' can therefore be fully employed in it without any assistance from the work of the cylinder.

"Further than this, the contemporary ships are also good because they contain such possibilities that in atmosphereless spaces an impetus can be given to them in any direction, and they can fall just where desired without the complicated manipulations necessary in ships of the system of Saint Venoma.

"In short, your Right Reverence, the convenience and simplicity of the contemporary ships are beyond comparison with former ships, which were often both very complicated and at the same time had none of the possibilities of the ships we use now."

---------------------------------- *72* ----------------------------------

which again in their turn revolve the fans attached to the sides and stern of the ship itself.

"Thus, Your Right Reverence, in spaces where there is no resistance, contemporary ships like ours simply fall toward the nearest 'stability'; but in spaces where there are any cosmic substances which offer resistance, these substances, whatever their density, with the aid of this cylinder enable the ship to move in any desired direction.

"It is interesting to remark that the denser the substance in any given part of the Universe, the better and more strongly the charging and discharging of this cylinder-barrel proceed and in consequence, of course, the force of the movement of the levers is also changed.

"But nevertheless, I repeat, a sphere without atmosphere, that is, a space containing only World-Etherokrilno, is for contemporary ships also the best, because in such a sphere there is no resistance at all, and the

'Law of Falling' can therefore be fully employed in it without any assistance from the work of the cylinder.

"Further than this, the contemporary ships are also good, because they contain such possibilities that in substanceless spaces an impetus can be given to them in any direction, and they can fall just where desired which was not possible for ships of the system of Saint Venoma without complicated manipulations.

"In short, Your Right Reverence, the convenience and simplicity of the contemporary ships are beyond comparison with former ships, which were often both very complicated, and at the same time, had none of the possibilities of the ships we use now."

Perpetual Motion

"W AIT! Wait!" Beelzebub interrupted the captain. "This—what you have just told us—must surely be just that short-lived idea which the strange three-brained beings breeding on the planet Earth called 'perpetual motion' and on account of which at one period a great many of them there went quite, as they themselves say, 'mad,' and many even perished entirely.

"It once happened there on that ill-fated planet that somebody in some way or another got into his head the, as they say, 'crazy notion' that he could make a 'mechanism' that would run forever without requiring any material from outside.

"This notion so took everybody's fancy that most of the queer fellows of that peculiar planet began thinking about it and trying to realize this miracle in practice.

"How many of them paid for this short-lived idea with all the material and spiritual welfare which they had previously with great difficulty acquired!

"For one reason or another they were all quite determined to invent what in their opinion was a 'simple matter.'

"External circumstances permitting, many took up the invention of this 'perpetual motion' without any inner data for such work; some from reliance upon their 'knowledge,' others upon 'luck,' but most of them just from their already complete psychopathy.

"In short, the invention of 'perpetual motion' was, as they say, 'the rage,' and every crank felt obliged to be interested in this question.

"I was once in one of the towns there where models of every kind and innumerable 'descriptions' of proposed

------------------------------- 73 -------------------------------

'mechanisms' for this 'perpetual motion' were assembled.

"What wasn't there? What 'ingenious' and complicated machines did I not see? In any single one of these mechanisms I saw there, there must have been more ideas and 'wiseacrings' than in all the laws of World-creation and World-existence.

"I noted at the time that in these innumerable models and descriptions of proposed mechanisms, the idea of using what is called the 'force of weight' predominated. And the idea of employing the 'force of weight' they explained thus: a very complicated mechanism was to lift 'some' weight and this latter was then to fall and by its fall set the whole mechanism in motion, which motion would again lift the weight, and so on, and so on.

"The result of it all was that thousands were shut up in 'lunatic asylums,' thousands more, having made this idea their dream, either began to fail altogether to fulfill even those being-duties of theirs which had somehow or other in the course of many years been established there, or to fulfill them in such a way as 'couldn't be worse.'

"I don't know how it would all have ended if some quite demented being there,

CHAPTER VI

Perpetual Motion

W AIT! . . . WAIT!" Beelzebub interrupted the captain, "This that you have just told us must surely be just that flimsy idea, which the strange three-brained beings breeding on the planet Earth call 'Perpetual Motion,' and on account of which at one period very many of them there went as they themselves say quite 'mad,' and many even quite perished.

"It happened that somebody once there on that ill-starred planet in some way or other got into his head, as they say, the crazy notion that he could create a 'mechanism' that would work forever without needing any material from outside.

"This notion so took everybody's fancy that most of the queer fellows of that peculiar planet thought about it and tried to realize this miracle in practice.

"How many of them paid for this flimsy idea with their material and spiritual welfare which they had acquired previously with great difficulty!

"And everyone wished for one or another reason absolutely to invent what, in their opinion, was this 'trifle.'

"External circumstances permitting, many took up the invention of this 'Perpetual Motion' without any inner data for such work; some from reliance upon their 'knowledge,' others upon 'luck' but most of them just from their already fulfilled psychopathy.

"In short, the invention of 'Perpetual Motion' was, as they say, the 'rage,' and everyone of these freaks was expected to be interested in this question.

"I was once in one of the towns there where 'models' of every kind, and innumerable 'descriptions' of proposed

'mechanisms' for this 'Perpetual Motion' were assembled.

"What, what only was not there! . . . what 'ingenious' and complicated machines did I not see there . . . In any single one of the 'mechanisms' I saw, there must have been more ideas and 'wiseacrings' than in all the laws of the World-creation and World-existence.

"I noted at the time that in these innumerable models and descriptions of proposed mechanisms, the idea of using what is called the 'force of weight' predominated. And the idea of employing the 'force of weight' they explained thus: a very complicated mechanism was to lift 'some' weight and this latter was then to fall and by its fall set the whole mechanism in motion, which motion would again lift this weight and so on and so on.

"The result of it all was, that thousands were shut up in 'lunatic asylums'; thousands more, having made this idea their dream, already either began to fail to fulfil even those being duties of theirs which had somehow or other in the course of many years been established there, or did them already quite atrociously.

"I don't know how it all would have ended if some quite demented being there with one foot already in the grave, such a one as they themselves call an 'old dot-ard,' and who had previously somehow acquired a certain authority, had not proved by 'calculations' known only to himself that it was absolutely impossible to invent 'perpetual motion.'

"Now, after your explanation, I can well understand how the cylinder of the system of Archangel Hariton works. It is the very thing of which these unfortunates there dreamed.

"Indeed, of the 'cylinder' of the system of the Archangel Hariton it can safely be said that, with atmosphere alone given, it will work perpetually without needing the expenditure of any outside materials.

"And since the world without planets and hence without

— 74 —

atmospheres cannot exist, then it follows that as long as the world exists and, in consequence, atmospheres, the cylinder-barrels invented by the great Archangel Hariton will always work.

"Now just one question occurs to me—about the material from which this cylinder-barrel is made.

"I wish very much, my dear Captain, that you would roughly tell me what materials it is made of and how long they can last," requested Beelzebub.

To this question of Beelzebub's the captain replied as follows: "Although the cylinder-barrel does not last forever, it can certainly last a very long time.

"Its chief part is made of 'amber' with 'platinum' hoops, and the interior panels of the walls are made of 'anthracite,' 'copper,' and 'ivory,' and a very strong 'mastic' unaffectable either by (1) 'paischakir' or by (2) 'tainolair' or by (3) 'saliakooriapa'* or even by the radiations of cosmic concentrations.

"But the other parts," the captain continued, "both the exterior 'levers' and the 'cogwheels,' must certainly be renewed from time to time, for though they are made of the strongest metal, yet long use will wear them out.

"And as for the body of the ship itself, its long existence can certainly not be guaranteed."

The captain intended to say still more, but at that moment a sound like the vibrations of a long minor chord of a far-off orchestra of wind instruments resounded through the ship.

With an apology the captain rose to leave, explaining as he did so that he must be needed on very important business, since everybody knew that he was with his Right Reverence and would not venture to trouble the ears of his Right Reverence for anything trifling.

— 75 —

---

* (1) Cold, (2) heat, and (3) water.

already with one foot in the grave, such a one as they themselves call an 'old codger' and who had previously acquired somehow a certain authority, had not 'proved' by 'calculations' known only to himself that it was absolutely impossible to invent 'Perpetual Motion.'

"Now after your explanation, I can well understand how the cylinder of the system of Archangel Hariton works. It is the very thing of which these unfortunates dreamed there.

"Indeed, of the cylinder of the system of Archangel Hariton, it can be safely said that, with atmosphere alone given, it will work perpetually without needing the expenditure of any outside materials.

"And since the World without planets and hence without

atmospheres cannot exist, then it follows that as long as the World exists and, in consequence, atmospheres, the cylinder-barrels invented by the great Archangel Hariton will always work.

"Now one question occurs to me personally just about the material from which this cylinder-barrel is made.

"I very much wish, my dear captain, that you would roughly tell me what materials it is made of and how long they can last," asked Beelzebub.

To this question of Beelzebub's the captain replied as follows:

"Although this cylinder-barrel does not last forever, it can certainly last a very long time.

"Its chief part is made of 'amber' with 'Platinum' hoops, and the interior panels of the walls are made of 'coal,' 'copper' and 'ivory,' and a very strong mastic unaffectable either by 'paischakir,' or by 'tainolair,' or by 'saliakooriapa,' or even by the radiations of cosmic concentrations.

"But the other parts," the captain continued, "both the exterior 'levers' and the 'cog-wheels,' must certainly be renewed from time to time, for although they are made of the strongest metal, yet long use will wear them out.

"And concerning the body of the ship itself, its long existence can certainly not be guaranteed."

The captain intended to say still more, but at that moment a sound like the vibrations of a long minor chord of a far off orchestra of wind instruments resounded through the ship.

With an apology the captain rose to leave, explaining as he did so, that he must be needed on very important business, since everybody knew that he was with his Right Reverence and would not venture to trouble the ears of his Right Reverence for anything trifling.

Becoming Aware of Genuine Being-Duty

AFTER the captain had gone, Beelzebub glanced at his grandson and, noticing his unusual state, asked him solicitously and with some anxiety:

"What is the matter, my dear boy? What are you thinking so deeply about?"

Looking up at his Grandfather with eyes full of sorrow, Hassein said thoughtfully:

"I don't know what is the matter with me, my dear Grandfather, but your talk with the captain of the ship has brought me to some exceedingly melancholy thoughts.

"Things of which I have never before thought are now a-thinking in me.

"Thanks to your talk, it has gradually become very clear to my consciousness that in the Universe of our ENDLESSNESS everything has not always been such as I now see and understand.

"Formerly, for instance, I should never have allowed such thoughts associatively to proceed in me, as that this ship on which we are now flying has not always been as it is at this moment.

"Only now have I come very clearly to understand that everything we have at the present time and everything we use—in a word, all the contemporary amenities and everything necessary for our comfort and welfare—have not always existed and did not make their appearance so easily.

"It seems that certain beings in the past have during very long periods labored and suffered very much for this, and endured a great deal which perhaps they even need not have endured.

------------------------------ 76 ------------------------------

"They labored and suffered only in order that we might now have all this and use it for our welfare.

"And all this they did, either consciously or unconsciously, just for us, that is to say, for beings quite unknown and entirely indifferent to them.

"And now not only do we not thank them, but we do not even know a thing about them, but take it all as in the natural order, and neither ponder nor trouble ourselves about this question at all.

"I, for instance, have already existed so many years in the Universe, yet the thought has never even entered my head that perhaps there was a time when everything I see and have did not exist, and that everything was not born with me like my nose.

"And so, my dear and kind Grandfather, now that owing to your conversation with the captain, I have gradually, with all my presence, become aware of all this, there has arisen in me, side by side with this, the need to make clear to my Reason why I personally have all the comforts which I now use, and what obligations I am under for them.

"It is just because of this that at the present moment there proceeds in me a 'process-of-remorse.'"

Becoming Aware Of Genuine Being-Duty

AFTER the captain had gone, Beelzebub glanced at his grandson and, noticing his unusual state, asked him solicitously and with some anxiety:

"What is the matter, my dear boy? What are you thinking so deeply about?"

Looking up at his grandfather with eyes full of sorrow Hassein said thoughtfully:

"I don't know what is the matter with me, my dear grandfather, but your talk with the captain of the ship has brought my thinking to some exceedingly melancholy thoughts.

"Things about which I have never before thought are now a-thinking in me.

"It has gradually become very clear to my consciousness during your talk that in the Universe of our ENDLESSNESS everything has not always been such as I now see and understand.

"Formerly, for instance, I should never have admitted such thoughts to associate in me, as that this ship on which we are now flying has not always been as it is at this moment.

"Only now have I come very clearly to understand that everything we have at the present time and everything we use—in a word, all the contemporary amenities and everything necessary for our comfort and welfare—have not always existed and did not appear so easily.

"It seems that certain beings in the past have during very long periods labored and suffered very much and for this endured a great deal, which perhaps they even need not have endured.

"They labored and suffered only that we might now have all this and use it for our welfare.

"And all this they did, either consciously or unconsciously, just for us, that is, just for beings quite unknown and absolutely indifferent to them.

"And now not only do we not thank them, but we even do not know a thing about them, but we take it all as in the natural order, and neither ponder nor trouble ourselves about the question at all.

"I, for instance, have already existed so many years in the Universe, yet the thought has never even entered my head, that perhaps there was a time when everything I see and have did not exist, and that everything was not born with me like my nose.

"And so, my dear and kind grandfather . . . Now, owing to your conversation with the captain, having gradually become aware of all this with all my 'presence,' there has arisen in me, side by side with this, the need to make clear to my reason just this, namely, why I personally have all the comforts which I now use, and what obligations I am under for them?

"It is just because of this that at the present time, there just proceeds in me a 'process-of-remorse.'"

Having said this, Hassein drooped his head and became silent; and Beelzebub, looking at him affectionately, began to speak as follows:

"I advise you, my dear Hassein, not to put such questions to yourself yet. Do not be impatient. Only when that period of your existence arrives which is proper for your becoming aware of such essence-questions, and you actively mentate about them, will you understand what you must do in return.

"Your present age does not yet oblige you to pay for your existence.

"The time of your present age is not given you in which to pay for your exist-

------------------------------ *77* ------------------------------

ence, but for preparing yourself for the future, for the obligations becoming to a responsible three-brained being.

"So in the meantime, exist as you exist. Only do not forget one thing, namely, at your age it is indispensably necessary that every day, at sunrise, while watching the reflection of its splendor, you bring about a contact between your consciousness and the various unconscious parts of your general presence. Try to make this state last and to convince the unconscious parts—not as if they were conscious— that if they hinder your general functioning, they, in the period of your responsible age, not only cannot fulfill the good that befits them, but your general presence of which they are part will not be able to be a good servant of our COMMON ENDLESS CREATOR and by that will not even be worthy to pay for your arising and existence.

"I repeat once more, my dear boy, try in the meantime not to think about these questions, which at your age it is still early for you to think about.

"Everything in its proper time!

"Now ask me to tell you whatever you wish, and I will do so.

"As the captain has not yet returned, he must be occupied there with his duties and will not be coming back so soon."

------------------------------ *78* ------------------------------

Having said this, Hassein drooped his head and became silent; and Beelzebub, looking at him affectionately, began to speak as follows:

"I advise you, my dear Hassein, not to put such questions to yourself yet. Be patient meanwhile.

"Only when the proper period of your existence arrives for your becoming aware of such an essence-question, and you actively think about it, will you understand what you must do far it in return.

"Your present age does not yet oblige you to pay for your existence.

"The time of your present age is given you not in which to pay for your exist-

ence, but for preparing yourself for the future, for the obligations becoming to a responsible three-brained being.

"So in the meantime exist as you exist. Only do not forget one thing and that is, very often with the consciousness you already have, persuade the unconscious parts of your general 'presence' that if these unconscious parts hinder their whole presence, then this whole presence when it becomes a responsible cosmic individuum will be unable to pay for its existence as it should, and in consequence unable to be a good servant to our COMMON ENDLESS CREATOR.

"I repeat, once more, my dear boy, try in the meantime not to think about these questions, about which it is still early far you at your age to think.

"Everything in its proper time!

"Now ask me what you like and I will reply. As the captain has not returned by now, he must be occupied there with his duties and will not be coming back so soon."

The Impudent Brat Hassein, Beelzebub's Grandson, Dares to Call Men "Slugs"

HASSEIN immediately sat down at Beelzebub's feet and coaxingly said: "Tell me anything you wish, my dear Grandfather. Anything you tell me will be the greatest joy for me, if only because it is you who relate it."

"No," objected Beelzebub, "you yourself ask what interests you most of all. It will give me at the present moment much pleasure to tell you about just whatever you particularly wish to know."

"Dear and kind Grandfather, tell me then something about those . . . how? . . . those . . . I forget . . . yes, about those 'slugs.'"

"What? About what slugs?" asked Beelzebub, not understanding the boy's question.

"Don't you remember, Grandfather, that a little while ago, when you spoke about the three-centered beings breeding on the various planets of that solar system where you existed for such a long time, you happened to say that on one planet—I forget how you called it—that on that planet exist three-centered beings who, on the whole, are like us, but whose skin is a little slimier than ours."

"Ah!" laughed Beelzebub. "You are surely asking about those beings who breed on the planet Earth and who call themselves 'men.'"

"Yes, Grandfather, yes, just that. Tell me about those 'men-beings,' a little more in detail. I should like to know more about them," concluded Hassein.

Then Beelzebub said: "About them I could tell you a great deal, for I often visited that planet and existed

--------------------------------- *79* ---------------------------------

among them for a long time and even made friends with many of those terrestrial three-brained beings.

"Indeed, you will find it very interesting to know more about these beings, for they are very peculiar.

"There are many things among them which you would not see among any other beings of any other planet of our Universe.

"I know them very well, because their arising, their further development, and their existence during many, many centuries, by their time calculation, have occurred before my eyes.

"And not only their own arising occurred before my eyes, but even the accomplished formation of the planet itself on which they arise and exist.

"When we first arrived on that solar system and settled on the planet Mars nothing yet existed on that planet Earth, which had not yet even had time to cool off completely after its concentration.

"From the very beginning, this same planet has been the cause of many serious troubles to our ENDLESSNESS.

"If you wish I will tell you first of all about the events of general cosmic character connected with this planet, which were the cause of the said troubles of our

The Impudent Brat Hassein, The Grandson Of Beelzebub, Dares To Call Us 'Slugs'

H ASSEIN immediately sat down at Beelzebub's feet and coaxingly said:
"Tell me anything you like, dear grandfather. Anything you tell me will be the greatest joy for me, only because it is just you who relate it.

"No," objected Beelzebub, "You yourself ask what interests you most of all. It will give me at the present moment much pleasure to tell you just about whatever you particularly wish to know."

"Dear and kind grandfather, tell me then something about those . . . how? . . . those . . . I forget . . . yes . . . about 'slugs.'"

"What, about what 'slugs'?" asked Beelzebub, not having understood the boy's question.

"Don't you remember, grandfather, that a little while ago, when you spoke about the three-centered beings breeding on various planets of that solar system where you existed for such a long time, you happened to say, that on one planet.. I forget how you called it.. on this very planet three-centered beings exist who are on the whole like us, but whose skin is a little slimier than ours."

"Ah . . . " laughed Beelzebub, "you surely are asking about those beings who breed on the planet "Earth" and who call themselves 'men.'"

"Yes! Grandfather, yes! . . . just about these 'men-beings,' relate a little more in detail. I wish to know more about them," concluded Hassein.

Then Beelzebub said; "I could tell you a great deal about them for I often visited that planet and existed

- -

among them and even made friends with many of those terrestrial three-brained beings.

"Indeed, you will find it very interesting to know more about these beings, for they are very peculiar.

"There are many things among them which you would not see among any other beings of any planet of our Universe.

"I know them very well for even their arising and their existence and self-perfecting during many, very many, centuries by their time-calculation have occurred before my eyes.

"And not only their own arising occurred before my eyes, but also even the completed formation of the planet itself on which they arise and exist.

"When we first arrived on this solar system and settled on the planet 'Mars,' nothing yet existed on this planet 'Earth,' which had not even yet had time to cool completely after its concentration.

"Quite from the beginning, this same planet has been the cause of many serious troubles to our ENDLESSNESS.

"If you wish I will tell you first of all about the events of general cosmic character connected with this planet which were the cause of the said cares of our

ENDLESSNESS.

"Yes, my dear Grandfather," said Hassein, "tell me first about this. It will surely be quite as interesting as everything you relate."

----------------------------- *80* -----------------------------

ENDLESSNESS.

"Yes, my dear grandfather, tell me first about this. It will surely be quite as interesting as anything you relate."

- -

The Cause of the Genesis of the Moon

B EELZEBUB began his tale as follows:
      "After we arrived on the planet Mars where we were directed to exist, we began slowly to settle down there.

"We were still fully absorbed in the bustle of organizing everything externally necessary for a more or less tolerable existence in the midst of that Nature absolutely foreign to us, when suddenly, on one of the very busiest days, the whole planet Mars was shaken, and a little later such an 'asphyxiating stink' arose that at first it seemed that everything in the Universe had been mixed up with something, one might say 'indescribable.'

"Only after a considerable time had passed and when the said stink had gone, did we recover and gradually make out what had happened.

"We understood that the cause of this terrible phenomenon was just that same planet Earth which from time to time approached very near to our planet Mars and which therefore we had possibilities of observing clearly, sometimes even without a 'Teskooano.'

"For reasons we could not yet comprehend, this planet, it transpired, had 'burst' and two fragments detached from it had flown off into space.

"I have already told you that this solar system was then still being formed and was not yet 'blended' completely with what is called 'The-Harmony-of-Reciprocal-Maintenance-of-All-Cosmic-Concentrations.'

"It was subsequently learned that in accordance with this said 'General-Cosmic-Harmony-of-Reciprocal-Maintenance-of-All-Cosmic-Concentrations' there had also to

-------------------------------- *81* --------------------------------

function in this system a comet of what is called 'vast orbit' still existing and named the comet 'Kondoor.'

"And just this very comet, although it was then already concentrated, was actualizing its 'full path' for only the first time.

"As certain competent Sacred Individuals also later confidentially explained to us, the line of the path of the said comet had to cross the line on which the path of that planet Earth also lay; but as a result of the erroneous calculations of a certain Sacred Individual concerned with the matters of World-creation and World-maintenance, the time of the passing of each of these concentrations through the point of intersection of the lines of their paths coincided, and owing to this error the planet Earth and the comet 'Kondoor' collided, and collided so violently that from this shock, as I have already told you, two large fragments were broken off from the planet Earth and flew into space.

"This shock entailed these serious consequences because on account of the recent arising of this planet, the atmosphere which might have served as a buffer in such a case had not yet had time to be completely formed upon it.

And, my boy, our ENDLESSNESS was also immediately informed of this gen-

The Cause Of The Genesis Of The Moon

BEELZEBUB began his tale as follows:

"After we arrived on the planet 'Mars,' where we were directed to exist, we began slowly to settle down there.

"We were still fully absorbed in the bustle of organizing everything externally necessary for a more or less tolerable existence amidst that Nature absolutely foreign to us, when suddenly, on one of the very busiest days, the whole planet 'Mars' was shaken, and a little later such a 'stupefying-odor' arose, that we thought at first that everything in the Universe had been mixed with something 'unmentionable.'

"Only after a considerable time had passed and when the said odor had disappeared did we recover and gradually make out what had happened.

"We understood that the cause of this terrible phenomenon was just that same planet 'Earth' which from time to time approached very near to our planet 'Mars' and which therefore we could observe very clearly, sometimes even without a 'Teskooano.'

"For reasons we could not yet comprehend, this planet, it transpired, had 'burst,' and two fragments separated from it had flown off into space.

"I have already told you, that this solar system had then only recently been formed and was not yet 'blended' completely with what is called 'The-Harmony-of-Reciprocal-Maintenance-of-all-Cosmic-Concentrations.'

"It was subsequently learned that in accordance with this said "General-Cosmic-Harmony-of-Reciprocal-Maintenance-of-all-Cosmic-Concentrations,' a comet of what is called 'vast orbit' still existing and named the comet 'Kondoor' had, also, to

- -

function in this system.

"And just that comet, although it was then already concentrated, was making its full appointed path for only the first time.

"As certain competent sacred Individuums also later explained confidentially to us, the line of the path of the said comet had to cross the line on which the path of that planet 'Earth' also lay; but as a result of the erroneous calculations of a certain sacred Individuum concerned with the affairs of World-building and World-maintenance, the time of passing through the point of intersection of the lines of the paths of both of these concentrations coincided, and owing to this error the planet 'Earth' and the comet 'Kondoor' collided, and collided so violently that from this shock, as I have already told you, two large fragments were broken off from the planet 'Earth' and flew into space.

"This shock entailed such serious consequences because on account of the recent arising of this planet, the atmosphere which usually serves us a buffer in such cases, had not yet had time to be completely formed upon it.

"So, my boy, our ENDLESSNESS was also immediately informed of this general cosmic misfortune.

"In consequence of this report, a whole commission consisting of Angels and Archangels, specialists in the work of World-creation and World-maintenance, under the direction of the Most Great Archangel Sakaki, was immediately sent from the Most Holy Sun Absolute to that solar system 'Ors.'

"The Most High Commission came to our planet Mars since it was the nearest to the planet Earth and from this planet of ours began its investigations.

"The sacred members of this Most High Commission at once quieted us by saying that the apprehended danger

------------------------------ 82 ------------------------------

of a catastrophe on a great cosmic scale had already passed.

"And the Arch-Engineer Archangel Algamatant was good enough to explain to us personally that in all probability what had happened was as follows:

"'The broken-off fragments of the planet Earth had lost the momentum they received from the shock before they had reached the limit of that part of space which is the sphere of this planet, and hence, according to the "Law of Falling," these fragments had begun to fall back towards their fundamental piece.

"'But they could no longer fall upon their fundamental piece, because in the meantime they had come under the cosmic law called "Law-of-Catching-Up" and were entirely subject to its influence, and they would therefore now make regular elliptic orbits around their fundamental piece, just as the fundamental piece, namely, the planet Earth, made and makes its orbit around its sun "Ors."

"'And so it will always continue, unless some new unforeseen catastrophe on a large scale changes it in one way or another.

"'Glory to Chance . . .' concluded His Pantemeasurability, 'the harmonious general-system movement was not destroyed by all this, and the peaceful existence of that system "Ors" was soon re-established.'

"But nevertheless, my boy, this Most High Commission, having then calculated all the facts at hand, and also all that might happen in the future, came to the conclusion that although the fragments of the planet Earth might maintain themselves for the time being in their existing positions, yet in view of certain so-called 'Tastartoonarian-displacements' conjectured by the Commission, they might in the future leave their position and bring about a large number of irreparable calamities both for this system 'Ors' and for other neighboring solar systems.

------------------------------ 83 ------------------------------

"Therefore the Most High Commission decided to take certain measures to avoid this eventuality.

"And they resolved that the best measure in the given case would be that the fundamental piece, namely, the planet Earth, should constantly send to its detached fragments, for their maintenance, the sacred vibrations 'Askokin.'

"This sacred substance can be formed on planets only when both fundamental cosmic laws operating in them, the sacred 'Heptaparaparshinokh' and the sacred 'Triamazikamno,' function, as is called, 'Ilnosoparno,' that is to say, when the said sacred cosmic laws in the given cosmic concentration are deflected independently and also manifest on its surface independently—of course independently

eral cosmic misfortune.

"In consequence of this report, a whole commission under the direction of the Most Great Archangel Sakaki, consisting of Angels and Archangels, specialists in the affairs of World-building and World-maintenance, was immediately sent from the Most Holy Sun Absolute to that solar system 'Ors.'

"The Most High Commission arrived on our planet 'Mars,' it being the nearest to the planet 'Earth,' and from this planet of ours began its investigations.

"The sacred members of this Most High Commission at once quieted us by saying that the apprehended danger

- -

of a catastrophe on a great cosmic scale had already passed.

"And the Arch-engineer Archangel Algamatant was good enough to explain to us personally that in all probability what had happened was as follows: "The broken off fragments of that planet 'Earth' had lost the momentum they received from the shock, before they had reached the limit of that part of the space which is the sphere of this planet, and hence according to the 'Law of Falling,' these fragments had begun to fall back towards their fundamental piece.

"But they could no longer fall upon their fundamental piece, because in the meantime they had come under the cosmic law called 'Law-of-Catching-Up' and were entirely subject to its influence, and they would therefore now make regular elliptic orbits around their fundamental piece, just as the fundamental piece, namely, the planet 'Earth,' made and makes its orbit ground its sun 'Ors.'

"And so it will continue until some fresh unforeseen catastrophe on a large scale changes it one way or another.

"Glory to the event' . . . concluded his Pantamensurability. The harmonious general-system-movement was not destroyed by all this, and the peaceful existence of that system 'Ors' was soon again reestablished.

"But nevertheless, my boy, this Most High Commission, having then calculated all the given facts at that time, and also all that might happen in the future, came to the conclusion that although the fragments of the planet 'Earth' might maintain themselves for the time being in their existing positions, yet in the future in view of certain so-called 'Tastartoonarian' transpositions conjectured by the Commission, they might leave their position and bring about a large number of irreparable calamities both for this system 'Ors' and for other neighboring solar systems.

- -

"The Most High Commission therefore decided to take certain measures beforehand to anticipate this eventuality.

"And they agreed that the best measure in the given case would be that the fundamental piece, namely, the planet 'Earth' should send constantly the sacred vibrations 'Askokin' to its separated fragments for their maintenance.

"This sacred substance can be formed on planets only when both fundamental cosmic laws operating in them, the sacred 'Heptaparaparshinokh' and the sacred 'Triamazikamno' function, as it is said, 'Ilnosoparno,' that is to say, when the said sacred cosmic laws in the given cosmic concentration are refracted and manifest on its Surface as well, independently—of course independently within certain

only within certain limits.

"And so, my boy, inasmuch as such a cosmic actualization was possible only with the sanction of HIS ENDLESSNESS, the Great Archangel Sakaki, accompanied by several other sacred members of that Most High Commission, set off immediately to HIS ENDLESSNESS to beseech Him to give the said sanction.

"And afterwards, when the said Sacred Individuals had obtained the sanction of HIS ENDLESSNESS for the actualization of the Ilnosoparnian process on that planet also, and when this process had been actualized under the direction of the same Great Archangel Sakaki, then from that time on, on that planet also, just as on many others, there began to arise the 'Corresponding,' owing to which the said detached fragments exist until now without constituting a menace for a catastrophe on a great scale.

"Of these two fragments, the larger was named 'Loonderperzo' and the smaller 'Anulios'; and the ordinary three-brained beings who afterwards arose and were formed on this planet also at first called them by these names; but the beings of later times called them differently at different

-------------------------------- 84 --------------------------------

periods, and in most recent times the larger fragment has come to be called Moon, but the name of the smaller has been gradually forgotten.

"As for the beings there now, not only have they no name at all for this smaller fragment, but they do not even suspect its existence.

"It is interesting to notice here that the beings of a continent on that planet called 'Atlantis,' which afterwards perished, still knew of this second fragment of their planet and also called it 'Anulios,' but the beings of the last period of the same continent, in whom the results of the consequences of the properties of that organ called 'Kundabuffer'—about which, it now seems, I shall have to explain to you even in great detail—had begun to be crystallized and to become part of their common presences, called it also 'Kimespai,' the meaning of which for them was 'Never-Allowing-One-to-Sleep-in-Peace.'

"Contemporary three-brained beings of this peculiar planet do not know of this former fragment of their planet, chiefly because its comparatively small size and the remoteness of the place of its movement make it quite invisible to their sight, and also because no 'grandmother' ever told them that once upon a time any such little satellite of their planet was known.

"And if any of them should by chance see it through their good, but nevertheless child's toy of theirs called a telescope, he would pay no attention to it, mistaking it simply for a big aerolite.

"The contemporary beings will probably never see it again, since it has become quite proper to their nature to see only unreality.

"Let us give them their due; during recent centuries they have really most artistically mechanized themselves to see nothing real.

"So, my boy, owing to all the aforesaid, there first arose

-------------------------------- 85 --------------------------------

on this planet Earth also, as there should, what are called 'Similitudes-of-the-

limits only.

"And so, my boy.

"Seeing that such a cosmic actualization was possible only with the sanction of HIS ENDLESSNESS, the Great Archangel Sakaki, accompanied by several other sacred members of that Most High Commission, set off immediately to HIS ENDLESSNESS to beg Him to give the said consent.

"And afterwards when the said sacred Individuums had obtained the sanction of HIS ENDLESSNESS for the actualization of the 'Ilnosoparnian' process on this planet also, and when this process was actualized under the direction of the same Great Archangel Sakaki, then from that time on on that planet also, just as on many others, there began to arise the 'Corresponding,' owing to which the said separated fragments exist until now without constituting a menace for a catastrophe on a great scale.

"Of these two fragments the larger was named 'Loonderperzo' and the smaller 'Anulios'; and the ordinary three-brained beings who afterwards arose on this planet also called them at first by these names; but the beings of later times called them differently at different

- -

periods, and the three-brained beings of the latest period there call the larger fragment 'Moon,' but the name of the smaller has been gradually forgotten.

"As for the beings there now, not only have they no name for this smaller fragment at all, but they do not even suspect its existence.

"It is interesting to notice here that the beings of a continent on that planet called 'Atlantis,' which afterwards perished, still knew of this second fragment of their planet and also called it 'Anulios,' but the beings of the last period of the same continent in whom the consequences of the properties of the organ Kundabuffer were crystallized and became part of their general presence, called it also 'Kimespai,' the meaning of which for them was 'One-That-Never-Allows-One-To-Sleep-In-Peace.'

"Contemporary three-brained beings of this peculiar planet are unaware of this former fragment of their planet, chiefly because its comparatively small size and the remoteness of the place of its movement, make it quite invisible to their sight, and also because no 'grandmother' ever told them that once upon a time such a small satellite of their planet was known.

"And if any of them should by chance see it through their good, but nevertheless children's toy, called a telescope, he would pay no attention to it, mistaking it simply for a big as they call it aerolite.

"The contemporary beings will probably never see it again since it has become a property of their nature to see only unreality.

"They must be given their due; during recent centuries they have indeed artistically mechanized themselves to see nothing real.

"So, my boy, owing to all the aforesaid, there first arose

- -

on this planet 'Earth' also, as they should, what are called 'Similarities of the

Whole,' or as they are also called 'Microcosmoses,' and further, there were formed from these 'Microcosmoses,' what are called 'Oduristelnian' and 'Polormedekhtic' vegetations.

"Still further, as also usually occurs, from the same 'Microcosmoses' there also began to be grouped various forms of what are called 'Tetartocosmoses' of all three brain-systems.

"And among these latter there then first arose just those biped 'Tetartocosmoses' whom you a while ago called 'slugs.'

"About how and why upon planets, during the transition of the fundamental sacred laws into 'Ilnosoparnian,' there arise 'Similitudes-of-the-Whole' and about what factors contribute to the formation of one or another of these, as they are called, 'systems of being-brains,' and also about all the laws of World-creation and World-maintenance in general, I will explain to you specially some other time.

"But meanwhile, know that these three-brained beings arising on the planet Earth, who interest you, had in them in the beginning the same possibilities for perfecting the functions for the acquisition of being-Reason as have all other forms of 'Tetartocosmoses' arising throughout the whole Universe.

"But afterwards, just in the period when they also, as it proceeds on other similar planets of our great Universe, were beginning gradually to be spiritualized by what is called 'being-instinct,' just then, unfortunately for them, there befell a misfortune which was unforeseen from Above and most grievous for them."

--------------------------------- 86 ---------------------------------

Whole,' or, as they are also called, 'Microcosmoses'; and, further, there were forced from these 'Microcosmoses' what are called 'Oduristolnian' and 'Polormedekhtic' vegetations.

"Still further, as it also usually proceeds, various forms of what are called 'Tetartocosmoses' of all three-brained systems also began to group themselves from the same 'Microcosmoses.'

"And among these latter there then first arose just those biped 'Tetartocosmoses' whom you a while ago called 'slugs.'

"About how and why upon planets where the fundamental sacred laws become 'Ilnosoparnian' there arise the 'Similarities of the Whole,' and about what factors contribute to the formation of one or another as they are called 'Systems of Being-Brains,' and concerning also all the laws of World-creation and World-existence in general I will specially explain to you some other time.

"But meanwhile know that these three-brained beings who interest you, arising on the planet 'Earth,' contained those same possibilities for perfecting the function of acquiring being-reason which possibilities all other forms of 'Tetartocosmoses' arising throughout the whole Universe.

"But afterwards, just during the period that they also were gradually being spiritualized by what is called being-instinct, as it proceeds on other similar planets of our great Universe, just then, unfortunately for them, there befell that misfortune which was unforeseen from Above and which was so deplorable for them."

- -

Why "Men" Are Not Men

B EELZEBUB sighed deeply and continued to speak as follows:
    "After the actualizing on this planet of the 'Ilnosoparnian' process, one year, by objective time-calculation, passed.

"During this period there had gradually been coordinated on this planet also the corresponding processes for the involution and evolution of everything arising there.

"And of course there began gradually to be crystallized in the three-brained beings there the corresponding data for the acquisition of objective Reason.

"In short, on this planet also everything had then already begun to proceed in the usual normal order.

"And therefore, my boy, if the Most High Commission under the supreme direction of the same Archangel Sakaki had not, at the end of a year, gone there again, perhaps all the subsequent misunderstandings connected with the three-brained beings arising on that ill-fated planet might not have occurred.

"This second descent of the Most High Commission to that planet was due to the fact that in spite of the measures they had taken, of which I have told you, there had not yet crystallized in the Reasons of the majority of its sacred members a complete assurance of the impossibility of any undesirable surprise in the future, and they now wished to verify on the spot the results of those measures.

"It was just during this second descent that the Most High Commission decided in any event, if only for the sake of their own reassurance, to actualize certain further special measures, among which was also that measure, the consequences of which have not only gradually turned

--------------------------------- 87 ---------------------------------

into a stupendous terror for the three-brained beings themselves who arise on this ill-fated planet, but have even become, so to say, a malignant sore for the whole of the great Universe.

"You must know that by the time of this second descent of the Most High Commission, there had already gradually been engendered in them—as is proper to three-brained beings—what is called 'mechanical instinct.'

"The sacred members of this Most High Commission then reasoned that if the said mechanical instinct in these biped three-brained beings of that planet should develop towards the attainment of Objective Reason—as usually occurs everywhere among three-brained beings—then it might quite possibly happen that they would prematurely comprehend the real cause of their arising and existence and make a great deal of trouble; it might happen that having understood the reason for their arising, namely, that by their existence they should maintain the detached fragments of their planet, and being convinced of this their slavery to circumstances utterly foreign to them, they would be unwilling to continue their existence and would on principle destroy themselves.

Why 'Men' Are Not Men

BEELZEBUB sighed deeply and continued to speak as follows:
"After the actualizing on this planet of the 'Ilnosoparnian' process, one year by objective time calculation passed.

"In the course of this period there had gradually been established on this planet also, the corresponding processes of the involution and evolution of everything arisen there.

"Naturally also, there began gradually to be crystallized in the three-brained beings there also, the corresponding function for their acquisition of objective reasoning.

"In short, on this planet also everything was then already following the usual order.

"And therefore, my boy, there perhaps would not have been all the subsequent eccentricities associated with the three-brained beings arising on that ill-starred planet, if, at the end of a year, the Most High Commission under the supreme direction of the same Archangel Sakaki had not again gone there.

"This second descent thereto of the Most High Commission was due to this, that in spite of the measures they had taken of which I have just told you, complete assurance of the impossibility of any unwelcome surprise in the future had not crystallized in the Reasons of a majority of its sacred members and they then wished to verify on the spot the results of the measures they had taken.

"It was just during this second descent that the Most High Commission decided if only for their peace of mind, to actualize in any event still certain other special measures, among which was that measure also whose consequences have been not only gradually transformed

- -

into a stupendous terror for the three-brained beings arising on this ill-starred planet themselves, but which have also become, so to say, a festering ulcer even for the whole of the great Universe.

"You must know that by the time of this second descent of the Most High Commission, there had already been gradually engendered in them—as is proper to three-brained beings—what is called 'mechanical instinct.'

"The sacred members of this Most High Commission thereupon then reasoned that if the said mechanical instinct in these biped three-brained beings of that planet should develop towards the attainment of objective Reason—as usually is the case everywhere among three-brained beings—then it might happen that they would prematurely grasp the real cause of their arising and existence and make a good deal of trouble; it might happen that having understood the reason for their arising, namely, that by their existence they should maintain the separated fragments of their planet, and being convinced of this their slavery to circumstances utterly foreign to them, they would protest against continuing their existence and destroy themselves on principle.

"So, my boy, in view of this the Most High Commission then decided among other things provisionally to implant into the common presences of the three-brained beings there a special organ with a property such that, first, they should perceive reality topsy-turvy and, secondly, that every repeated impression from outside should crystallize in them data which would engender factors for evoking in them sensations of 'pleasure' and 'enjoyment.'

"And then, in fact, with the help of the Chief-Common-Universal-Arch-Chemist-Physicist Angel Looisos, who was also among the members of this Most High Commission, they caused to grow in the three-brained beings there, in a special way, at the base of their spinal column, at the

- *88* -

root of their tail—which they also, at that time, still had, and which part of their common presences furthermore still had its normal exterior expressing the, so to say, 'fullness-of-its-inner-significance'—a 'something' which assisted the arising of the said properties in them.

"And this 'something' they then first called the 'organ Kundabuffer.'

"Having made this organ grow in the presences of the three-brained beings and having seen that it would work, the Most High Commission consisting of Sacred Individuals headed by the Archangel Sakaki, reassured and with good consciences, returned to the Center, while there, on the planet Earth which has taken your fancy, the action of this astonishing and exceedingly ingenious invention began from the first day to develop, and developed, as the wise Mullah Nassr Eddin would say—'like a Jericho-trumpet-in-crescendo.'

"Now, in order that you may have at least an approximate understanding of the results of the properties of the organ devised and actualized by the incomparable Angel Looisos—blessed be his name to all eternity—it is indispensable that you should know about the various manifestations of the three-brained beings of that planet, not only during the period when this organ Kundabuffer existed in their presences, but also during the later periods when, although this astonishing organ and its properties had been destroyed in them, nevertheless, owing to many causes, the consequences of its properties had begun to be crystallized in their presences.

"But this I will explain to you later.

"Meanwhile you must note that there was still a third descent of that Most High Commission to that planet, three years later according to objective time-calculations, but this time it was under the direction of the Most-Great-Arch-Seraph Sevohtartra, the Most Great Archangel Sakaki

- *89* -

having, in the meantime, become worthy to become the divine Individual he now is, namely, one of the four Quarter-Maintainers of the whole Universe.

"And during just this third descent there, when it was made clear by the thorough investigations of the sacred members of this third Most High Commission that for the maintenance of the existence of those said detached fragments there was no longer any need to continue to actualize the deliberately taken anticipatory measures, then among the other measures there was also destroyed, with the

"So, my boy, in view of this the Most High Commission then decided among other things provisionally to introject into the three-brained beings there such a special property that, firstly, they might perceive reality upside down and, secondly, that every repeated impression from outside should be a contributory factor in evoking in them sensations of 'pleasure' and 'satisfaction.'

"Thereupon, indeed, with the help of the Chief-Common-Universal-Arch-Physico-Chemist Angel Looisos, who also was among the members of this High Commission, they made grow in a special way in the three-brained beings there, at the base of their spinal column,

---

'something' which would enable the said properties to arise in them.

"And this 'something' they then first called the 'Organ Kundabuffer.'

"And having then made this organ grow in their 'presence' and practically assured themselves that it would work, the Most High Commission consisting of sacred Individuums headed by Archangel Sakaki, were content and returned to the center with a good conscience, while there on the planet which interests you, the action of this astonishing and exceedingly ingenious invention bloomed and blossomed from the very first day, as the wise Mullah Nassr Eddin would say— 'Like the trumpets of Jericho in full blast.'

"Now in order that you may have at least an approximate understanding of the results of the properties of the organ devised and actualized by the incomparable Angel Looisos—blessed be His Name forever!—you must assuredly know about certain manifestations of the three-brained beings of that planet, both during the period when this organ Kundabuffer existed in their 'presence' and during later periods when although this astonishing organ and its properties were destroyed in them, nevertheless owing to many causes, the consequences of its properties began to be crystallized in their 'presence.'

"But I shall explain this to you later

"You must note that the descent to that planet of that Most High Commission occurred there for the third time three years later, but this time it was under the supreme direction of the Most Great Archseraph-Sevohtartra, because the Most Great Archangel Sakaki

---

had in the meantime been raised to be the divine Individuum he even now is, namely, one of the four All-Quarters-Maintainers of the whole Universe.

"It was just on this third descent there, when owing to the thorough investigations of the sacred members of this third Most High Commission it was elucidated that for the maintenance of the existence of those said separated fragments, there was no longer any need to continue in force the measures that had previously been deliberately undertaken; that, in consequence, among other measures

help of the same Arch-Chemist-Physicist Angel Looisos, in the presences of the three-brained beings there, the said organ Kundabuffer with all its astonishing properties.

"But let us return to the tale I began.

"Now listen. When our confusion, caused by the recent catastrophe that had menaced that whole solar system, had passed off, we slowly, after this unexpected interruption, resumed the settlement of our new place on the planet Mars.

"Little by little we all of us made ourselves familiar with the local Nature and adapted ourselves to the existing conditions.

"As I have already said, many of us definitely settled down on the planet Mars; and others, by the ship *Occasion* which had been put at the disposal of the beings of our tribe for interplanetary communication, either went or prepared to go to exist on other planets of the same solar system.

"But I with my kinsmen and some of my near attendants remained to exist on that planet Mars.

"Yes, I must note that by the time to which my tale refers, my first Teskooano had already been set up in the observatory which I had constructed on the planet Mars and I was just then devoting myself entirely to

--------------------------------- 90 ---------------------------------

the further organization and development of this observatory of mine, for the more detailed observation of the remote concentrations of our great Universe and of the planets of this solar system.

"Among the objects of my observations, then, was also this planet Earth.

"Time passed.

"The process of existence on this planet also began gradually to be established and it seemed, from all appearances, that the process of existence was proceeding there just as on all other planets.

"But by close observation, first, it could be clearly seen that the numbers of these three-brained beings were gradually increasing and, secondly, it was possible sometimes to observe very strange manifestations of theirs; that is, from time to time they did something which was never done by three-brained beings on other planets, namely, they would suddenly, without rhyme or reason, begin destroying one another's existence.

"Sometimes this destruction of one another's existence proceeded there not in one region alone but in several, and would last not just one 'Dionosk' but many 'Dionosks' and sometimes even for whole 'Ornakras.' (Dionosk signifies 'day'; Ornakra signifies 'month.')

"It was sometimes very noticeable also that from this horrible process of theirs their numbers rapidly diminished; but on the other hand, during other periods, when there was a lull in these processes, their numbers also very noticeably increased.

"To this peculiarity of theirs we gradually got used, having explained it to ourselves that obviously, for certain higher considerations, these properties also must deliberately have been given to the organ Kundabuffer by the Most High

taken with the help of the same Arch-Chemist-Physicist Angel Looisos, there was also destroyed in the 'presence' of the three-brained beings there, the said organ Kundabuffer with all its astonishing properties. But now let us return to the tale I began.

"Then listen . . . when our confusion caused by the catastrophe that had occurred and that had menaced that whole solar system had calmed down, we slowly, after the unexpected interruption, resumed the settlement of our new place on the planet 'Mars.'

"Little by little we all of us became familiar with the Nature there and adapted ourselves to the existing conditions there.

"As I have already said, many of us settled on the planet 'Mars,' and others, by the ship 'Occasion' which had been put at the disposal of the beings of our tribe for interplanetary communication, either went or prepared to go to exist on some other planet of the same solar system.

"But with my kinsmen and some of my near attendants, I remained to exist on that planet 'Mars.'

"Yes, I must note that by the time to which my tale refers, my first 'Teskooano,' which I had had constructed on the planet 'Mars,' had already been set up in my observatory, and I was just then devoting myself entirely to

- -

the further organization and development of my observatory for the more detailed observation of the remote concentrations of our great Universe and of the planets of this Solar System. Among the objects of my observations then was this planet 'Earth' also.

"Time went on.

"The process of existence on this planet also was gradually established and it seemed, from all appearances, that the process of existence there was proceeding just as on all other planets.

"But by close observation, firstly, it could be clearly seen that the numbers of these three-brained beings increased, and, secondly, it was possible to observe some very strange occasional manifestation of theirs; they did something from time to time that was never done by three-brained beings on any other planet, namely, they would suddenly without any reason begin destroying each other's existence.

"This destruction of each other's existence, especially in masses, sometimes proceeded there not in one region only but in several at once, and would last not just one 'dionosk,' but many 'dionosks' and sometimes even for whole 'onakra.'

"It became also perceptible that from time to time, as a result of this horrible process of theirs, their numbers rapidly diminished; but on the other hand, during other periods when there was a respite from such processes, their numbers noticeably increased.

"We gradually got used to this peculiarity of theirs also, and explained it to ourselves, that for certain higher considerations these properties also must have been deliberately given to the organ Kundabuffer by the Most High Commission;

Commission; in other words, seeing the fecundity of these biped beings, we assumed that this had been

----------------------------------- *91* -----------------------------------

done with aforethought, in view of the necessity that they should exist in such large numbers for the needs of the maintenance of the common-cosmic Harmonious Movement.

"Had it not been for this strange peculiarity of theirs, it would never have entered anybody's head that there was anything 'queer' on that planet.

"During the period to which the aforesaid refers, I visited most of the planets of that solar system, the populated and the as yet unpopulated.

"Personally I liked best of all the three-centered beings breeding on the planet bearing the name Saturn, whose exterior is quite unlike ours, but resembles that of the being-bird raven.

"It is interesting, by the way, to remark that for some reason or other, the form of being-bird raven breeds not only on almost all the planets of this solar system, but also on most of those other planets of the whole of our great Universe upon which beings of various brain systems arise and are coated with planetary bodies of different forms.

"The verbal intercourse of these beings, ravens, of that planet Saturn is something like ours.

"But in regard to their utterance, it is in my opinion the most beautiful of any I have ever heard.

"It can be compared to the singing of our best singers when with all their Being they sing in a minor key.

"And as for their relations with others, they—I don't even know how to describe them—can be known only by existing among them and by experiencing them oneself.

"All that can be said is that these bird-beings have hearts exactly like those of the angels nearest our ENDLESS MAKER AND CREATOR.

"They exist strictly according to the ninth commandment

----------------------------------- *92* -----------------------------------

of our CREATOR, namely: 'Do unto another's as you would do unto your own.'

"Later, I must certainly tell you much more in detail about those three-brained beings also who arise and exist on the planet Saturn, since one of my real friends during the whole period of my exile in that solar system was a being of just that planet, who had the exterior coating of a raven and whose name was 'Harharkh.'"

----------------------------------- *93* -----------------------------------

in other words, seeing the fecundity of these biped beings we presumed that it had been done for a reason, because large numbers of them were needed and the

planet itself was not big enough.

"Had it not been for these strange peculiarities of theirs, then it would have entered nobody's head that there was anything 'fishy' about that planet.

"During the period to which what has been said refers, I had time to visit most of the planets of that solar system, both populated and unpopulated.

"I personally liked best of all the three-centered beings breeding on the planet bearing the name 'Saturn'; their appearance is quite unlike ours; but they resemble the large bird called the 'raven.'

"It is interesting to remark, by the way, that for some reason or other, the form of the bird-being raven breeds not only on almost all the planets of this solar system, but also on most of those other planets of the whole of the great Universe upon which beings of various brain-systems arise and are coated with planetary bodies of different forms.

"These bird-beings ravens of that planet 'Saturn' have verbal intercourse among themselves just as we have.

"It can be compared to the singing of our best singers when with all their being they sing in a minor key.

"And as for their mutual relations, they . . . I don't even know how to describe them—they can be understood only by existing among them and by personal experience.

"All that can be said is that these bird-beings have hearts like those of the angels nearest OUR ENDLESS MAKER AND CREATOR.

"They exist strictly according to the ninth commandment

of our CREATOR, namely: Represent another's as your own, and be so related.

"I will certainly tell you more in detail sometime later about those three-brained beings who arise and exist on the planet 'Saturn' and whose external coating is like that of the 'raven,' since one of my real friends during the whole of the period of my exile in that solar system was a being of just that planet who had the exterior coating of a 'raven' and whose name was 'Harharkh.'"

A Piquant Trait of the Peculiar Psyche of Contemporary Man

NOW let us return to those three-brained beings arising on the planet Earth, who have interested you most of all and whom you have called 'slugs.'

"I shall begin by saying how glad I am that you happen to be a long way from those three-centered beings whom you called by a word so 'insulting to their dignity' and that they are not likely ever to hear of it.

"Do you know, you poor thing, you small boy not yet aware of himself, what they would do to you, particularly the contemporary beings there, if they should hear what you called them?

"What they would have done to you if you had been there and if they had got hold of you—I am seized with horror at the very mention of it.

"At best they would have thrashed you so, that as our Mullah Nassr Eddin there says, 'you wouldn't have recovered your senses before the next crop of birches.'

"In any case, I advise you that, whenever you start anything new, you should always bless Fate and beseech her mercy, that she should always be on guard and prevent the beings of the planet Earth from ever suspecting that you, my beloved and only grandson, dared to call them 'slugs.'

"You must know that during the time of my observations of them from the planet Mars and during the periods of my existence among them, I studied the psyche of these strange three-brained beings very thoroughly, and so I already know very well what they would do to anybody who dared to give them such a nickname.

--------------------------------- 94 ---------------------------------

"To be sure, it was only in childish naiveté that you called them so; but the three-brained beings of that peculiar planet, especially the contemporary ones, do not discriminate such fine points.

"Who called them, why, and in what circumstances—it's all one. They have been called by a name they consider insulting—and that's quite enough.

"Discrimination in such matters is, according to the understanding of most of them, simply, as they express it, 'pouring from the empty into the void.'

"Be that as it may, you were in any case extremely rash to call the three-brained beings breeding on the planet Earth by such an offensive name; first, because you have made me anxious for you, and secondly, because you have laid up for yourself a menace for the future.

"The position is this: Though, as I have already said, you are a long way off, and they will be unable to get at you to punish you personally, yet nevertheless if they should somehow unexpectedly chance to learn even at twentieth hand how you insulted them, then you could at once be sure of their real 'anathema,' and the dimensions of this anathema would depend upon the interests with which they happened to be occupied at the given moment.

"Perhaps it is worth while describing to you how the beings of the Earth would behave if they should happen to learn that you had so insulted them. This descrip-

A Piquant Trait Of The Peculiarity Of Man's Psyche

L ET US talk again about those three-brained beings arising and existing on the planet Earth who have most interested you and whom you call 'slugs.'

"I shall begin by saying how glad I am that you are a long way from those three-centered beings whom you call 'slugs' and they are never likely to hear of it.

"Do you know, you poor thing—a mere chit of a boy who has not yet become aware of himself—what they, and particularly the contemporary beings there, would do to you if they should hear how you referred to them?

"What they would do to you if you were there, or if they should get hold of you—I'm seized with horror as I even mention it.

"At best they would so thrash you that as our Mullah Nassr Eddin there says: 'You wouldn't recover your senses before the next crop of birches.'

"In any case, I advise you that, whenever you start anything new, you should always bless and beseech Fate always to kindly watch out that beings of the planet Earth never suspect that just you, my beloved and only grandson, dared to call them 'slugs.'

"You must know that during the time of my observation of them from the planet Mars and during the periods of my existence among them, I studied the psyche of these strange three-brained beings very thoroughly, and I already know very well what they would do to anybody who dared to nickname them so.

- -

"Although it was only in boyish naïveté that you called them this, the three-brained beings of that peculiar planet, especially the contemporary ones, do not deal in such refinements.

"Who it was, why it was, in what circumstances it was—it's all the same! They were called by a name which they consider insulting—and that's quite enough.

"Discrimination is for most minds there simply, as they express it, 'pouring from the empty into the empty.'

"Be that as it may, you were, in any case, extremely rash to call the three-brained beings breeding on the planet Earth by such an offensive word; firstly, because you have made me anxious for you, and secondly, you have laid yourself up trouble for the future.

"The position is this: although, as I have already told you, being a long way off, they may be unable to get at you to punish you personally, yet nevertheless, if they should by remote chance learn even at twentieth hand how you insulted them, then you can certainly already be assured of their real 'anathema,' the dimensions of which will depend on the subject of interest at the given moment.

"Perhaps it is worth while describing to you how the beings of the Earth would behave if they happened to learn that you insulted them in this way. This description may serve as a very good example for the elucidation of the strangeness of the psyche of these three-brained beings who interest you.

"Provoked by such an incident as your thus insulting them, if everything was rather 'dull' with them at the given moment, owing to the absence of any other similar absurd interest, they would arrange somewhere in a previously chosen place, with previously invited people, all of

------------------------------- 95 -------------------------------

course dressed in costumes specially designed for such occasions, what is called a 'solemn council.'

"First of all, for this 'solemn council' of theirs, they would select from among themselves what is called a 'president' and only then would they proceed with their 'trial.'

"To begin with, they would, as they say there, 'pick you to pieces,' and not only you, but your father, your grandfather, and perhaps even all the way back to Adam.

"If they should then decide—of course, as always, by a majority of votes—that you are guilty, they would sentence you according to the indications of a code of laws collated on the basis of former similar 'puppet plays' by beings called 'old fossils.'

"But if they should happen, by a 'majority of votes' to find nothing criminal in your action at all—though this very seldom occurs among them—then this whole 'trial' of theirs, set out on paper in detail and signed by the whole lot of them, would be dispatched—you would think into the wastepaper basket? Oh, no!—to appropriate specialists; in the given instances to what is called the 'Hierarchy' or 'Holy Synod,' where the same procedure would be repeated; only in this case you would be tried by 'important' beings there.

"Only at the very end of this true 'pouring from the empty into the void' would they come to the main point, namely, that the accused is out of reach.

"But it is just here that arises the principal danger to your person, namely, that when they are quite certain beyond all doubt that they cannot get hold of you, they will then unanimously decide nothing more nor less than, as I have already said, to 'anathematize' you.

"And do you know what that is and how it is done?

"No!

"Then listen and shudder.

------------------------------- 96 -------------------------------

"The most 'important' beings will decree to all the other beings that in all their appointed establishments, such as what are called 'churches,' 'chapels,' 'synagogues,' 'town-halls,' and so on, special officials shall on special occasions with appointed ceremonies wish for you in thought something like the following:

"That you should lose your horns, or that your hair should turn prematurely gray, or that the food in your stomach should be turned into coffin nails, or that your future wife's tongue should be three times its size, or that whenever you take a bite of your pet pie it should be turned into 'soap,' and so on and so forth in the

tion may serve as a very good example for the elucidation of the strange psyche of these three-brained beings who interest you.

"Provoked by such an event, namely, your insulting them, if everything was rather 'dull' with them at the given moment, owing to the absence of any other similar absurd interest, they would arrange somewhere in a place previously chosen what is called a 'solemn council' consisting of people previously invited,

all, of course, dressed in special costumes for such occasions.

"For their 'solemn council' they would first select what is called a 'president' from among themselves and only then would they proceed with their 'trial.'

"To begin with, they would, as they say there, 'try you minutely,' and not only you, but your father, your grandfather, and perhaps even back to Adam.

"If they should then decide—certainly of course by a majority of votes—that you are guilty, they would sentence you according to a code of laws collated from former similar 'puppet plays' by beings called 'old fossils.'

"But if they should happen, by a 'majority of votes,' to find nothing criminal in your conduct at all—though this very seldom occurs among them—then this whole 'trial' of theirs, set out on paper in detail and signed by the whole lot of them would be dispatched . . . you think into the wastepaper basket . . . Not on your life . . . to appointed specialists, in the given instance, to what is called the 'Holy Synod' or 'Hierarchy' where the same procedure would again be repeated—only in this case you would be 'tried' by 'important' beings there.

"Only at the very end of this real 'pouring from the empty into the empty' would they come to the vital point, namely, that they couldn't get hold of the accused.

"Yes, but it is just at that point that the rub comes for you personally . . . namely, that when they are quite certain beyond all doubt, that they can't get hold of you, they will, then, unanimously decide neither more nor less than, as I have already said, to 'anathematize' you.

"And do you know what that is and how it is done?

"No?

"Then listen and shudder.

"The most 'important' beings will ordain that in all their appointed establishments called 'churches,' 'chapels,' 'Synagogues,' 'town-halls' and so on, special officials shall on special occasions with appointed ceremonies wish for you in their thoughts something like the following:

"That you should lose your horns, or that your hair should turn grey, or that the food in your stomach should become coffin-nails, or that your future wife's tongue should be three times its size, or that whenever you take a bite of your pet pie, it should taste like 'soap,' and so on and so forth in the same strain.

same strain.

"Do you now understand to what dangers you exposed yourself when you called these remote three-brained freaks 'slugs'?"

Having finished thus, Beelzebub looked with a smile on his favorite.

------------------------------- 97 -------------------------------

"Do you now understand to what dangers you exposed yourself when you called these remote three-brained freaks 'slugs'?"

Having finished thus, Beelzebub looked with a smile on his favorite.

The First "Growl"

A LITTLE later, Beelzebub began to speak as follows:
    "A story I have just recalled, connected with these 'anathemas' I have mentioned, may provide very useful material for beginning to comprehend the strangeness of the psyche of the three-brained beings of that planet which has taken your fancy; and furthermore, this story may reassure you a little and give you some hope that if these peculiar terrestrial beings should chance to learn how you had insulted them and should 'anathematize' you, then perhaps after all something 'not so very bad' might come of it for you.

    "The story I am going to tell you occurred quite recently among the contemporary three-brained beings there, and it arose from the following events:

    "In one of these large communities, there peaceably existed an ordinary being who was by profession what is there called a 'writer.'

    "You must here know, that in long-past ages one might still occasionally run across beings of that profession who still invented and wrote something really by themselves; but in these later epochs the 'writers' among the beings there, particularly among contemporary beings, have been of those that only copy from many already existing books all kinds of ideas, and by fitting them together make a 'new book.'

    "And they prefer books which have reached them from their very remote ancestors.

    "It is necessary to remark that the books written by contemporary 'writers' there are, all taken together, the principal cause that the Reason of all the other three-brained beings is becoming more and more what the

------------------------------ *98* ------------------------------

venerable Mullah Nassr Eddin calls 'stuff and nonsense.'

    "And so, my boy:

    "The contemporary writer of whom I began to speak was just a 'writer' like all the rest there, and nothing particular in himself.

    "Once when he had finished some book or other, he began to think what he should write about next, and with this in view, he decided to look for some new 'idea' in the books contained in his what is called 'library,' such as every writer there is bound to have.

    "As he was looking, a book called 'the Gospels' happened to fall into his hands.

    "'The Gospels' is the name given there to a book once written by certain persons called Matthew, Mark, Luke, and John about Jesus Christ, a Messenger from our ENDLESSNESS to that planet.

    "This book is widely circulated among those three-centered beings there who nominally exist according to the indications of this Messenger.

    "This book having chanced to fall into this writer's hands, the thought suddenly entered his head: Why should not I also make a 'Gospel'?

The First "Growl"

A LITTLE later Beelzebub spoke as follows:
    "A story I have just recalled connected with the 'anathema' I have just mentioned may provide very useful material for beginning to comprehend the strangeness of the psyche of the three-brained beings of that planet which has pleased you; and, furthermore, the story may reassure you a little and give you hope that if these peculiar terrestrial beings should chance to learn that you had insulted them and should 'anathematize' you, then perhaps after all something not so very 'bad' might come of it for you.

"The story I am going to tell you occurred quite recently amongst contemporary three-brained beings there.

"And it arose there from the following events:

"In one of those large communities, there peaceably existed an ordinary being who was by profession what is there called a 'writer.'

"Here you must know that, in previous ages, you might still occasionally run across beings of that profession who still invented and wrote something really by themselves; but in these later epochs the 'writers' among the beings there, particularly among contemporary beings, were of the kind that only plagiarize ideas from many already existing books, and make a 'new book' by fitting them together.

"As a rule, they prefer books which have reached them from their remote ancestors.

"It must further be particularly remarked that the books written by contemporary 'writers' there, are, taken all together, the principal cause that the Reasoning of the rest of the three-brained beings there becomes progressively what the

- -

venerable Mullah Nassr Eddin calls 'stuff and nonsense.'

"And so, my boy!

"The contemporary 'writer' of whom I began to speak, was just a 'writer' like all the rest there, and nothing particular in himself.

"Once when he had finished some book or other, he began to think what he should write about next, and with this in view, he decided to look for some new 'idea' or other in the books contained in what is called a 'library,' such as every writer there is bound to have.

"As he was looking, a book called the 'Gospels' happened to fall into his hands.

"The 'Gospels' is the name given there to a book written some time ago by a certain Matthew, Mark, Luke and John about Jesus Christ, a Messenger from our ENDLESSNESS to that planet.

"This book is widely circulated among the three-centered beings there, who, nominally, exist according to the indications of this Messenger.

"This book having chanced to fall into this writer's hands, the thought suddenly entered his head, 'Why shouldn't I also make a "Gospel"?'

"From investigations I had to make for quite different needs of mine, it turned out that he then further deliberated as follows:

"Am I any worse than those ancient barbarians, Matthew, Mark, Luke, and Johnnie?

"At least I am more "cultured" than they ever were; and I can write a much better "gospel" or my contemporaries.

"And very decidedly it is necessary to write just a "Gospel" because the contemporary people called "English" and "American" have a great weakness for this book, and the rate of exchange of their pounds and dollars is "not half bad" just now.'

99

"No sooner said than done.

"And from that very day he 'wiseacred' away at his new 'Gospel.' But it was only when he had finished it, however, and had given it to the printers, that all the further events connected with this new 'Gospel' of his began.

"At any other time, nothing perhaps would have happened, and this new 'Gospel' of his would simply have slipped into its niche in the libraries of the bibliomaniacs there, among the multitudes of other books expounding similar 'truths.'

"But fortunately or unfortunately for this writer, it happened that certain 'power-possessing' beings of that great community in which he existed had just been having rotten luck at what is called 'roulette' and 'baccarat' and they therefore kept on demanding what they called 'money' from the ordinary beings of their community, whereupon, thanks to these inordinate demands for money, the ordinary beings of that community at length awoke from their usual what is called torpor and 'began-to-sit-up.'

"Seeing this, the 'power-possessing' beings who remained at home became alarmed and took corresponding 'measures.'

"And among the 'measures' they took was also the immediate destruction from off the face of their planet of everything newly arising in their native land, such as could possibly keep the ordinary beings of their community from resuming their hibernation.

"And it was just at this time that the aforementioned 'Gospel' of this writer appeared.

"In the contents of this new 'Gospel' also, the 'power-possessing' beings found something which also to their understanding might keep the ordinary beings of their community from hibernating again; and they therefore decided almost immediately to 'get rid' of both the writer

100

himself and his 'Gospel'—because they had now become quite expert in 'getting rid' of these native 'upstarts' who did not mind their own business.

"But for certain reasons they could not treat this writer in this way, and so they got excited, and hemmed and hawed about what they should do.

"Some proposed that they should simply shut him up where many 'rats' and 'lice' breed; others proposed to send him to 'Timbuktu'; and so on and so forth;

"From the investigations I happened to make for quite different aims of mine, it seems that he then deliberated further in the following way:

"'I'm no worse than those ancient barbarians, John, Luke, Matthew and Mark!

"'And, at least, I am more cultured than they ever were; and I can write a much better 'Gospel' for my contemporaries.

"'And very decidedly it is necessary to write just a 'Gospel,' because the wealthiest people now existing—those called 'English' and 'American'—have a weakness for this book and the exchange rate of their pounds and dollars is 'not half bad' just now.

"No sooner thought than begun!

"And from that very day he 'wiseacred' away at his new 'Gospel.'

"It was just when he had finished it, however, and given it to the printers, only then it was that all the further events associated with this new 'Gospel' of his began.

"At any other time, nothing perhaps would have happened and this new 'Gospel' of his would simply have slipped into its niche in the libraries of the bibliophiles there, among the piles of other books expounding similar 'truths.'

"But fortunately or unfortunately for this writer, it happened that certain 'power-possessing' beings of that great community where he too existed had just had rotten luck at what is called 'roulette' and 'baccarat,' and they therefore kept on demanding what they call 'money' from the ordinary beings of their community, whereupon, thanks to these demands for money, inordinate for that time, the ordinary beings of that community at length began to wake from their usual torpor and to 'sit up.'

"Seeing this, the 'power-possessing' beings who remained at home, became alarmed and took corresponding 'measures.'

"And among the 'measures' they took was also the immediate destruction from the face of their planet of everything 'new' in their native land that could possibly keep the ordinary beings of their community from resuming their hibernation.

"It was just at this time that the aforementioned 'Gospels' of this writer appeared.

"In the contents of this new 'Gospel' also, the 'power-possessing' beings found something which to their understanding might also keep ordinary beings of their community from hibernating again; and they therefore decided almost immediately to 'bump off' both the writer

----

himself and his 'Gospel,' and especially because they had now become quite expert in 'bumping off' such native agitators as did not mind their own business.

"But for certain reasons, they couldn't treat this writer like that, and so they became much agitated and considered along time what they should do.

"Some proposed that he should just be confined there where breed many 'rats' and 'lice'; others proposed to send him to 'where Makkar had never driven his

but in the end they decided to anathematize this writer together with his 'Gospel,' publicly and punctiliously according to all the rules, and moreover with the very same 'anathema' with which no doubt they would have anathematized you also if they had learned how you had insulted them.

"And so, my boy, the strangeness of the psyche of the contemporary three-brained beings of this peculiar planet was revealed in the given instance in this, that when this writer and his 'Gospel' had been publicly anathematized with this 'anathema,' the result for him was, as the highly esteemed Mullah Nassr Eddin once again says: 'just roses, roses.'

"What occurred was as follows:

"The ordinary beings of the said community, seeing the fuss made about this writer by the power-possessing beings, became very greatly interested in him and avidly bought and read not only this new 'Gospel' of his but also all the books he had written before.

"Whereupon, as usually happens with the three-centered beings breeding on this peculiar planet, all the other interests of the beings of the said community gradually died down, and they talked and thought only of this writer.

"And as it also happens—whereas some praised him to the skies, others condemned him; and the result of these discussions and conversations was that the numbers interested in him grew not only among the beings of his own

- *101* -

community but among the beings of other communities also.

"And this occurred because some of the power-possessing beings of this community, usually with pockets full of money, still continued in their turn to go to other communities where 'roulette' and 'baccarat' proceeded and, carrying on their discussion there concerning this writer, they gradually infected the beings of other communities also with this affair.

"In short, owing to the strangeness of their psyche, it has gradually come about there that even at the present time, when this writer's 'Gospel' has been long forgotten, his name is known almost everywhere as that of an 'excellent writer.'

"Anything he writes now, they all seize upon and regard as full of indisputable truth.

"Everybody today looks upon his writings with the same veneration with which the ancient Kalkians there listened to the predictions of their sacred 'Pythoness.'

"It is interesting to notice here that if at the present time you ask any being there about this writer, he would know him and of course speak of him as an extraordinary being.

"But if you were then to ask what he wrote, it would turn out that most of them, if of course they confessed the truth, had never read a single one of his books.

"All the same they would talk about him, discuss him, and of course splutteringly insist that he was a being with an 'extraordinary mind' and phenomenally well acquainted with the psyche of the beings dwelling on the planet Earth."

- *102* -

calves,' that is, very far away, indeed; and so on and so forth; but in the end, they decided to anathematize this writer together with his 'Gospel' publicly and punctiliously according to all the rules, and with the self-same 'anathema' with which no doubt they would also anathematize you, if they learned how you had insulted them.

"And so, my boy; the strangeness of the psyche of the contemporary three-brained beings of this peculiar planet was revealed in the given instance in this, that when this writer and his 'Gospel' had been publicly anathematized with this 'anathema,' the result for him was as the highly esteemed Mullah Nassr Eddin once again says: 'simply roses, roses.'

"What further occurred was as follows:

"The ordinary beings of the said community, seeing the fuss made about this writer by the power-possessing beings, became very greatly interested in him and greedily bought and read, not only this new 'Gospel' of his, but also all the books he had written before.

"Whereupon, as usually happens with the three-centered beings breeding on this peculiar planet, all their other interests gradually died down and the beings of the said community all talked and thought only of this writer.

"And, as it also happens there—when some praised him extravagantly, others spoke against him; and the result of these discussions and conversations was that the numbers interested in him grew not only among the beings of his own

community, but among the beings of other communities also.

"And this occurred because some of the power-possessing beings of this community, usually with pockets full of money, still continued in their turn to go to other communities where 'roulette' and 'baccarat' proceeded, and, carrying on their discussions there concerning this writer, they gladly infected beings of other communities also with this affair.

"In short, owing to the strangeness of their psyche, it has gradually come about there that even at the present time, when the cause of the anathematizing of this writer has already long been forgotten, and even his 'Gospel' has been forgotten also, his name is still known almost everywhere as that of a 'very good writer.'

"Anything he writes now, they all seize upon and regard an indisputable truths.

"Everybody looks upon his writings with the same veneration with which the ancient Kalkians listened to the predictions of their sacred 'Pythias.'

"It is very interesting to notice here, that if you ask any being you like there about this writer, everybody would know him and, of course, speak of him as 'great.'

"But if you were then to ask them what he wrote, it would turn out that most of them—if, of course, they confessed the truth—had never even read a single one of his books.

"All the same they would discuss him, and of course, splutteringly insist that he was a being with an 'extraordinary mind' and phenomenally acquainted with the psyche of the beings dwelling on the planet Earth."

Why in Man's Reason Fantasy May Be Perceived as Reality

"M Y DEAR and kind Grandfather, be so kind as to explain to me, if only in a general way, why those beings there are such that they take the 'ephemeral' for the Real.'"

To this question of his grandson, Beelzebub replied thus:

"It was only during later periods that the three-brained beings of the planet Earth began to have this particularity in their psyche, and just this particularity arose in them only because their predominant part, which was formed in them as in all three-brained beings, gradually allowed other parts of their total presences to perceive every new impression without what is called 'being-Partkdolg-duty' but just merely as, in general, such impressions are perceived by the separate independent localizations existing under the name of being-centers present in the three-brained beings, or, as I should say in their language, they believe everything anybody says, and not solely that which they themselves have been able to recognize by their own sane deliberation.

"In general, any new understanding is crystallized in the presence of these strange beings only if Smith speaks of somebody or something in a certain way; and then if Brown says the same, the hearer is quite convinced it is just so and couldn't possibly be otherwise. Thanks merely to this particularity of their psyche and to the fact that the said writer was much spoken about in the said manner, most of the beings there at the present time are quite convinced that he is indeed a very great psychologist and

has an incomparable knowledge of the psyche of the beings of his planet.

"But, as a matter of fact, when I was on that planet for the last time and, having heard of the said writer, once went myself especially to see him, on quite another matter, he was according to my understanding not only like all the other contemporary writers there, that is to say, extremely limited, and as our dear Mullah Nassr Eddin would say: 'able to see no further than his nose,' but as regards any knowledge of the real psyche of the beings of his planet in real conditions, he might safely even be called 'totally illiterate.'

"I repeat that the story of this writer is a very characteristic example showing the extent to which, in the three-brained beings who have taken your fancy, particularly in the contemporary ones, the realization of 'being-Partkdolg-duty' is absent, and how their own subjective being-convictions formed by their own logical deliberations are never, as in general it is proper to three-brained beings, crystallized in them, but only those are crystallized which depend exclusively only upon what others say about the given question.

"It was only because they failed to realize 'being-Partkdolg-duty,' which realization alone enables a being to become aware of genuine reality, that they saw in the said writer some perfection or other which was not there at all.

"This strange trait of their general psyche, namely, of being satisfied with just

In Man's Reason, Fantasy May Be Perceived As Reality

"MY DEAR and kind grandfather," exclaimed Hassein "be so kind as to explain to me, if only roughly, why they there are such that they take the ephemeral for reality?"

To this question of his grandson, Beelzebub replied thus:

"It was only during later periods that the three-brained beings of the planet 'Earth' began to have this particularity of their psyche.

"Just that particularity arose in the beings there, only because their chief part, which was formed in them as in all three-brained beings, gradually allowed other parts of their total 'presence' to perceive new impressions without what is called 'being-Partkdolgduty,' but just merely as, in general, such impressions are perceived by the separate independent localizations existing under the name of being-centers present in the three-brained beings; or, as I should in their language say, they believe everything anybody says, and not solely that which they themselves could cognize with their own sane deliberation.

"In general, any new understanding in these strange beings becomes crystallized only if you say about somebody or something just what John Smith says, and then if only John Brown says the same, the hearer is now quite persuaded that it is just so and couldn't possibly be otherwise.

"Thanks merely to this particularity of their psyche and to the fact that the said writer was much spoken about in the said manner, most of the beings there at the present time are now persuaded that he is indeed a very great psychologist and

has an incomparable knowledge of the psyche of the beings of his planet.

"But, as a matter of fact, when I was on that planet for the last time and, having heard of the said writer, once went myself specially to see him, on quite another matter, he seemed to me to be not only like all the other contemporary writers there, that is to say, extremely limited, and also as our dear Mullah Nassr Eddin would say: 'seeing no further than his nose,' but as regards any knowledge of the real psyche of the beings of that planet in real conditions, he might safely be called 'totally illiterate.'

"I repeat that the story of this writer is a very characteristic example of the extent to which, in these three-brained beings who please you, particularly in the contemporary ones, the realization of the 'being-Partkdolgduty' is absent and how—as in general it is proper to the three-brained beings—their own subjective being-convictions formed by their own logical deliberations are never crystallized in them but only those are crystallized which depend exclusively only upon what others say about the given question.

"It was only because they failed to realize the 'being-Partkdolgduty,' which realization alone enables a being to become aware of genuine-reality, that they saw in the said writer some perfection or other that was not there.

"This strange trait of their general psyche, namely, of being satisfied with just what Smith or Brown says, without trying to know more, became rooted in them already long ago, and now they no longer strive at all to know anything cognizable by their own active deliberations alone.

"Concerning all this it must be said that neither the organ Kundabuffer which their ancestors had is to blame, nor its consequences which, owing to a mistake on the part of certain Sacred Individuals, were crystallized in

———————————————————————— 104 ————————————————————————

their ancestors and later began to pass by heredity from generation to generation.

"But they themselves were personally to blame for it, and just on account of the abnormal conditions of external ordinary being-existence which they themselves have gradually established and which have gradually formed in their common presence just what has now become their inner 'Evil-God,' called 'Self-Calming.'

"But all this you yourself, later on, will well understand, when I shall have given you, as I have already promised, more information about that planet which has taken your fancy.

"In any case, I strongly advise you to be very careful in the future in your references to the three-brained beings of that planet, not to offend them in any way; otherwise—as they also say there, 'With what may the Devil not joke?'—they might find out about your insulting them and, to use another of their expressions, 'lay you by the heels.'

"And in the present case there is no harm in recalling again one of the wise sentences of our dear Mullah Nassr Eddin, who says: 'Struth! What might not happen in this world. A flea might swallow an elephant.'"

Beelzebub intended to say something more, but at that moment a ship's servant entered and, approaching, handed him an "etherogram" in his name.

When Beelzebub had finished listening to the contents of the said "etherogram" and the ship's servant had gone, Hassein turned to Beelzebub again with the following words:

"Dear Grandfather, please go on talking about the three-centered beings arising and existing on that interesting planet called Earth."

Beelzebub having looked at his grandson again with a special smile, and having made a very strange gesture with his head, continued to speak as follows:

———————————————————————— 105 ————————————————————————

what John Smith or John Brown says, without trying to know more, became rooted in them already long ago, and now they no longer strive at all to know anything cognizable only by their own active deliberation.

"And it must be said concerning all this, that neither the organ Kundabuffer is to blame, which their ancestors had, nor its consequences, which owing to a mistake on the part of certain sacred Individuums, were crystallized in their ancest-

ors and later began to pass as an inheritance, from generation to generation.

"But they themselves are personally to blame for it, and just on that account of the abnormal conditions of external ordinary being-existence which they themselves have gradually established, and which gradually have formed in their general 'presence' just what has now become that inner 'Evil God' called 'Self Calming.'

"But you yourself, later on, will well understand when I shall have given you, as I have already promised, more information about that planet which pleases you.

"In any case, I strongly advise you to be very careful in the future in your references to the three-brained beings of that planet not to offend them in any way; otherwise, as they also say there, 'With what may the Devil not joke,' and they might find out some crime or other of yours and 'lay you by the heels'—to use another of their expressions.

"And as for the given case, there is no harm in recalling again one of the wise sentences of our dear Mullah Nassr Eddin who says:

"'Struth! What only may not happen in the world! A flea might swallow an elephant!'"

Beelzebub intended to say something still more, but at that moment a ship's servant entered and approached and handed him an 'etherogram' in his name. When Beelzebub had finished listening to the contents of the said 'etherogram' and the ship's servant had gone, Hassein turned to Beelzebub again with the following words:

"Dear Grandfather, please go on talking about the three-centered beings arising and existing on that interesting planet called 'Earth.'"

Beelzebub having looked at his grandson, again with a particular smile, and having made a very strange gesture with his head, continued to speak as follows:

The Beginnings of Perspectives Promising Nothing Very Cheerful

I MUST tell you first that the three-brained beings on that planet also had in the beginning presences similar to those possessed in general by all what are called 'Keschapmartnian' three-centered beings arising on all the corresponding planets of the whole of our great Universe; and they also had the same, as it is called, 'duration of existence' as all the other three-brained beings.

"All the various changes in their presences began for the most part after the second misfortune occurred to this planet, during which misfortune the chief continent of that ill-fated planet, then existing under the name 'Atlantis,' entered within the planet.

"And from that time on, as little by little they created for themselves all sorts of conditions of external being-existence thanks to which the quality of their radiations went steadily from bad to worse, Great Nature was compelled gradually to transform their common presences by means of various compromises and changes, in order to regulate the quality of the vibrations which they radiated and which were required chiefly for the preservation of the wellbeing of the former parts of that planet.

"For the same reason, Great Nature gradually so increased the numbers of the beings there that at the present time they are now breeding on all the lands formed on that planet.

"The exterior forms of their planetary bodies are all made alike, and of course in respect of size and in their other subjective particularities, they are each coated, just as we are, in accordance with the reflection of heredity,

- 106 -

with the conditions at the moment of conception and with the other factors that serve in general as the causes for the arising and formation of every being.

"They also differ among themselves in the color of their skin and in the conformation of their hair, and these latter particularities are determined in their presences, just as they are everywhere else, by the effects of that part of the planetary surface where the given beings arise and where they are formed until they reach the age of responsible beings, or as they say, until they become 'adult.'

"As regards their general 'psyche' itself and its fundamental traits, no matter upon what part of the surface of their planet they arise, these traits in all of them have precisely the same particularities, among them being also that property of the three-brained beings there, thanks to which on that strange planet alone in the whole of the Universe does that horrible process occur among three-brained beings which is called the 'process of the destruction of each other's existence,' or, as it is called on that ill-fated planet, 'war.'

"Besides this chief particularity of their common psyche, there are completely crystallized in them and there unfailingly become a part of their common presences—regardless of where they may arise and exist—functions which exist un-

The Beginnings Of Perspectives Promising Nothing Very Cheerful

I MUST first tell you that the three-brained beings on that planet also had in the beginning a 'presence' similar to that possessed in general by all what are called 'Keschapmartnian' three-centered beings arising on all the corresponding planets of the whole of our great Universe; and they also had the same, as it is called, 'duration of existence' as other three-brained beings.

"All the various changes in their 'presence' occurred for the most part after the second misfortune to this planet during which misfortune the principal continent of that ill-starred planet then existing under the name 'Atlantis' entered within the planet itself.

"And from that time forward, as, little by little they created for their existence every possible kind of condition of external being-existence, thanks to which the quality of their radiations went steadily from bad to worse, Great Nature was compelled gradually to regenerate their general 'presence' by means of various compromises and changes in order to regulate the quality of the vibrations which they radiated and which were chiefly required for the preservation of the well-being of the former parts of that planet.

"For the same reason, Great Nature gradually increased the numbers there, with the result that at the present time they are breeding on all the lands formed on the planet.

"The exterior forms of their planetary bodies are all much alike and, of course, in respect of size and in their subjective particularities they are each coated, just as we are, in accordance with the reflection of heredity,

the conditions at the moment of conception and with the rest of the factors that serve in general as the causes for the arising and formation of every being.

"They differ also among themselves in the color of their skin and in the conformation of the hair arising on them, and these latter particularities are also determined in each of their 'presences' just as they are everywhere else, by the effects of that part of the planetary surface where the given beings arise and where they are formed up to the age of a responsible being, or, as they say, until they become 'adult.'

"As regards their general psyche itself and its fundamental traits, no matter upon what part of the surface of their planet they arise, these traits in all of them have precisely the same particularities, among them being also that property of the three-brained beings there, thanks to which on that strange planet alone in the whole of the Universe does that horrible process occur among three-brained beings which is called the 'process of the destruction of the existence of each other,' or, as it is called on that ill-starred planet, 'war.'

"Besides this chief particularity of their common psyche, there are completely crystallized in them, regardless of where they may arise and exist, and there unfailingly become a part of their general 'presence,' functions which exist there under the names 'egoism,' 'self-love,' 'vanity,' 'pride,' 'self-conceit,' 'credulity,' 'suggestibility,' and many other properties quite abnormal and quite unbecoming to the essence of any three-brained beings whatsoever.

"Of these abnormal being-particularities, the particularity of their psyche the most terrible for them personally is that which is called 'suggestibility.'

"About this extremely strange and singular psychic particularity I shall specially explain to you sometime."

Having said this, Beelzebub was thoughtful, and this

------------------------------ *107* ------------------------------

time longer than usual, and then, turning again to his grandson, he said:

"I see that the three-brained beings arising and existing on the peculiar planet called Earth interest you very much, and as during our voyage on the ship *Karnak* we shall have willy-nilly to talk about many things just to pass away the time, I will tell you all I can just about these three-brained beings.

"I think it will be best for your clear understanding of the strangeness of the psyche of the three-brained beings arising on the planet Earth if I relate to you my personal descents to that planet in their order, and the events which occurred there during these descents of mine, of which I myself was a witness.

"I personally visited the surface of the planet Earth six times in all, and each of these personal visits of mine was brought about by a different set of circumstances.

"I shall begin with my first descent."

------------------------------ *108* ------------------------------

der the names, 'egoism,' 'self-love,' 'vanity,' 'pride,' 'self-conceit,' 'credulity,' 'suggestibility,' and many other properties quite abnormal and quite unbecoming to the essence of any three-brained beings whatsoever.

"Of the just named abnormal being-particularities, that particularity of their psyche, the most terrible for them personally, is called 'suggestibility.'

"About this extremely strange and singular psychic particularity I shall especially tell you some time."

Having said this Beelzebub became thoughtful

- -

and this time for longer than usual and then he resumed to his grandson as follows:

"I see that the three-brained beings arising and existing on the peculiar planet called 'Earth' interest you very much, and as, during our voyage on the ship 'Karnak' we shall have to talk about many things just to pass away the time, I will tell you all I can just about these three-brained beings.

"I think it will be best for your clear understanding of the strangeness of the psyche of the three-brained beings arising on the planet 'Earth' if I relate to you my personal descents to that planet in their order and the events which occurred there during these descents of mine and of which I was myself a witness.

"But I personally visited the surface of the planet 'Earth' only six times and each of these personal visits of mine was brought about by a different set of circumstances.

"I shall begin with my first descent."

- -

The First Descent of Beelzebub upon the Planet Earth

U PON that planet Earth," Beelzebub began to relate, "I descended for the first time on account of a young being of our tribe who had had the misfortune to become deeply involved with a three-brained being there, as a consequence of which he had got himself mixed up in a very stupid affair.

"There once came to my house on the planet Mars a number of beings of our tribe, also dwelling there on Mars, with the following request:

"They told me that one of their young kinsmen, 350 Martian years before, had migrated to exist on the planet Earth, and that a very disagreeable incident for all of us, his kinsmen, had recently occurred to him there.

"They told me further:

"'We, his kinsmen, both those existing there on the planet Earth and those existing here on the planet Mars, intended at first to deal with the unpleasant incident ourselves, with our own resources. But notwithstanding all our efforts and the measures we have adopted we have been unable so far to accomplish anything.

"'And being now finally convinced that we are unable to settle this unpleasant affair by ourselves independently, we venture to trouble you, your Right Reverence, and urgently beseech you to be so kind as not to withhold from us your wise advice how we may find a way out of our unhappy situation.'

"They told me further in detail in what the misfortune which had befallen them consisted.

"From all they told me I saw that the incident was

---------------------------- *109* ----------------------------

disagreeable not only for this young being's kinsmen, but that it might also prove disagreeable for the beings of all our tribe.

"So I could not help deciding at once to undertake to help them to settle this difficulty of theirs.

"At first I tried to help them while remaining on the planet Mars, but when I became certain that it would be impossible to do anything effective from the planet Mars, I decided to descend to the planet Earth and there, on the spot, to find some way out. The next day after this decision of mine, I took with me everything necessary which I had at hand and flew there on the ship *Occasion*.

"I may remind you that the ship *Occasion* was the ship on which all the beings of our tribe were transported to that solar system and, as I have already told you, it was left there for the use of the beings of our tribe for the purpose of interplanetary communication.

"The permanent port of this ship was on the planet Mars; and its supreme direction had been given me from Above.

"Thus it was on this same ship *Occasion* that I made my first descent to the planet Earth.

"Our ship landed on this first visit of mine, on the shores of just that continent which during the second catastrophe to this planet, disappeared entirely from its

The First Descent Of Beelzebub Upon The Earth

U PON THAT planet Earth," Beelzebub began to relate, "I descended for the first time on account of a young being of our tribe who had had the misfortune to become deeply involved with a three-brained being there, as a consequence of which he had got himself mixed up in a very stupid affair.

"There once came to my house on the planet Mars a number of beings of our tribe, also dwelling there on Mars, with the following request:

"They told me that one of their young kinsmen, 350 Martian years before, had migrated to exist on the planet Earth, and that a very disagreeable incident for all of us, his kinsmen, had recently occurred to him there.

"They told me further:

"'We, his kinsmen, both those existing there on the planet Earth and those existing here on the planet Mars, intended at first to deal with the unpleasant incident ourselves, with our own resources. But notwithstanding all our efforts and the measures we have adopted we have been unable so far to accomplish anything.

"'And being now finally convinced that we are unable to settle this unpleasant affair by ourselves independently, we venture to trouble you, Your Right Reverence, and urgently beseech you to be so kind as not to withhold from us your wise advice how we may find a way out of our unhappy situation.'

"They told me further in detail in what the misfortune which had befallen them consisted.

"From all they told me I saw that the incident was

- -

disagreeable not only for this young being's kinsmen, but that it might also prove disagreeable for the beings of all our tribe.

"So I could not help deciding at once to undertake to help them to settle this difficulty of theirs.

"At first I tried to help them while remaining on the planet Mars, but when I became certain that it would be impossible to do anything effective from the planet Mars, I decided to descend to the planet Earth and there, on the spot, to find some way out. The next day after this decision of mine I took with me everything necessary which I had 'at hand' and flew there on the ship 'Occasion.'

"I may remind you that the ship 'Occasion' was the ship on which all the beings of our tribe were transported to that solar system and as I have already told you, it was left there for the use of the beings of our tribe for the purpose of interplanetary communication.

"The permanent port of this ship was on the planet Mars; and its supreme direction had been given me from Above.

"Thus it was on this same ship 'Occasion' that I made my first descent to the planet Earth.

"Our ship landed on this first visit of mine, on the shores of just that continent which during the second catastrophe to this planet, disappeared entirely from its surface.

"This continent was called 'Atlantis' and most of the three-brained beings, and likewise most of the beings of our tribe, then existed only upon it.

"Having descended, I went straight from the ship *Occasion* to the city named 'Samlios,' situated on the said continent, where that unfortunate being of our tribe, who was the cause of this descent of mine, had the place of his existence.

"The city 'Samlios' was then a very large city, and was

- *110* -

the capital of the largest community then on the planet Earth.

"In this same city the head of this large community existed who was called 'King Appolis.'

"And it was with just this same King Appolis that our young, inexperienced countryman had become involved.

"And it was in this city of 'Samlios' itself that I learned all the details of this affair.

"I learned, namely, that before this incident our unfortunate countryman had for some reason been on friendly terms with this King Appolis, and was often at his house.

"As it transpired, our young countryman once, in the course of conversation during a visit to the house of King Appolis, made a 'wager' which was just the cause of all that followed.

"You must first of all know that both the community of which King Appolis was the head and the city of Samlios where he existed were at that period the greatest and richest of all the communities and cities then existing on the Earth.

"For the upkeep of all this wealth and grandeur King Appolis certainly needed both a great deal of what is called 'money' and a great deal of labor from the ordinary beings of that community.

"It is necessary to premise just here that at the period of my first descent in person onto this planet, the organ Kundabuffer was no longer in the three-brained beings who interest you.

"And it was only in some of the three-brained beings there that various consequences of the properties of that for them maleficent organ had already begun to be crystallized.

"In the period to which this tale of mine refers, one of the consequences of the properties of this organ which had already become thoroughly crystallized in a number

- *111* -

of beings there was that consequence of the property which, while the organ Kundabuffer itself was still functioning in them, had enabled them very easily and without any 'remorse-of-conscience' not to carry out voluntarily any duties taken upon themselves or given them by a superior. But every duty they fulfilled was fulfilled only from the fear and apprehension of 'threats' and 'menaces' from outside.

"It was in just this same consequence of this property already thoroughly crystallized in some beings of that period there, that the cause of this whole incident lay.

surface.

"This continent was called 'Atlantis' and most of the three-brained beings and likewise most of the beings of our tribe then existed only upon it.

"Having descended, I went straight from the ship 'Occasion' to the city named 'Samlios,' situated on the said continent, where that unfortunate being of our tribe, who was the cause of this descent of mine, had the place of his existence.

"The city 'Samlios' was then a very large city, and was

the capital of the largest community then on the planet Earth.

"In this same city the head of this large community existed who was called 'King Appolis.'

"And it was with just this same 'King Appolis' that our young inexperienced countryman had become involved.

"And it was in this city of 'Samlios' itself that I learned all the details of this affair.

"I learned, namely, that before this incident our unfortunate countryman had for some reason been on friendly terms with this King Appolis, and was often at his house.

"As it transpired, our young countryman once, in the course of conversation, during a visit to the house of King Appolis, made a 'wager' which was just the cause of all that followed.

"You must first of all know that both the community of which King Appolis was the head, and the city of Samlios where he existed were at that period the greatest and richest of all the communities and cities then existing on the Earth.

"For the upkeep of all this wealth and grandeur King Appolis certainly needed both a great deal of what is called 'money' and a great deal of labor from the ordinary beings of that community.

"It is necessary to premise just here that at the period of my first descent in person onto this planet, the organ Kundabuffer was no longer in three-brained beings who interest you.

"And it was only in some of the three-brained beings there that various consequences of the properties of that for them maleficent organ had already begun to be crystallized.

"In the period to which this tale of mine refers, one of the consequences of the properties of this organ which had already become thoroughly crystallized in a number

of beings there, was that consequence of the property which, while the organ Kundabuffer itself was still functioning in them had enabled them very easily and without any 'remorse-of-conscience' not to carry out voluntarily any duties taken upon themselves or given them by a superior. But every duty they fulfilled was fulfilled only from the fear and apprehension of 'threats' and 'menaces' from outside.

"It was in just this same consequence of this property already thoroughly crystallized in some beings of that period there, that the cause of this whole incident lay.

"And so, my boy, this is how it was. King Appolis, who had been extremely conscientious in respect of the duties he had taken upon himself for the maintenance of the greatness of the community entrusted to him, had spared neither his own labor nor wealth, and at the same time he demanded the same from all the beings of his community.

"But, as I have already said, the mentioned consequences of the organ Kundabuffer having by that time been thoroughly crystallized in certain of his subjects, he had to employ every possible kind of 'threat' and 'menace' in order to extract from everybody all that was required for the greatness of the community entrusted to him.

"His methods were so varied and at the same time so reasonable that even those of his 'subjects-beings' in whom the said consequences had already been crystallized could not help respecting him, although they added to his name, of course behind his back, the nickname 'Arch-cunning.'

"And so, my boy, these means by which King Appolis then obtained what was necessary from his subjects for the maintenance of the greatness of the community entrusted to him seemed to our young countryman, for some reason or other, unjust, and, as it was said, he often became

very indignant and restless whenever he happened to hear of some new device of King Appolis for getting what was necessary.

"And once, while talking with the King himself, our naive young countryman could not restrain himself, but expressed to his face his indignation and his views of this 'unconscionable' conduct of King Appolis towards his subjects.

"Not only did King Appolis not fly into a temper, as usually happens on the planet Earth when somebody pokes his nose where he has no business, nor did he pitch him out by the scruff of his neck, but he even talked it over with him and discussed the reasons for his 'severity.'

"They talked a great deal and the result of the whole of their conversation was precisely a 'wager,' that is to say they made an agreement and set it down on paper, and each of them signed it with his own blood.

"Among other things there was included in this agreement that for the obtaining from his subjects of all that was necessary King Appolis should be obliged to employ thereafter only those measures and means which should be indicated by our countryman.

"And in the event that all his subjects should fail to contribute all that which according to custom was required, then our countryman would become responsible for everything, and he pledged himself to procure for the treasury of King Appolis as much as was necessary for the maintenance and further aggrandizement of the capital and of the whole community.

"And so, my boy, King Appolis did indeed, from the very next day, fulfill very honorably the obligation which according to the agreement he had assumed; and he conducted the whole government of the country exactly according to the indications of our young countryman. The results of a government of this kind, however, very soon

"And so, my boy, this is how it was. King Appolis who had been extremely conscientious in respect of the duties he had taken upon himself for the maintenance of the greatness of the community entrusted to him had spared neither his own labor nor wealth, and at the same time he demanded the same from all the beings of his community.

"But, as I have already said, the mentioned consequences of the organ Kundabuffer having by that time been thoroughly crystallized in certain of his subjects, he had to employ every possible kind of 'threat' and 'menace' in order to extract from everybody all that was required for the greatness of the community entrusted to him.

"His methods were so varied and at the same time so reasonable that even those subjects-beings in whom the said consequences had already been crystallized could not help respecting him, although they added to his name, of course behind his back, the nickname 'Arch-cunning.'

"And so, my boy, these means by which King Appolis then obtained what was necessary from his subjects for the maintenance of the greatness of the community entrusted to him seemed to our young countryman, for some reason or other, unjust, and, as it was said, he often became

---

very indignant and restless whenever he happened to hear of some new device of King Appolis for getting what was necessary.

"And once, while talking with the King himself, our naive young countryman could not restrain himself, but expressed to his face his indignation and his views of this 'unconscionable' conduct of King Appolis towards his subjects.

"Not only did King Appolis not fly into a temper, as usually happens on the planet Earth when somebody pokes his nose where he has no business, nor did he pitch him out by the scruff of his neck, but he even talked it over with him and discussed the reasons for his 'severity.'

"They talked a great deal and the result of the whole of their conversation was precisely a 'wager,' that is to say, they made an agreement and set it down on paper, and each of them signed it with his own blood.

"Among other things there was included in this agreement that for the obtaining from his subjects of all that was necessary King Appolis should be obliged to employ thereafter only those measures and means which should be indicated by our countryman.

"And in the event that all the subjects should fail to contribute all that which according to custom was required, then our countryman would become responsible for everything, and he pledged himself to procure for the treasury of King Appolis as much as was necessary for the maintenance and further aggrandizement of the capital and of the whole community.

"And so, my boy, King Apolis did indeed, already from the following day fulfil very honorably the obligation which according to the agreement he had assumed; and he conducted the whole government of the country exactly according to the indications of our young countryman. The results of a government of this kind, however, very soon

---

proved to be quite the opposite of those expected by our simpleton.

"The subjects of that community—principally, of course, those in whom the said consequences of the properties of the organ Kundabuffer had already been crystallized—not only ceased to pay into King Appolis' treasury what was required, but they even began gradually snatching back what had been put in before.

"As our countryman had undertaken to contribute what was needed and, furthermore, had signed his undertaking with his blood—and you know, don't you, what the voluntary undertaking of an obligation, especially when signed with his blood, means to one of our tribe—he had of course soon to begin making up to the treasury all that was short.

"He first put in everything he had himself, and afterwards everything he could get from his nearests, dwelling also there on the planet Earth. And when he had drained dry his nearests there, he addressed himself for assistance to his nearests dwelling on the planet Mars.

"But soon on the planet Mars also everything ran dry and still the treasury of the city of Samlios demanded more and again more; nor was the end of its needs in sight.

"It was just then that all the kinsmen of this countryman of ours became alarmed and thereupon they decided to address themselves to me with the request to help them out of their plight.

"So, my boy, when we arrived in the said city I was met by all the beings of our tribe, both old and young, who had remained on that planet.

"In the evening of the same day a general meeting was called to confer together to find some way out of the situation that had arisen.

"To this conference of ours there was also invited King Appolis himself with whom our elder countrymen had already previously had many talks on this matter with this aim in view.

---- *114* ----

"At this first general conference of ours, King Appolis, addressing himself to all, said as follows:

"'Impartial friends!'

"'I personally am deeply sorry for what has occurred and what has brought about so many troubles for those assembled here; and I am distressed in all my being that it is beyond my power to extricate you from your prospective difficulties.

"'You must know, indeed,' King Appolis continued, 'that the machinery of the government of my community which has been wound up and organized during many centuries, is at the present time already radically changed; and to revert to the old order is already impossible without serious consequences, namely, without those consequences which must doubtless evoke the indignation of the majority of my subjects. The present situation is such that I alone am not able to abolish what has been created without provoking the mentioned serious consequences, and I therefore beg you all in the name of Justice to help me to deal with it.

proved to be quite the opposite of those expected by our simpleton.

"The subjects of that community—principally, of course, those in whom the said consequences of the properties of the organ Kundabuffer had already been crystallized—not only ceased to pay into King Appolis' treasury what was required, but they even began gradually snatching back what had been put in before.

"As our countryman had undertaken to contribute what was needed, and furthermore, had signed his undertaking with his blood—and you know, don't you, what the voluntary undertaking of an obligation, especially when signed with his blood, means to one of our tribe—he had of course soon to begin making up to the treasury all that was short.

"He first put in everything he had himself, and afterwards everything he could get from his nearests, dwelling also there on the planet Earth. And when he had drained dry his nearests there, he addressed himself for assistance to his nearests dwelling on the planet Mars.

"But soon on the planet Mars also everything ran dry and still the treasury of the city of Samlios demanded more and again more; nor was the end of its needs in sight.

"It was just then that all the kinsmen of this countryman of ours became alarmed and thereupon they decided to address themselves to me with the request to help them out of their plight.

"So, my boy, when we arrived in the said city I was met by all the beings of our tribe, both old and young, who had remained on that planet.

"In the evening of the same day a general meeting was called to confer together to find some way out of the situation that had arisen.

"To this conference of ours there was also invited King Appolis himself with whom our elder countrymen had already previously had many talks on this matter with this aim in view.

"At this first general conference of ours, King Appolis, addressing himself to all, said as follows:

"'Impartial friends!

"'I personally am deeply sorry for what has occurred and what has brought about so many troubles for those assembled here; and I am distressed in all my being that it is beyond my power to extricate you from your prospective difficulties.'

"'You must know, indeed' King Appolis continued, 'that the machinery of the government of my community which has been wound up and organized during many centuries, is at the present time already radically changed; and to revert to the old order is already impossible without serious consequences, namely, without those consequences which must doubtless evoke the indignation of the majority of my subjects. The present situation is such that I alone am not able to abolish what has been created without provoking the mentioned serious consequences, and I therefore beg you all in the name of Justice to help me deal with it.'

"'Still further,' he then added, 'I bitterly reproach myself in the presence of you all, because I also am greatly to blame for all these misfortunes.

"'And I am to blame because I ought to have foreseen what has occurred, since I have existed in these conditions longer than my opponent and your kinsman, namely, he with whom I made the agreement known to you.

"'To tell the truth it was unpardonable of me to risk entering into such conditions with a being who, although he may be of much higher Reason than I, is, nevertheless, not so practiced in such affairs as I am.

"'Once more I beg all of you, and your Right Reverence in particular, to forgive me and to help me out of this sad plight, and enable me to find some issue from the situation that has been created.

- *115* -

"'With things as they now are, I can at present do only what you will indicate.'

"After King Appolis had left, we decided the same evening to select from among ourselves several experienced elderly beings who should weigh together, that same night, all the data and draw up a rough plan for further action.

"The rest of us then departed on the understanding that we should assemble the ensuing evening at the same place; but to this second conference of ours King Appolis was not invited.

"When we assembled the next day, one of the elder beings, elected the night before, first reported as follows:

"'We pondered and deliberated the whole night upon all the details of this lamentable event, and as a result we have unanimously come to the conclusion first of all that there is no way out but to revert to the former conditions of government.

"'Further, we all, and also unanimously, agree that to return to the former order of government must indeed inevitably provoke a revolt of the citizens of the community, and, of course, that there will certainly follow all those consequences of revolt which have already become inevitable in such circumstances during recent times on Earth.

"'And of course, as has also become usual here, many of those so-called "power-possessing" beings of this community will suffer terribly, even possibly to the degree of their complete destruction; and above all, it seemed impossible that King Appolis could escape such a fate.

"'Thereafter we deliberated in order, if possible, to devise some means of diverting the said unhappy consequences at least from King Appolis himself.

- *116* -

"'And we had every wish to devise such a means because at our general conference yesterday evening King Appolis himself was very frank and friendly towards us, and we should all be extremely sorry if he himself should suffer.

"'During our further prolonged deliberations we came to the conclusion that it would be possible to divert the blow from King Appolis only if during the said revolt the exhibition of the fury of the rebellious beings of this community was directed not against the King himself but against those around him, that is, those

"'Still further,' he then added, 'I bitterly reproach myself in the presence of you all, because I also am greatly to blame for all these misfortunes.'

"'And I am to blame because I ought to have foreseen what has occurred, since I have existed in these conditions longer than my opponent and your kinsman, namely, he with whom I made the agreement known to you.'

"'To tell the truth it was unpardonable of me to risk entering into such conditions with a being who, although he may be of much higher reason than I, is, nevertheless, not so practiced in such affairs as I am.'

"'Once more I beg all of you, and Your Reverence in particular, to forgive me and to help me out of this sad plight, and enable me to find some issue from the situation that has been created.'

- -

"'With things as they now are, I can at present do only what you will indicate.'"

"After King Appolis had left, we decided the same evening to select from among ourselves several experienced elderly beings who should weigh together, that same night, all the data and draw up a rough plan for further action.

"The rest of us then departed on the understanding that we should assemble the ensuing evening at the same place; but to this second conference of ours King Appolis was not invited.

"When we assembled the next day, one of the elder beings elected the night before, first reported as follows:

"'We pondered and deliberated the whole night upon all the details of this lamentable event, and as a result we have unanimously come to the conclusion first of all that there is no way out but to revert to the former conditions of government.

"'Further, we all, and also unanimously, agree that to return to the former order of government must indeed inevitably provoke a revolt of the citizens of the community, and, of course, that there will certainly follow all those consequences of revolt which have already became inevitable in such circumstances during recent times on Earth.

"'And of course, as it has also become usual here, many of those called 'power-possessing' beings of this community will suffer terribly, even possibly to the degree of their complete destruction; and above all, it seemed impossible that King Appolis could escape such a fate.

"'Thereafter we deliberated in order, if possible, to devise some means of diverting the said unhappy consequences at least from King Appolis himself.

- -

"'And we had every wish to devise such a means because at our general conference yesterday evening King Appolis himself was very frank and friendly towards us, and we should all be extremely sorry if he himself should suffer.

"'During our further prolonged deliberations we came to the conclusion that it would be possible to divert the blow from King Appolis only if during the said revolt the exhibition of the fury of the rebellious beings of this community were directed not against the King himself but against those around him, that is, those who are there called his "administration."

"'But then the question arose among us, would those near the King be willing to take upon themselves the consequences of all this?

"And we came to the categorical conclusion that they certainly would not agree, because they would assuredly consider that the King himself had been alone to blame for it all, and that therefore he himself should pay for it.

"'Having come to all these aforesaid conclusions we finally also unanimously decided as follows:

"'In order at least to save King Appolis from what is inevitably expected, we must with the consent of the King himself replace all the beings in this community who now hold responsible posts, by beings of our tribe, and each of these latter, during the climax of this "psychosis" of the masses, must take upon himself a share of the consequences anticipated.'

"When this elected being of ours had finished his report our opinion was quickly formed, and a unanimous resolution was carried to do just as the elder beings of our tribe had advised.

"And thereupon we first sent one of our elder beings to King Appolis to put our plan before him, to which the latter agreed, once more repeating his promise, namely, that he would do everything according to our directions.

- *117* -

"We then decided to delay no longer and from the following day to begin to replace all the officials by our own.

"But after two days it turned out that there were not sufficient beings of our tribe dwelling on the planet Earth to replace all the officials of that community; and we therefore immediately sent the Occasion back to the planet Mars for our beings there.

"And meanwhile King Appolis guided by two of our elder beings, began under different pretexts replacing various officials by our beings, at first in the capital of Samlios itself.

"And when several days later our ship *Occasion* arrived from the planet Mars with beings of our tribe, similar replacements were made in the provinces also, and soon everywhere in that community what are called the responsible posts were filled by the beings of our tribe.

"And when all had been changed in this way, King Appolis, always under the guidance of these elder beings of ours, began the restoration of the former code of regulations for the administration of the community.

"Almost from the very first days of the restoration of the old code, the effects upon the general psyche of the beings of that community in whom the consequences of the mentioned property of the maleficent organ Kundabuffer had already been thoroughly crystallized began, as it was expected, to manifest themselves.

"Thus the expected discontent grew thereupon from day to day, until one day, not long after, there occurred just that which has ever since been definitely proper to be present in the presence of the three-brained beings there of all ensuing periods, and that is, to produce from time to time the process which they themselves

who are there called his 'administration.'

"'But then the question arose among us, would those near the King be willing to take upon themselves the consequences of all this?'

"And we came to the categorical conclusion that they certainly would not agree, because they would assuredly consider that the King himself had been alone to blame for it all, and that therefore he himself should pay for it.

"'Having come to all these aforesaid conclusions we finally also unanimously decided as follows:

"'In order at least to save King Appolis from what is inevitably expected, we must with the consent of the King himself replace all the beings in this community who now hold responsible posts, by beings of our tribe, and each of these latter, during the climax of this 'psychosis' of the masses must take upon himself a share of the consequences anticipated.'"

"When this elected being of ours had finished his report, our opinion was quickly formed; and a unanimous resolution was carried to do just as the elder beings of our tribe had advised.

"And thereupon we first sent one of our elder beings to King Appolis to put our plan before him, to which the latter agreed, once more repeating his promise, namely, that he would do everything according to our directions.

- -

"We then decided to delay no longer and from the following day to begin to replace all the officials by our own.

"But after two days it turned out that there were not sufficient beings of or tribe dwelling on the planet Earth to replace all the officials of that community; and we therefore immediately sent the 'Occasion' back to the planet Mars for our beings there.

"And meanwhile King Appolis guided by two of our elder beings, began under different pretexts replacing various officials by our beings, at first in the capital of Samlios itself.

"And when several days later our ship 'Occasion' arrived from the planet Mars with beings of our tribe, similar replacements were made in the provinces also, and soon everywhere in that community what are called the responsible posts were filled by the beings of our tribe.

"And when all had been changed in this way, King Appolis, always under the guidance of these elder beings of ours, began the restoration of the former code of regulations for the administration of the community.

"Almost from the very first days of the restoration of the old code, the effects upon the general psyche of the beings of that community in whom the consequences of the mentioned property of the maleficent organ Kundabuffer had already been thoroughly crystallized, began as it was expected, to manifest themselves.

"Thus the expected discontent grew thereupon from day to day, until one day, not long after, there occurred just that which has ever since been definitely proper to be present in the presence of the three-brained beings there of all ensuing periods, and that is, to produce from time to time the process which they themselves nowadays call 'revolution.'

"And during their revolution of that time, as it has also

------------------------------- *118* -------------------------------

become proper there to these three-brained phenomena of our Great Universe, they destroyed a great deal of the property which they had accumulated during centuries, much of what is called the 'knowledge' which they had attained during centuries also was destroyed and lost forever, and the existence of those other beings similar to themselves who had already chanced upon the means of freeing themselves from the consequences of the properties of the organ Kundabuffer were also destroyed.

"It is extremely interesting to notice here one exceedingly astonishing and incomprehensible fact.

"And that is that during their later revolutions of this kind, almost all the three-brained beings there or at least the overwhelming majority who begin to fall into such a 'psychosis,' always destroy for some reason or other the existence of just such other beings like themselves, as have, for some reason or other, chanced to find themselves more or less on the track of the means of becoming free from the crystallization in themselves of the consequences of the properties of that maleficent organ Kundabuffer which unfortunately their ancestors possessed.

"So, my boy, while the process of this revolution of theirs was running its course, King Appolis himself existed in one of his suburban palaces of the city of Samlios.

"Nobody laid a finger on him, because our beings had arranged by their propaganda that the whole blame should be placed not upon King Appolis but upon those surrounding him, that is, as they are called, his administration.

"Moreover, the beings who had fallen into the said psychosis even 'suffered grief' and really pitied their king, saying that it was because their 'poor King' had been surrounded by such unconscionable and ungrateful subordinates that these undesirable revolutions had occurred.

"And when the revolutionary psychosis had quite died down, King Appolis returned to the city of Samlios and

------------------------------- *119* -------------------------------

again with the help of our elder beings, gradually began replacing our countrymen either by those of his old subordinates who were still alive, or by selecting absolutely new ones from among his other subjects.

"And when the earlier policy of King Appolis towards his subjects had been re-established, then the citizens of this community resumed filling the treasury with money as usual and carrying out the directions of their King, and the affairs of the community settled again into the former already established tempo.

"As for our naive, unfortunate countryman who was the cause of it all, it was so painful to him that he would no longer remain upon that planet that had proved so disastrous for him, but he returned with us to the planet Mars.

"And later on he became there an even excellent bailiff for all the beings of our tribe."

------------------------------- *120* -------------------------------

nowadays call 'revolution.'

"And during their 'revolution' of that time, as it has also become proper there

to these three-brained phenomena of our Great Universe, they destroyed a great deal of the property which they had accumulated during centuries, much of what is called the 'knowledge' which their kind attained during centuries also was destroyed and lost forever, and the existences of those other beings similar to themselves who had already chanced upon the means of freeing themselves from the consequences of the properties of the organ Kundabuffer, were also destroyed.

"It is extremely interesting to notice here one exceedingly astonishing and incomprehensible fact.

"And that is that during their later 'revolutions' of this kind, almost all the three-brained beings there or at least the overwhelming majority who begin to fall into such a 'psychosis,' always destroy for some reason or other, the existence of just such other beings like themselves, as have for some reason or other, chanced to find themselves more or less on the track of the means of becoming free from the crystallization in themselves of the consequences of the properties of that maleficent organ Kundabuffer which unfortunately their ancestors possessed.

"So, my boy, while the process of this 'revolution' of theirs was running its course, King Appolis himself existed in one of his what are called suburban palaces of the city of Samlios.

"Nobody laid a finger on him, because our beings had arranged by their propaganda that the whole blame should be placed not upon King Appolis but upon those surrounding him, that is as they are called his administration.

"Moreover, the beings who had fallen into the said 'psychosis' even 'suffered grief' and really pitied their king saying that it was because their 'poor King' had been surrounded by such unconscionable and ungrateful subordinates that these undesirable revolutions had occurred.

"And when the revolutionary psychosis had quite died down, King Appolis returned to the city of Samlios and

again with the help of our elder beings, gradually began replacing our countrymen either by those of his old subordinates who were still alive, or by selecting absolutely new ones from among his other subjects.

"And when the earlier policy of King Appolis towards his subjects had been reestablished, then the citizens of this community resumed filling the treasury with 'money' as usual and carrying out the directions of their King, and the affairs of the community settled again into the former already established tempo.

"As for our naive, unfortunate countryman who was the cause of it all, it was so painful to him that he would no longer remain upon that planet that had proved so disastrous for him, but he returned with us to the planet Mars.

"And later on he became there an even excellent bailiff for all the beings of our tribe."

The Relative Understanding of Time

A FTER a short pause Beelzebub continued thus:
   "Before telling you further about the three-brained beings who have taken your fancy and who breed on the planet Earth, it is in my opinion absolutely necessary for you, for a clear representation of the strangeness of their psyche and, in general, for a better understanding of everything concerning this peculiar planet, first of all to have an accurate representation of their time-calculation, and of how the being-sensation of what is called the 'process-of-the-flow-of-time' in the presences of the three-brained beings of that planet has gradually changed and also of how this process now flows in the presences of the contemporary three-brained beings there.

   "It must be made clear to you because only then will you have the possibility clearly to represent to yourself and understand the events there which I have already related and those I shall yet relate.

   "You must first know that for the definition of Time, the three-brained beings of that planet take the 'year' as the basic unit of their time-calculation, just as we do, and also, like us, they define the duration of their 'year' by the time of a certain movement of their planet in relation to another definite cosmic concentration; that is to say, they take that period in the course of which their planet, during its movement—that is, during the processes of 'Falling' and 'Catching-up'—makes what is called its 'Krentonalnian-revolution' in relation to its sun.

   "It is similar to our reckoning of a 'year' for our planet Karatas, which is the period of time between the nearest approach of the sun 'Samos' to the sun 'Selos' and its next similar approach.

- *121* -

   "A hundred of such 'years' of theirs, the beings of the Earth call a 'century.'

   "And they divide this 'year' of theirs into twelve parts and each part they call a 'month.'

   "For the definition of the duration of this 'month' of theirs, they take the time of that completed period during which that larger fragment—which was separated from their planet and which they now call Moon—makes, owing to the same cosmic law of 'Falling' and 'Catching-up,' its full 'Krentonalnian-revolution' in relation to their planet.

   "It must be noticed that the twelve 'Krentonalnian-revolutions' of the said Moon do not correspond exactly to a single 'Krentonalnian-revolution' of their planet round its sun and therefore they have made some compromise or other when calculating these months of theirs, so that in the sum total these may correspond more or less to reality.

   "Further, they divide these months of theirs into thirty 'diurnities,' or, as they usually say, 'days.'

   "And a diurnity they reckon as that span of time during which their planet makes its 'completed-rotation' during the actualizing of the said cosmic laws.

The Relative Understanding Of Time

AFTER a short pause Beelzebub continued thus:
   "Before telling you more about the three-brained beings who please you, breeding on the planet 'Earth,' I think that for a clear conspectus of the strangeness of their psyche and, in general, for a better understanding of everything concerning the peculiarity of that planet, it is indispensably necessary for you to have, first of all, an accurate conception of their time-calculation and of how the being-sensation of what is called the 'process-of-the-flow-of-Time' in the 'presence' of the three-brained beings of that planet has gradually undergone change and of how this process now flows in the 'presence' of the contemporary three-brained beings there.

"It must be made clear to you because only then can you have a clear view and understanding, both of those events there which I have already related and those I have still to relate.

"You must first know that for the definition of Time, the three-brained beings of that planet, just as we do, take the year as the fundamental unit of their Time-calculation, and also just as we do, they define the duration of their year by the time of a certain movement of their planet in relation to another definite cosmic concentration; namely, they take that period in the course of which their planet, during its movement—that is, during the process of 'Falling' and 'Catching Up'—makes what is called its 'Krentonalnian' revolution in relation to its sun.

"It is similar to our reckoning of a year for our planet 'Karatas,' which is the period of time between one nearest approach of the Sun 'Samos' to the Sun 'Selos' and its next similar approach.

"A hundred of such years of theirs, the beings of the 'Earth' call a 'century.'

"And they divide this 'year' into twelve parts and each part they call a 'month.'

"For the definition of the duration of this 'month' of theirs, they take the time of the complete period during which that larger fragment—which was separated from their planet and which they now call 'Moon'—makes, owing to the same cosmic law of 'Falling' and 'Catching Up,' its full 'Krentonalnian' revolution in relation to their planet.

"It must be noticed that the twelve 'Krentonalnian' revolutions of the said 'Moon' do not correspond exactly to a single 'Krentonalnian' revolution of their planet round its sun and therefore they have made some compromise or other when calculating these 'months' of theirs so that in the sum-total these may correspond more or less to reality.

"Further, they divide these 'months' of theirs into thirty 'diurnities,' or, as they usually say, 'days.'

"And a 'diurnity' they reckon as that period of time during which their planet makes its appointed rotation during the operation of the said cosmic laws.

"Bear in mind, by the way, that they also say 'it-is-day,' when in the atmosphere of their planet—just as in general on all the other planets on which, as I have already told you, the cosmic process called 'Ilnosoparnian' is actualized—that 'Trogoautoegocratic' process which we call 'kshtatsavacht' periodically proceeds; and they also call this cosmic phenomenon 'daylight.'

"As regards the other process, the opposite one, which we call 'kldatzacht,' they call it 'night' and refer to it as 'it-is-dark.'

"And thus the three-brained beings breeding on the planet Earth call the greatest period of the flow of time

-------------------------------- *122* --------------------------------

'century,' and this 'century' of theirs consists of a hundred 'years.'

"A 'year' has twelve 'months.'

"A 'month' has an average of thirty 'days,' that is, diurnities.

"Further, they divide their diurnity into twenty-four 'hours' and an 'hour' into sixty 'minutes.'

"And a 'minute' they divide into sixty 'seconds.'

"But as in general, my boy, you do not yet know of the exceptional peculiarity of this cosmic phenomenon Time, you must first be told that genuine Objective Science formulates this cosmic phenomenon thus:

"Time in itself does not exist; there is only the totality of the results ensuing from all the cosmic phenomena present in a given place.

"Time itself, no being can either understand by reason or sense by any outer or inner being-function. It cannot even be sensed by any gradation of instinct which arises and is present in every more or less independent cosmic concentration.

"It is possible to judge Time only if one compares real cosmic phenomena which proceed in the same place and under the same conditions, where Time is being constated and considered.

"It is necessary to notice that in the Great Universe all phenomena in general, without exception wherever they arise and manifest, are simply successively law-conformable 'Fractions' of some whole phenomenon which has its prime arising on the 'Most Holy Sun Absolute.'

"And in consequence, all cosmic phenomena, wherever they proceed, have a sense of 'objectivity.'

"And these successively law-conformable 'Fractions' are actualized in every respect, and even in the sense of their involution and evolution, owing to the chief cosmic law, the sacred 'Heptaparaparshinokh.'

-------------------------------- *123* --------------------------------

"Only Time alone has no sense of objectivity because it is not the result of the fractioning of any definite cosmic phenomena. And it does not issue from anything, but blends always with everything and becomes self-sufficiently independent; therefore, in the whole of the Universe, it alone can be called and extolled as the 'Ideally-Unique-Subjective-Phenomenon.'

"Thus, my boy, uniquely Time alone, or, as it is sometimes called, the 'Heropass,' has no source from which its arising should depend, but like 'Divine-Love'

"Bear in mind, by the way, that they also call it 'day'—when in the atmosphere of their planet—just as in general upon all the other planets on which, as I have already told you, the cosmic process called 'Ilnosoparnian' is actualized—that 'Trogoautoegocratic' process which we call 'Kshtatsavacht' periodically proceeds; and they also call this cosmic phenomenon 'daylight.'

"And concerning the other process, the opposite one, namely, that which we call 'Kldatzacht,' they call it 'night' or speak of it as 'the dark.'

"And thus the three-brained beings breeding on the planet 'Earth' call the greatest period of the flowing of Time

- -

a 'century,' and this century of theirs consists of one hundred years.

"A 'year' has 'twelve months.'

"A 'month' has an average of thirty 'diurnities.'

"Further they divide their 'diurnity' into twenty-four 'hours' and an 'hour' they divide into sixty 'minutes.'

"And a 'minute' in its turn they divide into sixty 'seconds.'

"But as you are aware in general, my boy, of the altogether exceptional peculiarity of this same cosmic phenomenon Time, you must first be told that genuine objective Science formulates this cosmic phenomenon thus:

"Time in itself does not in general exist; there is only the totality of the results arising from the cosmic phenomena of every kind present in the given place.

"Time in itself no being can either understand by reason, or sense by any outer or inner being-function. It cannot even be sensed by any gradation of instinct which arises and is generally present in every kind of more or less independent cosmic concentration.

"It is possible to judge Time only if one compares some or other of the real cosmic phenomena which proceed in the same place and in the same conditions where Time is being ascertained and investigated.

"It is necessary to notice that in the Great Universe all phenomena in general without exception wherever they arise and manifest, are simply successively lawful fractions of some whole phenomenon which receives its prime arising on the Most Holy Sun Absolute.

"And owing to all this, all cosmic phenomena wherever they proceed, receive a 'sense of objectivity.'

"And these successively lawful fractions are actualized in every respect, and even in the sense of their evolution and involution, very strictly according to the chief cosmic law, the sacred 'Heptaparaparshinokh.'

- -

"Only Time alone has no 'sense of objectivity,' because it is not the consequence of the functioning of any definite cosmic phenomenon; and as it does not issue from anything, but blends always with everything, and becomes predominantly independent; therefore, alone in all the Universe, it can be called and lauded as the 'Ideal Unique Subjective Phenomenon.'

"Thus, my boy, uniquely Time alone, or, as it is sometimes called, the 'Hero-pass,' has no source from which its arising should depend, but like Divine Love flows always, as I have already told you, independently by itself, and blends proportionately with all the phenomena present in the given place and in the given arisings of our Great Universe.

"Again I tell you, you will be able clearly to understand all that I have just told you only when, as I have already promised you, I shall specially explain to you sometime later all about the fundamental laws of World-creation and World-maintenance.

"Meanwhile, remember this also, that since Time has no source of its arising and cannot like all other cosmic phenomena in every cosmic sphere establish its exact presence, the already mentioned Objective Science therefore has, for its examination of Time, a standard unit, similar to that used for an exact definition of the density and quality—in the sense of the vivifyingness of their vibrations—of all cosmic substances in general present in every place and in every sphere of our Great Universe.

"And for the definition of Time this standard unit has from long ago been the moment of what is called the sacred 'Egokoolnatsnarnian-sensation' which always appears in the Most Holy Cosmic Individuals dwelling on the Most Holy Sun Absolute whenever the vision of our UNI-BEING ENDLESSNESS is directed into space and directly touches their presences.

- *124* -

"This standard unit has been established in Objective Science for the possibility of exactly defining and comparing the differences between the gradations of the processes of the subjective sensations of separate conscious Individuals, and also of what are called 'diverse-tempos' among various objective cosmic phenomena which are manifested in various spheres of our Great Universe and which actualize all cosmic arisings both large and small.

"The chief particularity of the process of the flow of Time in the presence of cosmic arisings of various scales consists in this, that all of them perceive it in the same way and in the same sequence.

"In order that you may meanwhile represent to yourself, if only approximately, what I have just said, let us take as an example the process of the flow of Time proceeding in any drop of the water in that decanter standing there on the table.

"Every drop of water in that decanter is in itself also a whole independent world, a world of 'Microcosmoses.'

"In that little world, as in other cosmoses, there also arise and exist relatively independent infinitesimal 'individuals' or 'beings.'

"For the beings of that infinitesimal world also, Time flows in the same sequence in which the flow of Time is sensed by all individuals in all other cosmoses. These infinitesimal beings also, like the beings of cosmoses of other 'scales,' have their experiences of a definite duration for all their perceptions and manifestations; and, also, like them, they sense the flow of Time by the comparison of the duration of the phenomena around them.

"Exactly like the beings of other cosmoses, they are born, they grow up, they unite and separate for what are called 'sex-results' and they also fall sick and

alone flows always, as I have already told you, independently by itself, and blends proportionally with all the phenomena present in the given place and in the given arisings of Our Great Universe.

"Again I tell you, you will be able clearly to understand all that I have just told you only when I shall, as I have already promised you, specially explain to you sometime later all about the fundamental laws of World-creation and World-existence.

"Meanwhile only remember this also, that since Time has no source of its arising and cannot like all other cosmic phenomena in every cosmic sphere establish its exact 'presence,' the already mentioned objective Science has therefore for its investigations a standard unit, similar to that used for an exact definition of the density and quality—in the sense of the vivifyingness of their vibrations—of all cosmic substances in general, present in each and every place and in every sphere of our Great Universe.

"And for the definition of Time this standard unit has from long ago been reckoned as the moment of what is called the sacred 'Egokoolnatsnarnian-sensation,' which 'Egokoolnatsnarnian-sensation' always appears in the Most Holy Sun Absolute whenever the vision of our ENDLESS UNI-BEING is directed into space and touches their 'presence' immediately.

- -

"Such a standard unit is established in Objective Science as a means to exact definition and to the comparison both of the difference between the gradations of the processes of the subjective sensations of separate conscious Individuums, and also of what are called 'differing tempos' among various objective cosmic phenomena which are manifested in various spheres of our Great Universe and which actualize all cosmic arisings both large and small.

"The chief particularity of the process of the flow of Time in the 'presence' of cosmic arisings of various scales consists in this, that all of them perceive it in the same way and in the same sequence.

"In order that you may meanwhile have, if only an approximate conspectus of what I have just said, let us take as an example the process of the flow of Time proceeding in any drop of water contained in that decanter standing there on the table.

"Every drop of water in that decanter represents in itself also a whole independent World, namely a World of 'Microcosmoses.'

"In that little world also, exactly as in other cosmoses, there arise and exist relatively independent infinitesimal 'individuums' or 'beings.'

"For the beings of that infinitesimal World also, Time flows in the same sequence in which the flow of Time is sensed by all individuums in all other cosmoses; these infinitesimal beings also, like the beings of cosmoses of other 'scales' have their experiences of a definite duration for all their perceptions and manifestations; and also, like them, sense the flow of Time by the comparing of the duration of the phenomena around them.

"Exactly like the beings of other cosmoses, they are born grow up and unite and separate for what are called 'sex results'; they also fall sick and suffer, and fi-

suffer, and ultimately like everything existing in which Objective Reason has not become fixed, they are destroyed forever.

------------------------------ *125* ----------------------------

"For the entire process of the existence of these infinitesimal beings of this smallest world, Time of a definite proportionate duration also ensues from all the surrounding phenomena which are manifested in the given 'cosmic-scale.'

"For them also, Time of definite length is required for the processes of their arising and formation as well as for various events in the process of their existence up to their complete final destruction.

"In the whole course of the process of existence of the beings of this drop of water also, corresponding sequential definite what are called 'passages' of the flow of Time are also required.

"A definite time is required for their joys and for their sorrows, and, in short, for every other kind of indispensable being-experiencing, down to what are called 'runs-of-bad-luck,' and even to 'periods-of-thirst-for-self-perfection.'

"I repeat, among them also, the process of the flow of Time has its harmonious sequence, and this sequence ensues from the totality of all the phenomena surrounding them.

"The duration of the process of the flow of Time is generally perceived and sensed in the same way by all the aforementioned cosmic Individuals and by the already completely formed what are called 'instinctivized' units but only with that difference which ensues from the difference in the presences and states, at the given moment, of these cosmic arisings.

"It must be noticed, however, my boy, that though for separate individuals existing in any independent cosmic unit, their definition of the flow of Time is not objective in the general sense, yet nevertheless for them themselves it acquires a sense of objectivity since the flow of Time is perceived by them according to the completeness of their own presence.

------------------------------ *126* ----------------------------

"The same drop of water which we have taken as an example can serve for a clearer understanding of this thought of mine.

"Although in the sense of general Universal Objectivity, the whole period of the process of the flow of Time in that same drop of water is for the whole of it subjective, yet for the beings existing in the drop of water itself, the said given flow of Time is perceived by them as objective.

"For the clarification of this, those beings called 'hypochondriacs' can serve, who exist among the three-brained beings of the planet Earth which has taken your fancy.

"To these terrestrial hypochondriacs it very often seems that Time passes infinitely slowly and long, and, as they express themselves, 'it-drags-phenomenally-tediously.'

"And so, exactly in the same way, it might also sometimes seem to some of the infinitesimal beings existing in that drop of water—assuming, of course, that there happen to be such hypochondriacs among them—that Time drags very

nally, like everything existing in which Objective Reason has not been conceived, they are, as such, destroyed forever.

- -

"For the whole process of the existence of these infinitesimal beings of this smallest World also, Time of definite proportionate duration is also required, and this duration just as in other Worlds also flows from all the surrounding phenomena which are manifested in the given 'cosmic scale.'

"For them also, Time of definite length is required for the processes of their arising and formation as well as for various events in the process of their existence down to their complete final destruction.

"In the whole course of the process of existence of the beings of this drop of water also, corresponding sequential definite, as they are called, 'stages' of the flow of Time are also required.

"A definite time is required for their joys and their sorrows and, in short, for every other kind of indispensable being-experiencings, down to what are called 'runs-of-bad-luck,' and even to the 'periods of thirst for self perfection.'

"I repeat, among them, too, the process of the flow of Time has its harmonious succession also, and this succession flows from the totality of all the phenomena surrounding them.

"By all the aforementioned cosmic individuums and by the already definitely formed, as they are called, 'instinctivized' units, the duration of the process of the flow of Time is generally perceived and sensed in the same way, but with only this difference, namely, that which in final sum depends on the difference in the 'presence' and states at the given moment of these said cosmic arisings.

"It must be noticed, however, my boy, that though for separate individuums existing in any independent cosmic unit, their definition of the flow of time is not objective in the general sense, yet nevertheless for them themselves it acquires a 'sense of objectivity' because it is perceived by them according to the completeness of their own 'presence.'

- -

"The same drop of water which we have taken as an example can serve for a clearer understanding of this thought of mine.

"Although, in the sense of general Universal Objectivity, the Whole period of the process of the flow of Time in that same drop of water, is for the whole of it subjective, yet for the beings existing in it—that is, in the drop of water itself—the said given flow of time is already perceived by them as objective.

"For the clarification of this, the beings called 'Hypochondriacs' can serve who exist among those three-brained beings of the planet Earth who please you.

"To these terrestrial 'hypochondriacs' it seems very often that time flows infinitely slowly and long, and, as they express themselves, 'it drags marvelously tediously.'

"So exactly in the same way, it might also sometimes seem to some of the infinitesimal beings existing in that drop of water—assuming of course, that there happens to be such hypochondriacs among them—that Time drags very slowly and

slowly and 'phenomenally-tediously.'

"But actually from the point of view of the sensation of the duration of Time by your favorites of the planet Earth, the whole length of the existence of the 'beings-Microcosmoses' lasts only a few of their 'minutes' and sometimes even only a few of their 'seconds.'

"Now, in order that you may still better understand Time and its peculiarities, we may as well compare your age with the corresponding age of a being existing on that planet Earth.

"And for this comparing of ours we too must take the same standard unit of Time, which, as I have already told you, Objective Science employs for such calculations.

"Bear in mind, first of all, that according to the data about which you will also learn when I shall later have specially explained to you the fundamental laws of World-creation and World-maintenance, it is also established

------------------------------ 127 ------------------------------

by the same Objective Science that in general all normal three-brained beings, and amongst them certainly even the beings arising on our planet Karatas, sense the sacred 'Egokoolnatsnarnian' action for the definition of Time forty-nine times more slowly than the same sacred action is sensed by the sacred Individuals dwelling on the Most Holy Sun Absolute.

"Consequently the process of the flow of Time for the three-brained beings of our Karatas flows forty-nine times more quickly than on the Sun Absolute, and thus it should flow also for the beings breeding on the planet Earth.

"And it is also calculated that during the period of Time in which the sun 'Samos' actualizes its nearest approach to the sun 'Selos,' which period of the flow of Time is considered a 'year' for the planet Karatas, the planet Earth actualizes in relation to its Sun 'Ors' three hundred and eighty-nine of its 'Krentonalnian-revolutions.'

"From which it follows that our 'year,' according to the conventionally objective time-calculation, is three hundred and eighty-nine times longer than that period of Time which your favorites consider and call their 'year.'

"It may not be without interest for you to know that all these calculations were partly explained to me by the Great Arch-Engineer of the Universe, His Measurability, Archangel Algamatant.

"MAY HE BE PERFECTED UNTO THE HOLY ANKLAD...

"He explained this to me when, on the occasion of the first great misfortune to this planet Earth, he came to the planet Mars as one of the sacred members of the third Most Great Commission; and the captain of the transspace ship *Omnipresent*, with whom I had several friendly talks during that journey, also partly explained it to me during my journey home.

"Now it must be further noticed that you, as a three-brained being who arose on the planet Karatas, are at

------------------------------ *128* ------------------------------

the present time still only a boy of twelve years, and in respect of Being and of Reason, you are exactly like a boy of twelve on the planet Earth who has not yet

'marvelously tediously.'

"But actually from the point of view of the sensation of the duration of Time by your favorites of the planet Earth, the whole length of the existence of the beings, the Microcosmoses, is only a few of their 'minutes' and sometimes even only a few of their 'seconds.'

"Now in order that you may still better understand Time and its peculiarities, we may as well compare your age with the corresponding age of a being existing on that planet Earth.

"For this comparing of ours also, we must take the same standard unit of Time, which as I have already told you, Objective Science employs for such calculations.

"Bear in mind first of all that according to what also you will learn when I shall specially explain to you later the fundamental laws of World-creation and World-existence, it is also established

by the same Objective Science that in general all normal three-brained beings, and amongst them certainly even the beings arising on our planet 'Karatas,' sense the sacred 'Egokoolnatsnarnian' action for the definition of Time forty-nine times more slowly than the same sacred action is sensed by the sacred Individuums dwelling on the Most Holy Sun Absolute.

"Consequently the process of the flow of Time for the three-brained beings of our 'Karatas' flows forty-nine times more quickly than on the Sun Absolute, and in this manner it should flow for the beings breeding on the planet Earth also.

"But, nevertheless, it is also further calculated that in the period of Time during which the Sun 'Samos' actualizes its most near approach to the Sun 'Selos'—which period of the flow of Time is considered a 'year' for the planet 'Karatas'—then during this period of the flow of Time the planet Earth actualizes in relation to its Sun 'Ors' three hundred and eighty-nine of its 'Krentonalnian' revolutions.

"As a deduction from this then, our 'year,' according to the conventionally objective Time-calculation, is three hundred and eighty-nine times longer than the period of time which your favorites consider and call their 'year.'

"It may not be without interest for you to know, that all these calculations were explained to me partly by the Great Arch-Engineer of the Universe, His Measurability Archangel Algamatant.

"May he be perfected unto the Sacred Anklad! . . .

"He explained this to me just when he had come to the planet Mars as one of the sacred members of the third Most Great Commission, on account of the first great misfortune to the planet Earth; and the captain of the trans-space ship 'Omnipresent,' with whom I had several friendly talks during that journey also explained it in part to me during my journey home.

"Now concerning this it must be noticed that you, as a three-brained being who arose on the planet 'Karatas,' are at

the present time still only a boy of twelve years, and in the sense of Being and Reason, you are exactly the same boy of twelve, not yet formed and not yet cog-

been formed and who is not yet cognizant of himself—through which being-age all the three-brained beings arising there also live during the process of their growing up to the Being of a responsible being.

"All the 'features' of the whole of your psyche—what are called your 'character,' 'temperament,' 'inclinations,' and, in short, all the particularities of your psyche which are manifested exteriorly—are exactly the same as those of a still immature and pliant three-brained being there of the age of twelve years.

"And so, it follows from all that has been said that although according to our time-calculations you are still only like a boy of twelve there on the planet Earth who is not yet formed and not yet cognizant of himself, yet according to their subjective understanding and their being-sensations of the flow of Time, you have already existed by their time-calculation, not twelve years but the whole of four thousand six hundred and sixty-eight years.

"Thanks to all I have said, you will have material for the clarification of certain of those factors which were later the cause that the average proper normal duration of their existence began gradually to diminish and that it has now already become in the objective sense almost 'nothing.'

"Strictly speaking, this gradual diminution of the average length of the existence of the three-brained beings of that ill-fated planet, which has finally brought the whole of the duration of their existence to 'nothing,' did not have one cause but many and very varied causes.

"And among these many and varied causes the first and the chief one is of course that Nature had to adapt Herself correspondingly gradually to change their presences to those they now have.

- *129* -

"And concerning all the rest of the causes, Justice demands that I should first of all emphasize that on that ill-fated planet these causes might never have arisen had that first cause not occurred there, from which, at least in my opinion, they all chiefly ensued, though of course very gradually.

"Concerning all this you will understand in the course of further talks of mine about these three-brained beings, and meanwhile I will tell you only of the first and chief cause, namely, why and how Great Nature Herself was compelled to take stock of their presences and to form them into such new presences.

"You must first be told that there exist in the Universe generally two 'kinds' or two 'principles' of the duration of being-existence.

"The first kind or first 'principle' of being-existence, which is called 'Fulasnit-amnian,' is proper to the existence of all three-brained beings arising on any planet of our Great Universe, and the fundamental aim and sense of the existence of these beings is that there must proceed through them the transmutation of cosmic substances necessary for what is called the 'common-cosmic Trogoautoego-cratic-process.'

"And it is according to the second principle of being-existence that all one-brained and two-brained beings in general exist wherever they may arise. . .

"And the sense and aim of the existence of these beings, also, consist in this,

nizant of himself, which being-age all the three-brained beings arising on the planet Earth also experience during the process of their growing to the being of a responsible being.

"All the 'features' of the whole of your psyche—what are called your 'character,' 'temperament,' 'inclinations' and, in short, all the particularities of your psyche which are manifested exteriorly are exactly the same as those of a still immature and pliant three-brained being there of the age of twelve years.

"And thus on the basis of all that has been said, it happens that, although according to our Time-calculation you are still only the same boy of twelve who is also there on the planet Earth and who is not yet formed and not yet cognizant of himself, yet according to their subjective understanding and their being-sensations of the flow of Time, you have already existed, according to their Time-calculation, not twelve years but all of four thousand six hundred and sixty-eight years.

"In all the aforesaid you will have in this connection material for the clarification of certain of those factors which later became the causes that the average normal duration of their existence began gradually to be shortened and has now already become in the objective sense almost 'nothing.'

"Strictly speaking, for this gradual contraction of the average length of the existence of the three-brained beings of that ill-starred planet, not one cause but many and very varied causes have finally brought the whole of the duration of their existence to 'nothing.'

"And among these many and varied causes the first and the chief one is of course that Nature herself had to adapt herself correspondingly to change gradually their 'presence' to that which they now have.

- -

"And concerning all the other various causes, Justice demands that I should first of all emphasize that on that ill-starred planet these many other causes might never have arisen had that first cause not occurred there from which, at least in my opinion, all the rest of the causes chiefly arose, though of course very gradually.

"Concerning all this you will understand in the course of further talks of mine about these three-brained beings, and meanwhile I will tell you only of the first and chief cause, namely, why and how great Nature herself was compelled to take stock of their 'presence' and to form it into such a new 'presence.'

"You must first be told that there exist in the Universe generally two kinds or two 'principles' of the duration of being-existence.

"The first kind or first 'principle' of 'being-existence' which is called 'Fulasnitamnian' is proper to the existence of all three-brained beings arising on any planet of our great Universe, and the fundamental aim and sense of the existence of these beings is that there must proceed through them the transmutation of cosmic substances necessary for what is called the 'common-cosmic-Trogoautoegocratic-process.'

"And it is according to the second principle of being-existence that all one-brained and two-brained beings in general exist wherever they may arise . . .

"And the sense and aim of the existence of these beings also, consists in this, that there are transmuted through them the cosmic substances required not for purposes of a common-cosmic character, but only for that solar system or even only for that planet alone, in which and upon which these one-brained and two-brained beings arise.

"In any case, for the further elucidation of the strangeness of the psyche of those three-brained beings who have taken your fancy, you must know this also, that

------------------------------ 130 ------------------------------

in the beginning, after the organ Kundabuffer with all its properties had been removed from their presences, the duration of their existence was according to the 'Fulasnitamnian' principle, that is to say, they were obliged to exist until there was coated in them and completely perfected by reason what is called the 'body-Kesdjan,' or, as they themselves later began to name this being-part of theirs—of which, by the way, contemporary beings know only by hearsay—the 'Astral-body.'

"And so, my boy, when later, for reasons of which you will learn in the course of my further tales, they began to exist already excessively abnormally, that is to say, quite unbecomingly for three-brained beings, and when in consequence of this they had on the one hand ceased to emanate the vibrations required by Nature for the maintenance of the separated fragments of their planet, and, on the other hand, had begun, owing to the chief peculiarity of their strange psyche, to destroy beings of other forms of their planet, thereby gradually diminishing the number of sources required for this purpose, then Nature Herself was compelled gradually to actualize the presences of these three-brained beings according to the second principle, namely, the principle 'Itoklanoz,' that is, to actualize them in the same way in which She actualizes one-brained and two-brained beings in order that the equilibrium of the vibrations required according to quality and quantity should be attained.

"As regards the meaning of the principle 'Itoklanoz,' I shall also specially explain it to you sometime.

"And meanwhile remember, that although the fundamental motives for the diminution of the duration of the existence of the three-brained beings of this planet were from causes not depending on them, yet nevertheless, subsequently, the main grounds for all the sad results were—and particularly now continue to be—the abnormal

------------------------------ 131 ------------------------------

conditions of external ordinary being-existence established by them themselves. Owing to these conditions the duration of their existence has, down to the present time, continued to become shorter and shorter, and now is already diminished to such a degree that, at the present time, the difference between the duration of the process of the existence of the three-brained beings of other planets in the whole of the Universe and the duration of the process of the existence of the three-brained beings of the planet Earth has become the same as the difference between the real duration of their existence and the duration of the existence of the infinitesimal beings in that drop of water we took as an example.

"You now understand, my boy, that even the Most Great Heropass of Time has

that there are transmuted through them the cosmic substances required not for purposes of a common cosmic character, but only for that solar system, or even only for that planet alone, in which and upon which these one-brained and two-brained beings arise.

"In any case for the further elucidation of the strangeness of the psyche of those three-brained beings who please you, you must know this also, that in the beginning,

- -

after the organ 'Kundabuffer' with all its properties had been removed from their 'presence,' the duration of their existence was according to the 'Fulasnitamnian' principle, that is to say, they also were obliged to exist until there was coated in them and completely perfected by Reason what is called the body 'Kesdjan,' or, as they themselves later began to name this being-part of theirs—of which, by the way, contemporary beings know only by hearsay—the 'Astral body.'

"And so, my boy, when afterwards for reasons of which you will learn in the course of my further tales, they began to exist already too abnormally—that is to say, entirely unbecomingly to three-brained beings—and having on the one hand in consequence of this ceased to emanate the vibrations needed by Nature for the maintenance of the separated fragments of their planet, and on the other hand, having begun on account of the chief peculiarity of their strange psyche to destroy beings of other forms of their planet, thereby diminishing gradually the number of sources necessary for the same purpose, it was just then that Nature herself was compelled gradually to actualize the 'presence' of these three-brained beings according to the second principle, namely, the principle 'Itoklanoz,' that is, in the same way in which Nature actualizes one-brained and two-brained beings in order that the equilibrium, in quality and quantity of necessary vibrations, should be attained.

"And concerning the significance of the principle 'Itoklanoz' I shall also specially explain it to you sometime.

"And meanwhile remember that although the fundamental motives for the diminution of the duration of the existence of the three-brained beings of this planet were from causes not depending on them, yet nevertheless, subsequently the main grounds for all the sad results were and particularly now continue to be the abnormal

- -

conditions of external ordinary being-existence established by them themselves, owing to which, down to the present time, the duration of their existence continues to become shorter and shorter, and is already contracted to such a degree that, at the present time, the difference between the duration of the process of the existence of the three-brained beings of other planets in the whole of the Universe and the duration of the process of the existence of the three-brained beings of the planet Earth has become similar to the difference between the real duration of their existence and the duration of the existence of the infinitesimal beings in that drop of water we took as an example.

"You understand now, my boy, that even the Most Great Heropass or Time has also been compelled to actualize obvious absurdities in the presences of these unfortunate three-brained beings who arise and exist on this ill-fated planet Earth.

"And thanks to all I have just explained to you, you can put yourself in the position of and understand the although merciless, yet always, and in everything, just Heropass."

Having said these last words Beelzebub became silent; and when he again spoke to his grandson, he said with a heavy sigh:

"Ekh . . . my dear boy!

"Later when I shall have told you more about the three-brained beings of that ill-fated planet Earth, you yourself will understand and form your own opinion about everything.

"You yourself will very well understand that although the fundamental causes of the whole chaos that now reigns on that ill-fated planet Earth were certain 'unforeseeingnesses,' coming from Above on the part of various Sacred Individuals, yet nevertheless the chief causes for the developing of further ills are only those abnormal conditions

- *132* -

of ordinary being-existence which they themselves gradually established and which they continue to establish down to the present time.

"In any case, my dear boy, when you learn more about these favorites of yours, not only, I repeat, will you clearly see how pitiably small the duration of the existence of these unfortunates has gradually become in comparison with that normal duration of existence which has already long ago been established as a law for every kind of three-centered being of the whole of our Universe, but you will also understand that in these unfortunates, for the same reasons, there has gradually begun to disappear and at the present time are quite absent in them, any normal being-sensations whatever concerning any cosmic phenomenon.

"Although the beings of that ill-fated planet arose, according to conventionally objective time-reckoning, many decades ago, not only have they not as yet any being-sensation of cosmic phenomena such as it is proper to all three-centered beings of the whole of our Universe to have, but there is not in the Reason of these unfortunates even an approximate representation of the genuine causes of these phenomena.

"They have not an approximately correct representation even of those cosmic phenomena that proceed on their own planet round about them."

- *133* -

also been compelled to actualize such plain absurdities in the 'presence' of these unfortunate three-brained beings arising and existing on this ill-starred planet Earth.

"And owing to all I have just explained to you, you can put yourself in the position and understand the although merciless yet always and in everything, just Heropass."

Having said these last words Beelzebub became silent; and when he again spoke to his grandson he said with a heavy sigh:

"Eh . . . my dear boy!

"Afterwards when I shall have told you more about the three-brained beings of that ill-starred planet Earth you will yourself understand and have your own opinion about everything.

"You yourself will very well understand that although the fundamental causes of the whole chaos that now reigns on that ill-starred planet Earth were certain 'oversights' coming from Above on the part of various sacred Individuums, yet nevertheless that the chief causes for the developing of further ills are only those abnormal conditions

- -

of ordinary being-existence which they themselves gradually established and which they continue to establish down to the present time.

"In any case, my dear boy, when you learn more about these favorites of yours, not only, I repeat, will you clearly see that the duration of the existence of these unfortunates has gradually become so pitiably small in comparison with that normal duration of existence which has already long ago been established as a Law for the three-centered beings of every kind of the whole of our Universe; but you will also understand that in these unfortunates for the same reasons, there began gradually to disappear and at the present time are quite absent in them, any normal being-sensations whatever concerning any cosmic phenomenon.

"Although the beings of that ill-starred planet had their rising according to conventionally objective Time-reckoning already many tens of years ago, not only have they not as yet any being-sensation of cosmic phenomena such as is proper to all three-centered beings of the whole of our Universe, but in the reasonings of these unfortunates there is not even an approximate notion of the genuine causes of these phenomena.

"They have not an approximately correct conception even of those cosmic phenomena that occur on their own planet round about them."

- -

The Arch-absurd

According to the Assertion of Beelzebub, Our Sun Neither Lights nor Heats

IN ORDER, my dear Hassein, that you should meanwhile have an approximate representation also of just how far that function called 'the instinctive sensing of reality,' which is proper to every three-brained being of the whole of our Great Universe, is already entirely lacking in the presences of the three-centered beings breeding on the planet Earth, and especially in those of the most recent periods, it will be enough, to begin with, I think, if I explain to you only about how they understand and explain to themselves the causes why there periodically proceed on their planet those cosmic phenomena which they call 'daylight,' 'darkness,' 'heat,' 'cold,' and so on.

"All, without exception, of the three-brained beings of that planet who have attained the age of a responsible being, and even those many and various 'wiseacrings' existing there which they call 'sciences,' are categorically certain that all the said phenomena arrive on their planet completely, so to say, ready-made, 'd-i-r-e-c-t-l-y' from their own Sun . . . and as Mullah Nassr Eddin would say in such cases, 'no more hokey-pokey about it.'

"What is most peculiar, in this case, is that, except for certain beings who existed before the second Transapalnian perturbation there, absolutely no doubt whatever concerning this certainty of theirs, has ever, as yet, crept into a single one of them.

"Not only has not a single one of them—having a Reason which, though strange, has nevertheless some resemblance

- *134* -

to sane logic—ever yet doubted the causes of the said phenomena, but not a single one of them has manifested concerning these cosmic phenomena even that strange special property of their common psyche, which also became proper to the three-brained beings of that planet alone, and which is called 'to fantasy.'"

Having said these last words, Beelzebub, after a little while, with a bitter smile, continued to talk as follows:

"You, for instance, have the normal presence of a three-brained being, and within your presence there is intentionally 'implanted' from without, 'Oskiano,' or as they say there on the Earth, 'education,' which is founded on a morality based solely on the commandments and indications of the UNI-BEING HIMSELF and the Most Holy Individuals near to Him. And yet, if you should chance to be there among them, you would be unable to prevent the process in yourself of the 'being-Nerhitrogool,' that is, the process which, again there on the Earth, is called 'irrepressible inner laughter'; that is to say, you would not be able to restrain yourself from such laughter, if in some way or another, they were suddenly clearly to sense and understand, without any doubt whatever, that not only does nothing

The Arch-Absurd: In The Opinion Of Beelzebub, Our Sun, It Appears, Neither Lights Nor Heats

IN ORDER, my dear Hassein, that you may meanwhile have a fair representation also of just how far that function called 'instinctive-feeling-of-reality,' which is proper to every three-brained being of the whole of our Great Universe, is already completely lacking in the 'presence' of the three-centered beings breeding on the planet 'Earth' and especially in those of the most recent periods, it will be enough to begin with, I think, if I explain to you only about this—how they understand and explain to themselves the causes why there periodically proceed on their planet those cosmic phenomena which they call 'daylight,' 'darkness,' 'heat,' 'cold,' and so on.

"All, without exception, of the three-brained beings of that planet who have attained the age of a responsible being, and even those many and various 'wiseacrings' existing there which they call 'sciences,' are categorically certain that all the said phenomena arrive on their planet, so to say, absolutely-ready-made, directly from their own Sun . . . and . . . no more hokey-pokey about it!

"What is most peculiar, in this case, is that absolutely no doubt whatever concerning this persuasion of theirs has ever as yet crept into a single one of them.

"Not only has no single one of them, having a Reason which, though strange has nevertheless some resemblance

- -

to sane logic, ever yet doubted the causes of the said phenomena, but not a single one of them has manifested, concerning these cosmic phenomena, even that strange special property of their common psyche which also has become proper to the three-brained beings of that planet alone, and which is called 'to fantasy.'"

Having said these last words, Beelzebub, after a little while, with a bitter smile, continued to talk as follows:

"You, for instance, have the normal 'presence' of a three-brained being; and within your 'presence' an intentionally externally 'grown' Oskiano, or, as they say there on the 'Earth,' 'education,' which is founded on a morality based solely on the commandments and indications of the UNI-BEING HIMSELF and the Most Holy Individuums nearest Him. And yet, if you should chance to be there among them, you would be unable to prevent the process in yourself of the 'being-Nerhitrogool,' that is, the process, which, again there on the 'Earth' is called 'choking-with-mirth'; in other words, you could not restrain yourself from such laughter, if only it were to come about that they should suddenly clearly sense, in some way or another, and understand without any doubt whatever, that to their planet from

like 'light,' 'darkness,' 'heat,' and so on, come to their planet from their Sun itself, but that their supposed 'source of heat and light' is itself almost always freezing cold like the 'hairless-dog' of our highly esteemed Mullah Nassr Eddin.

"In reality, the surface of their 'Source-of-Heat,' like that of all the ordinary suns of our Great Universe, is perhaps more covered with ice than the surface of what they call their 'North Pole.'

"Surely this 'hearth-of-heat' itself would rather borrow heat, if only a little, from some other source of 'cosmic-substance,' than send a part of its own heat to any other planet, especially to that planet which, though it belongs

------------------------------ *135* ------------------------------

to its system, yet in consequence of the splitting off from it of a whole side, became a 'lopsided monstrosity' and is now already a source of 'offensive-shame' for that poor system 'Ors.'

"But do you yourself know, my boy, in general how and why in the atmosphere of certain planets during Trogoautoegocratic processes, there proceed those 'kshtatsavacht,' 'kldatzacht,' 'tainolair,' 'paischakir,' and other such phenomena, which your favorites call 'daylight,' 'darkness,' 'cold,' 'heat,' and so on?" Beelzebub asked Hassein.

"If you don't clearly understand, I shall explain this also to you a little.

"Although I have promised to explain to you, only later, all the fundamental laws of World-creation and World-maintenance in detail, yet the necessity has here arisen, to touch upon, if only briefly, the questions concerning these cosmic laws, without waiting for that special talk I promised.

"And this is necessary, in order that you may be able better to take in all that we are now talking about, and also in order that what I have already told you may be transubstantiated in you in the right way.

"It is necessary to say, first of all, that everything in the Universe, both the intentionally created and the later automatically arisen, exists and is maintained exclusively on the basis of what is called the 'common-cosmic Trogoautoegocratic-process.'

"This Most Great common-cosmic Trogoautoegocratic-process was actualized by our ENDLESS UNI-BEING, when our Most Great and Most Holy Sun Absolute had already existed, on which our ALL-GRACIOUS ENDLESS CREATOR had and still has the chief place of His existence.

"This system, which maintains everything arisen and existing, was actualized by our ENDLESS CREATOR in order that what is called the 'exchange of substances' or the

------------------------------ *136* ------------------------------

'Reciprocal-feeding' of everything that exists, might proceed in the Universe and thereby that the merciless 'Heropass' might not have its maleficent effect on the Sun Absolute.

"This same Most Great common-cosmic Trogoautoegocratic-process is actualized always and in everything on the basis of the two fundamental cosmic laws, the first of which is called the 'Fundamental-First-degree-Sacred-Heptaparapar-

their Sun itself, not only does nothing of any such thing as 'light,' 'darkness,' 'heat,' and so on, come, but that their supposed source of heat and light is itself almost always freezing with cold like the hairless dog of our highly esteemed Mullah Nassr Eddin.

"In reality, this surface of their 'Source of Heat,' like that of all the ordinary suns of our great Universe in general, is perhaps more covered with ice than the surface of what they call their North Pole.

"Surely this 'hearth of heat' itself would like to borrow, if only a little heat, from some other source of cosmic substances, rather than send a part of its own heat to any planet whatever, and especially to that planet which, although it belongs

to its system, yet in consequence of the splitting off from it of a whole side became a 'lopsided-monstrosity' and is now already the occasion of 'offensive shame' for that system 'Ors.'

"But you yourself, my boy, do you know in general how and why in the atmosphere of certain planets during Trogoautoegocratic processes, there proceed those 'Kshtatsavacht,' 'Kldatzacht,' 'Tainolair,' 'Paischakir,' and other such phenomena, which, your favorites call 'daylight,' 'darkness,' 'cold,' 'heat' and so on?" Beelzebub asked Hassein.

"If you don't clearly understand, I shall explain this also to you a little.

"Although I have promised to explain to you later in every detail all the fundamental laws of World-creation and World-maintenance, yet the necessity has here arisen, to touch upon, if only briefly, the questions concerning these cosmic laws, without waiting for that special talk I promised.

"And this is necessary in order that you may be able better to take in all that we are now talking about, and also in order that what I have already told you may be transubstantiated in you in the right way.

"It is necessary to say, first of all, that everything in the Universe, both the intentionally created and the later automatically arisen, exists and is maintained exclusively on the basis of what is called the common-cosmic-Trogoautoegocratic-process.

"This Most Great common-cosmic-Trogoautoegocratic-process was actualized by our ENDLESS UNI-BEING when there already existed Our Most Great and Most Holy Sun Absolute, on which our ALL-GRACIOUS ENDLESS CREATOR had and still has the fundamental place of His existence.

"This system, which maintains everything arisen and existing, was actualized by our ENDLESS CREATOR in order that there might proceed in the Universe what is called the 'exchange of substances' or the

'Reciprocal-feeding' of everything that exists, and thereby that the merciless 'Heropass' might not exert its maleficent influence upon the Sun Absolute.

"This same Most Great 'common-cosmic-Trogoautoegocratic-process' is actualized always and in everything on the basis of the two fundamental cosmic laws, the first of which is called the fundamental first-order sacred Heptaparaparshinokh,' and the second the 'Fundamental-First-degree-Sacred-Triamazikamno.'

"Owing to these two fundamental sacred cosmic laws, there first arise from the substance called 'Etherokrilno,' under certain conditions, what are called 'crystallizations'; and from these crystallizations, but later, and also under certain conditions, there are formed various large and small, more or less independent, cosmic definite formations.

"It is just within and upon these cosmic definite formations that the processes of what are called the involution and evolution of the already formed concentrations and also of the said crystallizations take place—of course also according to the two said fundamental sacred laws—and all the results obtained from those processes in atmospheres, and further, by means of these atmospheres themselves, blend and go for the actualizing of the said 'exchange-of-matters' for the purposes of the Most Great common-cosmic Trogoautoegocrat.

"Etherokrilno is that prime-source substance with which the whole Universe is filled, and which is the basis for the arising and maintenance of everything existing.

"Not only is this Etherokrilno the basis for the arising of all cosmic concentrations without exception, both large and small, but also all cosmic phenomena in general proceed during some transformation in this same fundamental cosmic substance as well as during the processes

———————————————————————— 137 ————————————————————————

of the involution and evolution of various crystallizations—or, as your favorites say, of those active elements—which have obtained and still continue to obtain their prime arising from this same fundamental prime-source cosmic substance.

"Bear in mind, here, that it is just because of this that the mentioned Objective Science says that 'everything without exception in the Universe is material.'

"You must also know further, that only one cosmic crystallization, existing under the name 'Omnipresent-Okidanokh,' obtains its prime arising—although it also is crystallized from Etherokrilno—from the three Holy sources of the sacred Theomertmalogos, that is, from the emanation of the Most Holy Sun Absolute.

"Everywhere in the Universe, this 'Omnipresent-Okidanokh' or 'Omnipresent-Active-Element' takes part in the formation of all both great and small arisings, and is, in general, the fundamental cause of most of the cosmic phenomena and, in particular, of the phenomena proceeding in the atmospheres.

"In order that you may be able to understand, at least approximately, concerning this Omnipresent-Okidanokh also, I must tell you, first of all, that the second fundamental cosmic law—the Sacred Triamazikamno—consists of three independent forces, that is to say, this sacred law manifests in everything, without exception, and everywhere in the Universe, in three separate independent aspects.

"And these three aspects exist in the Universe under the following denominations:

"The first, under the denomination, the 'Holy-Affirming';

"The second, the 'Holy-Denying'; and

"The third, the 'Holy-Reconciling.'

"And this is also why, concerning this sacred law and its three independent

shinokh, and the second the fundamental first-order sacred Triamazikamno.

"Owing to these two fundamental sacred cosmic laws, there first arise from the substance called 'Etherokrilno,' under certain conditions, what are called crystallizations; and from these crystallizations, but later, and also under certain conditions, there are formed various large and small more or less independent cosmic definite formations.

"It is just within and upon these cosmic 'definite formations' that the processes of what are called the involution and evolution of both the already formed concentrations and of the said crystallizations take place—of course also according to the two said fundamental sacred laws; and all the results obtained from these processes both in atmospheres and also, further, by means of these atmospheres themselves, blend and go for the actualizing of the said 'exchange of matters' for the purposes of the Most Great common-cosmic Trogoautoegocrat.

"Etherokrilno is that prime-source substance with which the whole Universe is filled and which is the basis for the arising and maintenance of everything that exists.

"Not only is this Etherokrilno the foundation of the arising of, without exception, all cosmic concentrations, both large and small; but also all cosmic phenomena in general proceed, during any transformation both within the same fundamental cosmic substance and from the process

----

of the involution and evolution of various crystallizations—or, as your favorites say, from those active elements—which have obtained and still continue to obtain their prime arising from this same fundamental prime-source cosmic substance.

"Bear in mind here, that it is just because of this that the mentioned Objective Science says that 'Everything in the Universe without exception is material.'

"You must also know, further, that only one cosmic crystallization, existing under the name 'Omnipresent Okidanokh,' although it also is crystallized from Etherokrilno, owes its prime arising to the three Holy sources of the sacred Theomertmalogos, that is, to the emanation of the Most Holy Sun Absolute.

"Everywhere in the Universe this 'Omnipresent Okidanokh' or omnipresent active element, takes part in the formation of all both great and small arisings, and is in general the fundamental cause of most of the cosmic phenomena and, in particular, of the phenomena proceeding in the atmospheres.

"In order that you may be able to understand, at least approximately, concerning this 'Omnipresent Okidanokh' also, I must tell you first of all that the second fundamental cosmic law—the sacred Triamazikamno—consists of three independent forces, that is to say, this sacred law manifests in everything without exception and everywhere in the Universe, in three separate independent aspects.

"And these its three aspects exist in the Universe under the following denominations:
The first, under the denomination, the Holy Affirming.
The second, the Holy Denying.
The third, the Holy Reconciling.
"And this is also why, concerning this sacred law and its three independent

forces, the said Objective Science
- *138* -
has, among its formulations, specially concerning this sacred law, the following: 'A law which always flows into a consequence and becomes the cause of sub-sequent consequences, and always functions by three independent and quite op-posite characteristic manifestations, latent within it, in properties neither seen nor sensed.'

"Our sacred Theomertmalogos also, that is, the prime emanation of our Most Holy Sun Absolute, acquires just this same lawfulness at its prime arising; and, during its further actualizations, gives results in accordance with it.

"And so, my boy, the Omnipresent-Okidanokh obtains its prime arising in space outside of the Most Holy Sun Absolute itself, from the blending of these three independent forces into one, and during its further involutions it is corres-pondingly changed, in respect of what is called the 'Vivifyingness of Vibrations' according to its passage through what are called the 'Stopinders' or 'gravity cen-ters' of the fundamental 'common-cosmic sacred Heptaparaparshinokh.'

"I repeat, among the number of other already definite cosmic crystallizations, the Omnipresent-Okidanokh unfailingly always participates in both large and small cosmic formations, wherever and under whatever external surrounding conditions they may arise in the Universe.

"This 'common-cosmic Unique-Crystallization' or 'Active-Element' has several peculiarities proper to this element alone, and it is chiefly owing to these peculi-arities proper to it that the majority of cosmic phenomena proceed, including, among other things, the said phenomena that take place in the atmosphere of cer-tain planets.

"Of these peculiarities proper to the Omnipresent-Active-Element alone, there are several, but it is enough, for the theme of our talk, if we become acquainted just with two of them.
- *139* -
"The first peculiarity is that when a new cosmic unit is being concentrated, then the 'Omnipresent-Active-Element' does not blend, as a whole, with such a new arising, nor is it transformed as a whole in any definite corresponding place—as happens with every other cosmic crystallization in all the said cosmic formations—but immediately on entering as a whole into any cosmic unit, there immediately occurs in it what is called 'Djartklom,' that is to say, it is dispersed into the three fundamental sources from which it obtained its prime arising, and only then do these sources, each separately, give the beginning for an independ-ent concentration of three separate corresponding formations within the given cosmic unit. And in this way, this 'Omnipresent-Active-Element' actualizes at the outset, in every such new arising, the sources for the possible manifestation of its own sacred law of Triamazikamno.

"It must without fail be noticed also, that in every cosmic formation, the said separated sources, both for the perception and for the further utilization of this property of the 'Omnipresent-Active-Element' for the purpose of the corres-

forces, the said Objective Science

---

has the following among its other formulations specially concerning this sacred law: 'A law which always flows into a consequence and thereby becomes the cause of further consequences, and always functions by three independent and absolutely opposite characteristic manifestations concealed within it in invisible and non-sensible properties.'

"Our sacred Theomertmalogos also, that is, the prime emanation of our Most Holy Sun Absolute, acquires just this same legitimacy at its prime arising; and during its farther actualizations gives results in accordance with it.

"And so, my boy, the 'Omnipresent Okidanokh' receives its prime arising already in space, outside of the Most Holy Sun Absolute itself, from the blending into one, of these three independent forces, and during its further involutions, it is correspondingly changed in respect of what is called the 'Vivifyingness of Vibrations' just according to its passage through what are called the 'Stopinders' or 'gravitational centers' of the fundamental 'common-cosmic sacred Heptaparaparshinokh.'

"I repeat, among the number of other already definite cosmic crystallizations, the 'Omnipresent Okidanokh' unfailingly always participates in both large and small cosmic formations, wherever and under whatever external surrounding conditions they may arise in the Universe.

"This 'common cosmic unique crystallization' or 'active element' has several peculiarities proper to this element alone, and it is chiefly owing to these, its proper peculiarities, that the majority of cosmic phenomena proceed, including, among other things, the said phenomena that take place in the atmospheres of certain planets.

"Of these proper peculiarities of the 'Omnipresent Active Element' there are several, but it is enough for the theme of our talk if we become acquainted with just two of them.

"The first peculiarity is this, that when a new cosmic unit is being concentrated, then the 'Omnipresent Active Element' does not blend in such a new arising, as a whole, nor is it transformed as a whole in one definite corresponding place—as happens with every other cosmic crystallization in all the said cosmic forms—but immediately on entering any cosmic unit as a whole, there at once occurs in it what is called 'Djartklom,' that is, it scatters into the three fundamental sources from which it received its prime arising, and only then do these its sources, each separately, give the beginning for an independent concentration of three separate corresponding formations within the given cosmic unit. And in this way, the 'Omnipresent Active Element' actualizes, at the outset, in every such new arising, the sources for the possible manifestation of its own also sacred law of Triamazikamno.

"It must not fail to be noticed also, that in every cosmic formation the said separated sources, both for the perception and further utilization of this peculiar property of the 'Omnipresent Active Element' for the purpose of the correspondponding actualizing, exist and continue to have the possibility of functioning as long as the given cosmic unit exists.

"And only after the said cosmic unit has been completely destroyed do these holy sources of the sacred Triamazikamno, localized in the 'Omnipresent-Active-Element-Okidanokh,' reblend and they are again transformed into 'Okidanokh,' but having now another quality of Vivifyingness of Vibrations.

"As regards the second peculiarity of the 'Omnipresent-Okidanokh,' equally proper to it alone, and which it is also necessary for us to elucidate just now for the given theme of our talk, you will be able to understand about that, only if you know something concerning one fundamental

------------------------------ *140* ------------------------------

cosmic second-degree law, existing in the Universe, under the denomination of the 'Sacred Aieioiuoa.'

"And this cosmic law is, that there proceeds within every arising large and small, when in direct touch with the emanations either of the Sun Absolute itself or of any other sun, what is called 'Remorse,' that is, a process when every part that has arisen from the results of any one Holy Source of the Sacred Triamazikamno, as it were, 'revolts' and 'criticizes' the former unbecoming perceptions and the manifestations at the moment of another part of its whole—a part obtained from the results of another Holy Source of the same fundamental sacred Cosmic Law of Triamazikamno.

"And this sacred process Aieioiuoa or 'Remorse' always proceeds with the 'Omnipresent-Active-Element-Okidanokh' also.

"The peculiarity of this latter during this sacred process is that while the direct action either of the sacred Theomertmalogos or the emanation of any ordinary sun is round about the whole of its presence, this Active-Element is dispersed into its three prime parts which then exist almost independently, and when the said direct action ceases, these parts blend again and then continue to exist as a whole.

"Here you might as well, I think, be told, by the way, about an interesting fact I noticed, which occurred in the history of their existence concerning the strangeness of the psyche of the ordinary three-brained beings of that planet which has taken your fancy, in respect of what they call their 'scientific-speculations.'

"And that is, that during the period of my many-centuried observation and study of their psyche I had occasion to constate several times that though 'science' appeared among them almost from the very beginning of their arising, and, it may be said, periodically, like everything

------------------------------ *141* ------------------------------

else there, rose to a more or less high degree of perfection, and that though during these and other periods, many millions of three-brained beings called there 'scientists' must have arisen and been again destroyed, yet with the single exception of a certain Chinese man named Choon-Kil-Tez, about whom I shall tell you later in detail, not once has the thought entered the head of a single one of them there that between these two cosmic phenomena which they call 'emanation' and 'radiation' there is any difference whatever.

ing actualizing, exist and continue to be able to function as long as the given cosmic unit exists.

"And only after the said cosmic unit has been completely destroyed do these holy sources of the sacred Triamazikamno, localized in the 'Omnipresent Active Element Okidanokh,' reblend and are again transformed into 'Okidanokh,' but having now another quality of the 'Vivifyingness of Vibrations.'

"Concerning the second peculiarity of the 'Omnipresent Okidanokh,' equally proper to it alone, and which it is also necessary for us to elucidate just now for the given theme of our talk you will be able to understand about that, only if you know something concerning one fundamental

- -

cosmic second-order law existing in the Universe under the denomination of the 'Sacred Aieioiuoa.'

"And this cosmic law consists in this, that there proceeds within every arising large and small, when in immediate touch with the emanations either of the Sun Absolute itself or of any other Sun, what is called 'Remorse'; that is, such a process, when every part that has arisen from the results of any one Holy Source of the sacred Triamazikamno, revolts, as it were, and criticizes the former unbecoming perceptions and contemporary manifestations of another part of its whole—a part obtained from the results of another Holy Source of the same fundamental sacred Cosmic law Triamazikamno.

"And this sacred process 'Aieioiuoa' or 'Remorse' always proceeds within the 'Omnipresent Active Element Okidanokh' also.

"The peculiarity of this latter during this sacred process consists in this, that while the direct action either of the sacred Theomertmalogos or the emanation of any other ordinary Sun is round about the whole of its 'presence,' this 'active element' scatters into its three prime parts which then exist almost independently, and when the said immediate action ceases these parts blend again and then again exist as a whole.

"Here it will do no harm, I think, to tell you, by the way, an interesting fact concerning the strangeness of the psyche of the ordinary three-brained beings of that planet that pleases you, which occurred in the history of their existence and concerns what they call the 'scientific speculations.'

"And that is, that during the period of my many-centuried observation and study of their psyche I had occasion to ascertain several times that although science appeared among them almost from the very beginning of their arising—and, it may here be said, periodically, like everything

- -

else there, rose to a more or less high degree of perfection—yet, though during these periods and others, many millions of three-brained beings called there 'scientists' must have arisen and been again destroyed, yet—with the single exception of a certain Chinaman named Choon-Kil-Tez, about whom I shall tell you later in detail—not once has the thought entered the head of a single 'scientist' there that between these two cosmic phenomena which they call 'emanation' and 'radiation' there is any difference whatever.

"Not a single one of those 'sorry-scientists' has ever thought that the difference between these two cosmic processes is just about the same as that which the highly esteemed Mullah Nassr Eddin once expressed in the following words:

"'They are as much alike as the beard of the famous English Shakespeare and the no less famous French Armagnac.'

"For the further clarification of the phenomena taking place in the atmospheres and concerning the 'Omnipresent-Active-Element' in general, you must know and remember this also, that during the periods when, owing to the sacred process 'Aieioiuoa,' 'Djartklom' proceeds in the Okidanokh, then there is temporarily released from it the proportion of the pure—that is, absolutely unblended—Etherokrilno which unfailingly enters into all cosmic formations and there serves, as it were, for connecting all the active elements of these formations; and afterwards when its three fundamental parts reblend, then the said proportion of Etherokrilno is re-established.

"Now, it is necessary to touch also, of course again only briefly, on another question, namely, what relation the 'Omnipresent-Active-Element-Okidanokh' has to the common presence of beings of every kind, and what are the cosmic results actualized owing to it.

------------------------------ 142 ------------------------------

"It is chiefly necessary to touch upon this question because you will then have still another very striking and illuminating fact for the better understanding of the difference between the various brain-systems of beings, namely, the systems called 'one-brained,' 'two-brained,' and 'three-brained.'

"Know first that, in general, every such cosmic formation called 'brain' receives its formation from those crystallizations the affirming source for whose arising, according to the sacred Triamazikamno, is one or another of the corresponding holy forces of the fundamental sacred Triamazikamno, localized in the Omnipresent-Okidanokh. And the further actualizings of the same holy forces proceed by means of the presences of the beings, just through those localizations.

"I shall sometime in the future specially explain to you about the process itself of the arising of these corresponding being-brains in the presences of beings, but meanwhile let us talk, though not in detail, about the results the Omnipresent-Okidanokh actualizes by means of these being-brains.

"The Omnipresent-Active-Element-Okidanokh enters into the presences of beings through all the three kinds of being-food.

"And this proceeds because, as I have already told you, this same Okidanokh obligatorily participates in the formation of all kinds of products which serve as all three being-foods and is always contained in the presence of these products.

"And so, my boy, the chief peculiarity of the Omnipresent-Okidanokh, in the given case, is that the process of 'Djartklom' proceeds in it within the presence of every being also but not from being in contact with the emanations of any large cosmic concentration; but the factors for this process in the presences of beings are either the

------------------------------ 143 ------------------------------

results of the conscious processes of 'Partkdolg-duty' on the part of the beings

"Not a single one of those 'sorry scientists' has ever thought that the difference between these two cosmic processes is just about the same as that which the highly esteemed Mullah Nassr Eddin once expressed in the following words:

"'They are as much alike as the beard of the famous English Shakespeare and French Armagnac, no less famous.'

"For the further clarification of the phenomena taking place in the atmospheres, and concerning the 'Omnipresent Active Element' in general, you must know and remember this also, that during the periods when, owing to the sacred process 'Aieioiuoa,' there proceeds 'Djartklom' in the 'Okidanokh,' then there is temporarily released from it the proportion of the pure—that is, absolutely un-blended—Etherokrilno which unfailingly enters into all cosmic forms and there serves, as it were, for connecting all the active elements; and afterwards when its three fundamental parts reunite, then the said proportion of Etherokrilno is reestablished.

"It is necessary to touch also, though again only briefly, on another question, namely, what effect the Omnipresent Active Element Okidanokh has upon the common 'presence' of beings of every kind, and what are the cosmic results actualized owing to it.

"It is chiefly necessary to touch upon this question because you will then have still another very striking and illuminating fact for the better understanding of the difference between the various brain-systems of beings, namely, the systems called one-brained, two-brained, and three-brained.

"Know first that, in general, every such cosmic formation called 'brain' receives its formation from those crystallizations for whose arising according to the sacred Triamazikamno the Affirming source is one or other corresponding holy force of the fundamental sacred Triamazikamno localized in the 'Omnipresent Okidan-okh.' And the further actualizings of the same holy forces proceed in the 'presence' of the beings just through these three localizations.

"Sometime in the future I will specially explain to you about the process itself of the arising of these corresponding being-brains in the 'presence' of a being; but meanwhile let us talk, though not in detail, about this, namely, what results the 'Omnipresent Okidanokh' actualizes by means of these being-brains.

"The Omnipresent Active Element Okidanokh enters into the 'presence' of beings through all the three kinds of being-food.

"And this proceeds because, as I have already told you, this same 'Okidanokh' obligatorily participates in the formation of products of every kind which serve the purpose of all three being-feedings and is always contained in the actuality of these products.

"And so, my boy, the chief peculiarity of the 'Omnipresent Okidanokh consists, in the given case, in this, that the process of Djartklom proceeds in it, in the 'presence' itself of every being also, but not from being in touch with the emanations of large cosmic concentrations, but as factors, there are either the

----

results of the conscious processes of Partkdolgduty on the part of the beings themselves—about which processes I shall also explain to you in detail later—or of that process of Great Nature Herself which exists in the Universe under the name 'Kerkoolnonarnian-actualization,' which process means 'The-obtaining-of-the-required-totality-of-vibrations-by-adaptation.'

"This latter process proceeds in beings absolutely without the participation of their consciousness.

"In both cases when Okidanokh enters into the presence of a being and the process of Djartklom proceeds in it, then each of its fundamental parts blends with those perceptions which correspond with it according to what is called 'Kindred-vibrations' and which are present in the being at the moment, and further, these parts are concentrated upon the corresponding localization, that is, upon the corresponding brain.

"And these blendings are called 'being-Impulsakri.'

"It is necessary to notice further that these localizations or brains in beings serve not only as apparatuses for the transformation of corresponding cosmic substances for the purposes of the Most Great common-cosmic Trogoautoegocrat, but also as the means for beings whereby their conscious self-perfecting is possible.

"This latter aim depends upon the quality of the presence of the 'being-Impulsakri' concentrated, or, as is otherwise said, deposited, upon the said corresponding being-brains.

"Concerning the qualities of being-Impulsakri, there is among the direct commandments of our ALL-EMBRACING ENDLESSNESS even a special commandment, which is very strictly carried out by all three-brained beings of our Great Universe, and which is expressed in the following words: 'Always guard against such perceptions as may soil the purity of your brains.'

-------------------------------- *144* --------------------------------

"Three-brained beings have the possibility personally to perfect themselves, because in them there are localized three centers of their common presence or three brains, upon which afterwards, when the process of Djartklom proceeds in the Omnipresent-Okidanokh, the three holy forces of the sacred Triamazikamno are deposited and acquire the possibility for their further, this time, independent actualizings.

"Just in this is the point, that the beings having this three-brained system can, by the conscious and intentional fulfilling of being-Partkdolg-duty, utilize from this process of Djartklom in the Omnipresent-Okidanokh, its three holy forces for their own presences and bring their presences to what is called the 'Sekronoolanzaknian-state'; that is to say, they can become such individuals as have their own sacred law of Triamazikamno and thereby the possibility of consciously taking in and coating in their common presence all that 'Holy' which, incidentally, also aids the actualizing of the functioning in these cosmic units of Objective or Divine Reason.

"But the great terror of it, my boy, lies just in this, that although in those three-brained beings who have interested you and who breed on the planet Earth, there

themselves—about which processes I shall also explain to you in detail later—or that process of Great Nature herself which exists in the Universe under the name 'Kerkoolnonarnian actualization,' by which is meant the 'Obtaining-the-Necessary-Sum-Total-of-Vibrations-by-Adaptation.'

"This process proceeds in beings absolutely without the participation of their consciousness.

"In both cases when Okidanokh enters into the 'presence' of a being, and the process of Djartklom proceeds in it, then each of its fundamental parts blends with those perceptions contained in the being at that moment which correspond with it according to what is called 'Kindred-Vibrations,' and then is further concentrated upon the corresponding localization, that is, upon the corresponding brain.

"And just such blendings are called 'Being-Impulsakri.'

"It is necessary to notice further that these localizations or brains in beings serve not only as apparatuses for the transformation of corresponding cosmic substances for the purposes of the Most Great Common Cosmic Trogoautoegocrat, but also as the means for beings whereby their conscious self-perfecting is possible.

"Just this latter aim depends upon the quality of the 'presence' of the Being-Impulsakri concentrated, or, as it is otherwise said, deposited, upon the said corresponding being-brains.

"Concerning the qualities of Being-Impulsakri, there is among the direct commandments of OUR ENDLESS ALL EMBRACING even a special commandment, which is very strictly carried out by all the three-brained beings of our Great Universe, and which is expressed in the following words:

"'Always guard against such perceptions as may impair the purity of your brains.'

- -

"The possibility of a personal self-perfecting by the three-brained beings exists because three such centers of three such being-brains are localized in their common 'presence,' upon which afterwards, when the process of Djartklom proceeds in the Omnipresent Okidanokh the three holy sources of the sacred Triamazikamno are deposited and acquire the possibility for their further, this time, independent actualizings.

"Just in this is the point, that the beings having this three-brained system can, by the conscious and intentional fulfilling of Being-Partkdolgduty, utilize from this process of Djartklom in the Omnipresent Okidanokh, its three holy sources for their own 'presence,' and lead this their 'presence' to what is called the 'Sekronoolanzaknian state'; that is to say, they can become such Individuums as have their own sacred law of Triamazikamno and thereby the possibility of consciously perceiving and coating in their common 'presence' all that 'Holy' which, incidentally, also aids the actualizing of the functioning of Objective or Divine Reason in these cosmic units.

"But the great terror of it, my boy, lies just in this, that although in those three-brained beings who have interested you, breeding on the planet 'Earth,' there arise

arise and are present in them, up to the time of their complete destruction, these three independent localizations or three being-brains, through which separately all the three holy forces of the sacred Triamazikamno which they might also utilize for their own self-perfecting are transformed and go for further corresponding actualizations, yet, chiefly on account of the irregular conditions of ordinary being-existence established by them themselves, these possibilities beat their wings in vain.

"It is interesting to note that the said being-brains are found in the same parts of the planetary body of these

------------------------------ 145 ------------------------------

three-brained beings who arise on the planet Earth as in us, namely:

"1. The brain predetermined by Great Nature for the concentration and further actualizing of the first holy force of the sacred Triamazikamno, called the Holy-Affirming, is localized and found in the head.

"2. The second brain, which transforms and crystallizes the second holy force of the sacred Triamazikamno, namely, the Holy-Denying, is placed in their common presences, also as in us, along the whole of their back in what is called the 'spinal column.'

"3. But as regards the place of concentration and source for the further manifestation of the third holy force of the sacred Triamazikamno, namely, the Holy-Reconciling—the exterior form of this being-brain in the three-brained beings there bears no resemblance whatever to ours.

"It must be remarked that in the primordial three-brained beings there, this said being-brain was localized in the same part of their planetary body as in us and had an exterior form exactly similar to our own; but for many reasons which you will be able to understand for yourself during the course of my further talks, Great Nature was compelled little by little to regenerate this brain and to give it the form which it now has in the contemporary beings.

"This being-brain in the contemporary three-brained beings there is not localized in one common mass, as is proper to the presences of all the other three-brained beings of our Great Universe, but is localized in parts, according to what is called 'Specific Functioning,' and each such part is localized in a different place of their whole planetary body.

"But although, in its exterior form, this being-center of theirs has now variously placed concentrations, nevertheless all its separate functionings are correspondingly connected

------------------------------ 146 ------------------------------

with each other, so that the sum total of these scattered parts can function exactly as in general it is proper for it to function.

"They themselves call these separate localizations in their common presence 'nerve nodes.'

"It is interesting to notice that most of the separate parts of this being-brain are localized in them, just in that place of their planetary body where such a normal being-brain should be, namely, in the region of their breast, and the totality of these nerve-nodes in their breast, they call the 'Solar Plexus.'

and are present in them, up to the time of their complete destruction, these three independent localizations or three being-brains, through which are transformed and go for the further corresponding actualizations separately all the three holy sources of the sacred Triamazikamno, which they might also utilize for their own self-perfecting—yet, chiefly on account of the irregular conditions of ordinary being-existence established by them themselves, these possibilities beat their wings in vain.

"It is interesting to note that the said being-brains are found in the same parts of the planetary body of these

three-brained beings arising on the planet 'Earth' as in us, namely:

"The brain assigned by Great Nature for the concentration and further actualizing of the first holy force of the sacred Triamazikamno, denominated the Holy Affirming, is localized and found in their head.

"The second brain, which transforms and crystallizes the second holy force of the sacred Triamazikamno, namely, the Holy Denying, is placed in their common 'presences,' also as in us, along the whole of their back in what is called the 'spinal column.'

"But as regards the place of concentration and source for the future manifestation of the third holy force of the sacred Triamazikamno, namely, the Holy Reconciling, the exterior form of this being-brain in the three-brained beings there, bears no resemblance whatever to ours.

"It must be remarked that in the earliest three-brained beings there, this said being-brain was localized in the same part of their planetary body as in us, and had an exterior form exactly similar to our own; but for many reasons which you will be able to work out for yourself during the course of my further talks, Great Nature was compelled little by little to regenerate it and to give it the form which this brain now has in the contemporary beings.

"This being-brain in the contemporary three-brained beings there is not localized in a common mass, as it properly is in the 'presence' of all the other three-brained beings of our Great Universe, but in them it is localized in parts, according to what is called 'Specific Functioning,' and each such part is localized in a different place of their whole planetary body.

"But although, in its exterior form, this being-center of theirs has now such variously placed concentrations, nevertheless all its separate functionings have corresponding connections

among themselves, so that the sum-total of these scattered parts can function exactly as in general it is proper for it to function.

"They themselves call these separate localizations in their common 'presence' 'nerve-nodes.'

"It is interesting to notice that most of the separated parts of this being-brain are localized in them just in that place of their planetary body where a normal being-brain should be, namely, in the region of their breast, and the mass of these 'nerve-nodes' contained in their breast they call the 'Solar Plexus.'

"And so, my boy, the process of Djartklom in the Omnipresent-Okidanokh proceeds in the presence of each of these favorites of yours, and in them also, all its three holy forces are blended independently with other cosmic crystallizations, and go for the corresponding actualizations, but as, chiefly owing to the already mentioned abnormal conditions of being-existence gradually established by them themselves, they have entirely ceased to fulfill being-Partkdolg-duty, then, in consequence of this, none of those holy sources of everything existing, with the exception of the denying source alone, is transubstantiated for their own presences.

"The crystallizations arising in their presences from the first and from the third holy forces go almost entirely for the service only of the common-cosmic Trogoautoegocratic-process, while for the coating of their own presences there are only the crystallizations of the second part of the Omnipresent-Okidanokh, namely, of the 'Holy-Denying'; and hence it is that the majority of them remain with presences consisting of the planetary body alone, and thus are, for themselves, destroyed forever.

"As regards all the peculiarities proper to the Omnipresent everywhere-penetrating Active-Element-Okidanokh alone, and also as regards the further results which these

-------------------------------- *147* --------------------------------

peculiarities actualize, you will have a complete representation of them only after I shall have explained to you in more or less detail, as I have already promised, about the fundamental laws of World-creation and World-maintenance.

"But meanwhile I shall tell you about those elucidating experiments concerning this Omnipresent cosmic crystallization at which I was personally present.

"But I must tell you that I was an eyewitness of these said elucidating experiments, not on that planet Earth which has taken your fancy—nor did your favorites make them—but on the planet Saturn where they were made by that three-brained being who during almost the whole period of my exile in that solar system was my real friend, about whom I recently promised to tell you a little more in detail."

-------------------------------- *148* --------------------------------

"And so, my boy; in the 'presence' of each of these favorites of yours also, there proceeds the process of Djartklom in the Omnipresent Okidanokh; in them also, all its three holy sources are blended independently with other cosmic crystalliz-ations, and go for the corresponding actualizations, but because, owing chiefly to the already mentioned abnormal conditions of being-existence gradually estab-lished by them themselves, they have completely ceased to fulfill the Being-Partk-dolgduty—then, as a consequence of this, of all those three holy sources of everything existing, with the exception of the denying force alone, no other is transubstantiated for their own 'presence.'

"The crystallizations arising in their 'presence' from the first and from the third holy sources go almost entirely for the service only of the common cosmic Tro-goautoegocratic process, while for the coating of their own 'presence' there only serve the crystallizations of the second part of the Omnipresent Okidanokh, namely, of the Holy Denying; and hence it is that the majority of them remain with a 'presence' consisting of the planetary body alone, and thus they are for themselves destroyed forever.

"As regards all the peculiarities proper to the omnipresent everywhere-penet-rating Active Element Okidanokh alone, and also as regards the further results which these

peculiarities actualize, you will have a complete representation of them only after I have sometime explained to you, as I have already promised I would in more or less detail, about the fundamental laws of World-creation and World-mainten-ance.

"But meanwhile I will tell you about some elucidating experiments which were concerned with this Omnipresent cosmic crystallization and at which I was per-sonally present.

"But I must tell you that I was an eyewitness of these said elucidating experi-ments, not on that planet 'Earth' which pleases you, nor did your favorites make them, but on the planet 'Saturn' where just that three-brained being performed them who during almost the whole period of my exile within that Solar System was my real friend, and about whom I recently promised to tell you a little more in detail."

The Arch-preposterous

B EELZEBUB continued as follows:
     "The cause of my first meeting with that three-centered being who sub-sequently became my essence-friend and by whom I saw the said experiments with theOmnipresent-Okidanokh, was as follows.

"That you may better represent to yourself the events of this tale of mine, you must first of all know that at the beginning of my exile to that solar system, certain corresponding essence-friends of mine who had not taken part in those events from which the causes of my exile had issued, performed concerning my person-ality that sacred process which exists in the Universe under the name of the 'Sac-red Vznooshlitzval,' that is to say, concerning my personality there was implanted in the presences of those three-brained beings by means of another sacred pro-cess called 'Askalnooazar,' that which Objective Science defines by the notion, 'Trust-another-like-yourself.'

"Well, then, just after my arrival in that solar system Ors, when I began visiting its various planets and first descended upon the surface of the planet Saturn, it turned out in connection with the aforesaid, that one of the beings who had un-dergone the sacred action of 'Vznooshlitzval' regarding my person was what is called there the 'Harahrahroohry' of all the three-centered beings arising and ex-isting on the planet Saturn.

"On the planet Saturn a being is called the 'Harahrahroohry' who is the sole chief over all the other beings on that planet.

"Similar beings-chiefs exist also on all the other planets upon which three-brained beings breed; they are differently

-- 149 --

named on different planets; and on your planet Earth such a chief is called a 'King.'

"The only difference is that while everywhere else, even on all the other planets of the same system, there is one such king for the whole of the given planet, on your peculiar planet Earth there is a separate king for every accidentally segreg-ated group of these favorites of yours and sometimes even several.

"Well, then:

"When I first descended on the surface of the planet Saturn and mingled with the three-centered beings there, it chanced that I had occasion the next day to meet the Harahrahroohry himself of the planet Saturn; and during what is called our 'Exchange-of-subjective-opinions' he invited me to make his own 'Harhoory,' that is, his own palace, the chief place of my existence during the whole of my sojourn on their planet.

"And this I did.

"So, my boy, when we were once talking simply according to the flow of what is called 'being-associative-mentation,' and happened to touch on the question,

The Arch-preposterous

BEELZEBUB continued further thus:
    "The following served as the cause of my first meeting with that three-centered being who subsequently became my essence-friend, and through whom I saw the said experiments with the Omnipresent Okidanokh.

"That you may have a better understanding concerning the events of this tale of mine, you must first know this also—that at the beginning of my exile in that solar system, by certain correspondent essence-friends of mine, who had not taken part in those events from which had also issued the causes of my exile in that solar system, that sacred process concerning my personality had also been enacted which exists in the Universe under the name of the 'Sacred Vznooshlitzval,' that is to say there was implanted in the 'presence' of those three-brained beings concerning my personality by means of other sacred cosmic processes called 'Askalnooazar,' that certain 'is-ness' which objective science defines by the conception 'Other-Self-Trust.'

"So, just after my arrival in that solar system Ors, when I began visiting its various planets and first descended upon the surface of the planet Saturn, it turned out in connection with the aforesaid, that one of the beings who had undergone the sacred action of 'Vznooshlitzval' regarding my person, was also what is called there the Harahrahroohry himself of all the three-centered beings arising and existing on the planet Saturn.

"On the planet Saturn a being is called the Harahrahroohry who is the sole head over all the other beings on that planet.

"Similar head-beings exist also on all the other planets upon which three-brained beings breed; they are differently

- -

named on different planets; and upon your planet Earth such a head is called a 'king.'

"The only difference is that while everywhere else, even on all the other planets of the same system, there is one such king for the whole of the given planet, on your peculiar planet Earth there is one such king for every accidentally segregated group of these favorites of yours and sometimes even several.

"So...

"When I first descended on the surface of the planet Saturn and mingled with the three-centered beings there, it chanced that I had occasion the next day to meet the Harahrahroohry himself of the planet Saturn; and during what is called our 'Exchange-of-Subjective-Opinions' he invited me to make his own Harhoory, that is, his own palace, the fundamental place of my existence during the whole of my stay on their planet.

"And this I did.

"So, my boy, when we were once talking, simply according to the flow of what is called 'being-associative-mentation,' and happened to touch on the question, among other things, of the strange results actualized in the manifestations of the particularities of theOmnipresent-Okidanokh, the venerable Harahrahroohry of the planet Saturn first mentioned that one of his learned beings-subjects, by name Harharkh, had recently devised for the elucidation of many of the previously unexplained properties of that cosmic substance, an exceedingly interesting appliance which he called a 'Rhaharahr,' the chief demonstrating part of which he called a 'Hrhaharhtzaha.'

"And further, he offered to make, if I wished, the necessary arrangements for showing me all these new inventions and for giving me every possible explanation of them.

"The result of it all was that the following day, escorted by one of that venerable Harahrahroohry's court, I went

-------------------------------- 150 --------------------------------

to the place of existence of that Gornahoor Harharkh where I first saw those novel elucidatory experiments with the Omnipresent-Okidanokh.

"Gornahoor Harharkh, who afterwards, as I have already told you, became my essence-friend, was then considered one of the foremost scientists among the ordinary three-brained beings of the whole Universe, and all his constatations as well as the elucidatory apparatuses he had invented were everywhere widespread, and other learned beings on the various planets were using them more and more.

"Here it will do no harm to remark that I also, thanks only to his learning, had later in my observatory on the planet Mars that Teskooano which, when it was finally established, enabled my sight to perceive, or as is said, 'approach-the-visibility' of remote cosmic concentrations, 7,000,285 times.

"Strictly speaking, it was owing to just this Teskooano that my observatory was afterwards considered one of the best constructions of its kind in the whole Universe; and, most important of all, it was by means of this Teskooano that I myself thereafter could, even while staying at home on the planet Mars, relatively easily see and observe the processes of the existence occurring on the surfaces of those parts of the other planets of that solar system which, in accordance with what is called the 'common-cosmic Harmonious-Movement,' could be perceived by being-sight at the given moment.

"When Gornahoor Harharkh was informed who we were and why we had come, he approached us and forthwith very amiably began his explanations.

"Before beginning his explanations I think it not inadvisable to warn you once and for all that all my conversations with various three-centered beings arising and existing on various planets of that system where I was obliged

-------------------------------- 151 --------------------------------

to exist for the 'Sins of my youth'—as for instance in the present case, the conversations with this Gornahoor Harharkh which I am now about to relate to you while we travel on the space-ship *Karnak*—all proceeded in dialects still quite unknown to you, and sometimes even, by the way, in such dialects the consonances of which were quite 'indigestible' for perception by normal being-functions assigned for this purpose.

among other things, of the strange results realized in the manifestations of the particularities of the Omnipresent Okidanokh, it was just then that the venerable Harahrahroohry of the planet Saturn first mentioned that one of his learned-being subjects, by name Harharkh, had recently devised for the elucidation of many of the previously unexplained properties of that cosmic substance, an exceedingly interesting contrivance which is called a 'Rhaharahr,' the chief demonstrating part of which he called the Hrhaharhtzaha.

"And further, he offered to make if I wished, the necessary arrangements for showing me all these new inventions and for giving me every possible explanation of them.

"The result of it all was that the following day, escorted by one of that venerable Harahrahroohry's court, I went

to the place of existence of that Gornahoor Harharkh and there it was that I first saw those novel elucidatory experiments with the Omnipresent Okidanokh.

"Gornahoor Harharkh, who afterwards, as I have already told you, became my essence-friend, was then considered one of the foremost scientists among the ordinary three-brained beings of the whole Universe, and his ascertainments of all kinds as well as the elucidatory apparatuses he invented, were everywhere spread, and other learned beings on the various planets were more and more using them.

"Here it will do no harm to remark that I also, thanks only to his learning, had later in my observatory on the planet Mars that Teskooano which, when it was finally established, enabled my 'sight' to perceive, or, as it is said, to 'approach the visibility' of remote cosmic concentrations, seven million two hundred and eighty-five times.

"Strictly speaking, it was owing to just this Teskooano that my observatory was afterwards considered one of the best artifacts of its kind in the whole Universe; and, most important of all, it was by means of this Teskooano that I myself thereafter could, even while staying at home that is, on the planet Mars—relatively easily see and observe the processes of existence occurring on the surfaces of those parts of the other planets of that solar system which in accordance with what is called the 'Common-system-harmonious-movement' could be perceived by 'being-sight' at the given moment.

"When Gornahoor Harharkh was informed who we were and why we had come, he approached us and forthwith very amiably began his explanations:

"Before repeating his explanations I think it not inadvisable to warn you once and for all that all my conversations with various three-centered beings arising and existing on various planets of that system, where I was obliged

to exist for the 'sins of my youth,' as, for instance, in the present case, the conversation with this Gornahoor Harharkh which I am now just about to relate to you as we travel on the spaceship 'Karnak'—all proceeded in verbal dialects you have never heard, and in some cases whose consonance is utterly unassimilable by the normal being-functions assigned for this purpose.

"And so, my boy, in view of all this, I shall not repeat these conversations word for word but shall give you only their sense in our speech, continuing of course to employ those terms and 'specific-names' or rather those consonances produced by what are called 'being-vocal-chords,' which consonances are used by your favorites of the planet Earth and which have now become for you, owing to continued repetition during my tales about them, habitual and easily perceived.

"Yes . . . it must be noticed here that the word 'Gornahoor' is used by the three-brained beings on the planet Saturn in courtesy; they utter it before the name of one whom they are addressing.

"It is the same with your favorites on the planet Earth. They also have added to the name of every person the word 'Mister' or sometimes a whole meaningless phrase expressing the notion for which our honorable Mullah Nassr Eddin has the following sentence:

"And namely he says:

"'Nevertheless, there's more reality in it than in the wiseacrings of an "expert" in monkey-business.'

"Well, then, my boy . . .

"When this subsequent essence-friend of mine, Gornahoor Harharkh, was informed of what was required of him, he invited us by a sign to approach one of the special appliances which he had made and which, as it later turned out, was named by him 'Hrhaharhtzaha.'

------------------------- 152 -------------------------

"When we were nearer the said special and very strange construction, he pointed to it with a particular feather of his right wing and said:

"'This special appliance is the principal part of the whole of my new invention; and it is just in this that the results are revealed and shown of almost all the peculiarities of the Omnipresent-World-substance-Okidanokh.'

"And, pointing to all the other special appliances also present in the 'Khrh,' he added:

"'I succeeded in obtaining extremely important elucidations concerning the Omnipresent and everywhere penetrating Okidanokh, because thanks to all these separate special appliances of my invention, it became possible, first to obtain all three fundamental parts of the Omnipresent-Okidanokh from every kind of sur- and intraplanetary process and then artificially to blend them into a whole, and secondly, also artificially to disassociate them and elucidate the specific properties of each part separately in its manifestations.'

"Having said this, he again pointed to the Hrhaharhtzahaand added that by means of the elucidating apparatus, not only can any ordinary being clearly understand the details of the properties of the three absolutely independent parts—which in their manifestations have nothing in common—of the whole 'Unique-Active-Element,' the particularities of which are the chief cause of everything existing in the Universe, but also any ordinary being can become categorically convinced that no results of any kind normally obtained from the processes occurring through this Omnipresent World-substance can ever be perceived by beings or sensed by them; certain being-functions, however, can perceive only those res-

"So, my boy, in view of all this I shall not repeat these talks word for word, but will give you only their 'sense' in our 'common speech,' continuing of course to employ those terms and 'specific names' of every kind, or rather those consonants produced by what are called the 'being-vocal-chords' which are used by your favorites of the planet Earth and which have now become for you, owing to the continued repetition during my former tales about them, habitual and easily perceived.

"Yes . . . it must be noticed here that the word Gornahoor is used by the three-brained beings of the planet Saturn in courtesy; they pronounce it before the name of one whom they are addressing.

"It is the same with your favorites on the planet Earth. They also have invented the addition to the name of every other person the word 'mister' or sometimes a whole meaningless phrase expressing such conception as our honorable Mullah Nassr Eddin has the following sentence for:

"And namely, he says:

"'All the same, there is more reality in it than in the wiseacrings of an expert in monkey-business.'

"So, my boy . . .

"When this subsequent essence friend of mine Gornahoor Harharkh, was informed of what was required of him, he invited us by a sign to approach one of the separate special appliances of the whole he had created and which was named by him, as it later turned out, the Hrhaharhtzaha.

"When we were nearer the said special and very strange construction, he said, pointing to it with a particular feather of his right wing:

"'Just this special appliance is the principal part of the whole of my new invention; and it is just in this that the results are brought out and shown of almost all the peculiarities of the Omnipresent World-substance "Okidanokh."'

"And then, pointing to all the other separate appliances also present in the 'khrh,' he added:

"'I succeeded in the obtaining extremely important elucidations concerning the omnipresent and everywhere penetrating Okidanokh because, thanks to all these separate special appliances of my invention, it became possible, first to obtain all the three fundamental parts of the Omnipresent Okidanokh from every kind of sur- and intraplanetary process, and artificially to blend them into a whole, and secondly, also artificially, afterwards to dissociate them for the purpose of elucidating the specific properties of each part separately in its manifestations.'

"Having said this, he again pointed to the Hrhaharhtzaha and added that by means of the elucidating apparatus, not only can any ordinary being clearly understand the details of the properties of the three absolutely independent, and in their manifestations, uniquely different parts of the whole 'Unique Active Element,' whose peculiarities are the chief cause of everything existing in the Universe, but furthermore, that any ordinary being can become categorically convinced that results of every kind, normally obtained from the processes occurring through this Omnipresent World-substance, can never be perceived by beings or sensed by them; but only those results of the said processes can be perceived by

ults of the said processes which proceed for some reason or other abnormally, on account of causes coming from without and issuing either from conscious sources or from accidental mechanical results."

-------------------------------- *153* --------------------------------

The part of Gornahoor Harharkh's new invention which he himself called the Hrhaharhtzaha and regarded as the most important was in appearance very much like the 'Tirzikiano' or, as your favorites would say, a 'huge-electric-lamp.'

"The interior of this special structure was rather like a smallish room with a door that could be hermetically closed.

"The walls of this original construction were made of a certain transparent material, the appearance of which reminded me of that which on your planet is called 'glass.'

"As I learned later, the chief particularity of this said transparent material was that, although by means of the organ of sight beings could perceive through it the visibility of every kind of cosmic concentration, yet no rays of any kind, whatever the causes they may have arisen from, could pass through it, either from within out or from without in.

"As I looked at this part of this said astonishing being-invention, I could through its transparent walls clearly distinguish inside in the center what seemed to be a table and two chairs; hanging above the table, what is called an 'electric-lamp'; and underneath it three 'things' exactly alike, each resembling the 'Momonodooar.'

"On the table and by the side of it, stood or lay several different apparatuses and instruments unknown to me.

"Later it became clear that the said objects contained in this Hrhaharhtzaha, as well as everything we had later to put on, were made of special materials invented by this Gornahoor Harharkh.

"And as regards these materials also, I shall explain a little more in detail at the proper time in the course of my further explanations concerning Gornahoor Harharkh.

"Meanwhile bear in mind that in the enormous Khrh

-------------------------------- *154* --------------------------------

or workshop of Gornahoor Harharkh there were, besides the already mentioned Hrhaharhtzaha, several other large independent appliances, and among them two quite special what are called 'Lifechakans' which Gornahoor himself called 'Krhr-rhihirhi.'

"It is interesting to note that your favorites also have something like this 'Lifechakan' or 'Krhrrhihirhi'; and they name such an apparatus a 'dynamo.'

"There was also there, apart, another independent large appliance, which, as it afterwards appeared, was a 'Soloohnorahoona' of special construction, or as your favorites would say, a 'pump-of-complex-construction-for-exhausting-at-mosphere-to-the-point-of-absolute-vacuum.'

"While I was looking over all this with surprise, Gornahoor Harharkh himself approached the said pump of special construction and with his left wing moved one of its parts, owing to which a certain mechanism began to work in the pump.

certain being functions, which proceed, for one reason or other, abnormally on account of causes coming from outside and due either to conscious sources or to accidental mechanical results.

"The part of Gornahoor Harharkh's new invention which he himself called the Hrhaharhtzaha and regarded as the most important, was in appearance very much like the 'tirzikiano' or, as your favorites would say, a 'huge electric-lamp.'

"The interior of this special structure was rather like a smallish room with a door that could be hermetically closed.

"The walls of this peculiar construction were made of a certain transparent stuff which looked like what on your planet is called 'glass.'

"As I learned later, the chief particularity of this said transparent stuff consisted in this, that although by means of the organ of sight, beings could perceive through it the visibility of cosmic concentrations of every kind, the stuff nevertheless admitted no passage through it, from within or from without, of any rays arising from any causes whatsoever.

"As I looked at this part or this said astonishing being-invention, I could clearly distinguish through its transparent walls that inside, in the middle, stood something like a table and two chairs. Above the table hung what is called an 'electric lamp,' and underneath were three somethings exactly alike and each resembling the 'Momonodooar.'

"Upon and around the table, stood or lay several different apparatuses and instruments previously unknown to me.

"It subsequently also proved that the said objects contained in this Hrhaharhtzaha as well as everything we had later to put on were made of special materials invented by the same Gornahoor Harharkh.

"However, as regards these materials also, I shall explain it a little more in detail at the proper point in the course of my further explanations concerning Gornahoor Harharkh.

"And meanwhile bear in mind that in the enormous Khrh

------

or workshop of Gornahoor Harharkh there stood, besides the already mentioned Hrhaharhtzaha, several other large independent appliances, and, among them, two quite special called 'Lifechakan' which Gornahoor Harharkh himself called 'Krhrrhihirhi.'

"It is interesting to note that your favorites also have something like this 'Lifechakan' or 'Krhrrhihirhi,' and they name such an apparatus a 'Dynamo.'

"There also stood there separately another independent large contrivance which as it afterwards appeared, was a special 'Soloohnorahoona' of a special construction, or as your favorites would say, a 'pump-of-complex-construction-for-exhausting-atmosphere-to-the-point-of-an-absolute-vacuum.'

"While I was looking over all this with surprise, Gornahoor Harharkh himself approached the said pump of a special construction and with his left wing moved one of its parts, owing to which a certain mechanism began to work in the pump.

He then approached us again and, pointing with the same special feather of his right wing to the largest Lifechakan, or Krhrrhihirhi, or dynamo, further continued his explanations.

"He said, 'By means of this special appliance, there are first "sucked-in" separately from the atmosphere, or from any intra- or surplanetary formation, all the three independent parts of the Omnipresent-Active-Element-Okidanokh present in it, and only afterwards when in a certain way these separate independent parts artificially reblended in the Krhrrhihirhi into a single whole, does the Okidanokh, now in its usual state, flow and is it concentrated there, in that "container"'—saying which, he again with the same special feather pointed to something very much like what is called a 'generator.'

"'And then from there,' he said, 'Okidanokh flows here into another Krhrrhihirhi or dynamo where it undergoes the process of Djartklom, and each of its separate parts

- 155 -

is concentrated there in those other containers'—and this time he pointed to what resembled 'accumulators'—'and only then do I take from the secondary containers, by means of various artificial appliances, each active part of Okidanokh separately for my elucidatory experiments.

"'I shall first demonstrate to you,' he continued, 'one of the results which occur when, for some reason or other, one of the active parts of the Omnipresent-Okidanokh is absent during the process of their "striving-to-reblend" into a whole.

"'At the present moment this special construction contains a space which is indeed an absolute vacuum, obtained, it must be said, only owing firstly to the special construction of the suction pump and to the materials of special quality of which the instruments are made, which alone make experiments possible in an absolute vacuum; and secondly, to the properties and the strength of the material of which the walls of this part of my new invention are made.'

"Having said this, he pulled another lever and again continued:

"'Owing to the pulling of this lever, that process has begun in this vacuum whereby in the separate parts of the Omnipresent-Okidanokh there proceeds what is called the "striving-to-reblend-into-a-whole."

"'But since, intentionally by an "able-Reason"—in the present case myself—the participation of that third part of Okidanokh existing under the name of "Parijrahatnatiooose" is artificially excluded from the said process, then this process proceeds there just now between only two of its parts, namely, between those two independent parts which science names "Anodnatious" and "Cathodnatious." And in consequence, instead of the obligatory law-conformable results of the said process, that non-law-conformable result is now actualized which exists under the denomination of

- 156 -

"the-result-of-the-process-of-the-reciprocal-destruction-of-two-opposite-forces," or as ordinary beings express it, "the-cause-of-artificial-light."

"'The "striving-to-reblend-into-a-whole" of two active parts of the Omnipresent-Okidanokh, which is proceeding at the present moment there in this va-

He then approached us again, and pointing with the same special feather of his right wing to the largest Lifechakan or Krhrrhihirhi or, finally, dynamo, continued his explanations.

"And namely, he said that by means of this special appliance there are first 'drawn' separately from the atmosphere or from any intra- or surplanetary formation, all the three independent parts of the Omnipresent active element Okidanokh present in them, and only afterwards, when in a certain way, these separate independent parts are artificially reblended in the Krhrrhihirhi into a single whole, Okidanokh, now in its usual state, flows and is collected there—in that 'container'—saying which, he again with the same special feather pointed to something very much like what is called a 'Generator.'

"'And then from there,' he said, 'Okidanokh flows here into another Krhrrhihirhi or Dynamo where it undergoes the process of "Djartklom," and each of its separate parts

is concentrated—look!—in those other "containers"'—and this time he pointed to what resembled "accumulators"—'and only then do I take from the containers of the second order, by means of various artificial appliances, each active part of Okidanokh separately for my elucidatory experiments.'

"'I will first demonstrate to you,' he continued, 'one of the results occurring when, for one reason or other, one of the active parts of the Omnipresent Okidanokh is absent during the process of their striving to be reblended into a whole.

"'At the present moment this special construction contains a space which is indeed a vacuum; obtained it must be said, only owing firstly to the special construction of the suction pump and to the materials of special quality of which the instruments are made, which alone make experiments possible in an absolute vacuum, and secondly, to the property and rigidity of the staff of which the walls of this part of my new invention are made.'

"Having said this, he shifted still another lever and again continued:

"'Owing to this present shifting of one of the levers, that process has begun in this vacuum whereby in the separate parts of the Omnipresent Okidanokh there proceeds what is called the 'striving-to-be-reblended-into-a-whole.'

"'But because, intentionally by an 'able-Reason'—in the present case by myself—there is artificially excluded from the said process the participation of that part of Okidanokh existing under the name of 'Parijrahatnatioose,' the said process proceeds there just now between only two of its parts, namely, between those two independent parts which science names, the one Anodnatious, and the second Cathodnatious. And on account of all this, instead of the obligatory lawful results of the said process, that non-lawful result is then actualized which exists under the denomination of

'the-result-of-the-process-of-mutual-destruction-of-two-opposite-forces,' or as ordinary beings express it, 'the-cause-of-artificial-light.'

"'Proceeding there at the given moment, that is to say, in this vacuum, the "striving-to-be-reblended-into-a-whole" of two active parts of the Omnipresent

cuum, has a force, as calculated by objective science, of 3,040,000 what are called "volts," and this force is indicated by the needle of that special appliance there.'

"Pointing to a 'something' very much like the apparatus existing also on your planet and called there 'voltmeter' he said:

"'One of the advantages of this new invention of mine for the demonstration of the given phenomenon is that in spite of the unusual power of the process of the "force-of-striving," now proceeding there, the what are called "Salnichizinooar-nian-momentum-vibrations," which most beings consider also to be "rays," and which ought to be obtained and to issue from this process, do not issue out of the place of their arising, that is, out of this construction in which the particularities of the Omnipresent-Okidanokh are being elucidated.

"'And in order that the beings who are outside of this part of my invention may nevertheless also have the possibility of elucidating the force of the given process, I intentionally made the composition of the material of the wall in one place such that it has the property of permitting the passage through it of the said "Salnichiz-inooarnian-momentum-vibrations" or "rays." '

"Having said this, he approached nearer to the Hrahaharhtzaha and pressed a certain button. The result was that the whole of the enormous Khrh or 'workshop' was suddenly so strongly lit up that our organs of sight temporarily ceased to function, and only after a considerable

- *157* -

time had passed could we with great difficulty raise our eyelids and look around.

"When we had recovered and Gornahoor Harharkh had pulled still another lever, which resulted in the whole surrounding space being restored to its former usual appearance, he first, with his customary angel-voice, again drew our attention to the 'voltmeter,' the needle of which constantly indicated the same figure, and then continued:

"'You see that, although the process of the clash of two opposite component parts of the Omnipresent-Okidanokh, of the same power of "force-of-striving" still continues, and that the part of the surface of this construction which has the property of admitting the passage of the said "rays" is still open, yet in spite of all this there is no longer the phenomenon which ordinary beings define by the phrase "the-causes-of-artificial-light."

"'And this phenomenon is no longer there, only because by my last pulling of a certain lever, I introduced into the process of the clash of two component parts of Okidanokh, a current of the third independent component part of Okidan-okh, which began to blend proportionally with its other two parts, owing to which the result derived from this kind of blending of the three component parts of the Omnipresent-Okidanokh—unlike the process of the non-law-con-formable blending of its two parts—cannot be perceived by beings with any of their being-functions.'

"After all these explanations of his, Gornahoor Harharkh then proposed that I

Okidanokh has a force, as calculated by Objective Science, of what is called 3,040,000 "volts" and this force is indicated by the needle—look!—of that special appliance.'

"He pointed to a 'something' very much like the apparatus existing also on your planet and there called a 'voltmeter' and said as follows:

"'One of the advantages of this new invention of mine for the demonstration of the given phenomenon consists in this, that in spite of the unusual power of the process of the 'force-of-striving' now proceeding there, nevertheless the, as they are called, 'Salnichizinooarnian-momentum-vibrations' which, by the way, the majority of beings consider also to be 'rays,' and which ought to be obtained and to issue from this process ... do not issue out of the place of their arising, that is, out of this artificial-construction in which just the particularities of the Omnipresent Okidanokh are elucidated.

"'And in order that beings outside this part of my invention may nevertheless also have the possibility of elucidating the force of the given process, I purposely made the composition of the stuff, of the wall in one place such that it has the property of permitting the passage through itself of the said "Salnichizinooarnian-momentum-vibrations" or "rays."'

"Having said this, he approached nearer to the Hrhaharhtzaha and pressed a certain button. The result was that the whole of the enormous Khrh or 'workshop' was suddenly so strongly lit up that our organs of sight temporarily ceased to function and only after a considerable

- -

time had passed could we with great difficulty raise our eyelids and contrive to look around us.

"When we had recovered and Gornahoor Harharkh had shifted still another lever, the result of which was that the whole surrounding space was restored to its former usual appearance, he first, with his customary angel-voice, again drew our attention to the 'voltmeter' the needle of which indicated the same figure constantly, and then continued thus:

"'You see that although the process of the clash of two opposite integral parts of the Omnipresent Okidanokh of the same power of 'force-of-striving' still continues, and the part of the surface of the construction which has the property of admitting the passage of the said 'rays' is still open, yet, in spite of all this, the phenomenon which ordinary beings define by the phrase, 'the causes of artificial light' is no longer there.

"'And this phenomenon is no longer there only because of this, that by the final shifting of a certain lever, I introduced into the process of the clash of two integral parts of Okidanokh a current of the third independent integral part of Okidanokh which began to blend proportionately with its other two parts, owing to which the result derived from this kind of blending of the three integral parts of the Omnipresent Okidanokh, unlike the process of the non-lawful blending of its two parts, cannot be perceived by any of the functions of beings.

"After all these explanations of his, Gornahoor Harharkh then invited me to

should venture to enter with him that demonstrating part itself of his new invention, in order that I might become, there within, an eyewitness of many particular manifestations of the Omnipresent and everything-penetrating Active-Element.

"Of course, without thinking long about it, I immediately decided and gave him my consent.

"And I immediately decided, chiefly because I expected

------------------------------ 158 ------------------------------

to obtain in my being unchangeable and imperishable 'objective-essence-satisfaction.'

"When this future essence-friend of mine had my consent, he at once gave the necessary orders to one of his assistants.

"It appeared that for the actualization of what he proposed, various preparations had first to be made.

"First of all his assistants put on Gornahoor Harharkh and myself some special, very heavy suits, resembling those which your favorites call 'diving suits' but with many small heads of what are called 'bolts' projecting, and when these extremely peculiar suits had been put on us, his assistants screwed up the heads of these bolts in a certain order.

"On the inner side of these diving suits, at the ends of the bolts, there were, it appeared, special plates which pressed against parts of our planetary body in a certain way.

"It later also became quite clear to me that this was necessary, in order that there might not occur to our planetary bodies what is called 'Taranooranura,' or, as it might otherwise be said, in order that our planetary bodies should not fall to pieces as usually occurs to sur- and intraplanetary formations of every kind when they happen to come into an entirely atmosphereless space.

"In addition to these special suits, they placed on our heads a 'something' resembling what is called a 'diver's helmet,' but with very complicated, what are called 'connectors' projecting from them.

"One of these connectors, which was called the 'Harhrinhrarh,' meaning 'sustainer-of-the-pulsation,' was something long, like a rubber tube. One end of it, by means of complicated appliances on the helmet itself, was hermetically attached to the corresponding place of the helmet for the breathing organs, while the other end, after we

------------------------------ 159 ------------------------------

had already entered that strange Hrhaharhtzaha, was screwed to an apparatus there, which was connected in its turn with the space, the 'presence' of which corresponded to the second being-food.

"Between Gornahoor Harharkh and myself there was also a special connector, through which we could easily communicate with each other while we were inside the Hrhaharhtzaha, from which the atmosphere was pumped out to make a vacuum.

"One end of this connector also, by means of appliances that were on the helmets, was fitted in a certain way to what are called my organs of 'hearing' and

venture to enter with him into that demonstrating part itself of the whole of his new invention, in order that I might become, there within, an eyewitness of many particular manifestations of the Omnipresent and everything-penetrating active element.

"Of course without thinking long about it, I decided at once and gave him my consent.

"And I decided at once chiefly because I expected

to obtain thereby for my being a changeless and imperishable 'objective-essence-satisfaction.'

"When this future essence-friend of mine had my consent, he at once gave the necessary order to one of his assistants.

"It appeared that for the realization of this, various preparations had first to be made.

"Namely, his assistants first of all put on both myself and Gornahoor Harharkh some special very heavy costumes resembling those which your favorites call 'diving-suits,' but with many small heads of what are called 'bolts' projecting.

"And when these extremely peculiar costumes had been put on us, his assistants screwed up the heads of these bolts in a certain order.

"On the inner side of these said 'diving-suits,' and at the ends of the said bolts, there were, it appeared, special plates which pressed against parts of our planetary body in a certain way.

"It later also became quite clear to me why this was necessary, namely, that there might not occur to our planetary bodies what is called 'Taranooranura' or, as it might otherwise be said, in order that our planetary bodies should not fall to pieces as usually occurs to sur—and intraplanetary formations of every kind when they happen to find themselves in a vacuum.

"In addition to these special costumes, they placed on our heads a 'something' also resembling what are called 'diver's helmets,' but with very complicated, as they are called, 'connectors' projecting from them.

"One of these 'connectors' was called the 'Harhrinhrarh,' which meant 'supporter-of-the-pulsation,' and was a long thing like a rubber tube, one end of which, by means of complicated appliances on the helmet itself, was hermetically attached to the corresponding place of the helmet for the breathing organs, while the other end, after we

had already entered that strange Hrhaharhtzaha, was screwed to an apparatus, there present, which was connected in its turn with the space, the presence of which corresponded to the second being-food.

"Between myself and Gornahoor Harharkh a special connector also led, through which we could easily communicate with each other while we were inside the Hrhaharhtzaha, from which the atmosphere was pumped out to make a vacuum.

"One end of this connector also, by means of appliances present on the helmets, was fitted in a certain way to what are called my organs of 'hearing' and 'speech,' and the other end was fitted to the same organs of Gornahoor Harharkh.

"Thus, by means of this connector between my subsequent essence-friend and myself, there was set up, as again your favorites would say, a peculiar 'telephone.'

"Without this appliance we could not have communicated with each other in any way, chiefly because Gornahoor Harharkh was at that time still a being with a presence perfected only up to the state called the 'Sacred Inkozarno'; and a being with such a presence not only cannot manifest himself in an absolutely empty space, but he cannot even exist in it, even though the products of all the three being-foods be artificially introduced into him in such a space.

"But the most 'curious' and, as it is said, the most 'cunningly ingenious' of all the connectors there for various purposes on those strange diving suits and helmets was the connector created by that great scientist Gornahoor Harharkh to enable the 'organ-of-sight' of ordinary beings to perceive the visibility of all kinds of surrounding objects in an 'absolutely-empty-space.'

"One end of this astonishing connector was fitted in a certain way, also by means of appliances on the helmets,

------------------------------ *160* ------------------------------

to our temples, while the other end was joined to what is called the 'Amskomoutator,' which in its turn was joined in a certain way by means of what are called 'wires' to all the objects within the Hrhaharhtzaha as well as to those outside, namely, to those objects whose visibility was needed during the experiments.

"It is very interesting to notice here that to each end of that appliance—a creation almost incredible for ordinary three-centered-being-Reason—two independent connectors, also of wire, were led, and through them, what are called special magnetic currents flowed from outside.

"As it was afterwards explained to me in detail, these connectors and the said special 'magnetic-currents' had, it seems, been created by that truly great scientist Gornahoor Harharkh in order that the presences of learned three-centered beings—even those not perfected to the Sacred Inkozarno—might, owing to one property of the 'magnetic current,' be 'reflected' for their own essences and that, owing to another property of this current, the presence of the mentioned objects might also be 'reflected,' so that thereby the perception of the reality of the said objects might be actualized by their imperfect organs of being-sight in a vacuum containing none of these factors or those results of various cosmic concentrations which have received such vibrations, from the actualization of which alone the functioning of any being-organ whatsoever is possible.

"Having fitted upon us the said very heavy appliances for enabling beings to exist in a sphere not corresponding for them, the assistants of this, then still great all-universal scientist Gornahoor Harharkh, with the help again of special appliances, carried us into the Hrhaharhtzaha itself; and having screwed up all the free ends of the connectors projecting from us to the corresponding apparatuses in the Hrhaharhtzaha itself, went out and hermetically closed

------------------------------ *161* ------------------------------

behind them the only way by which it was still possible, if at all, to have any com-

'speech,' and the other end to the same organs of Gornahoor Harharkh.

"Thus, by means of this connector between myself and my subsequent essence-friend, there was set up, as again your favorites would say, a peculiar 'telephone.'

"Without this artificial appliance we could not communicate with each other in any way, and chiefly because Gornahoor Harharkh was at that time still a being with a presence perfected only up to the state called the 'sacred Inkozarno'; and a being with such a presence not only cannot manifest himself in a vacuum, but he cannot even exist in it, even though the products of all the three being-foods should be artificially introduced into him in such a space.

"But the strangest and, as it is said, most 'cunningly ingenious' of all the 'connectors' present for various purposes on those strange diving-suits and helmets, were the connectors created by that great scientist Gornahoor Harharkh to enable the organ of sight of ordinary beings to perceive the visibility of surrounding objects of all kinds in 'absolutely empty space.'

"One end of this astonishing connector was fitted in a certain way, also by means of appliances present on the helmets,

to our 'temples,' while to other end was joined to what is called the 'Amskomoutator,' which in its turn was joined in a certain way by means of what are called 'wires,' to all the objects within the Hrhaharhtzaha as well as with those outside, namely, with those objects whose visibility was needed during the experiments.

"It is very interesting to notice here, that to each end of that artificial appliance—a creation almost incredible for an ordinary three-reason-being-Reason—in their turn, two independent connectors also of wire were led, through which what are called special magnetic currents flowed from outside.

"As it was afterwards explained to me in detail, these connectors and the said special magnetic currents had, it seems, been created by that truly great scientist Gornahoor Harharkh in order that, in the case of learned three-centered beings not perfected even to the Sacred Inkozarno, thanks to one property of the 'magnetic current,' their own presence might be 'reflected' for their own essence; and thanks to another property of the 'magnetic current' there might be 'reflected' the presence of the mentioned objects; and so that thereby the perception of the reality of the said objects might be realized by their imperfect organs of being-sight also, in a vacuum containing none of those factors or those results of various cosmic concentrations which have received such vibrations, from the realization of which alone, the functioning of any being-organ whatsoever is possible.

"Having fitted upon us the said very heavy artificial appliances for enabling beings to exist in a sphere not proper to them, the assistants of this then still great all-universal scientist Gornahoor Harharkh, with the help once again of special appliances, carried us into the Hrhaharhtzaha itself; and having screwed up all the free ends of the artificial-connectors projecting from us to the corresponding apparatuses present in the Hrhaharhtzaha itself, went out, hermetically closing

behind them the only way by which it was still possible, if at all, to have any communication with what is called the 'everything-representing-one-world.'

"When we were alone in the Hrhaharhtzaha itself, Gornahoor Harharkh, after turning one of what are called 'switches' there, said:

"'The work of the "pump" has already begun, and soon it will have pumped out all the results here without exception of those cosmic processes, whatever they may be, the totality of the results of which is the basis and significance, as well as the process itself, of the maintenance of the existence of everything existing in the whole of this "Everything-representing-one-world."'

"And he added in a half-sarcastic tone: 'Soon we shall be absolutely isolated from everything existing and functioning in the whole of the Universe; but, on the other hand, owing firstly to my new invention, and secondly to the knowledge we have already attained for ourselves, we have not only now the possibility of returning to the said world, to become again a particle of all that exists, but also we shall soon be worthy to become nonparticipating eyewitnesses of certain of these World-laws, which for ordinary uninitiated three-centered beings are what they call "great-inscrutable-mysteries-of-Nature" but which in reality are only natural and very simple results automatically-flowing-one-from-the-other.

"While he was speaking, one could feel that this pump—another also very important part of the whole of his new invention—was perfectly actualizing the work assigned to it by this being with Reason.

"To enable you to represent to yourself and understand better the perfection of this part also of the whole of this new invention of Gornahoor Harharkh, I must not fail to tell you also about the following:

"Although I personally, as a three-brained being

---------------------------- *162* ----------------------------

also, had had occasion many times before, owing to certain quite particular reasons, to be in atmosphereless spaces and had had to exist, sometimes for a long time, by means of the Sacred 'Kreemboolazoomara' alone; and although from frequent repetition, a habit had been acquired in my presence of moving from one sphere to another gradually and almost without feeling any inconvenience from the change in the presence of the 'second-being-food' occurring with the change of the presences of cosmic substances undergoing transformation and which are always around both large and small cosmic concentrations; and also, although the causes themselves of my arising and the subsequent process of my being-existence were arranged in an entirely special way, in consequence of which the various being-functions contained within my common presence had perforce gradually become also special, yet nevertheless, in spite of it all, the pumping out of the atmosphere by the said 'pump' then proceeded with such force that such sensations were impressed on the separate parts of the whole of my presence that even today I can very clearly experience the process of the flow of my state at that time and relate it to you almost in detail.

"This extremely strange state began in me shortly after Gornahoor Harharkh had spoken in a half-sarcastic tone about our imminent situation.

"In all my three 'being-centers'—namely, in the three centers localized in the presence of every three-centered being, and which exist under the names of

munication with what is called the 'From-everything-one-representing-World.'

"When we were alone in the Hrhaharhtzaha itself, Gornahoor Harharkh after shifting one of the so-called 'contacts' present in that strange artifact said:

'The work of the 'pump' has already begun and soon it will have pumped out all without exception of the results present here of those cosmic processes whatever they may be, the totality of whose results is the basis and significance, as well as the process itself, of the maintenance of the existence of everything existing in the whole of this 'From-everything-one-representing-World.'

"And he added in a half sarcastic tone: 'Soon we shall be absolutely isolated from everything existing and functioning in the whole of the Universe; but, on the other hand, owing firstly to my new invention, and secondly, to the knowledge we have previously obtained for ourselves, we have not only now the possibility of returning to the said world, to become again a particle of all that exists, but also we shall soon be worthy to become non-participating eyewitnesses of certain of those World-laws, which for ordinary uninitiated three-centered beings are what they call the great inscrutable mysteries of Nature, but which in reality are only natural and very simple 'one-from-the-other-automatically-flowing-results.'

"While he was speaking, one could feel that this pump, that is, another and also very important part of the whole of this new invention, was perfectly realizing the work assigned to it by the being-Reason.

"To enable you to represent and understand better the excellencies of this part also of the whole of this new invention of Gornahoor Harharkh, I must not fail to tell you also about the following:

"Although I personally, as a three-brained being

- -

also, on account solely of certain quite particular reasons had had occasion many times before to be in atmosphereless spaces and had had to exist, sometimes for a long time, by means of the Sacred 'Kreemboolazoomara' alone; although from frequent repetition a habit had been acquired in my presence of moving from one sphere to another gradually and almost without feeling any inconvenience from the change of the presence of the sacred being-food, occurring with the charge of the presences of cosmic substances undergoing transformation and which are always around both large and small cosmic concentrations; although the causes themselves of my arising and the subsequent process of my being-existence were arranged in an entirely special way, in consequence of which the various being-functions contained within my general presence had perforce gradually become also special—nevertheless in spite of it all, the pumping out of the atmosphere by the said pump proceeded then with such force, that such sensations were impressed on the separate parts of the whole of my presence, that even today I can very clearly experience the process of the flow of my then state and relate it to you almost in detail.

"This extremely strange state began in me shortly after Gornahoor Harharkh had spoken in a half-sarcastic tone about our prospective situation.

"First, in all my three 'being-centers,' namely, in the three centers usually localized in the presence of every three-centered being, which exist under the names

'Thinking,' 'Feeling,' and 'Moving' centers—there began to be perceived separately and independently in each of them in a very strange and unusual way very definite impressions that there was taking place in the separate parts of my whole planetary body an independent process of the sacred 'Rascooarno,' and that the cosmic crystallizations

------------------------------ *163* ------------------------------

which composed the presences of these parts were flowing 'in vain.'

"At first, what is called my 'initiative-of-constatation' proceeded in the usual way, that is, according to what is called the 'center-of-gravity-of-associative-experiencing,' but later, when this initiative-of-constatation of everything proceeding in me gradually and almost imperceptibly became the function of my essence alone, the latter not only became the unique all-embracing initiator of the constating of everything proceeding in me, but also everything, without exception, of that which newly proceeded began to be perceived by and fixed in this essence of mine.

"From the moment that my essence began to perceive impressions directly and to constate independently that, from what was proceeding, there was being entirely destroyed, as it were, in my common presence, firstly, the parts of my planetary body, and then, little by little, also the localizations of the 'second' and 'third' being-centers. At the same time, a constatation was definitely made that the functioning of these latter centers passed gradually to my 'thinking-center' and became proper to it, with the consequence that the 'thinking-center,' with the increasing intensity of its functioning, became the 'unique-powerful-perceiver' of everything actualized outside of itself and the autonomous initiator of the constating of everything proceeding in the whole of my presence as well as outside of it.

"While this strange, and to my Reason then, still incomprehensible being-experiencing was proceeding in me, Gornahoor Harharkh himself was occupied in pulling some 'levers' and 'switches,' of which there were very many at the edges of the table where we were placed.

"An incident which happened to Gornahoor Harharkh himself changed all this being-experiencing of mine, and in my common presence the usual 'inner-being-experiencing' was resumed.

------------------------------ *164* ------------------------------

"The following is what happened:

"Gornahoor Harharkh, with all those unusual heavy appliances which had been put on him as well, suddenly found himself at a certain height above the chair and began to flounder, as our dear Mullah Nassr Eddin says, 'like-a-puppy-who-has-fallen-into-a-deep-pond.'

"As it afterwards proved, my friend Gornahoor Harharkh had made a mistake while pulling the mentioned levers and switches and had made certain parts of his planetary body more tense than was necessary. In consequence, his presence together with everything on him had received a shock and also the momentum given by the shock, and, owing to the 'tempo' proceeding in his presence from taking in the 'second-being-food' and to the absence of any resistance in that ab-

of the centers of Thinking, Feeling and Moving, in each of them separately and independently I had very definite impressions, in a very strange and unusual way, that there was taking place in separate parts of my whole planetary body an independent process of the sacred Rascooarno, and that the cosmic crystallizations

composing their 'presence' were again dissolved into the 'void.'

"At first, what is called my 'initiative-of-ascertaining' proceeded in the usual way, that is, according to what is called the 'center-of-gravity-of-associative-experiencing'; but, later, as my said 'initiative-of-ascertaining' of everything proceeding in me gradually and almost imperceptibly became the function of my essence alone, my essence not only became the unique all-embracing initiator of everything proceeding in me, but everything, without exception, of that which newly proceeded, began to be perceived by and fixed in my essence alone.

"From the moment that my essence began to perceive impressions directly and to ascertain independently that from what was proceeding, there was being entirely destroyed, as it were, in my general presence, first, the parts of my planetary body, and then, little by little, the localizations of the 'second' and 'third' being-centers also—at the same time, the ascertainment was definitely made that the functioning of these latter centers passed gradually to my 'thinking-center' and became proper to it, with the consequence the' the thinking-center, with the increasing intensity of its functioning, finally became the 'unique-powerful-perceiver' of everything realized outside of itself, and the autonomous initiator of the ascertaining of everything proceeding in the whole of my presence as well as outside of it.

"While this strange and still rationally incomprehensible being-experiencing was proceeding in me, Gornahoor Harharkh himself was occupied in shifting certain 'levers' and 'contacts' present in great numbers at the edges of the table at which we were placed.

"An incident which happened to Gornahoor Harharkh himself changed all this being-experiencing, and in my general presence the usual 'inner-being-experiencing' was resumed.

"The following is what happened:

"Gornahoor Harharkh with all those unusual heavy appliances which had been put on him as well, suddenly found himself at a certain height above the chair, where he began to wriggle, as our dear Mullah Nassr Eddin says, 'like a puppy in a well.'

"As it afterwards proved, my friend Gornahoor Harharkh had made a mistake during the shifting of the mentioned levers and contacts, and had made certain parts of his planetary body more tense than was necessary. As a consequence, his presence together with everything on him, having received a shock and afterwards the momentum given by the shock, and thanks to the 'tempo' proceeding in his presence from taking in the 'second being food' and to the absence of any

solutely empty space, he began to drift, or, as I have already said, to flounder like a 'puppy-who-has-fallen-into-a-deep-pond.'"

Having said this with a smile, Beelzebub became silent; a little later he made a very strange gesture with his left hand, and with an intonation not proper to his own voice, he continued:

"While I am gradually recalling and telling you about all this concerning the events of a period of my existence now long since past, the wish arises in me to make a sincere confession to you—just to you, one of my direct heirs who must inevitably represent the sum of all my deeds during the periods of the process of my past being-existence—and namely, I wish sincerely to confess to you that when my essence, with the participation of the parts of my presence, subject to it alone, had independently decided to take a personal part in those scientific elucidatory experiments with the demonstrating part of the new invention of Gornahoor Harharkh, and I had entered

---------------------------- 165 ----------------------------

into this demonstrating part without the least compulsion from outside, yet, in spite of it all, my essence allowed to creep into my being and to be developed, side by side with the said strange experiencings, a criminally egoistic anxiety for the safety of my personal existence.

"However, my boy, in order that you may not at this moment be too distressed, it is not superfluous to add that this happened in me then for the first and also for the last time during all the periods of my being-existence.

"But perhaps it would be better for the present not to touch on questions that concern exclusively only our family.

"Let us rather return to the tale I have begun about the Omnipresent-Okidanokh and my essence-friend Gornahoor Harharkh, who was, by the way, at one time considered everywhere among ordinary three-brained beings as a 'great-scientist,' and is now, though he still continues to exist, not only considered not 'great,' but thanks to his own result, that is to say, to his own son, is what our dear Mullah Nassr Eddin would call a 'has-been' or, as he sometimes says in such cases, 'He-is-already-sitting-in-an-old-American-galosh.'

"Well, then, while floundering, Gornahoor Harharkh, with great difficulty, and only by means of a special and very complicated maneuver which he made, finally managed to get his planetary body, burdened with the various unusually heavy appliances, down onto the chair again, and this time he fixed it all with the aid of special screws which were on the chair for that purpose; and when we were both more or less arranged and communication was possible between us by means of the said artificial-connectors, he first drew my attention to those apparatuses hanging over the table which I told you were very much like the Momonodooars.

"On close inspection all these were alike in appearance

---------------------------- 166 ----------------------------

and served as three identical 'sockets,' from the ends of each of which, 'carbon-candles' projected, such as are usually to be found in the apparatuses which your

resistance in that absolutely empty space, he began to drift, or, as I have already said, to wriggle like a 'puppy in a well.'"

Having said this with a smile, Beelzebub became silent; a little later he made a very strange gesture with his left hand, and with an intonation not proper to his voice, he continued thus:

"While I am gradually recalling and telling you about all this concerning the events of a period of my existence now long since past, the wish arises in me to wake an admission frankly to you—just to you, to one of those my direct heirs who must inevitably become the resultant of all my deeds during the periods of the process of my past being-existence; and namely, I wish to confess to you frankly that just while I was inside that principal demonstrating part of that novel invention of my subsequent essence-friend Gornahoor Harharkh—even although my essence itself, with the participation of the subordinate parts of my presence subject to it alone, had independently decided to take part in those sci-

entific elucidatory experiments with the demonstrating part of the new invention of Gornahoor Harharkh, and I had entered into this demonstrating part without the least compulsion from outside—nevertheless, in spite of all I have said, my essence allowed to creep into my being and to be developed side by side with the said strange experiencings, a criminally egoistic anxiety for the safety of my common personal existence.

"All the same, my boy, in order that you may not at this moment grieve too much, I see no harm in adding that this happened in me then both for the first and the last time during all the periods of my being-existence.

"It is better, however, not to touch on questions that concern only our family exclusively.

"Let us return to the tale I began concerning the Omnipresent Okidanokh and my essence-friend Gornahoor Harharkh, who, I must say, though once everywhere considered among ordinary three-brained beings as a 'great-scientist,' is now, though he still continues to exist, not only not considered as even great, but thanks to his own result, that is to say, to his own son, is what our dear Mullah Nassr Eddin would call a 'has-been,' or, as he sometimes says in such cases, 'He is now sitting in old American galoshes.'

"So, while thus wriggling, Gornahoor Harharkh with great difficulty and only by means of a special and very complicated maneuver which he made, managed finally to get his planetary body, burdened with the various unusual heavy appliances, down on to the chair again; and this time he fixed it all with the aid of special screws which were on the chair for that purpose; and when we were both more or less arranged and communication was possible between us by means of the said artificial-connectors, he first drew my attention to those apparatuses hanging over the table which I told you were very much like the 'Momonodooar.'

"On close inspection all these were alike in appearance

and resembled three identical 'sockets.'

"From the end of each of these sockets 'carbon candles' projected, such as are

favorites call 'electric-arc-lamps.'

"Having drawn my attention to these three socket-like Momonodooars, he said:

"'Each of these externally similar apparatuses has a direct connection with those secondary containers which I pointed out to you while we were still outside and in which, after the artificial Djartklom, each of the active parts of Okidanokh collects into a general mass.

"'I have adapted these three independent apparatuses in such a way that, there in this absolutely empty space, we can obtain from those secondary containers for the required experiment as much as we wish of every active part of Okidanokh in a pure state, and also we can at will change the force of the "striving-to-reblend-into-a-whole," which is acquired in them and which is proper to them according to the degree of density of the concentration of the mass.

"'And here, within this absolutely empty space, I shall first of all show you that same non-law-conformable phenomenon which we recently observed while we were outside the place where it proceeded. And namely, I shall again demonstrate to you this World-phenomenon which occurs when, after a law-conformable Djartklom, the separate parts of the whole Okidanokh meet in a space outside of a law-conformable arising and, without the participation of one part, "strive-to-reblend-into-a-whole."'

"Having said this, he first closed that part of the surface of the Hrhaharhtzaha, the composition of which had the property of allowing 'rays' to pass through it; then he pulled two switches and pressed a certain button, as a result of which the small plate lying on that table, composed of a certain special mastic, automatically moved

- *167* -

toward the mentioned carbon-candles; and then having again drawn my attention to the Ammeter and the Voltmeter, he added: 'I have again admitted the influx of parts of the Okidanokh, namely, the Anodnatious and the Cathodnatious of equal force of "striving-to-reblend."'

"When I looked at the Ammeter and the Voltmeter and indeed saw that their needles moved and stopped on the same figures I had noticed the first time we were still outside the Hrhaharhtzaha, I was greatly surprised, because in spite of the indications of the needles and the intimation of Gornahoor Harharkh himself, I had neither noticed nor sensed any change in the degree of my perception of the visibility of the surrounding objects.

"So, without waiting for his further explanations, I asked him:

"'But why then is there no result from this non-law-conformable "striving-to-reblend-into-a-whole," of the parts of the Okidanokh?'

"Before replying to this question, he turned off the only lamp, which worked from a special magnetic current. My astonishment increased still more, because in spite of the darkness which instantly ensued, it could clearly be seen through the walls of the Hrhaharhtzaha, that the needles of the Ammeter and Voltmeter still stood in their former places.

"Only after I had somehow got accustomed to such a surprising constatation,

usually to be found in the apparatuses which your favorites call 'electric-arc-lamps.'

"Having drawn my attention to these three socket-like Momonodooar, he said:

"'Each of these externally similar apparatuses has a direct connection with these 'containers' of the second order, which I pointed out to you, while we were still outside, in which each of the active parts of Okidanokh, after the artificial Djartklom, collects into a general mass.

"'I have adapted these three independent apparatuses in such a way that here in this vacuum, we can obtain from those second-order "containers," which I also pointed out to you, as much as you like for the required experiment, of every active part of Okidanokh in a pure state, and also we can at will change the 'force-of-the-striving-to-be-blended-again-into-a-whole,' which is acquired in them and is proper to them in the degree of density of the concentration of the mass.

"'And here within the vacuum, I will just show you the same non-lawful phenomenon which we recently observed while we were outside the place of its origin. And namely, I will again demonstrate to you this World phenomenon which occurs when after some lawful Djartklom, the separate parts of the whole Okidanokh meet in a space outside of some lawful arising, and without the participation of one part, "strive-to-be-reblended-into-a-whole."'

"Having said this, he first closed that part of the surface of the Hrhaharhtzaha whose stuff had the property of admitting 'rays' to pass through it and then he shifted two 'contacts' and pressed a certain button, from the pressing of which the small plate lying on that table, also composed of a certain special mastic, automatically moved

towards the mentioned 'carbon candles'; and then having again drawn my attention to the 'ammeter' and the 'voltmeter' he added: 'I have again admitted the confluence of parts of the Okidanokh, namely the Anodnatious and the Cathodnatious of equal "force-of-striving-to-be-reblended."'

"When I looked at the 'ammeter' and the 'voltmeter' and saw indeed that their needles moved and stopped on the same figures I had noticed the first time while we there still outside the Hrhaharhtzaha, I was greatly surprised, because in spite of the indications of the needles and the reminder of Gornahoor Harharkh himself, I had neither noticed nor sensed any charge in the degree of my perception of the visibility of the surrounding objects.

"So without waiting for his further explanations, I asked him: 'But why is there no result from such non-lawful "striving-to-be-reblended-into-a-whole" of the parts of the Okidanokh?'

"Before replying to this question, he turned off the only lamp which worked from a special magnetic current. My astonishment increased still more, because in spite of the darkness which instantly ensued, it could clearly be seen through the walls of the Hrhaharhtzaha, that the needles of the Ammeter and Voltmeter still stood in their former places.

"Only After I had somehow got accustomed to such a surprising ascertain-

Gornahoor Harharkh said:

"'I have already told you that the composition of the material of which the walls of this construction in which we are at this moment are made, possesses the property of not allowing any vibrations arising from any source whatsoever to pass through it, with the exception of certain vibrations arising from nearby concentrations; and these latter vibrations can be perceived by the organs of

------------------------------ 168 ------------------------------

sight of three-brained beings, and even then of course, only of normal beings.

"'Furthermore, according to the law called "Heteratogetar," "the "Salnichiz-inooarnian-momentum-vibrations" or "rays" acquire the property of acting on the organs of perception of beings only after they have passed a limit defined by science in the following formula: "the-result-of-the-manifestation-is-proportion-ate-to-the-force-of-striving-received-from-the-shock."

"'And so, as the given process of the clash of the two parts of the Okidanokh has the strength of great power, the result of the clash is manifested much further than the place of its arising.

"'Now look!'

"Having said this, he pressed some other button, and suddenly the whole interior of the Hrhaharhtzaha was filled with the same blinding light which, as I have already told you, I experienced when I was outside the Hrhaharhtzaha.

"It appeared that the said light was obtained because by pressing this button, Gornahoor Harharkh had again opened that part of the wall of the Hrhaharhtzaha which had the property of permitting 'rays' to pass through it.

"As he explained further, the light was only a consequence of the result of the 'striving-to-reblend-into-a-whole' of the parts of Okidanokh proceeding in that absolutely empty space within the Hrhaharhtzaha and manifested owing to what is called 'reflection' from outside back to the place of its arising.

"After this he continued as follows:

"'I shall now demonstrate to you how and by what combinations of the processes of Djartklom and of the striving-to-reblend-into-a-whole of the active parts of Okidanokh, there arise in planets from what are called the "minerals" which compose their interior presence, definite

------------------------------ 169 ------------------------------

formations of varying densities, as for instance, "mineraloids," "gases," "metalloids," "metals," and so on; how these latter are afterwards transformed owing to these same factors one into another; and how the vibrations flowing from these transformations constitute just that "totality-of-vibrations" which gives the planets themselves the possibility of stability in the process called the "Common-system-harmonious-movement."

"'For my proposed demonstrating I must obtain, as I always do, the necessary materials from outside, which my pupils will give me by means of appliances which I have prearranged.'

"It is interesting to remark that while he was speaking, he was at the same time tapping with his left foot on a certain 'something,' very much like what your favorites call the famous Morse transmission apparatus—famous be it said, of course,

ment, Gornahoor Harharkh said:

"'I have already told you that the composition of the stuff of which the walls of this artifact in which we are at this moment are made, possesses the property of not allowing vibrations arising from any sources whatever to pass through it, with the exception of certain vibrations arising from concentrations nearby; and furthermore, these vibrations can be perceived by the organs of

sight only of three-brained beings, and even then only, of course, of normal beings.

"'Further, according to the law called "Heteratogetar," the "Salnichizinooarnian-momentum-vibrations" or "rays" acquire the property of acting on the organs of perception of beings only after they have passed a limit defined by science in the following formula, "the-result-of-the-manifestation-is-proportionate-to-the-force-of-striving-received-from-the-shock."'

"'So because the given process of the clash of the two parts of the Okidanokh has the strength of high power, the result of the clash is manifested much further than the place of its arising.'

"'Now Look!'

"Having said this, he pressed some other button, and suddenly the whole interior of the Hrhaharhtzaha was filled with the same blinding light which, as I have told you, I experienced when I was outside the Hrhaharhtzaha.

"It appeared that the said light was obtained because by pressing this last button, Gornahoor Harharkh had again opened that part of the wall of the Hrhaharhtzaha which had the property of permitting rays to pass through itself.

"As he explained further, the light was only a consequence of the result of the 'striving-to-be-reblended-into-a-whole' of the parts of Okidanokh proceeding in that entirely empty space within the Hrhaharhtzaha and owing to what is called 'reflection,' it is manifested back to the place of its arising.

"After this he continued as follows:

"'I will now demonstrate to you how and by what combinations of the process of "Djartklom" and "striving-to-be-reblended-into-a-whole" of the active parts of Okidanokh there arise in planets, from what are called the "minerals" which compose their interior presence, definite

formations of varying densities, as for instance, "mineraloids," "gases," "metalloids," "metals," and so on; and how these latter are afterwards gradually transformed owing to the same factors one into another, and how thereby the vibrations flowing from these transformations form just that "totality of vibrations" which gives the planets themselves the possibility of stability in the process called the "Common-system-harmonious-motion."'

"'For the demonstration I propose, I must obtain the necessary materials as I always do, from outside; and these materials my people will give me by means of appliances which I have prearranged.'

"It is interesting to remark that at the same time that he was speaking, he was tapping with his left foot on a certain 'something' very much like what your favorites call the famous Morse transmission apparatus—famous, of course, only to the only on the planet Earth.

"And a little later there slowly ascended from the lower part of the Hrhahar-htzaha a small something like a box, also with transparent walls, within which, as it proved later, were certain minerals, metalloids, metals, and various gases in liquid and solid states.

"Then with the aid of various appliances which were at one side of the table, he first of all, with complicated manipulation, took out from the box some what is called 'red copper' and placed it on the mentioned plate, and then said:

"'This metal is a definite planetary crystallization and is one of the densities required for the said stability in the process called the Common-system-harmonious-movement. It is a formation from preceding processes of the action of the parts of the Omnipresent-Okidanokh; and at the present moment I wish to allow the subsequent transformation of this metal to proceed artificially and acceleratedly by means of the peculiarities of the same factors.

---------------------------------- *170* ----------------------------------

"'I wish to aid artificially the evolution and involution of its elements towards a greater density, or, on the contrary, towards their transformation back to a primal state.

"'To make the picture of the further elucidatory experiments clearer to you, I find I must first inform you, even if only briefly, of my first personal scientific deductions concerning the evidence of the causes and conditions owing to which there proceeds in the planets themselves the crystallizing of separate parts of the Okidanokh in these or the other said definite formations.

"'Evidently first of all from any non-law-conformable Djartklom of the Omnipresent-Okidanokh which is in the presence of every planet, its separate parts are localized in the medium of that part of the presence of the planet, that is to say, in that mineral which was at the given moment in the place where the said non-law-conformable Djartklom occurred.

"'And so if what is called the "vibration-of-the-density-of-the-elements-of-the-said-medium" has an "affinity-of-vibration" with the said active part of the Omnipresent-Okidanokh, then according to the World-law called "Symmetrical-entering," this active part blends with the presence of the said medium and becomes an inseparable part of it. And from that moment, the given parts of the Omnipresent-Okidanokh begin, together with the said elements of the said medium, to represent the corresponding densities required in planets, that is to say, various kinds of metalloids or even metals, as for instance, the metal I have placed in this sphere, and in which there will proceed artificially at this moment, at my wish, the action of striving-to-reblend-into-a-whole of the parts of the Okidanokh, and which metal, as I have already said, exists under the name of red-copper.

"And further, having arisen in the planets in this way, the said various metalloids and metals then begin according

---------------------------------- *171* ----------------------------------

to the common-universal-law called "Reciprocal-feeding-of-everything-existing"—as it is generally proper to arisings of every kind in which Okidanokh or any of its active parts participates—to radiate from their presences the results of

planet Earth.

"And a little later there slowly ascended from the lower part of the Hrhahar-htzaha a small 'something' like a box, also with the transparent walls, within which, as it proved later, were certain 'minerals,' 'metalloids,' 'metals,' and various 'gases' in liquid and solid states.

"Then with the aid of various appliances already present on one side of the table, he with complicated manipulation first took out from the 'box' some, what is called 'red Copper' and placed it on the mentioned plate, and then said:

"'This metal is a definite intraplanetary crystallization and is one of the densities required for the said stability. It is a formation from preceding processes of the action of the parts of the Omnipresent Okidanokh and at the given moment I wish to allow the subsequent transformations of this metal to be produced artificially and acceleratedly by means of the particularities of the same factors.

- -

"'I wish to assist artificially the evolution and involution of its elements towards a greater density or, on the other hand, towards their transformation back to their primal state.

"'To make the picture of the further elucidatory experiments clearer to you, I find I must inform you, even if only briefly, of my first personal scientific conclusions concerning the evidence of the causes and conditions from and under which there proceeds in the planets themselves the crystallizing of separate parts of the Okidanokh in these or the other mentioned definite formations.

"'Evidently, first of all, from some non-lawful "Djartklom" of the Omnipresent Okidanokh contained also in the presence of every planet, its separate parts are localized in the medium of that part of the presence of the planet, that is to say, in just that mineral which was just then properly in that place where the said non-lawful Djartklom occurred.

"'So, if what is called the "vibration-of-the-density-of-the-element" of the said medium has an "affinity-of-vibration" with the said active part of the Omnipresent Okidanokh, then according to the World-Law called "Symmetric-entering," this active part blends with the presence of the said medium and becomes an inseparable part of it. And from that moment the given parts of the Omnipresent Okidanokh begin, together with the said elements of the said medium, to represent the corresponding densities required in planets, namely, various kinds of metalloids or even metals, as for instance, the metal I have placed in this sphere, and in which there will proceed artificially at this moment, at my wish, the action of "striving-to-be-reblended-into-a-whole" of the parts of the Okidanokh, and which metal, as I have already said, exists under the name of "red copper."

"'And further, having arisen in the planets in this way, the said various metalloids and metals then begin,

- -

as it is generally proper to arisings of every kind in which Okidanokh or any of its active elements participates, and according to the common universal law called the "Reciprocal-feeding-of-everything-existing," to radiate from their presence their inner "Interchange-of-substances." And as is proper to radiations of every kind issuing from sur- and intraplanetary formations that have acquired in their vibrations the property of Okidanokh or of its active parts, and which are in what is called the "center-of-gravity" of every such said formation, the radiations of these metalloids and metals possess properties almost similar to the properties of Okidanokh itself or of one or another of its active parts.

"'When the said masses of different densities that have thus arisen in planets under normal surrounding conditions radiate from their common presences the vibrations required for the said World-law of Reciprocal-feeding-of-everything-existing, then, among these vibrations of various properties there is established, owing to the fundamental World-law "Troemedekhfe," a reciprocally acting contact.

"'And the result of this contact is the chief factor in the gradual change of the various densities in planets.

"'My observations over many years have almost fully convinced me that it is owing only to the said contact and its results that there is actualized the "Stability-of-harmonious-equilibrium-of-planets."

"'This metal red-copper which I have placed in the sphere of my proposed artificial actualization of the action of the active parts of Okidanokh, has at this moment what is called a "specific-density," reckoning from the unit of density of the sacred element Theomertmalogos, of 444, that is to say, the atom of this metal was 444 times more dense, and as much less vivifying, than the atom of the sacred Theomertmalogos.

------------------------------ *172* ------------------------------

"'Now see in what order its artificially accelerated transformations will proceed.'

"Having said this, he first fixed before my organ of sight the automatically moving Teskooano and then turned on and off various switches in a certain sequence; and as I looked through the Teskooano he explained to me as follows:

"'At this moment I admit the "influx" of all three parts of Okidanokh into the sphere containing this metal; and as all three parts have the same "density" and, hence, the same "force-of-striving," they reblend into a whole in this sphere without changing anything in the presence of the metal; and the Omnipresent-Okidanokh thus obtained flows in its usual state through a special connection out of the Hrhaharhtzaha and is reconcentrated in the first container which you have already seen.

"'Now look!

"'I deliberately increase the force-of-striving of only one of the active parts of the Okidanokh; for example, I increase the force called Cathodnatious. In consequence of this, you see that the elements composing the presence of that red copper begin to involve towards the quality of the substances that compose the ordinary presences of planets.'

"As he explained this, he at the same time turned on and off various switches in a certain sequence.

"Although, my boy, I then looked very attentively at everything proceeding,

the results of their inner "Interchange-of-matters." And as is proper to radiations of every kind issuing from sur—and intraplanetary formations that have acquired in their vibration the property of Okidanokh or of its active parts, and which reside in what is called the 'center-of-gravity' of each such said formation, the radiations of these metalloids and metals possess properties almost similar to the properties of Okidanokh itself or of one or another of its active parts.

"'When the said masses of different densities that have thus arisen in planets under normal surrounding conditions proceed to radiate from their presences the vibrations required for the said World-Law—the "Reciprocal-feeding-of-everything-existing"—then, among these vibrations of various properties, there is established on the basis of the World-Law "Troemedekhfe," a "contact-of-reciprocal-action."

"'And the result of just this contact is the chief factor in the gradual change of the various densities in planets.

"'My observations over many years have almost fully persuaded me that it is owing only to this said contact and its results that there is realized the "Stability-of-harmonious-equilibrium-of-planets."

"'The element of the metal "red copper" which I have placed in this sphere where I anticipate my artificial realization of the action of the active parts of the Okidanokh, has at this moment what is called a "specific density," reckoning from the unit of density of the sacred element "Theomertmalogos," of 444; that is to say, the atom of this metal is 444 times more dense, and as much less vivifying, than the atom of the sacred Theomertmalogos.

"'Now see in what order its artificially accelerated transformations will proceed.'

"Having said this, he first fixed before my organ of sight the automatically, moving 'Teskooano,' and then switched on and off various 'contacts' in a certain sequence; and he explained to me as follows as I looked through the Teskooano:

"'At this moment I admit the "confluence" of all three parts of Okidanokh into the sphere containing this metal; and because all three parts have the same "density" and, hence, the same "force-of-striving," they reblend into a whole in this sphere, without changing anything in the presence of the metal; and the Omnipresent Okidanokh thus obtained flows through a special connection in its usual state out of the Hrhaharhtzaha and is reconcentrated in the first container which you have already seen.

"'Now look:

"'I deliberately increase the "force-of-striving" of one only of the active parts of the Okidanokh for example, I increase the force called Cathodnatious. In consequence of this, you see that the elements composing the presence of that "red copper" begin to involve towards the quality of the substances that compose the usual presence of planets.'

"As he explained this, he at the same time switched on and off various contacts in a certain sequence.

"Although, my boy, I then looked very attentively at everything proceeding, and everything I saw was impressed in my essence 'Pestolnootiarly,' that is, forever, yet nevertheless, not even with my best wish could I now describe to you in words a hundredth part of what then proceeded in that small fragment of a definite intraplanetary formation.

"And I will not try to put into words for you what I then saw, because I have just thought of a possibility of

—————————————————————— *173* ——————————————————————

soon actually showing it all to you when you also can be an eyewitness of so strange and astonishing a cosmic process.

"But I will tell you meanwhile that there proceeded in that fragment of red copper something rather like those terrifying pictures which I occasionally observed among your favorites on the planet Earth through my Teskooano from Mars.

"I said 'rather-like' because what occasionally proceeded among your favorites had a visibility only possible of observation at its beginning, whereas in the fragment of red copper the visibility was continuous until the final completion of transformation.

"A rough parallel can be drawn between the occasional proceedings on your planet and the proceedings then in that small fragment of copper, if you imagine yourself high up and looking down upon a large public square, where thousands of your favorites, seized with the most intense form of their chief psychosis, are destroying each other's existence by all kinds of means invented by them themselves, and that in their places there immediately appear what are called their 'corpses,' which owing to the outrages done to them by the beings who are not yet destroyed, change color very perceptibly, as a result of which the general visibility of the surface of the said large square is gradually changed.

"Then, my boy, this subsequent essence-friend of mine, Gornahoor Harharkh, by means of switching on and off the influx of the three active parts of Okidanokh and changing their force-of-striving, also changed the density of the elements of the said metal and thereby transformed the red copper into all the other also definite intraplanetary metals of lower or higher degree of vivifyingness.

"And here, for the elucidation of the strangeness of the psyche of the three-brained beings who have taken your

—————————————————————— *174* ——————————————————————

fancy, it is very important and interesting to note that while Gornahoor Harharkh was, with the aid of his new invention, artificially and deliberately producing the evolution and involution of the density and vivifyingness of the elements of red copper, I noticed very clearly that this metal was transformed once upon the said plate into just that same definite metal about which the sorry-savants of your planet have been wiseacring during nearly the whole of their arising and existing, in the hope of transforming other metals into this metal, and thus constantly leading astray their already sufficiently erring brethren.

"This metal is called there—'gold.'

"Gold is no other than the metal we call 'Prtzathalavr,' the specific weight of which, reckoning from the element of the sacred Theomertmalogos, is 1439; that

and everything I saw was impressed in my essence 'Pestolnootiarly,' that is, in-delibly—all the same, not even with my best wish could I now describe to you in words a hundredth part of what then proceeded in that small fragment of a defin-ite intraplanetary formation.

"And I will not try to put into words for you what I then saw because, also, I have just thought of a possibility of

- -

soon actually showing it all to you when you also can be an eyewitness of so strange and astonishing a cosmic process.

"But I will tell you meanwhile that there proceeded in that fragment of 'red copper' something rather like those terrifying pictures which I occasionally ob-served from Mars through my Teskooano among your favorites on the planet Earth.

"I said 'rather like' because what occasionally proceeded among your favorites had a visibility only possible of observation at its beginning, whereas in the frag-ment of 'red copper,' the visibility was continuous to the final completion of trans-formation.

"A rough parallel can be drawn between the occasional proceedings on your planet and the proceedings in that small fragment of copper, if you imagine your-self high up and looking down an a large public square, where thousands of your favorites, under the most intense form of their chief psychosis, are destroying each other's existence by every means they have invented, that in their places there immediately appear what are called their 'corpses,' which 'corpses' on ac-count of the outrages done to them by those who were not yet destroyed, change color very perceptibly, with the consequence that the general visibility of the sur-face of the said square is gradually changed.

"Then, my boy, this subsequent essence-friend of mine, Gornahoor Harharkh, by means of switching on and off the confluences of the three active parts of Okid-anokh and changing their forces of striving, also changed the density of the ele-ments of the said metal and thereby transformed the 'red copper' into all the other also definite intraplanetary 'metals' of lower or higher degree of vivifyingness.

"And here, for the elucidation of the strangeness of the psyche of the three-brained beings who please

- -

you, it is very important and interesting to note that while Gornahoor Harharkh was artificially and deliberately, with the aid of his new invention, producing the evolution and involution of the density and vivifyingness of the elements of 'red copper,' I noticed very clearly that this metal was once transformed upon the said plate into just that same definite metal about which the 'sorry savants' of your planet have been 'wiseacring' during nearly the whole time of their arising and existence, in the hope of transforming other metals into this metal—thereby con-stantly leading astray their already sufficiently erring brethren.

"This metal is called there—'gold.'

"Gold is no other than the metal we call 'Przarhalavr' whose 'specific weight,' reckoning from the element of the sacred Theomertmalogos, is 1439; that is to is to say, its element is three and a fraction times less vivifying than the element of the metal red copper.

"Why I suddenly decided not to try to explain to you in detail in words all that then took place in the fragment of the said red copper, in view of my suggestion of the possibility of soon actually showing you in definite intraplanetary formations the processes of various combinations of the manifestations of the active parts of Okidanokh, was because I suddenly remembered the all-gracious promise given me by our All-Quarters-Maintainer, the Most Great Archcherub, Peshtvogner.

"And this all-gracious promise was given me, as soon as I returned from exile and had to present myself first of all to His All-Quarters-Maintainer, the Archcherub Peshtvogner, and prostrated myself to produce before him what is called the 'Essence-Sacred-Aliamizoornakalu.'

"This I had to do on account of the same sins of my youth. And I was obliged to do so, because when I was pardoned by HIS UNI-BEING ENDLESSNESS and allowed to return to my native land, certain Sacred Individuals decided

---------------------------------- *175* ----------------------------------

to demand of me, for any eventuality, to have performed over my essence this sacred process in order that I might not manifest myself as in the days of my youth, and that the same might not thereby occur again in the Reason of most individuals dwelling here at the center of the Great Universe.

"You probably do not know yet what the Sacred-Aliamizoornakalu over an essence means? I shall later explain it to you in detail but meanwhile I shall simply use the words of our dear Mullah Nassr Eddin who explains this process as 'giving-one's-word-of-honor-not-to-poke-one's-nose-into-the-affairs-of-the-authorities.'

"In short, when I presented myself to His All-Quarters-Maintainer, he deigned to ask me, among other things, whether I had taken with me all the being-productions which had interested me and which I had collected from various planets of that solar system where I existed during my exile.

"I replied that I had taken almost everything, except those cumbersome apparatuses which my friend Gornahoor Harharkh had constructed for me on the planet Mars.

"He at once promised to give orders that everything I should indicate should be taken at the first opportunity on the next trip of the space-ship *Omnipresent*.

"That is why, my boy, I hope that everything necessary will be brought to our planet Karatas so that, when we return there, you will be able to see it all with your own eyes, and I shall be able to explain everything in detail, practically.

"And meanwhile, during our traveling here on the space-ship *Karnak*, I shall, as I have already promised you, tell you in their order about my descents there to your planet and also about the causes of what is called my 'appearances-there-in-person.'"

---------------------------------- *176* ----------------------------------

say, its active element is three and a fraction times less vivifying than the element of the metal 'red copper.'

"Why I suddenly decided not to try to explain to you in detail in words all that then took place in the fragment of the said 'red copper,' in view of my suggestion of the possibility of soon practically showing you in definite intraplanetary formations the processes of various combinations of the manifestations of the active parts of Okidanokh, was because I suddenly remembered the all-gracious promise given me by our All-Quarters-Maintainer, the Most Great Arch-Cherub, Peshtvogner.

"And this all-gracious promise was given me, as soon as I had returned from exile and had to present myself first of all to His All-Quarters-Maintainer, the Arch-Cherub Peshtvogner, and had prostrated myself to produce before him what is called the 'Essence-Sacred-Aliamizoornakalu.'

"This I had to do on account of the same sins of my youth. And I was obliged to do so because, when I was pardoned by HIS ENDLESS UNI-BEING, and allowed to returned to my native land, certain sacred Individuums decided

to demand of me, in order to provide for any eventuality, to produce over my essence, this sacred process, so that I might not manifest myself, as in the days of my youth, and that the same might not thereby occur again in the reasons of the majority of the Individuums dwelling here at the center of the Great Universe.

"You probably do not know yet what the Sacred Aliamizoornakalu over an essence means? I will explain it to you in detail some time; but meanwhile I shall simply use the words of our dear Mullah Nassr Eddin who explains this process as 'giving-one's-word-of-honour-not-to-meddle-in-the-affairs-of-the-authorities.'

"Briefly, when presenting myself to his All-Quarters-Maintainer, he was good enough to ask me, among other things, whether I had taken with me all the being productions which had interested me and which I had collected from various planets of that solar system in which I had existed during my exile.

"I replied that I had taken almost everything, except those cumbersome apparatuses which my friend Gornahoor Harharkh had constructed for me on the planet Mars.

"He at once promised to give orders that everything I should indicate should be taken at the first opportunity on the next trip of the spaceship Omnipresent.

"That is why, my boy, I hope that everything necessary will be brought to our planet Karatas, and that when we return there, you will be able to see with your own eyes, and I shall be able to explain practically everything in detail.

"And meanwhile, during our traveling here on the spaceship Karnak, I will as I have already promised you, tell you in their order about my descents there to your planet, and also about the causes of what is called my 'appearance there in person.'"

Beelzebub's Tales About His Second Descent
on to the Planet Earth

B EELZEBUB began thus:
"I descended upon your planet Earth for the second time only eleven of their centuries after my first descent there.

"Shortly after my first descent onto the surface of that planet, the second serious catastrophe occurred to it; but this catastrophe was local in character and did not threaten disaster on a large cosmic scale.

"During this second serious catastrophe to that planet, the continent Atlantis, which had been the largest continent and the chief place of the being-existence of the three-brained beings of that planet during the period of my first descent, was engulfed together with other large and small terra firmas within the planet with all the three-brained beings existing upon it, and also with almost all that they had attained and acquired during many of their preceding centuries.

"In their place there then emerged from within the planet other terra firmas which formed other continents and islands, most of which still exist.

"It was just on the said continent of Atlantis that the city of Samlios was situated, where, do you remember, I once told you that young countryman of ours existed, on whose account my first 'Descent-in-person' took place.

"During the mentioned second great disaster to that planet, many of the three-brained beings who have taken your fancy survived owing to many and various events, and their now already excessively multiplied posterity descended just from them.

- *177* -

"By the time of my second Descent-in-person, they had already multiplied so greatly that they were breeding again upon almost all the newly formed terra firmas.

"And as regards the question of just which causes, ensuing according to law, brought about this excessive multiplication of theirs, you will understand this also in the course of my further tales.

"You might as well, I think, notice here in connection with this terrestrial catastrophe, something about the three-brained beings of our own tribe; namely, why all the beings of our tribe existing on that planet during the mentioned catastrophe escaped the inevitable what is called 'Apocalyptic-end.'

"They escaped it for the following reasons:

"I told you once, in the course of our previous talks, that most of those beings of our tribe who had chosen this planet of yours as their place of existence, existed during my first descent chiefly on the continent of Atlantis.

"It appears that a year before the said catastrophe, our, as she is called, 'Party-Pythoness' there, when prophesying, asked us all to leave the continent of Atlantis and migrate to another small continent not very far away, where we were to exist on that definite part of its surface she indicated.

Beelzebub's Tale about His Second Descent
on the Planet Earth

B EELZEBUB began thus:

    "I descended upon your planet Earth for the second time, only eleven of their centuries after my first descent upon it.

"It was shortly after my first descent on to the surface of that planet that the second serious catastrophe just occurred to it; but this catastrophe was local in character and did not threaten disaster on a large cosmic scale.

"During the second serious catastrophe to that planet, the continent Atlantis, together with other large and small terra-firmas also, which had been the largest continent and the chief place of the being-existence of the three-brained beings of that planet during the period of my first descent, was engulfed within the planet both with all the three-brained beings existing upon it, and with almost everything they had attained and acquired during their many preceding centuries.

"In their place there then emerged from within the planet, other terra-firmas which formed other continents and islands, most of which still exist until now.

"It was just on the said continent of Atlantis that the city of Samlios was situated, where existed—do you remember? I once told you—-our young countryman on whose account my first, as it is called, 'personal-descent' took place.

"During the mentioned second great disaster to that planet, many of the three-brained beings who please you, survived, owing to a great variety of accidents and their now already excessively multiplied posterity just descended from them.

- -

"By the time of my second 'personal-descent,' they had already multiplied so greatly, that they were breeding again upon almost all the newly formed terra-firmas.

"And as regards the question, namely what legitimately derived causes resulted in this excessive multiplication of theirs, you will also understand in the course of my further tales.

"There is no harm, I think, in noticing here, in connection with this terrestrial catastrophe, something about the three-brained beings of our own tribe, namely, why all the beings of our tribe, existing on that planet during the mentioned catastrophe to it, escaped the inevitable what is called 'Apocalyptic end.'

"They escaped it, for the following reasons:

"I told you once, in the course of our previous talks, that the greater number of the beings of our tribe who had chosen this planet of yours as their place of existence, existed during my first descent chiefly on the continent of Atlantis.

"It appears that a year before the said catastrophe, our, as she is called, 'Party-Pythoness' there, when prophesying, had required that we should all leave the continent of Atlantis and migrate to another small continent not very far away, where we should exist on that definite part of its surface which she indicated.

"This small continent was then called 'Grabontzi' and the part the Pythoness indicated did indeed escape the terrifying perturbation which then occurred to all the other parts of the common presence of that ill-fated planet.

"In consequence of the said perturbation, this small continent Grabontzi, which exists until now under the name of 'Africa,' became much larger, because other terra firmas which emerged from the water spaces of the planet were added to it.

"So, my boy, the Party-Pythoness there was able to warn those beings of our tribe who had been obliged to

------------------------------ 178 ------------------------------

exist on that planet, and thereby to save them, as I have already told you, from the inevitable 'Apocalyptic-fate,' owing only to one special being-property which, by the way, can be acquired by beings only intentionally, by means of what is called being-Partkdolg-duty, about which I shall tell you later.

"I descended in person to the surface of that planet for the second time, for reasons that ensued from the following events.

"Once, while on the planet Mars, we received an etherogram from the Center announcing the imminent reappearance there on the planet Mars of certain Most High Sacred Individuals; and indeed, within half a Martian year, a number of Archangels, Angels, Cherubim, and Seraphim did appear there, most of whom had been members of that Most Great Commission which had already appeared on our planet Mars during the first great catastrophe to that planet of yours.

"Among these Most High Sacred Individuals there was again His Conformity, the Angel—now already an Archangel—Looisos, of whom, do you remember, I recently told you that during the first great catastrophe to the planet Earth he had been one of the chief regulators in the matter of averting the consequences of that general cosmic misfortune.

"So, my boy! The day following this second appearance of the mentioned Sacred Individuals, His Conformity, escorted by one of the Seraphim, his second assistant, made His appearance at my house.

"After Te Deums with me, and after certain inquiries of mine concerning the Great Center, His Conformity then condescended to tell me, among other things, that after the collision of the comet Kondoor with the planet Earth, he, or other responsible cosmic Individuals, superintending the affairs of 'Harmonious-World-Existence,' had

------------------------------ 179 ------------------------------

frequently descended to this solar system to observe the actualizing of those measures they had taken in order to avert the consequences of that general cosmic accident.

"'And we descended,' His Conformity continued, 'because although we had then taken every possible measure and had assured everybody that everything would be quite all right, we ourselves were nevertheless not categorically convinced that no unexpectedness might occur there unforeseen.

"'Our apprehensions were justified, although, "Thanks-to-Chance," not in a serious form, that is to say, on a general cosmic scale, since this new catastrophe

"This small continent was then called 'Grabontzi' and the part the 'Pythoness' indicated did indeed escape the terrifying perturbation which then occurred to all the other parts of the general 'presence' of that ill-starred planet.

"In consequence of the said 'perturbation' this small continent 'Grabontzi,' which exists until now under the denomination of 'Africa' became even much larger, because other terra-firmas emerging from the water spaces of the planet were added to it.

"So, my boy, the 'Party-Pythoness' there was able to warn those beings of our tribe, who had been obliged to exist on that planet, and thereby to save them, as I

have already told you, from the inevitable 'Apocalyptic fate,' only owing to one special being-property which I must say, in this connection, can be acquired by beings only intentionally, by means of what is called 'Being-Partkdolg-duty,' about which I will tell you later.

"I descended personally to the surface of that planet for the second time for reasons that arose from the following events.

"Once, while on the planet Mars, we received an etherogram from the center announcing the impending reappearance there on the planet Mars of certain most High Sacred Individuums; and indeed, within half a Martian year, a number of Archangels, Angels, Cherubim and Seraphim did appear there, most of whom had been members of that most great Commission, which had already appeared on our planet Mars during the first great catastrophe to that planet of yours.

"Among these most High Sacred Individuums there was again His Conformity, the Angel—now already an Archangel—Looisos, of whom, do you remember, I recently told you that during the first great catastrophe to the planet Earth he had been one of the chief regulators in the matter of averting the consequences of that general cosmic misfortune.

"So, my boy! The day following this second appearance of the mentioned Sacred Individuums, His Conformity, escorted by one of the Seraphim, His second assistant, made His appearance in my house.

"After Te Deums with His Conformity and after certain inquiries of mine concerning the Great Center, His Conformity then condescended to tell me among other things that after the collision of the comet Kondoor with the planet Earth, He, or other responsible cosmic Individuums, superintending the affairs of 'Harmonious-World-Existence,' had

frequently descended to this Solar System to take stock of the actualizing of those measures they had put into operation for averting the consequences of that general cosmic accident.

"'And we descended,' His Conformity continued, 'because although we had then put into effect every possible measure and had assured everybody that everything would be quite all right, we ourselves nevertheless were not perfectly convinced that no unexpectedness might not occur there unforeseen.

"'Our apprehensions were partly realized, but, by Good Luck, not in a serious form, that is, on a general cosmic scale, since this new catastrophe affected only affected only the planet Earth itself.

"'This second catastrophe to the planet Earth,' continued His Conformity, 'occurred owing to the following:

"'When during the first disaster two considerable fragments had been separated from this planet, then for certain reasons, the what is called "center-of-gravity" of the whole of its presence had no time to shift immediately into a corresponding new place, with the result that right until the second catastrophe, this planet had existed with its "center-of-gravity" in a wrong position, owing to which its motion during that time was not "proportionately-harmonious" and there often occurred both within and upon it various commotions and considerable displacements.

"'But it was recently, when the center-of-gravity of the planet finally shifted to its true center, that the said second catastrophe occurred.

"'But now,' added His Conformity with a shade of self-satisfaction, 'the existence of this planet will be quite normal in respect of the common-cosmic harmony.

"'This second catastrophe to the planet Earth has finally quite pacified and convinced us also that a catastrophe on a great scale cannot again occur on account of this planet.

"'Not only has this planet itself now again acquired a normal movement in the general cosmic equilibrium, but its two detached fragments'—which, as I have already told you, are now called Moon and Anulios —'have also acquired a normal movement and have become, although small, yet independent "Kofensharnian," that is, additional, planets of that solar system Ors.'

"Having thought a little, His Conformity then told me:

"'Your Reverence, I have appeared to you just for the purpose of talking over the future welfare of the large fragment of that planet, which exists at the present time under the name of Moon.

"'This fragment,' His Conformity continued, 'has not only become an independent planet, but there has now begun on it the process of the formation of an atmosphere, which is necessary for every planet and which serves for the actualization of the Most Great common-cosmic Trogoautoegocrat.

"'And now, your Reverence, the regular process of the formation of the said atmosphere on this small, unforeseenly arisen planet is being hindered by an undesirable circumstance caused by the three-brained beings arisen and existing on the planet Earth.

"'And it is just about this that I have decided to apply to you, your Reverence, and to request you to consent to undertake in the Name of the UNI-BEING CREATOR, the task of trying to spare us the necessity of resorting to some extreme sacred process, unbecoming for three-centered beings, and to remove this undesirable phenomenon in some ordinary way through the "being-Reason" they have in their presences.'

"And in his further detailed explanations, His Conformity then said, among other things, that after the second

the planet Earth itself.

"'This second catastrophe to the planet Earth,' continued His Conformity, 'occurred owing to the following:

"'When during the first disaster two considerable fragments had been separated from this planet, then for certain reasons, the so-called "center of gravity" of the whole of its "presence" had no time to shift immediately into its corresponding new place, with the result that right until the second catastrophe, that planet had existed with an erratic "center of gravity," owing to which, its motion during that time being not "equally harmonious," there often occurred both within and upon it a number of commotions and considerable displacements.

"'But when the "center of gravity" of the planet recently finally shifted into its true center, it was then that the said second catastrophe just occurred.

"'But now,' added His Conformity with a shade of self-satisfaction, 'the existence of this planet will run already quite normally in Conformity with the common cosmic harmony.

"'This second catastrophe to the planet Earth has finally quite quieted and convinced us also that a catastrophe on a great scale cannot again occur on account of that planet.

"'Not only has this planet itself now reacquired a normal movement in the general cosmic balance, but its two detached fragments also, as I have already told you, of the now called "Moon" and "Anulios" have also reacquired a normal movement and have become, although small, yet independent 'Kofensharnian,' that is, additional planets of that solar system Ors.'

"Having thought a little, His Conformity then told me:

"'Your Reverence, I have appeared to you just for the purpose of discussing the future welfare of the large fragment of that planet which exists at the present time under the denomination of Moon.

"'This fragment,' His Conformity continued, 'has not only become an independent planet, but there has now begun on it a process of the formation of an atmosphere, necessary for every planet, which serves for the realization of the most great common cosmic Trogoautoegocrat.

"'So, Your Reverence, the regular process of the formation of the said atmosphere on this small, unforeseenly arisen planet, is just now being hindered by an undesirable circumstance caused by the three-brained beings, arisen and existing on the planet Earth.

"'Concerning what I have just said, I decided to apply myself to you, Your Reverence, and to ask you to consent to take upon yourself, in the name of the UNI-BEING CREATOR, the task of trying to spare us the necessity of resorting to some extreme sacred processes, unbecoming to be used for any three-centered being whatsoever, and to remove this undesirable phenomenon, in some ordinary way through their own "being-reason" contained in their "presence."'

"And in his extended detailed explanations, His Conformity then said among other things further, that after the second

---

catastrophe to the Earth, the biped three-brained beings who had accidentally survived had again multiplied; that now, the whole process of their being-existence was concentrated on another, newly formed, also large continent called 'Ashhark'; that three independent large groups had just been formed on this same large continent 'Ashhark,' the first of which existed in a locality then called 'Tikliamish,' the second in a place called 'Maralpleicie,' and the third in a still existing locality then called 'Gemchania' or 'Pearl-land'; and that in the general psyche of the beings belonging to all those three independent groups, certain peculiar 'Havatvernoni' had been formed, that is, certain psychic strivings, the totality of the process of which common-cosmic strivings they themselves had named 'Religion.'

"'Although these Havatvernoni or Religions have nothing in common,' continued His Conformity, 'yet nevertheless in these peculiar religions of theirs there is very widely spread among the beings of all three groups the same custom called among them "Sacrificial-Offerings."

"And this custom of theirs is based on the notion, which can be cognized only by their strange Reason alone, that if they destroy the existence of beings of other forms in honor of their gods and idols, then these imaginary gods and idols of theirs would find it very, very agreeable, and always and in everything unfailingly help and assist them in the actualization of all their fantastic and wild fancies.

"'This custom is at present so widespread there, and the destruction of the existence of beings of various forms for this maleficent purpose has reached such dimensions, that there is already a surplus of the "Sacred Askokin" required from the planet Earth for its former parts, that is to say, a surplus of those vibrations which arise during the sacred process of "Rascooarno" of beings of every

------------------------------ *182* ------------------------------

exterior form arising and existing on that planet from which the said sacred cosmic arising is required.

"'For the normal formation of the atmosphere of the newly arisen planet Moon, the said surplus of the Sacred Askokin has already begun seriously to hinder the correct exchange of matters between the planet Moon itself and its atmosphere, and the apprehension has already arisen that its atmosphere may in consequence be formed incorrectly and later become an obstacle to the harmonious movement of the whole system Ors, and perhaps again give rise to factors menacing a catastrophe on a greater common-cosmic scale.

"'So, your Reverence, my request to you, as I have already told you, is that you should consent, since you are in the habit of often visiting various planets of that solar system, to undertake the task of specially descending on the planet Earth and of trying there on the spot to instill into the consciousness of these strange three-brained beings some idea of the senselessness of this notion of theirs.'

"Having said a few more words, His Conformity ascended and, when He was fairly high up, added in a loud voice: 'By this, your Reverence, you will be rendering a great service to our UNI-BEING ALL-EMBRACING ENDLESSNESS.'

"After these Sacred Individuals had left the planet Mars, I decided to carry out the said task at all costs and to be worthy, if only by this explicit aid to our

catastrophe to the Earth, the chance surviving biped three-brained beings had again multiplied, and that now, the whole process of their being-existence was concentrated on another, newly formed, also large continent called 'Ashhark.'

"Three independent large groups had just been formed on this same large continent 'Ashhark,' the first of which existed in the locality then called 'Tikliamish,' the second in the place called 'Maralpleicie,' and the third in the still existing locality then called 'Gemchania.'

"'The matter is,' continued His Conformity, 'that in the general psyche of the beings, belonging to all those three independent groups, certain peculiar "Havatvernoni" have been formed, that is, certain psychic strivings, the totality of the process of which they themselves have named "Religion."'

"'Although these "Havatvernoni" or "Religions" have nothing in common with each other, yet, nevertheless there is very widely spread among the beings of all three groups in these peculiar religions of theirs the same custom called among them "Sacrificial-Offerings."

"'And this custom of theirs is founded on the notion, recognized by their strange reason alone, that if they destroy the existence of beings of other forms in honor of their gods and idols, these gods and idols would find it very agreeable, and always in everything unfailingly help and assist them in the realization of their various fantastic and absurd whims.

"'This custom is at present so widely spread there, and the destruction of the existence of beings of various forms for this maleficent purpose has reached such dimensions there, that already there is a surplus of the "Sacred Askokin" required from the planet Earth for its former parts, that is to say, a surplus of those vibrations which arise during the sacred process of "Rascooarno" with beings of every

exterior form, arising and existing on that planet, from which the said sacred cosmic arising is required.

"'For the normal formation of the atmosphere of the newly arisen planet "Moon," the said surplus of the "Sacred Askokin" has already begun seriously to hinder the regular exchange of matters between the planet Moon itself and its atmosphere, and the fear has already arisen that its atmosphere may be formed irregularly on account of this and later become an obstacle to the harmonious movement of the whole Ors system, and perhaps again give rise to the menace of a catastrophe on a general cosmic scale.

"'So, Your Reverence, my request to you consists in this, as I have already told you, that you should consent, since you are in the habit of often visiting various planets of that solar system, to undertake the task of descending on the planet Earth specially, and of trying there on the spot to instill into the consciousness of these strange three-brained beings some idea of the senselessness of this notion of theirs.'

"Having said a few more words His Conformity ascended and having risen sufficiently high, he added in a loud voice already from on high: 'Thereby, Your Reverence, you will be rendering a great service to our ENDLESS UNI-BEING.'

"After these sacred Individuums had left the planet Mars, I decided at whatever cost to carry out the said task, and if only by this explicit aid to our UNIQUE-

UNIQUE-BURDEN-BEARING-ENDLESSNESS, of becoming a particle, though an independent one, of everything existing in the Great Universe.

"So, my boy, imbued with this, I flew the next day on the same ship *Occasion* for the second time to your planet Earth.

"This time our ship *Occasion* alighted on the sea which

- *183* -

was newly formed by the perturbation during the second great disaster to that planet of yours, and which was called there in that period of the flow of time, 'Kolhidious.'

"This sea was situated on the northwest of that newly formed large continent Ashhark, which at that period was already the chief center of the existence of the three-brained beings there.

"The other shores of this sea were composed of those newly emerged terra firmas which had become joined to the continent Ashhark, and which all together were first called 'Frianktzanarali' and a little later 'Kolhidshissi.'

"It must be remarked that this sea and also the mentioned terra firmas exist until now, but of course they now already have other names; for instance, the continent Ashhark is now called Asia; the sea 'Kolhidious,' the 'Caspian Sea'; and all the Frianktzanarali together now exist under the name 'Caucasus.'

"The Occasion alighted on this sea Kolhidious or Caspian Sea because this sea was the most convenient for mooring our Occasion as well as for my further travels.

"And it was very convenient for my further travels because from the East a large river flowed into it, which watered almost the whole country of Tikliamish, and on the banks of which stood the capital of that country, the city 'Koorkalai.'

"As the greatest center of the existence of these favorites of yours was then the country Tikliamish, I decided to go there first.

"Here it might as well be remarked that although this large river then called 'Oksoseria' now still exists, yet it no longer flows into the present Caspian Sea, because after a minor planetary tremor at almost half way, it turned to the right and flowed into one of the hollows on the surface of the continent Ashhark, where it gradually formed a small sea, which still exists and is called the 'Aral Sea';

- *184* -

but the old bed of the former half of that large river which is now called the 'Amu Darya,' can still be seen by close observation.

"During the period of this second descent of mine in person, the country Tikliamish was considered to be and indeed was the richest and most fertile of all the terra firmas of that planet good for ordinary being-existence.

"But when a third great catastrophe occurred to the ill-fated planet, this then most fertile country of the surface of your planet, along with other more or less fertile terra firmas, was covered by 'Kashmanoon,' or, as they say, by 'Sands.'

"For long periods after this third catastrophe, this country Tikliamish was simply called 'bare desert,' and now, its parts have various names; its former principal part is called 'Karakoom,' that is, 'Black-sands.'

"During these periods the second also quite independent group of three-

BURDEN-BEARING ENDLESSNESS, to be worthy to become a particle, but already an independent one, of everything existing in the Great Universe.

"So, my boy, imbued with this, I flew the next day for the second time to your planet Earth on the same ship Occasion.

"This time our ship Occasion alighted on the sea called there in that period of

the flow of time, 'Kolhidious.' This sea was also a new formation that had been caused by the perturbation during the second great disaster to that planet of yours.

"The said sea was situated on the north-west of that newly formed large continent Ashhark, which at that period was already the chief center of the existence of the three-brained beings there.

"The other shores of this sea were composed of those newly emerged terra-firmas which had become attached to the continent 'Ashhark,' and which all together were first called 'Frianktzanarali,' but a little later 'Kolhidshissi.'

"It must be remarked that both the said sea and the enumerated terra-firmas exist until now, but naturally they now already have other names; namely the continent Ashhark is now called 'Asia,' the sea 'Kolhidious,' the 'Caspian' sea, and all the 'Frianktzanarali' together exist now under the name 'Caucasus.'

"The Occasion' alighted on this sea 'Kolhidious' or 'Caspian' Sea, furthermore, because this sea was the most convenient, both for mooring our Occasion, and for my further travels.

"And it was very convenient for my further travels because from its Eastern side a large river flowed into it, which watered almost the whole country of 'Tikliamish,' and just on the banks of which there stood the capital of that country, the city 'Koorkalai.'

"As the greatest center of the existence of those favorites of yours was then the country 'Tikliamish,' I decided to go there first.

"Here there is no harm in noticing that although the mentioned large river then called 'Oksoseria' also still exists, yet it no longer flows into the present Caspian Sea. After a minor planet-quake at almost about the middle of its course, it turned to the right and flowed into one of the hollows on the surface of the continent Ashhark, where it gradually formed a small sea, still existing and called the

'Aral Sea'; but the old bed of the former half of that large river, now already called the 'Amu Darya' can be seen by close observation even at the present time.

"During the period of this second personal descent of mine, the country Tikliamish was considered to be and indeed was the richest and most prosperous of all the terra-firmas, good for the ordinary being-existence then existing on that planet.

"But when a third great catastrophe occurred to that ill-starred planet, this then most prosperous country on the surface of your planet, along with other more or less prosperous terra-firmas, was covered by 'Kashmanoon,' or, as they say, by 'Sands.'

"For long periods after this third catastrophe, this country Tikliamish was simply called 'bare desert.' At present its parts have various names; and its former principal part is called 'Karakoom,' that is, 'Black Sands.'

"On this same continent during that period there also dwelt the second, equally

brained beings of your planet also dwelt on that continent Ashhark, on that part which was then called the country Maralpleicie.

"Later when this second group also began to have a center point of their existence they called it the 'city Gob' and the whole country was for a long time called 'Goblandia.'

"This locality also was afterwards covered by Kashmanoon and now the former principal part of this also once flourishing country is called simply 'The Gobi Desert.'

"And as for the third group of the three-brained beings of that time of the planet Earth, this also quite independent group had the place of its existence on the southeastern side of the continent Ashhark, opposite to Tikliamish, quite on the other side of those abnormal projections of the continent Ashhark which also were formed during the second perturbation to this ill-fated planet.

-------------------------------- 185 --------------------------------

"This region of the existence of this third group was then called, as I have already told you 'Pearl-land.'

"Later the name of this locality also changed many times and the whole of this terra firma region of the surface of the planet Earth now exists under the name of 'Hindustan' or 'India.'

"It must without fail be remarked that at that period, that is, during this second descent of mine in person onto the surface of your planet, there was present and already thoroughly crystallized in all these three-brained beings who have taken your fancy, belonging to the three enumerated independent groups, instead of that function called 'the needful-striving-for-self-perfection,' which should be in every three-brained being, also a 'needful' but very strange 'striving' that all the other beings of their planet should call and consider their country the 'Center-of-Culture' for the whole planet.

"This strange 'needful-striving' was then present in all the three-centered beings of your planet and was for each of them, as it were, the principal sense and aim of his existence. And in consequence, among the beings of these three independent groups at that period, bitter struggles, both material and psychic, were constantly proceeding for the attainment of the mentioned aim.

"Well, then, my boy.

"We then set off from the sea Kolhidious, or as it is now called, the Caspian Sea, on 'Selchans,' that is to say, on rafts of a special kind, up the river Oksoseria, or as it is now called, the Amu Darya. We sailed for fifteen terrestrial days and finally arrived at the capital of the beings of the first Asiatic group.

"On arriving there and after arranging the place of our permanent existence there, I first began visiting the 'Kaltaani' of the city Koorkalai, that is, those establishments there which on the continent Ashhark were later

-------------------------------- 185 --------------------------------

called 'Chaihana,' 'Ashhana,' 'Caravanseray,' and so on, and which the contemporary beings there, especially those breeding on the continent called 'Europe,' call 'Cafes,' 'Restaurants,' 'Clubs,' 'Dance Halls,' 'Meeting Places,' and so on.

quite independent group of three-brained beings on your planet. And that part of the continent Ashhark was then called 'The Country Maralpleicie.'

"When this second group later on also had a central point of their existence which they called the 'City Gob,' the whole country was for a long time called 'Goblandia.'

"This locality also was afterwards covered by 'Kashmanoon,' and at present the former principal part of this also once flourishing country is called simply 'The Gobi Desert.'

"And as for the third group of the three-brained beings then of the planet Earth, this also quite independent group had the place of its existence on the South-Eastern side of the continent Ashhark, in the direction opposite to Tikliamish, quite on the other side of those abnormal projections of the continent Ashhark which also were formed during the second perturbation to this ill-starred planet.

"Just that region of the existence of this third group was then called, as have already told you, 'Gemchania.'

"The name of this locality also changed many times afterwards and the whole of this terra-firma region of the surface of the planet Earth exists at the present time under the name of 'Hindustan' or 'India.'

"It is quite necessary to notice also, that at that period, that is, during this second 'Personal descent' of mine on the surface of your planet there was present and already thoroughly crystallized in all these three-brained beings who please you, belonging to each of the three enumerated independent groups, in place of that function called 'the need-to-strive-to-be-perfected,' which should be in every three-brained being, a very strange, also a 'need to strive,' but towards this, that all the other beings of their planet should call and consider their country as the 'Culture-center' for the whole planet.

"This strange 'need to strive' was then present in all three-centered beings of your planet and was for each of them, as it were, the principal sense and aim of his existence. And in consequence, among the beings of these three independent groups at that period, bitter struggles, both material and psychic, were constantly proceeding for the attainments of the mentioned aim.

"And so, my boy.

"We then set off from the sea 'Kolhidious,' or as it is now called, 'Caspian Sea,' on 'Selchans,' that is to say, on rafts of a special kind, up the river 'Oksoseria,' or as it is now called, the 'Amu Darya.' We sailed for fifteen Earth-days and finally arrived at the capital of the beings of the first Asiatic group.

"On arriving there and after arranging the place of our permanent existence there, I first began visiting the 'Kaltaani' of the city 'Koorkalai,' that is, those establishments there which later,

there on the continent Ashhark, came to be called 'Chaihana,' 'Ashhana,' 'Caravansary,' and so on, and which the contemporary beings there, especially those breeding on the continent called 'Europe,' call 'Cafes,' 'Restaurants,' 'Clubs,' 'Dance-halls,' 'Assembly-rooms' and so on.

"I first began visiting these establishments of theirs because there on the planet Earth, at present just as formerly, nowhere can one observe and study the specific peculiarities of the psyche of the beings of the locality so well as in just such gathering places of theirs; and this was just what I needed to make clear to myself their real inner essence-attitude to their custom of sacrificial offerings and to enable me more readily and more easily to draw up a plan of action for the attainment of that aim for which I made this second sojourn of mine there in person.

"During my visits to the Kaltaani there, I met a number of beings, among whom was one I happened to meet rather often.

"This three-brained being there, whom I chanced to meet frequently, belonged to the profession of 'priest' and was called 'Abdil.'

"As almost all my personal activities, my boy, during that second descent of mine were connected with the external circumstances of this priest Abdil and as I happened to have during this descent of mine a great deal of trouble on his account, I shall tell you more or less in detail about this three-brained being there; and, moreover, you will at the same time understand from these tales about him the results I then attained for the purpose of uprooting from the strange psyche of your favorites the need to destroy the existence of beings of other forms in order to 'please' and 'appease' their gods and revered idols.

"Although this terrestrial being, who afterwards became

------------------------------ *187* ------------------------------

for me like one of my kinsmen, was not a priest of the highest rank, yet he was well versed in all the details of the teaching of the religion then dominant in the whole country Tikliamish; and he also knew the psyche of the followers of that religion, particularly, of course, the psyche of the beings belonging to his what is called 'congregation' for whom he was 'priest.'

"Soon after we were on 'good terms' with each other, I discovered that in the Being of this priest Abdil—owing to very many external circumstances, among which were also heredity and the conditions under which he had been prepared for a responsible being—the function called 'conscience' which ought to be present in every three-centered being, had not yet been quite atrophied in him, so that after he had cognized with his Reason certain cosmic truths I had explained to him, he immediately acquired in his presence towards the beings around him, similar to him, almost that attitude which should be in all normal three-brained beings of the whole Universe, that is to say, he became, as it is also said there, 'compassionate,' and 'sensitive' towards the beings surrounding him.

"Before telling you more about this priest Abdil, I must make clear to your Reason that there on the continent of Ashhark the mentioned terrible custom of Sacrificial-Offerings was at that time, as it is said, at its 'height,' and the destruction of various weak one-brained and two-brained beings proceeded everywhere in incalculable numbers.

"At that period, if anybody had occasion in any house to appeal to one or another of their imaginary gods or fantastic 'saints,' they invariably promised that in the event of good fortune, they would destroy in honor of their gods and saints

"I began visiting just these establishments of theirs first because there, on the planet Earth, at present, just as formerly, nowhere else so well as in just such gatherings of theirs is it possible to observe and study the specific peculiarities of the psyche of the beings of the locality; which was just what I needed for clearing up for myself their real inner essence-attitude to the custom of sacrifice and to enable me more readily and more easily to draw up a plan of action for the attainment of that aim for which I had made that second 'Personal-stay' of mine there.

"During my wanderings around the 'Kaltaani' there I met a number of beings, among whom was one whom I happened to meet rather often.

"This three-brained being there, whom I chanced to meet frequently, belonged to the profession of 'priest' and was called 'Abdil.'

"As, my boy, almost all my personal activities during that second descent of mine were connected with the external circumstances of this priest Abdil, and as I was obliged to have during this descent of mine a great deal of trouble on his account, I shall tell you more or less in detail about this three-brained being there; and, moreover, you will at the same time understand from these tales about him what, namely, were the results I then attained for my aim of uprooting from the strange psyche of your favorites the need to destroy the existence of beings of other forms for the 'appeasing' and 'pleasing' of their Gods and revered idols.

"Although this terrestrial being, who afterward became

- -

for me like one of my intimates, was not a priest of the highest rank, yet he was familiar with all the details of the teaching of the religion then dominant in the whole country Tikliamish; and he also knew the psyche of the followers of that religion, particularly, of course, the psyche of the beings belonging to his 'flock' for whom he was a 'priest.'

"Soon after we had become on good terms with each other, I discovered that in the Being of this priest Abdil, owing to very many external circumstances, among which there were also heredity and the conditions under which he had been prepared for a responsible being, the function called 'conscience' which ought to be present in every three-centered being was not yet quite atrophied in him, so that after he had cognized with his reason certain cosmic truths I explained to him, he immediately acquired in his 'presence' towards the beings around him, similar to him, almost that attitude which is proper to be present in all normal three-brained beings of the whole Universe; that is to say, he became as it is also said there, 'compassionate,' and 'sympathetic' towards the beings surrounding him.

"Before telling you more about this priest Abdil, I must clear up for your reason, that there, that is on the continent of Ashhark, the mentioned cruel custom of 'sacrificial offerings' was, as it is said, at its 'height' at that time, and the destruction of various 'one-brained' and 'two-brained' weak beings proceeded everywhere in incalculable numbers.

"At that period, if anybody had occasion in any house to appeal to one or other of their imaginary Gods, or fantastic 'Saints,' they invariably promised, that in the event of good fortune, they would destroy in honor of their Gods and Saints the

the existence of some being or other, or of several at once; and if by chance good fortune befell them, then they carried out their promise with the utmost

veneration, while, if it were otherwise, they increased their slaughter in order eventually to win the favor of their said imaginary patron.

"With the same aim, these favorites of yours of that period even divided the beings of all other forms into 'clean' and 'unclean.'

"'Unclean' they called those forms of being, the destruction of whose existence was presumably not pleasing to their gods; and 'clean,' those beings, the destruction of whose existence was, presumably, extremely agreeable to those various imaginary idols whom they revered.

"These Sacrificial-Offerings were made not only in their own houses by private beings, but were also made by whole groups, and sometimes even in public. There even then existed special places for slaughterings of this kind which were situated mostly near buildings in memory of something or somebody, chiefly of saints—of course, of the saints they themselves had elevated to 'sainthood.'

"Several such special public places, where the destruction of the beings of different exterior form was carried out, then existed in the country of Tikliamish; and among them was one most celebrated, situated on a small mountain from whence a certain thaumaturgist Aliman was supposed once upon a time to have been 'taken-alive' up to 'some-Heaven-or-other.'

"In that place, as well as in other similar places, especially at definite times of the year, they destroyed an innumerable number of beings called 'oxen,' 'sheep,' 'doves,' and so on, and even beings similar to them themselves.

"In the latter case, the strong usually brought the less strong to be sacrificed; as for instance, a father brought his son, a husband his wife, an elder brother his younger brother, and so on. But, for the most part, 'sacrifices' were offered up of 'slaves,' who then as now were usually what are called 'captives,' that is to say, beings of a conquered

community, which according to the law of what is called 'Solioonensius,' had at the given period—that is, at the period when their needful tendency to reciprocal destruction was more intensely manifested in their presences—a lesser significance in respect of this chief peculiarity of theirs.

"The custom of 'pleasing-their-gods' by destroying the existence of other beings is followed there, on your planet, until now, only not on the scale on which these abominations were practiced by your favorites at that time on the continent Ashhark.

"Well, then, my boy, during the early days of my sojourn in the town Koorkalai, I often talked on various subjects with this mentioned friend of mine, the priest Abdil, but, of course, I never spoke with him about such questions as might reveal my real nature.

"Like almost all the three-brained beings of your planet whom I met during all my descents, he also took me for a being of his own planet, but considered me very learned and an authority on the psyche of beings similar to himself.

existence of some or other being, or of several at once. And if by chance good fortune befell them, then they fulfilled their promise with the utmost

veneration, while, if it were otherwise, then they multiplied their slaughters in order eventually to win the favor of their said imaginary patron.

"With the same aim, these favorites of yours of that period even divided the beings of all other forms into 'clean' and 'unclean.'

"'Unclean' they called those forms of being, the destruction of whose existence was not pleasing, as it were, to their Gods, and 'clean'—those beings the destruction of whose existence, was, as it were, extremely agreeable to those various imaginary idols whom they revered.

"These sacrifices they made not only in their own houses, nor only as private beings, but they were made by whole groups, and sometimes even, in public. There even existed then special places for slaughterings of this kind; these were situated mostly near buildings in memory of something or somebody, chiefly of 'Saints'—naturally, of course, of the 'Saints' they themselves had elevated to 'Sainthood.'

"Several such special public places, where the destruction of the beings of different exterior forms was carried out, then existed in the country of Tikliamish; and among them was then one most celebrated, situated on a small mountain, whence, as it were, a certain thaumaturgist Aliman had once upon a time been 'taken' alive up to 'some' Heaven.

"In that place, just as in others like it, especially at defined times of year, an innumerable number of beings called 'oxen,' 'sheep,' 'doves' and so on were destroyed, and even beings similar to themselves.

"In the latter case, the strong usually sacrificed the less strong, as, for instance, a father his son, a husband his wife, an elder brother his younger brother and so on. But for the most part, 'sacrifices' were offered up of 'slaves,' who then as now were usually what are called 'captives'; that is, beings of a conquered

community, or beings of that caste, which, according to the law of what is called 'Solioonensius,' had at the given period a lesser value in respect of their chief particularity, namely, when their needful tendency to mutual destruction there is more intensely manifested in their 'presence.'

"The custom of pleasing their Gods by destroying the existence of other beings is followed there, on your planet, until now, only not on the same scale upon which this same abominable custom was practiced by your favorites then, on the continent Ashhark.

"So, my boy, during the early days of my stay in the town 'Koorkalai,' I often talked on various subjects with this mentioned friend of mine, the priest Abdil, though, of course, I never spoke with him about such questions as might reveal my real nature.

"Like almost all the three-brained beings of your planet during all my descents he also took me for a being of his own planet and looked upon me as very learned and as an authority on the psyche of beings similar to himself.

"From our earliest meetings, whenever we chanced to speak about other beings similar to himself, his responsiveness and experiencings about them always touched me deeply. And when my Reason made it quite clear to me that the function of conscience, fundamental for three-centered beings, which had been transmitted to his presence by heredity, had not yet become quite atrophied in him, then there gradually began from that moment to arise in my presence and as a result to be crystallized, a 'really-functioning-needful-striving' towards him as towards a kinsman of my own nature.

"Thereafter, he also, according to the cosmic law 'every-cause-gives-birth-to-its-corresponding-result,' of course began to have towards me 'Silnooyegordpana,' or, as your

favorites would say there, 'a-feeling-of-trusting-another-like-yourself.'

"Well, then, my boy, no sooner was this clearly constated in my Reason, than the idea occurred to me to actualize through this first terrestrial friend of mine, the task for which this second descent of mine in person had been made.

"I therefore intentionally began to lead all our conversation towards the question of the custom of Sacrificial-Offerings.

"Although, my boy, considerable time has flowed since I talked with that terrestrial friend of mine, I could, perhaps, now recall word for word and repeat one of our talks we had at that time.

"I wish to recall and repeat just that talk of ours which was the last, and which served as the starting point of all the subsequent events, which though they brought the planetary existence of this terrestrial friend of mine to a painful end, brought him nevertheless to the beginning of the possibility of continuing the task of self-perfecting.

"This last talk took place in his house.

"I then explained to him frankly the utter stupidity and absurdity of this custom of Sacrificial-Offerings.

"I said to him as follows:

"'Good.

"'You have a religion, a faith in something. It is excellent to have faith in something, in whatever it might be, even if you don't exactly know in whom or in what, nor can represent to yourself the significance and the possibilities of what you have faith in. To have faith, whether consciously or even quite unconsciously, is for every being very necessary and desirable.

"'And it is desirable because owing to faith alone does there appear in a being, the intensity of being-self-consciousness necessary for every being, and also the

valuation of personal Being as of a particle of Everything Existing in the Universe.

"'But what has the existence of another being, which you destroy, to do with this, and, moreover, one whose existence you destroy in the name of its CREATOR?

"During our earliest meetings, whenever we chanced to speak about other beings similar to himself, his responsiveness and experiencings about them touched me deeply, but when my Reason cleared up definitively that the function of 'conscience,' fundamental for three-centered beings, which had passed to his 'presence' by heredity had not yet become quite atrophied in him, then there began gradually from that moment to arise—and in the end to be crystallized in my 'presence'—a 'really-functioning-needful-striving' towards him as towards an intimate of my own nature.

"Thereafter, he also, according to the cosmic law 'every-cause-gives-birth-to-a-corresponding-result,' naturally began to have towards me 'Silnooyegordpana,' as your favorites say there, a 'feeling-of-other-self-trust.'

"So, my boy.

"No sooner was this clearly ascertained in my reason, than the idea just then occurred to me to realize through this first Earth-friend of mine, the task, on account of which this second 'Personal descent' of mine had been made.

"I therefore intentionally directed all our conversations towards the question of the custom of sacrifice-offering.

"Although, my boy, a very considerable 'flow of time' has passed since I talked with that Earth friend of mine, I could, perhaps, now recall word for word and repeat one of our talks then.

"I particularly wish to recall and repeat just that talk of ours which was our last, and which served as a starting point of all further sad events which brought the existence, though only the planetary existence, of this Earth friend of mine, to a painful end, nevertheless to the beginning of the possibility of an external universal existence.

"This last talk took place in his house.

"I explained to him already openly at that time the utter absurdity and stupidity of this custom of sacrifice offerings.

"I said to him as follows:

"'Good . . .

"'You have a religion, a faith in something! It is excellent to have faith in something, no matter in what; and even if you don't exactly know in whom or in what, nor can represent to yourself the significance and possibilities of what you believe—to have a faith, whether consciously or even quite unconsciously, is very necessary and desirable for every being.

"'And it is desirable because, owing to faith and to faith alone, there appears in the being, an intensity of being-self-consciousness necessary for every being, and

the valuation of personal being-hood, as of a particle of the All existing in the Universe.

"'But what has the existence of another being, which you destroy, to do with this, and, above all, one whose existence you destroy in the name of its CREATOR?

"'Is not that "life" just the same as yours for the CREATOR Who created you as well as this other being?

"'Thanks to your psychic strength and cunning, that is to say, to those data, proper to you, with which our same COMMON CREATOR has endowed you for the perfecting of your Reason, you profit by the psychic weakness of other beings and destroy their existence.

"'Do you understand, you unfortunate creature, what—in an objective sense—an indeed evil deed you commit by this?

"'Firstly, by destroying the existence of other beings, you reduce for yourself the number of factors of that totality of results which alone can form the requisite conditions for the power of self-perfecting of beings similar to yourself; and secondly, you thereby definitely diminish or completely destroy the hopes of our COMMON FATHER CREATOR in those possibilities which have been put into you as a three-brained being and upon whom He counts, as a help for Him later.

"'The obvious absurdity of such a terrible being-action is already clearly shown by your imagining that by destroying the existence of other beings, you do something pleasing just to that ONE who has intentionally created those beings also.

"'Can it be that the thought has never even entered your head that if our COMMON FATHER CREATOR has created that same life also, then He probably did so for some definite purpose?

"'Think,' I told him further, 'think a little, not as you have been accustomed to think during the whole of your

- *192* -

existence, like a "Khorassanian-donkey," but think a little honestly and sincerely, as it is proper to think for a being as you call yourself, "in-the-likeness-of-God."

"'When GOD created you and these beings whose existence you destroy, could our CREATOR then have written on the foreheads of certain of His creatures that they were to be destroyed in His honor and glory?

"'If anyone, even an idiot from "Albion's Isles," were to think seriously and sincerely about it, he would understand that this could never be.

"'This was invented only by people who say they are "in-the-likeness-of-God," and not by Him, Who created people and these other beings of different form whom they destroy, as they fancy, for His pleasure and satisfaction.

"'For Him there is no difference between the life of men and the life of beings of any other form.

"'Man is life, and the beings of other exterior forms are life.

"'It is most wisely foreseen by Him that Nature should adapt the difference of exterior form of beings in accordance with those conditions and circumstances under which the process of existence of various forms of life are pre-ordained to flow.

"'Take yourself as an example; with your internal and external organs, could you go now and jump into the water and swim like a fish?

"'Of course not, because you have neither the "gills," "fins," nor "tail" a fish has,

"'That life, for the CREATOR both of its and of your life, is just the same as yours.

"'Thanks to your psychic strength and cunning, namely, to those functions, proper to you, which our same COMMON CREATOR has granted you for the perfecting of your reason, you profit by the psychic weakness of other beings and destroy their existence.

"'Do you understand, you wretch, what—in an objective sense—an indeed evil deed you commit in this?

"'Firstly—by destroying the existence of other beings, you reduce for yourself the number of factors in that totality of results which alone can form the necessary conditions for the self-perfection of beings similar to yourself.

"'And secondly, you thereby definitely diminish or completely destroy the hopes of our COMMON FATHER CREATOR, based on those possibilities which have been put into you, yourself, as a three-brained being and upon which He counts, as a help for Him later.

"'The patent senselessness of such a terrible being action is clear already merely in this, that you imagine that by destroying the existence of other beings you do something pleasing just to that ONE who has intentionally created those beings also.

"'Can it be that even the thought has never entered you head, that if our COMMON FATHER CREATOR has created that same life also, then he probably did so for some definite purpose?

"'Think, I told him further, think a little, not as you have been accustomed to think during the whole of your

- -

existence, like a "Khorassanian donkey," but think a little honestly and sincerely, as it is proper to think, for a "God-like being" as you call yourself.

"'When GOD created you and these beings, whose existence you destroy, could our CREATOR then have written on the foreheads of certain of His creatures, that they were to be destroyed in His honor and glory?

"'Anybody, if he thinks seriously and sincerely about it, even an idiot from "Albion's Isles," can understand that this could never be.

"'It was invented by men only, by men who call themselves "God-like," but only not by Him, who created men and these other beings of different form whom men destroy, as it were, for His pleasure and satisfaction.

"'For Him there is no difference between the 'life' of man and the 'life' of beings of any other form.

"'Man is "life," and the beings of other exterior forms are "life."

"'It is most wisely foreseen by Him, that Nature should adapt the difference of exterior form of beings in accordance with those conditions and circumstances, under which the process of existence of this or the other form of 'life' is designed to flow.

"'Take yourself as an example; with these your internal and external organs, could you go and jump into the water and swim like a fish?

"'Of course not, because you have neither the 'gills' 'fins,' nor 'tail' a fish has, that

that is, a life which is preordained to exist in such a sphere as "water."

"'If it occurred to you to go and jump into the water, you would instantly choke and drop to the bottom and become hors d'oeuvre for those same fishes, who, in that sphere, proper for them, would naturally be infinitely stronger than you.

"'It is the same with the fishes themselves; could one

---------------------------- 193 ----------------------------

of them now come to us, sit with us at this table and drink in our company the "Green tea" we are now drinking?

"'Also, of course not! Because it has not the corresponding organs for manifest-ations of this kind.

"'It was created for the water and its internal and also external organs are adap-ted for the manifestations required in the water. It can manifest itself effectively and successfully and fulfill the purpose of its existence, preordained by the CRE-ATOR, only in that sphere appropriate to it.

"'In exactly the same way, your external and all your internal organs are also created by our COMMON CREATOR in a corresponding manner. You are given legs to walk; hands to prepare and take the necessary food; your nose and the or-gans connected with it are so adapted that you may take in and transform in your-self those World-substances by which there are coated in the three-brained beings similar to yourself both higher-being bodies, on one of which rests the hope of our COMMON ALL-EMBRACING CREATOR for help in His needs, for the purpose of actualizations foreseen by Him for the good of Everything Existing.

"'In short, the corresponding principle is foreseen and given to Nature by our COMMON CREATOR, so that He might coat and adapt all your internal and external organs in accordance with that sphere in which the process of the exist-ence of beings of such a brain-system as yours is preordained to flow.

"'A very good example for the clarification of this is your "own-donkey" now standing tied up in your stable.

"'Even as regards this own-donkey of yours, you abuse the possibilities given you by our COMMON CREATOR, since if this donkey is now compelled to stand unwillingly in your stable, it does so only because it is created two-brained; and this again is because such an organization

---------------------------- 194 ----------------------------

of the whole of its presence is necessary for common-cosmic existence upon planets.

"'And therefore, according to law, there is absent from the presence of your donkey the possibility of logical-mentation, and consequently, according to law, he must be what you call "senseless," or "stupid."

"'Although you were created for the purpose of the common-cosmic existence on planets, and although you were created also as "a-field-of-hope" for the future expectations of our COMMON ALL-GRACIOUS CREATOR—that is to say, cre-ated with the possibilities of coating in your presence that "Higher-Sacred" for the possible arising of which the whole of our now existing World was just created— and in spite of the said possibilities given to you, that is to say, in spite of your

is, "the life" for which it is designed to exist in that sphere which is the "water."

"'If it occurred to you to go and jump into the water, you would at once choke and drop to the bottom for the meal of those same fishes, who, in that sphere, appropriate for them, would naturally be infinitely stronger than you.

"'In a similar situation are the fishes themselves.

"'Could one of them come now to us, and sit with us at this table and drink in our "company" the "Green tea" we are now drinking?

"'Also, of course not! Because it has not the appropriate organs for manifestations of this kind.

"'It was created for the water and both its internal and external organs are adapted for the manifestations required in the water. It can manifest itself effectively and successfully, and fulfill the purpose of its existence, predesigned by the CREATOR, only in the sphere appropriate to it.

"'In exactly the same way, your external and all your internal organs are also created by our COMMON CREATOR in a corresponding manner. You are given legs to walk, you are given hands to prepare and take the necessary food; your nose and the organs connected with it are so adapted that you may perceive and transform in yourself those World-substances by means of which there are coated in the three-brained beings, similar to yourself there, both the higher being-bodies, on one of which the hope of our COMMON ALL-EMBRACING CREATOR is placed for help in His needs, for the purpose of realizations foreseen by him for the good of everything existing.

"'In short, the corresponding principle is foreseen and given to Nature by our COMMON CREATOR, so that it might coat and adapt all your internal and external organs, in accordance with that sphere, in which the process of the existence of such a brain-system as yours is preordained to flow.

"'A very good example for the clarification of this is your "own donkey" standing tied up in your stable.

"'Even as regards this "own donkey" of yours, you abuse the possibilities given you by our COMMON CREATOR, since if this donkey now stands under slavish compulsion there in your stable, it does so only because it is created two-brained; and this again is because just such an organization

---

of the whole of its "presence" is necessary for the common cosmic existence upon planets.

"'And therefore, there is absent from the "presence" of your donkey, according to law, the possibility of "logical mentation," and consequently, according to law, he must be what you call "senseless"—"stupid."

"'And although you are created both for this and for still another purpose also, namely, as a "field of hope" for the hopes for the future of our COMMON ALL-GRACIOUS CREATOR —that is to say, you are created with the possibilities of coating in your "presence" that "Higher Sacred" for the possible arising of which the whole of our now existing World was just created; yet in spite of the said possibilities given to you, that is to say, in spite of your having been created three-

having been created three-brained with possibilities of a logical mentation, yet you do not use this sacred property of yours for the purpose for which it was fore-ordained, but manifest it as "cunning" towards His other creations, as, for instance, towards your own-donkey.

"Apart from the possibilities present in you of consciously coating in your presence the mentioned Higher-Sacred, this donkey of yours is of the same value for the common-cosmic process and consequently for our COMMON CREATOR, as you yourself, since each of you is predestined for some definite purpose, and these distinct definite purposes, in their totality, actualize the sense of Everything Existing.

"'The difference between you and your own-donkey is merely in the form and quality of functioning of the internal and external organization of your common presences.

"'For instance, you have only two legs, whereas the donkey has as many as four, any one of which, moreover, is infinitely stronger than yours.

- 195 -

"'Can you, for instance, carry on those two weak legs of yours as much as that donkey can?

"'Certainly not, because your legs are given you only for carrying yourself and the little that is necessary for the normal existence of a three-brained being as foreseen by Nature.

"'Such a distribution of forces and strength, which at first sight appears unjust on the part of our MOST JUST CREATOR, was made by Great Nature simply because the surplus of cosmic substances foreseeingly given you by the CREATOR and by Nature to use for the purpose of your personal self-perfecting is not given to your donkey, but in place of this, Great Nature Herself transforms the same surplus of cosmic substances in your donkey's presence for the power and strength of certain of its organs for its present existence only, but of course without the personal cognition of the donkey itself, thus enabling it to manifest the said power incomparably better than you.

"'And these variously powered manifestations of beings of diverse forms actualize in their totality just those exterior conditions in which alone it is possible for those similar to you—that is, for three-brained beings—consciously to perfect the "germ-of-Reason" placed in their presences, to the necessary gradation of Pure Objective Reason.

"'I repeat, all beings, of all brain systems, without exception, large and small, arising and existing on the Earth or within the Earth, in the air or beneath the waters, are all equally necessary for our COMMON CREATOR, for the common harmony of the existence of Everything Existing.

"'And as all the enumerated forms of beings actualize all together the form of the process required by our CREATOR for the existence of Everything Existing, the essences of all beings are to Him equally valuable and dear.

- 196 -

"'For our COMMON CREATOR all beings are only parts of the existence of a whole essence spiritualized by Himself.

brained with the possibilities of a "logic-mentation," you do not use this sacred property of yours for the purpose for which it was designed, but you manifest it as "cunning" towards His other creations, as, for instance, towards your "own donkey."

"'Apart from the possibilities present in you of consciously coating in your "presence" the mentioned "Higher Sacred," this donkey of yours is of the same value for the common cosmic process, and consequently for our COMMON CREATOR, as you yourself, since each of you is designed for some definite purpose, and these separate definite purposes, in their totality, just realize the sense of everything existing.

"'The difference between you and your "own donkey" is merely in the form and quality of functioning of the internal and external organization in your general "presence."

"'For instance, you have two legs only, whereas the donkey has as many as four, any one of which, moreover, is infinitely stronger than yours.

- -

"'Can you, for instance, carry on those two weak legs of yours as much as that donkey can?

"'Certainly not, because your legs are given you only for carrying yourself and the little that is necessary for the normal existence of a three-brained being as foreseen by Nature.

"'Such a distribution of forces and strength which at first sight appears a piece of injustice on the part of a MOST JUST CREATOR through great Nature, is made simply because the surplus of cosmic substance foreseeingly given you to use by the CREATOR and by Nature for the purpose of your personal perfection, is not given to your donkey; but in place of this, great Nature herself transforms the same surplus of cosmic substances in your donkey's "presence" for the forces and strength of certain of its organs, only for its present existence, but of course without the personal cognition of the donkey itself; thus enabling it to manifest the said strength more and better than you.

"'And these differently-powered manifestations of beings of diverse forms realize in their totality, just those exterior conditions in which alone there is possible for those similar to you—that is, for three-brained beings—the conscious perfecting of the "germ of Reason" placed in their "presence," to the necessary gradation of the pure Objective Reason.

"'I repeat, all beings, of all brain systems, without exception, large and small, arisen and existing on the Earth or within the Earth or in the water or in the air are all equally necessary—for our COMMON CREATOR—for the general harmony of the existence of everything existing.

"'And as all the enumerated forms of beings actualize in their common totality the form of process required by our CREATOR, for the existence of everything existing, the essences of all beings are equally valuable and dear to Him.

- -

"'For our COMMON CREATOR all beings are only parts of the existence of a whole essence, spiritualized by Himself.

"'But what do we see here now?

"'One form of beings created by Him, in whose presences He has placed all His hopes and expectations for the future welfare of Everything Existing, taking advantage of their superiorities, lord it over other forms and destroy their existence right and left and, what is more, they do so presumably "in His name."

"'The whole terror of it is that although such phenomenal anti-God acts take place here in every house and on every square, nevertheless it never enters the head of any of these unfortunates that these beings whose existence I or we are now destroying are equally dear to that ONE, Who has created them, and that if He created these other forms of beings as well as ourselves, it must also have been for some purpose.'

"Having said all this to my friend, the priest Abdil, I said further:

"'And what is most distressing is that every man who destroys the existence of other beings, in honor of his honored idols, does so with all his heart and is convinced beyond all doubt that he is doing a "good" deed.

"'I am quite sure that if any one of them should become aware that in destroying another's existence he is not only committing an evil deed against the true GOD and every real Saint, but is even causing them, in their essences, sorrow and grief that there should exist in the great Universe "in-the-likeness-of-God" beings-monsters who can manifest towards other creations of our COMMON CREATOR so consciencelessly and pitilessly; I repeat, if any of them should become aware of this, then certainly not one among them could with all his heart ever again destroy the existence of beings of other forms for Sacrificial-Offerings.

---------------------------------- *197* ----------------------------------

"'Then perhaps on the Earth also would begin to exist the eighteenth personal commandment of our COMMON CREATOR which declared: "Love everything that breathes."

"'This offering to God of sacrifices by destroying the existence of His other creations is just as if somebody from the street should now break into your house and wantonly destroy all the "goods" there, which have taken you years to collect, and cost you years of labor and suffering.

"'Think, but again think sincerely, and picture to yourself what I have just said, and then answer : Would you like it and thank the impudent thief who broke into your house?

"'Certainly not!! A million times not!!!!

"'On the contrary, your whole being would be indignant and would wish to punish this thief, and with every fibre of your psyche you would try to find a means of revenge.

"'In all probability, you would now reply that although it is indeed so . . ."I am, however, only a man. . . ."

"'That is true, you are only a man. It is good that GOD is GOD and is not so vindictive and evil as man.

"'Certainly He will not punish you nor will He revenge Himself upon you, as you would punish the mentioned robber who destroyed the property and goods it had taken you years to collect.

"'But what do we see here now?

"'One form of beings created by Him, namely, that form of being just in whose 'presence' He has placed all His hope for the future welfare of everything existing, taking advantage of their privileges, lord it over other forms and destroy their existence indiscriminately, and, what is more, they do this, as it were, "in His name."

"'The horror of it is that although these phenomenal anti-God actions take place here in every house and on every square, nevertheless it never enters one of these wretches' heads to think that these beings whose existence I or we are now destroying, are equally dear to that ONE, Who has created them, and that if He created these other forms of beings as well as ourselves, it must have been also for some purpose.

"Having said all this to my friend, the priest Abdil, I said further:

"'And what is most distressing is that the very man who destroys the existence of other beings, in honor of his honored idols, does so with all his heart, and in the complete persuasion that he is doing a "good" deed.

"'I am quite sure, that if one of them should become aware, that in destroying another's existence, he is not only committing a crime against the true GOD and every genuine Saint, but even causing thereby sorrow and grief in their essence that there exist in the great Universe God-like being-monsters who can manifest towards other creations of our COMMON CREATOR so heartlessly and pitilessly; if, I repeat, any of them should become conscious of this, then certainly not one among them, could with all his heart, ever again destroy the existence of beings of other forms for sacrificial offering.

- -

"'Then perhaps on the Earth also, would begin to run the 18th personal commandment of our COMMON CREATOR, which declares: "Love every breathing thing."

"'This offering to God of sacrifices by destroying the existence of His other creations is just the same as if somebody from the street should now break into your house and wantonly destroy all the "goods" there, which have taken you years to collect, and cost you years of labor and suffering.

"'Think, and once more, think sincerely, and represent to yourself what I have just said, and answer: would you like it and thank the impudent thief who broke into your house?

"'Certainly not!! . . . A thousand times not!!!!!

"'On the contrary, your whole being would be indignant and would wish to punish this thief, and with every ounce of your psyche, you would try to find a means of revenge.

"'In all probability, you would now reply, that although it is indeed so . . . however, I am only a man . . .

"'That is true, you are only a man. It is good that GOD is GOD and is not so vindictive and base as man.

"'Certainly he will not punish you nor will He revenge Himself upon you, as you would punish the mentioned robber who destroyed the property and goods it had taken you years to collect.

"'It goes without saying, GOD forgives everything—this has even become a law in the World.

"'But His creations—in this case, people—must not abuse this All-Gracious and Everywhere-Penetrating; Goodness of His; they must not only care for, but even maintain all He has created.

------------------------------ 198 ------------------------------

"'But here on Earth, men have even divided beings of all other forms into the clean and the unclean.

"'Tell me what guided them when they made this division?

"'Why, for instance, is a sheep clean, and a lion unclean? Are they both not equally beings?

"'This also was invented by people. . . . And why have they invented it, and made this division? Simply because a sheep is a very weak being and moreover stupid, and they can do to it just what they like.

"'But people call the lion unclean simply because they dare not do to it what they like.

"'A lion is cleverer and, what is more, stronger than they.

"'A lion will not only not allow itself to be destroyed, but will not even permit people to approach near. If any man should venture to approach near to it, then this "Mister Lion" would give him such a crack on the noddle that our valiant's life would at once fly off to where "people from Albion's Isles" have not yet been.

"'I repeat . . . a lion is unclean simply because men are afraid of it; it is a hundred times higher and stronger than they; a sheep is clean merely because it is much weaker than they and again I repeat, much more stupid.

"'Every being, according to its nature and to the gradation of its Reason attained by its ancestors and transmitted by heredity, occupies its definite place among beings of other forms.

"A good example for clarifying what I have just said is the difference between the already definitely crystallized presences of the psyche of your dog and of your cat.

"'If you pet your dog a little and get it used to anything you please, it will become obedient and affectionate to the point of abasement.

------------------------------ 199 ------------------------------

"'It will run after you and cut every sort of caper before you just to please you all the more.

"'You can be familiar with it, you can beat it, you can hurt it; it will never turn on you, but will always humiliate itself still more before you.

"'But try the same on your cat.

"'What do you think? Will it respond to your indignities as your dog did, and cut the same humble capers for your amusement? Of course not. . . .

"'Even if the cat is not strong enough to retaliate immediately, it will remember this attitude of yours toward it for a long time, and at some time or other will get its revenge.

"'For instance, it is said that it has often happened that a cat has bitten the throat of a man while he was asleep. I can quite believe it, knowing what may have

"'There is no question about it, GOD forgives everything—this has even become a law in the World.

"'But HIS creations—men in this given case—must not abuse this all-gracious and everywhere penetrating Goodness of HIS; they must not only care for, but even maintain all HE has created.

- -

"'Here on Earth, however, men have even divided beings of all other forms—into the "clean" and the "unclean."

"'Tell me what led them, when they made that division?

"'Why, for instance, is a sheep "clean" and a lion "unclean"? Are they not equal beings?

"'This was also invented by men . . . And why have they invented this, and made this division? Simply because a sheep is a very weak being and moreover, stupid, so that they can do just what they like with it.

"'But men call the lion "unclean" simply because they can't do what they like with it.

"'A lion is cleverer and, above all, stronger than they.

"'A lion will not only not allow itself to be destroyed, but will not even permit men to come near it. If any man should once venture to approach it, then this "Mister Lion" would give him such a smack on the sconce that our valiant's life would at once take wings where the Russian Makar has not yet driven his flocks.

"'No . . . a lion is "unclean" simply because men are afraid of it.

"'It is a hundred times higher and stronger than they; a sheep is "clean" merely because it is much weaker than they and moreover—I repeat—much more stupid.

"'Every being according to its nature and to the gradation of its reason attained by its ancestors and passed to it by heredity, occupies its definite place among beings of other forms.

"'A good example for clarifying what I have just said is the difference between the already definitely crystallized "presences" of the psyche of your dog and cat.

"'If you pet a dog a little and get it used to anything you please, it will become obedient and affectionate to the point of humiliation.

- -

"'It will run after you and cut every sort of caper before you just to tickle your fancy.

"'You can be familiar with it, you can beat it, you can aggravate it; it will never turn on you, but will always humiliate itself still more before you.

"'But try the same on your cat.

"'What do you think? Will it respond to your indignities as your dog did, and cut the same humble capers for your amusement? Not much . . .

"'Even if the cat is not strong enough to retaliate at once, it will remember this attitude of yours against you for a long time, and one day or another, it will get its own back.

"'For instance, it has often happened that a cat has torn the throat of a man while he was asleep. I can quite believe it, knowing what may have been the cat's been the cat's reasons for it.

"'No, the cat will stand up for itself, it knows its own value, it is proud, and this is merely because it is a cat and its nature is on that gradation of Reason where according to the merits of its ancestors it just should be.

"'In any case, no being, and no man, should be angry with a cat for this.

"'Is it its fault that it is a cat and that, owing to the merits of its ancestors, its presence occupies such a gradation of "consciousness-of-self"?

"'It must neither be despised for this, nor beaten, nor ill-treated; on the contrary, one must give it its due, as one occupying a higher rung on the ladder of the evolution of "consciousness-of-self."

"By the way, my dear boy, concerning the reciprocal relations of beings, a former famous prophet from the planet 'Desagroanskrad,' the great 'Arhoonilo,' now already the assistant to the chief investigator of the whole Universe in respect of the details of Objective Morality, once said:

---------------------------- *200* ----------------------------

"'If by his Reason a being is higher than you, you must always bow down before him and try to imitate him in everything; but if he is lower than you, you must be just towards him, because you once occupied the same place according to the sacred Measure of the gradation of Reason of our CREATOR and ALL-MAINTAINER.'

"So, my dear boy, this last conversation with that Earth friend of mine produced such a strong impression on him, that for two days thereafter he did nothing but think and think.

"In short, the final outcome of it all was that this priest Abdil eventually began to cognize and sense concerning the custom of Sacrificial-Offerings almost as in reality he should have done.

"Several days after this conversation of ours, there occurred one of the two large religious festivals of the whole of Tikliamish, called 'Zadik'; and in the temple where my friend Abdil was the chief priest, instead of delivering the usual sermon after the temple ceremony, he suddenly began speaking about Sacrificial-Offerings.

"I chanced to be also in that large temple that day and was one of those who heard his speech.

"Although the theme of his speech was unusual for such an occasion and for such a place, yet it shocked nobody, because he spoke unprecedentedly well and beautifully.

"Indeed, he spoke so well and so sincerely, and cited in his beautiful speech so many persuasive and illustrative examples, that as he spoke many of the beings of Koorkalai there even began sobbing bitterly.

"What he said produced so strong an impression on all his congregation that although his speech lasted till the next day instead of the customary half-hour or hour, nevertheless even when it was over, nobody wished to leave and all stood for a long time as if spellbound.

---------------------------- *201* ----------------------------

"Thereafter, fragments from his speech began to be spread among those who

reasons for it.

"'No, the cat will stick up for itself, it knows its value, it is proud; and this merely because it is a cat and its nature is on that gradation of Reason where according to the merits of its ancestors it just should be.

"'In any case, no being, and no man, should be angry with a cat for this.

"'Is it its fault that it is a cat, and that owing to the merits of its ancestors, its "presence" occupies such a gradation of "self-consciousness"?

"'It must neither be despised for this, nor beaten nor maltreated; on the contrary one must give it its due, as one occupying a higher degree on the ladder of the evolution of "self-consciousness."

"By the way, my dear Hassein, keep in mind that concerning the reciprocal relations of beings, a former famous prophet from the planet 'Desagroanskrad,' the great 'Arhoonilo,' now already the assistant of the chief investigator of the whole Universe in respect of the details of Objective Morality—once said:

"'If by his Reason a being is higher than you, you must bow before him and try to imitate him; but if he is lower than you, you must be just with him, because you once occupied the same place according to the scared Measure of gradation of Reason of our CREATOR and ALL-MAINTAINER.'

"So, my dear boy, this particular conversation with that Earth friend of mine produced such a strong impression on him, that for two days thereafter he did nothing but think about it.

"And, briefly, the final outcome of it all was this, that this priest Abdil eventually became conscious and felt about the custom of 'sacrifice' almost as it is proper to feel in reality.

"Several days after this conversation of ours, there occurred one of the two large religious festivals of the whole of Tikliamish, called 'Zadik'; and in the temple where my friend Abdil was the chief priest, instead of delivering the usual address after the temple ceremony, he suddenly began speaking about 'sacrificial-offerings.'

"I chanced to be also in that large temple that day and was among the number of those who heard his sermon.

"Although the theme of his sermon, both for such an occasion and for such a place, was unusual, it shocked nobody, because the priest Abdil spoke extraordinarily well and beautifully.

"Indeed he spoke so well and so sincerely, and cited in his beautiful speech so many persuasive and picturesque examples that as he spoke many of the beings of 'Koorkalai' present there, even began sobbing bitterly.

"What he said produced so strong an impression on all his flock, that although his sermon lasted, instead of the customary, half an hour or an hour, until the next day, nevertheless even when it was over, nobody wanted to leave and everybody stood for a long time as if spellbound.

"Thereafter fragments from his sermon began to be spread among those who had not personally heard it.

"It is interesting to notice that it was the custom then for priests to exist simply on the offerings of their parishioners, and this priest Abdil had also been in the habit of receiving from parishioners all kinds of food for his ordinary existence, as for instance roast and boiled 'corpses' of beings of various exterior forms, such as 'chickens,' 'sheep,' 'geese,' and so on. But after this famous speech of his, nobody brought him any of these customary offerings but brought or sent him only fruits, flowers, handiwork, and so on.

"The day following his speech, this Earth friend of mine at once became for all the citizens of the town Koorkalai what is called the 'fashionable-priest,' and not only was the temple where he officiated always crammed with beings of the town Koorkalai, but he was also pressed to speak in other temples.

"He delivered many such speeches concerning Sacrificial-Offerings, and each time the number of his admirers grew and grew, so that he soon became popular not only among the beings of the town Koorkalai, but also of the whole of Tikliamish.

"I do not know how it would all have ended if the whole priesthood, that is, men-beings of the same profession as my friend, had not become alarmed and anxious on account of his popularity, and had not opposed everything he preached.

"Evidently these colleagues of his were afraid that if the custom of Sacrificial-Offerings were to disappear, their own excellent incomes would, disappear also, and that their authority would first totter and finally crumble.

"Day by day the number of this priest Abdil's enemies increased, and they spread new slanders and innuendoes

-------------------------------- *202* --------------------------------

about him in order to lower or destroy his popularity and significance.

"His colleagues began delivering addresses in their temples proving exactly the opposite of all that the priest Abdil had preached.

"At last it came to the point that the priesthood began to bribe various beings who had 'Hasnamuss' properties to plan and commit every kind of outrage upon this poor Abdil; and, indeed, these terrestrial nullities with the properties mentioned even tried on several occasions to destroy his existence by sprinkling poison on the various edible offerings brought to him.

"In spite of all this, the number of sincere admirers of his preaching daily increased.

"Finally, the whole corporation of the priesthood could stand it no longer; and on a sad day for my friend, a general ecumenical trial was held, which lasted four days.

"By the sentence of this general ecumenical council, not only was this Earth friend of mine completely excommunicated from the priesthood, but, at the same council, his colleagues also organized means for his further persecution.

"All this, of course, had little by little a strong effect on the psyche of the ordinary beings, so that even those around him who had formerly esteemed him also began gradually to avoid him and to repeat every kind of calumny about him.

had not personally heard it.

"It is interesting to notice, that it was the custom then, for priests to exist simply on the gifts of their parishioners; this priest Abdil had also been in the habit of receiving from the parishioners every kind of product for his ordinary exist-ence—gifts of the roast and boiled 'corpses' of beings of various exterior forms, for instance, 'chickens,' 'sheep,' 'geese,' and so on. But, after this famous sermon of his nobody brought him any of these customary gifts; they brought or sent him only fruits, flowers, handiwork, and so on.

"The day following his sermon, this Earth friend of mine, at once found himself what is called the 'fashionable priest' for all the citizens of the town 'Koorkalai'; and not only was the temple where he officiated always crammed with beings of the town 'Koorkalai,' but he was also in demand to speak in other temples.

"Such sermons concerning Sacrificial offerings he delivered many times, and every time the number of his admirers grew and grew, so that he became popular not only among the beings of the town 'Koorkalai,' but also of the whole of Tik-liamish.

"How it would all have ended I do not know, if the whole priesthood, that is, men-beings of the same profession as my friend, had not become alarmed and anxious on account of his popularity, and had not opposed everything he preached.

"These colleagues of his were obviously afraid, that if the custom of 'sacrifice' should disappear, their own excellent incomes would go with it, and that their authority would first totter and finally shake all to nothing.

"As day by day the number of this priest Abdil's enemies thereupon increased, fresh slanders and innuendoes

appeared, designed to lower or destroy his popularity and significance.

"His colleagues began delivering addresses in their temples, conclusively prov-ing the opposite of all that the priest Abdil had said in his sermon.

"At last it came to the point that the priesthood already began paying various beings with 'Hasnamuss' properties to plan and carry out every kind of outrage upon this poor Abdil; and in fact, these earth nullities with the properties men-tioned, came to such a point, that they even tried on several occasions to destroy his existence by sprinkling poison on the various edible gifts brought to him.

"Notwithstanding all this, the number of sincere admirers of his preaching also daily increased.

"Finally, the whole corporation of the priesthood could stand it no longer and on a sad day for my friend, a general ecumenical trial was held, which lasted four days.

"By the sentence of this general ecumenical trial, this Earth friend of mine was not only absolutely excommunicated from the priesthood, but at the same coun-cil, his colleagues also organized his further prosecution.

"Little by little, all this, of course, had a strong effect upon the psyche of ordin-ary beings, so that even those around him, who had formerly esteemed him, then also began gradually avoiding him and repeating every kind of calumny about

Even those who only a day before had sent him flowers and various other offerings and had almost worshiped him also soon became such bitter enemies of his, owing to the constant gossip, that it was as if he had not only injured them personally, but had slaughtered and butchered all their near and dear ones.

"Such is the psyche of the beings of that peculiar planet.

"In short, owing to his sincere good will to those around him, this good friend of mine endured a great deal. Even

--------------------------------- *203* ---------------------------------

this would have been, perhaps, nothing, if the climax of unconscionableness on the part of the colleagues of my friend and the other terrestrial 'God-like' beings around him had not brought all this to an end; that is to say, they killed him.

"And this occurred in the following way:

"My friend had no relatives at all in the city Koorkalai, having been born in some distant place.

"And as for the hundreds of servants and other ordinary terrestrial nullities who had been around him owing to his former importance, they, by this time, had gradually left him, naturally because my friend was no longer important.

"Toward the end there remained with him only one very old being who had been with him quite a long time.

"To tell the truth, this old man had remained with him only on account of old age which, owing to abnormal being-existence, most of the beings there reach; that is to say, on account of his complete uselessness for anything required under the conditions of being-existence there.

"He simply had no other place to go to, and that was why he did not desert my friend, but stayed with him even when he had lost his importance and was being persecuted.

"Going into my friend's room one sad morning, this old man saw that he had been killed and that his planetary body had been hacked to pieces.

"Knowing that I was his friend, he at once ran to me to tell me about it.

"I have already told you, that I had begun to love him as one of my nearests. So when I learned about this terrible fact, there almost occurred in my whole presence a 'Skinikoonartzino,' that is to say, the connection between my separate being-centers was almost shattered.

--------------------------------- *204* ---------------------------------

"But during the day I feared that the same or other unconscionable beings might commit further outrages on my friend's planetary body, so I decided at least to prevent the possible actualization of what I feared.

"I therefore immediately hired several suitable beings for a great sum of money and, unbeknown to anybody else, had his planetary body removed and temporarily placed in my Selchan, that is, on my raft which was moored not far away on the river Oksoseria, and which I had not disposed of because I had intended to sail on it from there to the sea Kolhidious to our ship *Occasion*.

"This sad end of my friend's existence did not prevent his preachings and persuasions about the cessation of Sacrificial-Offerings having a strong effect on many, even on a great many.

him. Those who only a day before had been sending him flowers and various other gifts and almost worshipping him, owing to the constant gossip, even they also soon became his bitter enemies. It was as if he had not only injured them personally, but had cut the throats of and slaughtered all their kith and kin.

"Such is the psyche of the beings of that peculiar planet. In short, thanks to his sincere goodwill to those around him, this good friend of mine underwent a great deal. But even

this might have been nothing, if the climax of baseness on the part of the colleagues of my friend and his other Earth 'god-like' beings around him had not put the lid on it; namely, they killed him.

"And this occurred in the following way:

"My friend had no relatives at all in the city 'Koorkalai,' having been born in some distant place.

"And as for the hundreds of servants and other ordinary terrestrial ciphers who surrounded him when he was important, they of course trickled away from him during this period, since my friend was important no longer.

"Towards the end there remained with him only one very old being who had been with him for a very long time.

"To tell the truth, this old man had remained with him only on account of that old age which, owing to the abnormal being-existence most of the beings there reach, that is to say, on account of his complete uselessness for anything required under the conditions of being-existence there.

"Having no other place to go to, he did not desert my friend, but stayed to exist with him even during the time when he had lost his importance and during his persecution.

"This same old man on going into my friend's room one sad morning saw that he had been killed and that his planetary body had been hacked to pieces.

"Knowing that I was friends with him, he at once ran to me to tell me about it.

"I have already told you, that I had begun to love him as one of my nearest, so that when I learned about this terrible event, there almost occurred in my whole 'presence' a 'Skinikoonartzino,' that is to say, the connection between my separate being-centers was almost shattered.

"But during the day I felt afraid that the same or some similar unconscionable beings like them might commit further outrages on the parts of my friend's planetary body, so I decided at least to prevent the possibility of this fear being realized.

"I therefore, unbeknown to anybody else, immediately hired several suitable beings for a great sum of money and had his planetary body removed and placed temporarily in my 'Selchan,' that is, on my raft which was moored not far away on the river 'Oksoseria.' I had not disposed of it because I had it in mind to sail on it from there to the Sea Kolhidious to our ship 'Occasion.'

"This sad end of my friend's existence did not prevent his preachings and persuasions about the cessation of sacrifices having a strong effect upon many, even upon very many.

"And indeed, the quantity of slaughterings for Sacrificial-Offerings began very perceptibly to diminish and one could see that even if the custom were not abolished completely with time, it would at least be considerably mitigated.

"And, for the time being, that was sufficient for me.

"As there was no reason for me to stay there any longer, I decided to return immediately to the sea Kolhidious and there to consider what to do further with the planetary body of my friend.

"When I arrived on our ship *Occasion* I found an etherogram for me from Mars in which I was informed of the arrival there of another party of beings from the planet Karatas, and that speedy return there was desired.

"Thanks to this etherogram a very strange idea came into my head—namely, I thought that instead of disposing of the planetary body of my friend on the planet Earth, I might take it with me and give it to the presence of the planet Mars.

"I decided to carry out this idea of mine as I was

-------------------------------- 205 --------------------------------

afraid that my friend's enemies who hated him might make a search for his planetary body, and if they had chanced to learn where it had been given to the presence of that planet, or, as your favorites say, 'buried,' then doubtless they would have found it and perpetrated some atrocity on it.

"And so, from the sea Kolhidious, I soon ascended on the ship *Occasion* to the planet Mars, where our beings and several kind Martians, who had already learned of the events which had taken place on the planet Earth, paid due respect to the planetary body I had taken with me.

"They buried him with the ceremonies customary on the planet Mars, and over the spot they erected a corresponding construction.

"Anyhow, this was the first and surely will be the last what your favorites call 'grave,' for a being of the planet Earth on this so near yet so far and, for the terrestrial beings, quite inaccessible planet Mars.

"I learned afterwards that this story reached His All-Quarters-Maintainer, the Most Great Archangel 'Setrenotzinarco,' the All-Quarters-Maintainer of that part of the Universe to which that system Ors belongs, and that He manifested his pleasure by giving to whom it was proper, a command concerning the soul of this terrestrial friend of mine.

"On the planet Mars I was indeed expected by several beings of our tribe who had newly arrived from the planet Karatas. Among them, by the way, was also your grandmother who, according to the indications of the chief Zirlikners of the planet Karatas, had been assigned to me as the passive half for the continuance of my line."

-------------------------------- 206 --------------------------------

"And indeed, the quantity of such slaughterings began very perceptibly to diminish and one could see that with time even if the custom were not abolished completely, at least it would be considerably mitigated.

"And that was enough for me for the time being. As there was no reason for me to stay there any longer, I decided to return immediately to the Sea 'Kolhidious' and there to consider what further to do with the planetary body of my friend.

"When I arrived on our ship 'Occasion,' an etherogram from Mars awaited me in which I was informed of the arrival there of still another party of beings from the planet Karatas, and that my earliest return there was desired.

"Thanks to this etherogram a very strange notion came into my mind, namely, I thought that instead of disposing of the planetary body of my friend on the Planet Earth, I might take it with me and return it to the 'presence' of the planet Mars.

"I decided to carry out this idea of mine as I was

afraid that my friend's enemies who hated him might make a search for his planetary body, and if they should chance to learn where it had been returned to the 'presence' of that planet, or as your favorites say—'buried,' then doubtless they would find it and perpetrate some or other atrocity upon it.

"Soon from the Sea Kolhidious I indeed ascended to the planet Mars on the ship 'Occasion.'

"Already there on the planet Mars, our beings and several kind Martians, having learned of the events which had taken place on the planet Earth, paid due respect to the planetary body I had taken with me.

"They 'buried' him with the ceremonies customary on the planet Mars, and over the spot they erected a suitable construction.

"Anyhow, this was the first and surely it will be the last, as your favorites call it 'grave' for a being of the planet Earth, on this at once so near and so far, and, for the terrestrial beings, quite inaccessible planet Mars.

"I learned afterwards that this story reached His All-Quarters-Maintainer Most Great Archangel 'Setrenotzinarco,' the All-Quarters-Maintainer of that part of the Universe to which that system Ors also belongs, and that He manifested His pleasure by giving to whom it was proper a command concerning the soul of this terrestrial friend of mine.

"On the planet Mars I was indeed awaited by several newly arrived beings of our tribe from the planet Karatas. Incidentally, among them was also your grandmother, who, according to the indications of the chief Zirlikners of the planet Karatas, had been assigned to me as a passive half for the continuance of my line."

The Third Flight of Beelzebub to the Planet Earth

A FTER a brief pause Beelzebub continued to speak further as follows:
"This time I remained at home, that is, on the planet Mars, only a short while, just long enough to see and talk with those who had newly arrived, and to give certain directions of a common tribal character.

"Having disposed of the said affairs, I descended again to your planet with the intention of continuing the pursuit of my aim, that is, the uprooting among these strange three-centered beings of their terrifying custom of doing as it were Divine work by destroying the existence of beings of other brain-systems.

"On this third descent of mine to the planet Earth our ship *Occasion* did not alight on the sea Kolhidious, which is now called there Caspian Sea, but on the sea called at that period the 'Sea of Beneficence.'

"We decided to alight on this sea because I wished this time to go to the capital of the beings of the second group of the continent Ashhark, then named the City Gob, which was situated on the southeastern shore of that sea.

"At that time, the City Gob was already a large city, and was well known over the whole planet for its production of the best 'fabrics' and the best what are called 'precious ornaments.'

"The City Gob was situated on both banks of the mouth of a large river called the 'Keria-chi' which flowed into the Sea of Beneficence and which had its rise in the eastern heights of this country.

"Into this Sea of Beneficence, on its western side, another large river flowed called the 'Naria-chi.'

"And it was in the valleys of these two large rivers that

------------------------------ *207* ------------------------------

the beings of the second group of the continent Ashhark chiefly existed.

"If you wish, my dear boy, I shall also tell you a little of the history of the rise of this group of beings of the continent Ashhark," Beelzebub said to Hassein.

"Yes, Grandfather, yes. I shall listen to you with great interest and much gratitude," replied his grandson.

Then Beelzebub began:

"A long, long time before that period to which my present tale relates, namely, long before that second great catastrophe to that ill-fated planet, while the continent Atlantis was still existing and at the height of its splendor, one of the ordinary three-centered beings of that continent 'invented'—as my latest detailed investigations and researches cleared up—that the powdered horn of a being of that particular exterior form then called a 'Pirmaral' was very effective against what they call 'diseases' of every kind. His 'invention' was afterwards widely spread by various 'freaks' on your planet, and also there was gradually crystallized in the Reason of the ordinary beings there an illusory directing factor, from which, by the way, there is formed in the whole of the presence of each of your favorites, especially of the contemporary ones, the Reason of what is called their 'waking-existence,'

The Third Flight of Beelzebub to the Planet Earth

A FTER a brief pause Beelzebub continued to speak further thus . . . He said:
"This time I remained at home, that is, on the planet Mars, only a short while, just long enough to see and talk with the newly arrived, and to give certain directions of a general tribal character.

"Having disposed of the said affairs, I descended again to your planet with the intention of continuing the pursuit of my aim, that is, the uprooting from among these strange three-centered beings, of their horrible custom of doing good as it were, by destroying the existence of beings of other brain-systems than their own.

"On this third descent of mine to the planet Earth our ship Occasion landed not on the Sea 'Kolhidious,' which, in contemporary times is there called the Caspian Sea, but on the Sea, called at that period, the 'Sea of Beneficence.'

"We decided to land on this sea, because I proposed to visit this time the capital of the beings of the second group of the continent Ashhark, then named the 'City Gob,' which was situated on the south eastern shore of that sea.

"At that time, the 'City Gob' also was a considerable city, and it was well known over the whole planet as a place that produced the best fabrics and the best as they are called 'precious ornaments.'

"The 'City Gob' was situated on both banks of the mouth of a large river called the 'Keria-chi' which flowed into the Sea of Beneficence and which had its rise in the eastern heights of this country.

"Into this Sea of Beneficence, on its western side, still another large river called the 'Naria-chi' flowed.

"And it was just in the valleys of these two large rivers that

---

the beings of the second group of the continent Ashhark mainly existed.

"If you wish, my dear boy, I will also tell you a little of the history of the rise of this group of beings of the continent Ashhark," Beelzebub asked Hassein.

"Yes, Grandfather, yes . . . I shall listen to you with great interest and great gratitude," replied his Grandson.

Then Beelzebub began thus:

"A very long time before that period there to which my present tale relates, namely, long before that second great catastrophe to that ill-starred planet, and while the continent Atlantis was still existing and flourishing, a certain one of the ordinary three-centered beings of that continent 'invented,' as my latest detailed investigation and researches cleared up, that the powdered horn of a being of a particular exterior form, then called a 'Pirmaral' was very effective against what they called 'diseases' of every kind; and his 'invention' afterwards was widely spread by various 'freaks' there on your planet, and also there was gradually crystallized in the reason of the ordinary beings there, an ephemeral governing factor, of which factor, I must here say, there is just formed in the whole of the 'presence' of every one of your favorites, especially of the contemporary ones, the Reasonab-

which factor is the chief cause of the frequent change in convictions accumulated in them.

"Owing to just this factor, crystallized in the presences of the three-brained beings of your planet of that period, it became the rule that anyone, as they say, who 'fell ill' of some disease or other invariably had to be given this powdered horn to swallow.

"It is not without interest to remark that Pirmarals breed there at the present time also; but, since contemporary beings take them merely for one of the species of being they collectively call 'deer,' they have no special name for them.

------------------------------ *208* ------------------------------

"So, my boy, as the beings of the continent Atlantis destroyed very many beings of that form for the sake of these horns, they very soon became extinct.

"Then a number of beings of that continent, who had by this time already made a profession of hunting these beings, went hunting for them on other continents and islands.

"This hunting was very difficult, because for the capture of these Pirmarals a great many of these hunter beings were required; so these professional hunters always took their whole families with them for assistance.

"Once several of these hunter families joined together and set off to hunt the Pirmarals on a very remote continent then called 'Iranan,' which later, after having been changed owing to the second catastrophe, was called 'the continent Ashhark.'

"This was the same continent your contemporary favorites now call 'Asia.'

"For my further tales concerning these three-brained beings who have taken your fancy, it will be very useful for you, I think, if I emphasize here that on account of various disturbances during the second terrestrial catastrophe, several parts of the continent Iranan entered within the planet, and other terra firmas emerged in their place and attached themselves to this continent, which in consequence became considerably changed and became in size almost what the continent Atlantis had been for the planet Earth before the catastrophe.

"Well, then, my boy, while this said group of hunters were once with their families pursuing a herd of these Pirmarals, they reached the shores of the water-space which was later called the Sea of Beneficence.

"Both the sea itself and its rich and fertile shores so

------------------------------ *209* ------------------------------

greatly pleased this group of hunters that they did not wish to return to the continent Atlantis, and from that time on they remained to exist there, on those shores.

"That country was at that time indeed so excellent and so 'Sooptaninalnian' for ordinary being-existence that no being who could think at all could help liking it.

"On that 'terra firma' part of the surface of your planet, not only did there exist at that period multitudes of two-brained beings of the said exterior form, namely, Pirmarals, but around this water-space were also multitudes of various kinds of 'fruit trees,' whose fruit then still served for your favorites as the principal product for their 'first being-food.'

ility of what is called their 'waking existence,' and which factor is the chief cause of frequent change in the convictions forming in them.

"Owing just to this factor, crystallized in the presences of the three-brained beings of your planet of that period, it became the rule that anyone, as they say, falling ill of this or that disease, should invariably be given this powdered horn to swallow.

"It is not without interest to remark that 'Pirmarals' breed there at the present time also; but, since contemporary beings look upon them merely as one of the species of being they call collectively 'deer,' they have no special name for them.

- -

"So, my boy, as the beings of the continent Atlantis destroyed very many beings of that form for the sake of these horns, very soon they became extinct.

"A number of the beings of that continent who had by this time already made a profession of such hunting, then went hunting for these beings on other continents and islands.

"This hunting being very difficult, because for the capture of these deer a host of these hunter-beings was required, these professional hunters always took their whole families with them for assistance.

"It happened once that several of these hunter families, having joined together, set off for hunting the 'Pirmaral-beings' to a very remote continent then called 'Iranan' though later, after having been changed, owing to the second catastrophe, it was called 'the continent Ashhark.'

"This was just the continent which you contemporary favorites now call Asia.

"For my further tales concerning these three-brained beings, who please you, it will be very useful for you I think, if I emphasize here that on account of various disturbances during the second terrestrial catastrophe, several parts of the continent 'Iranan' entered within the planet, and there emerged in their place, and attached themselves to it other terra-firma, whereby the continent was considerably changed and became almost the equal in size of the continent Atlantis, before the catastrophe.

"So, my boy, this said group of hunters while once with their families pursuing a herd of these 'Pirmarals,' came unawares upon the shores of the water-space that afterwards was called the Sea of Beneficence.

"Both the sea itself and its rich and fertile shores so

- -

greatly delighted this group of hunters that they had no wish to return to the continent Atlantis, but from that time on they remained to exist there.

"That country was indeed so excellent in those days and so 'Sooptaninalnian' for ordinary being-existence, that no being who could think at all could help liking it.

"On that terra-firma part of the surface of your planet, not only at this period did there exist among others, multitudes of the 'two-brained' beings of the said exterior form, namely, 'Pirmaral,' but around this water-space multitudes of various kinds of 'fruit trees' were also formed, whose fruit then still served for your favorites as the principal product of their 'first-being-food.'

"There were then also so many of the one-brained and two-brained beings which your favorites call 'birds' that when they flew in droves it became, as your favorites say, 'quite dark.'

"The water-space situated in the middle of that country and then named the Sea of Beneficence so abounded with fish that they could almost be caught, as they also say, with one's bare hands.

"As for the soil of the shores of the Sea of Beneficence and also of the valleys of the two large rivers flowing into it, any part of them could be adapted for growing anything you like.

"In short, both the climate of this country and everything else so delighted the hunters and their families that none of them, as I have already said, had any desire to return to the continent Atlantis, and from that time on they remained there, and soon adapting themselves to everything, multiplied and existed, as is said, 'on-a-bed-of-roses.'

"At this place in my tale I must tell you about an extraordinary coincidence which later had great consequences

---------------------------- *210* ----------------------------

both for the first beings of this second group and for their descendants of most recent times.

"It seems that at the time when the said hunters from the continent Atlantis reached the Sea of Beneficence and decided to settle there, there was already existing on the shores of the same sea a being from the continent Atlantis who was at that time very important and who belonged to the sect of 'astrosovors' and who was a member of a learned society, the like of which has never since appeared on that planet Earth and probably never will.

"This learned society then existed under the name of 'Akhaldan.'

"And this member of the Akhaldans reached the shores of the Sea of Beneficence on account of the following:

"Just before the second great catastrophe those genuine learned beings then existing on the continent Atlantis, who had organized that truly great learned society there, somehow became aware that something very serious had to happen in Nature, so they began to observe very carefully all the natural phenomena of their continent; but however hard they tried, they could in no way find out what precisely had to happen.

"A little later on and with the same aim, they sent some of their members to other continents and islands, in order, by means of these common observations, perhaps to be able to find out what was impending.

"The members sent were to observe not only Nature on the planet Earth, but also every kind of, as they then expressed themselves there, 'heavenly-phenomena.'

"One of these members, namely, the mentioned important being, had chosen the continent Iranan for his observations and, having migrated there with his servants, had settled on the shores of the said water-space later called the Sea of Beneficence.

"It was just this same learned member of the society

---------------------------- *211* ----------------------------

"There bred there then, also, so many of the one-brained and two-brained-beings which your favorites call 'birds,' that when they flew in a drove, it became, as your favorites say, 'quite dark.'

"The water-space situated in the middle of that country and then named the Sea of Beneficence, so abounded with fish, that they could almost be taken, as they also say, with bare hands.

"As for the soil both of the shores of the Sea of Beneficence and of the valleys of the two large rivers flowing into it, any part of it could be adapted for growing anything you like.

"In short, both the climate of this country and everything else so delighted the hunters and their families, that not one of them, as I have already said, had any desire to return to the continent Atlantis, and from that time on they remained there, and were soon adapted to everything and existing and multiplying as it is said, 'like a merry-go-round.'

"At this place in my tale I must tell you about an extraordinary coincidence of events, which later had great consequences

----

both for the first beings of this second group and for their remotest descendants.

"It seems, that at the time when the said hunters from the continent Atlantis reached the Sea of Beneficence and decided to settle there for good, there was already existing on the shores of the same sea a being from the continent Atlantis and a very important one for those times, who was a member there of a 'learned society,' the like of which there has never again been on that planet Earth and probably never will be.

"This 'learned society' existed then under the name of 'Akhaldan.'

"And this 'Akhaldan' member had gone there to the shores of the Sea of Beneficence for the following reason:

"Just before the second great catastrophe those genuine learned beings then existing on the continent Atlantis who had organized that truly great learned society there, once became aware that something very serious was about to happen in nature, and they set themselves to observe very carefully all the natural phenomena occurring on their continent; but however hard they tried, they could in no way find out what precisely it was that was impending.

"A little later on and with the same object, they sent numbers of their members to other continents and islands, in order, if possible, by means of these common observations, to be able perhaps to learn what awaited them.

"The members who were so sent were to observe not only nature on the planet Earth, but also every kind, as they expressed themselves there, of 'celestial' phenomenon.

"One of their members, namely, the mentioned important being, had chosen as a place for his observations the continent Iranan and having migrated there with his servants, had settled on the shores of just the said water-space later called the Sea of Beneficence.

"It was just this same learned member of the society

Akhaldan who once chanced to meet certain of the mentioned hunters on the shores of the said Sea of Beneficence, and having learned that they had also come from the continent Atlantis, was naturally very glad, and began to establish relations with them.

"And when, shortly afterwards, the continent Atlantis entered within the planet and this learned Akhaldan member had no longer any place to return to, he remained to exist with these hunters in that future Maralpleicie.

"A little later this group of hunters chose this learned being, as the cleverest, to be their chief, and still later . . . this member of the great society Akhaldan married the daughter named Rimala of one of the hunters, and afterwards shared fully in the lives of the founders of the beings of that second group of the continent Iranan, or, as it is called at the present time, 'Asia.'

"A long time passed.

"The beings of this place on the planet Earth were also born and were again destroyed; and the general level of the psyche of this kind of Earth-beings was thereby changed, of course at times for the better, at times for the worse.

"Multiplying, these beings gradually spread over this country more and more widely, although always preferring the shores of the Sea of Beneficence and the valleys of those two large rivers which flowed into it.

"Only much later the center of their common existence was formed on the southeastern shore of the sea; and this place they called the city Gob. This city became the chief place of existence for the head of this second group of beings of the continent Ashhark, whom they called 'king.'

"The duties of this king were here also hereditary and this inheritance began with the first chosen chief, who was the said learned member of the learned society Akhaldan.

"At the time to which the tale I began refers, the king

—————————————————— 212 ——————————————————

for the beings of that second group was the grandson of his great grandson, and his name was 'Konuzion.'

"My latest detailed investigations and researches showed that there had been actualized by that same King Konuzion exceedingly wise and most beneficent measures for uprooting a terrifying evil which had arisen among the beings who by the will of Fate had become his subjects. And he had actualized these said most wise and beneficent measures for the following reason:

"This same King Konuzion once constated that the beings of his community were becoming less and less capable of work, and that crimes, robberies, and violence and many other such things as had never occurred before were on the increase among them, or, if they had occurred, had seemed to be quite exceptional phenomena.

"These constatations surprised and at the same time grieved King Konuzion, who after thinking deeply about it, decided to find out the causes of this sorrowful phenomenon.

"After long observations he finally cleared up for himself that the cause of the phenomenon was a new habit of the beings of his community, namely, their habit

Akhaldan who once chanced to meet certain of the mentioned hunters on the shores of the said Sea of Beneficence, and having learned that they also had come from the continent Atlantis, he was naturally very glad and began to associate with them.

"And when, shortly afterwards, the continent Atlantis was engulfed in the planet and this learned Akhaldan member had no longer any place to return to, he remained to exist with these hunters in that future 'Maralpleicie.'

"A little later this group of hunters chose this learned being, because of his greater reason, to be their chief, and still later . . . this member of the great society Akhaldan married the daughter of one of the hunters, by name 'Rimala,' and afterwards shared fully in the lives of the founders of the beings of that second group of the continent Iranan, or, as it is called at the present time, 'Asia.'

"A long time passed.

"The beings of this place on the planet Earth were also born and again destroyed; and the general level of the psyche of this group of Earth-beings was also naturally changed thereby, now for the better, now for the worse.

"Multiplying, these beings spread gradually over this country widely and ever more widely, although always preferring just the shores of the Sea of Beneficence and the valleys of the two said large rivers flowing into it.

"Only much later a place of common existence was formed on the south eastern shore of the sea; and this place they called the 'City Gob.' This city just became the chief place of existence for the head of this second group of beings of the continent Ashhark, whom they called a 'king.'

"The duties of this king became hereditary here also; and this inheritance began with the first chosen chief, who was just the said member of the learned society Akhaldan.

"At the time to which the tale I began refers, the king

- -

for the beings of that second group was already the grandson of his grandson. His name was 'Konuzion.'

"My latest detailed investigations and researches showed that there had been put into operation by that same King Konuzion exceedingly wise and most beneficent measures for uprooting a 'shocking' evil which had arisen among the beings, who by Fate, had become his subjects. And these said most wise and beneficent measures he had actualized for the following reason.

"This same King Konuzion once constated that the beings of his community were becoming less and less capable of work, and that hitherto unknown crimes, robberies and violence were on the increase among them, and many other such things as had never occurred before, or, if they had occurred, had formerly been quite exceptional.

"These constatations both surprised and at the same time grieved King Konuzion, who after thinking deeply about it, decided to find out the causes of the said sorry state of affairs.

"After long observations he finally cleared up for himself that the cause of the phenomenon lay in a new habit of the beings of his community, namely, their of chewing the seed of a plant then called 'Gulgulian.' This surplanetary formation also arises on the planet Earth at the present time, and those of your favorites who consider themselves 'educated' call it 'Papaveroon,' but the ordinary beings simply call it the 'poppy.'

"Here it must without fail be noticed that the beings of Maralpleicie then only had a passion for chewing those seeds of the mentioned surplanetary formation which had without fail to be gathered at the time of what is called 'ripeness.'

"In the course of his further close observations and impartial investigations King Konuzion clearly understood that these seeds contained a 'something' that could

------------------------------ 213 ------------------------------

completely change, for the time being, all the established habits of the psyche of those beings who introduced this something into themselves, with the result that they saw, understood, felt, sensed, and acted quite otherwise than they were previously accustomed to see, sense, act, and so on.

"For instance, a crow would appear to them to be a peacock; a trough of water, a sea; a harsh clatter, music; good will, enmity; insults, love; and so on and so forth.

"When King Konuzion became clearly convinced of all this, he immediately dispatched everywhere trusted and faithful subjects of his strictly to command in his name all beings of his community to cease chewing the seeds of the mentioned plant; he also arranged for the punishment and fine of those beings who should disobey this order.

"Thanks to these measures of his, the chewing of the said seeds seemed to diminish in the country of Maralpleicie; but after a very short time it was discovered that the number of those who chewed had only seemingly diminished; in reality, they were even more than before.

"Having understood this, the wise King Konuzion thereupon resolved to punish still more severely those who should continue chewing; and at the same time he strengthened the surveillance of his subjects and also the strictness of the enforcement of the punishment of the guilty.

"And he himself began going about everywhere in the city of Gob, personally examining the guilty and impressing them by various punishments, physical and moral.

"In spite of all this, however, the desired result was not obtained, as the number of those who chewed increased more and more in the city of Gob itself, and corresponding reports from other places in the territories subject to him also increased daily.

------------------------------ 214 ------------------------------

"It then became clear that the number of those who chewed had increased still more because many of the three-brained beings who had never previously chewed now began chewing merely out of what is called 'curiosity,' which is one of the peculiarities of the psyche of the three-brained beings of that planet which has taken your fancy, that is to say, curiosity to find out what effect those seeds

habit of chewing the seeds of a plant then called 'Gulgulian.' This surplanetary formation also arises on the planet Earth at the present time, and those of your favorites who consider themselves 'educated' call it 'Papaveroon,' but the ordinary among them simply call it the 'poppy.'

"Here it must without fail be noticed that the beings of Maralpleicie then developed a passion for chewing the seeds of the mentioned surplanetary formation, and these seeds were necessarily gathered at a certain moment of what is called 'ripeness.'

"In the course of his further close observations and impartial researches the King Konuzion clearly understood that these seeds contained 'something' that could

completely change for the time being, all the established habits of the psyche of those beings who introduced it into themselves, with the result that they saw, understood, felt, sensed and acted quite otherwise than they were previously accustomed to see, sense, act and so on.

"For instance, a crow would appear to them to be a peacock; a vessel of water— a sea; a harsh clatter—music; good will they would take for enmity; insults for love; and so on and so forth.

"When King Konuzion became clearly convinced of all this, he immediately dispatched everywhere numbers of those intimate subjected beings devoted to him, strictly to command in his name all beings of his community to cease the chewing of the seeds of the mentioned plant; he also arranged for the punishment and fine of those beings who should disobey this order of his.

"Thanks to these measures of his, the use of the said seeds for chewing showed signs of diminishing in the country of Maralpleicie.

"But it soon afterwards turned out that the number of those who chewed had diminished only apparently; in reality, they were more than before.

"Having understood this, the wise King Konuzion thereupon resolved to punish still more severely those who should continue chewing; and at the same time he strengthened both the surveillance or his subjects and also the strictness of the enforcement of the punishment of the guilty.

"And he himself began going everywhere in the city Gob itself, personally examining the guilty and impressing them by various punishments both physical and moral.

"In spite of it all, however, the desired result was not obtained; the number of those who chewed continued to increase in the city Gob itself; and the returns from other places also in the territories subject to him, correspondingly increased daily.

"It was shown, moreover, that the number of those who chewed had increased still more, because many of the three-brained beings who had never chewed before, then began chewing out of what is called 'curiosity,' which is one of the peculiarities of the psyche of the three-brained beings of that planet that pleases you; curiosity, namely, to try the effects of those seeds whose chewing was forbidden

had, the chewing of which was prohibited and punished by the king with such insistence and relentless severity.

"I must emphasize here, that though the said particularity of their psyche began to be crystallized in your favorites immediately after the loss of Atlantis, yet in none of the beings of former epochs did it function so blatantly as it does now in the contemporary three-brained beings there; they have more of it perhaps, than there are hairs on a 'Toosook.'

"So, my boy . . .

"When the wise King Konuzion finally became quite convinced that it was not possible by the described measures to extirpate the passion for chewing the seeds of Gulgulian, and saw that the only result of his measures was the death of several who were punished, he abrogated all the measures he had previously taken and again began to think seriously about a search for some other real means for destroying this evil, lamentable for his community.

"As I learned much later—owing to a very ancient surviving monument—the great King Konuzion then returned to his chamber and for eighteen days neither ate nor drank but only very seriously thought and thought.

"It must in any case be noticed here, that those latest researches of mine showed that King Konuzion was then particularly anxious to find a means of uprooting this evil, because all the affairs of his community were going from bad to worse.

------------------------------ 215 ------------------------------

"The beings who were addicted to this passion almost ceased to work; the flow of what is called money into the communal treasury entirely ceased and the ultimate ruin of the community seemed to be inevitable.

"Finally the wise king decided to deal with this evil indirectly, namely, by playing on the weaknesses in the psyche of the beings of his community. With this aim he invented a very original 'religious doctrine' corresponding to the psyche of the beings of that time; and this invention of his he spread broadcast among all his subjects by every means at his disposal.

"In this religious doctrine it was said, among other things, that far from our continent Ashhark was a larger island where existed our 'Mister God.'

"I must tell you that in those days not one of the ordinary beings knew that, besides their planet Earth, other cosmic concentrations existed.

"The beings of the planet Earth of those days were even certain that the scarcely visible 'white-points' far away in space were nothing more than the pattern on the 'veil' of the 'world,' that is to say, just of their planet; as, in their notions then, the 'whole-world' consisted, as I have said, of their planet alone.

"They were also convinced that this veil was supported like a canopy on special pillars, the ends of which rested on their planet.

"In that ingeniously original 'religious doctrine' of the wise King Konuzion it was said that Mister God had intentionally attached to our souls the organs and limbs we now have to protect us against our environment, and to enable us effi-

and pushed by the king with such insistence and relentless severity.

"I must emphasize here that though that said particularity of their psyche was crystallized in your favorites immediately after the perishing of the continent Atlantis, yet in none of the beings of former epochs did it function so blatantly as it does now in the contemporary three-brained beings there; they have more of it perhaps, than there are hairs on a 'Toosook.'

"So, my boy . . .

"When the wise King Konuzion became finally quite convinced that by the described measures it was impossible to uproot the passion for chewing the seeds of 'Gulgulian,' and saw that the only result of his measures was the death of several who were punished, he abandoned all the measures he had previously taken and again pondered on the search for some other real means for destroying this evil, lamentable for his community.

"As I learned much later—and I learned it through a very ancient surviving monument—the great King Konuzion then returned to his chamber and for eighteen days neither ate nor drank but only very seriously thought and thought.

"You must notice here, in any case, that those latest researches of mine showed that King Konuzion was then, particularly anxious to find a means of uprooting this evil, also because all the affairs of his community were going from bad to worse.

- -

"The beings who abandoned themselves to this passion almost ceased to work; what is called the money revenue, entirely ceased flowing into the communal treasury; and the ultimate ruin of the community seemed to be inevitable.

"Finally the wise king decided to deal with this evil indirectly, namely, by playing on the weaknesses in the psyche of the beings of his community; and he then first invented for that purpose that which later existed under the denomination 'Religion.' Namely, he invented and formulated a certain what is called 'religious doctrine' adapted to the psyche of the beings then; and this invention of his he spread broadcast among his subjects by every means at his disposal.

"In this first of 'religions doctrines' on the planet Earth, it was said, among other things, that far from our continent Ashhark was a large island where existed our 'Mister God.'

"I must tell you that in those days not one of the ordinary beings was as yet aware that besides their planet Earth still other cosmic concentrations existed.

"The beings of the planet Earth of those days were even certain that the scarcely visible 'white points' far away in space were nothing more than the pattern on the veil of the 'world'; that is to say, just of their planet; since in their notions then the 'whole world' consisted, as I have said, of their planet only.

"They were also convinced that this veil was supported like a canopy on special pillars, whose ends rested on their planet.

"In that ingeniously strange 'religious doctrine' of the wise King Konuzion it was said, that 'Mister God' had intentionally attached to our souls these organs and limbs we now have to protect us against our surroundings, and to enable us ciently and profitably to serve both himself personally and the 'souls' already taken to that island of His.

"And when we die and our soul is liberated from all these specially attached organs and limbs,

- *216* -

it becomes what it should really be, and is then immediately taken just to this island of His, where our Mister God, in accordance with how our soul with its added parts has existed here on our continent Ashhark, assigns to it an appropriate place for its further existence.

"If the soul has fulfilled its duties honestly and conscientiously, Mister God leaves it, for its further existence, on His island; but the soul that here on the continent Ashhark has idled or discharged its duties indolently and negligently, that has in short, existed only for the gratification of the desires of the parts attached to it, or finally, that has not kept His commandments—such a soul our Mister God sends for its further existence to a neighboring island of smaller size.

"Here, on the continent Ashhark, exist many 'spirits' attendant upon Him, who walk among us in 'caps-of-invisibility,' thanks to which they can constantly watch us unnoticed and either inform our Mister God of all our doings or report them to Him on the 'Day-of-Judgment.'

"We cannot in any way conceal from them, either any of our doings, or any of our thoughts.

"It was still further said that just like our continent Ashhark, all the other continents and islands of the world had been created by our Mister God and now existed as I have said, only to serve Him and the deserving 'souls' already dwelling on His island.

"The continents and islands of the world are all places, as it were, for preparation, and storehouses for everything necessary for this island of His.

"That island on which Mister God Himself and the deserving souls exist is called 'Paradise,' and existence there is just 'Roses, Roses.'

"All its rivers are of milk, their banks of honey; nobody needs to toil or work there; everything necessary for a happy, carefree, and blissful existence is there, because

- *217* -

everything requisite is supplied there in superabundance from our own and the other continents and islands of the world.

"This island Paradise is full of young and lovely women, of all the peoples and races of the world; and each of them belongs for the asking to the 'soul' that desires her.

"In certain public squares of that superb island, mountains of various articles of adornment are always kept, from the most brilliant diamonds to the deepest turquoise; and every 'soul' can take anything he likes, also without the least hindrance.

"In other public squares of that beatific island are piled huge mountains of sweetmeats specially prepared with essence of 'poppy' and 'hemp'; and every 'soul' may take as much as he pleases at any time of the day or night.

efficiently and profitably to serve both himself personally and the 'souls' already taken to that island of His.

"At our death, our soul is liberated from these specially attached organs and limbs

- -

and becoming what it should really be, is just then immediately taken to this island of His, where our 'Mister God' according to how our soul has existed with the added parts here, on our continent Ashhark, there assigns to it an appropriate place for its further existence.

"If the soul has honestly and conscientiously fulfilled its duties, 'Mister God' leaves it, for its further existence, on his island; but the soul that here on the continent Ashhark has loafed or has discharged its duties idly and negligently, that has in short, existed only for the gratification of the desires of the parts attached to it, or, finally, that has not kept his commandments—such a soul our 'Mister God' sends for its further existence to a neighboring island of smaller size.

"Here, on the continent Ashhark, exist many 'Spirits' attendant upon Him, who walk among us in 'caps of darkness,' thanks to which they can constantly watch us and either inform our 'Mister God' of all our doings or report them to Him on the day of 'Judgment.'

"We cannot by any means conceal from them, either any of our doings, or any of our thoughts either.

"It was still further said that just like our continent Ashhark, all the other continents and islands of the 'world' were created by our 'Mister God' and now exist as I have said, only to serve Him and the deserving 'souls' already dwelling on His island.

"The continents and islands of the 'world' are all places, as it were, of preparation, and storehouses for everything necessary for this island of His.

"That island on which 'Mister God' Himself and the deserving souls exist is called 'Paradise,' and existence thereon is just 'Roses, Roses.'

"All its rivers are of milk, their banks of honey; nobody needs to work or toil there; everything necessary for a happy, carefree, and blissful existence is there, because

- -

everything demanded is supplied there from our own and the other continents and islands of the 'world' in superabundance.

"This island 'Paradise' is full of young and lovely women, collected from all the peoples and races of the world; and each of them belongs for the asking to the 'soul' that fancies her.

"In certain public squares of that superb island mountains of various articles of adornment are always kept, from the most brilliant diamonds to the deepest turquoise; and every 'soul' can take anything he likes, also without the least hindrance.

"In other public squares of that beatific island are piled huge mountains of sweetmeats specially prepared with essence of 'poppy' and 'hemp'; and every soul may take as much as he pleases at any time of the day or night.

"There are no diseases there; and of course, none of those 'lice' or 'flies' that give us all no peace here, and blight our whole existence.

"The other, smaller island, to which our Mister God sends for their further existence the 'souls' whose temporary physical parts have been idle here and have not existed according to His commandments, is called 'Hell.'

"All the rivers of this island are of burning pitch; the whole air stinks like a skunk at bay. Swarms of horrible beings blow police-whistles in every square; and all the 'furniture,' 'carpets,' 'beds,' and so on there, are made of fine needles with their points sticking out.

"One very salted cake is given once a day to every 'soul' on this island; and there is not a single drop of drinking water there. Many other things are also there of a kind that the beings of Earth not only would not like to encounter, but not even experience in thought.

"When I first came to the country of Maralpleicie, all the three-brained beings of that country were followers of a 'religion' based on the just-mentioned ingenious

------------------------------ 218 ------------------------------

'religious-doctrine,' and this 'religion' was then in full bloom.

"To the inventor himself of this ingenious 'religious-doctrine,' namely, the wise King Konuzion, the sacred 'Rascooarno' had occurred long before this time, that is to say, he had long previously 'died.'

"But of course owing once again to the strangeness of the psyche of your favorites, his invention had taken such a strong hold there that not a single being in the whole country of Maralpleicie then doubted the truth of its peculiar tenets.

"Here also in the city Gob, from the first day of my arrival, I began visiting the 'Kaltaani,' which were already called 'Chaihana.'

"It must be noticed that although the custom of Sacrificial-Offerings was also flourishing at that period in the country of Maralpleicie, it was not on the large scale on which it had flourished in the country Tikliamish.

"There in the city Gob I began deliberately looking for a corresponding being, in order to make friends with him, as I had in the city Koorkalai.

"And indeed I soon found such a friend here also, but this time he was not a 'priest' by profession.

"My friend here turned out to be the proprietor of a large Chaihana; and although I became, as it is said there, on very good terms with him, nevertheless I never had that strange 'tie' with him which arose in my essence towards the priest Abdil in the city Koorkalai.

"Although I had already existed a whole month in the city Gob, I had neither decided upon nor undertaken anything practical for my aim. I simply wandered about the city Gob, visiting first the various Chaihana, and only later the Chaihana of my new friend there.

"During this time I became familiar with many of the manners and customs of this second group and

------------------------------ 219 ------------------------------

also with the fine points of their religion; and at the end of the month I decided to attain my aim here also, through their religion.

"There are no diseases there; and, of course, none of those 'lice' or 'flies' that give us all no peace here, and blight our whole existence.

"The other island, that rather small island, to which our 'Mister God' sends for their further existence the souls whose temporary physical parts have been idle here, have loafed and failed to exist according to His commandments, is called 'Hell.'

"All the rivers of this island are of burning pitch; the whole air stinks like a skunk at bay, swarms of horrible beings blow police whistles in every square; and all the 'furniture,' 'carpets,' 'beds' and so on there present, are made of fine needles with their points sticking out.

"To every soul on this island a single very salted cake is given once a day; and there is not a drop of drinking water there. Still many other things also are there of the kind, that the beings of Earth would not only wish not to encounter, but not even to imagine.

"When I first came to the country of Maralpleicie, all the three-brained beings of that country were followers of the 'religion' based on the just mentioned in-

genious 'religious-doctrine,' and this 'religion' was then at its zenith.

"To the inventor himself of this ingenious 'religious-doctrine,' namely, the wise King Konuzion, the sacred 'Rascooarno' had long before occurred, that is to say, he had 'died' already long previously.

"But owing once again to the strangeness of the psyche of your favorites, his invention had naturally taken such deep hold there, that not a single being in the whole country of Maralpleicie then doubted the truth of its peculiar tenets.

"Here also in the City Gob, from the first day of my arrival, I began visiting the 'Kaltaani'—or, as they were now called, 'Chaihana.'

"It must be noticed that although there also, in the country Maralpleicie, the custom of sacrificing was flourishing at that period, it was not on the large scale on which it had flourished in the country Tikliamish.

"There in the City Gob I began deliberately looking for a suitable being, in order to make friends with him, as I had in the city Koorkalai.

"And indeed I soon found such a friend here also, but this time he was not a 'priest' by profession.

"My friend here turned out to be the proprietor of a large 'Chaihana'; and although I became, as it is said there, on very good terms with him, nevertheless I never felt that strange 'tie' with him which my essence had experienced toward the priest Abdil in the city Koorkalai.

"Although I had already existed a whole month in the City Gob, I had neither decided upon nor undertaken anything practical for my aim. I simply wandered about the City Gob, visiting first the various 'Chaihana,' and only later the 'Chaihana' of my new friend there.

"During this time I became familiar with the manners and customs of this second group and

also with the niceties of their religion; and in the course of a month I decided to attain my aim here also, through their religion.

"After serious pondering I found it necessary to add something to the 'religious-doctrine' existing there, and I counted on being able, like the wise King Konuzion, to spread this addition of mine effectively among them.

"Just then I invented that those spirits in 'caps-of-invisibility' who, as it was said in that great religion, watch our deeds and thoughts in order to report them later to our Mister God, are none other than just the beings of other forms, which exist among us.

"It is just they who watch us and report everything to our Mister God.

"But we people not only fail to pay them their due honor and respect, but we even destroy their existences for our food as well as for our Sacrificial-Offerings.

"I particularly emphasized in my preaching that not only ought we not to destroy the existence of the beings of other forms in honor of Mister God, but that, on the contrary, we ought to try to win their favor and to beseech them at least not to report to Mister God those little evil acts of ours which we do involuntarily.

"And this addition of mine I began to spread by every possible means; of course, very cautiously.

"At first, I spread this invention of mine through my new friend there, the proprietor of the Chaihana.

"I must tell you that his Chaihana was almost the largest in the whole city Gob; and it was very famous for its reddish liquid, of which the beings of the planet Earth are very fond.

"So there were always a great many customers there, and it was open day and night.

"Not only did the inhabitants of the city itself go there, but also all the visitors from the whole of Maralpleicie.

--------------------------------- *220* ---------------------------------

"I soon became quite expert in talking with and persuading individual customers as well as all those present in the Chaihana.

"My new friend himself, the proprietor of the Chaihana, believed my invention so firmly that he didn't know what to do with himself, for repentance for his past.

"He was in constant agitation and bitterly repented his previous disrespectful attitude and his treatment of the various beings of other forms.

"Becoming day by day a more ardent preacher of my invention, he thereby not only helped to spread it in his own Chaihana, but he even began of his own accord to visit other Chaihana in the city Gob, in order to spread the truth which had so agitated him.

"He preached in the market places, and several times made special visits to the holy places, of which there were then already many in the outskirts of the city Gob, and which had been established in honor or in memory of somebody or something.

"It is very interesting to remark here that the information that serves on the planet Earth for the rise of a holy place is usually due to certain Earth beings called 'Liars.'

"This disease of 'lying' is also very widespread there.

"After careful pondering I decided to add something 'to the 'religious-doctrine' existing there, and like the wise King Konuzion, I counted on being able to spread this addition of mine effectively among them.

"Just then I invented as follows: that those spirits with the 'cap of darkness' who, as it was said, in that great religion, observe our deeds and thoughts, to report them later to our 'Mister God,' are none other than just those beings of other forms, which exist among us.

"It is they who watch us and report everything to our 'Mister God.'

"But we people, not only fail to pay them proper honor and respect, but we even destroy their existence, both for our food and as sacrifices.

"I particularly emphasized in my preaching that not only ought we not to destroy the existence of the beings of other forms in honor of 'Mister God,' but that an the contrary, we ought to try to earn their favor and to beseech them not to report to 'Mister God' at least those petty evil acts of ours which we involuntarily do.

"And this addition of mine I began to spread by every possible means, of course, very cautiously.

"At first, I spread this invention of mine through my said new friend there, the proprietor of the 'Chaihana.'

"I must tell you that his 'Chaihana' was almost the largest in the whole City Gob; and it was very famous for a certain reddish liquid of which the beings of the planet Earth are very fond.

"So there were always a great many customers there, and it was open day and night.

"Not only the residents of the city itself went there, but also all the visitors from the whole of Maralpleicie.

- -

"I soon became quite expert in talking with and persuading both single customers and also any company of them present in the 'Chaihana.'

"My new friend himself, the proprietor of the 'Chaihana' was so deeply impressed by my invention, that he didn't know what to do with himself for remorse for his past.

"He was in constant distress and bitterly deplored his previous contemptuous attitude and his treatment of the various beings of other forms.

"Becoming day by day a more enthusiastic preacher of my invention, he thereby helped to spread it not only in his own 'Chaihana,' but he even began of his own accord visiting other 'Chaihana' in the City Gob, in order to spread the truth which had so impressed him.

"He preached in the market places, and several times made special visits to the holy places, of which there then already were many in the outskirts of the City Gob. They also had been established in honor of somebody or in memory of something or other.

"It is very interesting to remark here that the information that serves on the planet Earth for the rise of a holy place is usually due to certain Earth beings called 'Humbugs.'

"This disease of 'Humbugging' also is very widely spread there.

"On the planet Earth people lie consciously and unconsciously.

"And they consciously lie there when they can obtain some personal material advantage by lying; and they unconsciously lie there when they fall ill with the disease called 'Hysteria.'

"In addition to the proprietor of the Chaihana there in the city Gob, a number of other beings very soon began unconsciously to assist me, who, like the proprietor of the Chaihana, had meanwhile become ardent supporters of my invention; and all the beings of that second group of Asiatic beings were soon eagerly spreading this invention

---------------------------------- 221 ----------------------------------

of mine and persuading each other of it as an indubitable 'truth' that had suddenly been revealed.

"The result of it all was that there in the country of Maralpleicie, not only were Sacrificial-Offerings indeed diminished, but they even began to treat the beings of other forms with unprecedented attention.

"Such comical farces very soon began there that though I myself was the author of the invention, I nevertheless found it very difficult to refrain from laughter.

"Such comical farces occurred as, for instance, the following: a highly respectable and wealthy merchant of the city Gob would be riding in the morning on his donkey to his own shop and on the way a motley crowd of beings would drag this respectable merchant off his donkey and thoroughly maul him because he had dared to ride on it; and then the crowd, bowing low, would escort the donkey on which the merchant had been riding, wherever it chose to go.

"Or, what is called a 'woodcutter' would be hauling wood to market with his own oxen from the forest to the town.

"A mob of citizens would drag him also off his cart and after mauling him, very gently unyoke the oxen and escort them wherever they wished to go.

"And if the cart were seen in a part of the city where it might hold up the traffic, the mob of citizens would themselves drag the cart to the market and leave it there to its fate.

"Thanks to this invention of mine, various quite new customs were very soon created in the city Gob.

"As, for instance, the custom was established there of placing troughs in all the squares, public places, and at the crossroads of the town, where residents of the city Gob could in the morning throw their choicest morsels of food for dogs and other stray beings of various forms; and

---------------------------------- 222 ----------------------------------

at sunrise, throw into the Sea of Beneficence every kind of food for the beings called 'fishes.'

"But the most peculiar of all was the custom of paying attention to the voices of beings of various forms.

"As soon as they heard the voice of a being of any form, they immediately began to praise the names of their gods and to await their blessing.

"It might be the crowing of a cock, the barking of a dog, the mewing of a cat, the squealing of an ape, or so on. . . . It would always startle them.

"On the planet Earth, consciously and unconsciously, they lie.

"And they consciously lie there when there is some personal material advantage to be got by lying; and, unconsciously they lie there when they fall ill of the disease called 'hysteria.'

"In addition to the proprietor of the 'Chaihana' there in the City Gob, I was very soon unconsciously assisted by still a number of other beings, who, like the proprietor of the 'Chaihana,' had in the meanwhile become ardent supporters of my invention; and soon, all the beings of that second group of Asiatic beings were spreading this invention

of mine and persuading each other of it as an indubitable truth that had been suddenly revealed.

"The result of it all was, that there in that country of Maralpleicie, not only indeed were 'sacrifices' diminished, but they even began giving unprecedentedly good treatment to the beings of other forms.

"Such comic farces very soon began there that though I was myself the author of the invention, I nevertheless found it very hard not to laugh.

"Such comic farces, for instance, as the following, began: a highly respectable and wealthy merchant of the City Gob would be riding in the morning on his own donkey to his own shop; on the way a motley crowd of beings drag this respectable merchant off his ass and maul him thoroughly because he has dared to ride upon it; whereupon the said crowd, with profound bows, escort the ass on which the merchant had been riding, wherever it chooses to go.

"Or, what is called a 'woodcutter,' with his own oxen, is hauling wood to market from the forest to the town.

"A mob of citizens drag him also off his cart and after mauling him, very tenderly unyoke the oxen and escort them where they wish to go.

"And if the cart should be met in a part of the city where it might hold up the traffic, the mob of citizens itself would drag the cart to the market and leave it there to its fate.

"Thanks to this invention of mine, very soon various quite new customs were created in the City Gob.

"So, for instance, the custom was established there of placing troughs in all the squares and public places and at the cross-roads of the town, where every morning, every resident of the City Gob could throw his choicest morsels of food for dogs and other stray beings of various forms;

at 'sunrise,' of throwing into the Sea of Beneficence every kind of food for the beings called 'fishes.'

"But most peculiar of all was the custom of paying attention to the voices of beings of various forms.

"As soon as they heard the voice of a being of any form, they began immediately to praise the names of their gods and to invite their blessing.

"It might be the crowing of a cock or the barking of a dog, or the mewing of a cat, or the squeal of an ape, or so on . . . it always brought them to attention.

"Here it is interesting to notice that for some reason or other they would always on these occasions raise their heads and look upwards, even though, according to the teaching of their religion, their god and his assistants were supposed to exist on the same level as themselves, and not where they directed their eyes and prayers.

"It was extremely interesting at these moments to watch their faces."

"Pardon me, your Right Reverence," interrupted at that moment Beelzebub's old devoted servant Ahoon, who had also been listening with great interest to his tales.

"Do you remember, your Right Reverence, how many times in that same city Gob we ourselves had to flop down in the streets during the cries of beings of different forms?"

To this remark, Beelzebub said:

"Certainly I remember, dear Ahoon. How could I forget such comical impressions?

"You must know," he then continued, turning to Hassein again, "that the beings of the planet Earth are inconceivably proud and touchy. If someone does not share their views or agree to do as they do, or criticizes their manifestations, they are, oh, very indignant and offended.

"If one had the power, he would order whoever dared not to do as he did, or who criticized his conduct, to be

---------------------------- 223 ----------------------------

shut up in the kind of room which is usually infested by innumerable what are called 'rats' and 'lice.'

"And at times, if the offended one had greater physical strength, and an important power-possessing being with whom he was not on very good terms was not watching him, he would simply maul the offender as the Russian Sidor once mauled his favorite goat.

"Very well knowing this aspect also of their strange psyche, I had no desire to offend them and to incur their wrath; furthermore, I was always profoundly aware that to outrage anybody's religious feeling is contrary to all morality, so, when existing among them, I always tried to do as they did, in order not to be conspicuous and attract their attention.

"Here it does no harm to notice that owing to the existing abnormal conditions of ordinary existence there among your favorites, the three-brained beings of that strange planet Earth, especially during recent centuries, only those beings who manifest themselves, not as the majority of them do, but somehow or other, more absurdly, become noticed and consequently honored by the rest; and the more absurd their manifestations and the more stupid, mean, and insolent the 'tricks' they play, the more noticed and famous they become, and the greater is the number of the beings on the given continent and even on other continents who know them personally or at least by name.

"On the other hand, no honest being who does not manifest himself absurdly will ever become famous among other beings or even be simply noticed, however good-natured and sensible he may be in himself.

"And so, my boy, what our Ahoon so mischievously reminded me about con-

"Here it is interesting to notice that for some reason or other they always raised their heads on these occasions and looked upwards, even though, according to the teachings of their religion, their god and his assistants were supposed to exist on the same level with themselves, and not where they directed their eyes and prayers.

"It was extremely interesting at these moments to watch their faces."

"Pardon me, Your Right Reverence," at that moment interrupted Beelzebub's old devoted servant Ahoon who had also been listening with great interest to his tales.

"Do you remember, Your Right Reverence, how many times, we ourselves, in that same City Gob had to flop down on its streets during the cries of beings of different forms?"

To this remark Beelzebub said:

"Certainly I remember, dear Ahoon.

"How could I forget such comic impressions.

"You must know," he then continued, turning to Hassein again, "that the beings of the planet Earth are inconceivably prone and touchy, and if someone does not share their views or agree to do as they do, or criticizes their manifestations, they are, Oh—very, very indignant and offended.

"If one of them had the power, he would order whoever had dared not to do as he does, or who criticized his conduct, to be

immured in the sort of room which is usually infested by innumerable what are called 'rats' and 'lice.'

"And sometimes if he happened to be stronger, and a superior power-holding being with whom he is not on very good terms is not watching him, he will simply maul the offender, as the Russian Sidor once mauled his favorite goat.

"Knowing thoroughly this aspect also of their strange psyche, I had no desire to offend them and to incur their wrath; furthermore, I was always profoundly aware that to outrage anybody's religious feeling is contrary to every morality. When existing among them, therefore, I always tried to do as they did, in order to avoid attracting their attention.

"Here it does no harm to notice that on account of the prevailing abnormal conditions of ordinary existence there, just those beings only indeed among your favorites, the three-brained beings of that strange planet Earth, and especially during recent centuries, become notorious and consequently honored by the rest, who manifest themselves, not as the majority of them do, but somehow or other, more absurdly; and the more absurd their manifestations and the more stupid, mean, and insolent the tricks they perform, the more notorious and famous such beings become, and the greater the number of the beings on the given continent and even on other continents who know them personally or at least by name.

"On the other hand, no honest being, without ridiculous manifestations, will ever become famous among other beings or even barely noticed, however good natured and sensible he may be in himself.

"So, my boy, that about which our Ahoon so mischievously reminded me con-

cerned just that custom, which developed there in the city Gob, of attaching significance to the voices of beings of various forms and particularly to the voice of
what are called 'donkeys,' of which there

------------------------------ *224* ------------------------------

were then, for some reason or other, a great many in the city Gob.

"The beings of all other forms of that planet also manifest themselves by voice,
but at a definite time. For instance, the cock cries at midnight, an ape in the morning when it is hungry, and so on, but donkeys there bray whenever it enters their
heads to do so, and in consequence you may hear the voice of that silly being there
at any time of the day or night.

"So, my boy, it was established there in the city Gob that as soon as the sound
of the voice of the donkey was heard, all who heard it had to flop down immediately and offer up prayers to their god and to their revered idols and, I must add,
these donkeys usually have a very loud voice by nature and their voices carry a
long way.

"Well, then, as we walked along the streets of the city Gob and saw the citizens
flopping down at the braying of every donkey, we had to flop down likewise so as
not to be distinguished from the others; and it was just this comical custom, I see
now, that tickled our old Ahoon so much.

"You noticed, my dear Hassein, with what venomous satisfaction our old man
reminded me, after so many centuries, of that comical situation of mine."

Having said this, Beelzebub, smiling, went on with the tale he had begun.

"It is needless to say," he continued, "that there also, in this second center of
culture of the three-brained beings of your planet, breeding there on the continent of Ashhark, the destruction of beings of other forms for Sacrificial-Offerings
entirely ceased; and, if isolated instances occurred, the beings of that group themselves settled accounts with the offenders without compunction.

"Having thus become convinced that there also, among that second group of
beings of the continent Ashhark, I

------------------------------ *225* ------------------------------

had succeeded so easily in uprooting, for a long time, the custom of Sacrificial-
Offerings, I decided to leave; but I had it in mind, in any event, to visit also the
nearest large points where the beings of the same second group were breeding;
and I chose for this purpose the region of the course of the river 'Naria-Chi.'

"Soon after this decision, I sailed with Ahoon to the mouth of this river, and
began to sail up against its current, having become persuaded that there had
already passed from the beings of the city Gob to the beings of this group populating these large centers the same new customs and the same notions concerning
Sacrificial-Offerings by the destruction of the existence of other beings.

"We finally arrived at a small town called 'Arguenia,' which in those days was
considered the most remote point of the country Maralpleicie.

"Here also there existed a fair number of beings of this second Asiatic group
who were engaged chiefly in obtaining from Nature what is called 'turquoise.'

"There in the small town of Arguenia I began, as usual, to visit their various
Chaihana, and there also I continued my usual procedure."

------------------------------ *226* ------------------------------

cerned just that custom, established there in the City Gob, of attaching significance to the voices of beings of various forms and particularly to the voice of what
are called 'donkeys,' of which,

for some reason or other, there were a great many in the City Gob.

"The beings of all other forms of that planet also manifest themselves by voice,
but at a definite time. For instance, the cock cries at midnight, an ape in the morning when it is hungry, and so on, but donkeys there bray whenever it enters their
heads, in consequence you may hear the voice of that silly being there at any time
of the day or night.

"So, my boy, it was established there in the City Gob that as soon as the sound
of the voice of the donkey brayed out, all who heard it had at once to flop down
and offer up prayers to their god and to the idols they revered; and these donkeys,
I may say, usually have a very loud voice by nature, and their voices carry a long
way.

"So, as we walked along the streets of the City Gob and saw the citizens flopping down at the bray of every donkey, we had to flop down too, in order not to
be distinguished from the rest; and it was just this comic custom, I see now, that
gave our old Ahoon so much relish.

"You noticed, dear Hassein, with what wicked satisfaction our old man, after so
many centuries . . . reminded me of that comic situation of mine then?"

Having said this, Beelzebub, smiling, went on with the tale he had begun.

"It is needless to say that there also, in this second culture-center of the three-
brained beings of your planet, breeding there on the continent of Ashhark, the
destruction of beings of other forms in sacrifice entirely ceased; and, if isolated
instances occurred, the beings of that group themselves settled accounts with the
offenders without compunction.

"Having thus become convinced that there also, among that second group of
beings of the continent Ashhark, I

had succeeded so easily in uprooting, for a long time, the custom of 'sacrifices,' I
decided to leave; but I had it in mind, in any event, to pay a visit to the nearest
large centers also where the beings of the same second group were breeding; and
I chose for this purpose the region of the course of the river 'Naria-Chi.'

"Soon after this decision, I sailed with Ahoon to the mouth of this river, having
become persuaded that there had already passed from the beings of the City Gob
to the beings of this group populating these large centers the same new customs
and the same notions concerning sacrifices by the destruction of the existence of
other beings.

"We arrived at length at a small town called 'Arguenia,' which in those days was
considered the most remote town of the country Maralpleicie.

"Here also there existed a fair number of beings of this second Asiatic group;
they were engaged in mining what is called 'turquoise' from Nature.

"There in the small town of 'Arguenia' I began, as usual, visiting their various
'Chaihana,' continuing there also my usual procedure.

The First Visit of Beelzebub to India

BEELZEBUB continued to speak as follows:

"Sitting in a Chaihana in this small town of Arguenia, I once overheard a conversation among several beings seated not far from me.

"They were talking and deciding when and how they should go by caravan to Pearl-land.

"Having listened to their conversation, I gathered that they intended to go there for the purpose of exchanging their 'turquoises' for what are called 'pearls.'

"I must here, by the way, draw your attention also to the fact that your favorites of former as well as of contemporary epochs liked and still like to wear pearls and also the said turquoise, as well as many other what are called 'precious-trinkets' for the purpose, as they say, of 'adorning' their exteriors. But if you would like to know my opinion, they do so, of course instinctively, in order to offset, so to say, the 'value-of-their-inner-insignificance.'

"At that period to which my present tale refers, the said pearls were very rare among the beings of the second Asiatic group and commanded a high price among them. But in the country Pearl-land there was at the same time a great number of these pearls, and there, on the contrary, they were very cheap, because pearls at that time were exclusively obtained only from the water-spaces surrounding that country.

"The mentioned conversation of the beings who sat near me in the Chaihana in the small town Arguenia then immediately interested me, because at that time I already had the intention of going to that same Pearl-land where the three-brained beings of the continent Ashhark of the third group bred.

--------- *227* ---------

"And the conversation I then heard at once evoked in my mentation an association to the effect that it might be better to go to the country Pearl-land directly from here with this large caravan of these beings, rather than return the same way to the Sea of Beneficence, and from there, by means of the same ship *Occasion*, to reach this country.

"Although this journey, which in those days was almost impossible for the beings of the Earth, would take us a good deal of time, yet I thought that the journey back to the Sea of Beneficence with its unforeseeable contingencies would perhaps not take much less time.

"This association then arose in my mentation chiefly because I had long before heard a great deal about the rare peculiarities of those parts of the nature of that peculiar planet through which the proposed route of the caravan lay and, in consequence, what is called a 'being-love-of-knowledge' which was already crystallized in me, having received a shock for functioning from all that had been overheard, immediately dictated to my common presence the need to be persuaded of everything personally, directly through my own perceptive organs.

"So, my boy, owing to what I have said, I intentionally sat with the conversing

The First Visit of Beelzebub to India

BEELZEBUB continued to speak as follows:
"Sitting in a 'Chaihana' in this small town of 'Arguenia,' I once over heard a conversation among several beings seated not far from me.

"They were talking and deciding when and how they should go by caravan to 'Pearl-Land.'

"Having listened to their conversation, I gathered that they intended to go there for the purpose of exchanging their 'turquoises' for what are called 'pearls.'

"I must here, by the way, draw your attention also to the fact that your favorites of former as well as of contemporary epochs liked and still like to wear 'pearls' and also the said 'turquoise,' as well as many other what are called 'precious-trinkets' for the purpose, as they say, of 'adorning' their exteriors. But if you would like to know my opinion, they do so of course, instinctively, in order, if only by this, to offset, so to say, the 'value-of-their-inner-insignificance.'

"At that period to which my present tale refers, the said 'pearls' were a great rarity among the beings of the second Asiatic group and commanded a high price among them. But in the country 'Pearl-Land' there was at the same time a great number of these pearls, and there, on the contrary, they were very cheap, because pearls at that time were exclusively obtained only from the water spaces surrounding that country.

"The mentioned conversation of the beings sitting near me in the 'Chaihana' in the small town 'Arguenia' then at once interested me because at that time I had already had the intention of going to that same 'Pearl-Land' where the three-brained beings of the continent Ashhark of the third group bred.

- -

"And the conversation I then heard at once evoked in my mentation an association to the effect that it might be better to go to the country 'Pearl-Land' directly from here with this large caravan of these beings, rather than return by the way we had come to the 'Sea of Beneficence,' and from there, by means of the same ship 'Occasion,' to reach this country.

"Although this journey which in those days was almost impossible for the beings of the Earth would take us a good deal of time, yet I thought that the journey back to the 'Sea of Beneficence' with its unforeseeable contingencies, would perhaps not take much less time.

"This association then arose in my mentation chiefly because I had long before heard a great deal about the rare peculiarities of those parts of the nature of that peculiar planet through which the proposed route of the caravan lay, and in consequence, what is called a 'being-love-of-knowledge' already formed in me, having received a shock for functioning, from all that had been overheard, immediately dictated to my common presence the need to be persuaded of everything personally, directly through my own perceptive organs.

"So, my boy, owing to what I have said, I purposely sat with the conversing be-

beings and joined in their deliberations.

"As a result of it all, we also were then included in the company of their caravan, and two days later we set off together with them.

"I and Ahoon then passed through indeed very unusual places, unusual even for the general nature of this peculiar planet, certain parts of which, by the way, only became so because before that period this ill-fated planet had already undergone two what are called Transapalnian-perturbations, almost unprecedented in the Universe.

"From the first day we had to pass exclusively through

---------------------------------- *228* ----------------------------------

a region of various 'terra-firma-projections' of unusual forms, which had conglomerations of all kinds of 'intraplanetary-minerals.'

"And only after a month's travel, according to their time-calculation, did our caravan from Arguenia come to places where in the soil the possibility had not yet been quite destroyed of Nature's forming surplanetary formations and creating corresponding conditions for the arising and existing of various one-brained and two-brained beings.

"After every kind of difficulty we at last, one rainy morning, on ascending a height, suddenly saw on the horizon the outline of a large water-space bordering the edges of the continent Ashhark, which was then called Pearl-land.

"And four days later we came to the chief point of the existence of the beings of that third group, then the city 'Kaimon.'

"Having arranged there the place of our permanent existence, we did nothing during our first days there but stroll about the streets of the town, observing the specific manifestations of the beings of that third group in the process of their ordinary existence.

"It cannot be helped, my dear Hassein. Now that I have told you the history of the arising of the second group of the three-brained beings of the continent Ashhark, I must tell you also about the history of the arising of the third group."

"You must indeed tell me, my dear and beloved Grandfather," eagerly exclaimed Hassein; and, this time with great reverence, extending his hands upwards, he sincerely said:

"May my dear and kind Grandfather become worthy to be perfected to the degree of the sacred 'Anklad'!"

Without saying anything to this, Beelzebub merely smiled and continued to relate as follows:

---------------------------------- *229* ----------------------------------

"The history of the arising of this third group of Asiatic beings begins only a little later than that period when the families of hunters for Pirmarals first came to the shores of the Sea of Beneficence from the continent Atlantis and, having settled there, founded the second group of Asiatic beings.

"It was just in those, for your contemporary favorites, infinitely remote days, that is, not long before the second Transapalnian perturbation occurred to this ill-fated planet, that there had already begun to be crystallized in the presences of the three-centered beings then of the continent Atlantis certain consequences of

ings and joined in their deliberations.

"As a result of it all, we also were then included in the company of their caravan, and two days later we set off together with them.

"I and Ahhoon then passed through indeed very unusual places, unusual even for the general nature of this peculiar planet, certain parts of which, by the way, only became so because before that period, this ill-fated planet had already undergone two, what are called 'Transapalnian-perturbations,' almost unprecedented in the Universe.

"From the first day we had to pass exclusively through

a region of various 'terra-firma-projections' of unusual forms, which had conglomerations of all kinds of 'intraplanetary-minerals.'

"And only after a month's travel, according to their time-calculation, did our caravan from Arguenia come to places in whose soil the possibility had not yet been quite destroyed, of Nature's forming surplanetary formations and creating corresponding conditions for the arising and existing of various one-brained and two-brained beings.

"After difficulties of every kind we at last, one rainy morning, on ascending a height, suddenly saw on the horizon the outline of a large water-space bordering the edges of the continent Ashhark, which just then was called 'Pearl-Land.'

"And in four days more we came to the chief place of the existence of the beings of that third group, then the city 'Kaimon.'

"Having arranged there the place of our permanent existence, we did nothing else during our first days there but stroll about the streets of the town, observing the specific manifestations of the beings of that third group in the process of their ordinary existence.

"It cannot be helped, my dear Hassein—having told you the history of the arising of the second group of three-brained beings of the continent Ashhark, I must already tell you also the history of the arising of the third group.

"You must indeed tell me, my dear and beloved Grandfather," exclaimed Hassein eagerly; and this time with great reverence, extending his hands upwards, he sincerely said:

"May my dear and kind Grandfather be worthy to be perfected to the degree of the sacred 'Anklad'!"

Without saying anything to this, Beelzebub only smiled and continued to relate as follows:

"The history of the arising of this third group of Asiatic beings begins only a little later than that period when the families of hunters for Pirmarals first came to the shores of the 'Sea-of-Beneficence' from the continent Atlantis and, having settled there, founded the second group of Asiatic beings.

"It was just in those, for your contemporary favorites, infinitely remote days, that is, not long before the second 'Transapalnian-perturbation' occurred to this ill-fated planet, that there had already begun to be crystallized in the presences of the three-centered beings then of the continent Atlantis certain consequences of the properties of the organ Kundabuffer, on account of which the need—among other needs unbecoming to three-brained beings—began to arise in them to wear, as I have already told you, various trinkets as it were for their adornment, and also a kind of famous what is called 'Talisman' which they had invented.

"One of these trinkets, then on the continent Atlantis, just as now on the other continents of the planet Earth, was and is this same pearl.

"The said pearl is formed in one-brained beings which breed in the 'Saliakooriap' of your planet Earth, that is to say, in that part of it which is called 'Hentralispana,' or, as your favorites might express it, the blood of the planet, which is present in the common presence of every planet and which serves the actualizing of the process of the Most Great common-cosmic Trogoautoegocrat; and there on your planet this part is called 'water.'

"This one-brained being in which the said pearl is formed used to breed in the 'Saliakooriapnian,' or water-areas, surrounding the continent Atlantis; but in consequence of the great demand for the said pearl and therefore of the great destruction of these one-brained 'pearl-bearing beings,' soon none were left near this continent. Thereupon, when those beings there who made the aim and sense of their existence the destruction of these pearl-bearing beings, that is to say, who destroyed their existence only in order to procure that part of their common presence called pearl merely for the gratification of their quite absurd egoism, found no more of these said pearl-bearing beings in the water-area nearest to the continent Atlantis, they, that is, these 'professionals,' then began to look for them in other water-areas and gradually moved further and further away from their own continent.

----------------------------------- 230 -----------------------------------

"Once during these searches of theirs, owing to what are called 'Saliakoori-apnian-displacements,' or as they say, prolonged 'storms,' their rafts came unexpectedly to a place where there proved to be a great number of these pearl-bearing beings; and the place itself was extremely convenient for their destruction.

"These water-areas where the destroyers of the pearl-bearing beings then chanced to come and where these beings bred in large numbers, were just those water-areas which surround the place then called Pearl-land and now called Hindustan or India.

"For the first days, the aforementioned terrestrial professionals of that time who had chanced to arrive there did nothing but gratify to the full their inclinations, which had already become inherent to their presences in respect of the destruction of these one-brained beings of their planet; and it was only later, after they had also by chance found out that almost everything required for ordinary existence arose in abundance on the neighboring terra firma, that they decided never to return to Atlantis but to settle there for their permanent existence.

"A few of these destroyers of pearl-bearing beings then sailed to the continent Atlantis, and having exchanged their pearls for various articles which were still lacking in the new place, they returned, bringing with them their

----------------------------------- 231 -----------------------------------

own families as well as the families of those who had remained.

the properties of the organ Kundabuffer, on account of which the need—among other needs unbecoming to three-brained beings—began to arise in them to wear, as I have already told you, various trinkets as it were for their adornment, and also a kind of famous what is called 'Talisman' which they had invented.

"One of these trinkets, then on the continent Atlantis, just as now on the other continents of the planet Earth, was and is this same 'pearl.'

"The said pearl is formed in one-brained beings which breed in the 'Saliakooriap' also of your planet Earth, that is to say, in that part of it which is called 'Hentralispana,' or, as your favorites might express it, the blood of the planet which is present in the common presence of every planet and which serves the actualizing of the process of the Most Great Common Cosmic Trogoautoegocrat; and this part, there on your planet, is called 'water.'

"This one-brained being in which the said 'pearl' is formed, used to breed in the 'Saliakooriapnian,' or water-areas surrounding the continent Atlantis; but in consequence of the great demand for the said pearl and therefore of the great destruction of these one-brained 'pearl-bearing' beings, there were soon none left near this continent. Thereupon, when those beings there who made the aim and sense of their existence the destruction of these 'pearl-bearing' beings; that is to say, who destroyed their existence only in order to procure that part of their common presence called 'pearl' merely for the gratification of their quite absurd egoism, found no more of these said 'pearl-bearing' beings in the water area nearest to the continent Atlantis, they, that is these 'professionals,' then began to look for them in other water-areas and gradually moved further and further away from their own continent.

- -

"Once during these searches of theirs, their rafts, because of what are called 'Saliakooriapnian displacements,' or as they say, prolonged 'storms,' came unexpectedly upon a place where there proved to be a great number of these pearl-bearing beings; and the place itself was extremely convenient for their destruction.

"These water-areas to which the destroyers of the pearl-bearing beings then chanced to come and where these beings bred in large numbered, were just those water-areas which surround the place then called Pearl-Land and now called 'Hindustan' or 'India.'

"For the first days the mentioned terrestrial professionals of that time who had chanced to arrive there did nothing but gratify to the full their inclinations, which had already become inherent to their presences in respect of the destruction of these one-brained beings of their planet; and it was only later, after they had also by chance found out that almost everything required for ordinary existence arose in abundance on the neighboring terra-firma, that they decided never to return to Atlantis but to settle there for their permanent existence.

"A few of these destroyers of pearl-bearing beings then sailed to the continent Atlantis, and having exchanged their pearls for various articles which were still lacking in the new place, they returned, taking with them their

- -

own families as well as the families of those who had remained.

"Later several of these first settlers of this—for the beings then of that time—'new' country visited their native land from time to time for the purpose of exchanging pearls for articles required by them there; and each time they took back with them a further number of beings, either their relatives or their kinsmen or just laborers indispensable to their extensive work.

"So, my boy, from that time on, that part also of the surface of the planet Earth became known to all the three-brained beings there under the name of 'Land-of-Beneficence.'

"In this way, before the second great catastrophe to the planet Earth, many beings of the continent Atlantis already existed on this part of the continent Ashhark also, and when that second catastrophe occurred to your planet, then many of the beings who chanced to be saved from the continent Atlantis, chiefly those who already had relatives and kinsmen in that Pearl-land, also gradually collected there.

"Owing, as always, to their 'fecundity,' they gradually multiplied there and began to populate this part of the terra firma of their planet, more and more.

"At first they populated there in Pearl-land only two definite regions, namely, the regions around the mouths of the two large rivers which flowed from the interior of Pearl-land into the large water-space, just in those places near which many of the mentioned pearl-bearing beings bred.

"But when the population there greatly increased, they began to populate also the interior of that part of the continent Ashhark; but nevertheless their favorite regions continued to be the valleys of the two mentioned rivers.

"Well, then, my boy, when I first arrived in Pearl-land,

------------------------------ 232 ------------------------------

I decided to attain my aim there also by means of the 'Havatvernoni' which existed there, that is, through their Religion.

"But it turned out that amongst the beings of this third group of the continent Ashhark, there were at that time several peculiar 'Havatvernonis' or 'Religions' all based on different, quite independent what are called 'religious-teachings,' having nothing in common with each other.

"In view of this, I first began seriously studying these religious-teachings there, and having in the course of my studies constated that one of them, founded on the teaching of a genuine Messenger of our COMMON ENDLESS CREATOR, afterwards called Saint Buddha, had the most followers, I, on becoming acquainted with it, devoted most of my attention to its study.

"Before continuing to tell you about the three-brained beings breeding just on that part of the surface of the planet Earth, it is, I think, necessary to remark, even if briefly, that there existed and still exist, ever since the time when the practice of having peculiar being-Havatvernonis or Religions began to arise and exist among your favorites, two basic kinds of religious-teachings.

"One kind was invented by those three-brained beings there themselves, in whom, for some reason or other, there arises the functioning of a psyche proper to Hasrnamusses; and the other kind of religious-teaching is founded there upon those detailed instructions which have been preached, as it were, by genuine Mes-

"Later several of these first settlers of this—for the beings then at that time—'new' country, visited their native land from time to time for the purpose of exchanging 'pearls' for articles required by them there; and each time they took back with them a further number of beings, either their relatives or their kinsmen or just laborers indispensable to their big work.

"So, my boy, from that time on, that part also of the surface of the planet Earth became known to all the three-brained beings there under the name of 'Land-of-Beneficence.'

"In this way, before the second great catastrophe to the planet Earth, many beings of the continent Atlantis already existed on this part of the continent Ashhark also, and when that second catastrophe occurred to your planet, then many of the beings who chanced to be saved from the continent Atlantis, chiefly those who already had relatives and kinsmen in that Pearl-Land, also gradually collected there.

"Owing as always to their 'fecundity' they gradually multiplied there and began to populate this part also of the terra-firma surface of their planet, more and more.

"At first they populated there in Pearl-Land only two definite regions, namely, the regions around the mouths of the two large rivers which flowed from the interior of Pearl-Land into the large water-space, just in those places near which many of the mentioned pearl-bearing beings bred.

"But when the population there was greatly increased, they began populating also the interior of that part of the continent Ashhark; but nevertheless their favorite regions continued to be the valleys of the two mentioned rivers.

"Well then, my boy, when I first arrived in Pearl-Land,

- -

I decided to attain my aim there also by means of the 'Havatvernoni' existing there, that is, through their 'Religion.'

"But it turned out that amongst the beings of this third group of the continent Ashhark, there were at that time several peculiar 'Havatvernonis' or 'Religions' all based on different, quite independent, what are called 'religious-teachings,' having nothing in common with each other.

"In view of this, I first began seriously studying these 'religious-teachings' existing there, and having in the course of my studies constated that one of them—founded on the teaching of a genuine Messenger of OUR COMMON ENDLESS CREATOR, afterwards called Saint Buddha—had the most followers, I, on becoming acquainted with it, devoted most of my attention to its study.

"Before continuing to tell you merely about the three-brained beings breeding just on that part of the surface of the planet Earth, it is, I think, necessary to remark, even if briefly, that there existed and still exist, ever since the time when the custom of having peculiar being 'Havatvernoni' or 'Religions' began to arise and exist among your favorites, two basic kinds of 'religious teachings.'

"One kind was invented by those three-brained beings there themselves, in whom for some reason or other, there arises the functioning of a psyche proper to Hasnamusses; and the other kind of religious teaching is founded there upon those detailed instructions which have been preached, as it were, by genuine Messengers from Above, who indeed are from time to time sent by certain nearest helpers of our COMMON FATHER, for the purpose of aiding the three-brained beings of your planet in destroying in their presences the crystallized consequences of the properties of the organ Kundabuffer.

"The religion which was then followed by most of the beings of the country Pearl-land and to become acquainted

------------------------------- 233 ------------------------------

with which I then devoted my attention, and about which I find it necessary to tell you a little, arose there in the following way:

"As I later learned, with the multiplication of the three-brained beings of that third group, many beings among them with the properties of Hasnamusses were formed into responsible beings; and when these latter began spreading ideas more maleficent than usual among the beings of that group, there was crystallized in the presences of the majority of the three-centered beings of the third group, that special psychic property, which, in its totality, already engendered a factor which greatly hindered the normal 'exchange-of-substances' actualized by the Most Great common-cosmic Trogoautoegocrat. Well, then, as soon as this lamentable result, also issuing from this planet, was noticed by certain Most Most Sacred Individuals, it was sanctioned that a corresponding Sacred Individual should be sent there, specially to that group of beings, for the more or less tolerable regulation of their being-existence in accordance with the existence of the whole of that solar system.

"It was just then that the aforementioned Sacred Individual was sent to them who, having been coated with the planetary body of a terrestrial being, was called, as I have said, Saint Buddha.

"The coating of the said Sacred Individual with a planetary body of a terrestrial three-brained being was actualized there several centuries before my first visit to the country Pearl-land."

At this point in Beelzebub's tales, Hassein turned to him and said:

"My dear Grandfather, during your tales you have already many times used the expression Hasnamuss. I have until now understood only from the intonation of your voice and from the consonance of the word itself, that by

------------------------------- 234 ------------------------------

this expression you defined those three-brained beings whom you always set apart from others as if they deserved 'Objective-Contempt.'

"Be so kind as always and explain to me the real meaning and exact sense of this word."

Whereupon Beelzebub, with a smile inherent to him, said as follows:

"Concerning the 'typicality' of the three-brained beings for whom I have adopted this verbal definition, I shall explain it to you at the proper time, but meanwhile know that this word designates every already 'definitized' common presence of a three-brained being, both those consisting only of the single planetary body as well as those whose higher being-bodies are already coated in them, and in which for some reason or other, data have not been crystallized for the Divine impulse of 'Objective-Conscience.'"

sengers from Above, who indeed are from time to time sent by certain nearest helpers from our COMMON FATHER, for the purpose of aiding the three-brained beings of your planet in destroying in their presences the crystallized consequences of the properties of the organ Kundabuffer.

"The religion whose followers were then the majority of the beings of the country Pearl-Land and to become acquainted

- -

with which I then devoted my attention and about which I find it necessary to tell you a little, arose there in the following way:

"As I later learned, with the multiplication of the three-brained beings of that third group, many beings among them with the properties of Hasnamusses were formed into responsible beings; and when these latter began spreading more than usually maleficent ideas among the beings of that group, there was crystallized in the presences of the majority of three-centered beings of that third group, that special psychic property, which, in its totality, already engendered a factor very hindering to the normal 'exchange-of-substances' actualized by the 'Most Great Common Cosmic Trogoautoegocrat.' Well then, as soon as this lamentable result, also issuing from this planet, was noticed by certain most most Sacred Individuals, it was sanctioned that a corresponding Sacred Individual should be sent there, specially to that group of beings, for the more or less tolerable regulation of their being-existence in accordance with the existence of the whole of that solar system.

"It was just then that the aforementioned Sacred Individual was sent to them who, having been coated with the planetary body of a terrestrial being, was called, as I have said, 'Saint Buddha.'

"The coating of the said Sacred Individual with a planetary body of a terrestrial three-brained being was actualized there several centuries before my first visit to the country 'Pearl-Land.'"

At this point in Beelzebub's tales, Hassein turned to him and said:

"My dear Grandfather, during your tales you have already many times used the expression 'Hasnamuss.' I have until now understood only from the intonation of your voice and from the consonance of this word itself, that by

- -

this expression you defined those three-brained beings whom you always set apart from others as if they deserved 'objective-contempt.'

"Be so kind as always and explain to me the real meaning and exact sense of this word."

Whereupon Beelzebub, with a smile inherent to him, said as follows:

"Concerning the 'typicality' of the three-brained beings for whom I have adopted this verbal definition, I will explain it to you at the proper time, but meanwhile know that this word designates every already 'definitized' common presence of a three-brained being, both those consisting only of the single planetary body as well as those whose higher being-bodies are already coated in them, and in which for some reason or other, data have not been crystallized for the Divine impulse of 'Objective-Conscience.'"

Having said only this in defining the word Hasnamuss, Beelzebub continued to speak:

"During my detailed studies of the mentioned religious teaching I also clarified that after this Sacred Individual had become finally coated with the presence of a three-brained being there and had seriously pondered how to fulfill the task that had been laid upon him from Above, he decided to attain this by means of the enlightenment of their Reason.

"Here it must without fail be noticed that by that time there had already been crystallized in the presence of Saint Buddha, as the same detailed researches of mine had made clear, a very clear understanding that in the process of its abnormal formation, the Reason of the three-centered beings of the planet Earth results in a Reason called 'instincto-terebelnian,' that is, a Reason which functions only from corresponding shocks from without; yet in spite of this, Saint Buddha decided to carry out his task by means

------------------------------ 235 ------------------------------

of this peculiar Reason of theirs, that is, this Reason peculiar to the three-centered beings there; and therefore, he first of all began informing their peculiar Reason with objective truths of every kind.

"Saint Buddha first assembled many of the chiefs of that group and spoke to them as follows:

"'Beings possessing presences similar to that of the ALL-CREATOR HIMSELF!

"'By certain all-enlightened and all-justly guiding most sacred final results of the actualization of everything existing in the Universe, my essence has been sent to you to serve as a helping factor in the striving of each of you to free yourselves from the consequences of those abnormal being-properties which, in view of highly important common cosmic needs, were implanted in the presences of your ancestors and, passing by heredity from generation to generation, have reached you also!'

"Saint Buddha spoke again about this a little more in detail but only to certain beings there initiated by him.

"This second time, as it turned out, he then expressed himself in the following words:

"'Beings with presences for actualizing the hope of our COMMON FATHER!

"'Almost at the beginning of the rise of your race, there occurred in the process of the normal existence of the whole of this solar system, an unforeseen accident which threatened serious consequences for everything existing.

"'For the regulation of that common universal misfortune there was then required, among other measures, according to the explanations of certain Most High, Most Most Sacred Individuals, a certain change in the functioning of the common presences of your ancestors, namely, there was implanted into their presences a certain organ with special properties, owing to which everything external perceived by their whole presences and transformed for

------------------------------ 236 ------------------------------

their own coating was afterwards manifested not in accordance with reality.

Having said only this in defining the word Hasnamuss, Beelzebub continued to speak:

"During my detailed studies of the mentioned religious teaching I also clarified that after this Sacred Individual had become finally coated with the presence of a three-brained being there and had seriously pondered how to fulfill the task that had been laid upon him from Above, he decided to attain this by means of the enlightenment of their Reason.

"Here it must without fail be noticed that by that time there had already been crystallized in the presence of Saint Buddha, as the same detailed researches of mine made clear, a very clear understanding that in the process of its abnormal formation, the Reason of the three-centered beings the planet Earth results in a Reason called 'instincto-terebelnian,' that is, a Reason which functions only from corresponding shocks from without; yet in spite of this, Saint Buddha decided to carry out his task by means

of this peculiar Reason of theirs, that is, this Reason peculiar to the three-centered beings there; and therefore, he first of all began informing their peculiar Reason with objective truths of every kind.

"Saint Buddha first assembled many of the chiefs of that group and told them the following:

"'Beings possessing presences similar to that of the ALL CREATOR himself:

"'By certain all-enlightened and all-justly guiding most most sacred final results of the actualization of everything existing in the Universe, my essence has been sent to you to serve as a helping factor in the striving of each of you to free yourselves from the consequences of those abnormal being-properties which, in view of highly important common cosmic needs, were implanted in the presences of your ancestors, and, passing by heredity from generation to generation, have reached you also'!

"Saint Buddha spoke again about this a little more in detail but only to certain beings there initiated by him.

"This second time, as it turned out, he then expressed himself in the following words:

"'Beings with presences for actualizing the hope of our COMMON FATHER.

"'Almost at the beginning of the rise of your race, there occurred in the process of the normal existence of the whole of our solar system, an unforeseen accident which portended serious consequences for everything existing.

"'For the regulation of that common universal mishap there was then required, among other measures, according to the explanations of certain Most High, Most Most Sacred Individuals, a certain change in the functioning of the common presences of your ancestors, namely, there was implanted into their presences a certain organ with special properties, owing to which everything external was perceived by their whole presence, transformed for

their own coating, and afterwards manifested, not in accordance with reality.

"'A little later, when the normal existence of this solar system was stabilized and the necessity for certain intentionally created abnormal actualizations had passed, our MOST ALL-GRACIOUS COMMON FATHER did not fail to give the command immediately to annul certain artificial measures, among which was the removal from the common presences of your ancestors of the now already superfluous organ Kundabuffer with all its special artificial properties; and this command was immediately executed by corresponding Sacred Individuals who superintend such cosmic actualizations

"'After a considerable time had passed it was suddenly revealed that, although all the properties of the said organ had indeed been removed from the presences of your ancestors by the mentioned Most Sacred Individuals, yet nevertheless, a certain lawfully flowing cosmic result, existing under the name of "predisposition," and arising in every more or less independent cosmic presence owing to the repeated action in it of any function, had not been foreseen and destroyed in their presences.

"'And so it turned out that owing to this predisposition, which began to pass by heredity to the succeeding generations, the consequences of many of the properties of the organ Kundabuffer began gradually to be crystallized in their presences.

"'No sooner was this lamentable fact which proceeded in the presences of the three-brained beings breeding on this planet Earth first made clear, than by All-Gracious sanction of our COMMON FATHER, a suitable Sacred Individual was immediately sent here, so that, being coated with a presence like your own and having become perfected by Objective Reason under the conditions already established here, he might better explain and show you

------------------------------ 237 ------------------------------

the way of eradicating from your presences the already crystallized consequences of the properties of the organ Kundabuffer as well as your inherited predispositions to new crystallizations.

"'During the period when the said Sacred Individual, coated with a presence like your own and who had already attained to the age of a responsible three-centered being similar to yourselves, directly guided the ordinary process of the being-existence of your ancestors, many of them did indeed completely free themselves from the consequences of the properties of the organ Kundabuffer and either thereby acquired Being personally for themselves or became normal sources for the arising of normal presences of succeeding beings similar to themselves.

"'But in consequence of the fact that before the period of the said Sacred Individual's appearance here, the duration of your existence had, owing to very many firmly fixed abnormal conditions of ordinary existence created by yourselves, already become abnormally short, and therefore the process of sacred Rascooarno had also very soon to occur to this Sacred Individual, that is to say, he also had, like you, to die prematurely, then after his death, the former conditions were gradually re-established there owing on the one hand to the established abnormal conditions of ordinary being-existence and, on the other hand, to that

"'A little later, when the normal existence of your solar system was stabilized and the necessity for certain intentionally created abnormal actualizations had passed, our MOST ALL-GRACIOUS COMMON FATHER did not fail to give the command immediately to annul certain artificial measures among which was the removal from the common presences of your ancestors of the now already super-fluous organ Kundabuffer with all its special artificial properties, and this command was immediately executed by corresponding Sacred Individuals, who superintend such cosmic actualizations.

"'After a considerable time had passed, it was suddenly brought to light that although all the properties of the said organ had indeed been removed from the presences of your ancestors by the mentioned Most Sacred Individuals, yet nevertheless, a certain lawfully flowing cosmic result, existing under the name of 'predisposition,' and arising in every more or less independent cosmic presence owing to the repeated action in it of any function, had not been foreseen and destroyed in their presences.

"'And so, it turned out that owing to this 'predisposition' which began to pass by heredity to the succeeding generations, the consequences of many of the properties of the organ Kundabuffer began gradually to be crystallized in their presences.

"'No sooner was this lamentable fact which proceeded in the presences of the three-brained beings breeding on this planet Earth first made clear, than, by the All-Gracious sanction of our COMMON FATHER, a suitable Sacred Individual was immediately sent here, so that, being coated with a presence like your own and having become perfected by Objective Reason under the conditions already established here, he might better explain and show you

----

the way of out-rooting from your presences the already crystallized consequences of the properties of the organ Kundabuffer as well as your inherited predispositions to new crystallizations.

"'During the period when the said Sacred Individual, coated with a presence like your own and who had already attained to the age of a responsible three-centered being similar to yourselves, directly guided the ordinary process of the being-existence of your ancestors, many of them did indeed completely free themselves from the consequences of the properties of the organ Kundabuffer, and either thereby acquired 'Being' personally for themselves or became normal sources for the arising of normal presences of succeeding beings similar to themselves.

"'But in consequence of the fact that before the period of the said Sacred Individual's appearance here, the duration of your existence had, owing to very many firmly fixed abnormal conditions of ordinary existence created by yourselves, already become abnormally short, and therefore the process of the 'Sacred Rascooarno' had also very soon to occur to this Sacred Individual, that is to say, he also had, like you, to die prematurely, then after his death, the former conditions were gradually reestablished there owing on the one hand to the established abnormal conditions of ordinary being-existence and, on the other hand, to that maleficent particularity in your psyche, called Wiseacring.

"'Owing to this said particularity in your psyche, the beings here already of the second generation after the contemporaries of the mentioned Sacred Individual who had been sent from Above began gradually to change everything he had explained and indicated, and the whole of it was finally completely destroyed.

"'Again and again the same was actualized by the Most

------------------------------ 238 ------------------------------

Most High Common Cosmic Final Results, and each time the same fruitless results were obtained.

"'In this present period of the flow of time, when the abnormal being-existence of the three-brained beings of your planet, particularly of the beings arising and existing on that part of the surface of the Earth which is called Pearl-land, is already beginning seriously to hinder the normal harmonious existence of the whole of this solar system, my essence is manifested among you from Above, in order that here on the spot, it may together with your own essences find ways and means, under the conditions already fixed here, of freeing your presences from the said consequences, now present in them, owing to the absence of foresight on the part of certain Most Saintly Final Cosmic Results.'

"After having said all this, Saint Buddha thereafter, just by means of talks with them, first cleared up for Himself and afterwards explained to them how the process of their existence must be conducted and the order in which their positive part should consciously guide the manifestations of their unconscious parts, so that the crystallized consequences of the properties of the organ Kundabuffer and also the inherited predisposition to them might gradually disappear from their common presences.

"As the same detailed researches of mine made clear to me—at that period when the inner psyche of the beings of that part of the surface of the Earth was guided by this genuine Messenger from Above, Saint Buddha—the said, for them very maleficent, consequences indeed again began gradually to disappear from the presences of many of them.

"But to the grief of every Individual with Pure Reason of any gradation whatsoever and to the misfortune of the three-brained beings of all succeeding generations who arise on that planet, the first succeeding generation of the

------------------------------ 239 ------------------------------

contemporaries of this genuine Messenger from Above, Saint Buddha, also began, owing once again to that same particularity of their psyche, namely, of wiseacring—which until now is one of the chief results of the conditions of the ordinary being-existence abnormally established there—to wiseacre with all His indications and counsels, and this time to 'superwiseacre' so thoroughly that there reached the beings of the third and fourth generations nothing else but what our Honorable Mullah Nassr Eddin defines by the words:

"'Only-information-about-its-specific-smell.'

"Little by little they so changed these indications and counsels of His that if their Saintly Author Himself should chance to appear there and for some reason or other should wish to make Himself acquainted with them, He would not be

maleficent particularity in your psyche, called 'Wiseacring.'

"'Owing to this said particularity in your psyche, the beings here already of the second generation after the contemporaries of the mentioned Sacred Individual who had been sent from Above, began gradually to change everything he had explained and indicated, and the whole of it was finally completely destroyed.

"'Again and again the same was actualized by the Most

Most High Common Cosmic Final Results, and each time the same sterile results were obtained.

"'In this present period of the flow of time, when the abnormal being-existence of the three-brained beings of your planet, particularly of the beings arising and existing on that part of the surface of the Earth which is called Pearl-Land, is already beginning seriously to hinder the normal harmonious existence of the whole of this solar system, my essence is manifested among you from Above, in order that here on the spot, it may, together with your own essences, find ways and means under the conditions already fixed here of freeing your presences from the said consequences now present in them, owing to the absence of foresight on the part of certain Most Saintly Final Cosmic Results.'

"After having said all this, Saint Buddha thereafter, just by means of talks with them, first cleared up for himself and afterwards explained to them how the process of their existence must be conducted and the order in which their positive part should consciously guide the manifestations of their unconscious parts, so that the crystallized consequences of the properties of the organ Kundabuffer and also the inherited predisposition to them might gradually disappear from their common presences.

"As the same detailed researches of mine made clear to me—at that period when the inner psyche of the beings of that part of the surface of the Earth was guided by this genuine Messenger from Above, Saint Buddha, the said, for them very maleficent, consequences indeed again began gradually to disappear from the presences of many of them.

"But to the grief of every Individual with Pure Reason of any gradation whatsoever and to the misfortune of the three-brained beings of all succeeding generations who arise on that planet, the first succeeding generation of the

contemporaries of this genuine Messenger from Above, Saint Buddha, already also began, owing once again to that same particularity of their psyche, namely, of wiseacring, which until now is one of the chief results of the conditions of the ordinary being-existence abnormally established there—to wiseacre with all His indications and counsels, and this time to 'superwiseacre' so thoroughly that there reached the beings of the third and fourth generations no more than what our Honorable Mullah Nassr Eddin defines by the words:

"'Only-information-about-its-specific-smell.'

"Little by little they so changed these indications and counsels of His that if their Saintly Author himself should chance to appear there and for some reason or other should wish to make himself acquainted with them, he would not be able

able even to suspect that these indications and counsels were made by Him Himself.

"Here I cannot refrain from expressing my essence-grief at that strange practice of these favorites of yours there, which in the course of many of their centuries during the process of their ordinary existence has gradually become, as it were, conformable to law.

"And in the given case also the same established and already fixed peculiar practice there served for the modification of all the true indications and exact counsels of Saint Buddha and for the creation thereby of yet another factor for a still greater dilution of their psyche.

"This already long-established practice there consists in this, that a small, sometimes an almost trifling, cause is enough to bring about a change for the worse or even the complete destruction of any and every objectively good outer and inner previously established, what is called, 'tempo-of-ordinary-existence.'

"Because, my boy, the clarification of certain details of the arising of such a trivial cause, which was in this

------------------------------ 240 ------------------------------

instance a basis for the distortion of all the true explanations and exact indications also of this genuine Messenger from Above, Saint Buddha, may provide you with excellent material for a better sensing and understanding of the strangeness of the psyche of those three-brained beings who have taken your fancy, I shall tell you about this in as great detail as possible and shall explain to you just in what sequence the said practice then arose there which led to the following sad misunderstanding which began to exist there, and which is still manifested particularly clearly.

"I must inform you first of the two following facts:

"The first is this: that I cleared up this misunderstanding much later than the period to which my present tale refers; among other things I made it clear to myself only during the period of my sixth descent there when in connection with a question concerning the Saint Ashiata Shiemash, about whom I shall soon tell you in detail, it became necessary for me to find out about the activities of that genuine Messenger from Above, Saint Buddha.

"And the second fact is this: that unfortunately the basis of the lamentable misunderstanding was certain authentic words contained in one of the explanations of Saint Buddha, Himself.

"It turned out, indeed, that Saint Buddha Himself had, in the course of His explanations to some of His closest initiates initiated by Himself, very definitely expressed Himself concerning the means of the possible destruction in their nature of the mentioned consequences of the properties of the organ Kundabuffer transmitted to them by heredity.

"He then, among other things, told them very definitely the following:

"'One of the best means of rendering ineffective the predisposition present in your nature of the crystallization of the consequences of the properties of the organ

------------------------------ 241 ------------------------------

Kundabuffer is "intentional-suffering"; and the greatest intentional-suffering can

even to suspect that these indications and counsels were made by him himself.

"Here I cannot refrain from expressing essence-grief at that strange practice of these favorites of yours there, which in the course of many of their centuries during the process of their ordinary existence has gradually become, as it were, conformable to law.

"And in the given case also the same established and already fixed peculiar practice there served for the modification of all the true indications and exact counsels of Saint Buddha and for the creation thereby of yet another factor for a still greater dilution of their psyche.

"This already long established practice there consists in this, that a small, sometimes an almost trifling, cause, is enough to bring about a change for the worse or even the complete destruction of any and every objectively good outer and inner previously established what is called, 'tempo-of-ordinary-existence.'

"Because, my boy, the clarification of certain details of the arising of such a trivial cause, which served in this

instance as a basis for the distortion of all the true explanations and exact indications also of this genuine Messenger from Above, Saint Buddha, may provide you with excellent material for a better sensing and understanding of the strangeness of the psyche of these three-brained beings who have taken your fancy, I shall tell you about this in as great detail as possible and shall explain to you just in what sequence the said practice then arose there which led to the following sad misunderstanding which began to exist there and which is still manifested particularly clearly.

"I must inform you first of the two following facts:

"The first is this: that I cleared up this misunderstanding much later than the period to which my present tale refers; among other things I made it clear to myself only during the period of my sixth descent there, when in connection with a question concerning the Saint Ashiata Shiemash, about whom also I shall soon tell you in detail, it became necessary for me to find out about the activities of that genuine Messenger from Above, Saint Buddha.

"And the second fact is this; that unfortunately the basis of the lamentable misunderstanding was certain authentic words contained in one of the explanations of Saint Buddha himself.

"It turned out, indeed, that Saint Buddha himself had in the course of his explanations to some of his closest initiates, initiated by himself, very definitely expressed himself concerning the means of the possible destruction in their nature of the mentioned consequences of the properties of the organ Kundabuffer transmitted to them by heredity.

"He then, among other things, told them very definitely the following:

"'One of the best means of rendering ineffective the predisposition present in your nature for the crystallization of the consequences of the properties of the

organ Kundabuffer is "intentional suffering"; and the greatest "intentional suffer-

be obtained in your presences if you compel yourselves to be able to endure the "displeasing-manifestations-of-others-towards-yourselves."

"This explanation of Saint Buddha together with other definite indications of His was spread by His nearest initiates among the ordinary beings there; and after the process of the sacred Rascooarno had occurred to Him, it also began to pass from generation to generation.

"So, my boy, when, as I have already told you, those three-centered beings there among the second and third generation of the contemporaries of Saint Buddha in whose psyche, already from the time of the loss of Atlantis, that peculiarity had been fixed, called the 'organic-psychic need to wiseacre,' began—unfortunately for the ordinary three-centered beings of that period and unfortunately also for the beings of all succeeding generations and even for those of the present time—to wiseacre and superwiseacre concerning these counsels of Saint Buddha, then as a result a very definite notion became fixed and also began to pass from generation to generation, that this same 'endurance' should without fail be produced in complete solitude.

"Here that strangeness of the psyche of your favorites then manifested itself just as it now manifests itself, by their not having considered and not considering the obvious fact—obvious, that is, to every more or less sane Reason—that the Divine Teacher, Saint Buddha, in advising them to employ that kind of 'endurance,' of course had in view that they should produce this 'endurance' while existing among other beings similar to themselves, and so that by frequently producing in their presences this sacred being-actualization toward the manifestations displeasing to them of other beings similar to themselves, there might thereby be evoked in them what are called

------------------------------ *242* ------------------------------

those 'Trentroodianos,' or, as they themselves would say, those 'psychic-chemical-results' which, in general, in the presence of every three-centered being, form those sacred being-data, which actualize in the common presences of the three-centered beings one of the three holy forces of the sacred being-Triamazikamno; and this holy force in beings always becomes affirming towards all the denying properties already present in them.

"So, my boy, from that time when the mentioned definite notion had begun to exist, your favorites began leaving those already established conditions of being-existence on account of which the predisposition to the crystallization of the consequences of the properties of the organ Kundabuffer had become intense in their presences, and in which conditions, as the Divine Teacher Buddha supposed, the said 'endurance' towards others' manifestations displeasing to oneself could alone crystallize in their common presences that 'Partkdolg-duty' which in general is necessary for all three-centered beings.

"And so, for the purpose of this famous 'suffering' of theirs, many of the three-centered beings of that planet of yours, either singly or in groups, that is to say, with others who thought as they did, began from then on to go away from amongst beings similar to themselves.

"They even organized special colonies for this purpose, where, although exist-

ing" can be obtained in your presences if you compel yourself to be able to endure the "displeasing manifestations of others towards yourself"!'"

"This explanation of Saint Buddha together with other definite indications of his was spread by his nearest initiates among the ordinary beings there; and after the process of the sacred 'Rascooarno' had occurred to him, it also began to pass from generation to generation.

"So, my boy, when, as I have already told you, those three-centered beings there among the second and third generations of the contemporaries of Saint Buddha in whose psyche, already from the time of the loss of Atlantis, there had been fixed that peculiarity called the 'organic-psychic-need-to-wiseacre' began—unfortunately, for the ordinary three-centered beings of that period and unfortunately also for the beings of all succeeding generations and even for those of the present time—to 'wiseacre' and 'superwiseacre' concerning these counsels of Saint Buddha, then as a result a very definite action became fixed and also began to pass from generation to generation, that this same 'endurance' should without fail be produced in complete solitude.

"Here that strangeness of the psyche of your favorites then manifested itself just as it now manifests itself, in this, that they did not consider and do not consider the obvious fact—obvious, that is, to every more or less sane Reason—that the divine Teacher, Saint Buddha, in advising them to employ that kind of 'endurance' while existing among other beings similar to themselves, in order that by frequently producing in their presences this sacred being-actualization towards the manifestations displeasing to them of other beings similar to themselves, there might thereby be evoked in them what are called those 'Trentroodianos' or, as they themselves would say, those 'psychic-chemical-results,' which, in general, in

the presence of every three-centered being form those sacred being-data, which actualize in the common presences of the three-centered beings, one of the three holy forces of the sacred 'being-Triamazikamno'; and this holy force in beings always becomes affirming towards all the denying properties already present in them.

"So, my boy, from that time when the mentioned definite notion had begun to exist, your favorites began leaving those already established conditions of being-existence on account of which the predisposition to the crystallization of the consequences of the properties of the organ Kundabuffer became intense in their presences, and in which conditions, as the Divine Teacher Buddha supposed, the said 'endurance towards others' manifestations displeasing to oneself,' could alone crystallize in their common presences that 'Partkdolgduty' which in general is necessary for all three-centered beings.

"So, for the purpose of this famous 'suffering' of theirs, many of the three-centered beings of that planet of yours, either singly or in groups, that is to say, with others who thought as they did, began from then on to go away from amongst beings similar to themselves.

"They even organized special colonies for this purpose, where although existing together, they nevertheless arranged everything so as to produce this 'endurance' of theirs in solitude.

"It was just then that their famous what are called 'monasteries' came into existence, which exist down to the present time and in which, as it were, certain of your contemporary favorites as they say, 'save their souls.'

"When I first visited that Pearl-land, most of the three-brained beings there, as I have already said, were followers of that same religion which was based, as it were, on

------------------------------ 243 ------------------------------

the exact counsels and indications of Saint Buddha Himself, and the faith of every one of these beings in this religion was unshakably firm.

"At the outset of my investigations into the doctrinal subtleties of that religion there, I had as yet come to no definite decision how exactly to utilize it to attain my aim; but when in the course of my investigations I clarified one very definite comprehension—proper to all the followers of that religion—which arose there again, owing to a misunderstanding, from the words that had indeed been spoken by Saint Buddha Himself, I then at once decided how just to act there through this peculiar Havatvernoni or Religion of theirs.

"It transpired that in His explanations to them about cosmic truths, Saint Buddha had, among other things, told them also that in general the three-centered beings existing on various planets of our Great Universe—and of course the three-centered beings of the Earth also—were nothing else but part of that Most Great Greatness which is the All-embracing of all that exists; and that the foundation of this Most Great Greatness is there Above, for the convenience of the embracing of the essence of everything existing.

"This Most Great Foundation of the All-embracing of everything that exists constantly emanates throughout the whole of the Universe and coats itself from its particles upon planets—in certain three-centered beings who attain in their common presences the capacity to have their own functioning of both fundamental cosmic laws of the sacred Heptaparaparshinokh and the sacred Triamazikamno—into a definite unit in which alone Objective Divine Reason acquires the possibility of becoming concentrated and fixed.

"And this has been foreseen and created in this manner by our COMMON CREATOR in order that when these certain

------------------------------ 244 ------------------------------

parts of the Great All-embracing, already spiritualized by Divine Reason, return and reblend with the great Prime Source of the All-embracing, they should compose that Whole which in the hopes of our COMMON ENDLESS UNI-BEING may actualize the sense and the striving of all that exists in the whole of the Universe.

"Further, it seems Saint Buddha also told them:

"'You, three-centered beings of the planet Earth, having the possibility of acquiring in yourselves both chief fundamental, universal, sacred laws, have the full possibility also of coating yourselves with this most sacred part of the Great All-embracing of everything existing and of perfecting it by the required Divine

ing together, they nevertheless arranged everything so as to produce this 'endurance' of theirs in solitude.

"It was just then that their famous what are called 'monasteries' came into existence, which exist down to the present time and in which, as it were, certain of your contemporary favorites, as they say, 'save their souls.'

"When I first visited that 'Pearl-Land,' most of the three-brained beings there, as I have already said, were followers of that same religion which was based, as it were, on

the exact counsels and indications of Saint Buddha himself, and the faith of everyone of these beings in this religion was unshakably firm.

"At the outset of my investigations into the doctrinal subtleties of that religion there, I had as yet come to no definite decision how exactly to utilize it to attain my aim; but when in the course of my investigations I clarified one very definite comprehending—proper to all the followers of that religion—which arose there again owing to a misunderstanding, from the words that had indeed been spoken by Saint Buddha himself, I then at once decided how just to act there through this peculiar 'Havatvernoni' or 'Religion' of theirs.

"It transpired that in his explanations to them about cosmic truths, Saint Buddha had, among other things, told them also that in general the three-centered beings existing on various planets of our Great Universe—and of course the three-centered beings of the Earth also—were in result nothing else but part of that Most Great Greatness which is the All-embracing of all that exists; and that the foundation of this Most Great Greatness is there Above, for the convenience of the embracing of the essence of everything existing.

"This Most Great Foundation of the All-embracing of everything that exists, constantly emanates throughout the whole of the Universe and coats itself from its particles upon planets—in certain three-centered beings who attain in their common presence the capacity to have their own functioning of both fundamental cosmic laws of the sacred Heptaparaparshinokh and the sacred Triamazikamno—into a definite unit, in which alone Objective Divine Reason acquires the possibility of becoming concentrated and fixed.

"And this had been foreseen and created in this manner by our COMMON CREATOR in order that when these certain

parts of the Great All-embracing, already spiritualized by Divine Reason, return and reblend with the great Prime Source of the All-embracing, they should compose that whole which our COMMON ENDLESS UNI-BEING has the hope may just actualize the sense and the striving of all that exists in the whole of the Universe.

"Further it seems Saint Buddha had also told them:

"'You, three-centered beings of the planet Earth, having the possibility of acquiring in yourselves both chief fundamental, universal sacred laws, have the full possibility also of coating yourselves with this most sacred part of the Great All-embracing of everything existing and of perfecting it by the required Divine

Reason.

"And this Great All-embracing of all that is embraced, is called "Holy Prana.""

"This quite definite explanation of Saint Buddha was well understood by his contemporaries and many of them began, as I have already said, to strive with eagerness, first to absorb and to coat in their presences the particle of this Most Great Greatness and afterwards to 'make-inherent' to it Divine Objective Reason.

"But when the second and third generations of the contemporaries of Saint Buddha began wiseacring with His explanations of cosmic truths, they just wiseacred with their peculiar Reason and fixed—for its transmission—a very definite notion to the effect that that same 'Mister Prana' already begins to be in them immediately upon their arising.

"Thanks to this misunderstanding, the beings of that period and of all subsequent generations including the contemporary, have imagined and still imagine that without any being-Partkdolg-duty they are already parts of that Most Great Greatness, which Saint Buddha Himself had personally very definitely explained.

"So, my boy, as soon as I had made this misunderstanding

clear to myself and had clearly constated that the beings of that country Pearl-land were all, without exception, convinced that they were already particles of Mister Prana himself, I then at once decided to use this misunderstanding, and there also to attain my aim through that religion of theirs.

"Before saying more about this, it must without fail be noticed that concerning these same explanations of Saint Buddha's, namely, that He had supposedly said that beings already have in themselves, at their arising, a particle of the Most Great Greatness, my personal detailed investigations quite clearly showed me that He never could possibly have said just that.

"And He could not have said it because, as the same detailed investigations of mine have cleared up to me, when Saint Buddha once happened to be among His devoted disciples in the locality 'Senkoo-ori,' He definitely said:

"'If this most sacred Prana is crystallized in you, consciously or unconsciously on the part of your "I," you must without fail bring the perfecting of the individual Reason of the totality of its most holy atoms to the required gradations; otherwise this most holy coating will, changing various exterior coatings, suffer and languish eternally.'

"Here it is interesting to notice that concerning this they were warned by still another Saint-Individual, also a genuine Messenger from Above, namely, the Saint Kirmininasha.

"And this Saint and genuine Messenger gave this warning to them in the following words:

"'Blessed is he that hath a soul; blessed also is he that hath none; but grief and sorrow are to him that hath in himself its conception.'

"So, my boy, when I made this clear to myself there

in Pearl-land, I at once decided to use this error of theirs for the accomplishment of my aim.

Reason.'

"'And this Great All-embracing of all that is embraced, is called 'Holy Prana.'"

"This quite definite explanation of Saint Buddha was well understood by his contemporaries and many of them began, as I have already said, to strive with eagerness, first to absorb and to coat in their presences the particle of this Most Great Greatness and afterwards to 'make inherent' to it, Divine Objective Reason.

"But when the second and third generations of the contemporaries of Saint Buddha began 'wiseacring' with his explanations of cosmic truths, they just wiseacred with their peculiar 'Reason' and fixed—for its transmission—a very definite notion to the effect, that that same 'Mister Prana' already begins to be in them immediately upon their arising.

"Thanks to this misunderstanding, the beings of that period and of all sub-sequent generations, including the contemporary, have imagined and still imagine, that without any being-Partkdolgduty they are already parts of that Most Great Greatness, which Saint Buddha himself had personally very definitely explained.

"So, my boy, as soon as I had made this misunderstanding

clear to myself and had clearly constated that the beings of that country Pearl-Land were all, without exception, convinced that they were already particles of 'Mister Prana' himself, I then at once decided to use this misunderstanding, and there also to attain my aim through that religion of theirs.

"Before saying more about this, it must without fail be noticed that, concerning these same explanations of Saint Buddha's, namely, that he, as it were, had said that beings already have in themselves a particle of the Most Great Greatness at their very arising, my personal detailed investigations quite clearly showed me that he never could possibly have said just that.

"And he could not have said it because, as the same detailed investigations of mine have cleared up to me, that when Saint Buddha once happened to be among his devoted disciples in the locality 'Senkoo-ori,' he definitely said:

"'If this most sacred Prana is crystallized in you, consciously or unconsciously on the part of your "I," you must without fail bring the perfecting of the individual Reason of the totality of its most holy atoms to the required gradations; otherwise this most holy coating will, changing various exterior coatings, suffer and lan-guish eternally.'

"Here it is interesting to notice that concerning this they were warned by still another Saint-Individual, also a genuine Messenger from Above, namely, the Saint Kirmininasha.

"And this Saint and genuine Messenger gave this warning to them in the fol-lowing words:

"'Blessed is he that hath a soul; blessed also is he that hath none; but grief and sorrow are to him that hath in himself its conception.'

"So, my boy, when I made this clear to myself there

in Pearl-Land, I at once decided to use this error of theirs for the accomplishment of my aim.

"There in Pearl-land also, just as in the city Gob, I first 'invented-a-detailed-ad-dition' to the mentioned religious teaching, and afterwards by every possible means I began spreading this invention of mine.

"I began to spread there in Pearl-land that that 'Most-Sacred-Prana,' about which our Divine Teacher Saint Buddha had explained, is already present not only in people, but also in all the other beings that arise and exist on our planet Earth.

"A particle of that fundamental Most Great Great All-embracing, namely, the Most-Sacred-Prana, has already from the very beginning settled in every form of being of every scale, breeding on the surface of the planet, in the water, and also in the atmosphere.

"I regret to have to say here, my boy, that I was then constrained more than once to emphasize that these words had been uttered by the very lips of Saint Buddha Himself.

"The several beings there with whom I had meanwhile established 'friendly' relations, and whom without any discussion I first of all persuaded there of that invention, not only immediately fully believed it, but afterwards also very effectu-ally helped me, of course unconsciously, in spreading this new invention of mine.

"Here also these friends of mine always and everywhere very zealously and passionately proved to other beings like themselves, that this was just so and could not possibly be otherwise.

"In short, there in Pearl-land, owing to this second invention of mine, the de-sired results were unexpectedly rapidly brought about.

"And there in Pearl-land, owing simply to my invention, your favorites so greatly changed their essence-relations towards the beings of other forms, that they not only

---------------------------------- *247* ----------------------------------

ceased to destroy the existence of these beings for their famous Sacrificial-Offer-ings, but even began very sincerely with the whole of their being to regard these beings of other forms as beings like themselves.

"If only it had all continued like that, it would have been very good; but here as well, just as in the country Maralpleicie, they soon began, as is proper to them, to wiseacre and to manifest all kinds of comical aspects of their Havatvernoni.

"For instance, only a quarter of their year after the commencement of my preaching, you could see when strolling down the street of the city Kaimon, al-most at every step, beings there walking on what are called 'stilts.'

"And they walked on stilts in order not to risk crushing some insect or other, a 'little being,' as they thought, just like themselves.

"Many of them were afraid to drink water that had not been freshly taken from a spring or stream, because they thought that if the water had been a long time out of the spring or stream, 'little-beings' might have got into the water, and without seeing them, they might suddenly swallow these 'poor-little-creatures-like-themselves.'

"Many of them took the precaution to wear what are called 'veils,' lest poor-little-beings-like-themselves in the air might chance to enter mouths or noses,

"There in Pearl-Land also just as in the city Gob, I first 'invented' a detailed addition to the mentioned religious teaching, and afterwards by every possible means I began spreading this invention of mine.

"I began to spread there in Pearl-Land that that 'Most-Sacred-Prana,' about which our Divine Teacher Saint Buddha had explained, is already present not only in people, but in all the other beings that arise and exist on our planet Earth.

"A particle of that fundamental Most Great Great All-embracing, namely, the 'Most-Sacred-Prana,' has already from the very beginning settled in every form of being of every scale, breeding both on the surface of the planet itself and within it, and in the water as well as in the atmosphere.

"I regret to have to say here, my boy, that I was then constrained more than once to emphasize that these words had been uttered by the very lips of Saint Buddha himself.

"These several beings there with whom I had meanwhile established 'friendly' relations and whom without any discussion I first of all persuaded there of that invention, immediately not only completely believed it, but afterwards also very effectually helped me, of course unconsciously, in spreading this new invention of mine.

"Here also these friends of mine always and everywhere very zealously and passionately proved to other beings like themselves, that this was just so and could not possibly be otherwise.

"In short, there in Pearl-Land, owing to this second invention of mine, the desired results were unexpectedly rapidly brought about.

"And there in Pearl-Land, owing simply to my invention, your favorites so greatly changed their essence relations towards the beings of other forms, that they not only

---

ceased to destroy the existence of these beings for their famous 'sacrifices,' but even began very sincerely with the whole of their Being to regard these beings of other forms as beings like themselves.

"If only it had all continued like that, it would have been good; but here as well, just as in the country Maralpleicie, they soon began, as is proper to them, to 'wiseacre' and to manifest all kinds of comical aspects of their 'Havatvernoni.'

"For instance, only a quarter of their year after the commencement of my preaching, strolling down the street of the city Kaimon you could see, almost at every step, beings there walking on what are called 'stilts.'

"And they walked on 'stilts' in order not to risk crushing some insect or other, a 'little being,' as they thought, just like themselves.

"Many of them were afraid to drink water that had not been freshly taken from a spring or stream, because they thought that if the water had been a long time out of the spring or stream, 'little-beings' might have got into it, and without seeing them, they might suddenly swallow these 'poor-little-creatures-like-themselves.'

"Many of them took the precaution to wear what are called 'veils,' lest poor little beings like themselves, found in the air, might chance to enter their mouths or

and so on and so forth.

"From that time on, various societies began to arise there in Pearl-land in the city of Kaimon and its outskirts, whose aim was to protect 'defenseless' beings of various forms, both those existing among them and those they called 'wild.'

"Rules existed in all such societies prohibiting not only their destruction for Sacrificial-Offerings, but also the use of their planetary bodies for the 'first-being-food.'

"E-h-h-h-hkh . . . my boy.

------------------------------ 248 ------------------------------

"Owing once again merely to the strangeness of their psyche, the intentional suffering and conscious labors of this Sacred Individual, Saint Buddha, who had been specially actualized for them with a planetary presence similar to theirs, have ever since hovered and still hover in vain; nor have they yet actualized any lawfully expected real results whatsoever, but have engendered and until now continue to engender only all kinds of 'pseudo-teachings' there, like those existing there in recent times under the names of 'Occultism,' 'Theosophy,' 'Spiritualism,' 'Psychoanalysis,' and so on, which before as now, are means only for the obscuring of their already, without this, obscured psyche.

"It is needless to say that from the truths indicated by Saint Buddha Himself absolutely nothing has survived and reached the beings of the present time.

"Half of one of the words, however, managed to reach even the contemporary beings of that unparalleled planet.

"And this half of a word reached them in the following way:

"Saint Buddha among other things explained to the beings of Pearl-land how and to what part of the body of their ancestors the said famous organ Kundabuffer had been attached.

"He told them that the Archangel Looisos had by a special means made this organ grow in their ancestors at the extremity of that brain which in them, just as in you, Nature has placed along their back in what is called the 'spinal column.'

"Saint Buddha, as I also made clear, then also said that though the properties of this organ had been entirely destroyed in their ancestors, yet the material formation of this organ had remained at the lower extremities of this brain; and this material formation, being transmitted from generation to generation, had also reached them.

------------------------------ 249 ------------------------------

"'This material formation,' he said, 'now has no significance whatever in you, and it can be completely destroyed in the course of time, if your being-existence proceeds as is becoming to three-centered beings.'

"It was just when they began wiseacring and inventing various forms of that famous 'suffering' of theirs that they also played their usual 'tricks' with this word.

"Namely, first of all, as the root of the second half of this word chanced to coincide with a word in the language of that time which meant 'Reflection,' and as they had also invented a means for destroying this material formation rapidly and not merely in the course of time as Saint Buddha had told them, they also wiseacred about this word according to the following rumination of their bobtailed Reason.

noses, and so on and so forth.

"From that time on there began to arise there in Pearl-Land, both in the city Kaimon and in its outskirts, various societies whose aim was to protect 'defenseless' beings of various form, both those existing among them and those they called 'wild.'

"Rules existed in all such societies prohibiting not only their destruction for 'sacrifices' but also the use of their planetary bodies for the 'first-being-food.'

"Eh-h-h-h-h-h-kh! . . . my boy.

- -

"Owing once again merely to the strangeness of their psyche, the intentional sufferings and conscious labors of this Sacred Individual Saint Buddha, who had been specially actualized for them with a planetary presence similar to theirs, have hovered ever since and still hover in vain; nor have they yet actualized any lawfully expected real results whatsoever, but have engendered and until now continue to engender only all kinds of 'pseudo-teachings' there, like those existing there in recent times under the names of 'Occultism,' 'Theosophy,' 'Spiritualism,' 'Psychoanalysis,' and so on, which, before as now, are means only for the obscuring of their already, without this, obscured psyche.

"It is needless to say that from the truths indicated by Saint Buddha himself, absolutely nothing has survived and reached the beings of the present time.

"Half of one of the words, however, managed to reach even the contemporary beings of that unparalleled planet.

"And this half of a word reached them in the following way:

"Saint Buddha among other things explained to the beings of Pearl Land, how and to what part of the body of their ancestors the said famous organ Kundabuffer had been attached.

"He told them that the Archangel Looisos had by a special means made this organ grow in their ancestors at the extremity of that brain which in them, just as in you, Nature has placed along their back in what is called the 'spinal-column.'

"Saint Buddha, as I also made clear, then also said that though the properties of this organ had been absolutely destroyed in their ancestors, yet the material formation of this organ had remained at the lower extremities of this brain. And this material formation, being transmitted from generation to generation, had also reached them

- -

"'This material formation,' he said, 'now has no significance whatever in you, and it can be completely destroyed in the course of time, if your being-existence proceeds as is becoming to three-centered beings.'

"It was just when they began 'wiseacring' and inventing various forms of that famous 'suffering' of theirs that they also played then usual 'tricks' with this word.

"Namely, first of all, as the root of the second half of this word chanced to coincide with a word in the language of that time which meant 'Reflection' and as they had also invented a means for destroying this material formation rapidly, and not merely in the course of time as Saint Buddha had told them, they also wiseacred about this word according to the following rumination of their bobtailed Reason.

Of course, when this organ is in action, it ought to have in its name also the root of the word to 'reflect'; now, since we are destroying even its material basis, the name must end with a word whose root means 'former,' and because 'former' in their current language was then pronounced 'lina,' they changed the second half of this word, and instead of 'reflection,' they stuck in the mentioned 'lina,' so that instead of the word Kundabuffer, they obtained the word 'Kundalina.'

"Thus it was that a half of the word Kundabuffer survived and, being transmitted from generation to generation, finally reached your contemporary favorites also, accompanied, of course, by a thousand and one different explanations.

"Even the contemporary 'learned beings' also have a name made up of very abstruse Latin roots for that part of the spinal marrow.

"The whole of what is called 'Indian-philosophy' now existing there is based also on this famous Kundalina, and about the word itself there exist thousands of various occult, secret, and revealed 'sciences' which explain nothing.

--------------------------------- 250 ----------------------------

"And as regards the way in which the contemporary terrestrial learned beings of what are called the exact sciences define the significance of this part of the spinal marrow, that, my dear boy, is a profound secret.

"And it became a secret because several centuries ago, this 'explanation' suddenly for no reason whatever entered the favorite mole of the famous 'Scheherazade,' which that incomparable Arabian fantasist chanced to have on the right side of her adorable navel.

"And there this 'learned-explanation' remains perfectly preserved down to the present day.

"When I was quite convinced that I had succeeded so easily in the destruction, perhaps for a long time, of that terrible practice among the beings of that group there in Pearl-land, I decided to stay there no longer but to return to the Sea of Beneficence to our ship *Occasion*.

"When we were quite ready to leave that Pearl-land, the intention suddenly arose in me not to return to the Sea of Beneficence by the way we had come, but by another way quite unusual in those days.

"Namely, I decided to return through the locality which was later called 'Tibet.'"

--------------------------------- 251 ----------------------------

Of course, when this organ is in action, it ought to have in its name, also the root of the word to 'reflect'; now, since we are destroying even its material basis, the name must end with a word whose root means 'former'; and because 'former' in their current language was then pronounced 'lina,' they changed the second half of this word, and instead of 'reflection,' they stuck in the mentioned 'lina,' so that instead of the word Kundabuffer, they obtained the word 'Kundalina.'

"Thus it as that a half of the word Kundabuffer survived, and being transmitted from generation to generation, finally reached your contemporary favorites also, accompanied, of course, by a thousand and one different explanations.

"Even the contemporary 'learned-beings' also have a name for that part of the spinal-marrow, made up of very abstruse Latin roots.

"The whole of what is called 'Indian-philosophy' now existing there, is based also on this famous 'Kundalina,' and about the word itself there exist thousands of various occult, secret and revealed 'sciences' which explain nothing.

- -

"And as regards the way in which the contemporary terrestrial learned beings of what are called the exact 'sciences' define the significance of this part of the spinal marrow, that my boy, is a profound secret.

"And it became a secret because several centuries ago, this 'explanation' suddenly for no reason whatever, entered the favorite mole of the famous 'Scheherazade' which that incomparable Arabian fantasist chanced to have on the right side of her adorable navel.

"And there this 'learned-explanation' remains perfectly preserved down to the present day.

"When I was quite convinced that I had succeeded so easily in the destruction, perhaps for a long time, of that terrible practice among the beings of that group there in Pearl-Land, I decided to stay there no longer but to return to the 'Sea-of-Beneficence' to our ship 'Occasion.'

"When we were quite ready to leave that Pearl-Land, the intention suddenly arose in me not to return to the 'Sea-of-Beneficence' by the way we had come, but by another way quite unusual in those days.

"Namely, I decided to return through the locality which was later called 'Tibet.'"

- -

Beelzebub for the First Time in Tibet

A S THE route proposed this time was most uncommon for the terrestrial three-brained beings of those days and accordingly we could not count on the possibility of joining any 'caravan' of theirs, I had, then, to organize my own caravan, and I began the same day preparing and procuring everything necessary for this purpose.

"I then procured some score of the quadruped beings called 'horses,' 'mules,' 'asses,' and 'Chamianian' goats and so on, and hired a number of your biped favorites to look after the said beings and to do the semiconscious work required on the way for this mode of travel.

"Having procured everything necessary, I set off, accompanied by Ahoon.

"This time we passed through places still more peculiar, and through still more uncommon parts of the general Nature of that ill-fated planet; and we also encountered this time, or there came within the sphere of our vision, a much greater number of those one-brained and two-brained beings, of various forms, which are called 'wild,' and which in those days came there from very remote parts of the continent Ashhark for the purpose, as it is said there, of 'hunting.'

"The said 'wild' beings there, were at that period particularly 'dangerous' both for the three-brained beings there, and for those forms of quadruped beings which your favorites, with the 'cunning' proper to them, had already been able to make their slaves, compelling them to work exclusively for the satisfaction of their egoistic needs.

"And the said wild beings were then particularly dangerous because just at that period there was being crystallized

----------------------- *252* -----------------------

in the presences of these wild beings that special function which arose in them, again, owing to the abnormally established conditions of the being-existence of the three-brained beings there; and about this special function I shall later explain to you in detail.

"The places through which our way went this time were then almost inaccessible to the three-brained beings of that period, chiefly on account of these wild beings.

"In those days it was possible for the three-brained beings to pass through these places only, as they say, 'by day,' that is to say, when in the atmosphere of their planet the process of 'aieioiuoa' proceeds in the Active Element Okidanokh.

"And they could pass by day because during this time of the Krentonalnian position of their planet in relation to the rays of their sun, almost all the wild terrestrial beings are in the being-state called 'sleep,' that is to say, in a state of automatic elaboration in their presences of that energy which is necessary for their ordinary existence, which elaboration of energy proceeds in them during just this time, whereas in the three-centered beings there, on the contrary, the same is elaborated only when the said sacred property is not proceeding in the atmo-

Beelzebub in Tibet for the First Time

A S THE MODE of travel then planned was still quite uncommon in those days for the three-brained beings there, we could not count on the chance of joining some 'caravan.' So, having to organize my own 'caravan' I began the same day preparing and procuring everything necessary for this purpose.

"I then procured some tens of the quadruped beings called 'horses,' 'mules,' 'asses' and 'Chamianian goats,' and so on, and hired a number of your biped favorites to look after the said beings and to do the semiconscious labor required on the way during this mode of travel.

"Having procured everything necessary, accompanied by Ahoon, I set off.

"This time we passed through places still more peculiar, and still more uncommon parts of the general Nature of that ill-starred planet; and we also encountered this time, or there came within the sphere of our sight, a greater number of the one-brained and two-brained beings of various forms, which are there called 'wild' and which in those days came there from very remote parts of the continent Ashhark for the purpose, as it is said there, of 'hunting.'

"The said 'wild' beings there were at that period particularly 'dangerous' both for the three-brained beings there, and also for those forms of quadruped beings which your favorites, with the 'cunning' proper to them, had already been able to make their slaves, compelling them to work exclusively for the satisfaction of their egoistic needs.

"And the said 'wild beings' were particularly, dangerous then only because there was being crystallized

just at that period, in the presence of such 'wild beings,' that special function which arose in them also owing to the abnormally established conditions of being-existence of the three-brained beings there, and about which special function I shall explain to you in detail.

"The places through which our way went this time were at that period almost inaccessible for the three-brained beings then, chiefly on account of such 'wild beings.'

"In those days it was perhaps possible for the three-brained beings to pass through these places only, as they say, during the 'day,' that is to say, when in the atmosphere of their planet there, the process of 'Aieioiuoa' proceeds with the active element 'Okidanokh.'

"And they could pass during the 'day' because during this time of 'Krentonalnian' position of their planet in relation to the rays of their sun almost all the 'wild' terrestrial beings are in the state called 'sleep,' that is to say, in a state of the automatic elaboration in their presence of that energy, which is necessary to their ordinary existence and which elaboration of energy just then proceeds in them; whereas, on the contrary, in the three-centered beings there, the same is elabor-

sphere, that is, during the period of the diurnity which they call 'night.'

"So, my boy, because of this it was possible for your favorites of those times to pass through these places only by day. At night, great vigilance and the use of various artificial shelters was required as a defense against these wild beings, both for themselves and for their 'goods.'

"During the period of the aforesaid Krentonalnian position of the planet Earth, these wild beings there are wide awake and take their first being-food; and since, by that time, they had already become accustomed to use for this purpose almost exclusively the planetary bodies of weaker beings of other forms arising on their planet, they were

- 253 -

always trying, during that period, to get hold of such a being in order to use his planetary body for the satisfaction of that need of theirs.

"These wild beings, particularly the smallest of them, were at that time already—also, of course, owing to the abnormally established conditions of the ordinary being-existence of the three-brained beings there—perfected as regards apprehendingness and cunning up to the ideal.

"In consequence of this, all along this second route of ours, we, and especially our work men for the semiconscious work, had to be extremely watchful and alert at night in order to guard ourselves, our quadruped beings, and our supplies.

"A whole 'gathering' of these wild beings would form round our camp at night, having come there to provide themselves with something suitable for their first food, a meeting rather like an 'assembly' of your favorites during what is called the 'quotation of stock prices' or during their 'election' of representatives to some society or other, the nominal purpose of which is the joint pursuit of a means to the happy existence of all beings like themselves without distinction of their notorious castes.

"Although we kept logs burning brightly all night, to scare these wild beings, and although our biped workers, notwithstanding that they were forbidden, destroyed with the help of the, as they are called, poisoned arrows of 'Elnapara' those beings that came too near our camp, yet not a single night passed upon which what are there called 'tigers,' 'lions,' and 'hyenas' did not carry off one or more of our quadruped beings; the number of which in consequence diminished daily.

"Although, my boy, this way back to the Sea of Beneficence took us far longer than the way by which we had come here, all that we then saw and heard about the strangeness of the psyche of your favorites, during our

- 254 -

passage through these places, fully justified the extra time spent.

"We traveled under these conditions more than a month of their time, and finally we came upon a small settlement of the three-brained beings who, as it appeared later, had only recently migrated there from Pearl-land.

"As we afterwards learned, this settlement was called 'Sincratorza'; and when this region was subsequently populated and this same place became the principal center for all the beings of that region, the whole country also came to be called

ated only when the said sacred property is not proceeding in the atmosphere, the period of the diurnity which they call 'night.'

"So, my boy, for the said reason it was possible for your favorites in those days to pass through these places only by 'day.' At night, great vigilance and the use of various artificial shelters were required as a defense against these wild beings, both for themselves and for their 'goods.'

"During the period of the mentioned 'Krentonalnian' position of the planet Earth, these 'wild' beings there are wide awake and take their first being-food; and because, by that time, they had already become accustomed to use for this purpose almost only the planetary bodies of weaker beings of other forms arising on their planet, they were

always trying, during that period, to get hold of such a being in order to use his planetary body to satisfy that need of theirs.

"These 'wild' beings, particularly the smallest of them, were already at that time, owing also, of course, to the abnormally established conditions of the ordinary being-existence of the three-brained beings, perfected in point of ruminating and cunning up to the ideal.

"In consequence of this, throughout our whole route, we, and especially our workmen for the semiconscious work, had to be extremely careful and on the watch in order to guard ourselves, our quadruped workers and our supplies.

"A whole 'meeting' of these 'wild' beings would form around our camp at night, that had come there to provide themselves with something suitable for their first food, a gathering rather like an 'assembly' of your favorites during what is called the 'quotation of stock prices' or during their 'election' of representatives to some society or other whose nominal purpose is the joint pursuit of a means to the happy existence of all beings like themselves without distinction of their notorious castes there.

"Although we kept logs burning brightly all night, to scare these 'wild' beings, and although our biped workers, notwithstanding that they were forbidden, destroyed with the help of the so-called poisoned arrows of 'Elnapara,' those beings that came too near our camp, yet not a single night passed upon which what are there called 'tigers,' 'lions' and 'hyenas' did not carry off one or more of our quadruped beings; whose number in consequence diminished daily.

"Although, my boy, this way back to the 'Sea of Beneficence' then took us far longer than the way by which we had come there, all that we then saw and heard during our passage over those places, concerning the strangeness of the psyche of

your favorites, fully justified the extra time spent.

"We travelled under these conditions more than a month of their time, and finally we came upon a small settlement of three-brained beings, who, as it appeared later, had only recently migrated there from Gemchania.

"As we afterwards learned, this settlement was called 'Sincratorza'; and when this region was subsequently populated and this same place became the principal center for all the beings of that region, the whole country was called by the same

by the same name.

"The name of this place was afterwards changed several times and now it is called 'Tibet.'

"As we chanced to meet the said beings just as night was coming on, we asked them for, as it is said, a 'night's lodging.'

"And when they gave us permission to pass the night under their shelter we were very glad at the prospect of a night's rest, since, indeed, we were all so exhausted by the constant warfare with these wild beings that, both for ourselves and especially for our biped workers, it was now imperative to pass at least one night in peace.

"In the course of the evening talk, it transpired that all the beings of this settlement belonged to the sect then famous in Pearl-land under the name 'The Self-tamers,' which had been formed from among the followers of just that religion which, as I have already told you, purported to be based on the direct instructions of Saint Buddha.

"There is no harm in noticing in this connection that the beings of that planet had still another peculiarity which had long before become proper to them alone, and which consists in this, that no sooner does a new common Havatvernoni, or religion, arise among them than its followers immediately begin to split up into different parties each of which very soon creates its own, as it is called, 'sect.'

---------------------------- 255 ----------------------------

"The particular strangeness of this peculiarity of theirs consists in this, that those who belong to any such sect never call themselves 'sectarians,' the name being considered offensive; they are named 'sectarians' only by those beings who do not belong to their sect.

"And the adherents of any sect are sectarian for other beings only as long as they have no 'guns' and 'ships,' but as soon as they get hold of a sufficient number of 'guns' and 'ships,' then what had been a peculiar sect at once becomes the dominant religion.

"The beings both of this settlement and of many other regions of Pearl-land became sectarians, having separated just from the religion the doctrine of which, as I have already told you, I studied there in detail and which later was called 'Buddhism.'

"These sectarians who called themselves the Self-tamers arose owing to that distorted understanding of the Buddhist religion which, as I have already told you, they called 'suffering-in-solitude.'

"And it was in order to produce upon themselves the said famous 'suffering,' without hindrance from other beings similar to themselves, that these beings with whom we passed the night had settled so far away from their own people.

"Now, my boy, because everything I learned that night and saw the next day of the followers of that sect then produced so painful an impression upon me that for very many of their centuries I could never recall it all without, as is said, 'shuddering'—not that is until very much later, when I had made perfectly clear to myself all the causes of the strangeness of the psyche of those favorites of yours—I wish to tell you in greater detail about all I then saw and learned.

---------------------------- 256 ----------------------------

name.

"The name of this place was afterwards changed several times and at present it is called 'Tibet.'

"As we chanced to meet the said beings just as night was coming on, we asked them for, as it is said, a 'night's lodging.'

"And when they gave us permission to pass the night under their shelter we were very glad at the prospect of a night's rest, since, indeed, we were all so exhausted by the constant warfare with these wild beings, that both for ourselves and especially for our biped workers, it was already urgent to pass at least one night in peace.

"In the course of the evening talk, it was made clear that all the beings of this settlement belonged to the sect known then in Gemchania under the name 'The Self-tamers,' which had been formed from among the followers of just that religion which, as I have already told you, purported to be based on the direct instructions of Saint Buddha.

"There is no harm in noticing in this connection that the beings of that planet had still another peculiarity which had long before become proper to them alone; it consists in this, that no sooner does a new common 'Havatvernoni' or 'religion' arise among them, than its followers immediately begin to split up into different parties, each of which very soon creates its own, as it is called, 'sect.'

"The particular strangeness of this peculiarity of theirs consists in this, that those who belong to a sect never call themselves 'sectarians,' the name being considered offensive; they are named 'sectarians' only by these beings who do not belong to the same sect.

"And the adherents of any sect are sectarian for other beings only as long as they have no 'guns' and 'ships'; but as soon as they get hold of a sufficient number of 'guns' and 'ships' their particular sect at once becomes the dominant religion.

"The beings both of this settlement and of many other regions of Gemchania became sectarians, having separated just from the religion, the doctrine of which, as I have already told you, I studied in detail and which later was called 'Buddhism.'

"These sectarians of the Buddhist religion who called themselves the 'Self-tamers' arose owing to the same misconception, which, as I have already told you, they 'wiseacred' and named 'suffering-in-solitude.'

"And those beings with whom we passed the night, had settled so far away from their own people, in order to produce upon themselves the said notorious 'suffering,' without hindrance from others like themselves.

"Because, my boy, everything I learned that night and saw the next day of the followers of that sect, then produced so painful an impression upon me that for very many of their centuries I could never recall it all without what is called 'shuddering,' it was not until already long afterwards that I made perfectly clear to myself all of the causes of the strangeness of the psyche of these favorites of yours. It is for this reason that I wish to tell you all I then saw and learned in greater detail.

"As I then made clear to myself during the night's conversation, before the migration of the followers of that sect to this isolated place they had already invented in Pearl-land a special form of 'suffering,' namely, they had decided to settle somewhere in some inaccessible place where other beings similar to themselves, not belonging to the sect and not initiated into its 'arcana,' should not prevent them from producing upon themselves this same 'suffering' of special form which they had invented.

"When after long searching they finally found this same place which we had happened to come upon—a place well suited for such a purpose as theirs—they, already solidly organized and materially secured, migrated together with their families, with great difficulties, there to that place almost inaccessible to their ordinary countrymen; and this place they then first called, as I have already told you, 'Sincratorza.'

"At first, while they were settling down in this new place, they more or less agreed among themselves; but when they began carrying out in practice the special form of 'suffering' they had invented, their families and especially their wives, having learned what this special form of suffering consisted in, rebelled, and made a great outcry about it, with the result that a schism occurred.

"The said schism among them had occurred not long before our chance meeting with them, and at the time when we came upon that Sincratorza, they were already beginning little by little to migrate to other places which they had recently found and which were even more suitable for an isolated existence.

"For a clear understanding of what follows, you must know about the fundamental cause of the schism among these sectarians.

"It turned out that the leaders of that sect, while they were still in Pearl-land, had agreed among themselves to

---------------------------------- 257 ----------------------------------

go quite away from beings like themselves, and to stop at nothing in order to attain their deliverance from the consequences of that organ of which the divine Teacher Saint Buddha had spoken.

"In their agreement it was included that they should exist in a certain way until their final planetary destruction or, as they say, until their death, in order by this special form of existence to purify their, as they said, 'soul' of all the alien growths due to that organ Kundabuffer which, as Saint Buddha told them, their ancestors had, and, being freed from these consequences, thereby acquire the possibility, as the Divine Teacher Saint Buddha had said, of reblending with the All-embracing Holy Prana.

"But when, as I have already said, they, having settled down, set about carrying out in practice the special form of 'suffering' which they had invented, and their wives, having learned its true nature, rebelled, then many of them, having fallen under the influence of their wives, declined to carry out the obligations they had undertaken while still in Pearl-land—and as a result, they then divided into two independent parties.

"As I then cleared up during the night-talk, even before the migration of the followers of that new sect there of the Buddhist religion, there had been invented by its leaders in Gemchania a 'suffering' of a special form, namely: they had decided to settle somewhere in some inaccessible place where other beings like themselves, not belonging to the sect and not initiated into its 'arcana,' might not prevent them from producing upon themselves this same 'suffering' of special form which they had invented.

"When after long search they finally found this same place to which we also had chanced to come—a place well suited for such a purpose as theirs, they, already solidly organized and materially secured, migrated with great difficulties, together with their families, there to that place almost inaccessible to their ordinary countrymen; and this place they then at first called, as I have already told you, 'Sincratorza.'

"While they were still only settling in this new place, they more or less agreed among themselves; but when they began practically carrying into effect the special form of 'sufferings' they had invented, their families and especially their wives, having learned of what it consisted, protested, and made a great outcry about it, with the result that schism arose among them.

"The said schism had taken place among them shortly before our chance encounter with them.

"Although at that time when we arrived in that 'Sincratorza,' all these migrants from Gemchania still existed there together, yet they had already begun little by little to migrate to other places which they had newly found and which were suitable for an isolated existence.

"For a clear understanding of what follows, you must know about the fundamental cause of the schism among those sectarians.

"It seems that the leaders of that sect, while they were still in Gemchania, had agreed among themselves to

leave the beings like themselves, and to stick at nothing in order to attain their deliverance from the consequences of that organ of which the divine Teacher Saint Buddha had spoken.

"Among their conditions the agreement was included that they would exist in a certain way until their final planetary destruction or, as they say, until their death, in order that, as they said, their 'soul' might be cleansed by this special form of existence of alien growths of every kind, due to that organ Kundabuffer which, as Saint Buddha told them, their ancestors had, and, being freed from these consequences, to acquire thereby, the possibility, as the divine Saint Buddha had said, of reblending with the 'All-embracing Holy Prana.'

"But when, as I have already said, they, being settled, set about practically effecting the special form of 'suffering' which they had invented, and their wives, having learned its true nature, protested, then many of them, having fallen under the influence of their wives, declined to carry out the obligations they had undertaken while still in Gemchania, with the result that they just divided into two independent parties.

"From this time on, these sectarians, formerly called the Self-tamers, now began to be called by various names; those of the Self-tamers who remained faithful to the obligations they had taken upon themselves were called 'Orthodoxhydooraki,' while the rest, who had renounced the several obligations they had undertaken in their native country, were called 'Katoshkihydooraki.'

"It transpired that at the time of our arrival in Sincratorza those of the sectarians who were named Orthodoxhydooraki had their well-organized what is called 'monastery' not far from this original settling place of theirs, and there the said special form of suffering was already proceeding.

---------------------------------- 258 ----------------------------------

"On resuming our journey the next day after a restful night, we passed very near the monastery of these sectarians of the Buddhist religion of the Orthodox-hydooraki doctrine.

"At that time of the day we usually made a halt to feed our quadruped workers, and so we asked the monks to allow us to make our necessary halt in the shelter of their monastery.

"Strange and unusual as it may seem, the beings there bearing the name monks did not refuse our objectively just request, but at once, and without any of the 'swaggering' that had become proper there to monks of all centuries and of all doctrines, admitted us. And we thereupon entered the very center of the sphere of the arcana of this doctrine, the kind of sphere which, from the very beginning of their arising, the beings of the planet Earth came to be very skillful in concealing from the observation even of Individuals with pure Reason. In other words, they became skillful in wiseacring something or other and in making of it, as they say, a 'mystery,' and in so thoroughly concealing this mystery of theirs from others by all sorts of means that even beings with Pure Reason cannot penetrate them.

"The monastery of the Orthodoxhydooraki sect of the Buddhist religion occupied a large square with a strongly built wall around it, which protected everything within, both from beings similar to themselves and from wild beings.

"In the middle of this enormous walled enclosure stood a large structure, also strongly built, which constituted the main part of the monastery.

"In one half of this large structure their ordinary being-existence was carried on, and in the other they practiced those special manipulations of theirs which were just

---------------------------------- 259 ----------------------------------

the particularity of the form of belief of the followers of their sect and which to others were arcana.

"Around the outside wall, on its inner side, stood a row of small, strongly built, closely adjoining compartments, like cells.

"It was just these same 'cells' that represented the difference between this monastery and other monasteries in general on the planet Earth.

"These sentry-box structures were entirely walled in on all sides, except that near the bottom they had a small aperture through which, with great difficulty, a hand could be thrust.

"Thereafter these sectarians, before called the 'Self-tamers,' began already to be called by various names, namely; those of the 'Self-tamers' who remained faithful to the obligations they had taken upon themselves were called 'Orthodoxhy-dooraki,' while the rest, who had renounced the certain obligations they had undertaken there in their native country, were called 'Katoshkihydooraki.'

"By the time of our arrival in 'Sincratorza' those of the sectarians who were named 'Orthodoxhydooraki' had their well-organized so-called monastery not very far from their original settling-place, and therein the said special form of 'suffering' was in full process.

- -

"On resuming our journey the next day after a restful night, we passed quite near the monastery of these sectarians of the Buddhist religion of the 'Orthodox-hydooraki' doctrine.

"As we made our usual halt at this time of day, for feeding our quadruped workers, we asked the monks to allow us to make our camp under the covers of their monastery.

"Strange and unusual as it may seem, the beings there bearing the name monks, did not refuse our objectively just request, but at once, without any of the 'swaggering' that had become proper to the monks there of all centuries and of all doctrines, admitted us, whereupon we unexpectedly then entered the very center of that region which, from the very beginning of their arising, the beings of the planet Earth have, from time to time, become very skillful in concealing from the observation and understanding even of Individuums of pure Reason—in the present instance, into the sphere of the arcana of this doctrine. In other words, they had become skillful in 'wiseacring' something and making what they call a 'mystery' of it, and in so thoroughly concealing this mystery of theirs from others by every means, that even beings with pure Reason could not discover it.

"The monastery of this sect 'Orthodoxhydooraki' of the Buddhist religion occupied a large square with a strongly fortified wall around it, that protected everything within both from beings like themselves and from 'wild' beings.

"In the middle of this enormous walled enclosure stood a large, also strongly boarded, construction, which constituted just the main part of the monastery.

"In one half of this large edifice their ordinary being existence was carried on, and in the other, they practiced those special manipulations of theirs which were just

- -

the peculiarity of the form of belief of the followers of their sect and which were arcana to the rest.

"Around the outer wall on its inner side stood, in a row, small, strongly boarded sections like cells.

"It was just these same cells that represented the difference between this monastery and other monasteries on the planet Earth in general.

"These sentry box shapes were entirely boarded in on all sides, save that near the bottom was a small opening through which, with great difficulty, a hand could be thrust.

"These strong sentry-box structures were for the perpetual immurement of the already 'deserving' beings of that sect—and they were to occupy themselves with their famous manipulation of what they call their 'emotions' and 'thoughts'—until the total destruction of their planetary existence.

"And so, it was when the wives of these 'self-tamer-sectarians' learned of just this that they made the said great outcry.

"In the fundamental religious teaching of this sect there was a full explanation of just what manipulations and for how long a time it is necessary to produce them upon oneself in order to merit being immured in one of the strongly built cells, there to receive every twenty-four hours a piece of bread and a small jug of water.

"At that time when we came within the walls of that terrible monastery, all these monstrous cells were already occupied; and the care of the immured, that is, giving them once in twenty-four hours, through the aforementioned tiny apertures, a piece of bread and a small jug of water, was carried out with great reverence by those sectarians who were candidates for that immurement,

------------------------------ *260* ------------------------------

and who, while waiting their turn, existed in the said large building that stood in the monastery square.

"Your immured favorites did indeed exist in the said monastery sepulchres until their existence, so full of deprivations, half-starved and motionless, came quite to an end.

"When the companions of the immured learned of the cessation of the existence of any one of them, his planetary body was removed from the improvised sepulchre and immediately, in the place of the being thus self-destroyed, another similar unfortunate fanatic of that maleficent religious teaching of theirs was immured; and the ranks of these unfortunate 'fanatic monks' were being filled up by other members of that peculiar sect, constantly coming from Pearl-land.

"In Pearl-land itself all the adherents of that sect already knew of the existence of that special 'convenient' place for the actualization of the finale of their religious doctrine, purporting to have been based on the exact instructions of Saint Buddha; and in every big center they even had what are called agents who helped them to get there.

"Having rested and fed our biped and quadruped workers, we left that melancholy place of sacrifice to the same wretched organ which, in the ruminations of certain Most High Cosmic Individuals had had for some reason or other, without fail, to be implanted into the presences of the earliest three-brained beings of that ill-fated planet.

"Eh! Eh! Eh! my boy, we left there, as you can well believe, scarcely with agreeable sensations and happy reflections.

"Continuing our route in the direction of the Sea of Beneficence, we again passed through terra firmas of very many different forms, also with conglomerations of

------------------------------ *261* ------------------------------

intraplanetary minerals, but which had oozed to the surface of the planet from

"These strong constructions, of sentry box shape, were for the perpetual immurement of those already deserving beings of that sect whose occupation until the complete destruction of their planetary existence, was a certain manipulation of what they call their emotions and thoughts.

"And it was when the wives of these 'sectarian-self-tamers' learned of this that they just made the said great outcry.

"In the fundamental religious teaching of this sect, there was a complete explanation of how long a time and namely which manipulations it is necessary to produce upon oneself in order to merit being immured in one of those strongly constructed cells, there to receive every diurnity a morsel of bread and a small jug of water.

"On our visit to that enclosure of that terrible monastery, all these monstrous cells were already occupied; and the care of the immured, that is giving them once a diurnity, through the mentioned tiny openings, a morsel of bread and a small jug of water, was discharged with great reverence by the sectarians, who were candidates for that immurement,

and who, while waiting their turn, existed in the said building that stood in the middle of the monastery square.

"Your immured favorites did indeed exist in the said monstrous sepulchers until their half-starved motionless existence, full of deprivations, came to an end.

"When the companions of the immured learned of the ceasing to exist of one of their number, his planetary body was removed from the improvised sepulcher and immediately in the place of the self-destroyed being, another similar unfortunate fanatic of that maleficent religious doctrine of theirs was immured, their ranks being filled up by other members of that peculiar sect, dribbling in from Gemchania.

"In Gemchania itself all the adherents of that sect already knew of the existence of that special 'convenient' place for the actualization of the finale of their 'religious doctrine,' purporting to have been based on the exact instructions of the Saint Buddha; and in every big center they even had what are called agents who helped them to get there.

"Having rested and fed our biped and quadruped workers, we left that melancholy place of sacrifices to that same wretched organ which, in the ruminations of certain most high cosmic individuums had for some reason or other, without fail, to be introjected into the presence of the earliest three-brained beings of that ill-starred planet.

"Eh! Eh! Eh!, my boy, we left there, as you can well believe, scarcely with agreeable sensations and happy reflections.

"Continuing our route in the direction of the 'Sea-of-Beneficence,' we again passed through terra-firma of very many different forms, also with conglomerations of

intraplanetary minerals, but which had oozed to the surface of the planet from still greater depths.

"Here I must say something about an exceedingly strange thing, which I constated, closely connected with just that part of the surface of your planet which is now called Tibet.

"At that period when I was passing through Tibet for the first time, its heights were indeed also unusually far above the surface of the Earth, but they did not differ particularly from similar elevations on other continents and on the same continent Ashhark or Asia, of which Tibet was a part.

"But when during my sixth and last personal stay on the planet Earth there, my way again took me through those, for me, extremely memorable places, I just then constated that in the interval of the few score of their centuries, the whole of that locality had projected so far from the planet that no heights on any of the other continents could even be compared with them.

"For instance, the chief range of that elevated region through which we had then passed, namely, the range of elevations which the beings there call a 'mountain-range,' had in the interval projected so far from the planet that some of its peaks are now the loftiest among all the abnormal projections of that vainly-long-suffering-planet. And if you climbed them, you could possibly with the aid of a Teskooano 'see clearly' the center of the opposite side of that peculiar planet.

"When I first constated that strange phenomenon occurring on that remarkably peculiar planet of yours, I at once thought that in all probability it contained the germ for the arising of some subsequent misfortune on a great common cosmic scale, and when I afterwards collected statistics concerning that abnormal phenomenon, this first

------------------------------ *262* ------------------------------

apprehension of mine very soon more and more grew in me. "And it grew chiefly because, in my statistics, one item concerning that phenomenon there showed an increase in every decade.

"The said item concerning those Tibetan elevations referred just to this: which of the terrestrial, as they are called 'planetary tremors,' or as this is expressed by your favorites, 'earthquakes,' occur to that planet due to these excessively lofty elevations.

"Although planetary tremors or earthquakes frequently occur to that planet of yours from other interplanetary disharmonies also that have arisen in consequence of the two already mentioned great Transapalnian perturbations, the causes of which I shall sometime explain to you, nevertheless most of the planetary tremors there, and especially during recent centuries, have occurred solely on account of those excessive elevations.

"And they occur because, in consequence of those excessive elevations, the atmosphere also of that planet has acquired and continues to acquire in its presence the same . . . that is to say, what is called the 'Blastegoklornian-circumference' of the atmosphere of the planet Earth has acquired in certain places and continues to acquire an excessively projecting materialized presence for what is called the 'reciprocal-blending-of-the-results-of-all-the-planets-of-the-given-system'; with

still greater depths.

"Here I must say something about an exceedingly strange thing, which I constated, closely connected with just that part of the surface of your planet which is now called Tibet.

"At that period when I was passing through Tibet for the first time, its elevations were indeed also unusually far above the surface of the Earth, but they did not differ particularly from similar elevations on other continents and on the same continent Ashhark or Asia, of which Tibet was a part.

"But when during my sixth and last personal stay on the planet Earth there, my way again took me through these, for me, extremely memorable places, I just then constated that in the interval of the few tens of their centuries, the whole of that locality had projected so far from the planet that no heights on any of the other continents could even be compared with them.

"For instance, the chief range of that elevated region through which we had then passed, namely, the range of elevations which the beings there call a 'mountain range,' had in the interval projected so far from the planet that some of its peaks are now the loftiest among all the abnormal projections of that vainly-long-suffering-planet. And supposing you could climb them, you could possibly with the aid of a Teskooano, 'see clearly' the center of the opposite side of that peculiar planet.

"When I first constated that strange phenomenon occurring on that remarkably peculiar planet of yours, I at once thought that in all probability it contained the germ for the arising of some subsequent misfortune on a great common cosmic scale, and when I afterwards collected statistics concerning that abnormal phenomenon, this first

- -

apprehension of mine very soon more and more grew in me.

"And it grew chiefly, because, in my statistics one item concerning phenomenon there, showed an increase every decade.

"The said item concerning those Tibetan elevations referred just to this, which of the terrestrial, as they are called, 'planetary tremors,' or as they are otherwise called 'earthquakes,' occur to that planet, and when, on account of these excessively lofty elevations.

"Although 'planetary-tremors' or 'earthquakes' frequently occur to that planet of yours from other intraplanetary disharmonies also, that have arisen in consequence of the two already mentioned great Transapalnian-perturbations, the causes of which I shall sometime explain to you, nevertheless most of the planetary-tremors there, and especially during recent centuries, have occurred solely on account of those excessive elevations.

"And they occur because, in consequence of those excessive elevations, the atmosphere also of that planet has acquired and continues to acquire in its presence the same—that is to say, what is called the 'Blastegoklornian-circumference' of the atmosphere of the planet Earth has acquired in certain places and continues to acquire an excessively projecting materialized presence, for what is called the 'reciprocal-blending-of-the-results-of-all-planets-of-the-given-system'; with the

the result that during the motion of that planet, and in the presence of what is called 'common-system-harmony,' its atmosphere at certain times 'hooks on,' as it were, to the atmosphere of other planets or comets of the same system.

"And owing to these 'hookings on' there occur in the corresponding places of the common presence of that planet of yours just those said planetary tremors or quakes.

"I must also explain to you that the region of the

- 263 -

common presence of the planet where such planetary tremors occur on this account, depends upon the position occupied by the planet itself in the process of the common-system-harmonious-movement, in relation to other concentrations belonging to the same system.

"Be that as it may, if this abnormal growth of the Tibetan mountains continues thus in the future, a great catastrophe on a general cosmic scale is sooner or later inevitable.

"However, when the menace I see becomes already evident, no doubt the Most High, Most Sacred Cosmic Individuals will at the proper time take the proper precautions."

"If you please, if you please, your Right Reverence," Ahoon interrupted Beelzebub, and rattled off the following:

"Allow me to report to you, your Right Reverence, some information which I happened to pick up concerning just that growth of those same Tibetan mountains about which you have deigned to speak.

"Just before our flight from the planet Karatas," continued Ahoon, "I had the pleasure of meeting the Archangel Viloyer, the Governor of our solar system, and His Splendiferousness condescended to recognize me and to speak to me.

"Perhaps you remember, your Right Reverence, that while we were existing on the planet Zernakoor, His Splendiferousness Archangel Viloyer was still an ordinary angel, and used often to drop in to see us?

"So when His Splendiferousness, during our conversation, heard the name of that solar system where we were exiled, he told me that at the last most high and most sacred reception of finally returned cosmic results, a certain Individual, Saint Lama, had had the privilege of personally presenting at the feet of our END-LESS UNI-BEING,

- 264 -

in the presence of all the Most High Individuals, a certain petition regarding the abnormal growth of the elevations of some planet—it seems just of that solar system—and having received this request, our ALL-GRACIOUS-ENDLESSNESS immediately ordered Archangel Looisos to be dispatched to that solar system where, as one familiar with that system, he might there on the spot clarify the causes of the manifestation of the said projections and take appropriate measures.

"That is why His Conformity Archangel Looisos is at the present time hastily winding up his current affairs in order to set off there."

"So, dear Ahoon," commented Beelzebub, and he added, "Thank you for this information. . . . Glory be to our CREATOR . . . what you have just said will prob-

result that during the motion of that planet, and in the process of what is called 'common-system-harmony,' its atmosphere at certain times 'hooks on,' as it were, to the atmosphere of other planets or comets of the same system.

"And owing to these 'hookings on,' there occurs in the corresponding places of the general presence of that planet of yours just those said 'planetary tremors' or 'quakes.'

"I must also explain to you that the region of the

general presence of the planet where such 'planetary tremors' occur on this account, depends upon the position occupied by the planet itself in the process of the common-system-harmonious-movement, in relation to other concentrations belonging to the same system.

"Be that as it may, if this abnormal growth of the Tibetan mountains continues thus in the future, a great catastrophe on a general cosmic scale is sooner or later inevitable.

"However, when the menace I foresee becomes already evident, no doubt the most high, most sacred cosmic Individuums will, at the proper time, take the proper precautions."

"If you please, if you please, your Right Reverence," Ahoon thus interrupted Beelzebub, and rattled off the following:

"Allow me to report to you, Your Right Reverence, some information which I happened to pick up concerning just that growth of these same Tibetan mountains about which you have deigned to speak.

"Just before our flight from the planet Karatas," continued Ahoon, "I had the pleasure of meeting the Archangel Viloyer, the Governor of our solar system, and His Splendiferousness condescended to recognize me and to speak with me.

"Perhaps you remember, Your Right Reverence, that while we were existing on the planet Zernakoor, His Splendiferousness, Archangel Viloyer, was still an ordinary angel, and used often to drop in to see us.

"So when His Splendiferousness, during our conversation, heard the name of that solar system where we were exiled, he told me that at the last most high and most most sacred reception of final cosmic results who had returned, a certain Individuum, Saint Lama, had had the privilege of personally presenting at the feet of our ENDLESS UNI-BEING,

in the presence of all the most high Individuums, a certain petition regarding the abnormal growth of some elevations of some planet—it seems just of that solar system—and having received this request our ALL-GRACIOUS ENDLESSNESS immediately ordered Archangel Looisos to be dispatched to that solar system where, as one familiar with that system, he might there on the spot clarify the causes of the manifestation of the said projections and take appropriate measures.

"That is why His Conformity Archangel Looisos is at the present time hastily winding up his current affairs in order to set off there."

"So, dear Ahoon . . . " commented Beelzebub; and he added, "Thank you for this information . . . Glory be to our CREATOR . . . what you have just said will ably help to destroy in my presence the anxiety which arose in me when I first constated the abnormal growth of those said Tibetan mountains, namely, my anxiety for the complete disappearance from the Universe of the precious memory of our Endlessly Revered Wisest of the Wise, Mullah Nassr Eddin."

Having said this, and giving his face its usual expression, Beelzebub continued thus:

"Through that region now called Tibet, we then continued our route, encountering hardships of every kind, and finally came to the source of the river called the Keria-chi and a few days later, sailing down to the Sea of Beneficence, we came to our ship *Occasion*.

"Although after this third descent of mine to your planet Earth, I did not go there in person for a considerable time, nevertheless, from time to time I attentively observed these favorites of yours, through my big Teskooano.

"And I had no reason for a long time to go there personally on account of the following:

"After returning to the planet Mars I soon became

----------------------------- *265* -----------------------------

interested there in a work which the three-brained beings of the planet Mars were just then carrying out on the surface of their planet.

"Clearly to understand in what work it was there that I became interested, you must know, first of all, that the planet Mars is for the system Ors, to which it belongs, what is called a 'Mdnel-outian' link in the transformation of cosmic substances, in consequence of which it has what is called a 'Keskestasantnian-firmsurface,' that is to say, one half of its surface consists of land-presence and the other of 'Saliakooriapnian' masses; or, as your favorites would say, one half of it is land or one continuous continent, and the other half is covered with water.

"So, my boy, as the three-brained beings of the planet Mars use for their first being-food exclusively only 'prosphora'—or as your favorites call it, 'bread'—they, for the purpose of obtaining it, sow on the land of half of their planet what is called 'wheat,' and as this wheat derives the moisture it needs, for what is called evolving Djartklom, only from what is called 'dew,' the result is that a grain of wheat yields only a seventh part of the accomplished process of the sacred Heptaparaparshinokh, that is to say, what is called the 'yield' of the harvest is only a seventh.

"As this amount of wheat was insufficient for their needs, while to get more of it they would have to utilize the presence of the planetary Saliakooriap, the three-centered beings there from the very beginning of our arrival there were always talking of conducting that same Saliakooriap in the requisite quantity, from the opposite side of their planet to that side on which their being-existence proceeded.

"And when several of their years later they finally decided the question and began making every preparation, they began operations just before my return from the planet

----------------------------- *266* -----------------------------

Earth, that is to say, they began digging special canals for conducting the

probably help destroy in my presence the anxiety which arose in me when I first constated the abnormal growth of those said Tibetan mountains, namely, my anxiety for the complete disappearance from the Universe of the precious memory of our Endlessly Revered Wisest of the Wise, Mullah Nassr Eddin."

Having said this and giving his face its usual expression, Beelzebub continued thus:

"Through that region at present called Tibet, we then continued our route, encountering hardships of every kind; and finally we came to the source of the river called the Keria-Chi and a few days later, sailing down it to the Sea of Beneficence, we came to our ship Occasion.

"Although after this third descent of mine to your planet Earth, I did not go there in person for a considerable time, nevertheless, from time to time, I attentively observed those favorites of yours, through my big 'Teskooano.'

"And I had no reason for a long time to go there personally on account of the following.

"After returning to the planet Mars I soon became

- -

interested there in a work which the three-brained beings of the planet Mars were just then carrying out on the surface of their planet.

"Clearly to understand in what work there it was that I became interested, you must know, first of all, that the planet Mars is for the system Ors, to which it belongs, what is called a 'Mdnel-outian-link' in the transformation of cosmic substances, in consequence of which it has, what is called, a 'Keskestasantnian-firm-surface,' that is to say, one half of its surface consists of land-presence and the other of 'Saliakooriapnian' masses; or, as your favorites would say, one half of its land or one continuous continent, and the other half is covered with water.

"So, my boy, as the three-brained beings of the planet Mars use for their first being-food exclusively only 'prosphora'—or as your favorites call it, 'bread'—they, for the purpose of obtaining it, sow on the land half of their planet, what is called 'wheat,' and as this 'wheat' derives the moisture it needs for what is called evolving Djartklom, only from what is called 'dew,' the result is that a grain of wheat there yields only a seventh part of the fulfilled process of the sacred Heptaparaparshinokh, that is to say, what is called 'the yield' of the harvest is only a seventh.

"As this amount of wheat was insufficient for their needs, while to get more of it, they would have to utilize the presence of the planetary 'Saliakooriap,' the three-centered beings there from the very beginning of our arrival there, were always talking of conducting that same 'Saliakooriap' in the requisite quantity, from the opposite side of their planet to that side on which their being-existence proceeded.

"And when several of their years later they finally decided the question and began making every preparation, they began operations just before my return from the planet

- -

Earth, that is to say, they began digging special canals for conducting the

Saliakooriap.

"So, my boy, this work being extremely complicated, the beings of the planet Mars had invented and continued to invent for the work every kind of machine and appliance.

"And as there were very many peculiar and interesting ones among these machines and appliances they invented, I, being always interested in every kind of new invention, was very much taken by the said work of the beings of the planet Mars.

"By the courtesy of the kind Martians I then spent nearly all my time at these works, and that is why during that period I very seldom descended to the other planets of that solar system.

"Only sometimes I flew to the planet Saturn to rest, to Gornahoor Harharkh, who, during this time, had already become my real essence-friend, and thanks to whom I had such a marvel as that big Teskooano of mine which, as I have already told you, brought remote visibilities 7,000,285 times nearer."

------------------------------ *267* ------------------------------

'Saliakooriap.'

"So, my boy, this work thing extremely complicated, the beings of the planet Mars had invented and continued to invent for the work, every kind of machine and appliance . . .

"And as there were very many peculiar and interesting ones among those machines and appliances they invented, I, being always interested in every kind of new invention, was very much taken by the said work of the beings of the planet Mars.

"By the courtesy of the kind Martians, then, I then spent nearly all my time at these works, and that is why during that period I very seldom descended to the other planets of that solar system.

"Only sometimes I flew to the planet Saturn to rest, to Gornahoor Harharkh, who during this time, had already become my real essence-friend, and thanks to whom I had such a marvel as that big Teskooano of mine which, as I have already told you, brought remote visibilities, seven million, two hundred and eighty-five times nearer."

- -

The Fourth Personal Sojourn of Beelzebub on the Planet Earth

BEELZEBUB continued thus:
"I descended for the fourth time to that planet Earth owing to the request of my essence-friend Gornahoor Harharkh.

"I must first of all tell you that after I had met this Gornahoor Harharkh and had become friendly with him, I always, during our 'subjective exchange of opinions,' whenever we again met, shared my impressions with him about the strange psyche of the three-centered beings of that planet of yours.

"And the result of these exchanges of opinion of ours concerning your favorites was that he finally also became so interested in them that he once even very seriously asked me to keep him always informed, even if only approximately, of my observations of them, and thereafter I sent to him, just as I did to your uncle Tooilan, copies of all my brief-notes concerning the strange particularities of their psyche.

"And how Gornahoor Harharkh came to be the cause of this descent of mine ensued from the following:

"I have already told you that after my third personal descent to your planet, I occasionally for a rest ascended to the planet Saturn to this friend of mine.

"When during these flights to him I had become convinced of his great learning, the idea once arose in me to invite him to descend on our ship *Occasion* to the planet Mars, in order there, on the spot, to help me personally with his knowledge in the details of arranging my observatory which was just then being completed.

------------------------------- *268* -------------------------------

"Here I might as well emphasize the fact that if this observatory of mine afterwards became famous and indeed the best of all the constructions of its kind in the whole of the Universe, I am chiefly indebted to the learning of this same essence-friend of mine.

"Well, then, when I spoke to Gornahoor Harharkh about this, he, without thinking long about it, agreed, and together we immediately began to deliberate how to carry out our intention.

"The problem was that our route from the planet Saturn to the planet Mars would cross such cosmic spheres as did not correspond to the presence of Gornahoor Harharkh, a being who had as yet the possibilities only for an ordinary planetary existence.

"The result of our deliberations, then, was that on the following day his chief assistant began, under his direction, to arrange a special compartment in our ship *Occasion* itself, and to furnish it with every kind of adaptation and apparatus for elaborating those substances of which the atmosphere of the planet Saturn consists, and to which Gornahoor Harharkh was adapted by Nature for existence.

The Fourth Personal Sojourn Of Beelzebub On The Planet Earth

BEELZEBUB continued thus:

"I descended for the fourth time to that planet Earth owing to the request of my essence-friend Gornahoor Harharkh.

"I must first of all tell you that after I had met this Gornahoor Harharkh and had become friendly with him, I always, whenever we again met and during our 'subjective-exchange-of-opinions,' shared my impressions with him about the strange psyche of the three-brained beings of that planet of yours.

"And the result of these exchanges of opinion of ours concerning your favorites was that he finally also became interested in them and moreover, to such a degree, that once he even very seriously asked me to keep him always informed, even if only partially, of my observation on them, and thereafter, I sent him, just as I did to your uncle Tooilan, copies of all my brief notes concerning the strange particularities of their psyche.

"And how Gornahoor Harharkh came to be the cause of this descent of mine ensued from the following:

"I have already once told you that after my third personal descent to your planet, I occasionally, just for a rest, ascended only to the planet Saturn to this friend of mine.

"When during these flights I had become convinced of his great learning, the idea once arose in me to invite him to descend on our ship 'Occasion' to the planet Mars, in order there, on the spot, to help me personally with his knowledge in arranging the details of my observatory which was just then being completed.

"Here I might as well emphasize the fact that if this observatory of mine afterwards became famous and indeed the best among all the artificial constructions of its kind in the whole of the Universe, I am chiefly indebted just to the learning of this same essence friend of mine.

"Well then, when I spoke to Gornahoor Harharkh about this, he, without thinking long about it, agreed, and together we immediately began considering how to carry out our intention.

"The problem was that our route from the planet Saturn to the planet Mars would cross such cosmic spheres as did not correspond to the presence of Gornahoor Harharkh, that is to say, of a being who had as yet the possibilities only for an ordinary planetary existence.

"The result of our deliberations then was that on the following day his chief assistants, under his direction, began to arrange a special compartment in our ship 'Occasion' itself, and to furnish it with every kind of adaptation and apparatus for generating those substances of which the atmosphere of the planet Saturn consists, and to which Gornahoor Harharkh was adapted by Nature for existence.

"When all these preparations had been completed, we one Hrkh-hr-hoo later set out on our journey in the direction of the planet Mars and descended there at my house.

"And there, on the planet Mars, which had almost the same atmosphere as the planet Saturn, my essence-friend Gornahoor Harharkh very soon became acclimatized and began to exist almost freely.

"It was just during his stay on Mars that he devised that Teskooano, or, as your favorites call it, a 'telescope,' thanks chiefly to which, as I have already said, my observatory afterwards became particularly famous through the whole of the Universe.

"The Teskooano he constructed is indeed a marvel of being-Reason, as it increases the visibility of remote cosmic

---------------------------------- 269 ----------------------------------

concentrations up to 7,000,285 times, during certain processes in cosmic substances proceeding in the atmospheres surrounding almost all cosmic concentrations, as well as during certain processes in the cosmic Etherokrilno of interspatial spheres.

"Thanks to this Teskooano I was sometimes fully able, while seated in my house on Mars, to observe almost everything that proceeded on those parts of the surface of other planets of this solar system which, in the process of what is called the general-system-movement, were at the given time within the sphere of vision of my observatory.

"Well then, my dear boy, while Gornahoor Harharkh was then staying with me as my guest and we were once together observing the existence of these favorites of yours, a certain fact which we happened to notice was the cause of a very serious exchange of opinions between us concerning the three-centered beings of that peculiar planet of yours.

"The result of this 'exchange of opinions' of ours was that I undertook to descend onto the surface of that planet and to bring back to the planet Saturn a certain number of the beings called there 'apes,' in order to carry out certain elucidating experiments with them concerning the fact we had noticed and which had then surprised us."

At this point of Beelzebub's tales, he was given a "Leitoochanbros," that is, a special metal plate on which is recorded the text of an etherogram received from somewhere or other, the addressee having only to hold it to his perceptive hearing organ to hear everything communicated in it.

When Beelzebub had in this way heard the contents of the Leitoochanbros handed to him, he turned to his grandson and said:

---------------------------------- 270 ----------------------------------

"You see, my boy, what coincidences occur in our Great Universe.

"The contents of this etherogram concern just your favorites in connection with these terrestrial beings I have just mentioned, that is, these apes.

"It has been sent to me from the planet Mars, and among other things there is communicated in it that the three-centered beings of the planet Earth have again begun to revive what is called the 'Ape question.'

"When all these preparations had been completed, we, in one Hrkh-hr-hoo, set out on our journey in the direction of the planet Mars and successfully descended there at my house.

"And there on the planet Mars, which had almost the same atmosphere as the planet Saturn, my essence-friend Gornahoor Harharkh, very soon became acclimatized and existed fairly freely.

"It was just during his stay on Mars that he invented that 'Teskooano' or, as your favorites call it, that 'telescope,' thanks chiefly to which, as I have already said, my observatory afterwards became particularly famous throughout the whole of the Universe.

"The 'Teskooano' he constructed is indeed a marvel of being-Reason, as it increases the visibility of remote cosmic

concentrations up to seven million and two hundred and eighty-five times, both during certain processes in cosmic substances proceeding in the atmosphere surrounding almost all the cosmic concentrations, and also during certain processes in the cosmic Etherokrilno of interspatial spheres.

"Thanks to this 'Teskooano' I was sometimes fully able, while seated in my house on Mars, to observe almost everything that proceeded on those parts of the surface of other planets of this Solar System, which in the process of what is called the general-system-movement, were at the given time within the sphere of vision of my observatory.

"Well then, my dear boy, while Gornahoor Harharkh was then staying with me as my guest and we were once observing together the existence of these favorites of yours, a certain fact which we happened to notice was the cause of a very serious exchange of opinions between us concerning the three-centered beings of that peculiar planet of yours.

"The result of this 'exchange-of-opinions' of ours was that I undertook to descend upon the surface of that planet and to bring back a certain number of beings there called apes, in order to carry out certain elucidating experiments with them concerning that fact we had noticed and which had then surprised us.

At this point of Beelzebub's tales he was given a 'Leitoochanbros,' that is, a special metal plate on which the text is recorded of an etherogram received from somewhere or other; the addressee has only to hold it to his perceptive hearing organ to hear everything communicated in it. When Beelzebub had in this way heard the contents of the 'Leitoochanbros' handed to him, he turned to his grandson and said:

"You see, my boy, what coincidences occur in our Great Universe.

"The contents of this etherogram just concern your favorites in regard to these terrestrial beings I just mentioned, that is to these 'apes.'

"It has been sent to me from the planet Mars, and among other things there is communicated in it, that the three-centered beings of the planet Earth are again excited by what is called the 'Ape-question.'

"I must tell you first of all, that on account of a cause also ensuing from the abnormal being-existence there, there was long ago crystallized, and there is periodically intensified in its functioning in the presences of those strange three-brained beings arising and existing on the planet Earth, a strange factor which from time to time produces in their presences a 'crescendo impulse,' owing to which, during the periods of its action, they wish at all costs to find out whether they have descended from these apes or whether these apes have descended from them.

"Judging from the etherogram, this question is this time agitating chiefly those biped beings who breed there on the continent called America.

"Although this question always agitates them from time to time, yet every once in a while it becomes there for a long time, as they express it, 'the burning question of the day.'

"I very well remember that this 'agitation of mind' concerning the origin of these apes occurred there among them for the first time when, as they also like to express it, their 'center of culture' was Tikliamish.

"The beginning of that 'agitation of mind' there was the wiseacring of a certain 'learned being' of new formation there named Menitkel.

"This Menitkel then became a learned being,

firstly because his childless aunt was an excellent what is called matchmaker and mixed a great deal with power-possessing beings, and secondly, because when by age he was approaching the 'threshold of the being' of a responsible being, he received on his birthday a gift of a book entitled *Manual of Bon Ton and Love Letter Writing*. Being materially secure and therefore quite free, thanks to an inheritance left him by his uncle, a former pawnshop proprietor, he out of boredom compiled a massive and erudite work in which he 'spun out,' concerning the origin of these apes, an elaborate theory with every kind of 'logical proof,' but of course with such 'logical proofs' as could be perceived and crystallized only in the Reasons of those freaks who have taken your fancy.

"This Menitkel then 'proved' by his theory that these 'fellow apes' of theirs had descended neither more nor less than from what are called 'people who became wild.'

"And the other terrestrial beings of that period, as it had already become proper to them, implicitly believed this 'Auntie's darling' without any essence-criticism whatsoever, and from that time on, this question which had then agitated the strange Reason of your favorites, became a subject of discussion and fantasying, and existed right up to what is called the 'seventh-in-turn great general planetary process of reciprocal destruction.'

"Thanks to this maleficent idea, there was even fixed in the instincts of most of these unfortunates at that period still another abnormal what is called 'dictatory factor,' which began to engender in their common presences the false feeling that these ape-beings were presumably 'sacred'; and the abnormal factor engendering this sacrilegious impulse, also passing by inheritance from generation to generation, has reached the instincts of very many beings even of the present time.

"I must tell you, first of all, that on account of a cause also ensuing from the abnormal being-existence there, an extraordinary factor which became periodically intensified in its functioning was long ago crystallized in the presences of those strange three-brained beings arising and existing on the planet Earth, and every now and then produces in their presences a crescendo-impulse, owing to which, during periods of its action, they wish to find out at all costs, whether it is they who have descended from these apes or whether these same apes have descended from them.

"Judging from the etherogram, this question is, this time, agitating chiefly those biped beings there who breed on the continent called 'America.'

"Although this question always agitates them from time to time, yet every once in a while it becomes there for a long time, as they express it, the 'burning-question-of-the-day.'

"I very well remember that this 'agitation-of-mind' among them concerning the origin of these same apes occurred there for the first time when, as they also like to express it, their 'center-of-culture' was Tikliamish.

"The beginning of that 'agitation-of-mind' there was the wiseacring of a certain 'learned-being' of 'new formation' there named Menitkel.

"This Menitkel then became a learned being,

---

firstly, because his childless aunt was an excellent what is called matchmaker and mixed a great deal with power-possessing beings, and, secondly, because when, by age, he was approaching the 'threshold-of-Being' of a responsible being, he received on his birthday the gift of a book entitled 'Guide-to-etiquette-and-love-letter-writing.' Being materially provided for, and therefore quite free, thanks to an inheritance left him by his uncle, a former pawn-shop proprietor, he, out of boredom, then compiled a massive and erudite work in which he spun out an elaborate theory with every kind of 'logical proof' concerning the origin of these apes, but, of course, with such 'logical-proofs' as could be perceived and crystallized only in the Reasons of those queer ducks who have taken your fancy.

"This Menitkel then 'proved' by his theory that these 'fellow-apes' of theirs had descended neither more nor less than from what are called 'people-run-wild.'

"The other beings of that period, as it had already become proper to them, implicitly believed this 'Auntie's-darling' without any essence-criticism whatever, and so from that time on, this question which then agitated the strange Reason of your favorites, became a subject of discussion and fantasying, and existed up to what is called, the 'seventh-in-turn-great-general-planetary-process-of-reciprocal-destruction.'

"Thanks to this maleficent idea, there was even fixed in the instincts of most of these unfortunates at that period still another abnormal what is called 'dictatory factor,' which began to engender in their common presences the false feeling that these ape-beings were, so to say, sacred; and this abnormal factor for engendering such a sacrilegious impulse, also passing by inheritance from generation to generation, has reached the instincts of very many beings even of the present time.

"This false idea that arose and was fixed there owing

---------------------------- *272* ----------------------------

to the said 'pawnshop progeny' existed during nearly two of their centuries, and became an inseparable part of the Reason of the majority of them; and only various events proceeding from the mentioned general planetary process effaced it until it ultimately completely disappeared from their common presences.

"But when what is called their 'cultured existence' was concentrated on the continent named Europe, and when the time of the maximum intense manifestation of the peculiar illness there named 'to-wiseacre,' had again come round—which illness by the way had already long before become subject to the fundamental cosmic law of Heptaparaparshinokh, according to which it had, in respect of intensity, also to function with a certain periodicity—then, to the grief of three-brained beings of the whole of the universe, that Ape question, namely, the question who is descended from whom, again arose, and having become crystallized, again became a part of the presence of the abnormal Reason of your favorites.

"The stimulus for the revival there of this Ape question was this time also a 'learned' being, and of course also 'great,' but now a 'learned' being of quite a 'new formation' named Darwin.

"And this 'great' learned being, basing his theory on that same logic of theirs, began to 'prove' exactly the opposite of what Menitkel had said, namely, that it was they themselves who were descended from these Mister Apes.

"And as for the objective reality of the theories of both these 'great' terrestrial 'learned beings,' I am reminded of one of the wise sayings of our esteemed Mullah Nassr Eddin, namely:

"'They were both very successful, though of course not without luck, in finding the authentic godmother of the incomparable Scheherazade on an old dunghill.'

---------------------------- *273* ----------------------------

"In any case you must know and bear in mind that for many centuries just this question among similar ephemeral questions has provided material for the kind of mentation which is considered among your favorites as the 'highest manifestation of Reason.'

"These favorites of yours would in my opinion get quite a correct answer to this question which always excites them, that is, the question how the apes arose, if they were able in the given case to apply one of these sayings again of our dear Mullah Nassr Eddin, who on many occasions used to say: 'The cause of every misunderstanding must be sought only in woman.'

"If they had attempted the solution of this enigmatic question with that wisdom of his, then perhaps they would have finally discovered whence and how these countrymen of theirs had originated.

"As this question of the genealogy of these apes there is indeed exceedingly abstruse and unusual, I shall inform your Reason about this also as far as possible from every aspect.

"In fact, neither have they descended from apes nor have apes descended from them, but . . . the cause of the origin of these apes is in this case, just as in every other misunderstanding there, also—their women.

"This false idea that arose and was fixed there owing

to the said 'pawn-shop-progeny,' existed during nearly two of their centuries, and became an inseparable part of the Reason of the majority of them; and only various events proceeding from the mentioned general planetary process of reciprocal destruction which lasted nearly half a century gradually effaced it until it ultimately completely disappeared from their common presences.

"But when what is called their 'cultured-existence' was concentrated on the continent named Europe, and when the time of the maximum intense manifestation of the peculiar illness there, namely, 'to wiseacre,' had come round again, which illness, by the way, had already long before become subject to the fundamental cosmic law of Heptaparaparshinokh, according to which it had, in respect of intensity, to function also with a certain periodicity, then, to the grief of three-brained beings of the whole of the Universe, that 'Ape-question,' namely the question who is descended from which, again arose, and having become crystallized, again became a part of the presence of the abnormal Reason of your favorites.

"The stimulus for the revival there of this 'Ape-question' was this time also a 'learned' being, and of course also 'great,' but 'learned' of quite a 'new formation'—named Darwin.

"And this 'great-learned' being, basing his theory on that same logic of theirs, 'proved' that it was they themselves who were descended from these Mister Apes.

"And as for the objective reality of the theories of both these 'great' terrestrial 'learned-beings,' I am reminded and willy-nilly impelled to utter one of the wise sayings of our esteemed Mullah Nassr Eddin, namely:

"'They both succeeded, though of course not without luck, in finding the authentic god-mother of the incomparable Scheherazade on an old dung-hill.'

"In any case you must know and bear in mind that for many centuries just this question among similar ephemeral questions, provides material for the kind of mentation which is considered among your favorites as the 'highest-manifestation-of-Reason.'

"These favorites of yours would in my opinion get quite a correct answer to this question which always excites them, that is, the question how the apes arose, if they were able in the given case to apply one of those sayings again of our dear Mullah Nassr Eddin, who often used to say:

"'The-cause-of-every-misunderstanding-must-be-sought-only-in-woman.'

"If with that wisdom of his they had attempted the solution of this enigmatic question, then perhaps they would have finally discovered whence and how these countrymen of theirs originated.

"As the question of the genealogy of these apes there, is indeed exceedingly abstruse and unusual, I shall inform your Reason about this also as far as possible from every aspect.

"In fact, neither have they descended from apes nor have apes descended from them, but . . . the cause of the origin of these apes is in this case, just as in every other misunderstanding there, also . . . their women.

"I must tell you first of all that the species of terrestrial ape-beings now arising there under several different exterior forms, never existed at all before the second 'Transapalnian perturbation'; only afterwards did the genealogy of their species begin.

"The causes of the arising of this 'misconceived' being as well as the cause of all the other events more or less serious in an objective sense, which occur on the surface of that ill-fated planet, ensue from two sources, totally independent of each other.

"The first of them, as always, was the same lack of

- *274* -

foresight on the part of certain Most High, Most Very Saintly Cosmic Individuals, and the second was, in the given case, also the same abnormal conditions of ordinary being-existence established by them themselves.

"The point is that when the second Transapalnian perturbation occurred to that ill-fated planet, then, besides its chief continent Atlantis, many other large and small terra firmas entered within the planet and, in their place, new terra firmas appeared on the surface of the planet.

"These displacements of the parts of the common presence of that ill-fated planet then continued for several days, with repeated planetary tremors and with such manifestations as could not fail to evoke terror in the consciousness and feelings of beings of every kind.

"During that same period many of your three-brained favorites who chanced to survive, together with various one-brained and two-brained beings of other forms, unexpectedly struck upon other newly-formed terra firmas in entirely new places unfamiliar to them.

"It was just at this period that many of these strange Keschapmartnian three-brained beings of active and passive sex, or, as they say, 'men' and 'women,' were compelled to exist for some years there apart, that is to say, without the opposite sex.

"Before relating how this then further occurred, I must explain to you a little more in detail concerning that sacred substance which is the final result of the evolving transformations of every kind of being-food formed in the presence of every being without distinction of brain system.

"This sacred substance which arises in the presences of beings of every kind is almost everywhere called 'Exioëhary'; but your favorites on the planet Earth call it 'sperm.'

"Thanks to the all-gracious foresight and command of our COMMON FATHER AND CREATOR and according to the

- *275* -

actualization of Great Nature, this sacred substance arises in the presences of all beings without distinction of brain system and exterior coating, chiefly in order that by its means they might, consciously or automatically, fulfill that part of their being-duty which consists in the continuation of their species; but in the presences of three-brained beings it arises also in order that it might be consciously transformed in their common presences for coating their highest being-bodies

"I must tell you first of all that the species of terrestrial ape-beings now arising there under several different exterior forms never existed at all before the second 'Transapalnian-perturbation'; only afterwards did the genealogy of their species begin.

"The cause of this arising of this 'Misconceived' being as well as the causes of all the other events more or less serious in an objective sense, which occur on the surface of that ill-fated planet, are two circumstances totally independent of each other.

"The first of them, as always, was the same want of

foresight on the part of certain Most High, Most Very Saintly Cosmic Individuals, and the second was, in the given case, also the same abnormal conditions of ordinary being-existence established by them themselves.

"The point is that when the second 'Transapalnian-perturbation' occurred to that ill-fated planet, then, besides its chief continent Atlantis, many other both large and small terra-firmas entered within the planet, and in their place, new terra-firmas appeared on the surface of the planet.

"These displacements of the parts of the common presence of that ill-fated planet then continued for several days there, with repeated planetary tremors and with such manifestations, that they could not fail to evoke terror in the consciousness and feelings of beings of every kind.

"During that same period many of our three-brained favorites who chanced to survive together with various one-brained and two-brained beings of other forms, unexpectedly struck upon other newly formed terra-firmas in entirely new places unfamiliar to them.

"It was just at this period that many of these strange Keschapmartnian three-brained beings of active and passive sex, or as they say, 'men' and 'women,' were compelled to exist for some years there apart, that is to say, without the opposite sex.

"Before relating how this then further occurred, I must explain to you a little more in detail concerning that sacred substance which is the final result of the evolving transformations of every kind of being-food formed in the presence of every being without distinction of 'brain-system.'

"This sacred substance which arises in the presences of beings of every kind is almost everywhere called 'Exioëhary'; but your favorites on the planet Earth call it 'sperm.'

"Thanks to the all-gracious foresight and command of our COMMON FATHER CREATOR and according to the

actualization of Great Nature, this sacred substance arises in the presences of all beings without distinction of brain system and exterior coating, chiefly in order that by its means they might, consciously or automatically, fulfill that part of their being-duty which consists in the continuation of their species; but in the presences of three-brained beings it arises also in order that it might be consciously transformed in their common presences for coating their highest being-bodies for their own Being.

"Before the second Transapalnian perturbation there, which period of their planet the contemporary three-brained beings define by the words, 'Before the loss of the continent Atlantis,' when various consequences of the properties of the organ Kundabuffer had already begun to be crystallized in their presences, a being impulse began to be formed in them which later became predominant.

"This impulse is now called 'pleasure'; and in order to satisfy it they had already begun to exist in a way unbecoming to three-centered beings, namely, most of them gradually began to remove this same sacred being-substance from themselves only for the satisfaction of the said impulse.

"Well, then, my boy. Owing to the fact that most of the three-brained beings of the planet Earth thereafter carried out the process of the removal from themselves of this sacred substance—which is constantly formed in them—not at certain periods normally established by Great Nature for beings in accordance with their organization, simply for the purpose of the continuation of their species, and also owing to the fact that most of them ceased to utilize this sacred substance consciously for coating their higher being-bodies, the result was obtained that when they do not remove it from themselves by ways which had then already become mechanical, they naturally must experience a sensation called 'Sirkliniamen,' or as your

favorites there would say, the state defined by the words 'out of sorts,' which state is invariably accompanied by what is called 'mechanical suffering.'

"Remind me at some opportune moment about the said periods fixed by Nature for the normal process of the utilization of Exioëhary by beings of different brain systems for the purpose of the continuation of their species, and I shall explain it to you in detail.

"Well then, in consequence of the aforesaid, and because just like us they are also only Keschapmartnian beings, and the normal removal from their presences of this sacred substance which constantly and inevitably arises in them can proceed exclusively only with the opposite sex when they utilize it for the continuation of the species by means of the sacred process 'Elmooarno'; and also because they were not in the habit of utilizing it for the purpose of coating their higher being-bodies; these chance surviving three-brained beings there—namely, those who had already been existing as it is not becoming for three-brained beings to exist, that is to say, when during several of their years they had existed without beings of the opposite sex—began to turn to various antinatural means for the removal from themselves of the sacred substance Exioëhary formed in them.

"The beings of the male sex then turned to the antinatural means called 'Moordoorten' and 'Androperasty,' or, as the contemporary beings would say, 'onanism' and 'pederasty,' and these antinatural means fully satisfied them.

"But for the three-brained beings of the passive sex, or, as they are called, 'women,' the said antinatural methods proved to be not sufficiently satisfying, and so the poor 'women orphans' of that time, being already then more cunning and inventive than the men there, began to seek

for their own Being.

"Before the second 'Transapalnian-perturbation' there, which period of their planet the contemporary three-brained beings define by the words: 'Before-the-loss-of-the-continent-Atlantis,' when various consequences of the properties of the organ Kundabuffer had already begun to be crystallized in their presences, a being-impulse began to be formed in them which later became predominant.

"This impulse is now called 'pleasure'; and in order to satisfy it they had already begun to exist in a way that is not becoming to three-centered beings, namely, the majority of them gradually adapted the removal for themselves of this same sacred being-substance only for the satisfaction of the said impulse.

"So my boy! On account of the fact that the majority of the three-brained beings of the planet Earth thereafter carried out the process of the removal from themselves of this substance—which is constantly formed in them—not at certain periods normally established by Great Nature for beings in accordance with their organization simply for the purpose of the continuation of their species, and also because the majority of them ceased to utilize it consciously for coating their highest being-bodies, the result was obtained that when not removing it from themselves by ways which had then already become mechanical, they naturally must experience a sensation called 'Sirkliniamen,' or as your favorites there would say,

the state defined by the words 'out-of-sorts,' which state is invariably accompanied by what is called 'mechanical-suffering.'

"Remind me at some opportune moment about the said periods fixed by Nature for the normal process of the utilization of 'Exioëhary' by beings of different brain systems for the purpose of the continuation of their species, and I will explain it to you in detail.

"Well then, in consequence of the aforesaid, and also because just like us they are also Keschapmartnian beings, and the normal removal from their presences of this sacred substance which constantly and inevitably arises in them, can proceed exclusively only with the opposite sex when they utilize it for the continuation of the species by means of the sacred process 'Elmooarno,' and also because they were not in the habit of utilizing it for the purpose of coating their higher being-bodies, these chance surviving three-brained beings there—namely, those who had already been existing as it is not becoming for three-brained beings to exist, that is to say, when during several of their years they had existed without beings of the opposite sex—began to turn to various anti-natural means for the removal from themselves of the sacred substance 'Exioëhary' formed in them.

"The beings of the male sex then turned to the anti-natural means called 'Moordoorten' and 'Androperasty,' or as the contemporary beings would say, 'Onanism' and 'Pederasty,' and these anti-natural means fully satisfied them.

"But for the three-brained beings of the passive sex, or, as they are called, 'women,' the said anti-natural methods proved to be not sufficiently satisfying, and so the poor 'women-orphans' of that time, being already then more cunning and inventive than the men there, began to seek out and accustom beings of other forms of the given place to be their 'partners.'

"Well then, it was after these 'partnerships' that those kinds of beings also began to appear in our Great Universe who in themselves are, as our dear Mullah Nassr Eddin would say, 'neither one thing nor the other.'

"Concerning the possibility of this abnormal blending of two different kinds of Exioëharies for the conception and arising of a new planetary body of a being, it is necessary to explain to you also the following.

"On the planet Earth, just as on other planets of our Universe where Keschapmartnian three-brained beings breed and exist, that is to say, those three-brained beings the formation of whose Exioëhary for the purpose of creating a new being must obligatorily proceed in the presences of two distinct independent sexes, the fundamental difference between the sacred Exioëharies formed in the presences of the distinct and opposite sexes of Keschapmartnian beings, that is to say, in 'men' and 'women,' is that in the Exioëhary formed in the presences of beings of the male sex the localized sacred 'affirming' or 'positive' force of the sacred Triamazikamno participates; while for the completed formation of the Exioëhary in the presences of beings of the female sex, there participates the localized sacred 'denying' or 'negative' force of the same sacred law.

"And owing to the same all-gracious foresight and command of our FATHER of Everything Existing in the Great Universe, and according to the actualizations of Great Mother Nature, then in certain surrounding conditions and with the participation of the third separately localized holy force of the sacred Triamazikamno, namely, the holy force called 'Reconciling,' the blending of these two Exioëharies arising in two distinct independent different beings just gives, owing to the process called 'the process of the sacred Elmooarno' which proceeds between

---------------------------------- *278* ----------------------------------

those beings of opposite sex, the beginning for the arising of a new being.

"And the possibility in the given case of such an abnormal blending of two different kinds of Exioëhary then occurred owing only to a certain cosmic law called the 'affinity of the number of the totality of vibrations,' which proceeded owing to the second Transapalnian perturbation to this ill-fated planet and which then still continued to act for its own common presence.

"Concerning this cosmic law just mentioned, it is now absolutely necessary to tell you that it arose and began to exist in the Universe after the fundamental sacred law of Triamazikamno was changed by OUR CREATOR for the purpose of rendering the Heropass harmless, and after its previously totally independent holy parts had begun to be dependent upon forces coming from outside.

"You will understand this cosmic law also in all its aspects when, as I have already promised you, I shall explain to you in detail all the fundamental laws in general of World-creation and World-existence.

"Meanwhile know, concerning this question, that in general everywhere on normally existing planets of our Great Universe the Exioëhary formed in the presence of a three-brained being who has perceptive and transformative organs for localizing the holy affirming part of the sacred Triamazikamno, that is to say,

out and accustom beings of other forms of the given place to be their 'partners.'

"Well then, it was after these 'partnerships' that those kinds of beings also began to appear in our Great Universe who in themselves are, as our dear Mullah Nassr Eddin would say, 'Neither-one-thing-nor-the-other.'

"Concerning the possibility of this abnormal blending of two different kinds of Exioëharies for the conception and arising of a new planetary body of a being, it is necessary to explain to you also the following:

"On the planet Earth, just as on other planets of our Universe where Keschap-martnian three-brained beings breed and exist, that is to say, those three-brained beings the formation of whose Exioëhary for the purpose of creating a new being must obligatorily proceed in the presences of two distinct independent sexes, the fundamental differences between the sacred Exioëharies formed in the presences of the distinct and opposite sexes of Keschapmartnian beings, that is to say, in 'man' and 'woman,' is, that in the Exioëhary formed in the presences of beings of the male sex, there participates the localized sacred 'affirming' or 'positive' force of the sacred Triamazikamno; while for the completed formation of the Ex-ioëhary of the presences of beings of the female sex, there participates the local-ized sacred 'denying' or 'negative' force of the same sacred law.

"And owing to the same all-gracious foresight and command of our FATHER OF EVERYTHING EXISTING IN THE GREAT UNIVERSE, and according to the actualization of Great Mother Nature, then in certain surrounding conditions and with the participation of the third separately localized holy force of the sacred Triamazikamno, namely, the holy force called 'Reconciling,' the blending of these two Exioëharies arising in the two distinct independent beings, different in kind, just give, owing to the process called 'the-process-of-the-sacred-Elmooarno' pro-ceeding between

---

these beings of opposite sex, the beginning for the arising of a new being.

"And the possibility in the given case of such an abnormal blending of two different kinds of Exioëhary then occurred owing only to a certain cosmic law called the 'affinity-of-the-number-of-the-totality-of-vibrations,' which proceeded owing to the second 'Transapalnian-perturbation' to this ill-fated planet and which then still continued to act for its common presence.

"Concerning this cosmic law just mentioned, it is now absolutely necessary to tell you that it arose and began to exist in the Universe after the fundamental sacred law of Triamazikamno was changed by our CREATOR for the purpose of rendering the Heropass harmless, and after its previously totally independ-ent holy parts had begun to be dependent upon forces coming from outside.

"Moreover you will understand this cosmic law also in all its aspects when, as I have already promised you, I shall explain to you in detail all the fundamental laws in general of World-Creation and World-Existence.

"Meanwhile, concerning this question, know that in general everywhere on normally existing planets of our Great Universe, the Exioëhary formed in the presence of a three-brained being who has perceptive and transformative organs for localizing the holy affirming part of the sacred Triamazikamno, that is to say, a Keschapmartnian being of the male sex, can, owing to the just-mentioned cosmic law, never be blended with the Exioëhary formed in the presence of a Keschapmartnian two-brained being of the opposite sex.

"At the same time, the Exioëhary formed in the three-brained Keschapmartnian being of the female sex can sometimes—in those cases when a special combination of the blending of cosmic forces is obtained and the mentioned law comes into effect—be completely blended under

--------------------------------- *279* ---------------------------------

certain surrounding conditions with the Exioëhary formed in two-brained Keschapmartnian beings of the male sex, but only as the active factor in such an actualizing process of the fundamental sacred Triamazikamno.

"In short, during the said terrible years on this planet of yours, a result very rare in the Universe was obtained, that is to say, there was obtained the blending of the Exioëharies of two Keschapmartnian beings of different brain systems of opposite sexes; and as a result, there arose the ancestors of these terrestrial 'misconceived' beings now called apes, who give your favorites no peace and who from time to time agitate their strange Reason.

"But when after the mentioned terrible period there on your planet, when the relatively normal process of ordinary existence was re-established and your favorites of different sexes again began to find each other and to exist together, then the continuation of the species of the ape beings was thereafter actualized also among beings similar to themselves.

"And this continuation of their species by these abnormally arisen ape-beings there could be further continued among themselves because the conception for the arising of the first of these abnormal beings had also proceeded owing to those same mentioned external conditions, thanks to which the presences of future Keschapmartnian beings of active or of passive sex are generally determined.

"The most interesting result of this already excessively abnormal manifestation of the three-brained beings of your planet is that there now exist a great many species of generations of ape-beings differing in exterior form, and each of these varied species bears a very definite resemblance to some form of a two-brained quadruped being still existing there.

"This came about because the blending of the Exioëhary of the Keschapmartnian three-brained beings there of the

--------------------------------- *280* ---------------------------------

'female sex,' which served as a beginning for the arising of the ancestors of these apes, then proceeded with the active Exioëhary of those same varied quadruped beings existing there up to the present time.

"And indeed, my boy, when during the period of my last personal stay on the planet Earth, I chanced during my travels to meet with the said various independent species of apes, and when, by a habit which has become second nature, I also observed them, I constated very definitely that the whole of the inner functioning and what are called the 'automatic posture' of each separate species of these contemporary apes there are exactly like those present in the whole of the presences of some normally arisen quadruped being there, and that even what are called

in the presence of a Keschapmartnian being of the male sex, can, on the basis of the just mentioned cosmic law, never be blended with the Exioëhary formed in the presence of a Keschapmartnian two-brained being of the opposite sex.

"At the same time, the Exioëhary formed in a three-brained Keschapmartnian being of the female sex can sometimes—in those cases, when a special combination of the blending of cosmic forces is obtained and the mentioned law comes into effect—be completely blended under

certain surrounding conditions with the Exioëhary formed in two-brained Keschapmartnian beings of the male sex, but only as the active factor in such an actualizing process of the fundamental sacred Triamazikamno.

"In short, during the said terrible years on this planet of yours, a result very rare in the Universe was obtained, that is to say, there was obtained the blending of the Exioëharies of two Keschapmartnian beings of different brain systems of opposite sexes; and as a result, there arose the ancestors of these terrestrial sportive beings now called apes, who give your favorites no peace and from time to time agitate their strange Reason.

"But when after the mentioned terrible period there on your planet, when the relatively normal process of ordinary existence was reestablished and your favorites of different sexes again began to find each other and to exist together, then the continuation of their species among the ape-beings was thereafter actualized also among beings similar to themselves.

"And this continuation of their species by these abnormally arisen ape-beings there could be further continued among themselves because the conception for the arising of the first of these abnormal beings had also proceeded on the basis of those same mentioned external conditions, thanks to which the presence of future Keschapmartnian beings of active or of passive sex is generally determined.

"The most interesting result of this already excessively abnormal manifestation of the three-brained beings of your planet is that there now exist very many species of generations of ape-beings differing in exterior form, and each of these varied species bears a very definite resemblance to some form of a two-brained quadruped being still existing there.

"This came about because the blending of the Exioëhary of the Keschapmartnian three-brained beings there of the

'female sex' which served as a beginning for the arising of the ancestors of these apes, then proceeded with the active Exioëhary of these same varied quadruped beings existing there up to the present time.

"And indeed my boy, when during the period of my last personal stay on the planet Earth, I chanced during my travels to meet with the said various independent species of apes, and when by a habit which has become second nature, I also observed them, I constated very definitely that the whole of the inner functioning and what are called the 'automatic-postures' of each separate species of these contemporary apes there, are exactly like those present in the whole of the presence of any normally arisen quadruped being there, and that even what are called their

their 'facial features' very definitely resemble those of the said quadrupeds; but on the other hand that what are called the 'psychic features' of all the separate species of these apes there are absolutely identical, even down to details, with those of the psyche of the three-brained beings there of the 'female sex.'"

At this point of his tales, Beelzebub made a long pause and looking at his favorite Hassein with a smile which very clearly expressed a double meaning, he, continuing to smile, said:

"In the text of the etherogram which I have just received, it is further said that in order this time finally to settle who has descended from whom—whether they from the apes or the apes from them—these freaks, your favorites, have even decided to carry out 'scientific experiments,' and furthermore that several of them have already left for the continent of Africa where many of these apes breed, with the object of bringing back from there the number required for these 'scientific investigations' of theirs.

"To judge by this etherogram, the beings of the planet

Earth who have taken your fancy are again, in their turn, up to their 'extraordinary tricks.'

"From all I have learned about them during my observations, I foresee that this 'scientific experiment' will, of course, very greatly interest other of your favorites also, and will serve for a time as material to their strange Reason for endless discussion and talks.

"And all this will be quite in the order of things there.

"Concerning the 'scientific experiment' itself, which they propose to carry out with the apes taken back from Africa, I can with certainty say beforehand, that at any rate the first part of it will without any doubt, succeed 'wonderfully well.'

"And it will succeed wonderfully well, because the apes themselves, as beings of what is called a 'Terbelnian result,' are already, owing to their nature, extremely fond of occupying themselves with 'titillation' and before the day is out, will no doubt participate in and greatly assist your favorites in this 'scientific experiment' of theirs.

"As for those beings there who are going to carry out this 'scientific experiment,' and as for any benefit from it for the other three-brained beings there, it can all be pictured to oneself if one remembers the profoundly wise saying of our same honorable Mullah Nassr Eddin, in which he says: 'Happy is that father whose son is even busy with murder and robbery, for he himself will then have no time to get accustomed to occupy himself with "titillation."'"

"Yes, my boy, it seems that I have not yet told you why and by whom, since I left the solar system Ors, I am kept informed by etherogram of the most important events which proceed on various planets of that system, and, of course, also about events proceeding on your planet Earth.

"You remember I told you that my first descent in person upon the surface of that planet of yours took place

'facial-features' very definitely resemble those of the said quadrupeds; but on the other hand, that what are called the 'psychic-features' of all the separate species of these apes there are absolutely identical, even down to the details, with those of the psyche of the three-brained beings there of the 'female sex.'"

At this point of his tales, Beelzebub made a long pause and looking at this favorite Hassein, with a smile which very clearly expressed a double meaning, he, continuing to smile, said:

"In the text of the etherogram which I have just received, it is further said that in order this time finally to settle who has descended from which—whether they from the apes or the apes from them—these freaks, your favorites, have even decided to carry out 'scientific-experiments,' and furthermore that several of them have already left for the continent of Africa where many of these apes breed, with the object of bringing back from there the number required for these 'scientific-investigations' of theirs.

"To judge by this etherogram, the beings of the planet Earth

who have taken your fancy are again, in their turn, up to their 'extraordinary tricks.'

"From all I have learned about them during my observations, I foresee that this 'scientific-experiment' will, of course, very greatly interest other of your favorites also, and will serve for a time as material to their strange Reason for endless discussion and talks.

"And all this will be quite in the order of things there.

"Concerning the 'scientific-experiment' itself, which they propose to carry out with the apes taken back from Africa, I can with certainly say beforehand, that at any rate the first part of it will without any doubt, succeed wonderfully well.

"And it will succeed wonderfully well, because the apes themselves, as beings of what is called a 'Terbelnian-result' are already, owing to their nature, extremely fond of occupying themselves with 'titillation,' and before the day is out, will no doubt participate in and greatly assist your favorites in this 'scientific experiment' of theirs.

"As for those beings there who are going to carry out this 'scientific-experiment,' and as for any benefit from it for the other three-brained beings there, it can all be pictured if one remembers the profoundly wise saying of our same honorable Mullah Nassr Eddin, in which he says:

"'Happy is that father whose son is even busy with murder and robbery, for he himself will then have no time to get accustomed to occupy himself with "titillation."'

"Yes, my boy, it seems that I have not yet told you why and by whom, since I left the Solar System Ors, I am kept informed by etherograms of the most important events which proceed on various planets of that system, and, of course, also about events proceeding on your planet Earth.

"You remember I told you, that my first personal descent upon the surface of that planet of yours took place on account of one of the young beings of our tribe, who then had no desire to stay there any longer but returned with us to the planet Mars, where he later became a very good chief over all the beings of our tribe existing on that planet, and who is now already the chief over all the beings in general of our tribe who for various reasons still exist on certain planets of that system Ors.

"Well then, my boy, when I left that system, I presented my famous observatory to him with everything in it, and in gratitude for this he promised to report every month, according to the time-calculation of the planet Mars, all the more important events occurring on the planets of that system.

"And now this chief keeps me very accurately informed of the most important events proceeding on all the planets on which there is a being-existence; and, knowing my great interest in the three-brained beings breeding on the planet Earth, he does his best, as I now see, to elucidate and send me information concerning all those manifestations of theirs which can give me now also the possibility of being constantly informed of the whole process of the ordinary existence of these three-brained beings, even though I find myself already inaccessibly remote even for their featherweight thoughts.

"That chief of our beings who remains there collects the various kinds of information he communicates concerning the three-brained beings of the planet Earth, either by means of his own observations of them through the great Teskooano which I left him, or from reports which, in their turn, are communicated to him by those three beings of our own tribe who chose to exist forever on the planet Earth, and all three of whom have at the present time on the continent of Europe different substantial independent undertakings indispensable for everyone existing there under the prevailing conditions.

------------------------------ 283 ------------------------------

"One of them has in one of the large cities, an 'undertaker's business'; the second, in another large city, has a bureau for what are called matchmaking and divorce; and the third is the proprietor of many offices founded by himself in various cities for what is called 'money exchange.'

"However, my boy, owing to this etherogram, I have wandered a long way from my original tale.

"Let us go back to our former theme.

"Well, then, upon this the fourth flight of mine to the planet Earth, our ship *Occasion* descended onto the sea called the 'Red Sea.'

"And we descended upon this Sea because it washed the Eastern shores of that continent where I wished to go, namely, to that continent then called Grabontzi and now called Africa, on which those ape-beings I needed then bred more than on any other of the terra firma parts of the surface of that planet of yours; and also because this sea was at that period particularly convenient for the mooring of our ship *Occasion*; but what was still more important was that on one of its sides that country was situated which was then called 'Nilia' and is now called Egypt, where those beings of our tribe then existed who wished to remain on that planet and with whose help I intended to collect the apes.

"Well, then, having descended upon the Red Sea, we sailed from the ship *Occa-*

on account of one of the young beings of our tribe, who then had no desire to stay there any longer but returned with us to the planet Mars, where he later became a very good chief over all the beings of our tribe existing on that planet, and who is now already the chief over all the beings in general of our tribe who for various reasons still exist on certain planets of that system Ors.

"Well then my boy, when I left that system, I presented my famous observatory to him with everything in it, and in gratitude for this he promised to report every month, according to the time-calculation of the planet Mars, all the more important events occurring on the planets of that system.

"And now this chief keeps me very accurately informed of the most important events proceeding on all the planets on which there is a being-existence; and, knowing my great interest in the three-brained beings breeding on the planet Earth, he does his best, as I now see, to elucidate and send me information concerning all those manifestations of theirs which give me now also the possibility of being constantly informed of the whole process of the ordinary existence of these three-brained beings, even though I find myself already inaccessibly remote even for their featherweight thoughts.

"That chief of our beings remaining there, collects the various information he communicates concerning the three-brained beings of the planet Earth either by means of his own observations of them through the great Teskooano which I left him, or from the reports which, in their turn, are communicated to him by those three-brained beings of our own tribe who chose to exist forever on the planet Earth, and all three of whom have at the present time on the continent of Europe, different substantial independent undertakings indispensable for everyone existing there under the prevailing conditions.

- -

"One of them has in one of the large cities, an 'undertaker's-business'; the second, in another large city, has a bureau for what are called, match-making and divorce; and the third is the proprietor of many offices founded by himself in various cities for what is called, 'money-exchange.'

"However my boy, owing to this etherogram, I have wandered a long way from my original tale.

"Let us go back to our former theme.

"Well then, upon this fourth flight of mine to the planet Earth, our ship 'Occasion' descended on to the sea called 'Red-Sea.'

"And we descended upon this Sea because it washed the eastern shores of that continent where I wished to go, namely to that continent then called Grabontzi and now called Africa, on which those ape-like beings I needed then bred more than on any other of the terra-firma parts of the surface of that planet of yours; and also because this sea was at that period particularly convenient for the mooring of our ship 'Occasion'; but what was still more important was that on one of is sides that country was situated which was then called 'Nilia' and is now called Egypt, where those beings of our tribe still existed then, who wished to remain on that planet and with whose help I intended to collect the apes.

"Well then, having descended upon the 'Red-Sea,' we sailed from the ship 'Oc-

sion on 'Epodrenekhs' to the shore; and afterwards, on camels we came to that town where our beings existed and which was then the capital of the future Egypt.

"This capital city was then called Thebes.

"On the very first day of my arrival in the city of Thebes, one of the beings of our tribe existing there told me among other things, in the course of our conversation, that the beings of the Earth of that locality

------------------------------ *284* ------------------------------

had devised a new system for observing other cosmic concentrations from their planet, and that they were then constructing what was required in order to carry it into effect; and also, as everybody there said, that the convenience and possibilities of this new system were excellent and until then unparalleled on the Earth.

"And when he had related all he had himself seen with his own eyes, I immediately became greatly interested, because from his description of certain details of this new construction there, it seemed to me that these terrestrial beings had perhaps found a means of overcoming that inconvenience about which I myself had just previously been thinking a great deal while I was completing the construction of my observatory on the planet Mars.

"And so I decided to postpone for a while my first intention of immediately going further south on that continent to collect the apes I needed, and instead, to go first where the said construction was being made, in order on the spot to become personally acquainted with it from every aspect, and to find out all about it.

"Well then, the day following our arrival in the city Thebes, accompanied by one of the beings of our tribe who already had many friends there, and also by the chief constructor of the said construction, and of course by our Ahoon also, I went this time on what is called a 'Choortetev' down the tributary of that great river now called the 'Nile.'

"Near where this river flowed into a large 'Saliakooriapnian area' those constructions were just being completed, one part of which then interested me.

"The district itself, where the work was being carried on both for this new, what they called 'observatory,' and for several other constructions for the welfare of their being existence, was then called 'Avazlin'; a few years

------------------------------ *285* ------------------------------

later it came to be called there 'Caironana,' and at the present time it is simply called the 'outskirts of Cairo.'

"The mentioned constructions had been begun long before by one of what are called there 'Pharaohs,' the name by which the beings of that region called their kings; and at the time of my fourth flight to the Earth and my first visit to this place, the special constructions he had begun were already being completed by his grandson, also a Pharaoh.

"Although the observatory which interested me was not yet quite finished, nevertheless observations of the exterior visibility of cosmic concentrations could be made from it, and the results issuing from them and the reciprocal action of these results could be studied.

"Those beings who were occupied with such observations and studies were

casion' on 'Epodrenekhs' to the shore; and afterwards, on camels we came to that town where our beings existed and which was then the capital of the future Egypt.

"This capital city was then called Thebes.

"On the very first day of my arrival in the city of Thebes, one of the beings of our tribe existing there told me among other things, in the course of our conversation, that the beings of the Earth of that locality

- -

had devised a new system for observing other cosmic concentrations from their planet, and that they were then constructing what was required in order to carry it into effect; also, as everybody there said, that the convenience and possibilities of this new system were excellent and until then unparalleled on the Earth.

"And when he had related all he had himself seen with his own eyes, I immediately became greatly interested, because from his description of certain details of this new construction there, it seemed to me that these terrestrial beings had perhaps found a means of overcoming that inconvenience about which I myself had just previously been thinking a great deal while I was completing the construction of my observatory on the planet Mars.

"And so I decided to postpone for a while my first intention of immediately going further south on that continent to collect the apes I needed, and instead, to go first to where the said construction was being made, in order on the spot to become personally acquainted with it from every aspect, and to find out all about it.

"So then, the day following our arrival in the city Thebes, accompanied by one of the beings of our tribe who already had many friends there, and also by the chief constructor of the said construction, and of course by our Ah-hoon also, I went this time on what is called a 'Choortetev' down the tributary of that great river now called the 'Nile.'

"Near where this river flowed into a large "Saliakooriapnian-area," those artificial constructions were just being completed of which just one part then interested me.

"The district itself, where the work was being carried on both from this new, what they called 'observatory,' and for several other constructions for the welfare of their being-existence, was then called 'Avazlin' a few years

- -

later it came to be called there 'Caironana,' and at the present time it is simply called the 'outskirts-of-Cairo.'

"The mentioned artificial constructions had been begun long before by one of what are called there 'Pharaohs,' the name by which the beings of that region called their kings; and at the time of my fourth flight to the Earth and my first visit to this place, the special constructions he had begun were already being completed by his grandson, also a Pharaoh.

"Although the observatory which interested me was not yet quite finished, nevertheless observations of the exterior visibility of cosmic concentrations could be made from it, and the results issuing from them and the reciprocal action of these results, could be studied.

"Those beings there who were occupied with such observations and studies called, at that period on the Earth, 'Astrologers.'

"But when afterwards that psychic disease of theirs called wiseacring became finally fixed there, owing to which these specialists of theirs also 'shriveled and shrank' and became specialists only in giving names to remote cosmic concentrations, they came to be called 'Astronomers.'

"Inasmuch as the difference in significance and sense, in relation to surrounding beings, between those from among the three-brained beings who have taken your fancy who at that time were such professionals, and those who have now, as it were, the same occupation, might show you, so to say, 'the obviousness of the steady deterioration of the degree of crystallization' of data engendering the 'sane logical mentation,' which ought to be present in the common presences of your favorites as three-brained beings, I therefore find it necessary to explain to you and to help you to have an approximate

-------------------------------- 286 --------------------------------

understanding of this difference, which is also changing for the worse.

"At that period, these terrestrial three-brained beings, already of responsible age, whom the others named 'Astrologers,' besides making the said observations and investigations of various other cosmic concentrations for the purpose of a greater, as is said, 'detailizing' of that branch of general learning of which they were representatives, fulfilled several further definite essence-obligations taken upon themselves towards surrounding beings similar to themselves.

"Among their fundamental definite obligations was that they also, like our Zirlikners, had to advise all the conjugal pairs in their what was then called 'flock,' according to the types of those pairs, about the time and form of the process of the sacred 'Elmooarno' for the purpose of a desirable and corresponding conception of their results, and when such results were actualized, or, as they themselves say, 'newly born,' they had to draw up their 'Oblekioonerish' which is the same as what your favorites call 'horoscope'; and later either they themselves or their substitutes had—during the whole period of the formation of the newly born for responsible existence and of their subsequent responsible existence—to guide them and give corresponding indications on the basis of the said Oblekioonerish and also on the basis of the cosmic laws, constantly explained by them, flowing from the actions of the results of other large cosmic concentrations in general on the process of being-existence of beings on all planets.

"These indications of theirs, and also their, so to say, 'warning counsels' consisted in the following:

"When a function became disharmonized or only began to be disharmonized in the presence of any being of their flock, then this being applied to the Astrologer of his

-------------------------------- 287 --------------------------------

district, who, on the basis of the said Oblekioonerish made by him, and on the basis of the changes expected, according to his calculations, in the processes proceeding in the atmosphere, flowing in their turn from the action of the other planets of their solar system, indicated just what he had to do to his planetary body, at which definite periods of the Krentonalnian movements of their planet—

were called, at that period on the Earth, 'Astrologers.'

"But when afterwards that psychic illness of theirs called 'wiseacring' became finally fixed there, owing to which these specialists of theirs also shriveled and shrunk and became specialists only in giving names to remote cosmic concentrations, they came to be called 'Astronomers.'

"Owing to the fact that for surrounding beings, the difference in the meaning and good sense between those professionals of that time among the three-brained beings who have taken your fancy and those who have now, as it were, the same occupation, might show you, so to say, the 'obviousness-of-the-infallible-deterioration-of-the-degree-of-the-crystallisation' of the data engendering 'sane-logical-mentation' which ought to be present in the common presences of those favorites of yours as three-brained beings, I therefore find it necessary to explain to you and to help you to have an approximate

understanding just about this difference, which is also changing for the worse.

"At that period, these terrestrial three-brained beings who are already at responsible age and whom the others named 'Astrologers,' besides making the said observations and investigations of various other cosmic concentrations for the purpose of a greater, as is said, 'detailizing' of that branch of general learning of which they were representatives, fulfilled several further definite essence-obligations taken upon themselves towards surrounding beings similar to themselves.

"One of their fundamental definite obligations was that they, also like our Zirlikners, had to advise all the conjugal pairs of their, as it was then said, 'flock,' about the time and form of the process of the sacred 'Elmooarno' for the purpose of a desirable and corresponding conception of their result, and when such results were actualized, or as they themselves say, 'newly-born,' they had to draw up their 'Oblekioonerish' which is the same as what your contemporary favorites call 'horoscope'; and later, they themselves or their substitutes had—during the whole period of the formation of the newly-born into responsible existence—to guide them and give corresponding indications on the basis of the said 'Oblekioonerish' and also on the basis of cosmic laws constantly explained by them flowing from the actions of the results of other cosmic large concentrations in general during the process of being-existence of beings on all planets.

"These indications of theirs and also their, so to say, 'warning-counsels' proceeded just in the following manner:

"When a function became disharmonized or only began to be disharmonized in the presence of any being of their flock, then the latter applied to the Astrologer of his

district, who, on the basis of the said 'Oblekioonerish' made by him, and on the basis of the changes expected, according to his calculations, of the processes proceeding in the atmosphere and ensuing in their turn from the action of the other planets of their solar system, indicated just what they had to do to their own planetary body at which definite periods of the Krentonalnian movements of their

as for instance, in which direction to lie, how to breathe, what movements preferably to make, with which types to avoid relations, and many things of the same kind.

"In addition to all this, they assigned to the beings at the seventh year of their existence, likewise on the basis of these Oblekioonerishes, corresponding mates of the opposite sex for the purpose of fulfilling one of the chief being-duties, that is, continuation of the race, or as your favorites would say, they assigned them 'husbands' and 'wives.'

"Justice must be done to your favorites of the period when these Astrologers existed among them; they then indeed very strictly carried out the indications of these Astrologers and made their conjugal unions exclusively only according to their indications.

"Therefore, at that period, in regard to their conjugal unions, they always corresponded according to their type, just as such pairs correspond everywhere on planets on which Keschapmartnian beings also breed.

"These ancient terrestrial Astrologers made these matches successfully because even if they were very far from the knowledge of many cosmic Trogoautoegocratic truths, yet they at least already very well knew the laws of the influence of different planets of their solar system on the beings breeding on their own planet, namely, the influence of these planets on a being at the moment of his conception, for further formation, as well as for his complete acquisition of the Being of a responsible being.

------------------------------ 288 ------------------------------

"Having, thanks to the information transmitted to them from generation to generation, a many-centuried practical knowledge, they already knew which types of the passive sex can correspond to which of the active sex.

"Owing to all this, the pairs matched according to their indications almost always turned out to be corresponding, and not as it proceeds there at the present time; and that is to say they are now united in conjugal pairs who nearly always do not correspond in type; in consequence of which during the continuation of the entire existence of these couples there, about half of their, as they say, 'inner life' is spent only on what our esteemed Mullah Nassr Eddin expresses in one of his sayings by the following words:

"'What a good husband he is, or what a good wife she is, whose whole inner world is not busy with the constant "nagging of the other half."'

"In any case, my boy, if these Astrologers had continued to exist there, then surely, thanks to their further practicing, the existence of the beings of this unfortunate planet would by now have gradually become such that their family relations would at least have been a little like the existence of similar beings on other planets of our Great Universe.

"But all this which was beneficently established in the process of their existence they have also sent, like all their other good attainments, without even having had time to make good use of it, 'to the gluttonous swine' of our respected Mullah Nassr Eddin.

"And these 'Astrologers' of theirs, as usually happens there, also at first began

planet—as for instance, in which direction to lie, how to breathe, which movements to make in preference, with which types to avoid relations and many things of the same kind.

"In addition to all this, they assigned beings at the seventh year of their existence, likewise on the basis of these 'Oblekioonerishes,' to corresponding mates of the opposite sex for the purpose of fulfilling one of the chief being-duties, that is, the continuation of the race, or as your favorites would say, they assigned 'husbands' and 'wives.'

"Justice must be given to your Favorites of that period, when these 'Astrologers' existed among them they then indeed very strictly followed the counsels of these 'Astrologers' and accomplished their conjugal unions exclusively only according to their indications.

"Therefore at that period they always responded to each other in respect of their conjugal unions according to type, just as the said pairs correspond everywhere on those planets on which Keschapmartnian beings also breed.

"These ancient 'Astrologers' there made these matches successfully because, even if they were very far from the knowledge of many cosmic 'Trogoautoegocratic' truths, yet they at least already very well knew the laws of the influence of the different planets of their solar system on the beings breeding on their own planets, namely—the influence of these planets on a being at the moment of his conception for further formation as well as for his complete acquisition of the Being of a responsible being.

- -

"Having, thanks to the information transmitted to them from generation to generation, a many-centuried practical knowledge, they already knew which type of the passive sex can correspond to which type of the active sex.

"And owing to all of this, the pairs matched according to their indications almost always turned out to be corresponding and not as it proceeds there at the present time, and that is to say, they are now united into conjugal pairs who almost always do not correspond with each other in type, in consequence of which during the continuation of the entire existence of these couples there, about half of their as is said 'inner life' is spent only for what our esteemed Mullah Nassr Eddin expresses in one of his sayings by the following words:

"'What a good husband he is, or what a good wife she is, if the whole of their inner life is not occupied with the constant "nagging" of their other halves.'

"In any case my boy, if these Astrologers had continued to exist there, then surely, thanks to their further practice, the existence of the beings of this unfortunate planet would have by now gradually become such, that at least their family relations would have been a little like the existence of similar beings on other planets of our Great Universe.

"But no, this beneficent practice established in the process of their existence, they also sent, just like all their other good attainments—without even having had time to utilize it properly—'to-the-gluttonous-swine' of our respected Mullah Nassr Eddin.

"And these 'Astrologers,' as usually happens there, also began from the begin-

gradually to 'shrink' and then entirely, as is said, 'vanished.'

"After the total abolition among them of the duties of these Astrologers, other professionals in the same sphere appeared in their place, but this time from among the 'learned beings of new formation' who also began to

observe and study, as it were, the results issuing from various large cosmic concentrations and their influence on the existence of the beings of their planet; but as the ordinary beings around these professionals soon noticed that their 'observations' and 'studies' consisted merely in inventing names for various remote suns and planets meaning nothing to them, existing in milliards in the Universe, and in measuring, as it were, by a method known to them alone, and which constituted their professional secret, the distance between the cosmic points seen from their planets through their 'child's toys' called by them 'telescopes,' they began to call them, as I have already told you, Astronomers.

"Now, my boy, that we have spoken also about these contemporary 'ultra fantasists' from among your favorites, we might as well, again imitating the form of mentation and the verbal exposition of our dear teacher Mullah Nassr Eddin, also 'illuminatingly' enlighten you about their significance, so esteemed by your favorites.

"First of all, you should know about that ordinary cosmic something actualized for these same terrestrial types, which is in general always actualized of itself for every cosmic unit and which serves for beings with Objective Reason as what is called an 'issuing source' for pondering about the explanation of the sense and meaning of any given cosmic result.

"This same something which serves as an issuing source for discovering the significance of these terrestrial contemporary types, is a wiseacring map named by them themselves—of course unconsciously—the 'map inventory of the heavenly spaces.'

"There is no need for us to draw any other logical conclusion from this issuing source specially actualized for them; it will be sufficient merely to say that the name itself of this map of theirs shows that the designations

made on it cannot in any way be other than entirely relative, because with the possibilities at their disposal—though they break their esteemed heads over devising names and calculating various kinds of measurements—they can see from the surface of their planet only those suns and planets which to their good fortune do not very quickly change the course of their falling in relation to their own planet and thus give them the possibility during a long period of time—of course long as compared with the brevity of their own existence—to observe them and, as they bombastically express themselves, 'mark down their positions.'

"In any case, my boy, however worthless the results of the activities of these contemporary representatives of 'learning' among your favorites, please don't be angry with them. If they do not bring any benefit at all to your favorites, they at least do not do them any great harm.

"After all, they must be occupied with something.

ning gradually to 'dwindle' and later, entirely, as is said, 'vanished.'

"After the complete abolition among them of the duties of these Astrologers, others appeared in their places in this same professional sphere, but this time among the 'learned-beings-of-new-formation,' who, as it were, also began to

observe and study the results ensuing from various cosmic large concentrations and their influence on the existence of beings of their planet; and their 'studies' consisted only in inventing names for different remote suns and planets meaning nothing to them and existing in milliards in the Universe, and also in measuring, as it were, by a method known to them alone and which was their professional secret, the distance between the cosmic points which they see from their planet through their 'childish-toys' called by them 'telescopes,' they then therefore came to be called, as I have already told you, 'Astronomers.'

"Now my boy that we have spoken also about these contemporary 'ultra-fantasists' from among your favorites, we might as well, imitating the form of mentation and verbal exposition of our dear teacher Mullah Nassr Eddin, also 'illuminatingly' enlighten you about their significance, so esteemed by your favorites.

"First of all, you should know about that ordinary cosmic 'something' actualized just for these same terrestrial types, which is in general always actualized of itself for every cosmic unit and which serves for beings with Objective Reason as what is called an 'issuing-source' for pondering about the explanation of the sense and meaning of any given cosmic 'result.'

"This same 'something' which serves as an 'issuing source' for discovering the significance of these terrestrial contemporary types, is a 'wiseacring-map' named by them themselves—of course unconsciously, the 'map-inventory-of-the-heavenly-spaces.'

"There is no need for us to draw any other logical conclusion from this 'Issuing-source' specially actualized for them; it will be sufficient only to say that the name itself of this map of theirs shows that the designations

made on it cannot at all be any other than only relative, because from the surface of their planet, with only these possibilities at their disposal, and breaking their 'esteemed-heads' over the names devised and the calculations of various kinds of measurements, they can see only that sun and those planets, which to their good fortune, do not very quickly change the course of their falling in relation to their own planet, and thus give them the possibility during a long period of time—of course long, comparatively with the shortness of the duration of their own existence—to observe them and as they magniloquently express themselves 'mark-down-their-positions.'

"In any case my boy, however much matters do not go well with the results of the activities of these contemporary representatives of 'learning' among your favorites, please don't get angry with them. If they do not bring any benefit at all to your favorites, they at least do not do them any great harm.

"After all they must be occupied with something!

"It is not for nothing that they wear spectacles of German origin and special smocks sewed in England.

"Let them! Let them be occupied with this! God bless them!

"Otherwise like most of the other freaks there who are occupied with, as they say there, 'higher matters,' they will busy themselves, out of boredom, 'leading the struggle of five against one.'

"And it is known to all that the beings who are occupied with these matters always radiate from themselves vibrations very harmful for beings around them similar to themselves.

"Well enough! Leave these contemporary 'titillators' in peace and let us continue our interrupted definite theme.

"In view of the fact, my boy, that this conscious ability expressed in the creation of such a construction unparalleled both before and after this period, of which I was

--------------------------------- *291* ---------------------------------

then an eyewitness, was also the result of the attainments of the beings, members of the learned society Akhaldan, which was formed on the continent of Atlantis before the second great terrestrial catastrophe, I think it will be best, if, before continuing to explain to you further about the mentioned observatory and other constructions erected there for the welfare of being-existence, I should tell you, even though briefly, about the history of the arising there of such an indeed great learned society consisting of ordinary three-brained beings, as this learned society Akhaldan then was on the continent of Atlantis.

"It is imperatively necessary to inform you of this because in the course of my further explanations concerning these three-brained beings of the planet Earth who have taken your fancy I shall in all probability have to refer more than once to that society of learned beings there.

"I must also tell you about the history of the arising and existence of that society there on the continent Atlantis, so that you may also know that if the three-brained beings there on your planet—thanks to their being-Partkdolg-duty, that is to say, thanks to their conscious labors and intentional sufferings—ever attain anything, then not only do they utilize these for the good of their own Being, but also a certain part of these attainments is transmitted as with us by inheritance and becomes the property of their direct descendants.

"You can perceive such a law-conformable result there from the fact that although towards the end of the existence of the continent Atlantis abnormal conditions of ordinary being-existence had already begun to be established and that after the second great catastrophe they deteriorated at such a rate that they soon finally 'crushed' all their ableness to manifest the possibilities proper to the presences of three-brained beings, nevertheless their 'attainments of learning' passed by inheritance, at least

--------------------------------- *292* ---------------------------------

partly, even though mechanically, to their remote direct descendants.

"I must first tell you that I learned about this history, thanks to what are called 'Teleoghinooras' which are at present in the atmosphere also of that planet Earth

"It is not for nothing that they wear spectacles of German origin and special smocks sewn in England.

"Let them! Let them be occupied with this! God bless them!

"Like most of the other freaks there who are occupied with, as is said there, 'higher-matters,' they will out of boredom get busy as 'leaders-of-the-struggle-of-five-against-one.'

"And it is known to all that the beings who are occupied with these matters, always radiate from themselves very harmful radiations for beings around them similar to themselves.

"Well enough! Leave these contemporary 'titillators' in peace and let us continue our interrupted definite theme.

"In view of the fact my boy that this 'conscious-ability' expressed in the creation of such an artificial construction unparalleled both before and after this period, of which I was

then an eyewitness, was also the result of the attainments of the beings, members of the learned society Akhaldan, which was already formed on the continent of Atlantis before the second large terrestrial catastrophe, I think it will be best, if, before continuing to explain to you further about the mentioned observatory and other constructions erected there for the welfare of being-existence, I should tell you, even though briefly, about the history of the arising there of such an indeed great learned society consisting of ordinary three-brained beings, as this learned society Akhaldan then was on the continent Atlantis.

"It is imperatively necessary to inform you of this because in the course of my further explanations concerning these three-brained beings of the planet Earth who have taken your fancy, I shall in all probability have to refer more than once to that society of learned beings there.

"I must also tell you the history of the arising and existence of that society there on the continent Atlantis, in order that you may have a notion also about this, that if something is attained by three-brained beings there also on your planet, thanks to their 'being-Partkdolgduty,' that is to say, thanks to their conscious labors and intentional sufferings, then these attainments are not only utilized by themselves for the good of their own Being, but also a certain part, of them, as with us, is transmitted by inheritance and becomes the property of their direct descendants.

"Such a lawful result present there, you can see from the fact, that although towards the end of the existence of the continent Atlantis, abnormal conditions of ordinary being-existence had already begun to be established and that after the second great catastrophe they deteriorated at such a rate that they soon finally crushed all the 'potency' to manifest the possibilities present in the presences of every three-brained being, nevertheless their 'attainments-of-learning' passed by inheritance, at least,

partially even though mechanically, to their remote direct descendants.

"I must first tell you that I got to know this history, thanks to what are called 'Teleoghinooras,' which are present in the atmosphere also of that planet Earth of of yours.

"As you probably do not yet know exactly what a Teleoghinooras is, try to transubstantiate in the corresponding parts of your common presence the information concerning this cosmic actualization.

"A Teleoghinoora is a materialized idea or thought which after its arising exists almost eternally in the atmosphere of that planet on which it arises.

"Teleoghinooras can be formed from such a quality of being-contemplation as only those three-brained beings have and can actualize, who have coated their higher being bodies in their presences and who have brought the perfecting of the Reason of their higher being part up to the degree of the sacred 'Martfotai.'

"And the sequential series of being-ideas, materialized in this way, concerning any given event, are called 'Korkaptilnian thought tapes.'

"It seems that the said Korkaptilnian thought tapes concerning the history of the arising of the learned society Akhaldan were, as I found out much later, deliberately fixed by a certain 'Eternal Individual,' Asoochilon, now a saint, who became coated in the common presence of a three-brained being named Tetetos who arose on your planet on the continent of Atlantis and who had existed there four centuries before the second great 'Transapalnian perturbation.'

"These Korkaptilnian thought tapes are never destroyed as long as the given planet exists, which is in what is called the 'tempo of movement of the prime arising'; and they are subject to none of those transformations from

_293_

any cosmic causes whatsoever to which all other cosmic substances and cosmic crystallizations are periodically subject.

"And however long a time may have already passed, every three-brained being in whose presence there has been acquired the ability to enter into the being-state called 'Soorptakalknian contemplation' can perceive and cognize the texts of these Korkaptilnian thought tapes.

"And so, my boy, I myself learned about the details of the arising there of the society Akhaldan partly from the text of the just-mentioned Teleoghinoora and partly from many data which I learned much later, namely, when, having become interested also in this highly important factor there, I made my usual detailed investigations.

"According to the text of the mentioned Teleoghinoora and to data which I subsequently learned, it became clear and definitely known to me that this learned society Akhaldan which arose then on the continent Atlantis and which was composed of three-brained beings of the Earth, was formed 735 years before the second 'Transapalnian perturbation' there.

"It was founded on the initiative of a being there named Belcultassi, who was then able to bring the perfecting of his higher being part to the Being of a Saint 'Eternal Individual'; and this higher part of his now already dwells on the holy planet Purgatory.

"My elucidation of all those inner and outer being-impulses and manifestations which caused this Belcultassi then to found that truly great society of ordinary three-brained beings—a society which in its time was throughout the whole Uni-

yours.

"As you probably do not yet know exactly what a 'Teleoghinoora' is, try to transubstantiate in the corresponding parts of your common presence the information concerning just this cosmic actualization.

"'Teleoghinooras' can be formed from such a quality of being-contemplation which only those three-brained beings have and can actualize, who have coated their higher bodies in their presences and who have brought the perfecting of the Reason of their higher being-part up to the degree of the sacred 'Martfotai.'

"And the sequential series of being-ideas, materialized in this way, concerning any given event, are called 'Korkaptilnian-thought-tapes.'

"It seems that the said 'Korkaptilnian-thought-tapes' concerning the history of the arising of the learned society Akhaldan were, as I found out already much later, deliberately fixed by a certain 'Eternal-Individual,' Asoochilon, now a Saint who became coated in the common presence of a three-brained being named Tetetos who arose on your planet just on the continent of Atlantis and who had existed there four centuries before the second great 'Transapalnian-perturbation.'

"These 'Korkaptilnian-thought-tapes' are never destroyed as long as the given planet exists which is in what is called the 'tempo-of-movement-of-the-prime-arising'; and they are subject to none of those transformations from

any cosmic causes whatever to which all other cosmic substances and cosmic crystallizations are periodically subject.

"And however long a time may have already passed, every three-brained being in whose presences there is acquired the ableness to enter into the being-state called 'Soorptakalknian-contemplation' can perceive and cognize the text of these 'Korkaptilnian-thought-tapes.'

"And so my boy, I myself learned about the details of the arising there of the society Akhaldan partly from the text of the just mentioned 'Teleoghinoora' and partly from the many data which I learnt much later, namely when, having become interested also in this highly important factor there, I made my usual detailed investigations.

"According to the text of the mentioned 'Teleoghinoora' and to the data I subsequently learned, it became clear and definitely known to me that this learned society Akhaldan which arose then on the continent Atlantis and which was composed of the three-brained beings of the Earth, was formed seven hundred and thirty-five years before the second 'Transapalnian-perturbation' there.

"It was founded on the initiative of a being there named Belcultassi, who was then able to bring the perfecting of his higher being-part to the Being of a Saint 'Eternal-Individual'; and this higher-part of his now already dwells on the holy planet Purgatory.

"My elucidations of all those inner and outer being-impulses and manifestations which were the cause of this Belcultassi having then founded that truly great society of ordinary three-brained beings—a society which in its time was

verse called 'envied for imitation'—showed that when this same later Saint Individual Belcultassi was once contemplating, according to the practice of every normal being, and his thoughts were by association concentrated on himself, that is to say, on the sense

— *294* —

and aim of his existence, he suddenly sensed and cognized that the process of the functioning of the whole of him had until then proceeded not as it should have proceeded according to sane logic.

"This unexpected constatation shocked him so profoundly that thereafter he devoted the whole of himself exclusively to be able at any cost to unravel this and understand.

"First of all he decided to attain without delay such a 'potency' as would give him the strength and possibility to be quite sincere with himself, that is to say, to be able to conquer those impulses which had become habitual in the functioning of his common presence from the many heterogeneous associations arising and proceeding in him and which were started in him by all sorts of accidental shocks coming from outside and also engendered within him, namely, the impulses called 'self-love,' 'pride,' 'vanity,' and so on.

"And when, after incredible what are called 'organic' and 'psychic' efforts, he attained to this, he then without any mercy for these being-impulses which had become inherent in his presence, began to think and recall just when and what various being-impulses had arisen in his presence during the period preceding all this, and how he had consciously or unconsciously reacted to them.

"Analyzing himself in this manner, he began to recall just which impulses evoked which reactions in him, in his independently spiritualized parts, that is to say, in his body, in his feelings and in his thoughts, and the state of his essence when he reacted to anything more or less attentively, and how and when, in consequence of such reactions of his, he had manifested consciously with his "I" or had acted automatically under the direction of his instinct alone.

"And it was just then that this bearer of the later Saint

— *295* —

Individual Belcultassi, recalling in this way all his former perceptions, experiencings, and manifestations, clearly constated in consequence, that his exterior manifestations did not at all correspond either to the perceptions or to the impulses definitely formed in him.

"Further, he then began to make similar sincere observations of the impressions coming from outside as well as those formed within himself, which were perceived by his common presence; and he made them all with the same exhaustive, conscious verifications of how these impressions were perceived by his separate spiritualized parts, how and on what occasions they were experienced by the whole of his presence and for what manifestations they became impulses.

"These exhaustive conscious observations and impartial constatations finally convinced Belcultassi that something proceeded in his own common presence not as it should have proceeded according to sane being-logic.

"As it became clear to me during my subsequent detailed investigations, al-

throughout the whole Universe called 'envied-to-be-imitated'—showed that when this same later Saint Individual Belcultassi was once contemplating, according to the practice of every normal being, and his thoughts were by association concentrated on himself, that is to say, on the sense

and aim of his own existence, he suddenly sensed and cognized that the process of the functioning of his whole presence had hitherto proceeded not as it should have proceeded according to sane logic.

"So unexpectedly a constatation shocked him so profoundly that he thereafter devoted the whole of himself only to be able at any cost to unravel it all and understand.

"First of all he decided to attain without delay such a 'potency' as would give him the strength and possibility to be quite sincere with himself, that is to say, to be able to conquer those impulses which had become habitual in the functioning of his common presence from the many varied associations which arose in him and which were started in him by every kind of accidental shock proceeding from without and also by those arising within him, namely, the impulses called 'self-love,' 'pride,' 'vanity' and so on.

"And when after incredible what are called 'organic' and 'psychic' efforts, he attained to this, he then, without any compunction for those being-impulses which had become inherent in his presence, began to think and recall when and what various being-impulses had ever arisen in his presence during the period of his preceding existence and how he had consciously or unconsciously reacted to them.

"Analyzing himself in this manner, he recalled the impulses which evoked in him one or another reaction in his independently-spiritualized parts, that is to say, in his body, his feelings and his thoughts, and what his general essence had become when he reacted to something more or less attentively, and how and when, in consequence of such reactions of his, he had manifested consciously with his 'I' or had acted automatically under the direction only of his instinct.

"Recalling in this way all his former perceptions, experiencings, and manifest-

ations, this bearer of the later Saint Individual Belcultassi just then clearly constated, in consequence, that his external manifestations had no correspondence whatever with either the perceptions or with the impulses definitely formed in him.

"Further, he made the same sincere observations of his of the impressions proceeding from without and also formed within himself, which were perceived by his common presence; and he made them with always the same exhaustive, conscious verifications of how these impressions were received by his separate spiritualized parts, how on what occasions they were experienced by the whole of his presence and for what manifestations they became impulses.

"These exhaustive conscious observations and impartial constatations finally convinced Belcultassi that something proceeded in his own common presence not as it should have proceeded according to sane being-logic.

"As my subsequent detailed investigations made clear, although Belcultassi had

though Belcultassi had become indubitably convinced of the accuracy of his observations on himself, yet he doubted the correctness of his own sensations and understandings and also the normalness of his own psychic organization; and he therefore set himself the task of elucidating, first of all, whether he was in general normal in sensing and understanding all this just in this way and not otherwise.

"To carry out this task of his, he decided to find out how the same would be sensed and cognized by others.

"With that aim he began inquiring among his friends and acquaintances to try to find out from them how they sensed it all and how they cognized their past and present perceptions and manifestations, doing this, of course, very discreetly, so as not to touch the aforementioned

- 296 -

impulses inherent in them, namely, 'self-love,' 'pride,' and so on, which are unbecoming to three-brained beings.

"Thanks to these inquiries, Belcultassi gradually succeeded in evoking sincerity in his friends and acquaintances, and as a result it turned out that all of them sensed and saw in themselves everything just the same as he did.

"Now among these friends and acquaintances of Belcultassi, there were several earnest beings who were not yet entirely slaves to the action of the consequences of the properties of the organ Kundabuffer, and who, having penetrated to the gist of the matter also became very seriously interested in it and began to verify that which proceeded in themselves, and independently to observe those around them.

"Soon after, on the initiative of the same Belcultassi, they began to meet together from time to time, and to share their observations and new constatations.

"After prolonged verifications, observations, and impartial constatations, this entire group of terrestrial beings also became categorically convinced, just like Belcultassi himself, that they were not as they ought to be.

"Not long after, many others also having such presences joined that group of terrestrial beings.

"And later they founded that society which they named the 'Society of Akhaldans.'

"By the word Akhaldan the following conception was then expressed:

"'The striving to become aware of the sense and aim of the Being of beings.'

"From the very beginning of the foundation of this society, Belcultassi himself stood at its head, and the subsequent actions of the beings of this society proceeded under his general guidance.

"For many terrestrial years this society existed under the said name, and its member-beings were then called

- 297 -

'Akhaldansovors'; but later, when the members of this society, for purposes of a general character, were divided into a number of independent groups, the members belonging to different groups came to be called by different names.

"And this division of theirs into groups occurred for the following reason:

"When they had finally become convinced that there was something very un-

become convinced 'beyond-all-doubt' of the accuracy of his observations on himself, yet he doubted the correctness of his own sensations and understandings and also of the normality of his psychic organization; and he therefore set himself the task of elucidating, first of all, whether he was in general normal while sensing and understanding everything just in this way and not otherwise.

"To carry out this task of his he decided to find out how others sensed and cognized the aforesaid.

"With that aim he began inquiring among his friends and acquaintances to try to find out from them how they sensed it all and how they cognized their former and current perceptions and manifestations, doing this of course, very discreetly in order to avoid touching the mentioned

- -

impulses inherent in them of 'self-love,' 'pride' and so on, unbecoming to be present in three-brained beings.

"Thanks to these inquiries Belcultassi was gradually able to evoke sincerity among his friends and acquaintances, and the result proved that all of them sensed and saw themselves just as he did.

"There proved to be, just among these friends and acquaintances of Belcultassi, several serious beings who were not yet entirely slaves to the action of the consequences of the properties of the organ Kundabuffer, and who, having penetrated to the essence of the matter also became very seriously interested in it and began to verify that which proceeded in themselves, and independently to observe those around them.

"Soon after, on the initiative of the same Belcultassi, they began to meet together from time to time, and to share their observations and new constatations.

"After prolonged verifications, observations and impartial constatations this whole group of terrestrial beings also became categorically convinced, just like Belcultassi himself, that they were not as they ought to be.

"Not long after, many others having also the said presences, joined this group of terrestrial beings there.

"And later they founded this society which they named the 'Society-of-Akhaldans.'

"By the word 'Akhaldan,' the following conception was then expressed:

"'The-striving-to-become-aware-of-the-sense-and-aim-of-the-Being-of-beings.'

"From the very beginning of the foundation of this society, Belcultassi himself stood at its head, and the subsequent actions of the beings of this society proceeded under his general guidance.

"For many years there this society existed under the said name, and its member-beings were called

- -

'Akhaldansovors'; but later, when the members of this society, for purposes of a general character, were divided into a number of independent groups, the members belonging to different groups were called differently.

"And the division into groups occurred then for the following reason.

"When they had become finally convinced that there was something undesirdesirable in their presences and they had begun to seek means and possibilities of achieving its removal in order to become such as, according to sane logic, they ought to have been, corresponding to the sense and aim of their existence, the elucidation of which, whatever it might cost them, they made the basis of their task, and when they proceeded to actualize in practice this task previously decided upon by their Reason, it very soon became clear that it was imperatively necessary for its fulfillment to have in their Reason more detailed information of various special branches of knowledge.

"But as it proved impossible for each and every one of them to acquire the necessary special knowledge, they divided themselves for convenience into a number of groups so that each group might separately study one of these special branches of knowledge required for their common aim.

"Here, my boy, you should notice that genuine objective science just then arose and began to exist there for the first time, and developed normally up to the time of the second great catastrophe to their planet; also that the rate of the development of some of its separate branches then progressed at an indeed unprecedented tempo.

"And in consequence many great and small cosmic, what are called 'objective truths' gradually began at that period to become evident also to those three-brained beings who have taken your fancy.

- *298* -

"The learned members of this first and perhaps last great terrestrial learned society were then divided into seven independent groups, or as it is otherwise said, 'sections,' and each of these groups or sections received its definite designation.

"The members of the first group of the society Akhaldan were called 'Akhaldanfokhsovors,' which meant that the beings belonging to that section studied the presence of their own planet as well as the reciprocal action of its separate parts.

"The members of the second section were called 'Akhaldanstrassovors,' and this meant that the beings belonging to that section studied what are called the radiations of all the other planets of their solar system and the reciprocal action of these radiations.

"The members of the third section were called 'Akhaldanmetrosovors,' which meant beings occupied with the study of that branch of knowledge similar to that branch of our general knowledge we call 'Silkoornano,' and which partly corresponded to what your contemporary favorites call 'mathematics.'

"The members of the fourth group were called 'Akhaldanpsychosovors,' and by this name they then defined those members of the society Akhaldan who made their observations of the perceptions, experiencings, and manifestations of beings like themselves and verified their observations by statistics.

"The members of the fifth group were called 'Akhaldanharnosovors,' which meant that they were occupied with the study of that branch of knowledge which combined those two branches of contemporary science there which your favorites call 'chemistry' and 'physics.'

"The members belonging to the sixth section were called 'Akhaldanmistesso-

able in their presences and had begun to search for means and possibilities of removing it in order to become such as, according to sane logic, they had to be, that is to say, correspondent to the sense and aim of their existence, the elucidation of which, whatever it might cost them, they made the basis of their task, and when they began to actualize in practice this task previously decided upon by their Reason, it very soon became clear that it was imperatively necessary for its fulfillment to have more detailed information in their Reasons concerning various special branches of knowledge.

"But as it proved impossible for each and every one of them to acquire the necessary special knowledge, they divided themselves for convenience into a number of groups, in order that each group might separately study one of these special branches of knowledge required for their common aim.

"Here my boy, you should notice that genuine objective knowledge just then arose there for the first time and began to exist and developed normally up to the time of the second great catastrophe to their planet; also that the growth of the development of its branches then progressed even at an unprecedented rate.

"And in consequence a considerable number of great and small what are called cosmic 'objective-truths' gradually began at that period to become evident also to these three-brained beings who have taken your fancy.

"The learned beings of this great first and probably last terrestrial learned society were then divided into seven independent groups, or as it is otherwise said, 'sections'; and each of these groups or sections received a definite name.

"Members of the first group of the society Akhaldan were called 'Akhaldanfokhsovors,' which meant that the beings belonging to that section studied the presence as well as the reciprocal action of separate parts of their common planet.

"The members of the second section were called 'Akhaldanstrassovers,' and this meant that the beings belonging to that section studied what are called the 'radiations' and their reciprocal action of all the other planets of their solar system.

"Members of the third section were called 'Akhaldanmetrosovors,' which meant beings occupied with the study of that branch of knowledge, which was like that branch of our general knowledge we call 'Silkoornano,' and which partly corresponded to what your contemporary favorites call 'mathematics.'

"The members of the fourth group were called 'Akhaldanpsychosovors,' and by this name those members of the society Akhaldan were then denoted who made their observations of the perceptions, experiencings and manifestations of beings like themselves and verified their observations by statistics.

"Members of the fifth group were called 'Akhaldanharnosovors,' which meant that they were occupied with the study of that branch of knowledge which combined those two branches of contemporary science there, which your favorites called 'chemistry' and 'physics.'

"Members belonging to the sixth section were called 'Akhaldanmistessovors,'

vors,' that is to say, beings who studied every kind of fact arising outside of themselves, those actualized consciously from without and also those

-------------------------------- *299* --------------------------------

arising spontaneously, and which of them, and in what cases, are erroneously perceived by beings.

"And as regards the members of the seventh and last group, they were called 'Akhaldangezpoodjnisovors'; these members of the society Akhaldan devoted themselves to the study of those manifestations in the presences of the three-brained beings of their planet which proceeded in them not in consequence of various functionings issuing from different kinds of qualities of impulses engendered owing to data already present in them, but from cosmic actions coming from outside and not depending on them themselves.

"The three-brained beings of your planet who became members of this society actually did a great deal in respect of approaching objective knowledge which had never been done there before and which perhaps will never be repeated.

"And here it is impossible not to express regret and to repeat that to the most great misfortune of all terrestrial three-brained beings of all later epochs, it was just then—when after incredible being-labors by members of that great society the required tempo of work had already been established with regard to discernment, conscious on their part, and also with regard to their unconscious preparation for the welfare of their descendants—that, in the heat of it all, certain of them constated, as I have already told you, that something serious was to occur to their planet in the near future.

"For the purpose of discerning the character of the anticipated serious event, they dispersed over the whole planet and shortly afterwards, as I have already told you, the aforesaid second 'Transapalnian perturbation' occurred to that ill-fated planet of yours.

-------------------------------- *300* --------------------------------

"Well then, my boy, when after this catastrophe, a number of the surviving beings, members of that great learned society, gradually came together again, they, no longer having their native country, first settled together with most of the other surviving beings in the center of the continent Grabontzi, but later, when they had, on the continent Grabontzi, 'come to themselves' a little after the 'cataclysm not according to law,' which had occurred, they decided jointly to try to re-establish, and perhaps to continue to actualize in practice, all those tasks which had formed the basis of their last society.

"As the manifestations of those abnormal conditions of being-existence of most of the three-brained beings there which had already been established before the catastrophe had by this time already begun to 'boil' furiously on the said part of the surface of the continent Grabontzi, these surviving members of the society Akhaldan looked for another place on the same continent for their permanent existence more suitable for this work of theirs which demanded complete separateness.

"Such a suitable place they found in the valley of the large river flowing on the north of the said continent and there indeed they all migrated together with their

that is to say, beings who studied every kind of event arising outside of themselves, actualized consciously from without and also

arising by themselves, and in what circumstances which of them are erroneously
perceived by beings.

"And as regards the members of the seventh and last group, they were called
'Akhaldangezpoodjnisovors'; these members of the society Akhaldan devoted
themselves to the study of those manifestations in the presences of the three-
brained beings of their planet which proceeded in them not in consequence of
various functionings issuing from different kinds of impulses engendered owing
to data already present in them, but from cosmic actions coming from without
and not depending upon them themselves.

"The three-brained beings of your planet who then became members of this
society did indeed many things in respect of approaching objective knowledge as
had never been done there before and probably never will be again.

"And it is impossible not to express regret and to repeat that it was just then,
when to the most great misfortune of the three-brained beings there of all later
epochs, owing to the incredible being-labors of the member-beings of that great
society, the required tempo of work had already been established in respect of
conscious discrimination for them themselves and also in respect of their unconscious preparation for the welfare of their descendants, that, in the heat of it all, a
number of them constated, as I have already told you, that something serious had
to occur to their planet in the near future.

"For the purpose of discovering the nature of the anticipated serious event,
they dispersed over the whole planet, and it was shortly afterwards as I have also
already told you, that the mentioned second 'Transapalnian-perturbation' occurred to that ill-fated planet of yours.

"Well then my boy, when after this catastrophe, a number of the surviving
member-beings of that great learned society gradually came together again, they,
having no longer their native country, first settled together with the majority of
the other surviving beings in the center of the continent Grabontzi, but later,
when they had, on the continent Grabontzi, 'come-to-themselves,' a little after the
'cataclysm-not-according-to-law,' which had occurred, they decided jointly to try
to reestablish and perhaps to continue to actualize in practice, all those tasks
which had formed the basis of their last society.

"As the manifestations of those abnormal conditions of being-existence of most
of the three-brained beings there on the said part of the surface of the continent
Grabontzi, which had already been established before the catastrophe, had
already begun to 'boil' furiously, these surviving members of the society
Akhaldan looked for another place on the same continent for their permanent
existence more suitable for this work of theirs which demanded complete separateness.

"Such a suitable place they found in the valley of the large river flowing on the
northern side of the said continent, and there indeed they all together migrated

families to continue in isolation the attainment of the tasks set by their society.

"This entire region, through which the said large river flowed, they first named 'Sakronakari.'

"But this name was afterwards several times changed and at the present time this region is called 'Egypt' while the said large river, then called 'Nipilhooatchi,' is now, as I have already said, called the Nile.

"Soon after certain former members of the learned society Akhaldan had settled on this part of the surface of the planet Earth, all the beings of our tribe, who then

------------------------------ *301* ------------------------------

existed on the surface of that planet which has taken your fancy, migrated to the same place.

"And the relations of our tribe with that part of your planet and also with the first migration there of the chance surviving former members of the society Akhaldan were as follows:

"I told you once that just before the second 'Transapalnian perturbation' our Party-Pythoness, while prophesying, insisted that all the beings of our tribe should, without delay, migrate for the continuation of their existence on that planet, to a definite part of the surface of that same continent now called Africa.

"This definite part of the surface of the continent which the Pythoness indicated, lay just at the source of the said large river Nipilhooatchi where the beings of our tribe existed all the time the said second Transapalnian perturbation lasted, as well as later when everything had gradually resumed its relatively normal state and when most of the surviving beings had then almost forgotten what had happened and had again formed—just as if nothing had occurred to them—one of their famous 'centers of culture' in the very center of that future Africa. And it was just when the former members of the society Akhaldan were searching for a suitable place for their permanent existence, that they chanced to meet a number of the beings of our tribe who advised them to migrate to the country further down the said river.

"Our acquaintanceship and our friendly relations with many of the former members of the society Akhaldan had already begun on the continent Atlantis almost from the founding of that society.

"Do you remember I told you that when I descended to that planet for the first time and the beings of our tribe assembled in the city of Samlios with my participation in order together to find a way out of the difficult situation

------------------------------ *302* ------------------------------

that had been created, those general meetings of ours were held in one of the sections of the principal cathedral of the society Akhaldan; and from that time on, good relations were established between many beings of our tribe and certain members of this society?

"And there in that future Egypt whither both had migrated in the said way, the relations of the beings of our tribe with the authentic former members themselves who chanced to be saved, and also with the descendants of other authentic mem-

with their families in order to continue in isolation the attainment of the tasks set by their society.

"This whole region through which the said large river flowed, they first named 'Sakronakari.'

"But this name was afterwards several times changed and at the present time this region is called 'Egypt,' while the said large river, then called 'Nipilhooatchi,' is now, as I have already said, called the 'Nile.'

"Soon after, certain former members of the learned society Akhaldan settled on this part of the surface of the Planet Earth, all the beings of our tribe then existing

- -

on the surface of that planet which has taken your fancy, migrated to the same place.

"And the facts concerning the real relations of the beings of our tribe with that part of your planet and also with the first migration there of the chance surviving former members of the society Akhaldan are as follows:

"I told you once that just before the second 'Transapalnian-perturbation,' our party-Pythoness, while prophesying, insisted that all the beings of our tribe should, without delay, migrate for the continuation of their existence on that planet, to a definite part of the surface of that same continent which is now called Africa.

"This definite part of the surface of the continent which the Pythoness indicated, lay just at the source of the said large river, 'Nipilhooatchi,' where the beings of our tribe existed the whole time the said second 'Transapalnian-perturbation' lasted as well as afterwards when everything had gradually resumed its relatively normal state and when most of the surviving beings had then almost forgotten what had happened and had again formed—just as if nothing had occurred to them—one of their famous 'centers-of-culture' in the very middle of that future Africa. Just at the time when the former members of the society Akhaldan were searching for a suitable place for their permanent existence, and chanced to meet a number of the beings of our tribe, they advised them to migrate to the country further down the said river.

"Our acquaintanceship and our friendly relations with many of the former members of the society Akhaldan, had already been begun on the continent Atlantis almost from the founding of that society.

"Do you remember I told you, that when I descended to that planet for the first time and the beings of our tribe assembled in the city of Samlios with my participation in order together to find a way out of the difficult situation

- -

that had been created—well, those general meetings of ours were held just in one of the sections of the principal cathedral of the society Akhaldan; and already, from that time on, good relations were established between many beings of our tribe and certain members of this society.

"And there in that future Egypt whither both had migrated in the said way, the relations of the beings of our tribe with the genuine former members themselves who had chanced to be saved and also with the descendants of other genuine bers, remained uninterrupted and continued almost until the departure of our tribe from your planet.

"Although the hope of the few chance surviving members of the society Akhaldan that they would be able to resume the actualizing of the task of their society was not fulfilled, nevertheless, thanks to them alone, there still continued to be present in the presences of beings of several subsequent generations after the loss of Atlantis, the 'instinctive conviction' concerning the sense of what is called there 'completed personal Being.'

"In addition, thanks to them, something of what had been attained by the Reason of the three-brained beings there also nevertheless survived when that Reason was still normal in them; and after a while this something began mechanically to be transmitted by inheritance from generation to generation and reached the beings of quite recent periods, even to several beings of contemporary times.

"Among those results of the learned attainments of the members of the society Akhaldan which were transmitted by inheritance, were also, without question, those ingenious and solid constructions which I saw being erected during this fourth descent of mine to your planet by the beings of whom I am just going to inform you, who were

--------------------------------- 303 ---------------------------------

breeding on that part of the surface of the continent of the present Africa.

"Although the expectations that I had formed from all that our countrymen had told me concerning the mentioned new observatory there, before I had seen it with my own eyes, were not justified, nevertheless, the observatory itself and also the other constructions of the beings then of that region proved to be exceedingly ingenious and provided data for the enrichment of my common presence by a great deal of productive information for my consciousness.

"And in order that you may clearly represent to yourself and understand how these various constructions were then erected by the three-brained beings of this region for the welfare of their being-existence, I think it will be enough if I explain to you in as great detail as possible, how the particularity of their ingenious practical invention was manifested in respect of their new observatory on account of which I had decided to visit that region.

"For this purpose I must first of all inform you of two facts connected with the change in the common presences of these three-brained beings who have taken your fancy.

"The first fact is that at the outset, while they were still existing normally, that is, as it is in general becoming to all three-brained beings to exist, and while they had what is called 'Olooestesnokhnian sight,' they could also perceive, at a distance proper to be perceived by ordinary three-brained beings, the visibility of all great as well as small cosmic concentrations existing beyond them during every process of the Omnipresent-Okidanokh which proceeded in their atmosphere.

"In addition, those of them who were consciously perfected and had thereby brought the sensibility of the perception of their organ of sight—like three-brained beings everywhere else—up to what is called the

--------------------------------- 304 ---------------------------------

members, remained uninterrupted and continued almost down to the time of the departure of our tribe from your planet.

"Although the hope of the few chance surviving members of the society Akhaldan that they would be able to resume the actualizing of the tasks of their society was not fulfilled, nevertheless, thanks to them alone, there still continued to be present in the presences of several subsequent generations after the loss of Atlantis, the 'instinctive-conviction' concerning the sense of what is there called 'completed-personal-Being.'

"In addition to this, thanks to them, something of what had been attained by the Reason of the three-brained beings there also nevertheless survived when that Reason was still normal in them; and after a while this something began mechanically to be transmitted by inheritance from generation to generation and reached the beings of quite recent periods, even to several beings of contemporary times.

"Among these results of the learned attainments of the members of the society Akhaldan which were transmitted by inheritance, were also, without question, those ingenious and solid 'artificial-constructions' which I saw being erected during this fourth descent of mine to your planet, by the beings of whom I am just going to inform you, who were

- -

breeding on that part of the surface of the continent of the present Africa.

"Although the expectations that I had formed from all that our countrymen had told me concerning the mentioned new observatory there, before I had seen it with my own eyes, were not justified, nevertheless the observatory itself and also the other 'artificial-constructions' of the beings then of that region proved to be exceedingly ingenious and provided data for my common presence to become enriched by a great deal of productive information for my consciousness.

"And in order that you may clearly represent to yourself and understand how these various 'artificial constructions' were then erected by the three-brained beings of this region for the welfare of their being-existence, I think it will be enough if I explain to you in as great detail as possible, how the particularity of their ingenious, practical invention was manifested in respect just of their new observatory, on account of which I had decided to visit that region.

"For this purpose I must first of all inform you of two facts connected with the change in the common presences of these three-brained beings who have taken your fancy.

"The first fact is that at the outset, while they still existed normally, that is, as it is in general becoming to all three-brained beings to exist, and while they had what is called 'Olooestesnokhnian-sight,' they also could perceive at a distance proper to be perceived by ordinary three-brained beings, the visibility of all both great and small cosmic concentrations existing beyond them during every process of the Omnipresent Okidanokh proceeding in their atmosphere.

"In addition, those of them who were consciously perfected and had thereby brought the sensibility of the perception of their organ of sight—like three-brained beings everywhere—up to what is called the

- -

'Olooessultratesnokhnian state,' acquired the possibility of perceiving also the visibility of all these cosmic units situated at the same distance, which arise and have their further existence dependent upon the crystallizations localized directly from the sacred Theomertmalogos, that is to say, from the emanations of our most holy Sun Absolute.

"And later, when the same constant abnormal conditions of ordinary being-existence were finally established, as a consequence of which Great Nature was compelled, for reasons of which I have already once told you, among other limitations, also to degenerate the functioning of their organ of sight into what is called 'Koritesnokhnian,' that is to say, into the sight proper to the presences of one-brained and two-brained beings, then thereafter they were able to perceive the visibility of their great as well as their small concentrations situated beyond them only when the sacred process 'Aieioiuoa' proceeded in the Omnipresent Active Element Okidanokh in the atmosphere of their planet, or, as they themselves say—according to their understanding and their own perceptions—'on dark nights.'

"And the second fact, by virtue of the same degeneration of their sight into Koritesnokhnian, is based on that law common to all beings, namely, that the results obtained from every manifestation of the Omnipresent Okidanokh are perceived by the organs of sight only when in immediate contact with those vibrations which are formed in beings and which actualize the functioning of the being-organ for perceiving, at the given moment, the visibility of cosmic concentrations situated beyond them; that is to say, only when the said results of the manifestation of the Omnipresent-Okidanokh proceed up to the limit beyond which, according to the quality of the given organ for perceiving visibility, what is called the 'momentum of the impulse' dies down, or to put it otherwise, they

— *305* —

perceive the visibility of objects only when almost next to them.

"But if these results take place beyond the mentioned limit, then this manifestation does not at all extend to those beings in whose presences there are organs for the perception of visibility, formed only by the results of the totality of 'Itoklanoz.'

"Here it is very opportune to repeat one of the profound sayings, seldom used there, of our Mullah Nassr Eddin, which very neatly defines the given case, that is, this degree of the limitation of the perception of visibility of your contemporary favorites.

"This wise saying of his, seldom used there, consists of the following words:

"'Show me the elephant the blind man has seen, and only then will I believe that you have really seen a fly.'

"Well then, my boy, thanks to that artificial adaptation which I had then seen for the observation of other cosmic concentrations, and which was being constructed in that future Egypt on the initiative issuing from the Reasons of the remote descendants of the member beings of the learned society Akhaldan, any one of these unfortunate favorites of yours, in spite of the Koritesnokhnian sight which had long before become inherent to them, could nevertheless acquire the

'Olooessultratesnokhnian-state,' acquired the possibility of perceiving also the visibility of all these cosmic units situated at the same distance, which arise and have their further existence dependent upon the crystallizations localized directly from the sacred Theomertmalogos, that is to say, upon the emanations of our most holy Sun Absolute.

"And later, when the same constant abnormal conditions of ordinary being-existence were finally established, as a consequence of which Great Nature was compelled, for reasons of which I have already told you, among other limitations, also to remold the functioning of their organ of sight into what is called 'Koritesnokhnian,' that is to say, into the sight proper to the presences of one-brained and two-brained beings, then thereafter they were already able to perceive the visibility, both of their great and small concentrations situated beyond them, only when there proceeded in the Omnipresent active element Okidanokh in the atmosphere of their planet, the sacred process 'Aieioiuoa,' that is, as they themselves say—according to their understanding and their own perceptions—'on-dark-nights.'

"And the second fact, by virtue of the same degeneration of their sight into a 'Koritesnokhnian' one, is based on that law common to all beings, namely, that the results obtained from every manifestation of the Omnipresent Okidanokh are perceived by the organs of sight only when in immediate contact with those vibrations which are formed in beings and which actualize the functioning of the being-organ for perceiving at the given moment the visibility of cosmic concentrations situated beyond them; that is to say, only when the said results of the manifestation of the Omnipresent Okidanokh take place up to the point beyond which, according to the quality of the given organ for perceiving visibility, what is called the 'momentum-of-the-impulse' dies down; or to put it otherwise, they

perceive the visibility of objects only when almost next to them.

"But if these results take place beyond the mentioned limit, then this manifestation does not at all reach those beings in whose presence are organs for the perception of visibility, formed only by the results of the totality of 'Itoklanoz.'

"Here it is very opportune to repeat one of the profound sayings seldom used there, of our Mullah Nassr Eddin, which very nearly defines the given case, that is, this degree of the limitation of the perception of visibility of your contemporary favorites.

"This wise saying of his, seldom used there, consists of the following words:

"'Show me the elephant the blind man has seen, and only then will I believe that you have really seen a fly.'

"Well then, my boy, thanks to that artificial adaptation which I then saw, for the observation of other cosmic concentrations, and which was being constructed in that future Egypt on the initiative issuing from the Reasons of the remote descendants of the member-beings of the learned society Akhaldan, any one of these unfortunate favorites of yours, in spite of the 'Koritesnokhnian-sight' which had long before become inherent to them, nevertheless acquired the potency to per-

ability to perceive freely at any time, as they say, 'of the day and night,' the visibility of all those remote cosmic concentrations which in the process of the general 'cosmic harmonious movement' come within the sphere of the horizon of their observation.

"In order to overcome this limitation of their organ of the perception of visibility, they then invented the following:

"Their Teskooano or telescope, the construction of which, it must here be said, passed to them also from their remote ancestors, they did not fix on the surface of their

------------------------------ 306 ------------------------------

planet, as was usually done there and is still done now—but they placed this Teskooano very deeply within the planet, and they carried out their observations of the cosmic concentrations found beyond the atmosphere of their planet through specially bored, pipe-like hollows.

"The observatory, I then saw, had five of these hollows.

"They began, in relation to the horizon, from different places of the surface of the planet occupied by the observatory, but they all met at a small underground common hollow which was something like a cave. From there, the specialists, then called Astrologers, made their observations for the purpose of studying, as I have already told you, the visible presences and results of the reciprocal action of other cosmic concentrations belonging to their own solar system as well as to other systems of the Great Universe.

"They made these observations of theirs through any one of the mentioned hollows which looked out in different directions onto their horizon, according to the given position of their planet relative to the cosmic concentration observed in the process of the 'common cosmic harmonious movement.'

"I repeat, my boy, that although the chief peculiarity of the observatory constructed there by the three-brained beings of the future Egypt proved not to be new to me, since this principle had also been utilized in my observatory on Mars, with only this difference, that my seven long pipes were fixed not within the planet but on it, nevertheless all their innovations were so interesting in detail that, for any case that might arise, I even made, during my stay there, a detailed sketch of everything I saw, and later even used something of it for my own observatory.

"And as regards the other 'constructions' there, I shall perhaps tell you about them in detail sometime later, but

------------------------------ 307 ------------------------------

meanwhile, I will only say that all these independent constructions which were then not quite finished were situated not far from the observatory itself, and were intended—as I elucidated during my inspection under the guidance of the constructor who accompanied us and who was a friend of one of our tribe—partly for the same purpose of observing other suns and planets of our Great Universe, and partly for determining and intentionally directing the course of the surrounding atmosphere in order to obtain the 'climate' desired.

"All these 'constructions' of theirs occupied a fairly large open space of that part

ceive freely at any time, as they say, 'of-the-day-and-night,' the visibility of all those remote cosmic concentrations which in the process of the general cosmic harmonious movement, come within the sphere of the horizon of their observation.

"In order to overcome this limitation of their organ of the perception of visibility, they then invented the following:

"Their 'Teskooano' or 'telescope,' the construction of which, it must be here said, passed to them also from their remote ancestors, they did not fix on the surface of their planet, as was usually done there and is still done now—but they

placed this 'Teskooano' very deeply within the planet, and they carried out their observations of the cosmic concentrations found beyond the atmosphere of their planet through specially-bored, pipe-like-hollows.

"The observatory I then saw had five of these hollows.

"They began in relation to the horizon, from different places of the surface of the planet occupied by the observatory, but they all met at a small underground common hollow which was something like a cave. From there the specialists, then called 'Astrologers,' made their observations for the purpose of studying, as I have already told you, the visible presences and results of the reciprocal action of other cosmic concentrations belonging both to their own solar system and to other systems of the Great Universe.

"They made these observations of theirs through any of the mentioned hollows which looked out in different directions on to their horizon, depending on the given position of their planet relative to the cosmic concentration observed in the process of the 'common-cosmic-harmonious-movement.'

"I repeat, my boy, that although the chief peculiarity of the observatory constructed there by the three-brained beings of the future Egypt proved not to be new to me, since this principle had also been utilized in my observatory on Mars, with only this difference, that my seven long pipes were fixed not within the planet but on it, nevertheless all their innovations were so interesting in detail that, for any case that might arise, I even made, during my stay there, a detailed sketch of everything I saw, and later even used something of it for my own observatory.

"And concerning the other 'artificial-constructions' there, I shall perhaps tell you about them in detail sometime later, but

meanwhile I will only say that all these independent constructions, not then quite finished, were situated not far from the observatory itself, and were intended, as I cleared up during my inspection under the guidance of the constructor who accompanied us and who was a friend of one of our tribe, partly for the same purposes of observing other suns and planets of our Great Universe, and partly for determining and intentionally directing the course of the surrounding atmosphere in order to obtain the 'climate' desired.

"All these 'artificial-constructions' of theirs occupied a fairly large open space of the said region, and were enclosed by a special lattice-work made of the plant then called there 'Zalnakatar.'

"It is extremely interesting to notice here that they erected at the chief entrance of that huge enclosure a rather large—large of course in comparison with the size of their presences—stone statue called 'Sphinx' which strongly reminded me of the statue I saw on my first descent in person to your planet in the city of Samlios, just opposite the enormous building belonging to the learned society Akhaldan and which was then called the 'chief cathedral of the society Akhaldan.'

"The statue I saw in the city of Samlios and which greatly interested me, was the emblem of this society, and was called 'Conscience.'

"It represented an allegorical being, each part of whose planetary body was composed of a part of the planetary body of some definite form of being existing there, but of the parts of those beings of other forms who, according to the crystallized notions of the three-brained beings there, had to perfection one or another being-function.

"The main mass of the planetary body of the said allegorical being was represented by the trunk of a being there of definite form, called 'Bull.'

------------------------------ 308 ------------------------------

"This Bull trunk rested on the four legs of another being existing there, also of a definite form, called 'Lion,' and to that part of the Bull trunk called its 'back' two large wings were attached similar in appearance to those of a strong bird-being breeding there, called 'Eagle.'

"And on the place where the head should be, there was fixed to the Bull trunk, by means of a piece of 'amber,' two breasts representing in themselves what are called 'Breasts of a virgin.'

"When I became interested on the continent Atlantis in this strange allegorical image, and then enquired about its meaning, one of the learned members of the Great Society of men-beings explained it to me as follows:

"'This allegorical figure is the emblem of the society Akhaldan and serves for all its members as a stimulus constantly to recall and awaken in them the corresponding impulses attributed to this allegorical figure.'

"Further he continued:

"'Each part of this allegorical figure gives to every member of our society in all the three independently associating parts of his common presence, namely, in the body, in the thoughts, and in the feelings, a shock for corresponding associations for those separate cognizances which in their totality can alone give us the possibility of gradually getting rid of those undesirable factors present in every one of us, both those transmitted to us by heredity as well as those acquired by ourselves personally, which gradually engender within us impulses undesirable for us, and as a consequence of which we are not as we might be.

"'This emblem of ours constantly reminds and indicates to us that it is possible to attain freedom from what I have mentioned only if we compel our common presence always to think, feel, and act in corresponding

------------------------------ 309 ------------------------------

circumstances according to that which is expressed in this emblem of ours.

of that part of the said region, and were enclosed by a special lattice-work made of the plant then called there 'Zalnakatar.'

"It is extremely interesting to notice here that they erected at the chief entrance of that huge enclosure a rather large—large of course in comparison with the size of their presences—stone statue called 'Sphinx,' which strongly reminded me of the statue I saw on my first personal descent to your planet in the city of Samlios, just opposite the enormous building belonging to the learned society Akhaldan and which was then called the 'chief-cathedral-of-the-society-Akhaldan.'

"The statue I saw in the city of Samlios and which greatly interested me, was the emblem of this Society, and was called 'Conscience.'

"It represented an allegorical being, each part of whose planetary body was composed of a part of the planetary body of some definite form of being existing there, but of the parts of those beings of various forms in whom, according to the crystallized conceptions of the three-brained beings there, one or another being-function was present in a superlative degree.

"The main mass of the planetary body of the said allegorical being was represented by the 'trunk' of a being there of definite form, called 'Bull.'

- -

"This bull-trunk rested on the four legs of another being existing there, also of a definite form, called 'Lion,' and to that part of the bull-trunk called its 'back,' two large wings were attached similar in appearance to those of a strong bird-being breeding there, called 'Eagle.'

"And on the place where the head should be, there were fixed to the bull-trunk, by means of a piece of 'amber,' two breasts representing in themselves what are called, 'breasts-of-a-virgin.'

"When I became interested on the continent Atlantis in this strange allegorical image, and then enquired about its meaning, one of the learned members of the Great Society of men-beings explained it to me as follows:

"'This allegorical figure is the emblem of the society Akhaldan and serves for all its members as a stimulus constantly to recall and awaken in them the corresponding impulses attributed to this allegorical figure.'

"Further he continued:

"'Each part of this allegorical figure gives to every member of our society in all, three independently associating parts of his common presence, namely, in the body, in the thoughts and in the feelings, a shock for corresponding associations for those separate cognizances which in their totality can alone give us the possibility of gradually getting rid of those undesirable factors present in every one of us, both those transmitted to us by heredity and those acquired by ourselves personally, which gradually engender within us impulses undesirable for us, and as a consequence of which we are not as we might be.

"'This emblem of ours constantly reminds and indicates to us that it is possible to attain freedom from what I have mentioned, only if we compel our common presences always to think, feel and act in corresponding

- -

circumstances according to that which is expressed in this emblem of ours.

"'And this emblem of ours is understood by all of us, members of the society Akhaldan, in the following way:

"'The trunk of this allegorical being, represented by the trunk of a "Bull," means that the factors crystallized in us and which engender in our presences the impulses maleficent for us, those we have inherited, as well as those we have personally acquired, can be regenerated only by indefatigable labors, namely, by those labors for which among the beings of our planet, the Bull is particularly fitted.

"'That this trunk rests on the legs of a "Lion" means that the said labors should be performed with that cognizance and feeling of courage and faith in one's "might," the property of which "might" is possessed among all the beings of the Earth in the highest degree by the possessor of these legs—the mighty Lion.

"'The wings of the strongest and the highest soaring of all birds, the Eagle, attached to the Bull trunk, constantly remind the members of our society, that during the said labors and with the mentioned inner psychic properties of self-respect, it is necessary to meditate continually on questions not related to the direct manifestations required for ordinary being-existence.

"'And as regards the strange image of the head of our allegorical being, in the form of the "Breasts of a virgin," this expresses that Love should predominate always and in everything during the inner and the outer functionings evoked by one's consciousness, such a Love as can arise and be present only in the presences of concentrations formed in the lawful parts of every whole responsible being in whom the hopes of our COMMON FATHER are placed.

"And that the head is fixed to the trunk of the Bull

- *310* -

with "amber" signifies that this Love should be strictly impartial, that is to say, completely separated from all the other functions proceeding in every whole responsible being.'

"In order, my boy, that the sense of this latter emblem put into the material called there amber, may become quite comprehensible to you, I must add that amber is one of those seven planetary formations, in the arising of which the Omnipresent Active Element Okidanokh takes part with all its three separate, independent, sacred parts, in equal proportion; and in the process of planetary actualization, these intraplanetary and surplanetary formations serve for what is called the 'impeding' of the independent flow of these three localized independent sacred parts."

At this point of his tale, Beelzebub made a short pause, as if he were thinking about something, and afterwards continued thus:

"During my narration of what I then saw on a still surviving terra firma part of the surface of your planet among the three-brained beings there, certain of whom were the direct descendants of members of the truly great learned society Akhaldan there, the result of the manifestations of my being-Reason was that, owing to various associative recollections of all kinds of impressions of the perceptions of the visibility of the exterior environment of the said region, which have become fixed in my common presence, there have been gradually revived in

"'And this emblem of ours is understood by all of us members of the society Akhaldan in the following way:

"'The trunk of this allegorical being, represented by the trunk of a 'bull', means that the factors crystallized in us and which bring forth in our presences maleficent for us, both those we have inherited and those we have personally acquired, can be regenerated only by indefatigable labors, namely, by such labors as, among the beings of our planet, the bull is particularly capable.

"'That this trunk rests on the legs of a 'Lion' means that the said labors should be performed with that cognizance and feeling of courage and faith in one's 'might', the property of which 'might' is possessed among all the beings of the Earth in the highest degree by the possessor of these legs—the mighty lion.

"'The wings of the strongest and highest soaring of all birds, the 'Eagle', attached to the bull-trunk, constantly remind the members of our society that during the said labors and with the mentioned inner psychic properties of self-respect, it is necessary to meditate continually on questions not related to the direct manifestations required for ordinary being-existence.

"'And as regards the strange image of the head of our allegorical being, in the form of the "breasts-of-a-virgin," this expresses that always and in everything during both the inner and outer functionings evoked by one's own consciousness, there should predominate such a "love" as can arise and be present only in the presences of concentrations formed in the lawful parts of every whole responsible being in whom the hopes of our COMMON FATHER are placed.

"'And that the head is fixed to the trunk of the bull

----

with "amber" signifies that the said love should be strictly impartial, that is to say, completely separated from all the other functions proceeding in every whole responsible being.'"

"In order, my boy, that the sense of this latter emblem, put into the material called there 'amber', may become quite comprehensible to you, I must add that 'amber' is one of those seven planetary formations, in the arising of which the Omnipresent Active Element Okidanokh takes part with all its three separate, independent, sacred parts in equal proportion; and in the process of planetary actualization these intraplanetary and surplanetary formations serve for what is called the 'impeding' of the independent flow of those three localized independent sacred parts.

At this point of his tale Beelzebub made a short pause, as if he were thinking about something, and afterwards continued thus:

"During my narration of what I then saw on a still surviving terra-firma part of the surface of your planet among the three-brained beings there, certain of whom were the direct descendants of members-beings of the truly great learned society Akhaldan there, the result of the manifestations of my being-Reason, owing to various associative recollections of all kinds of impressions of the perceptions of the visibility of the exterior environment of the said region, which became fixed in my common presence, has been that there has been gradually revived in me all me all the scenes and all the associative flow of thoughts of one of these being-experiencings of mine which occurred during my last stay there on my visit just to that same contemporary Egypt, when I once sat absorbed in thought at the foot of one of these constructions, which had chanced to survive from that period, and which is now called there 'Pyramids.'

------------------------------ *311* ------------------------------

"It was just then, that in the general functioning of my Reason there was also associated among other things the following:

"Good! . . . If none of the benefits already formerly attained by the Reason of the beings of the continent Atlantis for ordinary being-existence has become the possession of the contemporary beings of this planet, then this might perhaps be logically explained simply because for cosmic reasons, not issuing at all from and not depending upon the three-brained beings there, that second great 'cataclysm not according to law' occurred, during which, not only that continent itself perished, but also everything which existed on it.

"But this Egypt!

"Was not its magnificence still quite recent?

"There is no denying it . . . owing to the third small catastrophe to that ill-fated planet, and also to the fifth, about which I shall speak later, this part also of its surface, it is true, suffered, having been covered with sands. . . . Nevertheless, the three-brained beings dwelling there did not perish, but were only scattered over various other parts of the same continent, and consequently, whatever new exterior conditions may have ensued, there should have survived in their presences, it would seem, the crystallized results of the perfected factors, transmitted to them by inheritance for normal 'being-logical-mentation.'

"And so, my boy, being desirous after this distressful 'Alstoozori' of mine, or as your favorites would say, 'sorrowful reflections,' to clear up for myself the very essence of the cause also of this lamentable fact there, I understood at the end of my minute investigations, and became aware with all my being, that this abnormality there proceeds exclusively owing only to one remarkable aspect of the chief particularity of their strange psyche,

------------------------------ *312* ------------------------------

namely, that particularity which has become completely crystallized and is an inseparable part of their common presences and which serves as a factor for the periodic arising in them of what is called the 'urgent need to destroy everything outside of themselves.'

"The point is that when, during the apogee of the development of such a peculiarity—terrifying to every Reason—of the psyche of the three-brained beings, they began to manifest outside of themselves this phenomenal peculiarity of their common presences, that is to say, when they begin to carry out on some part of the surface of their planet the process of reciprocal destruction, then, at the same time, without any deliberate aim, and even without what is called 'organic need,' they also destroy everything which chances to come within the sphere of the perception of their organ of sight. During the periods of this 'phenomenal psychopathic apogee,' they destroy also all the objects in the given place and at the given

the scenes and all the associative flow of thoughts of one of those being-experiencings of mine which occurred during my last stay there, on my visit just to that
same contemporary Egypt, when I once sat absorbed in thought at the foot of one
of those 'artificial-constructions' that had chanced to survive from that period,
and is now already called there, the 'Pyramids.'

- -

"It was just then, that in the general function of my Reason there was also associated among other things, the following:

"Good! . . . If none of the benefits already formerly attained by the Reason of
the beings of the continent Atlantis for ordinary being-existence, has become the
possession of the contemporary beings of this planet—this might perhaps be logically explained simply because for cosmic causes, not issuing at all from and not
depending upon the three-brained beings there, that second great 'cataclysm-not-
according-to-law' occurred, during which not only that continent itself perished,
but also everything existing on it.

"But this Egypt! . . .

"Its magnificence was still recent . . .

"There is no denying it . . . owing to the third small catastrophe to that ill-fated
planet, and also to the fifth, about which I will speak later, this part also of its surface, it is true, suffered, having been covered with sands. Nevertheless, the three-
brained beings dwelling there did not perish, but were only scattered over various
other parts of the same continent, and consequently, whatever new exterior conditions may have ensued, there should have survived in their presence, it would
seem, the crystallized results of the perfected factors, transmitted to them by inheritance for normal 'being-logical-mentation.'

"And so, my boy, being desirous after this distressful 'Alstoozori' of mine, or as
your favorites would say, 'sorrowful-reflections,' to clear up for myself the very
essence of the causes also of this lamentable fact there, I understood at the end of
my minute investigations and became aware with all my Being, that this abnormality there proceeds exclusively owing only to one very remarkable aspect of the
chief particularity of their strange psyche,

- -

namely, that particularity which has become completely crystallized and an inseparable part of their common presences and which serves as a factor for the
periodical arising in them of what is called the 'urgent-need-to-destroy-
everything-outside-of-them.'

"The point is that when, during the apogee of the development of such a peculiarity—terrifying to every Reason—of the psyche of the three-brained beings,
they began to manifest outside of themselves this phenomenal peculiarity of their
common presence, that is to say, when they begin to carry out the process of reciprocal destruction on some part of the surface of their planet, then, at the same
time, without any deliberate aim, and even with what is called 'organic-need,' they
also destroy everything which chances to come within the sphere of the perception of their organ of sight. At the periods of this 'phenomenal-psychopathic-apo-
gee,' they destroy also all the objects present in the given place and at the given

time which these same beings themselves, between whom this terrifying process proceeds, have intentionally produced as well as the productions which have chanced to survive and to reach them from the beings of previous epochs.

"Well then, my boy, at the period of this fourth sojourn of mine in person on the surface of your planet, I first arrived in the country now called Egypt, and after having stayed there a few days among the remote descendants of the members of the great learned society Akhaldan, and becoming acquainted with certain surviving results of their 'being-Partkdolg-duty' for the welfare of their descendants, I afterwards, accompanied by two of our tribe, went to the southern countries of the same continent, and there, with the help of the local three-brained beings, caught the necessary number of ape-beings.

"Having accomplished this, I telepathically signaled our

- 313 -

ship *Occasion* which descended to us, it must be said on the first, very dark night; and when we had loaded these ape-beings into that special section of the ship *Occasion* which had been constructed for Gornahoor Harharkh under his directions, we at once reascended to the planet Mars; and three Martian days later, on the same ship and together with these apes, I ascended to the planet Saturn.

"Though we had previously decided to carry out the experiments with these apes only on the following year, when they would have become thoroughly acclimatized and orientated to existence under the new conditions, I ascended then to the planet Saturn so soon because at my last personal meeting with Gornahoor Harharkh, I had promised him to be present at his family solemnity which had soon to take place.

"And this family solemnity of Gornahoor Harharkh's was that beings like himself around him were to consecrate the first heir produced by him.

"I promised to attend this family solemnity Krik hrak hri in order to undertake, regarding his recently arisen heir, what is called the 'Alnatoorornian-being-duty.'

"Here it is interesting to remark that this kind of procedure for undertaking this being-duty, took place among the ancient three-brained beings of your planet also, and even reached your contemporary favorites, though these latter, just as in everything else, take only the external form of this serious and important procedure. The beings who undertake, as it were, these duties, are called by your contemporary favorites 'godfathers' and 'godmothers.'

"The heir of Gornahoor Harharkh was then called Rakhoorkh."

- 314 -

time, which these same beings themselves, between whom this terrifying process proceeds, have intentionally produced as well as the productions which have chanced to survive and to reach them from the beginnings of previous epochs.

"Well then my boy, at the period of this fourth personal sojourn of mine on the surface of your planet, I first arrived in the country now called Egypt, and after having stayed there a few days among the remote descendants of the member-beings of the great learned society Akhaldan, and having become acquainted with certain surviving results of their 'being-Partkdolgduty' for the welfare of their descendants, I, afterwards, accompanied by two of our tribe, went to the southern countries of the same continent, and there, with the help of the local three-brained beings, caught the necessary number of ape beings.

"Having accomplished this, I telepathically signaled our

ship 'Occasion' which descended to us on the first, it must be said, very dark night; and when we had loaded these ape-beings in that special section of the ship 'Occasion' which had been constructed for Gornahoor Harharkh under his directions, we at once reascended to the planet Mars; and three Martian days later, on the same ship and together with these apes, I ascended to the planet Saturn.

"Though we had previously decided to carry out the experiments with those apes only the following year, when they would have become thoroughly acclimatized and orientated to existence under the new conditions, I ascended then to the planet Saturn so soon because at my last personal meeting with Gornahoor Harharkh, I had promised him to be present at his family solemnity which had soon to take place.

"And this family solemnity of Gornahoor Harharkh's consisted in this, that beings like himself around him, would consecrate the first heir produced by him.

"I promised to attend this family solemnity "Krik-hrak-hri' in order to undertake, regarding his recently arisen heir, what is called the 'Atnatoorornian-being-duty.'

"Here it is interesting to remark that the kind of procedure for undertaking this being-duty, took place among the ancient three-brained beings of your planet also, and even reached your contemporary favorites, though these latter, just as in everything else, take only the external form of this serious and important procedure. The beings who undertake, as it were, these duties, are called by your contemporary favorites 'godfathers' and 'godmothers.'

"The heir of Gornahoor Harharkh was then called 'Rakhoorkh.'"

Beelzebub's Flight to the Planet Earth for the Fifth Time

B EELZEBUB continued to relate as follows:
      "After my fourth sojourn on the surface of the planet Earth many years again passed.

"During these years I of course, as before, sometimes attentively observed through my Teskooano the being-existence of these favorites of yours.

"During this time their number considerably increased and they had already populated almost all the large and small terra firma parts of the surface of this planet of yours; and of course there also continued to proceed among them their chief particularity, namely, from time to time they destroyed each other's existence.

"During this time, that is to say, between my fourth and fifth visits, great changes occurred to the surface of your planet; many changes also occurred there in the concentrations of the places of settlement of these favorites of yours. For example, all those centers-of-culture of theirs on the continent Ashhark where I had been in person during my previous descents upon the Earth, namely, the countries of Tikliamish and Maralpleicie, had by the time of my fifth arrival there entirely ceased to exist.

"The cause of the destruction of these centers-of-culture of theirs and of the changes on the surface of this planet in general, was again a misfortune, the third for this ill-fated planet.

"This third misfortune was entirely of a local character and occurred because during several years there had proceeded in its atmosphere unprecedented what are called 'accelerated-displacements-of-the-parts-of-the-atmosphere';

--------------------------- *315* ---------------------------

or, as your favorites there would say, 'great winds.'

"The cause of these abnormal displacements or great winds at that time was once again those two fragments which had been separated from this planet of yours during the first great calamity, and which afterwards became independent small planets of this solar system, and are now called Moon and Anulios.

"Strictly speaking, the main cause of this terrestrial misfortune was only the larger of these separated parts, namely, the Moon; the smaller fragment, Anulios, played no part in it whatsoever.

"The accelerated-displacements in the Earth's atmosphere resulted from the following:

"When the atmosphere on the small, accidentally arisen planet Moon had been finally formed, and the Moon, according to the already mentioned law of 'Catching-up,' continued to fall back upon its fundamental mass by the path already then established, and this newly arisen definite presence on the Moon had not yet acquired its own harmony within the common-system-harmony-of-movement, then the what is called 'Osmooalnian-friction' which was, so to say, not harmonized with the whole, evoked in the atmosphere of the Earth the mentioned accel-

Beelzebub's Flight To The Planet Earth For The Fifth Time

B EELZEBUB continued to relate as follows:
      "After my fourth stay on the surface of the planet Earth many years again passed.

"During these years I, of course, as before, sometimes observed attentively through my Teskooano the being-existence of these favorites of yours also.

"During this time their numbers considerably increased and they already populated almost all the large and small 'terra-firma-parts' of the surface of this planet of yours, and of course there also continued to proceed among them during the whole of certain periods, their chief particularity, namely, every so often they would destroy each other's existence.

"During this time, that is to say, between my fourth and fifth visits, great changes occurred to the surface of your planet.

"Many changes also occurred there in the concentration of the places of settlement of these favorites of yours. For example, all those 'centers-of-culture' of theirs on the continent Ashhark where I personally was during my previous descents upon the earth, namely, the countries of Tikliamish and Maralpleicie had by the time of my fifth arrival there, ceased altogether to exist.

"The cause of the destruction of the 'centers-of-culture' of theirs and of the changes on the surface of this planet in general, was again a misfortune, the third in number for this ill-starred planet.

"This third misfortune was entirely of a local character and occurred because there had proceeded in its atmosphere during several years unprecedented so-called 'accelerated-displacements-of-the-parts-of-the-atmosphere'

- -

or as your favorites there would say, 'great winds.'

"The cause of these abnormal 'displacements' or 'great winds' at that time was once again those two fragments which had been separated from this planet of yours during the first great calamity, and which afterwards became independent small planets of this solar system. They are now called 'Moon' and 'Anulios.' Strictly speaking, the main cause of this third terrestrial misfortune was only the larger of these separated parts, namely, the Moon; the smaller fragment, 'Anulios,' played no part in it whatever.

"The 'accelerated-displacements' in the earth's atmosphere resulted from this, that when the atmosphere on the small, chance-arisen planet Moon had been finally formed, and the Moon, according to the already mentioned law of 'catching-up,' continued to fall back upon its fundamental mass by the path already then established, and while this newly arisen definite presence of the Moon had not yet acquired its own harmony within the 'Common-system-harmony-of-movements,' then this, so to say, not harmonized on the whole, as it is called 'Osmooalnian friction' just evoked in the atmosphere of the Earth the mentioned 'accelerated-displacements' or 'great winds.' Then by the force of their currents these

erated-displacements or great winds.

"These unprecedented great winds then began, by the force of their currents, as it is said, to wear down the elevated 'terra-firma-parts' and to fill up the corresponding 'depressions.'

"Such depressions were also the two countries of the continent Ashhark upon which the process of existence was chiefly concentrated of the second and third groups of beings of contemporary Asia, that is to say, the main parts of the countries Tikliamish and Maralpleicie.

"At the same time sands also filled up certain parts of the country, Pearl-land, as well as that country in the

316

middle of the continent Grabontzi, where, as I have already told you, there was formed, after the loss of Atlantis, what they called the leading 'Center-of-Culture' for all the three-brained beings there, a country which at that time was the most flourishing part of the surface of this planet of yours, and which is now the desert called 'Sahara.'

"Bear in mind also, that during the abnormal winds of that time, besides the countries mentioned, several other smallish terra firma spaces of the surface of that hapless planet were also covered by sands.

"It is interesting to note here that your contemporary favorites have also by some means or other learned about the changes that then occurred in the places of the permanent existence of the three-centered beings, and having made a label for this as well, this time the 'Great-transmigration-of-races,' they stuck it onto what they call their 'knowledge.'

"A number of the 'learned' there now puff and blow with all their might to find out why and how it all occurred, so that they can tell everybody else about it.

"Just now there are several theories about the matter there, which although they have nothing in common with each other and are each in an objective sense more absurd than the other, are nevertheless accepted there by what is called 'official-knowledge.'

"But in fact, the real cause of the transmigration of the three-centered beings there was that as soon as the said abrasion began, the beings living on the continent Ashhark, fearing to be buried by the sands, began moving to other, more or less secure places. And these migrations of the three-brained beings there proceeded in the following order:

"Most of the three-brained beings populating Tikliamish moved to the south of the same continent Ashhark,

317

to the country which was later called 'Persia,' and the rest moved north, and settled in those regions which were afterwards called 'Kirkistcheri.'

"As for the beings populating the country Maralpleicie, one part wandered eastwards, while the rest, the major part, went towards the west.

"Having crossed the eastern heights, those who went east settled down on the shores of the large Saliakooriapnian spaces, and this country was later called 'China.'

unprecedented 'great winds' began, as it is said, to 'wear down' the elevated 'terra-firma-parts,' and to fill up the corresponding depressions.

"The two countries of the continent Ashhark upon which chiefly was concentrated the process of existence of the second and third groups of beings of contemporary Asia, that is to say, the fundamental parts of the countries Tikliamish and Maralpleicie, just happened to be also such depressions.

"At the same time sand also filled up certain parts of the country Gemchania as well as that country in the

middle of the continent Grabontzi, where, as I have already told you, there was formed after the sinking of Atlantis, what they called the leading 'center-of-culture' for all the three-brained beings there, a country which was at that time the most flourishing part of the surface of this planet of yours, and is already now the desert called 'Sahara.'

"Bear in mind also that during the abnormal winds of that time, besides the countries mentioned, several other inconsiderable terra-firma spaces of the surface of that unhappy planet were also covered by sands.

"It is interesting to note here, that concerning the changes that then occurred in the locale of the permanent existence of the three-centered beings, your contemporary favorites also, by some means or other, learned of it, and having made a label for this as well, this time 'the great migration of races,' they stuck it on what they call their knowledge.

"A number of the 'learned' there now mightily puff and blow to find out why and how it all occurred, so that they can tell everybody else.

"Just now there exist several theories about the matter there, and, although they have nothing in common with each other, and in an objective sense, each is more absurd than the other, nevertheless they are accepted there by what is called 'official knowledge.'

"But in fact the real cause of the migration of the three-centered beings then arose because as soon as the said abrasion began, the beings living on the continent Ashhark, fearing to be buried by the sand, began moving to other, more or less, secure places, and these migrations of the three-brained beings there proceeded in the following order.

"Most of the three-brained beings populating Tikliamish moved to the south of the same continent Ashhark,

to the country which was called later 'Persia'; and the rest moved north, and settled in those regions which were afterwards called 'Kirkistcheri.'

"As regards the beings populating the country Maralpleicie, one part wandered eastwards, while the rest, the major part, went west. Having crossed the eastern heights, those who went east settled down on the shores of the large 'saliakoori-apnian-spaces,' and this country was later called 'China.'

"And that part of the beings of Maralpleicie who sought safety by moving to the west, after wandering from place to place, ultimately reached the neighboring continent, later called 'Europe,' and the three-brained beings who then still existed in the middle of the continent Grabontzi dispersed over the whole of the surface.

"And so, my boy, this fifth descent of mine in person to your planet belongs to the period of the time after this said redistribution of the groups of the communities of these favorites of yours.

"And the causes of my descent there in person were the following events:

"I must first tell you that the chief peculiarity of the psyche of your favorites, namely, the 'periodic-need-to-destroy-the-existence-of-others-like-oneself,' interested me more and more with every succeeding century of theirs, and side by side with it the irresistible desire increased in me to find out the exact causes of a particularity so phenomenal for three-brained beings.

"And so, my boy, in order to have more material for elucidating this question which interested me so intensely, I, in the interval between my fourth and fifth sojourn on the planet Earth, organized my observations through the Teskooano from the planet Mars of the existence of those peculiar three-brained beings in the following way:

"I deliberately kept under observation quite a number of

---------------------------- *318* ----------------------------

their beings from among your favorites and during many of their years either I personally or somebody whom I commissioned observed them attentively, trying as much as possible not to miss anything, and to clear up from every aspect all the particularities in their manifestations during the processes of their ordinary existence.

"And I must confess, my boy, that when I happened to be quite free, I sometimes during whole 'Sinonoums' or, as your favorites there approximately define the corresponding flow of time, 'hours,' followed with great interest the movements of the said three-brained beings there under observation, and tried to explain to myself logically their what are called 'psychic-experiencings.'

"And so, during these observations of mine from the planet Mars through my Teskooano, it once flashed upon me that the length of their existence was, century by century and even year by year, becoming shorter and shorter at a very definite and equally uniform rate, and this served as the beginning of my further quite serious study of the psyche of these three-brained beings who have taken your fancy.

"Of course when I first noticed this, I at once took into account not only the chief particularity of their psyche, that is their periodic reciprocal destruction, but also the innumerable what are called 'illnesses' which exist exclusively only on that planet, the majority of which, by the way, arose and continue to arise owing to the same abnormal external conditions of the ordinary being-existence established by them, which help to make it impossible for them to exist normally up to the sacred Rascooarno.

"When I first noticed this and began to recall my previous impression about it,

"And that part of the beings of Maralpleicie who sought safety by moving to the west, after wandering from place to place, ultimately reached the neighboring continent, later called 'Europe,' while the three-brained beings who then still remained existing in the middle of the continent 'Grabontzi' dispersed over the whole of its surface.

"And so, my boy, this my fifth personal flight to your planet already belongs to the period of time after this said redistribution of the groups of the communities of these favorites of yours. And the reasons of my personal descent there were the following events:

"I must first tell you that the chief peculiarity of the psyche of your favorites, namely, the 'periodic-need-to-destroy-the-existence-of-others-like-oneself,' interested me more and more with every succeeding century of theirs; and side by side with it the craving increased in me to ferret out the exact causes of a particularity so phenomenal in three-brained beings.

"And so, my boy, in order to have more material for elucidating this question that so intensely interested me, I, in the interval between my fourth and fifth stay on the planet Earth, organized through the Teskooano from the planet Mars my observation of the existence of those peculiar three-brained beings in the following way:

"I deliberately kept under observation quite a number of

separate beings from among your favorites and during many of their years either I personally, or somebody whom I specially commissioned, observed them attentively, taking pains not, if possible, to miss anything, and to clear up from every aspect every kind of particularity in their manifestations during the processes of their ordinary existence there.

"And I must confess, my boy, that when I happened to be otherwise free I sometimes during whole 'Sinonoums,' or, as your favorites there approximately define the corresponding flow of time, during whole 'hours,' observed with great interest the movements of the three-brained beings there under observation, and tried to explain to myself logically what are called their 'psychic experiencings.'

"And so, during these observations of mine from the planet Mars by means of my Teskooano, that once 'flashed' upon me which just served as the beginning of my further then quite serious study of the psyche of these three-brained beings who please you; namely, it 'flashed' upon me that the length of their existence was, century by century, and even year by year, becoming shorter and shorter, at a very definite and uniform rate.

"Of course, when I first noticed it, I at once took into account not only the chief particularity of their psyche, that is, their periodic reciprocal destruction, but also the innumerable what are called 'illnesses' which exist exclusively only on the planet, the majority of which, by the way, arose and continued to arise owing to the same abnormal external conditions of the ordinary being existence established by them, and which help to make it impossible for them normally to exist up to the sacred Rascooarno.

"When I first noticed this, and as my previous impressions concerning the

each of the separate independent spiritualized parts of my whole presence became filled with the conviction, and my essence perceived the mentioned

'flash,' that in truth these three-brained beings of your planet had in the beginning
existed according to their time calculation for about twelve centuries, and some
of them, even, for about fifteen centuries.

"To be able more or less clearly to represent to yourself the rate at which the
length of their existence declined during this time, it is enough for you to know
that when I left this solar system for ever, the maximum length of their existence
was already from seventy to ninety of their years.

"And latterly, if anybody should exist even as long as this, all the rest of the beings of that peculiar planet would already consider that he had existed quite 'a
good long time.'

"And if anybody happened to exist a little over a century he would be exhibited
in their museums, and of course all the rest of the beings there would know about
him because his photograph, and descriptions of the manner of his existence even
to the enumeration of each of his movements, would continually be found in all
their what are called 'newspapers.'

"And so, my boy, since, at the time when I suddenly constated such a fact there,
I had no special business on the planet Mars and it was quite impossible to try to
probe this novel peculiarity by means of the Teskooano, I therefore decided to go
there myself in order perhaps to clear up for myself there on the spot the causes
of this also.

"Several Martian days after my decision, I again ascended there on the ship *Occasion*.

"At the time of this fifth descent of mine in person to your planet, their 'center-
for-the-incoming-and-the-outgoing-results-of-the-perfecting-of-being-rumina-
tion' or, as they themselves call it, their 'Center-of-Culture' was

already the city of Babylon; so it was just there that I decided to go.

"This time our ship *Occasion* alighted on what is called the 'Persian Gulf' because we had ascertained through the Teskooano before our flight that for our
further traveling, that is, to reach the town of Babylon and also for the mooring
of our ship *Occasion* itself, the most convenient place would be that same
Saliakooriapnian space of the surface of your planet now existing there under the
name of the Persian Gulf.

"This water space was convenient for my further traveling because the large
river, on the banks of which the city of Babylon stood, flowed into it, and we proposed to sail up the stream of this river to get there.

"During that period of the flow of time this 'incomparably majestic' Babylon
was flourishing in every respect. It was a Center-of-Culture not only for the beings dwelling on the continent Ashhark, but also for all the beings of all those
other large and small terra firmas which were adapted to the needs of ordinary
being-existence on that planet.

"At the time of my first arrival there in this Center-of-Culture of theirs, they

same began to come back to me, each of the separate independent spiritualized parts of my whole presence become filled with the conviction, and my essence

perceived the mentioned 'flash,' that in truth these three-brained beings of your planet had, in the beginning, existed, according to their time calculation, for about twelve centuries, and some of them even, for about fifteen centuries.

"To be able more or less clearly to represent to yourself the rate at which the length of their existence declined during this time, it is enough for you to know that when I left this solar system forever, the maximum length of their existence was already from seventy to ninety of their years.

"And latterly if anybody should exist as long as this, all the rest of the beings of that peculiar planet would already consider that he had existed 'quite decently long,' while if anybody happened to exist a little over a century, he would be exhibited in their museums, and of course all the rest of the beings there would know about him, because his photographs and descriptions of the manner of his existence, even to the enumeration of each of his movements, would constantly be published in all their, what are called 'newspapers.'

"And so, my boy, having suddenly constated such a fact there, as I had no special business on the planet Mars, and it was quite impossible to try to probe this novel peculiarity by means of the Teskooano, I decided to go there myself with the aim of perhaps clearing up for myself, there on the spot, the causes of this also.

"Several Martian days after my resolve I again ascended there on the ship 'Occasion.'

"At the time of this fifth personal descent of mine on your planet their 'center-for-the-ingoing-and-outgoing-results-of-the-perfecting-of-the-being-rumination' or as they themselves call it, their 'center-of-culture,' was

already the city of Babylon, and it was just there that I decided to go.

"This time our ship 'Occasion' descended to what is called the 'Persian Gulf,' because we ascertained through the Teskooano before our flight that for my further traveling, that is to say, to get to the town of Babylon, and for the mooring of our ship 'Occasion' itself, the most convenient place would be that same 'saliakooriapnian-space' of the surface of your planet, now existing there under the name of the 'Persian Gulf.'

"This water space was convenient for my further traveling because the large river on the banks of which the city of Babylon stood, flowed into it, and we proposed to sail up the stream of this river in order to get there.

"During that period of the flow of time this 'Incomparably-majestic' Babylon flourished in every respect. It was a 'center-of-culture' not only for the beings dwelling on the continent Ashhark, but also for all the beings of all those other large and small terra-firmas which were adapted to the needs of the ordinary being existence on that planet.

"At the time of my first arrival there in this 'center-of-culture' of theirs, they were just preparing that which was afterwards the principal cause of the acceleration of the rate of the degeneration of their 'psychic-organization,' especially in the sense of the atrophy in them of the instinctive functioning of those three fundamental factors which ought to exist in the presence of every three-brained being—namely, those factors which give rise to the being-impulses existing under the names of 'Faith,' 'Hope,' and 'Love.'

"These being-factors degenerating by heredity from generation to generation has brought it about that instead of a real being-psyche, such as should exist in the presence of every kind of three-brained being, there now already

- *321* -

exists in the presences of your contemporary favorites, although a 'real-psyche' also, nevertheless one that can be very well defined by one of the wise sayings of our dear Mullah Nassr Eddin, which consists of the following words: 'There is everything in it except the core or even the kernel.'

"It is absolutely necessary to relate to you in as great detail as possible what occurred during that period in Babylon, as all this information may be valuable material for you for a better elucidation and transubstantiation in your Reason of all the causes which together have finally given rise to that strange psyche of the three-centered beings which your contemporary favorites already have.

"I must first of all tell you that I obtained the information concerning the events of that time which I am about to relate chiefly from those three-centered beings there whom the other beings called 'learned.'

"Before going any further, I must here dwell a little on just what kind of beings there on your planet the other beings call learned.

"The point is that, even before this fifth sojourn of mine there, that is to say before that period when Babylon, as I have told you, flourished in every respect, those beings who became learned and were regarded by others as learned were not such beings as become and are regarded as learned everywhere in the Universe, nor such as first became learned even on your planet, namely, such beings as acquire by their conscious labors and intentional sufferings the ability to contemplate the details of all that exists from the point of view of World-arising and World-existence, owing chiefly to which, they perfect their highest body to the corresponding gradation of the sacred measure of Objective Reason in order that they might later sense as much about cosmic truths as their higher being-body is perfected.

- *322* -

"But from the time of what is called the Tikliamishian civilization until now, those beings, especially the contemporary ones, chiefly became learned who 'learned-by-rote' as much as possible about every kind of vacuous information, such as old women love to relate about what was presumably said in olden times.

"Note, by the way, that for the definition of the importance of the learned there, our venerated Mullah Nassr Eddin also has a sentence expressed in the following words:

"'Everybody talks as if our learned know that half a hundred is fifty.'

were just preparing that . . . which was afterwards the principal cause of the acceleration of the rate of the degeneration of their 'psychic organization,' especially in
the sense of the atrophy in them of the instinctive functioning of those three fundamental factors which should exist in the presence of every kind of three-
brained being, namely, those factors which give rise to those being-impulses
which exist under the names of 'Faith,' 'Hope,' and 'Love.'

"The decline of those being-factors by inheritance from generation to generation has brought it about that instead of a real being-psyche, such as should exist
in the presence of every kind of three-brained being, there now already

exists in the presence of your contemporary favorites, although a 'real psyche'
also, nevertheless one that can be very well defined by the wise sayings of our dear
Mullah Nassr Eddin, which consists of the following words:

"'There is everything in it except core, or even kernel.'

"It is absolutely necessary to relate to you in as great detail as possible what occurred during that period in Babylon, since all this information may serve you as
valuable material for a better elucidation and transmutation in your reason of all
the causes which together have finally given rise to that strange psyche of the
three-centered beings, which psyche your contemporary favorites already have,
and which has so much interested you.

"I must first tell you that the information concerning the events of that time
which I am now about to relate I picked up among those three-centered beings
there whom the other beings call 'learned.'

"Here, before going any further, I must dwell a little on the beings there on your
planet whom the other beings call 'learned.'

"Even before this fifth stay of mine there, that is to say, before that period when
Babylon, as I have told you, flourished in every respect, there became and were
regarded as 'learned' by others, not such beings as become and are regarded as
learned everywhere in the Universe, and such as at first became learned even on
your planet, namely such beings as from the first bring themselves by their conscious labors and intentional sufferings to the ableness to contemplate the details
of all that exists, from the point of view of World-arising and World-existence,
and owing to which they chiefly perfect their highest body to the corresponding
gradation of the sacred measure of objective reason in order that by this means as
much about cosmic truths might later be sensed in them as their higher being-
body is perfected.

"But they mostly become 'learned,' from the time of what is called the Tikliamishian civilization until now, especially the contemporary ones, who 'learned by
rote' as much as possible of every kind of vacuous information such as 'old women' love to report about what was said, as it were, in olden times.

"Note, by the way, that for the definition of the importance of the scientists
there, our venerated Mullah Nassr Eddin also has a sentence expressed as follows:

"'Everybody talks as if our learned know that half a hundred is fifty.'

"There on your planet, the more of such information one of your favorites mechanically learns by rote, information he himself has never verified, and which moreover, he has never sensed, the more learned he is considered to be.

"And so, my boy, we reached the city of Babylon; there were indeed a great many learned beings there gathered from almost the whole of that planet of yours.

"As the causes of the gathering of these beings in the city of Babylon at that time are extremely interesting, I will tell you also about this a little more in detail.

"The point is, that most of the learned beings of the Earth had been then assembled there under compulsion by a most peculiar Persian king, under whose dominion at that period was also the city of Babylon.

"In order to understand thoroughly which fundamental aspect ensuing from the total results of the abnormally established conditions of ordinary being-existence there gave rise to the said peculiarity of this Persian king, I must first enlighten you in respect of two facts which had become fixed long before.

"The first fact is that almost from the time of the loss of the continent Atlantis, there gradually began to be

------------------------------- 323 -------------------------------

crystallized, and during later centuries became completely crystallized in the presence of every one of your favorites there, a particular 'inherency' thanks to which that being-sensation which is called 'happiness-for-one's-being'—which is experienced from time to time by every three-brained being from the satisfaction of his inner self-evaluation—appears in the presences of your favorites exclusively only when they acquire for their own possession a great deal of that popular metal there called 'gold.'

"A greater misfortune for them arising from this particular 'inherency' in their common presences is that the mentioned sensation due to the possession of the said metal is strengthened by the beings around the possessor and also by beings who learn about it only by what is called 'hearsay' and have not themselves been convinced by personal corresponding perceptions; and it is, moreover, the established custom there never to consider through which kind of being-manifestations he becomes the possessor of a great quantity of this metal, and such a being there becomes for all those around him one who evokes in their presences the functioning of that crystallized consequence of the property of the organ Kundabuffer called 'envy.'

"And the second fact is this, that when in the presences of your favorites their chief particularity functions 'crescendently' and, according to the established custom among their different communities, the process of the reciprocal destruction of each other's existence proceeds, then afterwards, when this property, only maleficent for them themselves, has run its course, and they temporarily cease these processes of theirs, then the king of that community in which a greater number of subjects survive, receiving the title of conqueror, usually takes for himself

------------------------------- 324 -------------------------------

everything belonging to the beings of the conquered community.

"There on your planet the more of such information one of your favorites mechanically learns by rote—information he himself has never verified and which moreover he has never sensed—the more learned he is thought to be.

"And so, my boy, when we reached the city of Babylon, there were indeed a great many learned beings. Scientific beings were then gathered there from almost the whole of that planet of yours.

"As the reasons for the original congregation of these beings in the city of Babylon at that time are extremely interesting I will tell you also about this a little more in detail. The truth is that most of the scientists of the Earth had been assembled there under the compulsion of a most peculiar Persian King, under whose dominion the city of Babylon was also at that period.

"Thoroughly to understand the fundamental aspects flowing from the total results of the abnormally established conditions of ordinary being-existence there, which gave rise to the said peculiarity of this Persian king, I must first enlighten you in regard to two facts which had long before that been fixed.

"The first fact is this, that from almost the time of the sinking of the continent Atlantis, a particular 'essence property' began gradually to be

crystallized and during the later centuries became already finally crystallized in the presence of every one of your favorites there, thanks to which that being-sensation which is called 'happiness-for-one's-being' which is experienced from time to time by every three-brained being from the satisfaction of his inner self-respect, appears in the presence of your favorites exclusively only when they acquire for their own possession a great deal of that popular metal, there called 'gold.'

"A further great misfortune for them arising from this particular 'essence-property' in their general presence consists in this, that the mentioned sensation due to the ownership of the said metal, is also strengthened by the beings surrounding the owner, even if they learn about it only by what is called 'hearsay,' and have not themselves been convinced by personal corresponding perceptions. At the same time it is the established custom there never to consider what kind of being-manifestations one made to become the owner of a great quantity of this metal. But such a being there becomes for all those around him an object which evokes in their presence the functioning of that crystallized consequence of the property of the organ Kundabuffer which is called 'envy.'

"And the second fact consists in this, that when in the presence of your favorites their chief particularity functions 'Crescendantly,' and according to the established custom among different communities of theirs, their process of the reciprocal destruction of each other's existence proceeds, then afterwards when this property only proper to themselves and maleficent for them themselves, has run its course, and they temporarily cease these processes of theirs, then the King of that community in which a greater number of subjects remains unharmed, receiving the title of conqueror, usually takes for himself

everything which is possessed by the beings of the conquered community.

"Such a 'king-conqueror' there usually orders his subjects to take from the conquered all their lands, all the young beings of female sex present in the conquered community, and all the what is called 'riches' accumulated by them during centuries.

"And so, my boy, when the subjects of that said peculiar Persian king conquered the beings of another community, he ordered them not to take and even not to touch any of these, but to take with them as what are called 'captives' only the learned beings of this conquered community.

"Clearly to represent and to substantiate in yourself the understanding just why such a peculiar craze arose in the individuality of that Persian king and became proper only to him, you must know that at the period of the Tikliamish civilization, in the town called 'Chiklaral' a three-brained learned being by name Harnahoom—whose essence later became crystallized into what is called an 'Eternal-Hasnamussian-individual'—invented that any old metal you like, abundant on the surface of that planet, could easily be turned into the rare metal 'gold' and all it was necessary to know for this was just one very small 'secret.'

"This maleficent fiction of his became widely spread there, and having become crystallized in the presences of the beings of that time, and being transmitted by inheritance from generation to generation, began to pass to the beings of subsequent generations as a gradually formed definite maleficent fantastic science there, under the name of 'alchemy,' under the name, that is, of that great science which had indeed existed there during those epochs long past, when in the presences of their ancestors the consequences of the properties of the organ Kundabuffer had

--------------------------- *325* ---------------------------

not yet been quite crystallized, and which branch of genuine knowledge might be useful and indeed necessary for the three-brained beings there even of contemporary times.

"And as at that period to which my tale relates, this Persian king needed for some or other of his undoubtedly Hasnamussian aims, a great deal of this metal, rare on the surface of the Earth, called 'gold,' and as the notion concerning this method that had been invented by the then existing 'Hasnamussian-individual,' Harnahoom, had also reached his presence, he was eager to get gold by so easy a means.

"When this Persian king had finally decided to get gold by 'alchemy,' he then and there for the first time cognized with the whole of his being that he did not as yet know that 'little secret' without which it was absolutely impossible to fulfill this desire of his. So he then pondered how to find out that 'little secret.'

"The result of this pondering was that he became aware of the following:

"As the learned already have knowledge of every other kind of 'mystery,' then this mystery must also be known to one of them.

"Having finally arrived at such a conclusion, he, with an intensified functioning of 'being-astonishment' at why such a simple idea had never entered his head before, called several of his attendant subjects and ordered them to find out which of the learned beings of his capital knew this mystery.

"Such a King-conqueror there usually orders his subjects to take from the conquered all their lands, all the young beings of female sex present in the conquered community, and all that which is called 'riches' accumulated by them during centuries.

"And so, my boy, when the subjects of that said peculiar Persian King conquered the beings of another community he ordered them not to take, and even not to touch any of these, but to take with them as what are called 'captives' only all the learned beings present in the conquered community.

"Clearly to represent and transmute in yourself the understanding why in the individuality of that Persian King such a peculiar craze arose and became proper only to him, you must know, that still at the period of the Tikliamishian civilization, there in the town called 'Chiklaral,' a three-brained learned, by name 'Harnahoom,' whose essence later became crystallized into what is called an 'eternal-Hasnamuss-individuum' invented, that any old metal you like abundant in that planet could easily be turned into the rare metal 'gold,' and all that was necessary to know for this, being just one very small 'secret.'

"This maleficent invention of his became widely spread there, and having become crystallized in the presence of the beings of that time, and being transmitted by inheritance from generation to generation, it began to pass to the beings of the subsequent generation as a gradually formed definite maleficent fantastic science there under the name of 'alchemy,' under the name, that is, of just that great science which indeed existed there during those epochs long past, when, in the presence of their ancestors, the consequences of the properties of the organ Kundabuffer had

not yet been crystallized and which branch of genuine knowledge might be really necessary and truly advantageous for the three-brained beings there even of contemporary times.

"And as at that period to which my tale relates, this Persian King needed for some or other of his undoubtedly Hasnamussian aims a great deal of this metal, rare on the surface of the Earth, called 'gold,' and as the notion concerning this method that had been invented by the then existing, now 'Hasnamussian individuum,' Harnahoom, had also reached his presence, he was anxious to get gold by so easy a means.

"When this Persian King had finally decided to get gold by 'Alchemy,' he for the first time with all his being realized that he as yet did not know that 'little secret' without which it was absolutely impossible to fulfill this wish of his. So he then pondered how to find out this little 'secret.'

"The result of his pondering was that he became aware of the following:

"'If the learned already have knowledge of every other kind of "mystery" then to one of them, perhaps, this mystery must also be known.'

"Having finally arrived at such a conclusion, he, with an intensified functioning of 'being-astonishment' at why such a simple idea had never entered his head before, called several of his attendant subjects and ordered them to find out to which of the learned beings of his capital this 'mystery' was known.

"When it was reported to him the following day that not a single one of the learned beings of the capital knew this mystery, he ordered inquiries to be made also of all the learned present among the beings of the whole of his subject-community, and when after several days he again

------------------------------ *326* ------------------------------

received the same negative reply, he once more began to ponder, and this time very seriously.

"His serious thinking first led his Reason to the understanding that, without any doubt, one or other of the learned beings of his community was aware of this 'secret' also, but since among beings of that clan, this strict keeping of a 'professional' mystery was very strongly developed, nobody, of course, was willing to reveal it.

"The result of his serious thinking was that he became aware that it was necessary not merely to question, but to examine the learned beings about this mystery.

"The same day, he gave appropriate instructions to his nearest corresponding assistants, and the latter already began to 'examine,' after the manner that had already long before been the way of power-possessing beings to examine ordinary beings.

"And when this peculiar Persian king became finally convinced that the learned beings of this community indeed knew nothing about this mystery, he began to look for learned beings in other communities to whom this mystery might be known.

"As the kings of the other communities were unwilling to offer their learned beings for 'examination,' he decided forcibly to compel these unconquered kings to do so. And from that time on, at the head of numerous hordes in subjection to him, he began with their help to make what are called 'military excursions.'

"This Persian king had many hordes in subjection to him because at that period, from the region of the surface of this planet of yours where that community was situated and over which he happened to be king, there had been intensified in the presences of the beings, even before this time, according to what is called the 'foreseeing-adaptation' of Great Nature, the what is called 'birth rate'; and at the given period, there was being actualized that

------------------------------ *327* ------------------------------

which was demanded for the common-cosmic Trogoautoegocratic process, that is to say, from this region of the surface of your planet there had to issue more of those vibrations arising from the destruction of being-existence."

During this last explanation Hassein interrupted Beelzebub with the following words:

"Dear Grandfather, I do not understand why the issuing of the required vibrations for the purpose of the actualization of this most great cosmic process should depend on a definite region of the surface of the planet."

To this question of his grandson, Beelzebub replied as follows:

"As before long I intend to make the special question of those terrifying processes of reciprocal destruction which they call 'wars' the theme of my tales con-

"When it was reported to him the following day that not one of the learned beings of the capital knew this 'mystery' he ordered enquiries to be made also of all the learned present among the beings of the whole of his subject-community; and when after several days he again

received the same negative reply he once more betook himself to thought, and this time very seriously.

"His serious thinking first led his reason to the understanding that no doubt whatever, one or other of the learned beings of his community was aware of this 'secret' also; but since among beings of that clan the strict keeping of a 'professional' mystery was very strongly developed, nobody, of course, was willing to reveal it.

"The result of his serious thinking was that he became aware that it was not enough merely to question, he must examine the learned beings about this 'Mystery.'

"The same day he gave suitable instructions to his nearest corresponding assistants, and the latter already began to 'examine' after the manner that had already long before been the way of power-possessing beings to 'examine' ordinary beings.

"And when this peculiar Persian King became finally convinced that the learned beings of this community indeed and in truth knew nothing about this mystery, he began to look for learned beings in other communities to whom this mystery might be known.

"As the kings of the other communities were unwilling to offer their learned beings for interrogation he just decided to compel the recalcitrant by force. And from that time on, at the head of numerous hordes in subject on to him, with their help he began to make what are called 'military excursions.'

"This Persian King had many hordes in subjection to him because at that period, from the region of the surface of this planet of yours where that community was situated and over which he happened to be King, there had been intensified in the presence of the beings even before this time, on the basis of what is called the 'Foreseeing-adaptation' of Great Nature, the, as it is called, 'birthrate'; and at the given period that

which was demanded for the common cosmic Trogoautoegocratic process was being effectuated, that is to say, in order that from this region of the surface of your planet there should issue more of those vibrations arising from the destruction of being-existence."

During this last explanation Hassein interrupted Beelzebub with the following words:

"Dear Grandfather, I do not understand why, for the purpose of the effectuation of this most great cosmic process, the issuing of the required vibrations should depend on any definite region of the surface of the planet."

To this question of his grandson Beelzebub replied as follows:

"As before long I intend to make the special question of those terrifying processes of reciprocal destruction which they call 'wars' the theme of my tales concerning the three-brained beings of the planet Earth, it is better to defer this question of yours also until this special tale, because then, I think, you will understand it well."

Having said this, Beelzebub again continued to relate about the Babylonian events.

"When the peculiar Persian king I mentioned began, thanks to the hordes in subjection to him, to conquer beings of other communities and to seize by force the learned among them, he assigned as a place for their congregation and existence the said city of Babylon, to which they were taken in order that this lord of half the then continent of Asia could thereafter freely examine them in the hope that one of them might perhaps happen to know the secret of turning cheap metal into the metal gold.

"With the same aim he even made at that time a special what is called 'campaign' into the country Egypt.

"He then made this special campaign there because the learned beings of all the continents of the planet were assembled there at that period, the opinion being widely spread there that more information for their various

— 328 —

'sciences' was to be obtained in this Egypt than anywhere else on their planet.

"This Persian king-conqueror then took from Egypt all the learned beings present there, both the native and those who had come from other communities; and among their number were then also several called 'Egyptian priests,' descendants of just those learned members of the society Akhaldan who had chanced to escape, and who had been the first to populate that country.

"When a little later a fresh craze arose in the presence of this peculiar Persian king, the craze for the process itself of the destruction of the existence of other beings similar to himself, and which supplanted the former craze, he forgot about the learned beings and they began to exist there freely in the city of Babylon awaiting his further directions.

"The learned beings collected in this way there in the city of Babylon from almost the whole of the planet used often to meet together and of course to discuss among themselves, as it is proper to the learned beings of the planet Earth, questions which were either immeasurably beyond their comprehension, or about which they could never elucidate anything useful whatsoever, either for themselves or for ordinary beings there.

"Well, it was just during these meetings and discussions that there arose among them, as it is in general proper to arise among learned beings there, what is called 'a-burning-question-of-the-day,' a question which in some way or other indeed interested them at that time to, as they say, 'their very marrow.'

"The question which chanced to become the-burning-question-of-the-day so vitally touched the whole being of every one of them, that they even 'climbed down' from their what are called 'pedestals' and began discussing it not only with the learned like themselves, but also here,

— 329 —

there and everywhere with anyone they chanced to come across.

cerning the three-brained beings of the planet Earth, it is better to defer this question of yours also until this special tale, because then, I think, you will understand it well."

Having said this Beelzebub again continued to relate about the Babylonian events.

"When the peculiar Persian King I mentioned began, thanks to the hordes in subjection to him, to conquer the beings of other communities and to seize by force the learned among them, he assigned as a place for their congregation and existence the said city of Babylon to which they were taken in order that this lord of half the then continent of Asia could thereafter freely interrogate them in the hope that one of them perhaps, might happen to know the secret of turning cheap metal into the metal gold.

"With the same aim he even made at that time a special what is called 'campaign' into the country Egypt.

"He then made this special 'campaign' there because the learned beings of all the continents of the planet were assembled there at that period, the opinion being widely spread there that more information for their various

'sciences' was to be got in this 'Egypt' than anywhere else on the planet.

"This Persian King-conqueror then took from Egypt all the learned beings present there, both the native and those who had come from other communities; and among the number were then also several called 'Egyptian Priests,' descendants of just those scientific members of the society Akhaldan who chanced to escape, and who were the first to populate that country.

"When a little later a fresh craze arose in the presence of this peculiar Persian King, just the craze for the process itself of the destruction of the existence of other beings similar to himself, and which thrust out the former craze, he forgot about the learned beings and they began to exist there freely in the city of Babylon awaiting his further directions.

"The neo-learned beings collected in this way there in the city of Babylon from almost the whole of the planet, used often to meet together; and of course, as it is proper to the learned beings of the planet Earth, they began discussing among themselves questions which were either immeasurably beyond their comprehension, or about which they could never elucidate anything useful whatsoever, either for themselves or for ordinary beings there.

"Well, it was just during these meetings and conversations that there arose among them, as it is in general proper to arise among 'learned beings' there what is called a 'burning-question-of-the-day,' a question which in some way or other indeed interested them at that time to, as they say, their very 'marrow.'

"The question which chanced to become the 'burning-question-of-the-day' so vitally touched the whole of everybody's essence that they even climbed down from their, what are called 'pedestals,' and began discussing it not only with the learned like themselves, but

with every Tom, Dick and Harry.

"The consequence was that an interest in this question gradually spread among all the ordinary three-brained beings then existing in Babylon, and by about the time we reached this city it had become the question-of-the-day for all the beings there.

"Not only did these learned themselves talk about and discuss this question, but similar conversations and fierce discussions proceeded like fury among the ordinary beings there also.

"It was talked about and discussed by the young and old, by men and women, and even by the Babylonian butchers. Exceedingly anxious were they, particularly the learned, to know about this question.

"Before our arrival there, many of the beings existing in Babylon had ultimately even lost their reason on account of this question, and many were already candidates for losing theirs.

"This burning-question-of-the-day was that both the 'sorry-learned' and also the ordinary beings of the city of Babylon were very anxious to know whether they had a 'soul.'

"Every possible kind of fantastic theory existed in Babylon upon this question; and more and more theories were being freshly cooked up; and every, as it is said there, 'catchy theory' had, of course, its followers.

"Although whole hosts of these various theories existed there, nevertheless they were one and all based upon only two, but two quite opposite assumptions.

"One of these was called the 'atheistic' and the other the 'idealistic' or 'dualistic.'

"All the dualistic theories maintained the existence of the soul, and of course its 'immortality,' and every

---------------------------- *330* ----------------------------

possible kind of 'perturbation' to it after the death of the being 'man.'

"And all the atheistic theories maintained just the opposite.

"In short, my boy, when we arrived in the city of Babylon there was then proceeding what is called the 'Building-of-the-Tower-of-Babel.'"

Having uttered these latter words, Beelzebub became a little thoughtful and then continued as follows:

"Now I wish to explain to you about the expression I just used, namely, the 'Building-of-the-Tower-of-Babel.' This expression is very often used on your planet by the contemporary three-brained beings there also.

"I wish to touch upon this expression frequently used there and to elucidate it to you chiefly because firstly I chanced to be a witness at that time of all the events which gave rise to it, and secondly because the history of the arising of this expression and its transubstantiation in the understanding of your contemporary favorites can very clearly and instructively elucidate to you that, thanks as always to the same abnormally established conditions of ordinary being-existence, no precise information of events there which have indeed occurred to beings of former epochs ever reaches beings of later generations. And if, by chance, something like this expression does reach them, then the fantastic Reason of your favorites constructs a whole theory on the basis of just one expression such as this, with the result that those illusory 'being-egoplastikoori,' or what they call

"The consequence was that interest in this question gradually spread among all the ordinary three-brained beings then existing in Babylon, and by about the time we reached this Babylon it had become the 'question-of-the-day' for all the beings there.

"Not only did these learned themselves talk and discuss this question, but similar conversations and fierce discussions proceeded like fury among the ordinary beings there also.

"It was talked about and discussed by young and old, both men and women, and even by the Babylonian butchers. They were all, and particularly learned, exceedingly anxious to know about this question.

"Before our arrival there, many of the beings then existing in Babylon had ultimately even lost their reason on account of this question, and many were already candidates for the same—to lose it.

"This 'burning-question-of-the-day' consisted in this, that both the 'neo-learned' and the ordinary beings of the city of Babylon were very anxious to know whether they had a 'soul.'

"Every possible variety of fantastic theory existed in Babylon upon this question; and more and more theories were being freshly cooked up; and every, as it is said there 'catchy theory' had of course its followers.

"Although a whole host of various theories existed there, nevertheless they were one and all based upon only two, but two quite opposite assumptions. One of these was called the 'atheistic' and the other the 'idealistic' or 'dualistic.'

"All the 'dualistic' theories maintained the existence of the 'soul,' and of course its immortality and every

---

possible kind of 'perturbation' to it after the death of the being 'man.'

"And all the 'atheistic' theories maintained just the opposite.

"In short, my boy, when we arrived in the city of Babylon there was then proceeding what is called the 'building-of-the-tower-of-Babel.'"

Having pronounced these latter words Beelzebub became a little thoughtful and then continued as follows:

"Now I wish to explain to you the expression I just used, namely, the 'building-of-the-tower-of-Babel.' This expression is very often used on your planet by the contemporary three-brained beings there also.

"I wish to touch upon this frequently there-used-expression and to elucidate it to you first of all, chiefly because I chanced to be a witness then of all the events which gave rise to it, and secondly because the history of the arising of this expression, and its transmutation in the understanding of the contemporary favorites of yours can very clearly and instructively elucidate to you that, thanks as always to the same abnormally established conditions of ordinary being-existence, no precise information of events there which have indeed occurred to beings of former epochs ever reach the beings of later generations; or if by chance something like this expression does even reach them, then the fantastic reason of your favorites constructs a whole theory on the basis of just one expression such as this, with the result that those baseless 'being-egoplastikoori,' or, as they call 'psychic-picturings' increase and multiply in their presences owing to which there has arisen in the Universe the strange 'unique-psyche' of three-brained beings which every one of your favorites has.

"Well then, when we arrived in the city of Babylon, and I began mixing with various beings there and making

----------------------------- *331* -----------------------------

my corresponding observations in order to elucidate the question which had interested me, then, because almost everywhere I ran across the said learned beings who had gathered and met there in great numbers, it so fell out that I began associating with them alone, and made my observations through them, and also through their individualities.

"Among the number of the learned beings whom I met for my mentioned aim, was also one named Hamolinadir who had also been brought there by compulsion from Egypt.

"Well, during these meetings of ours, almost the same relations were established between this terrestrial three-brained being Hamolinadir and myself as in general are established everywhere between three-brained beings who frequently meet.

"This Hamolinadir was one of those learned there in the common presence of whom the factors for the impulses of a three-brained being which had passed to him by heredity were not quite atrophied, and moreover it turned out that during his preparatory age the responsible beings around him had prepared him to be also more or less normally responsible.

"It is necessary to notice that many learned beings of this kind were then in the city of Babylon.

"Although this learned Hamolinadir had his arising and preparation for becoming a responsible being just there in the city of Babylon and descended from the race of beings there called 'Assyrian,' yet he became learned in Egypt where the highest school existing on Earth at that time was found, and which was called the 'School of Materializing-Thought.'

"At the age he was when I first met him he already had his "I"—in respect of rationally directing what is called the 'automatic-psychic-functioning' of his common

----------------------------- *332* -----------------------------

presence—at the maximum stability for three-centered beings of the planet Earth at that time, in consequence of which during what is called his 'waking-passive-state' he had very definitely expressed being-manifestations, as, for instance, those called 'self-consciousness,' 'impartiality,' 'sincerity,' 'sensibility of perception,' 'alertness,' and so forth.

"Soon after our arrival in Babylon, I began going with this Hamolinadir to various what are called 'meetings' of the mentioned learned beings, and listened to every kind of what they called 'reports' upon the very question which was then 'the-question-of-the-day,' and which was the cause of the 'agitation-of-the-minds-of-the-whole-of-Babylon.'

"This friend of mine, Hamolinadir, was also very much excited about the said

them, 'psychic representations,' increase and multiply in their presence from which, also as a result, there has arisen in the universe the strange and unique psyche of three-brained beings which is possessed by every one of your favorites.

"Well then, when we arrived in the city of Babylon, and with the aim of elucidating the question which had interested me I began mixing with various beings

- -

there and making my corresponding observations, then because almost everywhere I ran across only the said learned who had gathered and met there in great numbers, it so fell out that I, associating with them only, began making my observations both by means of them, and in their own individualities.

"Among the number of learned beings whom I met for my mentioned aim there, was also one named Hamolinadir who had also been brought there by compulsion from Egypt.

"Well, between this terrestrial three-brained being Hamolinadir and myself during these meetings of ours, almost the same relations were established which in general are established everywhere between three-brained beings who frequently meet.

"This Hamolinadir was one of those learned there in the total presence of whom the factors for the impulses of a three-brained being which had passed by inheritance were not yet quite atrophied, and moreover it turned out that during his corresponding age the responsible beings around him had prepared him to be also more or less normally responsible.

"It is necessary to notice that many scientific beings of this kind were then in the city of Babylon.

"Although this learned Hamolinadir had his arising and preparation for becoming a responsible being just there in the city of Babylon and descended from the race of beings there called 'Assyrian,' yet he became learned in Egypt where the highest school existing on the Earth at that time was found, and which was called 'Materializing Thought.'

"At the age he was when I first met him, he already had his 'I'—in the sense of rational directing, present in his general presence and which is called 'automatic-psychic-functioning'

- -

—of the maximum steadiness for three-centered beings of the planet Earth at that time, in consequence of which during what is called his 'waking-passive-state' he had very definitely expressed being-manifestations, as for instance those called 'self-consciousness,' 'impartiality,' 'sincerity,' 'impressionability,' 'rumination,' and so forth.

"Soon after our arrival in Babylon, I began going with this Hamolinadir to what are called the 'meetings' of the mentioned learned beings, and listening to every possible kind of what they called their 'reports' upon just the question which was then 'the-question-of-the-day,' and which was the reason for the 'agitation-of-mind' of all the Babylonians.

"This friend of mine, Hamolinadir, was also very much excited about the said 'burning question.'

"He was agitated and perplexed by the fact that both the already existing and the many newly appearing theories upon this question were all, in spite of their entirely contradictory proofs, equally convincing and equally plausible.

"He said that those theories in which it was proved that we have a soul were very logically and convincingly expounded; and, likewise, those theories in which quite the contrary was proved were expounded no less logically and convincingly.

"So that you may be able to put yourself in the place of that sympathetic Assyrian, I shall also explain to you that in general on your planet, then in the city of Babylon as well as at the present time, all the theories on such a question as they call it of 'the beyond,' or any other 'elucidation-of-details' of any definite 'fact,' are invented by those three-brained beings there in whom most of the consequences of the properties of the organ Kundabuffer are completely crystallized, in consequence of which there actively functions in their presence, that being-property,

-------------------------------- 333 --------------------------------

which they themselves call 'cunning.' Owing to this, they consciously—of course consciously only with the sort of reason which it has already become long ago proper for them alone to possess—and moreover, merely automatically, gradually acquire in their common presence the capacity for 'spotting' the weakness of the psyche of the surrounding beings like themselves; and this capacity gradually forms in them data which enable them at times to sense and even to understand the peculiar logic of the beings around them, and according to these data, they invent and propound one of their 'theories' concerning this or that question; and because, as I have already told you, in most of the three-brained beings there, owing to the abnormal conditions of ordinary being-existence established there by them themselves, the being-function called 'instinctively-to-sense-cosmic-truths' gradually atrophies, then, if any one of them happens to devote himself to the detailed study of any one of these 'theories,' he is bound, whether he wishes or not, to be persuaded by it with the whole of his presence.

"Well, my boy, already seven of their months after our arrival in the city of Babylon I once went with this friend of mine there, Hamolinadir, to what is called a 'general-learned-conference.'

"This 'general-learned-conference' had already been convened at that time by the learned beings previously brought there by force; and thus there were at this conference not only the learned forcibly assembled there by the mentioned Persian king who in the meantime had already got over his craze about the science of 'alchemy,' and forgotten all about it, but many other learned also from other communities who had voluntarily gathered as they then said 'for-the-sake-of-science.'

"At this 'general-learned-conference' that day, the reporters spoke by lot.

-------------------------------- 334 --------------------------------

"My friend, Hamolinadir, also had to report about some topic and therefore drew a lot; and it fell to him to speak fifth.

'burning-question.'

"He was agitated and perplexed by the fact that both the already existing and the many newly appearing theories upon this question were all, in spite of their entirely opposite proofs, equally convincing and equally veridical.

"He said that those theories in which it was proved that we have a 'soul' were very logically and convincingly expounded; and equally the theories in which quite the contrary was proved were expounded no less logically and convincingly.

"So that you may be able to put yourself in the place of that sympathetic Assyrian, I shall also explain to you that in general on your planet, then in the city of Babylon as also now at the present time, most of the various theories concerning such a question, as they call it, 'of the beyond,' or concerning any other 'elucidation-of-the-details' of any definite thesis whatever, are invented by those three-brained beings there in whom most of the consequences of the properties of the organ Kundabuffer are fulfilledly crystallized, in consequence of which there act-

ively functions in their presence that being-property which they themselves call 'cunning.' Owing to this they gradually and consciously acquire—of course consciously only with the sort of reason which it has already become long ago proper for them alone to possess—and moreover only automatically acquired in their general presence—capacity for 'spotting' the weak points of the psyche of the surrounding beings like themselves; and this capacity is gradually formed in them into data that enable them at times to sense and even to understand the peculiar logic present in the beings surrounding them, and according to these data they invent and propound one of their 'theories' concerning this or that question; and because, as I have already told you, in most of the three-brained beings there, owing to the abnormal conditions of ordinary being-existence established there by them themselves, the being-function called 'instinctively-to-sense-cosmic-truths' gradually atrophies, then, if any one of them happens to devote himself to the detailed study of any one of these 'theories' he is bound, whether he likes it or not, to be persuaded of it with the whole of his presence.

"Well my boy.

"Already seven of their months after our arrival in the city of Babylon I once went with this friend of mine there, Hamolinadir, to what is called a 'general learned conference.'

"This 'general learned conference' had already been convened at that time by the learned beings previously brought there by force; and thus there were at this conference not only the learned forcibly assembled there by the mentioned Persian King, who in the meantime had already got over his craze about the science of 'alchemy,' and forgotten all about it, but many other learned also from other communities who had voluntarily gathered together, as they then said 'for the sake of science.'

"At this 'general learned conference' the reporters spoke by lot.

"My friend, Hamolinadir, having also to report upon some topic, also drew a lot; and it fell to him to speak the fifth in order.

"The reporters who preceded him either reported upon new 'theories' they had invented or they criticized theories already existing and known to everybody.

"At last came the turn of this sympathetic Assyrian.

"He ascended what is called the 'rostrum,' and as he did so some attendants hung up a notice above it indicating on which subject the given reporter would speak.

"It was the custom at that time to do so.

"The notice announced that the reporter had taken as the theme of his report the 'Instability-of-Human-Reason.'

"Thereupon, this terrestrial friend of mine first expatiated on the kind of structure which, in his opinion, the human 'head-brain' has, and in which cases and in what manner various impressions are perceived by the other brains of man, and how only after definite what is called 'agreement' between all the brains are the total results impressed on this head-brain.

"He spoke calmly at first, but the longer he spoke, the more agitated he became, until his voice rose to a shout, and shouting he began to criticize the Reason in man.

"And at the same time, he mercilessly criticized his own Reason.

"Still continuing to shout, he very logically and convincingly demonstrated the instability and fickleness of man's Reason, and showed, in detail, how easy it is to prove and convince this Reason of anything you like.

"Although in the midst of the shouting of this terrestrial friend of mine, Hamolinadir, his sobbing could be heard, nevertheless, even while sobbing, he continued to shout. Further he said:

"'To every man, and also of course to me, it's quite easy to prove anything; all that is necessary to know is

---------------------------- 335 ----------------------------

which shocks and which associations to arouse in the other human brains while one or other "truth" is being proved. It is very easily possible even to prove to man that our whole World and of course the people in it, are nothing but an illusion, and that the authenticity and reality of the World are only a "corn" and moreover the corn growing on the big toe of our left foot. Besides this corn, absolutely nothing exists in the World; everything only seems, and even then only to "psychopaths-squared."'

"At this point in the speech of this sympathetic terrestrial three-brained being, an attendant offered him a bowl of water, and after he had eagerly drunk the water, he continued to speak, but now more calmly.

"He said further:

"'Take myself as an example: I am not an ordinary learned man. I am known by all Babylon and by people of many other towns as an exceedingly learned and wise man.

"'I finished the course of study higher than which has never yet existed on the Earth, and which it is almost impossible will ever exist again.

"'But what then has this highest development given to my Reason in respect of that question which, already during one or two years, is driving all Babylonians

"The reporters who preceded him reported either new theories they had invented, or they criticized theories already existing and known to everybody.

"At last came the turn of this sympathetic Assyrian.

"He ascended what is called the rostrum, and as he did so some attendants suspended a placard above it on which was indicated the subject of the given reporter's discourse.

"It was the custom at that time to do this.

"The placard announced that the reporter had taken as the theme of his report the 'instability of human reason.'

"Thereupon, this terrestrial friend of mine first expatiated on the kind of structure which in his opinion the human 'head brain' has, and in which cases and in what manner various impressions are perceived by the other brains of man, and how only after definite what is called 'agreement' between all the brains are the total results just impressed on this head brain.

"He spoke calmly at first, but the longer he spoke the more agitated he became, until his voice rose to a shout, and so it was that he criticized the reason present in man.

"Thereupon he also mercilessly criticized his own reason.

"Still continuing to shout, he very logically and convincingly demonstrated the instability and fickleness of man's reason and showed in detail how easy it is to prove and convince this reason of anything you like.

"Although signs of his sobbing could be heard now and then, in the midst of the shouting of this terrestrial friend of mine, Hamolinadir, nevertheless, even while sobbing, he continued to shout. Further he said:

"'To every man, and also of course to me, it's no trouble to prove anything; all it is necessary to know is

which shocks and just which associations to arouse in the other human brains, while one or other 'truth' is being proved. It is very easily possible even to prove to man that our whole world and also of course the people in it, are nothing but an illusion, and that the authenticity and reality of the World are only a 'corn,' and moreover the 'corn' growing on the big toe of our left foot. Other than this 'corn,' absolutely nothing exists in the world; everything only seems, and even then only to 'psychopaths squared.'

"At this point in the speech of this sympathetic terrestrial three-brained being, an attendant offered him a bowl of water, and after he had eagerly drunk the water, he continued to speak, but now more calmly.

"He said further:

"'Take myself as an example: I am not an ordinary learned man. I am known by all Babylon and by the people of many other towns as an exceedingly learned and able man.

"'I finished the course of study higher than which has never yet existed on the Earth, and which it is almost impossible will ever exist again.

"'But what has this highest development given to my Reason in respect of that question which, well, already during one or two years, is driving all Babylonians insane?

"'This Reason of mine which has received the highest development, has given me during this general dementia concerning the question of the soul nothing else but "five-Fridays-a-week."

"'During this time, I have very attentively and seriously followed all the old and new theories about the "soul" and there is not a single theory with the author of which I do not inwardly agree, since all of them are very logically and plausibly expounded, and such Reason as I have cannot but agree with their logic and plausibility.

"'During this time I have even myself written a very

- 336 -

lengthy work on this "question-of-the-beyond"; and many of those present here have surely become acquainted with my logical mentation and most probably there is not one of you here who does not envy this logical mentation of mine.

"'Yet at the same time I now honestly declare to you all, that concerning this "question-of-the-beyond" I myself, with the whole of the knowledge that has been accumulated in me, am neither more nor less than just an "idiot-cubed."

"'There is now proceeding among us in the city of Babylon the general public "building-of-a-tower" by means of which to ascend to "Heaven" and there to see with our own eyes what goes on there.

"'This tower is being built of bricks which outwardly all look alike, but which are made of quite different materials.

"'Among these bricks are bricks of iron and wood and also of "dough" and even of "eider down."

"'Well then, at the present time, a stupendously enormous tower is being built of such bricks right in the center of Babylon, and every more or less conscious person must bear in mind that sooner or later this tower will certainly fall and crush not only all the people of Babylon, but also everything else that is there.

"'As I personally still wish to live and have no desire to be crushed by this Babylonian tower, I shall therefore now immediately go away from here, and all of you, do as you please.'

"He uttered these last words while leaving, and ran off and since that time, I never saw that sympathetic Assyrian again.

"As I later learned, he left the city of Babylon the same day forever, and went to Nineveh and existed somewhere there to a ripe old age. I also ascertained that this

- 337 -

Hamolinadir was never again occupied with 'sciences' and that he spent his existence only in planting 'choongary' which in contemporary language is called 'maize.'

"Well, my boy, the speech of this Hamolinadir at first made such a deep impression upon the beings there that for almost a month they went about, as it is said there, 'down-in-the-mouth.'

"And when they met each other, they could speak of nothing else but only of the various passages from this speech which they remembered and repeated.

"They repeated them so often that several of Hamolinadir's phrases spread

insane? This Reason of mine which has received the highest development, has given me during this general dementia concerning the question of the 'soul' nothing else but 'five Fridays a week.'

"'During this time I have very attentively and seriously followed all the old and newly appearing theories about the 'soul' and there was not a single theory with the author of which I did not inwardly agree, since all of them were very logically and plausibly expounded, and such reason as I have, could not fail to agree with their logic and plausibility.

"'During this time I have even myself written a very

lengthy work on this 'Question of the beyond'; and many of those present here have surely become acquainted with this logical thinking of mine and most probably there was none of you but envied this logical mentation of mine.

"'Yet at the same time I now honestly declare to you all that concerning this 'question of the Beyond' I myself with the whole of the knowledge that has been accumulated in me, am neither more nor less than just an idiot cubed.

"'There is now proceeding among us in the city of Babylon the common public building of a Tower by means of which to ascend to 'heaven' and there to see with one's own eyes what goes on there.

"'This tower is being built of bricks which outwardly all look alike, but which are made of quite different materials.

"'Among these bricks are bricks of iron and wood and also of 'dough' and even of 'eiderdown.'

"'Well, of such bricks, a stupendously enormous tower is being built at the present time right in the center of Babylon, and every more or less conscious person is obliged to bear in mind that sooner or later this tower will certainly fall and crush not only all the people in Babylon, but also everything else that is there.

"'As I personally still wish to live, and have no fancy for being crushed by this Babylonian Tower, I shall therefore now immediately get away from here, leaving you to do as you please . . . '

"These last words he uttered while leaving, and ran off.

"And from that time I never saw that Sympathetic Assyrian again.

"As I later learned, he left the city of Babylon the same day forever, and went to Nineveh, and existed somewhere there to a ripe old age. I also ascertained that

this Hamolinadir was never again occupied with 'sciences,' and that he spent his existence only in planting 'choongary' which in contemporary language is called 'maize.'

"Well, my boy, the speech of this Hamolinadir at first made such a deep impression upon the beings there that for almost a month they went about as it is said there, like beings 'down-in-the-mouth.'

"And when they met each other, they could speak of nothing else but only the various passages from his speech which they remembered and repeated.

"They repeated them so often that several of Hamolinadir's phrases spread among the ordinary beings of Babylon and became sayings for ordinary daily existence.

"Some of his phrases reached even contemporary beings of the planet Earth, and among them there is also the phrase 'The-Building-of-the-Tower-of-Babel.'

"Contemporary beings now already quite clearly picture to themselves that once upon a time a certain tower was built in this said city of Babylon to enable beings to ascend in their planetary bodies to 'God Himself.'

"And the contemporary beings of the planet Earth also say and are quite persuaded that during the building of this 'Babylonian tower' a number of tongues were confused.

"In general there reached the contemporary beings of the planet Earth a great many of such isolated expressions, uttered or fixed by various sensible beings of former epochs concerning certain details of a complete understanding from the epoch when the Center-of-Culture was Babylon as well as from the other epochs; and your favorites of recent centuries, simply on the basis of these 'scraps,' have with their already quite 'nonsensical' Reason concocted such 'cock-and-bull' stories as our Arch-cunning Lucifer himself might envy.

"Among the many teachings then current in Babylon

— 338 —

concerning the 'question-of-the-beyond,' two had a large number of adherents though these teachings had nothing in common.

"And it was precisely these two teachings which began to pass from generation to generation, and to confuse their 'being-sane-mentation' which had already been confused enough without them.

"Although in the course of their transmission from generation to generation the details of both these teachings underwent change, nevertheless the fundamental ideas contained in them remained unchanged and have even reached down to contemporary times.

"One of these two teachings which then had many adherents in Babylon was just the 'dualistic' and the other, the 'atheistic'; so that in one of them it was proved that in beings there is the soul, and in the other, quite the opposite, namely, that they have nothing of the kind.

"In the dualist or idealist teaching, it was said that within the coarse body of the being-man, there is a fine and invisible body, which is just the soul.

"This 'fine body' of man is immortal, that is to say, it is never destroyed.

"This fine body or soul, it was said further, must make a corresponding payment for every action of the physical body whether voluntary or involuntary, and every man, already at birth, consists of these two bodies, namely, the physical body and the soul.

"Further it was said that as soon as a man is born, two invisible spirits immediately perch upon his shoulders.

"On his right shoulder sits a 'spirit-of-good' called an 'angel,' and on his left, a second spirit, a 'spirit-of-evil' called a 'devil.'

"From the very first day these spirits—the spirit-of-good and the spirit-of-evil—record in their 'notebooks' all the manifestations of the man, the spirit sit-

among the ordinary beings of Babylon and became sayings for ordinary daily existence.

"Some of his phrases even reached contemporary beings of the planet Earth, and among them was also this, namely, the 'Building of the Tower of Babel.'

"And contemporary beings now already quite clearly picture to themselves that once upon a time a certain tower was built in this said city of Babylon to enable beings to ascend to 'God Himself' in their planetary bodies.

"The contemporary beings of the planet Earth also say and are quite persuaded that during the building of this 'Babylonian Tower' a number of 'tongues' were confused.

"Altogether there reached the contemporary beings of the planet Earth a great many such isolated expressions, uttered or fixed by various reasonable beings of former epochs concerning certain details of a complete understanding from the epoch when the 'center-of-culture' was Babylon, and also from other epochs; and your favorites of recent centuries, simply on the basis of these 'scraps,' have with their already quite 'babelish' reason, concocted such 'cock and bull' stories as our Arch-cunning Lucifer might envy.

"Among the many teachings then current in Babylon

concerning the 'question of the Beyond,' two had a large number of adherents although these teachings had nothing in common.

"And it was precisely these two teachings which began to pass from generation to generation, and to confuse their being 'sane-mentation,' which had already been confused enough without them.

"Although in the course of their transmission from generation to generation the details of both these teachings underwent change, nevertheless the fundamental ideas contained in them, remained unchanged and have even reached down to contemporary times.

"Of these two teachings which then had many adherents in Babylon one was just the 'dualistic,' and the other the 'atheistic' so that in one of them it was proved that they do contain this 'soul' and in the other, quite the opposite, namely that they contain nothing of the kind.

"It was said in the 'dualistic' or 'idealistic' teaching that within the coarse body of the man-being is a fine and invisible body, and just this latter is the 'soul.'

"This fine body of man is immortal, that is to say, it is never destroyed.

"This 'fine body' or 'soul,' it was said further, must make a corresponding payment for every action of the 'physical body,' whether voluntary or involuntary, and every man already at birth consists of these two bodies, namely the 'physical body' and the 'soul.'

"Further it was said that when a man is born, two invisible spirits immediately perch upon his shoulders.

"On his right shoulder sits a 'spirit of good,' called an 'angel,' and on his left a second spirit, a 'spirit of evil,' called a 'Devil.'

"From the very first day these spirits, the 'spirit of good' and the 'spirit of evil,' record in their ledgers all the manifestations of the man, the spirit sitting on his

ting on his right

-------------------------------- *339* --------------------------------

shoulder recording all those called his 'good manifestations' or 'good deeds,' and the spirit sitting on his left shoulder, the 'evil.'

"Among the duties of these two spirits is that of suggesting to and compelling a man to do more of those manifestations which are in their respective domains.

"The spirit on the right constantly strives to make the man refrain from doing those actions which are in the domain of the opposite spirit, and, perforce, more of those in his own domain.

"And the spirit on the left does the same, but vice versa.

"In this strange teaching it was further said that these two 'spirit-rivals' are always combating each other, and that each strives with might and main that the man should do more of those actions which are in his domain.

"When the man dies, these spirits leave his physical body on the Earth and take his soul to God who exists somewhere 'up-in-Heaven.'

"There up-in-Heaven this God sits surrounded by his devoted archangels and angels, and suspended in front of him is a pair of scales.

"On each side of the scales, 'spirits' stand on duty. On the right, stand the spirits who are called 'servants of Paradise' and these are the angels; and on the left stand the 'servants of Hell' and these are the devils.

"The spirits which have sat on the man's shoulder all his life bring his soul after death to God, and God then takes from their hands the notebooks in which the notes have been recorded of all the man's actions; and He places them on the 'pans of the scales.'

"On the right pan He puts the notebook of the angel; and on the left pan the notebook of the devil, and, according to the pan which falls, God commands the spirits on duty standing on the given side to take this soul into their charge.

-------------------------------- *340* --------------------------------

"In the charge of the spirits standing on duty on the right is just that place called Paradise.

"It is a place of indescribable beauty and splendiferousness. In that Paradise are magnificent fruits in abundance and endless quantities of fragrant flowers, and enchanting sounds of cherubic songs and seraphic music constantly echo in the air; and many other things were also enumerated whose outer reactions according to the perceptions and cognitions abnormally inherent in the three-brained beings of that strange planet are likely to evoke in them, as they say, 'great-satisfaction,' that is to say, the satisfaction of those needs formed in their common presences, which are criminal for three-centered beings to possess, and the totality of which have driven out from their presences everything, without exception, that was put into them by our COMMON FATHER and which it is imperative for every three-brained being to possess.

"In the charge of the spirits standing on duty on the left of the scales, who, according to this Babylonian teaching, are the devils, there is what is called Hell.

"Concerning Hell it was said that it is a place without vegetation, always unimaginably hot, and without a single drop of water.

right

---

shoulder recording all those called his 'good manifestations' or 'good deeds' and the spirit sitting on had left shoulder, the 'evil.'

"Among the duties of these two spirits is that of tempting and compelling a man to do more of those manifestations which are in their respective domains.

"The spirit on the right constantly strives to make the man refrain from doing those actions which are in the domain of the opposite spirit and perform more of those in his own domain.

"And the spirit on the left does the same, but vice versa.

"In this strange teaching it was further said that these two 'spirit rivals' are always at odds with each other and that each strives with might and main that the man should perform more of those actions which are under his charge.

"When the man dies, these spirits leave his 'physical body' on the Earth and take his 'soul' to 'God' who exists somewhere there 'up in Heaven.'

"There in 'Heaven' this 'God' sits surrounded by his devoted Archangels and Angels and in front of him a pair of scales is suspended.

"On each side of the 'scales' 'spirits' stand on duty. On the right stand the spirits who are called 'servants of Paradise' and these are 'Angels'; and on the left stand the 'servants of Hell' and these are 'Devils.'

"The spirits which have sat on the man's shoulders all his life bring his 'soul' after death to 'God,' and 'God' then takes from their hands the 'ledgers' in which the notes have been recorded of all the man's 'doings'; and He places them on the 'pans of the scales.'

"On the right 'pan' He puts the ledger of the 'Angel'—and on the left 'pan' the ledger of the 'Devil'; and according to the 'pan' which falls, 'God' commands the spirits on duty standing on the given side to take this 'soul' into their charge.

"In the charge of the spirits standing on duty on the right is just that place called 'Paradise.'

"It is a place of indescribable beauty and splendiferousness. In that 'Paradise' are magnificent fruits in abundance, endless quantities of fragrant flowers, and enchanting sounds of cherubic songs and seraphic music constantly echo in the air; and many other things were also enumerated whose outer reactions, according to the perceptions and awareness abnormally present in the three-brained beings of that strange planet, are likely to evoke in them, as they say, 'delight,' that is the satisfaction of those needs formed in their general presence which are criminal for three-centered beings to possess, and the totality of which have just ousted from their presence everything, without exception, that was put into it by our COMMON FATHER and which it is imperative for every three-brained being to possess.

"But in charge of the spirits standing on duty on the left of the scales, who, according to this Babylonian teaching are the 'devils,' there is what is called 'Hell.'

"Concerning 'Hell' it was said that it is a place of no vegetation, but it is always unimaginably hot, and without a drop of water.

"In that Hell sounds constantly echo of fearful 'cacophony' and infuriated offensive 'abuse.'

"Everywhere there are instruments of every conceivable torture from the 'rack' and the 'wheel' to instruments for lacerating bodies and mechanically rubbing them with salt, and so on of the same kind.

"In the Babylonian idealistic teaching, it was minutely explained that in order that his soul should enter this Paradise, the man must constantly strive while on Earth to provide more material for the notebook of the spirit angel sitting on his right shoulder, otherwise there would be more material for the records of the spirit sitting on

- *341* -

the left shoulder, in which case, such a man's soul would inevitably go to this most awful Hell."

Here Hassein could not restrain himself, and suddenly interrupted with the following words:

"And which of their manifestations do they consider good, and which bad?"

Beelzebub looked at his grandson with a very strange look and, shaking his head, said as follows:

"Concerning this, which being-manifestations are there on your planet considered good and which bad—two independent understandings, having nothing in common with each other, have existed from the most ancient times up to the present period, having passed from generation to generation.

"The first of these understandings exists there and passes from one generation to another among such three-brained beings there as were those members of the society Akhaldan on the continent Atlantis, and such as those who, although of another kind, several centuries later after the Transapalnian perturbation acquired almost the same in the foundations of their common presences and who were called 'initiates.'

"The first of these understandings exists there under the following formulation:

"Every action of man is good in the objective sense, if it is done according to his conscience, and every action is bad, if from it he later experiences 'remorse.'

"And the second understanding arose there soon after the wise 'invention' of the Great King Konuzion, which invention, passing from generation to generation through ordinary beings there, gradually spread over almost the whole planet under the name of 'morality.'

"Here it will be very interesting to notice a particularity of this morality which was grafted upon it at the very

- *342* -

beginning of its arising and which ultimately became part and parcel of it.

"What this said particularity of terrestrial morality is, you can easily represent to yourself and understand if I tell you that, both inwardly and outwardly, it acquired exactly that 'unique property' which belongs to the being bearing the name 'chameleon.'

"And the oddity and peculiarity of this said particularity of the morality there,

"Sounds constantly echo in this 'Hell'—of fearful 'cacophony' and infuriatingly offensive 'abuse.'

"Everywhere there are instruments of every conceivable torture from the 'Rack' and the 'Wheel' to instruments for lacerating bodies and mechanically rubbing them with salt, and so on, of the same kind.

"In the Babylonian 'Idealist' teaching it was very minutely explained that in order for his 'soul' to enter this 'Paradise' the man must constantly strive while on Earth to provide most material for the ledger of the spirit 'Angel' sitting on his right shoulder, otherwise a superior amount would be provided for the records of the spirit sitting on

the left shoulder, in which case such a man's 'soul' would inevitably go to this most awful 'Hell.'

"Here Hassein could not restrain himself, and suddenly interrupted Beelzebub with the following words:

"And which of their manifestations do they consider good and which bad?"

Beelzebub looked at his grandson with a very strange look, and shaking his head said as follows:

"Concerning this, which being-manifestations are there on your planet considered good and which bad, two independent understandings, having nothing in common with each other, have existed right from the most ancient times up to the present period, having passed from generation to generation.

"The first of these understandings exists there and passes from one generation to another among such three-brained beings there, as those members of the society Akhaldan who were on the continent Atlantis, and such as those who after the second 'Transapalnian-perturbation' several centuries later again became beings, although of another kind, who acquired almost the same in the foundations of their general presence and who were called 'initiates.'

"The first of these understandings exists there under the following formulation:

"Every action of a man is good in the objective sense if it is done according to his conscience, and every action is bad if remorse will afterwards be experienced from it.

"And the second understanding arose there soon after the rational 'invention' of the Great King Konuzion, which invention, passing from generation to generation through ordinary beings there gradually spread over almost the whole planet under the name of 'Morality.'

"Here it will be very interesting to notice a particularity of this 'Morality' which was grafted upon it at the very

beginning of its arising and which ultimately became part and parcel of it.

"In what this said particularity of terrestrial 'Morality' just consists, you can easily represent to yourself and understand if I tell you that both within and without it acquired exactly that 'unique-property' which belongs to the beings bearing the name 'chameleon.'

"And the oddity and peculiarity of this said particularity of the 'morality' there, especially of contemporary morality, is that its functioning automatically depends entirely on the moods of the local authorities, which moods in their turn depend also automatically on the state of the four sources of action existing there under the names of 'mother-in-law,' 'digestion,' 'John Thomas,' and 'cash.'

"The second Babylonian teaching which then had many followers, and which, passing from generation to generation, also reached your contemporary favorites, was on the contrary one of the atheistic teachings of that period.

"In this teaching by the terrestrial Hasnamussian candidates of that time, it was stated that there is no God in the world, and moreover no soul in man, and hence that all those talks and discussions about the soul are nothing more than the deliriums of sick visionaries.

"It was further maintained that there exists in the World only one special law of mechanics, according to which everything that exists passes from one form into another; that is to say, the results which arise from certain preceding causes are gradually transformed and become causes for subsequent results.

"Man also is therefore only a consequence of some preceding cause and in his turn must, as a result, be a cause of certain consequences.

"Further, it was said that even what are called 'supernatural phenomena' really perceptible to most people, are

- *343* -

all nothing but these same results ensuing from the mentioned special law of mechanics.

"The full comprehension of this law by the pure Reason depends on the gradual impartial, all-round acquaintance with its numerous details which can be revealed to a pure Reason in proportion to its development.

"But as regards the Reason of man, this is only the sum of all the impressions perceived by him, from which there gradually arise in him data for comparisons, deductions, and conclusions.

"As a result of all this, he obtains more information concerning all kinds of similarly repeated facts around him, which in the general organization of man are in their turn material for the formation of definite convictions in him. Thus, from all this there is formed in man—Reason, that is to say, his own subjective psyche.

"Whatever may have been said in these two teachings about the soul, and whatever maleficent means had been prepared by those learned beings assembled there from almost the whole planet for the gradual transformation of the Reason of their descendants into a veritable mill of nonsense, it would not have been, in the objective sense, totally calamitous; but the whole objective terror is concealed in the fact that there later resulted from these teachings a great evil, not only for their descendants alone, but maybe even for everything existing.

"The point is, that during the mentioned 'agitation-of-minds' of that time in the city of Babylon, these learned beings, owing to their collective wiseacrings acquired in their presences, in addition to all they already had, a further mass of new data for Hasnamussian manifestations, and when they dispersed and went home to their own countries, they began everywhere, of course unconsciously, to

especially of contemporary morality, lies in this—that its functioning automatic-ally depends entirely on the humors of the 'local authorities,' which humors in their turn depend also automatically on the state of the four sources of action ex-isting there, bearing the names of 'mother-in-law,' 'digestion,' 'John Thomas,' and 'Cash.'

"The second Babylonian teaching which then had many followers, and which passing from generation to generation also reached your contemporary favorites, was on the contrary one of the 'atheistic' teachings of that period.

"In this teaching by the terrestrial Hasnamuss candidates of that time, it was flatly stated that there is no God in the world, and moreover no 'soul' in man, and hence that all those talks and discussions about the 'soul' are nothing more than the fancies of sick visionaries.

"It was further maintained that there exists in the World only one special law of mechanics according to which everything that exists passes from one species into another, that is to say, the results which arise from certain preceding causes are gradually transformed and become causes for subsequent results.

"Man is also therefore only a consequence of some preceding cause, and in his turn must as a result serve as a cause of certain consequences.

"Further it was said that even what are called 'supernatural-phenomena' really perceptible to most people are

- -

all nothing but these same results flowing out of the mentioned special law of mechanics.

"The full comprehension of this law by the pure reason depends on the gradual impartial, all-round acquaintance with its numerous details which can be re-vealed to a pure reason in proportion to its development.

"But as regards the reason of man, this is only the sum of all the impressions perceived by him from which there gradually arise in him data for comparisons, deductions, and conclusions.

"As a result of all this, he obtains a greater information concerning every pos-sible kind of similarly repeated fact around him, which facts in their turn serve in the general organization of man as material for forming definite convictions in him. Thus all this reason formed in man is merely his own subjective psyche.

"Whatever had been said in these two 'teachings' about the 'soul,' and whatever maleficent means had been prepared by these scientists assembled there from al-most the whole planet, for the gradual transformation of the reason of the beings of their descendants into a veritable 'Mill' of 'Babel,' it would not have been in the objective sense, completely calamitous; but the whole objective terror is con-cealed in this, that there later resulted from these teachings a great evil, not for their descendants alone, but possibly for everything that exists.

"The fact is that when, owing to their mutual 'wiseacrings' during the men-tioned 'agitation of minds' of that time in the city of Babylon, these learned beings acquired in their presences in addition to all they already had, a further mass of new data for Hasnamussian manifestations, and then went to their respective homes, they began everywhere, of course unconsciously, propagating like conta-

propagate like contagious bacilli all these notions which all together, ultimately, totally destroyed the last remnants

------------------------------ 344 ------------------------------

and even the traces of all the results of the holy labors of the Very Saintly Ashiata Shiemash.

"The remnants, that is to say, of those holy 'consciously-suffering-labors' which he intentionally actualized for the purpose of creating, just for three-centered beings, such special external conditions of ordinary being-existence in which alone the maleficent consequences of the properties of the organ Kundabuffer could gradually disappear from their presences, so that in their place there could be gradually acquired those properties proper to the presence of every kind of three-brained being, whose whole presence is an exact similitude of everything in the Universe.

"Another result of the diverse wiseacrings by those learned beings of the Earth then in the city of Babylon concerning the question of the soul, was that soon after my fifth appearance in person on the surface of that planet of yours this, in its turn, Center-of-Culture of theirs, the incomparable and indeed magnificent Babylon, was also, as it is said there, swept away from the face of the Earth to its very foundations.

"Not only was the city of Babylon itself destroyed but everything also that had been acquired and accomplished by the beings who had, during many of their centuries, formerly existed there.

"In the name of Justice, I must now say that the prime initiative for the destruction of the holy labors of Ashiata Shiemash did not spring, however, from these learned of the Earth who were then assembled in the city of Babylon, but from the invention of a learned being very well known there, who also existed there on the continent Asia several centuries before these Babylonian events, namely, from the invention of a being named 'Lentrohamsanin' who, having coated his higher-being-part into a definite unit, and having perfected himself by Reason up to the required gradation of Objective Reason, also became one

------------------------------ 345 ------------------------------

of those three hundred and thirteen Hasnamussian-Eternal-individuals who now exist on the small planet bearing the name of Retribution.

"About this Lentrohamsanin I shall also tell you, since the information concerning him will serve to elucidate for your understanding the strange psyche of those three-brained beings who exist on that peculiar remote planet.

"But I shall tell you about this Lentrohamsanin only when I have finished speaking about the Very Saintly Ashiata Shiemash, as the information relating to this now already Most Very Saintly Individual Ashiata Shiemash and his activities in connection with this planet of yours is most important and of the utmost value for your understanding of the peculiarities of the psyche of these three-brained beings who have taken your fancy and who breed on the planet Earth."

------------------------------ 346 ------------------------------

gious bacilli, all these notions which together finally and utterly destroyed the last remnants

- -

and even the traces of all the results of the holy labors of the very saintly Ashiata Shiemash.

"The remnant, that is to say, of those holy 'consciously suffering' labors which he intentionally performed for the creation, just for the three-centered beings, of such special external conditions of ordinary being-existence in which alone there could gradually disappear from their presence the maleficent consequences of the properties of the organ Kundabuffer, and in their place, there could be gradually acquired those properties proper to be possessed in the presence of every kind of three-brained being, whose whole presence is an exact counterpart of everything in the universe.

"Another result of these divers wiseacrings by these learned beings of the Earth then in the city of Babylon concerning the question of the 'soul' was this: that soon after my fifth personal appearance on the surface of that planet of yours, this, in its turn, 'center-of-culture' of theirs, the incomparable, and indeed Magnificent, Babylon was also, as it is said there, swept away from the face of the Earth to its very foundation.

"Not only was the city of Babylon itself then destroyed, but everything also that had been acquired and accomplished by the beings who had, during many of their centuries, formerly existed there. I must say for the sake of Justice that the prime initiative for the destruction of the holy labors of Ashiata Shiemash, did not spring, however, from these learned of the Earth who were then assembled in the city of Babylon, but from the invention of a 'learned' being very well known there, who, several centuries before these Babylonian events, also existed there on the continent Asia; namely, from the invention of a being named 'Lentrohamsanin' whose higher being part having coated itself into a definite unit, and having perfected itself by its reason up to the required gradation of objective reason, also became one

- -

of those three hundred and thirty-five Hasnamuss 'eternal individuums' who now exist on the small planet bearing the name 'Retribution.'

"About this 'Lentrohamsanin' I shall also tell you, since the information concerning him will serve to elucidate for your understanding the strange psyche of those three-brained beings. But I shall tell you about this 'Lentrohamsanin' only when I have finished speaking about the very saintly Ashiata Shiemash, as the information relating to this planet of yours concerning this now already most very saintly Individuum Ashiata Shiemash, is the most important and the most material for your understanding of the peculiarities of the psyche of these three-brained beings who please you and who breed on the planet Earth."

- -

The Very Saintly Ashiata Shiemash, Sent from Above to the Earth

"A ND so, my boy!"

"Now listen very attentively to the information concerning the Most Very Saintly, now already Common Cosmic Individual, Ashiata Shiemash and his activities connected with the existence of the three-brained beings arising and existing on that planet Earth which has taken your fancy.

"I have already more than once told you, that by the All Most Gracious Command of Our OMNI-LOVING COMMON FATHER ENDLESSNESS, our Cosmic Highest Most Very Saintly Individuals sometimes actualize within the presence of some terrestrial three-brained being, a 'definitized' conception of a sacred Individual in order that he, having become a terrestrial being with such a presence, may there on the spot 'orientate' himself and give to the process of their ordinary being-existence such a corresponding new direction, thanks to which the already crystallized consequences of the properties of the organ Kundabuffer, as well as the predispositions to such new crystallizations, might perhaps be removed from their presences.

"It was seven centuries before the Babylonian events I have spoken of, that there was actualized in the planetary body of a three-brained being there a 'definitized' conception of a sacred Individual named Ashiata Shiemash, who became there in his turn a Messenger from Above, and who is now already one of the Highest Most Very Saintly common-cosmic Sacred Individuals.

"Ashiata Shiemash had his conception in the planetary body of a boy of a poor family descended from what is

------------------------------ *347* ------------------------------

called the 'Sumerian Race,' in a small place then called 'Pispascana' situated not far from Babylon.

"He grew up and became a responsible being partly in this small place and partly in Babylon itself, which was at that time, although not yet magnificent, already a famous city.

"The Very Saintly Ashiata Shiemash was the only Messenger sent from Above to your planet who succeeded by His holy labors in creating on that planet conditions in which the existence of its unfortunate beings somewhat resembled for a certain time the existence of the three-brained beings of the other planets of our great Universe on which beings exist with the same possibilities; and He was also the first on that planet Earth, who for the mission preassigned to Him refused to employ for the three-brained beings of that planet the ordinary methods which had been established during centuries by all the other Messengers from Above.

"The Very Saintly Ashiata Shiemash taught nothing whatever to the ordinary three-brained beings of the Earth, nor did He preach anything to them, as was done before and after Him by all the Messengers sent there from Above with the

The Very Saintly Ashiata Shiemash Sent From Above To The Earth

A ND SO, my boy!
"Now listen very attentively to the information concerning the most Very Saintly now already Common Cosmic Individuum Ashiata Shiemash, relating to the three-brained beings arising and existing on that planet Earth which has pleased you.

"I have already more than once told you, that by the All-Gracious Command of Our OMNI-LOVING COMMON FATHER ENDLESSNESS, our Cosmic Highest Most Very Saintly Individuums sometimes actualize within the presence of some terrestrial three-brained being or other, a definitized conception of a sacred Individuum, in order that the latter, having become a terrestrial being with such a presence, might there on the spot 'orient himself' and give to the process of their ordinary being-existence, a corresponding new direction, just such a direction that thanks to it perhaps both the already crystallized consequences of the properties of the organ Kundabuffer and the predispositions to such new crystallizations could be removed from their presences.

"Well, namely, already seven centuries before the Babylonian events I have spoken of, there was just actualized in the planetary body of a three-brained being, a definitized conception of a sacred Individuum, named Ashiata Shiemash, who became there in his turn a Messenger from Above, and who is already now one of the Highest Most Very Saintly Common Cosmic Sacred Individuums.

"Ashiata Shiemash had his conception in the planetary body of a boy of a poor family descended from what is

- -

called the 'Sumerian Race,' in a small place then called 'Pispascana' and situated not far from Babylon.

"He grew up and became a responsible being partly in this small place and partly in Babylon itself, which was at that time, although not yet magnificent, even already an important city.

"The Very Saintly Ashiata Shiemash was the Unique Messenger from Above to your planet who firstly endeavored by his holy labors to create on that planet conditions in which the existence of its unfortunate beings for a certain time somewhat resembled the existence of the three-brained beings of the other planets of our great Universe on which beings exist with the same possibilities; and secondly, this Saint was the first on that planet Earth, who for the mission preassigned to him refused to employ the ordinary methods established during previous centuries for the three-brained beings of that planet by all the other Messengers sent from above.

"The Very Saintly Ashiata Shiemash taught nothing whatever to the ordinary three-brained beings of the Earth, nor did he preach anything to them, as was done before and after him by all the Messengers sent there from Above with the same aim.

"And in consequence chiefly of this, none of His teachings passed in any form from His contemporaries even to the third generation of ordinary beings there, not to mention the contemporary ordinary beings there.

"Definite information relating to His Very Saintly Activities passed from generation to generation from the contemporaries of the Very Saintly Ashiata Shiemash to the beings of the following generations through those called there 'initiates,' by means of a certain what is called 'Legominism' of His deliberations under the title of 'The Terror-of-the-Situation.'

"In addition to this, there has survived from the period

------------------------------ 348 ------------------------------

of His Very Saintly Activities and there still exists even till now, one of several what are called 'marble tablets' on which were engraved His 'counsels' and 'commandments' and 'sayings' to the beings contemporary with Him.

"And at the present time this surviving tablet is the chief sacred relic of a small group of initiated beings there, called the 'Brotherhood-Olbogmek,' whose place of existence is situated in the middle of the continent Asia.

"The name Olbogmek means, 'There are not different religions, there is only one God.'

"When I was personally on the surface of your planet for the last time, I happened by chance to become acquainted with the Legominism which transmits to the initiated men-beings of the planet Earth of remote generations these deliberations of the Saintly Ashiata Shiemash under the title of 'The Terror-of-the-Situation.'

"The Legominism was of great assistance to me in elucidating certain strange aspects of the psyche of these peculiar beings—just those strange aspects of their psyche which, with all my careful observations of them during tens of centuries, I had previously been unable to understand in any way whatsoever."

"My dear and beloved Grandfather, tell me, please, what does the word Legominism mean?" Hassein asked.

"This word Legominism," replied Beelzebub, "is given to one of the means existing there of transmitting from generation to generation information about certain events of long-past ages, through just those three-brained beings who are thought worthy to be and who are called initiates.

"This means of transmitting information from generation to generation had been devised by the beings of the continent Atlantis. For your better understanding of the said means of transmitting information to beings of succeeding generations by means of a Legominism, I must here

------------------------------ 349 ------------------------------

explain to you a little also about those beings there whom other beings called and call initiates.

"In former times there on the planet Earth, this word was always used in one sense only; and the three-brained beings there who were called initiates were those who had acquired in their presences almost equal objective data which could be sensed by other beings.

same aim.

"And in consequence of this, almost none of his teaching in any form passed from his contemporaries even to the third generation of ordinary beings there, not to mention the contemporary ordinary beings there.

"Definite information relating to his Very Saintly activities passed there from the contemporaries of the Very Saintly Ashiata Shiemash to the beings of the following generation, and from generation to generation thereafter through those there called 'Initiated' beings by means of a certain what is called 'Legominism' of his deliberations under the title of: 'The Terror of the Situation.'

"In addition to this, there has survived from the period

---

of his Very Saintly activities and there still exists even until now, what is called a marble tablet on which are graven his 'counsels and commandments' to the beings contemporary with him.

"Even at the present time this surviving tablet serves as the chief holy relic for a small group of initiated beings there, who are called the 'Olbogmek' Brotherhood, and whose place of existence is situated in the middle of the continent Asia.

"The name 'Olbogmek' means, 'There are not different religions, there is only one God.'

"With this 'Legominism' which transmits to the initiated men-beings of the planet Earth of remote generations these deliberations of the Saintly Ashiata Shiemash under the title of 'The Terror of the Situation,' I happened by chance to become acquainted when I was personally on the surface of your planet for the last time.

"This 'Legominism' was of great assistance to me in elucidating certain strange aspects of the psyche of these peculiar beings—just those strange aspects of their psyche which, with all my careful observations of them during tens of centuries, I had previously been unable to understand in any way whatsoever.

"My dear and beloved grandfather, tell me please what the word 'Legominism' means?" Hassein asked.

"This name 'Legominism,'" replied Beelzebub, "is given to one of the means existing there of transmitting from generation to generation information about certain events of long-past ages, through just those three-brained beings who are thought worthy to be and are called 'Initiates.'

"For your better understanding of the said means there, that is of transmitting information to beings of succeeding generations, by means of a 'Legominism,' I must here also tell a little about those beings there, whom other beings called and call 'Initiates.'

"In former times there on the planet Earth, this word was always used in one definite sense only; namely those three-brained beings there were called 'Initiates' who acquired in their presence almost the same objective data sensible to other beings. But during the last two centuries this word has come to be used there

"But during the last two centuries this word has come to be used there now in two senses:

"In one sense it is used for the same purpose as before, that is to say, those beings there are so named who became initiates thanks to their personal conscious labors and intentional sufferings; and thereby, as I have already told you, they acquire in themselves objective merits which can be sensed by other beings irrespective of brain-system, and which also evoke in others trust and respect.

"In the other sense, those beings call each other by this name who belong to those what are called there 'criminal gangs' which in the said period have greatly multiplied there and whose members have as their chief aim to 'steal' from those around them only 'essence-values.'

"Under the pretence of following 'supernatural' or 'mystic' sciences, these criminal gangs there are really occupied, and very successfully, with this kind of plunder.

"And so, any and every genuine member of such a gang there is called an initiate.

"There are even 'great-initiates' among these terrestrial initiates, and these great-initiates especially at the present time, are made out of those ordinary initiates of new formation who in their 'virtuoso-affairs' pass, as is said there, through 'fire-water-copper-pipes-and-even-through-all-the-roulette-halls-of-Monte-Carlo.'

"Well then, my boy, Legominism is the name given to the successive transmission of information about long-past events which have occurred on the planet Earth from

- *350* -

initiates to initiates of the first kind, that is, from really meritorious beings who have themselves received their information from similar meritorious beings.

"For having invented this means of transmitting information, we must give the beings of the continent Atlantis their due; this means was indeed very wise and did indeed attain their aim.

"This is the sole means by which information about certain events that proceeded in times long past has accurately reached the beings of remote later generations.

"As for the information which passed from generation to generation through the ordinary mass of beings of that planet, it has either completely disappeared, having been soon forgotten, or there remains of it, as our dear Mullah Nassr Eddin expresses it, only the 'tail-and-mane-and-food-for-Scheherazade.'

"Hence it is that when a few scraps of information about some event or other do happen to reach the beings of remote later generations, and the learned beings of new formation there concoct their 'hotchpotch' out of these scraps, there then occurs a most peculiar and most instructive 'phenomenon'; namely, when the cockroaches there chance to hear what is in this hotchpotch, 'the-evil-spirit-of-Saint-Vitus' existing there immediately enters their common presences and begins to rage quite merrily.

"How the contemporary learned beings of the planet Earth concoct their

already in two senses.

"In one sense it is used for the same purpose as before, that is, those beings there are so named who become initiates, thanks to their personal conscious labors and intentional sufferings, thanks also to which, as I have already told you, they acquire in themselves objective merits sensible to other beings, of any brain system, and which evoke trust and respect.

"In the other sense these beings call each other by this name who belong to what are there called robber gangs, which during the said period greatly multiplied there, and the members of which have as their chief aim to 'steal' from amongst their surroundings only 'essence values.'

"Under the pretence of following 'supernatural' or 'Mystic' sciences, these gangs of robbers there are really occupied, and very successfully, with this kind of plunder.

"And so it is any and every full-blown member of such a gang there, that is just called an 'Initiate.'

"There are even 'High Initiates' among them also, and these 'High Initiates,' especially at the present time, are made out of those ordinary 'Initiates' of 'new format,' who during their 'virtuoso' affairs, pass as it is also said there, through 'fire-water-copper-pipes-and-even-through-all-the-roulette-halls-of-Monte-Carlo.'

"Well then, my boy, a 'Legominism' is the name given to the transmission of information about long-past events which have occurred on the planet Earth from

- -

initiates to initiates of the first kind, that is, from really meritorious beings, who in their turn, have received the information from similar meritorious beings.

"This means of transmitting information was already invented by beings of the continent Atlantis, and, we must give them their due, this means was indeed very wise and did indeed attain their aim.

"This is the sole means by which information about certain events that proceeded in times long-past has correctly reached the beings of remote later generations.

"As for the information which passed from generation to generation through the ordinary mass of beings of that planet, it either completely disappeared, having been soon forgotten, or there remains of it, as our dear Mullah Nassr Eddin expressed himself, only the 'tail-and-mane-and-food-for-Scheherazade!'

"Hence it is that when a few scraps of information about some event or other do happen to reach the beings of remote later generations and the learned beings of 'new format' there, concoct their hotchpotch out of these scraps, there then occurs a most peculiar and most instructive 'phenomenon,' namely, when the cockroaches there chance to hear what is in this hotchpotch, there immediately enters into their general presence and starts off at full blast, what is called 'the-evil-spirit-of-Saint-Vitus,' which exists there.

"How the contemporary learned beings of the planet Earth concoct their hotchpotch from scraps of information which reach them is very well defined in one of the wise sentences of our dear Mullah Nassr Eddin, which consists of the following words: 'A flea exists in the World just for one thing—that when it sneezes, that deluge should occur with the description of which our learned beings love so much to busy themselves.'

"I must tell you that when I used to exist among your favorites it was always difficult for me to refrain, as your

------------------------------ *351* ------------------------------

favorites say, from 'laughter,' when one or another of the learned beings there delivered a 'lecture' or related to me personally about some past events, of which I had myself been an eyewitness.

"These lectures or 'stories' there are crammed with fictions so absurd that even if our Arch-cunning Lucifer or his assistants tried to invent them, they could not succeed."

------------------------------ *352* ------------------------------

hotchpotch from the scraps of information which reach them, is very well defined by one of the wise sentences of our dear Mullah Nassr Eddin; it consists of the following words: 'A flea exists in the world just for one thing . . . so that when it sneezes, that deluge should occur which our "learned beings" love so much the job of describing.'

"I must tell you that it was always difficult for me when I used to exist amongst your favorites to keep from laughing, as your

favorites say, when one or another of the 'learned beings' there delivered a 'lecture' or related to me personally about some past event of which I had myself been an eyewitness.

"These 'lectures' or stories there are crammed with fantasies so absurd that neither our arch-cunning Lucifer nor His staff could invent them if they tried."

The Legominism Concerning the Deliberations of the Very Saintly Ashiata Shiemash Under the Title of "The Terror-of-the-Situation"

THE 'Legominism,'" Beelzebub continued to speak, "through which the deliberations of the Very Saintly Ashiata Shiemash were transmitted, had the following contents:

"It began with the prayer:

"'In the name of the causes of my arising, I shall always strive to be just towards every already spiritualized origination, and towards all the originations of the future spiritualized manifestations of OUR COMMON CREATOR, ALMIGHTY AUTOCRAT ENDLESSNESS, Amen.

"'To me, a trifling particle of the whole of the GREAT WHOLE, it was commanded from Above to be coated with the planetary body of a three-centered being of this planet and to assist all other such beings arising and existing upon it to free themselves from the consequences of the properties of that organ which, for great and important reasons, was actualized in the presences of their ancestors.

"'All the sacred Individuals here before me, specially and intentionally actualized from Above, have always endeavored while striving for the same aim to accomplish the task laid upon them through one or other of those three sacred ways for self-perfecting, foreordained by OUR ENDLESS CREATOR HIMSELF, namely, through the sacred ways based on the being-impulses called "Faith," "Hope," and "Love."

"'When I completed my seventeenth year, I began as commanded from Above, to prepare my planetary body

------------------------------ *353* ------------------------------

in order, during my responsible existence, "to be able to be" impartial.

"'At this period of my "self-preparation," I had the intention upon reaching responsible age, of carrying out the task laid upon me, through one or other of the said three sacred being-impulses also.

"'But when during this period of my "self-preparation" I chanced to meet many beings of almost all "types" formed and existing here in the city of Babylon, and when during my impartial observations, I constated many traits of their being-manifestations, there crept into me and progressively increased an "essence-doubt" as to the possibilities of saving the three-centered beings of this planet by means of these three sacred ways.

"'The different manifestations of the beings I then encountered, which increased my doubts, gradually convinced me that these consequences of the properties of the organ Kundabuffer, having passed by heredity through a series of generations over a very long period of time, had ultimately so crystallized in their presences, that they now reached contemporary beings already as a lawful part of their essence, and hence these crystallized consequences of the properties of the

The Legominism Concerning The Deliberations Of The Very Saintly Ashiata Shiemash, Under The Title Of 'The Terror Of The Situation

"THE LEGOMINISM," Beelzebub continued to speak, "through which the deliberations of the Very Saintly Ashiata Shiemash were transmitted, had the following contents:

"It began with the following prayer:

"'In the Name of the causes of my arising, I shall strive always to be just towards every already spiritualized origination, and towards all the originations of the future spiritualized manifestations of OUR COMMON CREATOR, ALMIGHTY AUTOCRAT ENDLESSNESS, Amen.

"'To me, a trifling particle of the whole of the GREAT WHOLE, it was commanded from Above to be coated with the planetary body of a three-centered being of this planet and to assist all other such beings arising and existing upon it, in freeing themselves from the consequences of the properties of that organ which for great and important reasons was actualized in the presences of their ancestors.

"'All the sacred Individuums here before me, especially and intentionally actualized from Above, have always endeavored while striving for the same aim, to accomplish the task laid upon them through one or other of those three sacred paths for self-perfecting, foreordained by OUR ENDLESS CREATOR HIMSELF—namely, through the sacred paths based on the being-impulses called "Faith," "Hope" and "Love."

"'When I reached my seventeenth year, I began as commanded from Above, to prepare my planetary body

in order, during my responsible existence, 'to be able to be' impartial.

"'At this period of my self-preparation, I had the intention upon reaching responsible age, of carrying out the task laid upon me through one or other of the said three sacred being-impulses also.

"'But when during this period of my self-preparation, I chanced to meet many beings of almost all 'types' formed and existing here in the city of Babylon, and when during my impartial observations, I constated many traits of their being-manifestations, there crept into me and progressively increased a 'being-doubt' as to the possibilities of saving the three-centered beings of that planet by means of any of these three sacred paths.

"'The different manifestations of the beings I then encountered, which increased my doubts, gradually convinced me that these consequences of the properties of the organ Kundabuffer, having passed by inheritance through a series of generations over a very long period of time, had ultimately so crystallized in their presence, that they now reach contemporary beings already, as it were, as a lawful part of their essence, and hence these crystallized consequences of the properties

organ Kundabuffer are now, as it were, a "second nature" of their common presences.

"'So, when I finally became a responsible being, I decided that before making my choice among the mentioned sacred ways, I would bring my planetary body into the state of the sacred "Ksherknara," that is, into the state of "all-brained-balanced-being-perceptiveness," and only when already in that state, to choose the way for my further activities.

"'With this aim, I then ascended the mountain "Veziniama," where for forty days and nights I knelt on my knees and devoted myself to concentration.

"'A second forty days and nights I neither ate nor drank, but recalled and analyzed all the impressions present in me of all the perceptions I had acquired during my existence here, during the period of my "self-preparation."

- 354 -

"'A third forty days and nights I knelt on my knees and also neither ate nor drank, and every half-hour I plucked two hairs from my breast.

"'And only when, thereafter, I had finally attained complete freedom from all the bodily and spiritual associations of the impressions of ordinary life, I began to meditate how to BE.

"'These meditations of my purified Reason then made it categorically clear to me, that to save the contemporary beings by any of the sacred ways was already too late.

"'These meditations of mine made it categorically clear to me that all the genuine functions proper to man, being as they are, proper to all the three-centered beings of our Great Universe, had already degenerated in their remote ancestors into other functions, namely, into functions included among the properties of the organ Kundabuffer which were very similar to the genuine sacred being-functions of Faith, Love, and Hope.

"And this degeneration occurred in all probability in consequence of the fact that when the organ Kundabuffer had been destroyed in these ancestors, and they had also acquired in themselves factors for the genuine sacred being-impulses, then, as the taste of many of the properties of the organ Kundabuffer still remained in them, these properties of the organ Kundabuffer which resembled these three sacred impulses became gradually mixed with the latter, with the result that there were crystallized in their psyche the factors for the impulses Faith, Love, and Hope, which although similar to the genuine, were nevertheless somehow or other quite distinct.

"'The contemporary three-centered beings here do at times believe, love, and hope with their Reason

- 355 -

as well as with their feelings; but how they believe, how they love, and how they hope—ah, it is exactly in this that all the peculiarity of these three being-properties lies!

"'They also believe, but this sacred impulse in them does not function independently, as it does in general in all the three-centered beings existing on the various other planets of our Great Universe upon which beings with the same

of the organ Kundabuffer are now, as it were, a 'second nature' within their general presences.

"'So when I finally became a responsible being, I decided that before making my choice among the mentioned three sacred paths, I would bring my planetary body into the state of the sacred 'Ksherknara,' that is, into the state of all-brained-balanced-being-manifestation, and only when already in that state, to choose the path for my further actions.

"'With this aim, I then ascended the mountain "Veziniama," where for forty days and nights I knelt on my knees and devoted myself to concentration.

"'A second forty days and nights I neither ate nor drank, but recalled and analyzed all the impressions present in me of all the perceptions I had acquired during my existence here during the period of my self-preparation.

"'A third forty days and nights I knelt on my knees and also neither ate nor drank, and every half-hour I plucked two hairs from my breast.

"'And only when thereafter, I had finally attained complete freedom from all the bodily and spiritual associations of the impressions of ordinary life, I began to meditate how to be.

"'These meditations of my purified reason then made it categorically clear to me, that to save the contemporary beings by any one of the three sacred paths was already too late.

"'Just these meditations then made it categorically clear to me, that all the genuine functions proper to men being, as they are, proper to all the three-centered beings of Our Great Universe, had already in their remote ancestors degenerated into other functions, namely, into functions included in the number of the properties of the organ Kundabuffer which were very similar to the genuine sacred being-functions of "Faith," "Love" and "Hope."

"'And this degeneration occurred in all probability in consequence of this, that when the organ Kundabuffer had been destroyed in these ancestors and they had also acquired in themselves factors of the genuine sacred being-impulses, the taste of many of the properties of the organ Kundabuffer still remained in them and those properties of the organ Kundabuffer which resembled these three sacred impulses became gradually mixed with the latter, with the result that there were crystallized in their psyche the factors for the impulses "Faith," "Love" and "Hope," which although similar to the genuine, were nevertheless somehow or other utterly exotic.

"'The contemporary three-centered beings here do at times believe, they do love and they do hope, both with their

reason and with their feelings, but how they believe, how they love and how they hope—ah, it is exactly in this, that all the eccentricity of these three being-properties lies.

"'They also believe, but this impulse in them functions not independently, as in general it does in all the three-centered beings existing on the various other planets of our Great Universe, upon which beings with the same possibilities breed;

possibilities breed; but it arises dependent upon some or other factors, which have been formed in their common presences, owing as always to the same consequences of the properties of the organ Kundabuffer—as or instance, the particular properties arising in them which they call "vanity," "self-love," "pride," "self-conceit," and so forth.

"'In consequence of this, the three-brained beings here are for the most part subject just to the perceptions and fixations in their presences of all sorts of "Sinkrpoosarams" or, as it is expressed here, they "believe-any-old-tale."

"'It is perfectly easy to convince beings of this planet of anything you like, provided only during their perceptions of these "fictions," there is evoked in them and there proceeds, either consciously from without, or automatically by itself, the functioning of one or another corresponding consequence of the properties of the organ Kundabuffer crystallized in them from among those that form what is called the "subjectivity" of the given being, as for instance: "self-love," "vanity," "pride," "swagger," "imagination," "bragging," "arrogance," and so on.

"'From the influence of such actions upon their degenerated Reason and on the degenerated factors in their localizations, which factors actualize their being-sensations, not only is there crystallized a false conviction concerning the mentioned fictions, but thereafter in all sincerity and faith, they will even vehemently prove to those around them that it is just so and can in no way be otherwise.

------------------------------ *356* ------------------------------

"'In an equally abnormal form were data moulded in them for evoking the sacred impulse of love.

"'In the presences of the beings of contemporary times, there also arises and is present in them as much as you please of that strange impulse which they call love; but this love of theirs is firstly also the result of certain crystallized consequences of the properties of the same Kundabuffer; and secondly this impulse of theirs arises and manifests itself in the process of every one of them entirely subjectively; so subjectively and so differently that if ten of them were asked to explain how they sensed this inner impulse of theirs, then all ten of them—if, of course, they for once replied sincerely, and frankly confessed their genuine sensations and not those they had read about somewhere or had obtained from somebody else—all ten would reply differently and describe ten different sensations.

"'One would explain this sensation in the sexual sense; another in the sense of pity; a third in the sense of desire for submission; a fourth, in a common craze for outer things, and so on and so forth; but not one of the ten could describe even remotely, the sensation of genuine Love.

"'And none of them would, because in none of the ordinary beings-men here has there ever been, for a long time, any sensation of the sacred being-impulse of genuine Love. And without this "taste" they cannot even vaguely describe that most beatific sacred being-impulse in the presence of every three-centered being of the whole Universe, which, in accordance with the divine foresight of Great Nature, forms those data in us, from the result of the experiencing of which we can blissfully rest from the meritorious labors actualized by us for the purpose of

but it arises dependently upon these or other factors, which have been formed in their general presence, owing as always to the same consequences of the properties of the organ Kundabuffer; as for instance, the particular properties arising in them which they call "vanity," "self-love," "pride," "self-conceit," and so forth.

"'In consequence of this, the three-brained beings here are for the most part subject just to the perceptions and fixations in their presences of all sorts of 'Sinkrpoosarams' or, as it is expressed here, they 'believe-in-any-old-lie.'

"'It is perfectly easy to convince beings of this planet of anything you like, provided only that during their perceptions of these 'fictions,' there is evoked in them and there proceeds, either consciously from without, or automatically by itself, the functioning of one or another corresponding consequences of the properties of the organ Kundabuffer crystallized in them from among the number of those that formed what is called the 'personality' of the given being; as for instance, "self-love," "pride," "vanity," "swagger," "imagination," "bragging," "arrogance" and so on.

"'From the influence of such actions upon their degenerated reason and upon the localization of the degenerate factors which actualize their being-sensations, not only is there crystallized a false conviction concerning the mentioned fictions, but thereafter in all sincerity and faith, they will even vehemently prove to those around them that it is just so and can in no way be otherwise.

- -

"'In an equally abnormal form, the data were molded in them for evoking the sacred impulse, 'Love.'

"'In the presences of the beings of contemporary times, there also arises and is present in them as much as you please of that strange impulse which they call 'love'; but this strange love of theirs is firstly also the result of certain crystallized consequences of the properties of the same Kundabuffer; and secondly this impulse of theirs arises and manifests itself in the presence of every one of them entirely subjectively—so subjectively and so differently that if ten of them were asked to explain how they sensed this inner impulse of theirs, then all ten of them—if, of course, they for once replied sincerely and frankly confessed their genuine sensations and not those they had read about somewhere or had got from somebody else—then all ten would reply differently and describe ten different sensations.

"'One would explain this sensation in the sexual sense, another in the sense of pity, a third in the sense of desire for submission, a fourth, in common interests regarding outer things, and so on and so forth; but not one of the ten could describe even remotely the sensation of genuine love.

"'And none of them could, because in none of the ordinary men-beings here has there ever been, already for a long time, any sensation of the sacred being-impulse of genuine Love. And without this "taste" they cannot even vaguely describe that most beatific sacred being-impulse in the presence of every three-centered being of the whole Universe, which, in accordance with the divine foresight of Great Nature, forms those data in us from the results of the experiencing of which we can blissfully rest from the meritorious labors actualized by us

self-perfection.

"'Here, in these times, if one of those three-brained

------------------------------ *357* ------------------------------

beings "loves" somebody or other, then he loves him either because the latter always encourages and undeservingly flatters him; or because his nose is much like the nose of that female or male, with whom thanks to the cosmic law of "polarity" or "type" a relation has been established which has not yet been broken; or finally, he loves him only because the latter's uncle is in a big way of business and may one day give him a boost, and so on and so forth.

"'But never do beings-men here love with genuine, impartial and non-egoistic love.

"'Thanks to this kind of love in the contemporary beings here, their hereditary predispositions to the crystallizations of the consequences of the properties of the organ Kundabuffer are crystallized at the present time without hindrance, and finally become fixed in their nature as a lawful part of them.

"'And as regards the third sacred being-impulse, namely, "essence-hope," its plight in the presences of the three-centered beings here is even worse than with the first two.

"'Such a being-impulse has not only finally adapted itself in them to the whole of their presences in a distorted form, but this maleficent strange "hope" newly formed in them, which has taken the place of the being-impulse of Sacred Hope, is now already the principal reason why factors can no longer be acquired in them for the functioning of the genuine being-impulses of Faith, Love, and Hope.

"'In consequence of this newly-formed-abnormal hope of theirs, they always hope in something; and thereby all those possibilities are constantly being paralyzed in them, which arise in them either intentionally from without or accidentally by themselves, which possibilities could perhaps still destroy in their presences their hereditary

------------------------------ *358* ------------------------------

predispositions to the crystallizations of the consequences of the properties of the organ Kundabuffer.

"'When I returned from the mountain Veziniama to the city of Babylon, I continued my observations in order to make it clear whether it was not possible somehow or other to help these unfortunates in some other way.

"'During the period of my year of special observations on all of their manifestations and perceptions, I made it categorically clear to myself that although the factors for engendering in their presences the sacred being-impulses of Faith, Hope, and Love are already quite degenerated in the beings of this planet, nevertheless, the factor which ought to engender that being-impulse on which the whole psyche of beings of a three-brained system is in general based, and which impulse exists under the name of Objective-Conscience, is not yet atrophied in them, but remains in their presences almost in its primordial state.

"'Thanks to the abnormally established conditions of external ordinary being-existence existing here, this factor has gradually penetrated and become embed-

for the purpose of self-perfection.

"'Here, in these times, if one of these three-brained

beings "loves" somebody or other, then he "loves" him either because the latter always encourages and flatters him, or because his nose is much like the nose of that female or male, with whom, thanks to the cosmic law of "polarity" or "type," a relation has been established which has not yet been broken, or finally he "loves" him only because the latter's uncle is in a big way of business and may one day give him a boost, and so on and so forth.

"'But never do men-beings here love with genuine impartial and non-egoistic love.

"'Thanks to this kind of love present in the contemporary beings here, their hereditary predispositions to the crystallizations of the consequences of the properties of the organ Kundabuffer are crystallized at the present time already without hindrance, and finally become fixed in their nature as a lawful part of them.

"'And as regards the third sacred being-impulse, namely, "Hope," its plight in the presences of the three-centered beings here is even worse than with the first two.

"'Such a being-impulse has not only in its distorted form finally adapted itself in them to the whole of their presences, but this maleficent strange "hope" newly formed in them which has taken the place of the being-impulse of the sacred Hope, is now already the principal reason why they can no longer acquire in themselves the data for the functioning of the genuine being-impulses of "Faith," "Love" and "Hope."

"'In consequence of this, and owing to this newly formed abnormal "hope" of theirs they always hope in something; and on this account all those possibilities are constantly being paralyzed in them which arise in them either intentionally from without or accidentally by themselves; and which possibilities could perhaps still destroy in their presences their hereditary

predispositions to the crystallization of the consequences of the properties of the organ Kundabuffer.

"'When I returned from the mountain Veziniama to the city Babylon, I continued my observations in order to make it clear whether it was not possible somehow or other to help these unfortunates in some other way.

"'During the period of my year of special observations of every variety of their manifestations and perceptions, I made it categorically clear to myself, that although the data for evoking in their presences the sacred being-impulses of "Faith," "Hope" and "Love" are already quite degenerated in the beings of this planet, nevertheless the factor for producing that being-impulse on which the whole psyche of beings of a three-brained system is in general based, and which impulse exists under the name of "Objective-Conscience" is not yet atrophied in them, and it remains in their presence almost in its primordial state. Thanks to the abnormally established conditions of external ordinary being-existence here, this factor has gradually penetrated and become embedded in that consciousness ded in that consciousness which is here called "subconsciousness," in consequence of which it takes no part whatever in the functioning of their ordinary consciousness.

"'Well, then, it was just then that I indubitably understood with all the separate ruminating parts representing the whole of my "I," that if the functioning of that being-factor still surviving in their common presences were to participate in the general functioning of that consciousness of theirs in which they pass their daily, as they here say, "waking-existence," only then would it still be possible to save the contemporary three-brained beings here from the consequences of the properties of that organ which was intentionally implanted into their first ancestors.

"'My further meditations then confirmed for me that

- *359* -

it would be possible to attain this only if their general being-existence were to flow for a long time under foreseeingly-corresponding conditions.

"'When all the above-mentioned was completely transubstantiated in me, I decided to consecrate the whole of myself from that time on to the creation here of such conditions that the functioning of the "sacred-conscience" still surviving in their subconsciousness might gradually pass into the functioning of their ordinary consciousness.

"'May the blessing of OUR ALMIGHTY OMNI-LOVING COMMON FATHER UNI-BEING CREATOR ENDLESSNESS be upon my decision, Amen.'

"Thus ended the Legominism concerning the deliberations of the Very Saintly Incomparable Ashiata Shiemash, under the title of 'The Terror-of-the-Situation.'

"So, my boy, when, as I have already told you, early in my last descent in person onto the surface of your planet, I first became acquainted in detail with this Legominism which I have just repeated, and had at once become interested in the deductions of this later Most High Very Saintly Common Cosmic Individual Ashiata Shiemash, there existed neither any other Legominisms nor any other sources of information concerning His further Very Saintly Activities among those favorites of yours, so I then decided to investigate in detail and without fail to make clear to myself which were the measures He took and how He subsequently actualized them, in order to help these unfortunates to deliver themselves from the consequences of the properties of the organ Kundabuffer which had passed to them by heredity and were so maleficent for them.

"And so, as one of my chief tasks during this last sojourn of mine in person there, on the surface of your planet, I made a detailed investigation and elucidation of the whole of the further Very Saintly Activities there among your favorites of that Great Essence-loving now

- *360* -

Most High Very Saintly Common Cosmic Individual Ashiata Shiemash.

"And as regards that 'marble tablet' which has by chance survived since the time of the Very Saintly Activities of the Great Ashiata Shiemash, and is now there the principal sacred relic of the brotherhood of the initiated beings called the Brotherhood-Olbogmek, I happened to see and read the contents engraved on it during this last sojourn of mine there.

which is here called "subconsciousness," in consequence of which it takes no part whatever in the functioning of their ordinary consciousness.

"'Well, it was just then that I understood for a surety with all the separate ruminating parts representing the whole of my 'I,' that only if the functioning of this being-factor still surviving in the whole of their presence were to participate in the general functioning of that consciousness of theirs in which they pass their daily, as they here say, "waking-existence," only then would it still be possible to save the contemporary three-brained beings here from the consequences of the properties of that organ which was intentionally introjected into their first ancestors.

"'My further mediations then confirmed for me that

---

this would be possible only if their general being-existence were to flow for a long time under foreseeingly corresponding conditions.

"'When all the above-mentioned was completely transubstantiated in me, I decided to consecrate the whole of myself from that time forward to the creation here of such conditions, that the functioning of the "sacred-conscience" still safely surviving in their subconsciousness, might gradually pass into the functioning of their ordinary consciousness.

"'May the blessing of our ALMIGHTY OMNI-LOVING COMMON FATHER UNI-BEING ENDLESS CREATOR be upon my decision, Amen!'

"Thus ended the 'Legominism' concerning the deliberations of the Very Saintly Incomparable Ashiata Shiemash, under the title of 'The Terror of the Situation.'

"So, my boy, when, as I have already told you, early in my last personal descent on the surface of your planet, I first became acquainted in detail with this 'Legominism' which I have just repeated, and had at once become interested in the deductions of this later Most High Very Saintly Common Cosmic Individuum Ashiata Shiemash, as there existed neither any other 'Legominism' nor any other sources of information concerning his further Very Saintly activities among these favorites of yours—I then decided to investigate in detail and without fail to make clear to myself, which were the measures he took and how he subsequently actualized them, in order to help these unfortunates to deliver themselves from the consequences of the properties of the organ Kundabuffer which had passed to them by inheritance and were so maleficent for them.

"And so, as one of my chief tasks during this last personal stay of mine there on the surface of your planet, I made a detailed investigation and elucidation of the whole of the further Very Saintly activities there among your favorites, of that great essence-loving now

---

Most High very saintly common-cosmic Individuum Ashiata Shiemash.

"And as regards that 'marble tablet' which by chance has remained intact since the time of the Very Saintly activities of the great Ashiata Shiemash, and now serves there as the principal sacred relic of the brotherhood of the initiated beings there called the 'Olbogmek Brotherhood,' I happened to see and read, during this last stay of mine there, the contents of what was carved on that marble.

"During my subsequent elucidations it turned out that later on, when this Very Saintly Ashiata Shiemash had established there the particular conditions of ordinary being-existence which He had planned, several of these tablets were, on His advice and initiative, set up in corresponding places of many of the large towns, and there were engraved upon them all kinds of sayings and counsels for corresponding existence.

"But when their big wars later on again began, all these tablets were also destroyed by these strange beings themselves, and only one of them, namely, that one now with these brethren, somehow survived, as I have already told you, and is now the property of this Brotherhood.

"On this still surviving marble were inscriptions concerning the sacred being-impulses called Faith, Love, and Hope, namely:

"'Faith,' 'Love,' and 'Hope'

Faith of consciousness is freedom
Faith of feeling is weakness
Faith of body is stupidity.

Love of consciousness evokes the same in response
Love of feeling evokes the opposite
Love of body depends only on type and polarity.

Hope of consciousness is strength
Hope of feeling is slavery
Hope of body is disease.

---------------------------------- 361 ----------------------------------

"Before continuing to tell you more about the activities of the Very Saintly Ashiata Shiemash for the welfare of your favorites, I must, I think, elucidate to you, a little more in detail, that inner impulse which is called there by your favorites Hope, and concerning which the Very Saintly Ashiata Shiemash constated that the case is worse than with the other two.

"And the personal observations and investigations I later specially made, regarding this said strange impulse present in them, clearly showed me that in truth the factors for engendering this abnormal impulse in their presences are most maleficent for them themselves.

"Thanks to this abnormal hope of theirs a very singular and most strange disease, with a property of evolving, arose and exists among them there even until now—a disease called there 'tomorrow.'

"This strange disease 'tomorrow' brought with it terrifying consequences, and particularly for those unfortunate three-brained beings there who chance to learn and to become categorically convinced with the whole of their presence that they possess some very undesirable consequences for the deliverance from which they must make certain efforts, and which efforts moreover they even know just how to make, but owing to this maleficent disease 'tomorrow' they never succeed in making these required efforts.

"During my subsequent elucidations it proved that later on, after this Very Saintly Ashiata Shiemash had established there the particular conditions of ordinary being-existence which he had planned, several of these tablets were on his advice and initiative, then set up in corresponding places of many of the large towns, and carved upon them were all kinds of sayings and counsels for corresponding existence.

"But when their big wars later on again began, all these tablets were also destroyed by these strange beings themselves, and only one of them, namely that one now with these brethren, somehow remained intact, as I have already told you, and is now the property of this 'Brotherhood.'

"On this marble still surviving whole were inscriptions concerning the sacred being-impulses called 'Faith,' 'Love' and 'Hope.'

"On this marble there was carved as follows:

Faith, Love and Hope

Faith of consciousness is freedom,
Faith of feeling is weakness,
Faith of body is stupidity.

Love of consciousness evokes the same in response,
Love of feeling evokes the opposite,
Love of body depends on type and polarity.

Hope of consciousness is strength,
Hope of feeling is slavery,
Hope of body is disease.

- -

"Before continuing to tell you more about the activities of the Very Saintly Ashiata Shiemash for the welfare of your favorites, I must I think elucidate to you, a little more in detail, that inner impulse which is called there by your favorites, 'Hope,' and concerning which, the Very Saintly Ashiata Shiemash constated that the case is worse than with the two first ones.

"And the personal observations and investigations I later specially made regarding this said strange impulse present in them, clearly showed me that in truth the data for evoking in their presences this abnormal impulse are most maleficent for themselves.

"Thanks to this abnormal hope of theirs a very singular and most strange disease with its own property of evolving arose and exists among them there even until now—a disease called there 'tomorrow.'

"This strange disease 'tomorrow' brought with it terrible consequences and particularly for those unfortunate three-brained beings there, who chance to learn and to become categorically convinced with the whole of their presence that they contain some very undesirable consequences for the deliverance from which they must make certain efforts, and which efforts moreover they even know just how to make.

"And this is just the maleficent part of all that great terrifying evil, which, owing to various causes great and small, is concentrated in the process of the ordinary being-existence of these pitiable three-brained beings; and by putting off from 'tomorrow' till 'tomorrow,' those unfortunate beings there who do by chance learn all about what I have mentioned are also deprived of the possibility of ever attaining anything real.

"This strange and for your favorites maleficent disease

------------------------------ *362* ------------------------------

'tomorrow' has already become a hindrance for the beings of contemporary times, not only because they have been totally deprived of all possibilities of removing from their presences the crystallized consequences of the properties of the organ Kundabuffer, but it had also become a hindrance to most of them in honestly discharging at least those being-obligations of theirs which have become quite indispensable in the already established conditions of ordinary being-existence.

"Thanks to the disease 'tomorrow,' the three-brained beings there, particularly the contemporary ones, almost always put off till 'later' everything that needs to be done at the moment, being convinced that 'later' they will do better and more.

"Owing to the said maleficent disease 'tomorrow' most of those unfortunate beings there who accidentally or owing to a conscious influence from without, become aware through their Reason in them of their complete nullity and begin to sense it with all their separate spiritualized parts, and who also chance to learn which and in what way, being-efforts must be made in order to become such as it is proper for three-brained beings to be, also, by putting off from 'tomorrow' till 'tomorrow,' almost all arrive at the point that on one sorrowful day for themselves, there arise in them and begin to be manifest those forerunners of old age called 'feebleness' and 'infirmity,' which are the inevitable lot of all cosmic formations great and small toward the end of their completed existence.

"Here I must without fail tell you also about that strange phenomenon which I constated there during my observations and studies of the almost entirely degenerated presences of those favorites of yours; namely, I definitely constated that in many of them, toward the end of their planetary existence, most of the consequences of the properties

------------------------------ *363* ------------------------------

of that same organ which had become crystallized in their common presences begin to atrophy of their own accord and some of them even entirely disappear, in consequence of which these beings begin to see and sense reality a little better.

"In such cases a strong desire appears in the common presences of such favorites of yours, to work upon themselves, to work as they say, for the 'salvation-of-their-soul.'

"But needless to say, nothing can result from such desires of theirs just because it is already too late for them, the time given them for this purpose by Great

"But they too fail to make these required efforts and all on account of that maleficent disease 'tomorrow'; and this is just the maleficent part of all that great terrifying evil, which, owing to various causes great and small, is concentrated in the processes of the ordinary being-existence of these pitiable three-brained beings, since those unfortunate beings there who do by chance learn all about what I have mentioned, postponing from 'tomorrow' until 'tomorrow,' are also deprived of the possibility of ever attaining anything real.

"This strange and for your favorites maleficent disease

'tomorrow' has already become a hindrance for the beings of contemporary times, not only in regard to this, that these favorites of yours have finally lost any possibility of removing from their presences the crystallized consequences of the properties of the organ Kundabuffer, but it has also become a hindrance to most of them in honestly discharging at any rate those being-duties of theirs which have become indispensable in the already established conditions of ordinary being-existence.

"Thanks to the disease 'tomorrow,' the three-brained beings there, particularly the contemporary ones, almost always postpone until 'later' everything that needs to be done at the given moment, being convinced that 'later' they will do better and more.

"On account of the said maleficent disease 'tomorrow,' the majority of those unfortunate beings there who accidentally or owing to a conscious suggestion from without, become aware of their complete nothingness through the reason present in them and begin to sense it with all their separate spiritualized parts, and also chance to learn which and in what way, being-efforts must be made in order that they may become what it is proper for three-brained beings to be— then thanks also to the said maleficent disease of postponing from 'tomorrow' until 'tomorrow' they almost all arrive at the point that on one sorrowful day for themselves, there arise in them and begin to show those forerunners of old age called 'feebleness' and 'infirmity,' which are the inevitable lot of all cosmic formations great and small at the close of their fulfilled being.

"Here I must without fail tell you also about that strange phenomenon which I constated there during my observations and studies of the almost entirely degenerated presence of these favorites of yours; namely, I definitely constated that in many of them, towards the close of their planetary existence, most of the crystallized consequences of the properties of that same organ—which are consequently

present in the whole of their presence—begin to decay of their own accord and some of them even entirely disappear, in consequence of which these beings begin to see and sense reality a little more truly.

"In such cases a strong desire appears in the whole of the presence of such favorites of yours, to work upon themselves, to work as they say, for the 'salvation of their souls.'

"But needless to say, nothing can result from such desires of theirs just on account of this, that it is already too late for them, the time given then for this pur-

Nature having already passed; and although they see and feel the necessity of actualizing the required being-efforts, yet for the fulfillment of such desires of theirs, they have now only ineffectual yearnings and the 'lawful-infirmities-of-old-age.'

"And so, my boy, my researches and investigations concerning the further activities of the Very Saintly Ashiata Shiemash for the welfare of the three-brained beings arising and existing on this planet of yours eventually made the following clear to me.

"When this great and, by His Reason, almost incomparable Sacred Individual became fully convinced that the ordinary sacred ways which exist for the purpose of self-perfection for all the three-brained beings of the Universe, were no longer suitable for the beings of this planet, He then, after His year of special observation and studies of their psyche, again ascended to that same mountain Veziniama, and during several terrestrial months contemplatively pondered in which way He could actualize His decision, that is, to save the beings of this planet from those hereditary predispositions to the crystallizations of the consequences of the properties of the organ Kundabuffer, by means of those data which survived in their

- 364 -

subconsciousness for the fundamental sacred being-impulse, Conscience.

"These ponderings of His then first of all fully convinced Him that though it were indeed possible to save them by means of the data which survived in their common presences for engendering this sacred being-impulse, nevertheless, it would only be possible if the manifestations of these data which survived in their subconsciousness were to participate without fail in the functioning of that consciousness of theirs, under the direction of which their daily-waking existence flows, and furthermore if this being-impulse were to be manifested over a long period through every aspect of this consciousness of theirs."

- 365 -

pose by Great Nature having already passed; and although they see and feel the necessity of actualizing the required being-efforts, yet for the fulfillment of such desires of theirs, they have now only ineffectual yearnings and the lawful infirmities of old age.

"And so, my boy, my researches and investigations concerning the further activities of the Very Saintly Ashiata Shiemash for the welfare of the three-brained beings arising and existing on this planet of yours eventually made the following clear to me.

"When this great, and in point of Reason, almost incomparable sacred Individuum became finally convinced that the ordinary sacred paths which exist for the purpose of self-perfection for all the three-brained beings of the Universe, were already no longer suitable for the beings of this planet Earth, he then, after his year of now special observations and studies of their psyche, again ascended to that same mountain Veziniama, and during several terrestrial months pondered in which way he could actualize his decision; that is, to save the beings of this planet from those inherited predispositions to the crystallizations of the consequences of the properties of the organ Kundabuffer, by means of those data

which remained whole in their subconsciousness for the fundamental sacred being-impulse, Conscience.

"These ponderings of his then first of all finally convinced him, that although it was indeed possible to save them by means of those data which remained in the whole of their presence for bringing forth the sacred being-impulse, nevertheless it would only be possible in the event that the manifestations of that which remained whole in their subconsciousness should without fail participate in the functioning of that consciousness of theirs under the direction of which their daily waking existence flows, and furthermore if this being-impulse were to be manifested through every aspect of this consciousness of theirs over a long period."

The Organization for Man's Existence Created by the Very Saintly Ashiata Shiemash

BEELZEBUB continued to relate further as follows:
"My further researches and investigations also cleared up for me that after the Very Saintly Ashiata Shiemash had pondered on the mountain Veziniama and had formulated in his mind a definite plan for his further Most Saintly Activities, he did not again return to the city of Babylon but went straight to the capital city Djoolfapal of the country then called Kurlandtech, which was situated in the middle of the continent Asia.

"There he first of all established relations with the 'brethren' of the then existing brotherhood 'Tchaftantouri'—a name signifying 'To-be-or-not-to-be-at-all'—which had its quarters not far from that city.

"This said brotherhood was founded five of their years before the arrival there of the Very Saintly Ashiata Shiemash on the initiative of two genuine terrestrial initiates, who had become initiates according to the principles existing, as it was then said there, before the Ashiatian epoch.

"The name of one of these two terrestrial three-brained beings of that time, who had become genuine initiates there, was 'Poundolero' and of the other 'Sensimiriniko.'

"I must remark by the way, that both of these two terrestrial genuine initiates of that time had already by then 'coated' in their common presences their higher being-parts to the gradation called 'completion' and hence they had time during their further existence to perfect these higher parts of theirs to the required gradation of Sacred Objective Reason, and now their perfected higher being-parts have even 'become worthy' to have and already now have the place of their further existence on the holy planet Purgatory.

------------------------------ *366* ------------------------------

"According to my latest investigations, when, in all the separate spiritualized parts of the common presences of these two three-brained beings of that period, Poundolero and Sensimiriniko, there arose and was continuously sensed the suspicion, which later became a conviction, that, owing to some obviously nonlawful causes, 'something-very-undesirable' for them personally had been acquired and had begun to function in their general organization and that at the same time it was possible for this something-very-undesirable to be removed from themselves by means of their own data within themselves, they then sought several other beings like themselves who were striving for this same aim, in order together to try to achieve the removal from themselves of this said something-very-undesirable.

"And when they soon found beings responding to this aim amongst what are called the 'monks' of places called 'monasteries' of which there were already many of that period in the environs of the town Djoolfapal, they together with these monks chosen by them, founded the said 'brotherhood.'

The Kind Of Organization For Man's Existence Created By The Very Saintly Ashiata Shiemash

BEELZEBUB continued to relate further as follows:

"My further researches and investigations cleared up for me that after the Very Saintly Ashiata Shiemash had pondered on the Mountain Veziniama and formulated in his mind a definite plan for his further Most Saintly activities, he did not again return to the city Babylon but went straight to the capital city Djool-fapal of the country called Kurlandtech, which was situated in the middle of the continent Asia.

"There he first of all established relations with the 'brethren' of the then existing brotherhood 'Tchaftantouri,' a name signifying 'To-Be-or-To-Be-Not,' which had its quarters not far from that city.

"This said brotherhood was founded five of their years before the arrival there of the Very Saintly Ashiata Shiemash, on the initiative of two genuine terrestrial initiates, who had become initiates according to the principals existing, as it is said there, before the Ashiatian epoch.

"The name of one of these two terrestrial three-brained beings of that time, who had become genuine initiates there, was Poundolero and of the other, Sensimiriniko.

"Here it is necessary to notice also that just each of these two terrestrial genuine initiates of that time had already by that time the 'coating' in their general presences of their higher being-parts to the gradation called 'fulfillment,' and they had then time during their further existence to perfect these higher parts of theirs to the required gradation of the Holy Objective Reason, so that their perfected higher being-parts even became worthy to have, and also now have, the place of their further existence on the holy planet Purgatory.

- -

"Concerning these two initiated beings, my further detailed investigations cleared up for me, that when, in all the separate spiritualized parts of the general presence of these two three-brained beings of that period, namely Poundolero and Sensimiriniko, there arose and was continuously sensed the suspicion, which later became a conviction, that owing to some obviously non-lawful causes 'something very undesirable' for them personally had been acquired in their general organization and was functioning there, and at the same time that it was possible for this 'something very undesirable' to be removed from themselves by means of their own possibilities existing in them, they then decided to find other beings like themselves who were striving for this same aim, and together to try to achieve the removal from themselves of this said 'something very undesirable.'

"They soon found beings responding to this aim amongst what were called the monks of places called monasteries, of which there were already many at that period in the environs of the town Djoolfapal.

"And with these monks chosen by them they first founded the mentioned

"And so, after arriving in the town Djoolfapal, the Very Saintly Ashiata Shiemash established corresponding relations with these brethren of the mentioned brotherhood who were working upon that abnormally proceeding functioning of their psyche which they themselves had constated, and he began enlightening their Reason by means of objectively true information, and guiding their being-impulses in such a way that they could sense these truths without the participation either of the abnormally crystallized factors already within their presences, or of the factors which might newly arise from the results of

_____ 367 _____

the external perceptions they obtained from the abnormally established form of ordinary being-existence.

"While enlightening the brethren of the said brotherhood in the mentioned way and discussing his suppositions and intentions with them, the Very Saintly Ashiata Shiemash occupied himself at the same time in drawing up what are called the 'rules,' or, as it is also said there, 'statutes,' for this brotherhood, which he, in association with these brethren he initiated of the former brotherhood Tchaftantouri, founded in the town Djoolfapal and which later was called the brotherhood 'Heechtvori,' which signified 'Only-he-will-be-called-and-will-become-the-Son-of-God-who-acquires-in-himself-Conscience.'

"Later, when, with the participation of these brethren of the former brotherhood Tchaftantouri, everything had been worked out and organized, the Very Saintly Ashiata Shiemash sent these same brethren to various places and commissioned them under his general guidance to spread the information that in the subconsciousness of people there are crystallized and are always present the data manifested from Above for engendering in them the Divine impulse of genuine conscience, and that only he who acquires the 'ableness' that the actions of these data participate in the functioning of that consciousness of theirs in which they pass their everyday existence, has in the objective sense the honest right to be called and really to be a genuine son of our COMMON FATHER CREATOR of all that exists.

"These brethren then preached this objective truth at first chiefly among the monks of the mentioned monasteries—many of which, as I have already said, existed in the environs of the town itself.

"The result of these preachings of theirs was that they first of all selected thirty-five serious and well-prepared

_____ 368 _____

what are called 'novices' of this first brotherhood Heechtvori, which they founded in the city Djoolfapal.

"Thereafter, the Very Saintly Ashiata Shiemash, while continuing to enlighten the minds of the former brethren of the brotherhood Tchaftantouri, then began with the help of these brethren to enlighten the Reason of those thirty-five novices also.

"So it continued during the whole of one of their years; and only after this did

'brotherhood.'

"And so, after arriving in the town Djoolfapal, the Very Saintly Ashiata Shiemash established corresponding relations with these brethren of the mentioned brotherhood who were already working upon that abnormally proceeding functioning of their psyche which they themselves had constated, and he began enlightening their reason by means of objectively true information, and guiding their being-impulses in such a way that they could sense these truths without the participation either of the abnormally crystallized data already contained in their presences, or of the data newly arising from the results of

the exterior perceptions they received from the abnormally established form of ordinary being-existence.

"While enlightening the brethren of the said brotherhood in the mentioned way and discussing his suppositions and intentions with them, the Very Saintly Ashiata Shiemash was occupied at the same time in drawing up what are called the 'rules,' or, as it is said there, 'statutes,' for this brotherhood, which in association with those brethren he initiated, the former brethren of the brotherhood Tchaftantouri, founded in the town Djoolfapal, and which later was called the 'Brotherhood Heechtvori,' signifying 'Only he will be called and will become the Son of God who acquires Conscience in himself.'

"Later, when with the participation of these brethren of the former brotherhood Tchaftantouri, everything had been worked out and organized, the Very Saintly Ashiata Shiemash sent these same brethren to various places and commissioned them under his general guidance to spread the information that in people, namely, in their 'subconsciousness,' there are crystallized and are always present the data manifested from Above for giving birth in them to the divine impulse of genuine conscience, and that only he who acquires such 'ableness' that the activities of these 'data' participate in the functioning of that consciousness of theirs in which they pass their everyday existence, has in the objective sense, the honest right to be called and really to be a genuine Son of our COMMON FATHER CREATOR of all that exists.

"These brethren preached this objective truth at first chiefly among the monks of the mentioned monasteries, many of which, as I have already said, existed in the environs of the town Djoolfapal, and later among the ordinary inhabitants of the town itself.

"The first result of these preachings of theirs was that they selected thirty-five serious and well prepared

what are called 'novices' of this first brotherhood 'Heechtvori,' which they founded in the city of Djoolfapal.

"Thereafter, the Very Saintly Ashiata Shiemash while continuing to enlighten the minds of the former brethren of the brotherhood Tchaftantouri, then began with the help of these brethren, enlightening the reason of those thirty-five 'novices' also.

"So it continued during the whole of one of their years; and only after this did some of them from among the brethren of the former brotherhood Tchaftantouri, and from among the thirty-five said novices, gradually prove worthy to become what are called 'All-the-rights-possessing' brethren of this first brotherhood Heechtvori.

"According to the statutes drawn up by the Very Saintly Ashiata Shiemash, any brother could become an All-the-rights-possessing brother of the brotherhood Heechtvori, only when in addition to the other also foreseen definite objective attainments, he could bring himself—in the sense of 'ableness-of-conscious-direction-of-the-functioning-of-his-own-psyche'—to be able to know how to convince to perfection a hundred other beings and to prove to them that the impulse of being-objective-conscience exists in man, and secondly how it must be manifested in order that a man may respond to the real sense and aim of his existence, and moreover so to convince them that each of these others, in their turn, should acquire in themselves what is called the 'Required-intensity-of-ableness,' to be able to convince and persuade not less than a hundred others also.

"It was those who became worthy to become such an All-the-rights-possessing brother of the brotherhood Heechtvori who were first called by the name of 'priest.'

"For your complete elucidation concerning the Very Saintly Activities of Ashiata Shiemash, you must also know that afterwards, when all the results of the Very

------------------------------ 369 ------------------------------

Saintly Labors of the Very Saintly Ashiata Shiemash were destroyed, both this word priest there and also the word initiate about which I have already told you, were used and still continue to be used by your favorites down to the present time in two quite different senses. In one sense this word priest was since then and now still is commonly used, but only in certain places and for unimportant separate groups of those professionals existing there whom everybody now calls there 'confessors' or 'clergymen.'

"And in the other sense, those beings were called and are still called by this word priest who by their pious existence and by the merits of their acts performed for the good of those around them, stand out so much from the rank and file of the ordinary three-brained beings there, that whenever these ordinary beings there have occasion to remember them, there arises and proceeds in their presences the process called 'gratitude.'

"Already during that same period while the Very Saintly Ashiata Shiemash was enlightening the Reason of the brethren of the former brotherhood Tchaftantouri as well as of the newly collected thirty-five novices, there began to spread, among ordinary beings of the city Djoolfapal and its environs, the true idea that in the common presences of men-beings all the data exist for the manifestation of the Divine impulse conscience, but that this Divine impulse does not take part in their general consciousness; and that it takes no part because, although their manifestations bring them, certain what are called 'quite-late-repaying-satisfactions' and considerable material advantage, nevertheless they thereby gradually atrophy the data put into their presences by Nature for evoking in other beings around them, without distinction of brain system, the objective impulse of Di-

some of them from among the brethren of the former brotherhood Tchaftantouri, and from among the thirty-five said 'novices,' gradually prove worthy to become what are called 'All-the-rights-possessing' brethren of this first 'brotherhood-Heechtvori.'

"According to the 'statutes' drawn up by the Very Saintly Ashiata Shiemash, any brother could become an 'All-the-rights-possessing' brother of the 'brotherhood-Heechtvori,' only when, in addition to the other also foreseen definite objective attainments, he could bring himself—in the sense of 'ableness-of-conscious-direction of the functioning of his own psyche'—to the state of knowing how to convince a hundred other beings about self-perfecting, and moreover, so to convince them that each of these others, in their turn, should acquire in themselves what is called the 'required-intensity-of-ableness' to be able to convince and persuade not less than a hundred others, first, that the impulse of being-objective-conscience exists in man, and second, how it must be manifested in order that a man may respond to the real sense and aim of his existence.

"It was those who became worthy to become such an 'All-the-rights-possessing' brother of the 'Brotherhood-Heechtvori,' who were first called by the name 'priest.'

"For your complete elucidation concerning the Very Saintly activities of Ashiata Shiemash, you must also know that afterwards, when all the results of the Very

Saintly Labors of the Very Saintly Ashiata Shiemash were destroyed, both this word 'priest' there and also the word 'initiate' about which I have already told you, were used and still continue to be used by your favorites down to the present time in two quite different senses. In one sense, from then until now, this word 'priest' was and is still now commonly used, but only in certain places and for unimportant separate groups of those professionals existing there whom everybody now calls there 'confessors' or 'clergymen.'

"And in the other sense, those beings were called and are still called by this word 'priest,' who, by their pious existence and by the merits of their acts performed for the good of those around them, stand out so much from the rank and file of the ordinary three-brained beings there, that whenever these ordinary beings there have occasion to remember them, there arises and proceeds in their presences the process called 'gratitude.'

"Already during that same period while the Very Saintly Ashiata Shiemash was enlightening the reasons of the brethren of the former brotherhood 'Tchaftan-touri,' as well as of the newly collected thirty-five 'novices,' there began to spread among ordinary beings of the city Djoolfapal and it environs, the 'true idea' about this, namely, that in the general presences of man-beings all the data exist for the manifestation of the divine impulse conscience, but that this divine impulse does not take part in their general consciousness; and that it takes no part only because, although their manifestations bring them certain immediate what are called 'quite-late-repaying-satisfactions' and considerable material advantage, nevertheless they thereby gradually atrophy the data put into their presences by Nature for evoking in other beings around them without distinction of 'brain-sys-

vine-Love.

"This true information began to spread, thanks chiefly

------------------------------ *370* ------------------------------

to the superlatively wise provision of the Very Saintly Ashiata Shiemash which obliged everyone striving to become an All-the-rights-possessing brother of the brotherhood Heechtvori to attain, as I have already told you, in addition to all kinds of definite self-merits, the 'ableness' to know how to convince all the three separate spiritualized and associating parts of a further hundred three-brained beings there, concerning the Divine impulse conscience.

"When the organization of the first brotherhood Heechtvori in the city Djoolfapal had been more or less regulated and was so established that the further work could already be continued independently, by means only of the directions issuing from the Reason then present in the brotherhood, then the Very Saintly Ashiata Shiemash himself selected from among those who had become All-the-rights-possessing brothers of the brotherhood, those who had already sensed the said Divine impulse, consciously by their Reason and unconsciously by the feelings in their subconsciousness, and who had full confidence that by certain self-efforts this Divine being-impulse might become and forever remain an inseparable part of their ordinary consciousness. And those who had sensed and become aware of this Divine conscience, and who were called 'first-degree-initiates,' he set apart, and he began to enlighten their Reason separately concerning these 'objective truths,' which before that time were still quite unknown to the three-brained beings.

"It was just these outstanding 'first-degree-initiated-beings' who were then called 'Great Initiates.'

"Here it must be remarked that those principles of being of the initiated beings there, which were later on called there 'Ashiata's renewals,' were then renewed by the Very Saintly Ashiata Shiemash.

"Well, then, it was to those same Great Initiates who were first set apart that the Very Saintly Ashiata Shiemash,

------------------------------ *371* ------------------------------

now already the Most Very Saintly, then among other things also elucidated in detail what this being-impulse 'objective conscience' is, and how factors arise for its manifestation in the presences of the three-brained beings.

"And concerning this he once said as follows:

"'The factors for the being-impulse conscience arise in the presences of the three-brained beings from the localization of the particles of the "emanations-of-the-sorrow" of our OMNI-LOVING AND LONG-SUFFERING-ENDLESS-CREATOR; that is why the source of the manifestation of genuine conscience in three-centered beings is sometimes called the REPRESENTATIVE OF THE CREATOR.

"'And this sorrow is formed in our ALL-MAINTAINING COMMON FATHER from the struggle constantly proceeding in the Universe between joy and sorrow.'

"And he then also further said:

tem,' the objective impulse of Divine Love.

"This true information began to spread, thanks chiefly

- -

to that superlatively wise provision of the Very Saintly Ashiata Shiemash that obliged everyone striving to become an 'All-the-rights-possessing' brother of the brotherhood 'Heechtvori' to attain, in addition to all kinds of definite self-merits, the 'ableness' to know how to convince all the three separate spiritualized and associating parts of the total whole of a further hundred three-brained beings there, concerning the divine impulse conscience.

"When the organization of the first brotherhood 'Heechtvori' in the city Djoolfapal had been more or less regulated and was so established that the further work could already be continued independently, by means only of the directions issuing from the Reason then present in the brotherhood, then the Very Saintly Ashiata Shiemash himself selected from among those who had become 'All-the-rights-possessing' brothers of the brotherhood, those who had already sensed the said divine impulse, consciously by their reason and unconsciously by the feelings in their subconsciousness, and who had full confidence that by certain self-efforts this divine being-impulse might become and forever remain an inseparable part of their ordinary consciousness. And those who had sensed and become aware of this divine impulse conscience, and who were called 'first-degree-initiates,' he set apart, and he began to enlighten their Reasons separately concerning these 'objective truths' which before that time were still quite unknown by the three-brained beings.

"It was just these outstanding 'first degree initiated beings' there who were then first called 'Great-Initiates.'

"Here it must be remarked that those principles of Being of the initiated beings there, which later on just came to be called there 'Ashiata's-renewals,' were then renewed by the Very Saintly Ashiata Shiemash.

"Well then, it was to those same 'Great-Initiates' who were first set apart, that the Very Saintly Ashiata Shiemash,

- -

now already the Most Very Saintly, then among other things also elucidated in detail what, namely, this being-impulse 'objective conscience' is, and how factors arise for its manifestation in the presences of the three-brained beings. And concerning this he once said as follows:

"'The factors for the being-impulse conscience arise in the presences of the three-brained beings from the localization of the particles of the 'emanation-of-the-sorrow' of our OMNI-LOVING AND LONG-SUFFERING ENDLESS CREATOR; that is why the source of the manifestation of genuine conscience in three-centered beings is sometimes called REPRESENTATIVE OF THE CREATOR.

"'And this sorrow is formed in our ALL MAINTAINING FATHER from the struggle between the joy and the sorrow constantly proceeding in the Universe.'

"And he then also further said:

"'In all three-brained beings of the whole of our Universe without exception, among whom are also we men, owing to the data crystallized in our common presences for engendering in us the Divine impulse of conscience, "the-whole-of-us" and the whole of our essence, are, and must be, already in our foundation, only suffering.

"'And they must be suffering, because the completed actualizing of the manifestation of such a being-impulse in us can proceed only from the constant struggle of two quite opposite what are called "complexes-of-the-functioning"of those two sources which are of quite opposite origin, namely, between the processes of the functioning of our planetary body itself and the parallel functionings arising progressively from the coating and perfecting of our higher being-bodies within this planetary body of ours, which functionings in their totality actualize every kind of Reason in the three-centered beings.

"'In consequence of this, every three-centered being of our Great Universe, and also we men existing on the

------------------------------------ 372 ------------------------------------

Earth, must, owing to the presence in us also of the factors for engendering the Divine impulse of "Objective Conscience," always inevitably struggle with the arising and the proceeding within our common presences of two quite opposite functionings giving results always sensed by us either as "desires" or as "non-desires."

"'And so, only he, who consciously assists the process of this inner struggle and consciously assists the "non-desires" to predominate over the desires, behaves just in accordance with the essence of our COMMON FATHER CREATOR HIMSELF; whereas he who with his consciousness assists the contrary, only increases HIS sorrow.'

"Owing to all I have just said, my boy, at that period scarcely three years had passed when, on the one hand, all the ordinary beings of the town Djoolfapal and its environs and also of many other countries of the continent Asia, not only already knew that this Divine being-impulse of 'genuine conscience' was in them, and that it could take part in the functioning of their ordinary 'waking consciousness,' and that in all the brotherhoods of the great prophet Ashiata Shiemash all the initiates and priests elucidated and indicated how and what had to be done in order that such a Divine impulse should take part in the functioning of the mentioned ordinary waking consciousness, but furthermore, nearly everybody even began to strive and to exert himself to become priests of the brotherhood Heechtvori of which many brotherhoods were already founded during that period and functioned almost independently in many other countries of the continent Asia.

"And these almost independent brotherhoods arose there in the following order:

"When the common work of the brotherhood founded in the town Djoolfapal was finally established, the Very Saintly Ashiata Shiemash began sending the said great

------------------------------ 373 ------------------------------

"'In all without exception of the three-brained beings of the whole of our Universe, among whom are also we men, thanks to these data crystallized in our general presences for the bringing forth in us of the divine impulse conscience, 'the whole of us' and the whole of our essence, are, and must be, already in our foundation, only suffering.

"'And they must be suffering, because the appointed actualizing of the manifestation of such a being-impulse in us can proceed only from the constant struggle of two quite opposite, what are called "Complexes-of-the-functioning" of those two sources which are reciprocally of quite opposite origin; namely, between the processes of the functioning of our planetary body itself and the parallel functionings arising progressively from the coating and perfecting of our higher being-bodies within this planetary body of ours, which functionings in their totality, just actualize every kind of reason in the three-centered beings.

"'In consequence of this, every three-centered being of our great Universe, and also we, men, existing on the

Earth, must, owing to the presence in us, also, of the factors for the bringing forth of the divine impulse of "objective conscience," always inevitably struggle with the arising and the proceeding within our general presences of two quite opposite functionings, the results of which are always sensed by us either as "desires" or as "non-desires."

"'And so, he only who consciously assists the process of this inner struggle and consciously assists the "non-desires" to predominate over the "desires"—only he behaves just in accordance with the essence of our COMMON FATHER CREATOR HIMSELF; while he who with his consciousness assists the contrary, only increases His sorrow.'

"Owing to all this, which I have just said, my boy, at that period hardly three years had passed when, on the one hand, all the ordinary beings of the town Djoolfapal and its environs and also of many other countries of the continent Asia, not only already knew that this divine being-impulse of 'genuine conscience' was in them, and that it could take part in the functioning of their ordinary 'waking-consciousness,' also that in all the brotherhoods of the great Prophet Ashiata Shiemash, all the initiates and priests elucidated and indicated how and what had to be done in order that such a divine impulse should take part in the functioning of the mentioned ordinary 'waking-consciousness'—but furthermore, nearly everybody even began to strive and to exert themselves to become priests of the brotherhood 'Heechtvori,' of which many brotherhoods were already founded during that period, functioning almost independently in many other countries of the continent Asia.

"And these nearly independent brotherhoods arose there in the following order:

"When the common work of the brotherhood founded in the town Djoolfapal was finally established, the Very Saintly Ashiata Shiemash began sending the said 'Great-Initiates,'

initiates with corresponding directions to other countries and towns of the continent Asia, in order to organize similar brotherhoods there also, while he himself remained in the town Djoolfapal from where he guided the activities of these helpers of his.

"However it might have been, my boy, it then so turned out that almost all of your favorites—those strange three-brained beings—also wished and began to strive with all their spiritualized being-parts to have in their ordinary waking-consciousness the Divine genuine objective conscience, and in consequence, most of the beings of Asia at that time began to work upon themselves under the guidance of initiates and priests of the brotherhood Heechtvori, in order to transfer into their ordinary consciousness the results of the data present in their subconsciousness for engendering the impulse of genuine Divine conscience, and in order to have the possibility, by this means, on the one hand of completely removing from themselves, perhaps forever, the maleficent consequences of the properties of the organ Kundabuffer, both those personally acquired and those passed to them by heredity and, on the other hand, of consciously taking part in diminishing the sorrow of OUR COMMON ENDLESS FATHER.

"Owing to all this, the question of conscience already began to predominate at that period during the ordinary process of being-existence both in the waking-consciousness state and in the 'passive-instinctive' state among your favorites, particularly among those who existed on the continent Asia.

"Even those three-brained beings of that time in whose presences the taste of this Divine impulse had not yet been transubstantiated, but who had in their strange peculiar consciousness, proper to them alone, only empty information concerning this being-impulse which could be present in them as well, also exerted themselves to manifest in everything in accordance with this information.

--------------------------------- *374* ---------------------------------

"The total result, however, of everything I have mentioned, was that within ten terrestrial years there had disappeared of their own accord those two chief forms of ordinary being-existence abnormally established there, from which there chiefly flow and still continue to flow, most of the maleficent causes the totality of which engenders all kinds of trifling factors which prevent the establishment of conditions there for at least a normal outer being-existence for these unfortunate favorites of yours.

"And namely, firstly their division into numerous communities with various forms of organization for external and even internal existence, or as they themselves express it, 'state-organizations,' ceased to exist, and secondly in these said numerous communities there also disappeared equally, of their own accord, those various what are called 'castes' or 'classes' which had long before been established there.

with appropriate instructions, to other countries and towns of the continent Asia, in order to organize similar brotherhoods there also, while he himself remained to exist there in the town of Djoolfapal from where he guided the activities of these helpers of his.

"However it might have been, my boy, it then so turned out, that almost all of your favorites—those strange three-brained beings—also wished and began to strive with all their spiritualized being-parts to have in their ordinary waking-consciousness, the divine genuine objective conscience; with the consequence that most of the beings of Asia at that time began to work upon themselves under the guidance of 'initiates' and 'priests' of the brotherhood 'Heechtvori,' in order to transfer into their ordinary consciousness the results of the data present in their subconsciousness for bringing forth the impulse of genuine divine conscience, and in order to have the possibility, by this means, on the one hand of completely removing from themselves, perhaps forever, the maleficent consequences of the properties of the organ Kundabuffer, both those personally acquired and those passed to them by inheritance; and on the other hand, of consciously taking part in diminishing the sorrow of OUR COMMON ENDLESS FATHER.

"Owing to all this, the question of conscience already began to predominate both in the 'waking-consciousness' state and in the 'passive-instinctive' state among your favorites also, and particularly among those who existed on the continent Asia at that period during the ordinary process of being-existence.

"Even those three-brained beings of that time in whose presences the taste of this divine impulse had not yet been transubstantiated, but who had in their strange peculiar consciousness, proper to them alone, only empty information concerning this being-impulse which could be present in them as well, also exerted themselves to manifest in everything in accordance with this information.

"The total result, however, of everything I have mentioned, was that already within ten terrestrial years, there had disappeared of their own accord those two chief forms of ordinary being-existence abnormally established there, from which chiefly there flow and still continue to flow, most of the maleficent causes whose sum increasingly evokes every possible kind of insignificant factor which opposes obstacles to the establishment of conditions there—if only for a normal being-existence externally—for those favorites of yours.

"And, namely, their numerous communities with various forms of organization for external and even internal existence, or as they themselves express it, 'state organization,' first just ceased to exist, and secondly, in these said numerous communities, there also disappeared, equally just by themselves, those various what are called 'castes' or 'classes' which had long before been established there.

"These two chief maleficent forms of their ordinary existence, namely, their numerous independent communities and the practice of assigning each other to different 'castes,' ceased to exist on account of the following:

"At that period when thanks to the very saintly labors of Ashiata Shiemash the functioning in the presences of the majority of your favorites of the factors which

"And in my opinion, as you also will surely understand eventually, it was precisely this second of the two mentioned chief abnormally established forms of ordinary being-existence, namely, the assigning of each other to different classes or castes that had specially become there the basis for the gradual crystallization in the common presences of these unfortunate favorites of yours, of that particular psychic property which, in the whole of the Universe, is inherent exclusively only in the presences of those three-brained beings.

"This exclusively particular property was formed in them soon after the second Transapalnian perturbation there, and, gradually undergoing development and becoming strengthened in them, was passed from generation to generation by heredity, until it has now already

- *375* -

passed to the contemporary beings as a certain lawful and inseparable part of their general psyche, and this particular property of their psyche is called by themselves 'egoism.'

"Some time later, in its appropriate place, during my further tales concerning the three-brained beings existing on the planet Earth, I shall also explain to you in detail how thanks to those conditions of external being-existence which were established there, your favorites first began assigning each other to various castes, and how, thanks to subsequent similar abnormalities, this same maleficent form of mutual relationship then established there has continued even until now. But meanwhile, concerning this exceptionally particular property of their general psyche, namely, egoism, it is necessary for you to know that the cause of the possibility of the arising in their common presences of this particular property was that, owing always to the same abnormal conditions established from the very beginning after the said second Transapalnian-perturbation there, their general psyche had become dual.

had remained whole in their subconsciousness for the bringing forth of the sacred being-impulse 'conscience,' had begun to take part in the process of that consciousness of theirs under the direction of which it had become proper to them to pass their 'waking-state,' and when, thanks to this, the beings of that period began to exist and to have relations with each other and to take from each other only in accordance with conscience, and when every kind of mutual 'esteem' and 'aggrandizement' began to proceed only in accordance with the personally acquired obvious moral attainments, then, with such mutual relations prevalent among them, the caste distinctions which had formerly existed and which were afterwards reestablished, were, at first, simply dissipated; and in the same way there afterwards gradually began to dissolve and disappear what are called the 'pales of settlement' of their separate independent communities.

"And in my opinion, as you also will surely understand eventually, it was precisely this second of the two mentioned chief abnormally established forms of ordinary being-existence, namely, this assigning of each other to different castes—that has specially become there the basis for the crystallization in the general presences of these unfortunate favorites of yours, of that particular psychic property which, in the whole of the Universe, exists exclusively only in the presences of those three-brained beings.

"This exclusively particular property was formed in them soon after the second Transapalnian-perturbation there, and gradually undergoing development and becoming strengthened in them, was passed from generation to generation by inheritance, until it has now already

----

passed to the contemporary beings as a certain lawful and inseparable part of their general psyche; this particular property of their psyche being called by themselves, 'Egoism.'

←   *The paragraph opposite will be found on the next page of this version of* The Tales.

"Concerning this exclusively particular property itself of their general psyche, it must assuredly be elucidated to you also, that later during the period of my last personal stay on the surface of this planet of yours, when I became deeply interested in the mentioned 'Legominism' concerning the deliberations of the Very Saintly Ashiata Shiemash entitled the 'Terror of the Situation,' the question arose in me, in the course of my further detailed researches and investigations relating

"This became fully evident to me when, during the period of my last sojourn on the surface of this planet of yours, I became deeply interested in the mentioned Legominism concerning the deliberations of the Very Saintly Ashiata Shiemash entitled 'The Terror-of-the-Situation.' I began in the course of my further detailed researches and investigations relating to his subsequent Very Saintly Activities and their results, to investigate the causes in which way and why the crystallization of the mentioned factors obtained from the particles of the emanation of the Sorrow of OUR COMMON FATHER CREATOR for the actualizing of the Divine being-impulse of objective conscience, proceeded in their presences, that is to say, just in their said subconsciousness, and thus avoided that final degeneration to which are subject all the data

---------------------------------- *376* ----------------------------------

placed in them for engendering in their presences the being-impulses Faith, Love, and Hope, and I was convinced that this strange anomaly there fully justifies one of the numerous wise sentences of our highly esteemed, irreplaceable, and honorable Mullah Nassr Eddin which states:

"'Every-real-happiness-for-man-can-arise-exclusively-only-from-some-unhappiness-also-real-which-he-has-already-experienced.'"

The paragraph opposite will be found on the previous page in this version of The Tales.

"The mentioned duality of their general psyche proceeded because on the one hand various what are called 'individual-initiatives' began to issue from that localization arising in their presences, which is always predominant during their waking existence, and which localization is nothing else but only the result of the accidental perceptions of impressions coming from without, and engendered by their abnormal environment, which perceptions in totality are called by them their 'consciousness'; and on the other hand, similar individual-initiatives also began to issue in them, as it is proper to them, from that normal localization existing in the presences of every kind of being and which they call their subconsciousness.

"And because the mentioned individual-initiatives issue from such different

to his subsequent Very Saintly Activities and their results, in which way and why the crystallization of the mentioned factors obtained from the particles of the emanation of the sorrow of OUR COMMON FATHER CREATOR for the actualizing of the divine being-impulse of objective conscience, proceeded in their presences, that is, just in their said 'subconsciousness,' and thus avoided that final degeneration to which all the data placed in them for bringing forth in their presences the other sacred being-impulses, are subject.

"And concerning also this strange anomaly there, one of the numerous wise sentences of our highly esteemed, irreplaceable and honorable Mullah Nassr Eddin, can also be applied.

"In such cases he says:

— —

"'Every real happiness for man can arise exclusively only from some unhappiness—but also real—which he has already experienced.'

"Well, this said particular property of their general psyche, called 'Egoism,' was just gradually formed in them, only because of that mentioned abnormally established form in the process of their ordinary being-existence, namely, the assigning of each other to various 'classes' or 'castes.'

"Some time later, in its appropriate place, during my further tales concerning the three-brained beings existing on the planet Earth, I shall also explain to you in detail how, thanks to those conditions of external being-existence which were established there, you favorites first began assigning each other to various castes, and how, thanks to subsequent similar abnormalities, this same maleficent form of mutual relation then established there, has continued even until now. But meanwhile for my present tale it is necessary for you to know that the basis for the arising in their general presence of the mentioned particular property of their psyche, namely the property of egoism, has also been the reason, owing always to the same abnormal conditions established from the very beginning after the second Transapalnian-perturbation there, that their general psyche has become dual.

"And this happened because on the one hand, various what are called 'Individual-initiatives' began to issue from that localization arising in their presences, which is always predominant during their waking-existence, and which localization is nothing else but only the result of the accidental perceptions of impressions coming from without, brought forth by their abnormal environment, which perceptions in totality are called by them their 'consciousness'; and on the other hand, similar 'Individual-initiatives' also began to issue in them, as it is proper to them, from that normal localization existing in the presences of every kind of being and which they called their 'subconsciousness.'

"And because the mentioned 'Individual-initiatives' issue from such different localizations during their waking-existence, each of them, during the process of his daily existence is, as it were, divided into two independent personalities.

"Here it must be remarked that just this said duality was also the cause that there was gradually lost from their presences that impulse necessary to three-brained beings, which is called 'sincerity.'

"Later, the practice of deliberately destroying the just mentioned being-impulse called Sincerity even took root among them, and now, from the day of their arising, or, as they say, from the day of their 'birth,' the three-brained beings

--------------------------------- *377* ---------------------------------

there are accustomed by their producers—or, as they say, 'parents'—to an entirely contrary impulse, namely, 'deceit.'

"To teach and to suggest to their children how to be insincere with others and deceitful in everything, has become so ingrained in the beings of the planet Earth of the present time, that it has even become their conception of their duty towards their children; and this kind of conduct towards their children they call by the famous word 'education.'

"They 'educate' their children never to be able and never to dare to do as the 'conscience' present in them instinctively directs, but only that which is prescribed in the manuals of 'bon ton' usually drawn up there just by various candidates for 'Hasnamusses.'

"And of course when these children grow up and become responsible beings, they already automatically produce their manifestations and their acts; just as during their formation they were 'taught,' just as they were 'suggested to,' and just as they were 'wound up'; in a word, just as they were 'educated.'

"Thanks to all this, the conscience which might be in the consciousness of the beings of that planet is, from their earliest infancy, gradually 'driven-back-within,' so that by the time they are grown up the said conscience is already found only in what they call their subconsciousness.

"In consequence, the functioning of the mentioned data for engendering in their presences this said Divine impulse conscience, gradually ceased long ago to participate in that consciousness of theirs by means of which their waking-existence flows.

"That is why, my boy, the crystallization in their common presences of the Divine manifestation issuing from Above for the data of the arising of this sacred

--------------------------------- *378* ---------------------------------

being-impulse in them, proceeds only in their subconsciousness—which has ceased to participate in the process of their ordinary, daily existence—and that is why these data have escaped that 'degeneration' to which all the other sacred being-impulses were subject, and which they also ought to have in their presences, namely, the impulses Faith, Love, and Hope.

"Furthermore, if, for some reason or other, the actions of the Divine data, crystallized in their presences for the said being-impulse, should now begin to manifest themselves in them from their subconsciousness and should strive to participate in the functioning of their abnormally formed ordinary 'consciousness,'

localizations during their waking existence, each of them, during the process of his daily existence, is, as it were, divided into two independent personalities.

"Here it must be remarked that just this said duality was also the cause, that there was also gradually lost from their presences that impulse necessary to three-brained beings, which is called 'sincerity.'

"Later, the practice of deliberately destroying the just mentioned being-impulse called 'sincerity' even took root among them and, now from the day of their arising, or as they say, from the day of their 'birth,' the three-brained beings there

are accustomed by their producers—or, as they say, 'Parents'—to an entirely contrary impulse, namely, 'deceit.'

"To teach and to suggest to their children how to be insincere with others and deceitful in everything, has become so ingrained in the beings of the planet Earth of the present time, that it has even become their conception of their duty towards their children; and just this same they call by the notorious name, 'education.'

"They 'educate' their children to be never able and never to dare to do as the 'conscience' present in them instinctively directs, but only that which is prescribed in the manual of 'Bon-ton,' usually drawn up there just by various candidate 'Hasnamusses.'

"And of course when these children grow up and become responsible beings, they already automatically produce their manifestations and acts just as they were 'educated' during their formation, that is to say, just as they were 'taught,' just as they were 'suggested' and just as they were 'wound up.'

"Thanks to all this, the conscience which might be in the consciousness of the beings of that planet is, from their earliest infancy, gradually driven back within, so that by the time they are grown up the said conscience is already found only in what they call their 'subconsciousness.'

"As a consequence, the functioning of the mentioned data for the bringing forth in their presences of this said divine impulse conscience, gradually ceased long ago to participate in that consciousness of theirs, by means of which their 'waking-existence' flows.

"That is why, my boy, the crystallization in their general presence of the divine manifestation issuing from Above for the 'data' both of this arising and also of this

sacred being-impulse in them, proceeds only in their subconsciousness; and as this subconsciousness of theirs has ceased to participate in the process of their ordinary daily existence, that alone is the sole reason why these data have escaped that 'degeneration' to which all the other sacred being-impulses were subjected, namely, the impulses 'Faith,' 'Love' and 'Hope,' which also they ought to have in their presences.

"Furthermore, if for some reason or other the actions of the divine data crystallized in their presences for the said being-impulse should now begin to manifest themselves in them from their subconsciousness and should strive to participate in the functioning of their abnormally formed ordinary 'Consciousness,' no

then no sooner are they aware of it than they at once take measures to avoid it, because it has already become impossible in the conditions already existing there for anyone to exist with the functioning in their presences of this Divine impulse of genuine objective conscience.

"From the time when the said egoism had become completely 'inoculated' in the presences of your favorites, this particular being-property became, in its turn, the fundamental contributory factor in the gradual crystallization in their general psyche of the data for the arising of still several other quite exclusively-particular being-impulses now existing there under the names of 'cunning,' 'envy,' 'hate,' 'hypocrisy,' 'contempt,' 'haughtiness,' 'servility,' 'slyness,' 'ambition,' 'double-facedness,' and so on and so forth.

"These exclusively particular properties of their psyche which I have just named, utterly unbecoming to three-brained beings, were already fully crystallized in the presences of most of your favorites and were the inevitable attributes of the psyche of every one of them even before the period of the Very Saintly Ashiata Shiemash; but when there began to be fixed and to flow automatically

379

in the process of their being-existence the new form of existence intentionally implanted in them by Ashiata Shiemash himself, then these strange properties, previously present in their psyche, entirely disappeared from the presences of most of the three-brained beings there. Later, however, when they themselves destroyed all the results of the Very Saintly Labors of this Essence-Loving Ashiata Shiemash, these same psychic properties maleficent for themselves gradually again arose anew in all of them, and, for them the contemporary three-brained beings there, they are already the foundation of the whole of their essence.

"Well, then, my boy, when the data arose in the common presences of your favorites for engendering this 'unique-particular' being-impulse egoism and when gradually evolving and giving rise to factors ensuing from it for other also particular but now secondary strange being-impulses, this said 'unique-property' egoism usurped the place of the 'Unique-All-Autocratic-Ruler' in their general organization; then, not only every manifestation but even what is called the 'desire-for-the-arising' of such a Divine being-impulse became a hindrance to the actions of this 'All-Autocratic-Ruler.' And in consequence of this, when eventually your favorites had already, by force of necessity, both consciously and unconsciously, always and in everything, prevented it partaking in the functioning of that consciousness of theirs through the control of which it had become proper for them to actualize their waking-existence, the actions of those Divine data were gradually, as it were, removed from the functioning of their ordinary 'consciousness' and participated only in the functioning of their said subconsciousness.

"And it was only after my detailed researches and investigations had made all the foregoing clear to me, that I understood why there arose and why there still exists

380

that division of themselves there into various classes or castes which is particu-

sooner are they aware of it than they at once take measures to avoid it, because it has already become impossible in the conditions already existing there for anyone to exist with the functioning in their presences of this divine impulse of genuine objective conscience.

"From the time when the said 'egoism' had become finally 'inoculated' in the presences of your favorites, this particular being-property became, in its turn, the fundamental auxiliary in the gradual crystallization of the data of their general psyche for the arising of several other already quite exclusively-particular being-impulses now existing there under the names of 'cunning,' 'envy,' 'hate,' 'hypo-crisy,' 'contempt,' 'haughtiness,' 'servility,' 'slyness,' 'ambition,' 'double-facedness,' and so on and so forth.

"These exclusively-particular properties of their psyche which I have just named, utterly unbecoming to be possessed by three-brained beings, were already fully crystallized in the presences of the majority of your favorites, and were the inevitable attributes of the psyche of every one of them even before the period of the Very Saintly Ashiata Shiemash; but when there began to be fixed

and to flow automatically in the process of their being-existence the new forms of existence intentionally implanted in them by Ashiata Shiemash himself, then these strange properties, previously present in their psyche, entirely disappeared from the presences of most of the three-brained beings there. Later, however, when they themselves destroyed all the results of the Very Saintly Labors of this Essence Loving Ashiata Shiemash, these same psychic properties maleficent for them themselves, gradually again arose anew in all of them, and, for the contem-porary three-brained beings there, they are already the foundation of the whole of their essence.

"Well, my boy, when there arose the data in the general presences of your favor-ites for the bringing forth of this 'Unique-particular' being impulse 'egoism' and of gradually evolving and producing factors flowing from it for other also partic-ular but now secondary strange being-impulses, said 'unique-property' 'egoism' usurped the place of the 'Unique-All-Autocratic-Ruler' in their general organiza-tion, and then not only every manifestation but even what is called the 'desire-for-the-arising' of such a divine being-impulse became a hindrance to the actions of this 'All-Autocratic-Ruler.' And in consequence of this, when eventually your fa-vorites had already, by force of necessity, both consciously and unconsciously al-ways and in everything, prevented its partaking in the functioning of that con-sciousness of theirs through the control of which it had become proper for them to actualize their waking-existence, the actions of those divine data were gradu-ally, as it were, removed from the functioning of their said 'consciousness.'

"Well, it was only after my detailed researches and investigations had made all the foregoing clear to me, that I understood why there arose and why there still exists

that division of themselves there into various 'classes' or 'castes,' which is particularly maleficent for them.

"My later detailed researches and investigations very definitely and clearly showed me that, in that consciousness of theirs, which they call their subconsciousness, even in the beings of the present time, the said data for the acquisition in their presences of this fundamental Divine impulse conscience does indeed still continue to be crystallized and, hence, to be present during the whole of their existence.

"And, that these data of this Divine being-impulse are still crystallized and their manifestations still continue to participate in the process of their being-existence, was, apart from the said investigations, further confirmed by the fact that I frequently had a good deal of difficulty on account of it, during the periods of my observation of them from the planet Mars.

"The point is, that, through my Teskooano from the planet Mars, I could freely observe without any difficulty whatsoever, the existence proceeding on the surfaces of the other planets of that solar system, but making my observations of the process of the existence proceeding on the surface of your planet was, owing to the special coloration of its atmosphere, a real misery.

"And this special coloration occurred, as I later ascertained, because there appeared from time to time, in the presence of this atmosphere, large quantities of those crystallizations which were frequently radiated from the presences of these favorites of yours, owing to that particular inner impulse which they themselves call 'Remorse-of-Conscience.'

And this proceeded because in those of them who chance to receive and experience some kind of what is called 'shock-to-organic-shame,' the associations proceeding from their previous impressions almost always become

---------------------------------- *381* ----------------------------------

changed, calmed, and sometimes even for a time entirely cease in them, which associations as I have already told you, consist mostly of various kinds of what is called 'rubbish.'

"In consequence, there is then automatically obtained, in these three-brained beings there, such a combination of functioning in their common presences as temporarily frees the data present in their subconsciousness for the manifestation of the Divine impulse conscience and for its participation in the functioning of their ordinary consciousness, with the result that this said Remorse-of-Conscience proceeds in them.

"And as this Remorse-of-Conscience gives rise to the mentioned particular crystallizations which issue from them with their other radiations, the result is that the totality of all these radiations occasionally gives the atmosphere of this planet of yours that particular coloration which hinders the being-organ of sight from penetrating freely through it.

"Here it is necessary to say, that these favorites of yours, particularly the contemporary ones, become ideally expert in not allowing this inner impulse of theirs, called Remorse-of-Conscience, to linger long in their common presences.

"No sooner do they begin to sense the beginning, or even only, so to say, the 'prick' of the arising of the functioning in them of such a being-impulse, than they

larly maleficent for them on account of its consequences.

"My said later 'detailed researches' and investigations very definitely and clearly also showed me that, in that consciousness of theirs, which they call their 'subconsciousness,' even in the case of the beings of the present time, the said data for the acquisition in their presences of this fundamental divine impulse conscience does indeed still continue to be crystallized and, hence to be present during the whole of their existence.

"And, that these data of this divine being-impulse are still crystallized and their manifestations still continue to participate in the process of their being existence, was, apart from what I have already said, further confirmed by this—that I frequently had a good deal of difficulty on account of it, during the periods of my observation of them from the planet Mars.

"The truth is, that through my 'Teskooano' I could freely observe from the planet Mars without any difficulty whatever, the existence proceeding on the surfaces of the other planets of that solar system, but making my observations of the process of the existence proceeding on the surface of your planet was a real misery owing to the special coloration of its atmosphere.

"And this special coloration occurred, as I later ascertained, because there appeared from time to time, in the presence of this atmosphere, large quantities of these crystallizations frequently radiated from the presences of these favorites of yours, owing to that particular inner impulse which they themselves call 'Remorse of Conscience.'

"And this proceeded because in those of them who chance to receive and experience some kind of what is called 'moral shock,' the associations proceeding from their previous impressions almost always become changed and calm, and

sometimes even for a time entirely cease in them—associations which, as I have already told you, consist mostly of various kinds of what is called 'rubbish.'

"In consequence, there is then automatically obtained in these three-brained beings there, such a combination of functioning in their general presences, that temporarily frees the data present in their subconsciousness for the manifestation of the divine impulse conscience, and for its participation in the functioning of their ordinary consciousness, with the result that just this said 'Remorse of Conscience' proceeds in them.

"And as this 'Remorse of Conscience' carries with the arising of the mentioned particular crystallizations which issue from them with their other radiations, the result is that the totality of all these radiations occasionally gives the atmosphere of this planet of yours just that particular coloration which hinders the being-organ of sight from penetrating freely through it.

"Here it is necessary to say, that these favorites of yours, particularly the contemporary ones, become ideally expert in not allowing this inner impulse of theirs, called 'Remorse-of-Conscience,' to linger long in their general presence.

"No sooner do they begin to sense the beginning of the functioning in them of such a being-impulse, or even no more than what is called the 'prick' of its arising, immediately, as it is said 'squash' it, whereupon this impulse, not yet quite formed in them, at once calms down.

"For this 'squashing' of the beginning of any Remorse-of-Conscience in themselves, they have even invented some very efficient special means, which now exist there under the names of 'alcoholism,' 'cocainism,' 'morphinism,' 'nicotinism,' 'onanism,' 'monkism,' 'Athenianism,' and others with names also ending in 'ism.'

"I repeat, my boy, at a suitable occasion I shall explain

------------------------------ 382 ------------------------------

to you in detail also about those results issuing from the abnormally established conditions of ordinary existence there, which became factors for the arising and the permanent existence there of this for them maleficent assignment of themselves to various castes.

"I shall without fail explain this to you, because the information elucidating this abnormality there, may serve as very good data for your further logical comparisons for the purpose of better understanding the strangeness of the psyche of these three-brained beings who have taken your fancy.

"Meanwhile transubstantiate in yourself the following: when the mentioned particular psychic property of 'egoism' had been completely formed in the common presences of these favorites of yours, and, later, there had also been formed in them various other secondary impulses already mentioned by me which ensued and now still continue to ensue from it—and furthermore, in consequence of the total absence of the participation of the impulse of sacred conscience in their waking-consciousness—then these three-brained beings arising and existing on the planet Earth, both before the period of the Very Saintly Activities of Ashiata Shiemash and also since have always striven and still continue to strive to arrange their welfare during the process of their ordinary existence, exclusively for them themselves.

"And as in general, on none of the planets of our great Universe does there or can there exist enough of everything required for everybody's equal external welfare, irrespective of what are called 'objective-merits,' the result there is that the prosperity of one is always built on the adversity of many.

"It is just this exclusive regard for their own personal welfare that has gradually crystallized in them the already quite particularly unprecedented and peculiar properties

------------------------------ 383 ------------------------------

of their psyche which I cited, as for instance 'cunning,' 'contempt,' 'hate,' 'servility,' 'lying,' 'flattery,' and so on, which in their turn, on the one hand are factors for an outer manifestation unbecoming to three-brained beings, and on the other hand are the cause of the gradual destruction of all those inner possibilities of theirs, placed in them by Great Nature, of becoming particles of the whole of the 'Reasonable Whole.'

"Well then, my boy, at the time when the results of the Very Saintly Labors of the Essence-loving Ashiata Shiemash had already begun to blend with the pro-

than they immediately, as it is said, 'sit on it,' whereupon this impulse not yet quite formed in them, at once 'pipes down.'

"For this 'sitting on' the beginning of any 'Remorse-of-Conscience' in themselves, they have even invented some very efficient special means, which now exist there under the names of 'Alcoholism,' 'Cocainism,' 'Morphinism,' 'Nicotinism,' 'Onanism,' 'Monkism,' 'Athenianism' and others with names also ending in 'ism.'

"Sometime later, on a suitable occasion, I shall explain

- -

to you in detail also about those results issuing from the abnormally established conditions of ordinary existence there, which became factors for the arising and permanent existence there of this for them maleficent reciprocal assignment of themselves to various castes.

"I shall without fail explain this to you some time, because the information elucidating their abnormality there, may serve as very good data for your further logical comparisons for the purpose of understanding better the strangeness of the psyche of these three-brained beings who please you.

"Meanwhile listen attentively and transubstantiate in yourself the following: when the mentioned particular psychic property of 'egoism' had been fulfilledly formed in the general presences of these favorites of yours, and later, there had also been formed in them various other secondary also particular being-impulses never present in the presences of any other normal three-brained beings of the whole of our Universe, and which flowed out and now still continue to flow out from this particular psychic property of 'Egoism'—and, furthermore, in consequence of the total absence of the participation of the impulse of sacred conscience in their waking-consciousness—then these three-brained beings arising and existing on the planet Earth, both before the period of the Very Saintly activities of Ashiata Shiemash and also since, have always striven and continue still to strive to arrange their welfare during the process of their ordinary existence, exclusively only for them themselves.

"And as in general, on none of the planets of our Great Universe does there or can there exist enough of everything required for everybody's equal exterior welfare, without distinction of what are called 'objective merits,' the result there is that the prosperity of one is always built on the adversity of many.

"It is just this exclusive regard for their own personal welfare that has gradually crystallized in them the already quite particularly unprecedented and peculiar properties

- -

of their psyche which I cited, as for instance, 'cunning,' 'contempt,' 'hate,' 'servility,' 'lying,' 'flattery' and so on, which in their turn, on the one hand are factors for an exterior manifestation unbecoming to three-brained beings, and on the other hand are the causes of the gradual destruction of all those inner possibilities of theirs placed in them by great Nature, of becoming particles of the whole of the 'reasonable whole.'

"At the time when the results of the Very Saintly labors of the Essence Loving Ashiata Shiemash had already begun to blend with the processes of what is called

cesses of what is called their 'inner' and 'outer' being-existence, and when thanks to this, data for the Divine impulse conscience, surviving in their subconsciousness, gradually began to share in the functioning of their 'waking-consciousness', then the being-existence both personal and reciprocal began to proceed on this planet also, almost as it does on the other planets of our great Universe on which three-brained beings exist.

"These favorites of yours also then began to have relations towards each other only as towards the manifestations varying in degree of a UNIQUE COMMON CREATOR and to pay respect to each other only according to the merits personally attained by means of 'being-Partkdolg-duty', that is, by means of personal conscious labors and intentional sufferings.

"That is why, during that period, there ceased to exist there the said two chief maleficent forms of their ordinary existence, namely, their separate independent communities and the division of themselves in these communities into various castes or classes.

"At that time, also, there upon your planet, all the three-brained beings began to consider themselves and those like themselves merely as beings bearing in themselves

----------------------------- 384 -----------------------------

particles of the emanation of the Sorrow of our COMMON FATHER CREATOR.
"And all this then so happened because when the actions of the data of the Divine being-impulse began to participate in the functioning of their ordinary waking-consciousness, and the three-brained beings began manifesting themselves towards each other, solely in accordance with conscience, the consequence was that masters ceased to deprive their slaves of freedom, and various power-possessing beings of their own accord surrendered their unmerited rights, having become aware by conscience and sensing that they possessed and occupied these rights and positions not for the common welfare but only for the satisfaction of their various personal weaknesses, such for instance as 'vanity', 'self-love', 'self-calming', and so on.

"Of course, at that period also, there continued to be all kinds of chiefs, directors and 'adviser-specialists', who became such chiefly from difference of age and from what is called 'essence-power', just as there are everywhere on all planets of the Universe on which there breed three-brained beings of varying degrees of self-perfecting, and they then became such, neither by hereditary right nor by election, as was the case before this blissful Ashiatian epoch and as again afterwards became and even till now continues to be the case.

"All these chiefs, directors and advisers then became such in accordance with the objective merits they personally acquired, and which could be really sensed by all the beings around them.

"And it proceeded in the following way:

"All the beings of this planet then began to work in order to have in their consciousness this Divine function of genuine conscience, and for this purpose, as everywhere in the Universe, they transubstantiated in themselves

----------------------------- 385 -----------------------------

their 'inner' and 'outer' being-existence, and when thanks to this the data for the divine impulse conscience, surviving in their subconsciousness, began gradually to share in the functioning of their 'waking-consciousness,' then the being-existence both personal and reciprocal began to proceed on this planet also, almost as it does on the other planets of our great Universe on which three-brained beings exist.

"These favorites of yours also then began to have relations towards each other as only towards the manifestations varying in degree of a UNIQUE COMMON CREATOR and to pay respect to each other only according to the merits personally attained by means of 'being-Partkdolgduty,' that is, by means of personal conscious labors and intentional sufferings.

"That is why there just ceased to exist there during that period the said two chief maleficent forms of their ordinary existence, namely, their separate independent communities and the division of themselves in these communities into various 'castes,' or, as is still sometimes said there, into various 'classes.'

"At that time, also, there upon your planet, all the three-brained beings began to consider themselves and those like them merely only as beings bearing in themselves

---

particles of the emanation of the Sorrow of our COMMON FATHER CREATOR.

"And all this then so happened because when the actions of the data of the divine being-impulse began to share in the functioning of their ordinary waking-consciousness, and the three-brained beings began manifesting themselves in relation to each other, solely in accordance with conscience, the consequence was that masters ceased to deprive their slaves of freedom, and various power-possessing beings of their own accord surrendered the rights they had obtained without desert, having become aware by conscience and sensing that they actualized and occupied these rights and offices not for the common welfare but only for the satisfaction of their various personal weaknesses, such, for instance, as 'vanity,' 'self-love,' 'self-calming' and so on.

"Of course, there continued to be all kinds of chiefs, rulers, and 'adviser-specialists' at that period also, just as there are everywhere on all the planets of the Universe on which there breed three-brained beings of varying degrees of self-perfecting arising chiefly from difference of age and from what is called 'essence power,' but they then became such, neither by hereditary right nor by election, as was the case before this blissful 'Ashiatian-epoch' and as again afterwards became and even until now continues to be the case.

"All these chiefs, rulers and advisers then became such by themselves automatically, in accordance with the objective merits they personally acquired, and which were really sensible to all the beings around them.

"And it proceeded in the following way: All the beings of this planet also, then began to work in order to have in their consciousness this divine function of genuine conscience, and for this purpose as everywhere in the Universe, they transubstantiated in themselves

---

what are called the 'being-obligolnian-strivings' which consist of the following five, namely:

"The first striving: to have in their ordinary being-existence everything satisfying and really necessary for their planetary body.

"The second striving: to have a constant and unflagging instinctive need for self-perfection in the sense of being.

"The third: the conscious striving to know ever more and more concerning the laws of World-creation and World-maintenance.

"The fourth: the striving from the beginning of their existence to pay for their arising and their individuality as quickly as possible, in order afterwards to be free to lighten as much as possible the Sorrow of our COMMON FATHER.

"And the fifth: the striving always to assist the most rapid perfecting of other beings, both those similar to oneself and those of other forms, up to the degree of the sacred 'Martfotai,' that is, up to the degree of self-individuality.

"At this period when every terrestrial three-centered being existed and worked consciously upon himself in accordance with these five strivings, many of them thanks to this quickly arrived at results of objective attainments perceptible to others.

"Of course, these objective attainments then, as it is said, 'attracted-the-attention' of all around them, who thereupon made those who had attained stand out from their midst and paid them every kind of respect; they also strove with joy to merit the attention of these outstanding beings and to have for themselves their counsel and advice how they themselves could attain the same perfecting.

"And these outstanding beings of that period began in their turn to make the most attained among themselves stand out and this outstanding being thereby automatically became,

---------------------------------- 386 ----------------------------------

without either hereditary or other right, the chief of them all, and recognizing him as chief, his directings were spread correspondingly, and this recognition included not only the separate neighboring parts of the surface of your planet, but also even the neighboring continents and islands.

"At that period the counsel and guidance and in general every word of these chiefs became law for all the three-brained beings there and were fulfilled by them with devotion and joy; not as it had proceeded there before the results obtained by the Very Saintly Labors of Ashiata Shiemash, nor as it again proceeded and still continues to proceed since they themselves destroyed the fruits of his Very Saintly Labors.

"That is to say, these strange three-brained beings, your favorites, now carry out the various commands and orders of their 'chiefs' and, as they are called 'kings,' only from fear of what are called 'bayonets' and 'lousy cells,' of which there are a great many at the disposition of these chiefs and kings.

"The results of the Very Saintly Labors of Ashiata Shiemash were then also very definitely reflected in respect of that terrible peculiarity of the manifestation of the psyche of your favorites, namely, in their 'irresistible-urge-for-the-periodic-

what are called the 'being-obligolnian-strivings' and which consist of the following five, namely:

The first striving: to have in their ordinary being-existence everything satisfying for their planetary body.

The second striving: to have a constant and unflagging instinctive need for self-perfection in the sense of Being.

The third: the conscious striving to know ever more and more concerning the laws of World-creation and World-maintenance.

The fourth: the striving to discharge the debt of their arising and their individuality of existence as early and as possible in order afterwards to be free to lighten as much as possible the Sorrow of OUR COMMON FATHER.

And the fifth: the striving always to assist the most rapid perfecting of other beings, both those similar to oneself and those of other forms, up to the degree of the 'sacred Martfotai,' that is, up to the degree of self-individuality.

"At this period when every terrestrial three-centered being began to exist concordantly with these five strivings and work consciously upon himself, many of them, thanks to this, quickly arrived at results of objective attainments perceptible to others.

"Of course, these objective attainments then, as it is said, 'attracted the attention' of all around them who thereupon made those who had attained, stand out from their midst and paid them every kind of respect; they also strove with joy to merit the attention of these outstanding beings and to have for themselves their counsel and advice concerning how they themselves could attain the same perfecting.

"And these outstanding beings themselves of that period in their turn and from their own number, began to make the one most attained stand out, and this outstanding being thereby became

- -

mechanically, without either hereditary or other right, the chief of them all. Their directings were spread correspondingly with the occurrence of his recognition as chief, and this recognition included not only the separate neighboring parts of the terra-firma of the surface of your planet, but also even the neighboring continents and islands.

"At that period the counsel and guidance, and in general, every word of these chiefs, became law for all the three-brained beings there; and were fulfilled by them with devotion and joy; not as it had proceeded there before the results obtained by the Very Saintly Labors of Ashiata Shiemash, nor as it again proceeded and still continues since they themselves destroyed the fruits of his Very Saintly Labors.

"Namely, these strange three-brained beings, your favorites, now carry out the various commands and orders of their 'chiefs' and, as they are called 'kings,' only from fear of what are called 'bayonets' and 'lousy cells,' of which there are a great many at the disposition of these chiefs and kings.

"The results of the Very Saintly Labors of Ashiata Shiemash were then also very definitely reflected in respect of that terrible peculiarity of the manifestation of the psyche of your favorites, namely, in their 'needful-tendency-to-the-periodic-destruction-of-each-other's-existence.'

"The process of reciprocal destruction established there and ensuing from that terrible particularity of their psyche entirely ceased on the continent Asia, and only proceeded occasionally on those large and small parts of the surface of that planet of yours, which were far from the continent Asia. And this continued there only because owing to their distance the influence of the initiates and priests could not reach and be transubstantiated in the presence of the beings breeding on these parts of the surface of your planet.

------------------------------ 387 ------------------------------

"But the most astonishing and significant result of the Very Saintly Labors of Ashiata Shiemash was that at that period not only did the duration of the existence of these unfortunates become a little more normal, that is to say, it began to increase, but also what they call the 'death rate' also diminished, and at the same time the number of their results manifested for the prolongation of their generation, that is, as they say, their 'birth rate,' diminished to at least a fifth.

"Thereby there was even practically demonstrated one of the cosmic laws, namely, what is called 'the-law-of-the-equilibration-of-vibrations,' that is, of vibrations arising from the evolutions and involutions of the cosmic substances required for the Most Great Omnicosmic Trogoautoegocrat.

"The said decline in both their death rate and their birth rate proceeded because, as they approximated to an existence normal for the three-centered beings, they also began to radiate from themselves vibrations responding more closely to the requirements of Great Nature, thanks to which Nature needed less of those vibrations which are in general obtained from the destruction of the existence of beings.

"You will also understand well about this cosmic law 'equilibration-of-vibrations' when at the proper time I shall explain to you in detail, as I have already many times promised you, concerning all the general fundamental cosmic laws.

"It was just in this way, my boy, and in such a sequence that there in that period, thanks to the conscious labors of the Very Saintly Ashiata Shiemash, the said welfare unprecedented for your favorites was gradually created; but to the infinite sorrow of all more or less consciously thinking individuals of all gradations of Reason, shortly after the departure from this planet of the Very Saintly Ashiata

------------------------------ 388 ------------------------------

Shiemash, these unfortunates themselves, after the manner that had become in general proper to them before, in respect of every good attainment of their ancestors, totally destroyed it all; and thus it was they destroyed and thus it was they swept away from the surface of their planet all that welfare, so that even the rumor has failed to reach contemporary beings there that once upon a time such bliss existed.

"In certain inscriptions which have survived from ancient times and have reached the contemporary beings of that planet, there is, however, some information that there once existed on their planet, what is called a special kind of 'state-organization' and that at the head of every such state were beings of the highest attainments.

destruction-of-each-other's-existence.'

"The process of reciprocal destruction established there and flowing out from that terrible particularity of their psyche entirely ceased on the continent Asia, and only proceeded occasionally on those large and small terra-firma surfaces of that planet of yours, which were far from the continent of Asia. And this continued there only because owing to their distance, the influence of the 'initiates' and 'priests' could not reach and be transubstantiated in the presences of the beings breeding on these said terra-firmas.

"But the most astonishing and significant result of the Very Saintly labors of Ashiata Shiemash was that at that period not only did the length itself of the existence become a little more normal—that is to say, it began to increase—and also that what they called the 'death rate' itself was also diminished, but at the same time the number of their results manifested for the prolongation of their generation, that is as they say, their 'birth-rate,' diminished at least a fifth.

"Thereby there was even practically demonstrated one of the cosmic laws, namely, what is called 'the law-of-the-equilibration-of-vibrations'—that is, of vibrations arising from the evolutions and involutions of the cosmic substances required for the Most Great Omnicosmic Trogoautoegocrat.

"The said decline in both their 'death-rate' and their 'birth-rate' proceeded because as they approximated to an existence normal for the three-centered beings, they also began to radiate from themselves vibrations responding more closely to the requirements of Great Nature, thanks to which, there was less need in Nature for those vibrations which in general are obtained from the destruction of the existence of beings.

"About this cosmic law 'equilibration-of-vibrations' you will also understand well when at the proper time I shall explain to you in detail, as I have already many times promised you, concerning all the general fundamental cosmic laws.

"It was in just this way, my boy, and in such a sequence that there in that period, thanks to the conscious labors of the Very Saintly Ashiata Shiemash the said welfare unprecedented for your favorites was gradually created, but to the infinite sadness of all more or less consciously thinking individuums of all gradations of reason, shortly after the departure from this planet of the Very Saintly Ashiata

Shiemash, these unfortunates themselves, after the manner that had become in general proper to them before, in respect of every good attainment of their ancestors, totally destroyed it all; and thus it was they destroyed and thus it was they swept away from the surface of their planet all that welfare, so that even the rumor that once upon a time such a bliss existed, on their own planet, failed to reach the contemporary beings there.

"In certain inscriptions which have survived from ancient times and have reached the contemporary beings of that planet, there, is however, some information that there once existed on their planet, what is called a special kind of 'state-organization,' and that at the head of every such state were beings of the highest attainments.

"And on the basis of this information, the contemporary beings have invented just a mere name for this state-organization; they call it a 'priest-organization' and that is all.

"But what constituted this priest-organization, how and why it was? . . . is it not all the same to the contemporary beings of the planet Earth what ancient savages did!!! . . ."

"And on the basis of this information, the contemporary beings have invented just a mere name for this 'state organization'; they call it a 'priest-state-organization' and have done with it.

"But what constituted this 'priest-state-organization,' how it was and why it was . . . ? it's all the same to the contemporary beings of the planet what primitive savages did!

"And now, my boy, hear how these strange three-brained beings who please you, began and finally achieved the complete destruction of all the results obtained from the Very Saintly Labors of the Great Essence Loving now Omnicosmic Most Very Saintly Ashiata Shiemash.

- -

The Chief Culprit in the Destruction of All the Very Saintly Labors of Ashiata Shiemash

YOU remember that I have already told you that the basis of the initiative for the arising there of the factors which became the causes of the final destruction of the still surviving remains of the beneficent results of the conscious labors of the Very Saintly Ashiata Shiemash for the subsequent generations of your favorites did not issue from the learned beings who were then assembled from almost the whole of the surface of the Earth in the city of Babylon, but that these latter—as it had long before become proper to most of the terrestrial learned beings of new formation—were only like 'contagious bacilli,' the unconscious disseminators of every kind of then existing evil for their own and for subsequent generations.

"The basis for all the further great and small maleficent activities and unconscious maleficent manifestations of the learned beings of that time concerning the destruction of even the last remnants of the results, beneficent for the three-brained beings there, obtained from the very saintly conscious labors of the Essence-loving Ashiata Shiemash, was—as my later detailed researches concerning these further very saintly activities made clear to me—the 'invention' of a learned being, well known there in his time, also belonging to the number of learned beings of new formation and named Lentrohamsanin.

"As a result of his inner what is called 'double-gravity-centered' existence, the 'highest being-part' of the presence of this terrestrial three-brained being was coated and perfected up to the required gradation of Objective Reason, and later this 'highest being-part' became, as I

- 390 -

have once already told you, one of those three hundred and thirteen 'highest being-bodies' who are called 'Eternal-Hasnamuss-individuals' and who have the place of their further existence in the Universe on a small planet existing under the name of 'Eternal-Retribution.'

"Now, strictly speaking, about this terrestrial three-brained being Lentrohamsanin, I would have to fulfill my promise and to explain to you in detail about the expression Hasnamuss, but I prefer to do so a little later in the proper place of the sequence in this tale.

"The mentioned maleficent 'invention,' or as they themselves, that is, the contemporary terrestrial learned beings, name such an invention of a learned being there of 'new formation,' a 'composition,' or even a 'creation,' was actualized, as I have already told you, two or more centuries before the time when, during my fifth sojourn there, I first reached the city of Babylon, where partly by coercion and also partly voluntarily, learned beings had been assembled from the surface of almost the whole of the planet.

"The maleficent composition of that learned being of former centuries reached the learned beings of the said Babylonian epoch by means of what is called a 'Kashireitleer,' on which this invention was engrossed by the said learned Lentro-

The Chief Culprit Of The Destruction Of All The Very Saintly Labours Of Ashiata Shiemash

YOU REMEMBER that I have already told you that the basis of the initiative for the arising there of the factors which became the causes of the final destruction of the still surviving remains of the beneficent results for the subsequent generations of your favorites of the conscious labors of the Very Saintly Ashiata Shiemash did not issue from the scientific beings who were then assembled from almost the whole of the surface of the Earth, in the city of Babylon, but that these latter—as it had long before become proper to the majority of the terrestrial scientists of 'new format'—were only, like 'carrier-germs,' the unconscious disseminators of every kind of evil, already arisen before them, both for their own and for subsequent generations.

"As the basis for all the further great and small maleficent doings and unconscious maleficent manifestations of the scientific beings of that time, relative to the destruction of even the last remnants of the results, beneficent for the three-brained beings there, that were obtained from the very saintly conscious labors of the Essence Loving Ashiata Shiemash, there served—as my later detailed researches concerning his further very saintly activities made clear to me—the 'invention' of a scientific being, well known there in his time, also belonging to the number of the scientists of 'new format,' named Lentrohamsanin.

"In the presence of this terrestrial three-brained being, the 'highest-being-part' was coated and perfected up to the required gradation of objective reason, and he afterwards became, as I

have once already told you, one of the number of those 335 'highest-being-bodies' who are called 'eternal-Hasnamuss-individuums' and who have the place of their further existence in the Universe, on a small planet existing under the name of 'Retribution.'

"Now, strictly speaking, about this terrestrial three-brained being Lentrohamsanin, I would have to fulfill my promise and to explain to you in detail concerning the expression 'Hasnamuss,' but I prefer to do so a little later in the proper place of the sequence of my given tale.

"And so, my boy, the mentioned maleficent 'invention'—or as they themselves, that is, the contemporary terrestrial scientists, name such an invention of a scientist there of 'new format'—'composition' or even a 'creation'—was just actualized, as I have already told you, two or more centuries before the time when, during my fifth stay there, I first reached the city of Babylon, where partly by coercion and partly voluntarily, scientific beings had been assembled from the surface of almost the whole of the planet.

"That maleficent 'invention' of that scientist of former centuries reached the scientific beings of the said Babylonian epoch by means of what is called a 'Kashireitleer,' on which this invention was engrossed by the said learned Lentrohamsanin himself.

"I find it very necessary to inform you a little more in detail about the history of the arising of this Lentrohamsanin and also how, owing to which accidental circumstances of his environment, he later became there a great learned being and authority for his contemporary beings of almost the whole surface of your planet.

"In addition to this history itself being very characteristic, it can also serve as a good elucidatory example of that practice which has long ago become firmly established in the process of the existence of these three-brained beings who have taken your fancy, the result of which is

--------------------------------- *391* ---------------------------------

that several of them at first become so to say authorities for other learned beings of new formation and thereby later for all the unfortunate ordinary beings there.

"The details concerning the conditions of the arising and subsequent formation of this Lentrohamsanin into a responsible being chanced to become clear to me, by the way, during my investigations of which aspects of the strange psyche of your favorites were the basis for the gradual change and ultimately also for the total destruction of all those beneficent special forms and customs in the process of their being-existence, which had been introduced and firmly fixed in this process by the ideally foreseeing Reason of our now Omnicosmic Most Very Saintly Ashiata Shiemash during the period of his self-preparation to be that which he now is for the whole of the Universe.

"It was then that I learned that this Lentrohamsanin arose, or, as it is said there, 'was born,' on the continent Asia, in the capital of Nievia, the town Kronbookhon.

"The conception of his arising resulted from the blending of two heterogeneous Exioëharies formed in two already elderly three-brained Keschapmartnian beings there.

"His 'producers' or, as it is said there, his 'parents,' having chosen as the place for their permanent existence the capital of Nievia, moved there three terrestrial years before the arising of that later Universal Hasnamuss.

"For his elderly and very rich parents he was what is called a 'first-born,' for although the blending of their Exioëharies had been many times actualized between them before him, yet, as I found out, they, being deeply engaged in the business of acquiring riches and not wishing to have any hindrance for this, had recourse at each actualizing of this sacred blending to what is called 'Toosy,' or, as your contemporary favorites express themselves, 'abortion.'

--------------------------------- *392* ---------------------------------

"Towards the end of his activities in acquiring riches, 'the-source-of-the-active-principle-of-his-origin,' or, as it is said there, his father, had several of his own what are called 'caravans' and he also owned special 'caravansaries' for the exchange of goods in various cities of this same Nievia.

"And 'the-source-of-the-passive-principle-of-his-origin,' that is, his mother, was at first of the profession of what is called 'Toosidji,' but later, on a small mountain, she organized what is called a 'Holy-place' and published broadcast among other beings information concerning its supposed special significance, namely,

hamsanin himself.

"It will do no harm to relate to you a little more in detail the story of the arising of this Lentrohamsanin and also how, owing to which accidental circumstances of his environment, he later became there a 'great scientist' and 'authority' for his contemporary beings of almost the whole surface of your planet.

"This must be explained to you because this story by itself is very characteristic and can moreover serve as a clear indication of what three-brained beings in general there become what are called 'authorities' for other scientists of 'new format' there and hence for all the other unfortunate ordinary beings there.

"The details concerning the conditions of the arising and subsequent formation of this Lentrohamsanin into a responsible being chanced to become clear to me, by the way, during my investigations of, namely, which aspects taken together of the strange psyche of your favorites had served as the basis for the gradual change and ultimately also for the total destruction of all those beneficent special forms in the process of their being-existence, which had been grafted into that process of theirs by the ideally-foreseeing reason of our now Omnicosmic Most Very Saintly Ashiata Shiemash during the period of his self-preparation to be that which he now is for the whole of the Universe.

"It was then that I learned that this Lentrohamsanin arose, or, as it is said there, 'was born,' on the continent Asia, in the capital of Nievia, the town Kronbookhon.

"The conception of his arising resulted from the blending of two heterogeneous exioëharies formed in two already elderly three-brained Keschapmartnian beings there.

"His 'producers' or, as it is said there, his 'parents,' having chosen as the place for their permanent existence the capital of Nievia, moved there three terrestrial years before the arising of that later Universal Hasnamuss.

"For his elderly and very rich parents he was what is called 'a first-born' for although blendings of their Exioëharies had been many times actualized between them before him, yet, as I found, being deeply engaged in the business of acquiring riches and not wishing to have any hindrance for this, they, in each such instance, had recourse to what is called 'Toosy,' or as your contemporary favorites express themselves, 'abortion.'

"Towards the end of his activities in acquiring riches the source of the active beginning of his origin, or, as it is said there, his 'father,' had several of his own what are called 'Caravans' and he also owned special 'Caravansaries' for the exchange of goods in various cities of this same Nievia.

"And the source of the passive beginning of his origin, that is, his mother, was, at first, of the profession of what is called 'Toosidji,' and afterwards she organized on a small hill what is called a 'Holy place' and published broadcast among other beings information concerning its significance, namely, that beings of the female

that beings of the female sex, without children would, on visiting this place, acquire the possibility of having them.

"When this couple, in what is called 'the-decline-of-their-years,' had already become very rich, they moved to the capital city Kronbookhon in order to exist there, but only for their own pleasure.

"But soon they felt that without a real 'result' or as they say there 'in-childlessness,' there cannot be full pleasure, and from that time on, without sparing what is called 'money,' they took every kind of measure to obtain such a result.

"With this end in view, they visited various Holy-places existing there for that purpose, of course with the exception of their own 'Holy-mountain,' and resorted to every kind of what are called 'medical means' which purported to assist the blending of heterogeneous Exioëharies; and when eventually by chance such a blending was actualized, then there indeed arose, after a certain time, just that long-awaited result of theirs, later called Lentrohamsanin.

"From the very first day of his arising, the parents were, as it is said, completely wrapped up in what they described as their 'God-sent-result' or son; and they spent vast sums on his pleasures and on what was called his 'education.'

- 393 -

"To give their son the very best 'upbringing' and 'education' the Earth could provide, became for them, as it is said there, their 'Ideal.'

"With this aim, they hired for him various what are called 'tutors' and 'teachers,' both from among those existing in the country Nievia and from various distant lands.

"These latter, that is, these foreign 'tutors' and 'teachers,' they then invited chiefly from the country which at the present time is called 'Egypt.'

"Already by the time this terrestrial what is called 'Papa's-and-Mama's-darling' was approaching the age of a responsible being, he was, as it is said there, very well 'instructed' and 'educated,' that is, he had in his presence a great deal of data for all kinds of being 'egoplastikoori,' consisting, as it is usual there according to the abnormally established conditions of their existence, of various fantastic and dubious information; and later, when he became a responsible being he manifested himself automatically through all kinds of corresponding accidental shocks.

"When this later great learned being there reached the age of a responsible being, and although he had indeed a great deal of information or, as it is called there, 'knowledge,' nevertheless, he had absolutely no Being in regard to this information or knowledge which he had acquired.

"Well, when the said Mama's-and-Papa's-darling became a learned being there of new formation, then because on the one hand there was no Being whatsoever in his presence, and on the other hand because there had already by this time been thoroughly crystallized in him those consequences of the properties of the organ Kundabuffer which exist there under the names of 'vanity,' 'self-love,' 'swagger,' and so forth, the ambition arose in him to become a famous learned being not only among the beings

- 394 -

of Nievia, but also over the whole of the surface of their planet.

sex without children would, on visiting this place, acquire the possibility of having them.

"When this couple, in what is called 'the decline of their years' had already become very rich, they moved to Kronbookhon in order to exist there, already only for their own pleasure.

"But soon they felt that without a real result, or as they say there, 'in childlessness,' there cannot be full pleasure, and from that time on, without sparing what is called 'money,' they took every kind of measure in order to obtain such a result.

"They visited, with this object, every kind of 'holy place' existing there for that purpose, of course with the exception of their own 'holy mountain'; and resorted to every kind of what are called 'medical-means,' which purported to assist the blending of heterogeneous exioëharies; and when eventually by chance such a blending was actualized, then there indeed arose, after a certain time, just that long awaited result of theirs, later called Lentrohamsanin.

"From the very first day, the parents were completely wrapped up in what they described as their God-sent 'result' or 'son'; and they spent vast sums on his pleasures and on what is called his 'education.'

- -

"Their ambition was to give this son the best 'upbringing' and 'education' the Earth could provide.

"With this aim, they hired for him various what are called 'tutors' and 'teachers,' both from among those existing in the country Nievia and from various distant lands.

"These latter, that is, these foreign 'tutors' and 'teachers,' they then imported chiefly from the country which at the present time is called 'Egypt.'

"Already by the time this terrestrial what is called 'Papa's and Mama's darling' was approaching the age of a responsible being, he was, as it is said there, very well 'instructed' and 'educated,' that is, he already had in his presence a great deal of dubious information concerning this, that and the other, and could manifest himself automatically accurately conformably with the conditions of being-existence abnormally established there.

"But when he had already reached the age of a responsible being there—although he had indeed a great deal of information, or, as it is called there, 'knowledge'—nevertheless, in regard to this 'information' or 'knowledge' which he had acquired, there was as yet no corresponding Being in him.

"Well, when this said 'Mama's and Papa's darling' became a scientist of 'new-format' there, then because on the one hand there was no Being whatsoever in his presence and on the other hand, because there had already by this time been thoroughly crystallized in him those consequences of the properties of the organ Kundabuffer which exist there under the names of 'vanity,' 'self-love,' 'swagger' and so forth, the ambition arose in him to become a 'famous scientist' not only among the beings

- -

of Nievia, but over the whole surface of their planet as well.

"So, with all his presence he dreamed and ruminated how he could attain this.

"For many days he then thought seriously, and finally he decided first of all to invent a theory upon a topic which nobody before him had ever touched upon; and secondly, to inscribe this 'invention' of his upon such a Kashireitleer as nobody had ever before inscribed or would ever be able to in the future either.

"And from that day, he made preparations for the actualizing of that decision of his.

"With the help of his many slaves he first prepared a Kashireitleer such as had never before existed.

"At that period of the flow of time on the planet Earth, the Kashireitleers were generally made from one or another part of the hide of a quadruped being called there 'buffalo,' but Lentrohamsanin made his Kashireitleer from a hundred buffalo hides joined together.

"These Kashireitleers were replaced there later by what is called 'parchment.'

"Well, when this unprecedented Kashireitleer was ready, the subsequently great Lentrohamsanin inscribed upon it his invention concerning a topic which, indeed, it had occurred to nobody to discuss before, and for which, in truth, there was no reason why it should have been.

"Namely, in those wiseacrings of his, he then criticized in every way the existing order of collective existence.

"This Kashireitleer began thus:

"'Man's greatest happiness consists in not being dependent on any other personality whatsoever, and in being free from the influence of any other person, whoever he may be!'

"Some other time, I will explain to you how your

---------------------------------- *395* ----------------------------------

favorites, the strange three-brained beings there on the planet Earth, in general understand freedom.

"This subsequently Universal Hasnamuss inscribed further as follows:

"'Undeniably, life under the present state-organization is now far better for us than it used to be before; but where then is that real freedom of ours upon which our happiness must depend?

"'Don't we work and labor as much now as during all other former state-organizations?

"'Haven't we to labor and sweat to get the barley indispensable to us to live and not to starve to death like chained dogs?

"'Our chiefs, guides, and counselors are always telling us about some other sort of world, supposedly so much better than here among us on the Earth, and where life is in every respect beatific for the souls of those men who have lived worthily here on the Earth.

"'Don't we live here now "worthily"?

"'Don't we always labor and sweat for our daily bread?

"'If all that our chiefs and counselors tell us is true and their own way of living here on the Earth really corresponds to what is required of their souls for the other world, then of course God ought, and even must, in this world also, give

"So, with all his presence he dreamed and ruminated how he could attain it

"For many days he then thought very seriously; and finally he decided, first of all, to invent a theory upon a topic which nobody before him had ever discussed, and, secondly, to engross this 'invention' of his upon such a 'Kashireitleer' as nobody had ever before engrossed or would ever be able to in the future either.

"And from that day on he made preparations for the actualizing of that decision of his.

"With the help of many slaves, he first prepared a 'Kashireitleer' such as had never before existed, namely, of a hundred buffalo hides joined together.

"I must tell you that the 'Kashireitleers' were generally made on the planet Earth in those times from one or another part of a single buffalo hide, whereas Lentrohamsanin made his 'Kashireitleer' from a hundred buffalo hides.

"These 'Kashireitleers' were replaced there later by what is called 'Parchment.'

"Well, when this unprecedented 'Kashireitleer' was ready, the future great Lentrohamsanin engrossed upon it concerning a topic which indeed it had occurred to nobody to discuss before—and, in truth, there was no reason why it should.

"Namely, in those 'wiseacrings' of his, he then criticized in every possible way the existing what is called 'Political Organization of Society.'

"This 'Kashireitleer' began thus:

"'Man's greatest happiness consists in depending upon no other personality whatsoever, and in being free from all alien influences whatsoever.'

"Some other time I will explain to you how your

- -

favorites, the strange three-brained beings there on the planet Earth, in general understand freedom.

"This subsequent Universal Hasnamuss engrossed further as follows:

"'Undeniably, life under the present state-organization is now far better for us than it used to be; but where then is that real freedom of ours upon which our happiness must depend?

"'Don't we work and labor as much now as during any former state-organization?

"'Haven't we to labor and sweat to get the barley indispensable to enable us to live and not to starve to death like chained dogs?

"'Our lords and masters and pastors are always telling us about some other sort of world, which is purported to be so much better than here among us on the Earth, and where life is in every respect beatific for the souls of those men who live here on the Earth "worthily."

"'Don't we live here "worthily"?

"'Don't we always labor and sweat for our daily bread?

"'If what all our masters and pastors tell us is true and their own way of living here on the Earth really worthily corresponds to what is required of their souls for the other world, then of course God ought, and even must, in this world also, give more possibilities to them than to us ordinary mortals.

"'If all that our chiefs and counselors tell and try to make us believe is really true, let them prove it to us, ordinary mortals, by facts.

"'Let them prove it to us, for instance, that they can at least change a pinch of the common sand, in which, thanks to our sweat, our daily bread arises, into bread.

"'If our present chiefs and counselors do this, then I

---------------------------------- 396 ----------------------------------

myself will be the first to run and kneel and kiss their feet.

"'But meanwhile, as this is not so, we ourselves must struggle and we ourselves must strive hard for our real happiness and for our real freedom and also to free ourselves from the need of having to sweat.

"'It is true that for eight months of the year we now have no trouble in obtaining our daily bread; but then, how we must labor those four summer months and exhaust ourselves getting the barley we need!

"'Only he who sows and mows that barley knows the hard labor required.

"'True, for eight months we are free, but only from physical labors, and for this, our consciousness, namely, our dearest and highest part, must remain day and night in slavery to these illusory ideas which are always being dinned into us by our chiefs and counselors.

"'No, enough! We ourselves, without our present chiefs and counselors who have become such without our consent, must strive for our real freedom and our real happiness.

"'And we can only obtain real freedom and real happiness if we all act as one, that is to say, all for one and one for all. But for this, we must first destroy all that is old.

"'And we must do so to make room for the new life we shall ourselves create that will give us real freedom and real happiness.

"'Down with dependence on others!

"'We ourselves will be masters of our own circumstances and no longer they, who rule our lives and do so without our knowledge and without our consent.

"'Our lives must be governed and guided by those whom we ourselves shall elect from our midst, that is by men only from amongst those who themselves struggle for our daily barley.

---------------------------------- 397 ----------------------------------

"'And we must elect these governors and counselors on the basis of equal rights, without distinction of sex or age, by universal, direct, equal, and open ballot.'

"Thus ended the said famous Kashireitleer.

"When this subsequent Universal Hasnamuss, Lentrohamsanin, had finished inscribing this Kashireitleer, indeed unprecedented there, he arranged an enormous and costly banquet to which he invited all the learned beings from all Nievia, taking upon himself all their traveling expenses; and at the end of this banquet, he showed them his Kashireitleer.

more possibilities to them than to us ordinary mortals.

"'If all this, which our masters and pastors tell and try to make us believe, is really true, let them prove it to us ordinary mortals by facts.

"'Let them prove to us by facts at least this—that they can change a pinch of the common sand in which, thanks to our sweat, our daily bread arises, into bread.

"'Let our present masters and pastors do this, and I

myself will be the first to run and kneel and kiss their feet.

"'But meanwhile, as this is not so, we ourselves must struggle and we ourselves must strive for our real happiness and for our real freedom from the influence of strange personalities, and also to escape the need to sweat.

"'It is true that for eight months of the year we now have no trouble in obtaining our daily bread; but how do those four summer months go, when we have to spend our sweat to get the barley we need?

"'Only he who sows and mows that barley knows the difficulties of it.

"'For eight months we are free, but from physical labors only, and for this our consciousness, namely, our dearest and highest part, must remain subject night and day to these ephemeral ideas which are always being dinned into us by our pastors and masters.

"'No, enough! Without our present masters and pastors, who have become so without our leave, we ourselves must strive for our real freedom and our real happiness.

"'Only if we act all for each and each for all, can we obtain real freedom and real happiness.

"'To create a happy life for ourselves, we must first destroy all that is old.

"'And we must do so to make room for the new life we shall ourselves create that will give us real freedom and real happiness.

"'Down with dependence on others!

"'We will to be ourselves the masters of our own circumstances; and no longer they should be our masters and rule our lives who do so without our knowledge and without our consent.

"'Our lives must be governed and guided by those whom we ourselves shall elect from our midst, and namely, from amongst those men only who themselves struggle for our daily barley.

"'And these governors and counsellors we must elect from our midst on the basis of equal rights, without distinction of sex or age by universal, direct, equal and open ballot.'

"Thus ended the said famous 'Kashireitleer.'

"When this subsequent Universal Hasnamuss, Lentrohamsanin, had finished engrossing this 'Kashireitleer,' indeed unprecedented there, he arranged an enormous and costly banquet to which he invited all the 'learned' beings from all Nievia, taking upon himself all their traveling expenses; and at the end of this banquet he showed them his 'Kashireitleer.'

"When the learned beings then gathered at that free feast from almost the whole of Nievia saw that indeed unprecedented Kashireitleer, they were at first so astounded that they became, as it is said there, as if 'petrified' and only after a considerable time did they gradually begin looking at each other with dumbfounded glances, and exchanging opinions in whispers.

"Chiefly they asked one another how was it possible that not a single learned being nor a single ordinary being had known or guessed that there in their own country such a learned being with such knowledge existed.

"Suddenly one of them, namely, the oldest among them who enjoyed the greatest reputation, jumped up on the table like a boy, and in a loud voice and with the intonation which had already long before become proper to the learned beings there of new formation, and which has also reached the contemporary learned beings, uttered the following:

"'Listen, and all of you be aware that we, the representatives of terrestrial beings assembled here who have thanks to our great learning already attained independent individuality, have the happiness to be the first to behold with our own eyes the creation of a Messiah of Divine

---------------------------------- *398* ----------------------------------

consciousness sent from Above to reveal World-truths to us.'

"Thereupon began that usual maleficent what is called 'mutual inflation,' which had already long been practiced among the learned beings of new formation and chiefly on account of which no true knowledge which has chanced to reach them ever evolves there as it does everywhere else in the Universe, even merely from the passage of time itself; but, on the contrary, even the knowledge once already attained there is destroyed, and its possessors always become shallower and shallower.

"And the rest of the learned beings then began shouting and pushing each other in order to get near Lentrohamsanin; and addressing him as their 'long-awaited-Messiah' they conveyed to him by their admiring glances what is called their 'high-titillation.'

"The most interesting thing about it all is that the reason why all the other learned beings were so greatly amazed and so freely gave vent to what are called their 'learned snivellings' lay in a certain extremely strange conviction which had been formed in the psyche of your favorites, thanks as always to the same abnormally established conditions of ordinary existence, that if anybody becomes a follower of an already well-known and important being, he thereby seems to be to all other beings almost as well known and important himself.

"So it was on the strength of his being very rich, and what is more important, already very famous, that all the other learned beings of that time, of the country Nievia, immediately manifested themselves approvingly towards this Lentrohamsanin.

"Well then, my dear boy, when after the said banquet, the learned beings of

"When the 'scientists' then gathered at that free feast from almost the whole Nievia saw that 'Kashireitleer,' indeed unprecedented there, they were at first flabbergasted, and, as it is said there, 'knocked speechless,' and only after a considerable time did they gradually begin looking at each other with dumbfounded glances, and exchanging opinions in whispers.

"Chiefly they asked one another how it was possible that not one of the number of 'scientists' nor one or the ordinary beings had hitherto known or guessed that there in their own country such a scientist with such knowledge existed.

"Suddenly one of them, namely, the oldest among them, who enjoyed the greatest reputation, jumped up on the table like a boy, and in a loud voice and with the intonation which had already long before become proper to the scientists there of 'new forat,' and which has also reached the contemporary scientists, pronounced the following:

"'Listen, and all of you be aware that we, the representatives of terrestrial beings assembled here, who have, thanks to our great sciences, already attained independent individuality, have the happiness to be the first to behold with our own eyes the creation of a Messiah of divine

---

consciousness sent to us from Above to reveal "World-truths" to us!

"Thereupon began that usual maleficent what is called 'mutual-inflation,' which had already long been practiced among the scientific beings of 'new format,' and chiefly on account of which no objectively true knowledge ever evolves there as it does everywhere else, even merely from the passage of time itself; but, on the contrary, even the knowledge once already attained there is destroyed; and its keepers themselves are always becoming shallower and shallower.

"That is to say, the rest of the scientists then began shouting and pushing each other in order to get near Lentrohamsanin; and addressing him as their 'long-awaited Messiah' they conveyed to him by their admiring glances what are called their 'tributes of praise.'

"The most interesting thing about it all is this, namely, that the reason why all the other scientists ware so greatly amazed and so freely gave way to what are called their 'scientific whimpers,' lay in a very strange and particularly unconscious need which had been formed in the psyche of the scientists there.

"Namely, thanks as always to the same abnormally established conditions of ordinary existence, the notion had already arisen there long before—and is up until now an inseparable part of the general psyche of each and every one of your favorites—that if anybody is a follower of an already well known and important being, he thereby also becomes, or at least he will seem to be, almost as well known and important himself.

"So it was on the strength of this that all the other scientists of that time, of the country Nievia, immediately manifested themselves approvingly towards this Lentrohamsanin, because he was both very rich and what is most important, already famous.

"Well, my dear boy, when after the said banquet, the scientific beings of Nievia

Nievia returned home, they immediately began firstly to speak among their neighbors and later more and more widely, here, there and everywhere,

about that unprecedented Kashireitleer itself, and, secondly, already foaming at the mouth, to persuade and convince everybody of the truth of those 'revelations' which that great Lentrohamsanin had inscribed on this Kashireitleer.

"The result of it all was that the ordinary beings of the town Kronbookhon as well as of other parts of the country Nievia talked among themselves of nothing but these 'revelations.'

"And gradually, as it also usually happens there, almost everywhere beings became divided into two mutually opposing parties, one of which favored the 'invention' of the subsequent Universal Hasnamuss, and the other, the already existing and well-fixed forms of being-existence.

"Thus it continued during almost a whole terrestrial year, during which time the ranks of the contending parties increased everywhere and towards each other there grew one of their particular properties called 'hate'; the result of which was that one sorrowful day in the town of Kronbookhon itself, there suddenly began among the beings, who had become followers of one or the other of the two said mutually opposite currents, their process of what is called 'civil war.'

"'Civil war' is the same as 'war'; the difference is only that in ordinary war, beings of one community destroy the beings of another community, while in a civil war the process of reciprocal destruction proceeds among beings of one and the same community, as, for example, brother annihilates brother; father, son; uncle, nephew, and so on.

"At the outset, during the four days that the horrible process was at its height in Kronbookhon, and the attention of the other beings of the whole country of Nievia was concentrated on it, everything was still relatively quiet in the other towns, but here and there, small, what are called 'skirmishes' occasionally took place. When at the end of

the fourth day, those who were for the 'invention' of Lentrohamsanin, that is for the learned beings, were victorious in Kronbookhon, then, from that time on, the same process also began at all the large and small points of the whole surface of Nievia.

"That widespread terrifying process continued until there appeared 'hordes' of learned beings who, as it is said, 'feeling-firm-ground-beneath-their-feet' compelled all the surviving beings to accept the ideas of Lentrohamsanin and immediately destroyed everything, and from then on, all the three-brained beings of Nievia became followers of the 'invention' of Lentrohamsanin and soon after, in that community, there was established a special what is called 'Republic.'

"A little later, the community Nievia, being at that period great and what is called 'powerful,' began, as it also usually happens there, 'making war' on the neighboring communities for the purpose of imposing upon them also her new

returned home, then they were no sooner there than they began speaking first among their neighbors and later more and more widely, here, there and every-

where, firstly, about that unprecedented Kashireitleer itself, and secondly, already foaming at the mouth, to persuade and convince everybody of the truth of those revelations which that great Lentrohamsanin had engrossed on this 'Kashireitleer.'

"The result of it all was that the ordinary beings both of the town Kronbookhon and of other parts of the country Nievia talked among themselves of nothing but these revelations.

"And gradually, as it also usually happens there, almost everywhere beings became divided into two mutually opposing parties, one of which favored the 'invention' of the subsequent Universal Hasnamuss, and the other the already existing and well fixed forms of being existence.

"Thus it continued during almost a whole terrestrial year, during which time, both the ranks of the contending parties increased and towards each other there grew one of their particular properties called 'hate.'

"And one sorrowful day in the town Kronbookhon itself, there suddenly began among the beings, who already had become followers of one or the other of the two said mutually opposite currents, their process of what is called 'Civil War.'

"'Civil War'—this is the same as 'war'; the difference lies only in this, that in ordinary 'war,' beings of one community destroy the beings of another community, while in a 'civil war,' the process of reciprocal destruction proceeds among beings of one and the same community, as, for example: brother annihilates brother; father–son; uncle–nephew; and so on.

"At the outset, during the four days, while that horrible process was at its height in Kronbookhon, and the attention of the other beings of the country of all Nievia was concentrated on it, everything was still relatively quiet in the other towns, except that here and there, small, what are called, 'skirmishes' occasionally took place; but when at the end of

the fourth day, those who were for the 'invention' of Lentrohamsanin, that is, for the scientists, were victorious in Kronbookhon, then, from that time forward, the same process also began at all the large and small points of the whole of the surface of Nievia.

"That widespread horrible process which had nowhere existed before, continued until there already appeared quite powerful 'hordes' of scientists, who, compelling all the surviving beings to acknowledge the ideas of Lentrohamsanin, immediately destroyed everything.

"The result of all I have described was just that all the three-brained beings of Nievia became followers of the 'invention' of Lentrohamsanin and in that community there was established a particular what is called 'Republic.'

"A little later, the community Nievia, being at that period great and what is called 'powerful,' began, as it also usually happens there, 'making war' on the neighboring communities for the purpose of imposing upon them also her new form of state-organization.

"From that time on, my boy, on the largest continent of your planet, the processes of reciprocal destruction among these strange three-brained beings began to proceed as before; and at the same time, there were gradually changed and finally destroyed those various beneficent forms of their ordinary existence which had already been fixed thanks to the ideally foreseeing Reason of our now Most Very Saintly Ashiata Shiemash.

"Thereupon there again began to be formed on the surface of your planet—only to be destroyed anew and to give place to others—numerous separate distinct communities with every kind of 'form-of-inner-state-organization.'

"Although the direct effect of that maleficent invention of the now Universal Hasnamuss Lentrohamsanin was that among your favorites the practice was revived of existing in separate distinct communities and they again

resumed their periodic reciprocal destruction, yet within many of these newly arisen independent communities on the continent Asia, beings still continued to conform in their ordinary existence to many of the unprecedently wisely foreseen usages of the Very Saintly Ashiata Shiemash for their ordinary being-existence, which usages had already been inseparably fused into their automatically flowing process of daily existence.

"And those to blame for the final destruction of these said usages and customs that still remained in certain communities, were those learned beings who were then assembled in the city of Babylon.

"And they were then to blame in this respect owing to the following:

"When owing to that famous question of the Beyond, they organized the 'general-planetary-conference' of all the learned beings there, there happened to be also among the learned beings who went to Babylon on their own accord, the great-grandson of Lentrohamsanin himself, who had also become a learned being.

"And he took with him, there to the city of Babylon, an exact copy of the mentioned Kashireitleer, but made on papyrus, the original of which had been inscribed by his great-grandfather and which he had obtained by inheritance, and at the very height of the 'frenzy' concerning the 'question-of-the-soul' during one of the last big general meetings of the learned beings, he read aloud the contents of that maleficent 'invention' of his great-grandfather's; whereupon, it occurred—as it had also become proper to the 'sorry-learned-beings' of this planet, thanks to their strange Reason—that from one question which interested them, they at once passed to quite another, namely, from the question 'of-the-soul' to the question of what is called 'politics.'

"Thereupon in the city of Babylon, meetings and

discussions again began everywhere concerning the various kinds of already existing state-organizations and those which in their opinion ought to be formed.

"As the basis of all their discussions they took, of course, the 'truths' indicated

form of 'state-organization.'

"From that time on, my boy, on the then largest continent of your planet, their processes of reciprocal destruction among these strange three-brained beings began to proceed as before; and at the same time gradually were changed and finally were destroyed those various beneficent forms of their ordinary existence which had already been fixed in the process of their ordinary existence, thanks to the ideally foreseeing Reason of our now Most Very Saintly Ashiata Shiemash.

"Thereupon there again arose on the surface of your planet there—only to be destroyed anew and to give place to other arisings—their numerous separate communities with every possible, as it is expressed there, 'form-of-inner-state-organization.'

"Although the direct effect of that maleficent 'invention' of the now universal Hasnamuss Lentrohamsanin was that among your favorites the practice was revived of existing in separate communities and they again

resumed their periodic reciprocal destruction, yet within many of these newly arisen independent communities on the continent Asia, beings still continued to conform in their ordinary existence to many of the unprecedentedly-wisely-foreseen-details of the Very Saintly Ashiata Shiemash for their ordinary being-existence, those details which had already been inseparably grafted into, what is called their 'mechanical-daily-life.'

"Well, it was for the final destruction of these said details that still remained in certain communities that the said scientists then assembled in the city of Babylon were just to blame.

"And they were then to blame in this respect also owing to the following:

"When in connection with that notorious question of the Beyond, they organized the 'all-planetary-conference' of all the scientists, there happened to be also among the scientists who went to Babylon on their own accord, the great-grandson of Lentrohamsanin himself, who had also become a scientist.

"And he took with him, there to the city of Babylon, an exact copy of the mentioned Kashireitleer, but made on papyrus, the original of which had been engrossed by his great-grandfather and which he had obtained by inheritance.

"At the very height of the 'frenzy' concerning the 'question-of-the-soul,' during one of the last big general meetings of the 'scientists,' he read aloud the contents of that maleficent 'invention' of his great-grandfather's whereupon, thanks to the strange reason of these 'sorry scientists,' it occurred—as also it had become proper among the scientists of this peculiar planet—that from a question which interested them, they at once passed to quite another, namely, from the 'question-of-the-soul' to the question of what is called 'politics.'

"Thereupon in the city of Babylon meetings and

discussions again commenced everywhere concerning the various kinds of 'state-organization' already existing or which ought to be formed anew.

"As the basis of all their discussions they took, of course, the truths indicated in in the invention of Lentrohamsanin, this time expounded on what is called a papyrus that had been taken there by his great-grandson, and a copy of which almost every learned being who was then in Babylon carried in his pocket.

"For several months they discussed and argued, and as a result, they this time 'split' into parties; that is to say all the learned beings then in the city of Babylon split into two independent what are called 'sections,' under the following names:

"The first: 'Section of Neomothists.'

"The second: 'Section of Paleomothists.'

"Each of these sections of learned beings soon had its adherents from among the ordinary beings in the city of Babylon; and once again things would certainly have ended also with a civil war if the Persian king, hearing of it all, had not immediately 'cracked' them on their 'learned noddles.'

"A number of these learned beings were executed by him, others were imprisoned with lice, and still others were dispatched to places, where even now, as Mullah Nassr Eddin would say, 'French champagne' could not be taken. Only a few of those who were clearly shown to have been occupied with all this, only because, as it is said there, they were 'mad,' were permitted to return to their own countries, and those among them who had taken no part whatever in 'political-questions' were not only also given full liberty to return to their native land, but by the order of the mentioned Persian king, their return to their native land was even accompanied with every kind of honor.

------------------------------ 403 ------------------------------

"Well then, my boy, those Babylonian learned beings who, owing to various reasons, survived and were scattered everywhere over the surface of almost the whole of the planet, continued by momentum their wiseacring, the basis of which, they made—of course, not consciously but simply mechanically—those two leading questions which had arisen and which had been the 'questions-of-the-day' during the said Babylonian events, namely, the famous questions concerning the 'soul' of men and the 'inner-communal-organization.'

"The result of these wiseacrings of theirs was that over the whole continent of Asia civil wars again broke out in various communities, and the processes of mass reciprocal-destruction between different communities.

"The destruction which thus proceeded of the remnants of the results of the conscious labors of the Very Saintly Ashiata Shiemash, continued on the continent of Asia for about a century and a half; yet, in spite of this, in some places there were preserved and even by momentum were still carried out certain forms that had been created by Ashiata Shiemash for their beneficent being-existence.

"But when the three-brained beings there who arose and existed on the neighboring continent, now called Europe, then began taking part in the Asiatic wars, and when 'hordes' with the arch-vainglorious Greek called 'Alexander-of-Macedonia' at their head, were dispatched thence and passed almost everywhere over the continent of Asia, they made, as it is said, a 'clean sweep' from the surface of that ill-fated planet of everything that had been established and had still been preserved and carried out; so clean a sweep, that it left not even the trace of the

the invention of Lentrohamsanin and contained in what is called the 'Papyrus,' that had been taken there and a copy of which almost every scientist who was then in Babylon carried in his pocket.

"For several months they discussed and argued, and once again, as before, the 'split' into parties; that is to say, all the scientists then in the city of Babylon 'split' into three independent what are called 'sections,' under the following names:

the first—Section of 'Legominists'

the second—Section of 'Neomothists'

the third—Section of 'Paleomothists'

"Each of these sections soon had its adherents from among the ordinary beings there in the city of Babylon; and once again things would certainly have ended also with a 'civil' war, if the Persian King, hearing of it all, had not at once 'cracked' them on their 'scientific noddles.'

"A number of these scientists were executed by him, others were imprisoned with lice, still others were dispatched to places, where even now 'French champagne' could not be taken.

"Finally, certain of those left, who were clearly shown to have been occupied with all this, only because, as it is said there, they were 'obviously mad,' were permitted to return 'to their fatherlands' and those among them who had taken no part whatever in 'politics' were not only also given full liberty to return to their native land, but by the order of the mentioned Persian king, their return to their native land was even accompanied with every kind of what is called 'honor.'

- -

"So, my boy, those Babylonian scientists, who for various reasons survived and were scattered everywhere over the surface of almost the whole of the planet, then just continued wiseacring, as it were, and they took as the basis of their wiseacring—of course, not consciously, but simply mechanically—those two leading questions which had arisen and which had been the 'questions of the day' during the said Babylonian events, namely, the notorious questions concerning the 'soul' of man and the inner-state-organization.

"Well, the net result of these wiseacrings of theirs was that over the whole continent of Asia civil wars again broke out in various communities, and among the communities themselves the processes of mass reciprocal destruction.

"The destruction which thus proceeded of the remnants of the results of the conscious labors of the Very Saintly Ashiata Shiemash, continued on the continent of Asia for about a century and a half; nevertheless there were still in some places preserved and even by momentum were still in some places carried out certain forms that had been created by Ashiata Shiemash for their beneficent being-existence. But when the three-brained beings there, who arose and existed on the neighboring continent, hitherto called Europe, then began taking part in these Asiatic wars and civil wars, and when 'hordes' with the arch-vainglorious Greek called 'Alexander of Macedonia' at their head, were dispatched thence and passed almost everywhere over the continent of Asia, they now finally, as it is said, 'made a clean sweep' of everything from the surface of that ill-starred planet; so clean a sweep that it left not even the trace of the memory that there on the sur-

memory that there could once have existed on the surface of their planet such a 'bliss,' specially and intentionally created for their existence by such a Reason,

- 404 -

whose possessor is now one of our seven MOST VERY SAINTLY OMNICOS-MIC INDIVIDUALS, without whose participation even our UNI-BEING COMMON FATHER does not allow himself to actualize anything.

"And now, my boy, after my tale about this Lentrohamsanin—thanks to which you obtained to a certain degree a conspective account of the consequences for subsequent generations ensuing from the activities of such a typical representative of Eternal-Hasnamuss-individuals from among the three-brained beings of the planet Earth—it will now be quite opportune to explain to you, as I promised, a little more in detail about the significance of the word Hasnamuss.

"In general, those independent individuals are called and defined by the word Hasnamuss in whom, among what are called 'Individual-impulses,' a certain 'something' arises, which participates in what is called the 'completed formation' of independent individualities in the common presences of three-brained beings both of the highest possible coating as well as of those who consist only of the planetary body alone.

"This 'something' in these separate cosmic individuals arises and blends in the process of the transformation of substances in them with the crystallizations resulting from the action of the entire 'spectrum' of certain what are called 'Naloo-osnian-impulses.'

"This 'Naloo-osnian-spectrum-of-impulses' consists, on the basis of that chief cosmic law, the sacred Heptaparaparshinokh, according to the source of its essence in respect of the 'perception-of-engenderings' and the 'resulting-manifestations,' of seven heterogeneous aspects.

"If these separate aspects of the entire 'spectrum' of Naloo-osnian-impulses are described according to the notions of your favorites and expressed in their language, they might then be defined as follows:

- 405 -

(1) Every kind of depravity, conscious as well as unconscious

(2) The feeling of self-satisfaction from leading others astray

(3) The irresistible inclination to destroy the existence of other breathing creatures

(4) The urge to become free from the necessity of actualizing the being-efforts demanded by Nature

(5) The attempt by every kind of artificiality to conceal from others what in their opinion are one's physical defects

(6) The calm self-contentment in the use of what is not personally deserved

(7) The striving to be not what one is.

"This certain 'something' which arises in the presences of definite individuals

face of their planet there could once have existed such a 'bliss' specially and intentionally created for their existence by just such a Reason,

- -

whose bearer is now one of our seven Most Very Saintly Omni-Cosmic Individuums, without whose participation even our UNI-BEING COMMON FATHER
allows Himself to actualize nothing.

"I shall now elucidate rather more in detail concerning what I promised you a
little while ago, namely, concerning the expression 'Hasnamuss.'

"In general, those independent individuums are called and defined by the
Word 'Hasnamuss' in whom, among a number of other what are called 'Individual-impulses' a certain 'something' obtained from the total presence of every
three-brained being arises which participates in what is called their 'fulfilled-
formation'; that is to say, which participates in the forming both of the 'planetary-
body' itself and of the being and of his two higher being bodies at every stage of
the perfecting of these latter.

"This 'something' in these separate cosmic Individuums arises and interblends
in the process of crystallization from a certain, what is called 'Naloo-osnian-spectrum-of-impulses.'

"In addition to several very undesirable consequences for the said Individuums
themselves, in whom they arise—about which I shall later also explain to you in
detail—this said 'something' has still another particularity, namely, that as soon
as the action of what is called 'intense-effort' ceases in the presences of the given
arisings, it is always perceived and manifested according to some or other part of
the mentioned 'Naloo-osnian-spectrum-of-impulses,' as if there were not enough
of that something like the first and second being-foods, and it thus helps the totality of the whole given presence to manifest itself 'harmfully-actingly,' both for
itself and for other independent Individuums around.

- -

←   *The text opposite is found at the end of this chapter in* The 1931 Manu-
    script of The Tales.

owing to the enumerated Naloo-osnian-impulses, besides being the cause of what are called 'serious-retributive-suffering-consequences' for these individuals themselves, also has the particularity, that as soon as the action of what is called 'intense-effort' ceases in one of these individuals, the radiations proper to one or other of the aspects of the manifestations of this 'something' have a greater effect on those around him and become a factor for engendering the same in them.

"In the common presence of every kind of three-brained being, there can arise during the process of his planetary existence, four kinds of independent Hasnamuss-individuals.

"The first kind of Hasnamuss-individual is a three-brained being who, while acquiring in his common presence that something, still consists only of his planetary body and who, during the process of his sacred Rascooarno, is subject to the corresponding consequences of the presence in him of the properties of this something and is thus destroyed forever such as he is.

---------------------------------- *406* ----------------------------------

"The second kind of Hasnamuss-individual is that Kesdjan body of a three-brained being which is coated in his common presence with the participation of that same something and which, acquiring—as is proper to such a cosmic arising—the property of 'Toorinoorino,' that is, non-decomposition in any sphere of that planet on which he arose, has to exist, by being formed again and again in a certain way, such as he is, until this certain something will have been eliminated from him.

"The third kind of Hasnamuss-individual is the highest being-body or soul, during the coating of which in the common presence of a three-brained being this something arises and participates; and he also acquires the property of Toorinoorino, but this time proper to this highest being-body; that is to say, this arising is no longer subject to decomposition not only in the spheres of that planet on which he had his arising, but also in all other spheres of the Great Universe.

"The fourth kind of Hasnamuss-individual is similar to the third, but with this difference, that the Hasnamuss of the third kind has the possibility of at some time succeeding in becoming so to say 'cleansed' from this something, whereas for this fourth kind such a possibility is lost forever.

"That is why this fourth kind of Hasnamuss is called an 'Eternal-Hasnamuss-individual.'

"For these four kinds of Hasnamuss-individuals, owing to their having in their presences this something, the mentioned retributive-suffering-consequences are various and correspond both to the nature of each kind as well as to what is called 'objective-responsibilities' ensuing from the primordial providence and hopes and expectations of our COMMON FATHER concerning these cosmic actualizations.

"For the Hasnamuss of the first kind, namely, when this something is acquired

"From the total presence of every kind of three-brained being, there arises four kinds of the mentioned independent 'Hasnamuss Individuums.'

"The first kind arises, when the planetary body of a being becomes such a 'Hasnamuss-Individuum' during its planetary existence.

- -

"The second kind arises when there become 'Hasnamuss-Individuums' with the 'Kesdjan-bodies' of the three-brained beings which are 'fulfilledly' coated in the total presences of the beings, and which acquire in themselves the property of 'Toorinoorino,' that is, they are no longer subject to the property of decomposition in any sphere of that planet on which they arise.

"The third kind of 'Hasnamuss-Individuum' issues from amongst those three-brained beings' in whose presence the highest 'being-body' is already 'fulfilledly' coated and perfected, in the sense of objective reason, up to the corresponding gradation, and who have also acquired in themselves the property 'Toorinoorino' not only as regards the sphere of that planet on which they arise, but also in all the other spheres of the Universe, until that time when there proceeds in the presence of the given Individuum what is called the 'complete-transformation' of this said 'something.'

"The fourth kind of 'Hasnamuss-Individuum' is similar to the third, but with this difference, that for the Hasnamuss of the third kind there is a possibility of at some time obtaining the mentioned transformation, whereas for this fourth kind that possibility is already lost forever. Hence this fourth kind of Hasnamuss is called the 'Eternal-Hasnamuss-Individuum.'

"All the four said independent kinds of 'Hasnamuss-Individuum' who may have their arising in the total presence of any three-brained being, on account of the acquisition and the existence of the said 'something' in their presences, completely lose, firstly, any possibility of crystallizing in themselves the divine data for the arising of the sacred impulse of 'Objective-Conscience'; and secondly, after the sacred process of 'Rascooarno' and pending the elucidation from their presence of the action of the said 'something,' they must inevitably be subject to the corresponding.

"And, namely, in the Hasnamusses of the first kind, that is to say, when the said

by a being still consisting only of

------------------------------ *407* ------------------------------

just a planetary body alone, the decomposition of this planetary body of his does not proceed according to the general rule, that is to say, the cessation of the functioning in his organism of every kind of sensed-impulse does not proceed simultaneously with the approach of the 'sacred Rascooarno,' that is, death.

"But the process of the sacred Rascooarno begins in him still during his planetary existence and proceeds in parts, that is, one by one there gradually cease to participate in his common presence, the functioning of one or other of his separate independent spiritualized 'localizations'—or, as your favorites would say there, in such a being, first of all, one of his brains with all its appertaining functions dies; later on, the second one dies, and only then does the final death of the being approach.

"In addition to this, after the final death, the 'disintegration-of-all-the-active-elements' of which the given planetary body was formed, proceeds firstly much more slowly than usual, and secondly, with the inextinguishable action—only lessened in proportion to the volatilization of the active elements—of the mentioned 'sensed-impulses' he had during life.

"For the second kind of Hasnamuss-individual, that is, when the Kesdjan-body of a three-brained being becomes such, the corresponding consequences are that such an indeed unfortunate arising, freed from the planetary body of a three-brained being, on the one hand not having the possibility of perfecting himself independently of and without a planetary coating, does not succeed in eliminating from his presence this maleficent something even not always acquired by his own fault, which something is always and with everything in the Universe an obstacle for the correct flowing of the common cosmic Trogoautoegocratic process; on the other hand, owing to the property in him of Toorinoorino, that is, not being subject

------------------------------ *408* ------------------------------

to decomposition in any sphere of that solar system in which he is formed, he must inevitably be again coated in a planetary body and in most cases with the exterior form of a being of one- or two-brained system; and in view of the brevity in general of the duration of beings of these planetary forms and also not having time to adapt himself to a single exterior form, he must constantly begin all over again in the form of another being of the planet with the full uncertainty as to the result of this coating.

"And as regards the third kind of Hasnamuss-individual, namely, when the highest being-body of a three-brained being becomes such, and when this certain something participates in his coating in such a quality that he never loses the possibility of freeing himself from it, the matter is still more terrible, chiefly because he—as a higher cosmic arising, who according to the foreseeing FIRST-SOURCED-PRINCIPLE-OF-EVERYTHING-EXISTING was predetermined to serve the aim of helping the government of the whole increasing World, and on whom from the moment of the completion of his formation, even when he was not yet perfected in Reason, was placed the responsibility for every subjective

'something' is acquired by beings still consisting of only

- -

just a 'planetary-body' alone, the decomposition of their planetary body does not proceed according to the general rule. In other words, the ceasing to function of the various kinds of what are called, 'self-sensible impulses' does not simultaneously proceed in their presence with the approach of the sacred 'Rascooarno.'

"But in them the process of the sacred 'Rascooarno' begins still during their planetary existence and proceeds in parts, that is one by one there gradually cease to participate in their total presence the functioning of separate, what are called, 'Complexes' of some of their independent spiritualized 'localizations,' or, as your favorites would say there—in such a being, first, one of his brains with all its appertaining functionings dies, later on, the second dies, and only then does the final death of the being approach.

"This partial death as well as the final 'disintegration-of-the-active-element' of which the given 'planetary body' was formed, proceeds at first more slowly, and secondly, with the complete and inextinguishable action of the said 'self-sensible impulses' still possessed during life.

"The second kind of 'Hasnamuss-Individuum,' namely, such an indeed unfortunate arising, whose 'Kesdjan-body' as a three-brained being becomes such, contains no possibilities of independent self-perfection independently of the planetary coating, or, at least, no possibilities of succeeding in eradicating from his presence what is undesirable and what has not even always been acquired through his own fault.

- -

"And because every planetary formation has a defined duration of existence, and every such 'Kesdjan body' arisen in a three-brained being can be coated in a new exterior only of a one-brained or two-brained system and not in a three-brained one, this said unfortunate cosmic arising, in addition to the said permanent trial, is compelled having had no time to adapt himself to one exterior form— to begin all over again in the form of some one-brained or two-brained being of the given planet with the presence of the permanent impulse of 'Hope.'

"As regards the third kind of 'Hasnamuss-Individuum,' namely, those from amongst the three-brained beings who have perfected themselves up to the 'higher-being-bodies,' their presences are already never subject to decomposition in any sphere of the Universe; nor can any forces from without destroy that 'something' they acquired; but that 'something' can be destroyed in them exclusively by the actions of 'Partkdolgduty' formed in the presences themselves of these cosmic Individuums and which are called 'intentional suffering.'

voluntary as well as involuntary manifestation—has the possibility to succeed in eliminating from his presence this something, exclusively only by the action of the results of intentionally actualized Partkdolg-duty, that is to say, of 'conscious-labors-and-intentional-sufferings.'

"Hence such a higher being-body must inevitably always suffer correspondingly, having already acquired the gradation of what is called the 'degree-of-cognition-of-one's-own-individuality,' until this certain something is entirely eradicated from his common presence.

"As a place for the suffering existence of such a high order of Hasnamuss-individuals, the HIGHER-SACRED-INDIVIDUALS

---------------------------------- *409* ----------------------------

have intentionally allotted, from the totality of the large cosmic concentrations, four planets, disharmonized in their subjective functioning, situated in various most remote corners of our Great Universe.

"One of these four disharmonized planets called 'Eternal-Retribution' is specially prepared for the 'Eternal-Hasnamuss-individuals' and the other three for those 'Higher being-bodies' of Hasnamusses in whose common presences there is still the possibility of 'at some time or other' eliminating from themselves the mentioned maleficent something.

"The three small planets exist under the names of:

(1) 'Remorse-of-Conscience'

(2) 'Repentance'

(3) 'Self-Reproach.'

"Here it is interesting to notice that from among all the 'highest being-bodies' which have been coated and perfected in every kind of exterior form of three-brained being there have, so far, reached the planet 'Retribution' from the whole Universe, only three hundred and thirteen, two of whom had their arising on your planet and one of these is the 'highest being-body' of this Lentrohamsanin.

"On that planet Retribution, these Eternal-Hasnamuss-individuals must constantly endure those incredible sufferings called 'Inkiranoodel' which are like the sufferings called Remorse-of-Conscience but only much more painful.

"The chief torture of the state of these 'highest being-bodies' is that they must always experience these terrifying sufferings fully conscious of the utter hopelessness of their cessation."

---------------------------------- *410* ----------------------------

(1) Every kind of depravity, conscious as well as unconscious

(2) The feeling of self-satisfaction from leading others astray

(3) The irresistible inclination to destroy the existence of other breathing creatures

(4) The urge to become free from the necessity of actualizing the being-efforts demanded by Nature

(5) The attempt by every kind of artificiality to conceal from others what in their opinion are one's physical defects

(6) The calm self-contentment in the use of what is not personally deserved

(7) The striving to be not what one is.

"Such cosmic arisings, therefore, must inevitably suffer correspondingly, until the time when they shall have succeeded in eradicating this 'something' from their presence.

"For the existence and suffering of these 'Hasnamuss-Individuums' who arise from amongst the 'highest-being-bodies,' there are even

intentionally allotted and preserved in the Universe, four small planets situated in various most remote corners of our great Universe.

"One of these four small planets, called 'Retribution,' is specially prepared for the 'eternal-Hasnamuss-Individuums'; and the other three are for the 'highest-being-bodies' of those Hasnamusses in whose presences there is still the possibility of eliminating from themselves at some time or other, the said undesirable 'something.'
"These three small planets exist under the names of:
the first—'Remorse of Conscience'
the second—'Repentance'
the third—'Self-Reproach'
"Here it is interesting to notice that from among the number of all the highest-being-bodies which have been coated and perfected in every kind of exterior form of three-brained beings, there have, so far, reached the planet 'Retribution' from the whole Universe only three hundred and thirty five; and one of them is just the 'highest-being-part' of the said Lentrohamsanin of the planet Earth.
"On that planet 'Retribution' those 'eternal-Hasnamuss-Individuums' must constantly endure those incredible sufferings called 'Inkiranoodel' which are like the sufferings called 'Remorse of Conscience,' but still more terrible, their chief terror being this, that these 'highest-being-bodies' must always undergo those horrible sufferings with the consciousness of complete hopelessness.

"As regards the 'Naloo-osnian-spectrum-of-impulses' which I spoke of, on account of which certain separate cosmic arisings are transformed into Hasnamusses, then, on the basis of the chief cosmic law the sacred Heptaparaparshinokh, this spectrum has the essence to be the source of the 'perception-for-the-bringing-forth' and 'manifestation' of seven heterogeneous, what are called, 'aspects.' And these 'aspects,' if characterized according to the ideas of your favorites and defined in their conversational language, may be called as follows:
(1) Conscious and unconscious depravity of every kind.
(2) Self-satisfaction from leading others astray.
(3) The urge to destroy the existence of other breathing things.

"This certain 'something' which arises in the presences of definite individuals owing to the enumerated Naloo-osnian-impulses, besides being the cause of what are called 'serious-retributive-suffering-consequences' for these individuals themselves, also has the particularity, that as soon as the action of what is called 'intense-effort' ceases in one of these individuals, the radiations proper to one or other of the aspects of the manifestations of this 'something' have a greater effect on those around him and become a factor for engendering the same in them.

The text above which corresponds to the text on the opposite page is repeated from earlier in the 1950 version of The Tales. It appears on page 406 [513]

(4) The urge to succeed in never actualizing being-effort.

(5) The wish to conceal one's defects under the cloak of pretence.

(6) Calm self-content in the use of what is not personally deserved.

(7) The striving not to be what one is; and thus never to be aware or to sense one's real place in the Universe; and neither to give to others what is due, nor what corresponds, nor what is, in fact, deserved.

"And so, my boy, from the time that your favorites made a 'clean sweep' from the surface of their planet of every kind of result of the very saintly conscious labors of Ashiata Shiemash, their separate communities gradually arose again in great numbers as before, under those two forms of what is called 'subjective-ordering' which they themselves called 'hereditary monarchy' and 'republic.'

"And in connection with these 'state-organizations' established for these 'inner-subjective-orderings' there again began to exist there, terrors for all the beings of that ill-starred planet."

Other Books from the Karnak Press

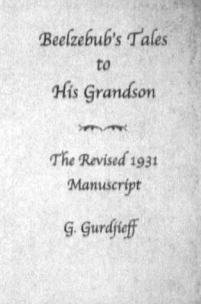

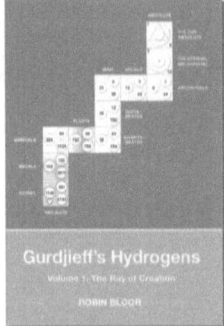

All of these books are available on Amazon or can be ordered direct from the Karnak Press via this URL: *https://tofathomthegist.com/buy-books-2/*
The titles are:

- **To Fathom The Gist Volume I: Approaches to the Writings of G. I. Gurdjieff** by Robin Bloor

- **To Fathom The Gist Volume II: The Arch-Absurd** by Robin Bloor

- **To Fathom The Gist Volume III: The Arousing Of Thought** by Robin Bloor

- **The 1931 Manuscript of Beelzebub's Tales to His Grandson** by G.I Gurdjieff, edited by Robin Bloor

- **Beelzebub's Tales to His Grandson: The Revised 1931 Manuscript** by G.I Gurdjieff, edited by Robin Bloor

- **Gurdjieff's Hydrogens Volume 1: The Ray of Creation** by Robin Bloor

- **Readings Prosaic And Poetic** edited by Paula Schmidt and Robin Bloor

- **Sayings From The Gurdjieff Work**

- **Gurdjieff & Kundabuffer Food For The Moon**

- **The Herald Of Coming Good [With Notes]** by G.I Gurdjieff, edited by Robin Bloor

- **The Search For Meaning And The Mystery Of Consciousness** by Stephen Aronson

- **Rodney Collin a man who wished to do something with his life** by Terje Tonne

- **SACRED DANCES The Gurdjieff Movements** by Nella Denzey Markoe Liska